THE NIV APPLICATION COMMENTARY

HAGGAI, ZECHARIAH

THE NIV APPLICATION COMMENTARY SERIES

THE NIV APPLICATION COMMENTARY

HAGGAI, ZECHARIAH

BRINGING THE ANCIENT
MESSAGE OF THE BIBLE
INTO YOUR WORLD

MARK J. BODA

ZONDERVAN
ACADEMIC

ZONDERVAN ACADEMIC

Haggai, Zechariah

Published in Grand Rapids, Michigan, by Zondervan. Zondervan is a registered trademark of The Zondervan Corporation, L.L.C., a wholly owned subsidiary of HarperCollins Christian Publishing, Inc.

Requests for information should be addressed to customercare@harpercollins.com.

Zondervan titles may be purchased in bulk for educational, business, fundraising, or sales promotional use. For information, please email SpecialMarkets@Zondervan.com.

ISBN 978-0-310-57157-5 (ebook)

Library of Congress Cataloging-in-Publication Data

Boda, Mark J.
Haggai, Zechariah / Mark. J. Boda.
p. cm. — (The NIV application commentary)
Includes bibliographical references and indexes.
ISBN-10: 0-310-20615-4
ISBN-13: 978-0-310-20615-6
1. Bible. O.T. Haggai — Commentaries. 2. Bible. O.T. Zechariah — Commentaries. I. Title. II. Series.
BS 1655.53.B63 2004
224'.97077—dc22 2004005204
CIP

Printed in the United States of America

---

26 27 28 29 30 31 33 34 35 /TRM/ 23 22 21 20 19 18 17 16 15 14

ad majorem Dei gloriam

To Rexford and Jean Boda

Contents

THE NIV APPLICATION COMMENTARY SERIES

Old Testament Volumes

Genesis, John H. Walton

Exodus, Peter Enns

Leviticus, Numbers, Roy Gane

Deuteronomy, Daniel I. Block

Joshua, Robert L. Hubbard Jr.

Judges, Ruth, K. Lawson Younger Jr.

1 and 2 Samuel, Bill T. Arnold

1 and 2 Kings, August H. Konkel

1 and 2 Chronicles, Andrew E. Hill

Ezra-Nehemiah,
Donna Petter and Thomas Petter

Esther, Karen H. Jobes

Job, John H. Walton

Psalms Volume 1, Gerald H. Wilson

Psalms Volume 2, W. Dennis Tucker Jr. and Jamie A. Grant

Proverbs, Paul E. Koptak

Ecclesiastes, Song of Songs, Iain Provan

Isaiah, John N. Oswalt

Jeremiah, Lamentations,
J. Andrew Dearman

Ezekiel, Iain M. Duguid

Daniel, Tremper Longman III

Hosea, Amos, Micah, Gary V. Smith

Jonah, Nahum, Habakkuk, Zephaniah,
James Bruckner

Joel, Obadiah, Malachi, David W. Baker

Haggai, Zechariah, Mark J. Boda

New Testament Volumes

Matthew, Michael J. Wilkins

Mark, David E. Garland

Luke, Darrell L. Bock

John, Gary M. Burge

Acts, Ajith Fernando

Romans, Douglas J. Moo

1 Corinthians, Craig L. Blomberg

2 Corinthians, Scott J. Hafemann

Galatians, Scot McKnight

Ephesians, Klyne Snodgrass

Philippians, Frank Thielman

Colossians, Philemon, David E. Garland

1 and 2 Thessalonians,
Michael W. Holmes

1 and 2 Timothy, Titus,
Walter L. Liefeld

Hebrews, George H. Guthrie

James, David P. Nystrom

1 Peter, Scot McKnight

2 Peter, Jude, Douglas J. Moo

Letters of John, Gary M. Burge

Revelation, Craig S. Keener

NIV Application Commentary
Series Introduction

THE NIV APPLICATION COMMENTARY SERIES is unique. Most commentaries help us make the journey from our world back to the world of the Bible. They enable us to cross the barriers of time, culture, language, and geography that separate us from the biblical world. Yet they only offer a one-way ticket to the past and assume that we can somehow make the return journey on our own. Once they have explained the *original meaning* of a book or passage, these commentaries give us little or no help in exploring its *contemporary significance*. The information they offer is valuable, but the job is only half done.

Recently, a few commentaries have included some contemporary application as *one* of their goals. Yet that application is often sketchy or moralistic, and some volumes sound more like printed sermons than commentaries.

The primary goal of the NIV Application Commentary Series is to help you with the difficult but vital task of bringing an ancient message into a modern context. The series not only focuses on application as a finished product but also helps you think through the *process* of moving from the original meaning of a passage to its contemporary significance. These are commentaries, not popular expositions. They are works of reference, not devotional literature.

The format of the series is designed to achieve the goals of the series. Each passage is treated in three sections: *Original Meaning*, *Bridging Contexts*, and *Contemporary Significance*.

Original Meaning

THIS SECTION HELPS you understand the meaning of the biblical text in its original context. All of the elements of traditional exegesis—in concise form—are discussed here. These include the historical, literary, and cultural context of the passage. The authors discuss matters related to grammar and syntax and the meaning of biblical words.[1] They also seek to explore the main ideas of the passage and how the biblical author develops those ideas.

1. Please note that in general, when the authors discuss words in the original bibilical languages, the series uses a general rather than a scholarly method of transliteration.

After reading this section, you will understand the problems, questions, and concerns of the *original audience* and how the biblical author addressed those issues. This understanding is foundational to any legitimate application of the text today.

Bridging Contexts

THIS SECTION BUILDS a bridge between the world of the Bible and the world of today, between the original context and the contemporary context, by focusing on both the timely and timeless aspects of the text.

God's Word is *timely*. The authors of Scripture spoke to specific situations, problems, and questions. The author of Joshua encouraged the faith of his original readers by narrating the destruction of Jericho, a seemingly impregnable city, at the hands of an angry warrior God (Josh. 6). Paul warned the Galatians about the consequences of circumcision and the dangers of trying to be justified by law (Gal. 5:2–5). The author of Hebrews tried to convince his readers that Christ is superior to Moses, the Aaronic priests, and the Old Testament sacrifices. John urged his readers to "test the spirits" of those who taught a form of incipient Gnosticism (1 John 4:1–6). In each of these cases, the timely nature of Scripture enables us to hear God's Word in situations that were *concrete* rather than abstract.

Yet the timely nature of Scripture also creates problems. Our situations, difficulties, and questions are not always directly related to those faced by the people in the Bible. Therefore, God's word to them does not always seem relevant to us. For example, when was the last time someone urged you to be circumcised, claiming that it was a necessary part of justification? How many people today care whether Christ is superior to the Aaronic priests? And how can a "test" designed to expose incipient Gnosticism be of any value in a modern culture?

Fortunately, Scripture is not only timely but *timeless*. Just as God spoke to the original audience, so he still speaks to us through the pages of Scripture. Because we share a common humanity with the people of the Bible, we discover a *universal dimension* in the problems they faced and the solutions God gave them. The timeless nature of Scripture enables it to speak with power in every time and in every culture.

Those who fail to recognize that Scripture is both timely and timeless run into a host of problems. For example, those who are intimidated by timely books such as Hebrews, Galatians, or Deuteronomy might avoid reading them because they seem meaningless today. At the other extreme, those who are convinced of the timeless nature of Scripture, but who fail to discern its timely element, may "wax eloquent" about the Melchizedekian priesthood to a sleeping congregation, or worse still, try to apply the holy wars of the Old Testament in a physical way to God's enemies today.

The purpose of this section, therefore, is to help you discern what is timeless in the timely pages of the Bible—and what is not. For example, how do the holy wars of the Old Testament relate to the spiritual warfare of the New? If Paul's primary concern is not circumcision (as he tells us in Gal. 5:6), what *is* he concerned about? If discussions about the Aaronic priesthood or Melchizedek seem irrelevant today, what is of abiding value in these passages? If people try to "test the spirits" today with a test designed for a specific first-century heresy, what other biblical test might be more appropriate?

Yet this section does not merely uncover that which is timeless in a passage but also helps you to see *how* it is uncovered. The authors of the commentaries seek to take what is implicit in the text and make it explicit, to take a process that normally is intuitive and explain it in a logical, orderly fashion. How do we know that circumcision is not Paul's primary concern? What clues in the text or its context help us realize that Paul's real concern is at a deeper level?

Of course, those passages in which the historical distance between us and the original readers is greatest require a longer treatment. Conversely, those passages in which the historical distance is smaller or seemingly nonexistent require less attention.

One final clarification. Because this section prepares the way for discussing the contemporary significance of the passage, there is not always a sharp distinction or a clear break between this section and the one that follows. Yet when both sections are read together, you should have a strong sense of moving from the world of the Bible to the world of today.

Contemporary Significance

THIS SECTION ALLOWS the biblical message to speak with as much power today as it did when it was first written. How can you apply what you learned about Jerusalem, Ephesus, or Corinth to our present-day needs in Toronto, Chicago, Los Angeles, or London? How can you take a message originally spoken in Greek, Hebrew, and Aramaic and communicate it clearly in our own language? How can you take the eternal truths originally spoken in a different time and culture and apply them to the similar-yet-different needs of our culture?

In order to achieve these goals, this section gives you help in several key areas.

(1) It helps you identify contemporary situations, problems, or questions that are truly comparable to those faced by the original audience. Because contemporary situations are seldom identical to those faced by the original audience, you must seek situations that are analogous if your applications are to be relevant.

(2) This section explores a variety of contexts in which the passage might be applied today. You will look at personal applications, but you will also be encouraged to think beyond private concerns to the society and culture at large.

(3) This section will alert you to any problems or difficulties you might encounter in seeking to apply the passage. And if there are several legitimate ways to apply a passage (areas in which Christians disagree), the author will bring these to your attention and help you think through the issues involved.

In seeking to achieve these goals, the contributors to this series attempt to avoid two extremes. They avoid making such specific applications that the commentary might quickly become dated. They also avoid discussing the significance of the passage in such a general way that it fails to engage contemporary life and culture.

Above all, contributors to this series have made a diligent effort not to sound moralistic or preachy. The NIV Application Commentary Series does not seek to provide ready-made sermon materials but rather tools, ideas, and insights that will help you communicate God's Word with power. If we help you to achieve that goal, then we have fulfilled the purpose for this series.

The Editors

General Editor's Preface

BEING A PROPHET IS COUNTERINTUITIVE. It means unquestioning obedience to God by saying unpopular things that usually leads to persecution from powerful people. Consider Haggai. On September 1, 520 B.C., God told him to go and confront his fellow Jews with their sluggishness in rebuilding the temple after returning from captivity. He went to the prince, Zerubbabel, and the high priest, Joshua. His compatriot, Zechariah, perhaps inspired by Haggai's courage, joined in the prophetic task two months later. Their basic message was: "You seem to have all the energy you need to build your own houses, but the temple, Yahweh's house, still lies in blackened ruins. Let's get busy."

Intriguingly, these confrontational messages didn't sow discord. They brought comfort. As Mark Boda shows us in his excellent commentary, the overall response of the leaders and the people to the prophets' calls to get busy and get connected with God again was action and renewed relationships. That result was counterintuitive also. How and why can a message so untactful, so politically incorrect, so socially inappropriate (at least by the standards of so-called civil society) produce such positive results? The temple got built, and the people were restored—personally, communally, and spiritually.

If both being a prophet and the results of prophetic work are counterintuitive, perhaps the problem is with our intuition. Perhaps we are not reading the signs right. Perhaps we do not have ears to hear. Perhaps we are not speaking the word of the Lord but are spouting conventional wisdom. Perhaps.

It may just be possible, however, that prophetic work and the results of prophecy are supposed to be counterintuitive. After all, not everyone is called to be a prophet. If the sociology of the Old Testament is any indication, it appears that prophets are odd ducks, a rare breed of religious fanatics who appear in certain times in certain places, do their thing, and then disappear again. We are all called to be missionaries of the word, but how long has it been since you met someone who was sure his or her calling was to be a prophet?

One way to make the uniqueness of the prophetic task more clear is to look at the question in modern terms. That is, let's consider this question: Who might be modern-day candidates for prophethood?

How about corporate whistleblowers? These are people who not only discover illegal behavior on the part of the corporations they work for (unfortunately, not too difficult a task these days) but decide to risk their careers by going public with their knowledge. Officially we endorse this behavior and try to protect such people through our laws. But do we succeed? Do we really like what they do? We sometimes are more sympathetic with the leaders who fall (there but for the grace of God go I) than the more moral whistleblowers. Can you name one of the whistleblowers of the last two or three years? So are whistleblowers prophets? It seems there is more to prophethood than merely the courage to act on moral indignation.

How about the leaders of various regulating agencies and groups? When Ralph Nadar fought for seatbelt laws, he wasn't combating illegalities but human ignorance. People's refusal to do what was good for them—or their persistence in continuing harmful behavior—was the problem he addressed. Is it a function of prophetic behavior to save us from our follies? Do we first need to ask about the relationship between our so-called follies and God's will?

And what about activists such as those concerned with degrading our environment? These are people who chose to address patterns of long-term, failed policies. We are using up our natural resources at unacceptable rates. Yet because that rate of consumption is part of what makes our lives so materially comfortable, we are as a society reluctant to cut back. Activists call us to do just that. Does this make them prophets?

There is more to being a prophet than doing what a group of people thinks is good. Prophets must do what *God* thinks is good—and what God calls them to do. Prophets aren't just doers of the Word—they must first be hearers of the Word. Like Haggai and Zechariah.

Terry C. Muck

Author's Preface

IT WAS WHILE I WAS DEVELOPING a hermeneutics course a decade ago in my first teaching post that I found a fascinating book by Stephen Fowl and Gregory Jones entitled *Reading in Communion: Scripture and Ethics in Christian Life*. As their title suggests, they challenged me, among other things, to move beyond a modern approach to interpretation with its focus on the centered self to one that seriously considers the role of the community. Now at the end of the long process of interpreting the books of Haggai and Zechariah, I can look back and say that this commentary is indeed the product of reading in communion.

My first serious encounter with the book of Zechariah was in my second year at Westminster Theological Seminary, where I sat under the teaching of the late Ray Dillard in his course on the Prophets, in which he focused his Hebrew translation on the early chapters of Zechariah. Since I also had a pastoral charge at the time, I was forced by time constraints to take his translations and interpret them immediately for my faith community in Flourtown, Pennsylvania. In many ways this early task of moving between scholarly reflection and contemporary application set the tone for the results you will find in this volume, but little did I know it was just the beginning.

I have taken seriously the role of the academic guild to sharpen my interpretations. As a result, I have read papers at various scholarly conferences and seminars (Society of Biblical Literature Regional, National, and International conferences, European Association of Biblical Studies, McMaster Theological Research Seminar), published articles in various peer-reviewed journals and volumes, and sponsored colloquia focused on the study of Haggai and Zechariah. Through these academic activities I have met countless people from graduate students to professors emeriti who have become iron to sharpen the iron of my ideas. I am especially thankful to friends like Michael Floyd, Lis Fried, John Kessler, Rex Mason, Paul Redditt, Wolter Rose, Al Wolters, and many more, who took the time to consider my ideas and offer their encouraging affirmations as well as gentle critique.

My reading has also taken place within communities of learning at a variety of educational institutions where I have had the privilege of teaching courses focused in varying degrees on Haggai and Zechariah, including Canadian Bible College (the infamous "supervisions"), Canadian Theological Seminary, Edmonton Baptist Seminary, ACTS at Trinity Western University, Asbury Theological Seminary, and McMaster Divinity College. In these communities students and faculty alike have challenged me to sharpen my exegesis and interpretation as well as to struggle with the relevance of these texts to our contemporary context. My two host institutions, Canadian Bible College/Canadian Theological Seminary and McMaster Divinity College, provided the research time and support that made this project possible. I am grateful to the Board of Governors and Trustees at these two institutions for their affirmation of research and writing. Through these institutions I was offered the resource of superb research assistants who have ordered and retrieved numerous articles and books and pored over later drafts of this book. This illustrious group includes Ken Symes, Mandy Ralph, and Joel Barker.

An essential part of the process of writing this commentary has been the opportunity to preach these texts in local churches. I am grateful to congregations in Regina, Saskatchewan (Pine Park, Hillsdale, Living Hope, Westside), Strathmore, Alberta (Strathmore Alliance), and Burlington, Ontario (North Burlington Baptist) for the opportunity to interpret in their faith communities. Furthermore, two young Canadian prairie pastors, Michael Yager (Alberta) and T. Earl Rysavy (Saskatchewan), did me a great service when they agreed to preach from my commentary notes in their early draft form.

As the manuscript reached its final stages, it was strengthened by two fine editors at Zondervan. Robert Hubbard's encouraging and challenging comments on the manuscript made the final product much stronger. Verlyn Verbrugge's suggestions helped shape the manuscript into a commentary useful for contemporary audiences.

There is one community of interpretation that lies at the core of my life, my own family. My three boys, David, Stephen, and Matthew, and especially my wife, Beth, created a space of safety and love in which I could joyfully live, reflect, and write.

Finally, I turn to those who shaped the first interpreting community I knew in this world—my parents, Rexford and Jean Boda. Within the application section of this commentary you will find many experiences that have been drawn from my life with these two godly people (and their tribe of seven children), who first awakened me to love the God of the Scriptures and to seek him through study and prayer. I dedicate this commentary to them for their faithful service to family, culture, and kingdom for over half a century.

Mark Boda
Hamilton, Ontario, Canada
April 14, 2004

Ego ex eorum numero me esse profiteor qui scribunt proficiendo, & scribendo proficiunt.

Augustine, *Letters* 153.2, via
Ioannes Calvinus

Abbreviations

AB	Anchor Bible
ABD	*Anchor Bible Dictionary*
ABR	*Australian Biblical Review*
ABL	*Assyrian and Babylonian Letters*, ed. R.F. Harper (14 vols.)
AJSL	*American Journal of Semitic Languages and Literature*
ANET	J. Pritchard, ed., *Ancient Near Eastern Texts Relating to the Old Testament*, 3d ed.
ATANT	Abhandlungen zur Theologie des Alten und Neuen Testaments
ATD	Das Alte Testament Deutsch
AUMSR	Andrews University Monographs: Studies in Religion
AUSS	*Andrews University Seminary Studies*
BASOR	*Bulletin of the American Schools of Oriental Research*
BHS	*Biblia Hebraica Stuttgartensia*
Bib	*Biblica*
BibOr	Biblica et orientalia
BSac	*Bibliotheca sacra*
BKAT	Biblischer Kommentar: Altes Testament
BRev	*Bible Review*
BST	Bible Speaks Today
BT	*Bible Translator*
BTB	*Biblical Theology Bulletin*
BZ	*Biblische Zeitschrift*
BZAW	Beihefte zur Zeitschrift für die alttestamentliche Wissenschaft
CAH	Cambridge Ancient History
CBC	Cambridge Bible Commentary
CBET	Contributions to Biblical Exegesis and Theology
CBQ	*Catholic Biblical Quarterly*
CC	Continental Commentaries
ch(s).	chapter(s)
cf.	*confer* (compare)
CurBR	*Currents in Biblical Research*
CurBS	*Currents in Research: Biblical Studies*
DBI	*Dictionary of Biblical Imagery*, ed. L. Ryken, J. C. Wilhoit, and T. Longman III

EBC	*Expositor's Bible Commentary*
ed(s).	editor(s)
ErIsr	*Eretz-Israel*
et al.	*et alii*, and others
EvQ	*Evangelical Quarterly*
ExpTim	*Expository Times*
GKC	*Gesenius' Hebrew Grammar*, ed. E. Kautzsch, trans. A. E. Cowley
GTJ	*Grace Theological Journal*
HAR	*Hebrew Annual Review*
HAT	Handbuch zum Alten Testament
HBT	*Horizons in Biblical Theology*
HeyJ	*Heythrop Journal*
HKAT	Handkommentar zum Alten Testament
HSM	Harvard Semitic Monographs
HSS	Harvard Semitic Studies
HTR	*Harvard Theological Review*
IBC	Interpretation: A Bible Commentary for Teaching and Preaching
IBHS	*An Introduction to Biblical Hebrew Syntax*, B. K. Waltke and M. O'Connor, eds.
ICC	International Critical Commentary
IDB	*Interpreter's Dictionary of the Bible*
IDBSup	*Interpreter's Dictionary of the Bible: Supplementary Volume*, ed. K. Crim
IEJ	*Israel Exploration Journal*
Int	*Interpretation*
ITC	International Theological Commentary
JANES	*Journal of the Ancient Near Eastern Society*
JAOS	*Journal of the American Oriental Society*
JBL	*Journal of Biblical Literature*
JETS	*Journal of the Evangelical Theological Society*
JHS	*Journal of Hebrew Scriptures*
JJS	*Journal of Jewish Studies*
JNES	*Journal of Near Eastern Studies*
JNSL	*Journal of Northwest Semitic Languages*
JSJ	*Journal for the Study of Judaism in the Persian, Hellenistic and Roman Periods*
JSJSup	Journal for the Study of Judaism Supplements
JSNTSup	Journal for the Study of the New Testament: Supplement Series
JSOT	*Journal for the Study of the Old Testament*

JSOTSup Journal for the Study of the Old Testament: Supplement Series
JSS *Journal of Semitic Studies*
JTS *Journal of Theological Studies*
KAT Kommentar zum Alten Testament
LXX Septuagint
m. *Mishnah*
MT Masoretic Text
n. note
NAC New American Commentary
NCB New Century Bible
NIB *New Interpreter's Bible*, ed. L. Keck, et al.
NIBC New International Biblical Commentary
NICNT New International Commentary on the New Testament
NICOT New International Commentary on the Old Testament
NIDOTTE *New International Dictionary of Old Testament Theology and Exegesis*, ed. W. VanGemeren
NIV New International Version
NIVAC NIV Application Commentary
NovT *Novum Testamentum*
NovTSup Novum Testamentum Supplements
NRSV New Revised Standard Version
NTTS New Testament Tools and Studies
OBT Overtures to Biblical Theology
OTE *Old Testament Essays*
OTG Old Testament Guides
OTL Old Testament Library
OTM Oxford Theological Monographs
OtSt *Oudtestamentische Studiën*
RB *Revue biblique*
RevExp *Review and Expositor*
RHR *Revue de l'histoire des religions*
RTR *Reformed Theological Review*
SBLABS Society of Biblical Literature Archaeology and Biblical Studies
SBLDS Society of Biblical Literature Dissertation Series
SBLEJL Society of Biblical Literature Early Judaism and Its Literature
SBLSP *Society of Biblical Literature Seminar Papers*
SBLMS Society of Biblical Literature Monograph Series
SBLSymS Society of Biblical Literature Symposium Series

ScrHier	Scripta Hierosolymitana
SHANE	Studies in the History of the Ancient Near East
SJOT	*Scandinavian Journal of the Old Testament*
SLJT	*St. Luke's Journal of Theology*
SOTBT	Studies in Old Testament Biblical Theology
TDOT	*Theological Dictionary of the Old Testament*, ed. G. J. Botterweck and H. Ringgren
TLOT	*Theological Lexicon of the Old Testament*, ed. E. Jenni and C. Westermann
TOTC	Tyndale Old Testament Commentaries
trans.	translation/translated by
TrinJ	*Trinity Journal*
TWOT	*A Theological Wordbook of the Old Testament*, ed. R. L. Harris, G. L. Archer, and B. K. Waltke
TynBul	*Tyndale Bulletin*
v(v).	verse(s)
VT	*Vetus Testamentum*
VTSup	Vetus Testamentum Supplements
WBC	Word Biblical Commentary
WMANT	Wissenschaftliche Monographien zum Alten und Neuen Testament
ZAW	*Zeitschrift für die alttestamentliche Wissenschaft*
ZWT	*Zeitschrift für wissenschaftliche Theologie*

Introduction to Haggai and Zechariah

IN HIS 1956 BOOK *Everyday Life in Old Testament Times*, E. W. Heaton provides an artistic illustration of the exiles of Judah marching under armed Babylonian guard through the famous Ishtar gate of Babylon.[1] Underneath the picture is the caption: "The Closing Scene of Old Testament Times: The Babylon of Nebuchadnezzar."[2] This title captures the sentiments of many readers of the Old Testament, that after the destruction of Jerusalem the story of redemption fades into the haze of exile only to reappear with the birth of Christ in the New Testament. There is no question that most of the events of Israel that are fixed in the cultural consciousness of the church happened prior to the fall of Jerusalem in 587 B.C.,[3] such as the call of Abraham, the rise of Joseph, the exploits of Samson, the victories of David, or the proclamations of Elijah.

The period in which Haggai and Zechariah lived and ministered, therefore, does not receive much attention in Christian circles. A preference for the earlier stories of Israel is apparent for several reasons. (1) With the fall of Jerusalem in 587 B.C. the Israelites did not regain independence from foreign powers until the Maccabean revolt. Even the province in which part of the Jewish remnant lived was a mere fraction of its size under David and Solomon. This does not make for great storytelling, although Daniel and Esther enjoy some popularity.

(2) The New Testament accounts of Jesus and Paul portray the leadership of the Jews (the Sadducees, Pharisees, and teachers of the law) in a negative light. These various groups arose in the period between the Babylonian destruction of Jerusalem and the birth of Christ, and thus the literature from this period is read through the lens of the New Testament critique of these groups. Books like Ezra and Nehemiah are disparaged for their close attention to the law.

1. I am thankful to P. R. Ackroyd for drawing my attention to this book; P. R. Ackroyd, *Exile and Restoration: A Study of Hebrew Thought of the Sixth Century B.C.* (OTL; Philadelphia: Westminster, 1968), 1.

2. E. W. Heaton, *Everyday Life in Old Testament Times* (New York: Scribner, 1956), 26.

3. For debate over whether Jerusalem fell in 587 or 586 B.C. see G. Galil, *The Chronology of the Kings of Israel and Judah* (SHANE 9; Leiden: Brill, 1996); G. Galil, "The Babylonian Calendar and the Chronology of the last Kings of Judah," *Bib* 72 (1991): 367–78; A. R. Green, "The Chronology of the Last Days of Judah: Two Apparent Discrepancies," *JBL* 101 (1982): 52–73.

(3) The rebuilding of the temple and the city of Jerusalem is seen as odd in light of Christ's coming. Why rebuild the temple only to have it rejected by Christ in his ministry?

These factors introduce us to some of the major hurdles for preaching and teaching on Haggai and Zechariah. In order to appropriate the rich theology of these books for contemporary audiences, we need to overcome these challenges. The purpose of this introduction is to provide historical-literary, biblical-theological, and contemporary orientation for the interpreter of Haggai and Zechariah. We will begin with a basic orientation to the history and literature of these books, ending with a summary of the basic theological message to their ancient audience (Original Meaning). Then we will offer a biblical-theological orientation so that Christian readers can appropriate the truth of Haggai and Zechariah for their lives today (Bridging Contexts). Finally, we will survey key implications of the theology of Haggai and Zechariah for church and society today (Contemporary Significance). In this way my desire is to strike a balance between history and theology, always sensitive to the fact that the theological truth of the Scriptures has been delivered within particular historical contexts through particular literary forms.

Original Meaning

BECAUSE THE PREVAILING historical approach to the Scriptures in the modern era has often turned the Bible into a museum piece, theologians are increasingly abandoning historical context in their search for theological truth. This shift is challenged in Tom Wright's parody of the prodigal son, in which the prodigal is the historical study of the Bible. Wright attacks theologians who have taken "off their historical sandals lest they tread on holy ground" and reminds us that "stripped of its arrogance, its desire to make off with half of the patrimony and never be seen again, history belongs at the family table. If theology, the older brother, pretends not to need or notice him it will be a sign that he has forgotten, after all, who his father is."[4] It will become evident throughout the commentary that I utilize a three-dimensional hermeneutic, one that seeks to interpret these texts in their ancient context (historical dimension) with sensitivity to their message encased in literary form (literary dimension), but also as texts with a relevant message appropriated by contemporary readers seeking to interpret and live faithfully as Christians (contemporary dimension). In this

4. N. T. Wright, *Jesus and the Victory of God* (Christian Origins and the Question of God 2; Minneapolis: Fortress, 1996), 661.

way my desire is to strike a balance between history and theology, always sensitive to the fact that the theological truth of the Scriptures has been delivered within particular historical contexts through particular literary forms

A. History of the Early Persian Period

NABONIDUS, ONE of the last emperors of Babylon, records a dream in which he receives instruction from the god Marduk to go to his mother's temple in Haran (which was under the control of the Medes) and rebuild it:

> In the beginning of my everlasting reign he made me to see a vision. Marduk, the great lord, and Sin, the light of heaven and earth, stood on either side. Marduk said to me: "Nabonidus, King of Babylon, haul bricks with your wagon-horses, rebuild E-hul-hul, and make Sin, the great lord, to take up his residence therein." Reverently I spoke to the lord of the gods, Marduk: "The Medes have encompassed that house, which you did command to rebuild, and their forces are mighty." But Marduk said to me: "The Medes of whom you have spoken—they, their country, and the kings who marched with them are no more." On the approach of the third year they instigated Cyrus, King of Anzan, his petty vassal, to attack them, and with his few troops he routed the numerous Medes. He seized Astyages, King of the Medes, and took him as a captive to his own country. (It was) the word of the great lord, Marduk, and Sin, the light of heaven and earth, whose command can not be annulled.[5]

This dream assembles a fascinating trio of leaders who rose to prominence in the final phase of the Neo-Babylonian empire in mid–sixth century B.C.: Nabonidus of Babylon, Astyages of Media, and Cyrus of Persia. To set the stage for this dream and the impact of these characters on the Jewish community, we need to return to the beginning of the sixth century and the reign of an earlier Babylonian emperor, Nebuchadnezzar.

Probably the ancient emperor most familiar to us is Nebuchadnezzar, ruler of the Neo-Babylonian empire from 605–562 B.C.[6] His father, Nabopolassar (626–605), in concert with Cyaxares of Media (625–585), wrested control of the ancient Near East from the Assyrians during an extended struggle that

5. R. F. Harper, "Inscription of a Clay Cylinder of Nabonidus," in *ABL*, ed. R. F. Harper (New York: D. Appleton and Company, 1901), 163–68, with slight revisions.

6. For details of this history see further H. W. F. Saggs, *The Might That Was Assyria*, rev. ed. (London: Sidgwick & Jackson, 1984); idem, *The Greatness That Was Babylon: A Survey of the Ancient Civilization of the Tigris-Euphrates Valley*, rev. ed. (London: Sidgwick & Jackson, 1988); P. A. Beaulieu, *The Reign of Nabonidus, King of Babylon 556–539 B.C.* (Yale Near Eastern

began in earnest with a three-month siege of Nineveh in 612. The following decade saw intense competition between the Babylonian-Median alliance and the Egypto-Assyrian coalition for supremacy in western Asia, with the Assyrians operating out of Haran, culminating in a famous battle at Carchemish in 609. The newly crowned Pharaoh Necho II had marched north to help the Assyrians retake Haran, but at Carchemish met the superior might of the Babylonian army.

The Babylonians, led by Nebuchadnezzar, routed the Egyptians first at Carchemish and soon after at Hamath. At that time Nebuchadnezzar received word that his father had died, so he returned to Babylon to secure the throne. Then he returned to his war along the Mediterranean coast, took the Philistine territory, and by the end of 601 B.C. pushed his way to the border of Egypt. A valiant Egyptian military force stopped him there.

The record of the reigns of the final kings of Judah reveals the impact of these larger movements on the ancient Near Eastern scene. King Josiah foolishly challenged Necho on his way to Carchemish in 609 B.C. and was killed in the battle (2 Kings 23:29–30). Necho's brief control of western Asia (609–605) is reflected in his punishment of Josiah's son Jehoahaz (23:32, 34) and the promotion of his brother Jehoiakim (Eliakim; 23:33, 35). Babylonian successes against Necho in 605 and the ensuing battles between the two world powers are reflected in Jehoiakim's vacillation in allegiance, beginning under Necho, then switching to Nebuchadnezzar (24:1a), back to the Egyptians (24:1b), before being bullied by Babylonian allies (24:2–6). After Nebuchadnezzar marched to the border of Egypt (24:7), Jehoiakim died, leaving his son Jehoiachin to face the fury of the Babylonian monarch, who besieged Jerusalem, deported its leadership, and placed Zedekiah on the throne in 598 (24:8–17). Zedekiah's disloyalty to Nebuchadnezzar, however, prompted his return in 587 to destroy the city (ch. 25).

These events had a devastating effect on the Jewish people. Many were killed, some fled to surrounding nations, some were exiled to Mesopotamia, while others remained in the land. Such disarray rendered doubtful any national hopes for the Jewish people.

Researches 10; New Haven, Conn.: Yale Univ. Press, 1989); J. Boardman et al., eds., *Persia, Greece and the Western Mediterranean c. 525 to 479 B.C.*, 2d ed. (CAH 4; Cambridge: Cambridge Univ. Press, 1988); J. Boardman et al., eds., *The Assyrian and Babylonian Empires and Other States of the Near East, from the Eighth to the Sixth Centuries B.C.* (CAH 3/2: Cambridge: Cambridge Univ. Press, 1991); I. Gershevitch, S. I. Grossman, and H. S. G. Darke, *The Cambridge History of Iran: The Median and Achamenian Periods* (Cambridge: Cambridge Univ. Press, 1993); P. Briant, *From Cyrus to Alexander: A History of the Persian Empire,* trans. P. T. Daniels (Winona Lake, Ind.: Eisenbrauns, 2002).

Nebuchadnezzar ruled the ancient Near East until 562 B.C., but as is typical in the ancient world, greatness is followed by upheaval as three different kings reigned in the short space of 562–556: Nebuchadnezzar's son Amel-Marduk (Evil-Merodach, 2 Kings 25:27–30), followed by Neriglissar (Amel-Marduk's brother-in-law), and finally Neriglissar's son Labashi-Marduk.

Such upheaval threatened the integrity of the empire, setting the stage for a strong leader. That man would be Nabonidus, who arose from the military ranks of the Babylonian army and whose dream was recorded at the outset of our discussion. As the dream indicates, when Nabonidus assumed power in 556 B.C. Astyages ruled as king in Media with control over the lesser kingdom of his grandson Cyrus in Persia. By 553, however, Cyrus revolted against Astyages, an action celebrated by Nabonidus because it freed him to rebuild his mother's temple in Haran. During the next decade, Nabonidus installed his son Belshazzar as king in Babylon and moved his base of operations to the oasis of Teima in the Arabian desert. This action led to dissatisfaction among the populace in Babylon, especially among the priests of Marduk, whose New Year's festival could not be held without the emperor.

While Nabonidus was in Teima, Cyrus was busy acquiring territory on the fringes of the Babylonian empire. In 547/546 B.C. he extended the former Median territories to the west, crossed the Halys river, and took control of Lydia from King Croesus, who was in alliance with Nabonidus. Then he turned to the east and extended his control to the Jaxartes river.

These actions prompted Nabonidus's return to Babylon, but the situation was grave. In the final months of his rule the emperor transported many gods to Babylon, enraging the priests of the various shrines in southern Mesopotamia. Although he did participate in the New Year's festival upon his return, his relationship with the priests was irreparable. In 539 B.C. Cyrus moved across the Zagros mountains, forded the Tigris at Opis, and marched with little resistance into Babylonia (see Dan. 5, esp. v. 39). At least in his mind, if not in reality, Cyrus was welcomed into the city of Babylon more as a liberator than a conqueror and assumed the territories of the Babylonians. A new day had dawned in the ancient Near East.

A key record of Cyrus's triumph over Babylon is recorded on a clay barrel called the Cyrus Cylinder, found in an archaeological expedition in Mesopotamia. In it he claims that Marduk raised him up to conquer Babylon and that he did so to the delight of its citizens. This resulted in the submission of rulers throughout the Babylonian empire who came to Babylon to bow before Cyrus. Key to Israel's destiny was his immediate move to reconstruct sanctuaries for the gods of his conquered nations and along with this to return their former inhabitants to their lands:

> ... As to the region from as far as Ashur and Susa, Agade, Eshnunna, the towns of Zamban, Me-Turnu, Der as well as the region of the Gutians, I returned to these sanctuaries on the other side of the Tigris, the sanctuaries of which had been ruins for a long time, the images which used to live therein and established for them permanent sanctuaries. I also gathered all their former inhabitants and returned to them their habitations. Furthermore, I resettled upon the command of Marduk, the great lord, all the gods of Sumer and Akkad whom Nabonidus had brought into Babylon to the anger of the lord of the gods, unharmed, in their former chapels, the places which make them happy. May all the gods whom I have resettled in their sacred cities ask daily Bel and Nebo for a long life for me and may they recommend me to him; to Marduk, my lord, they may say this: "Cyrus, the king who worships you, and Cambyses, his son *[lacuna]*." All gods I settled in a peaceful place.... I endeavoured to fortify/repair their dwelling places.[7]

This text attests Cyrus's claim not only to a peaceful transition from Babylonian to Persian rule, but also highlights his shrewd politico-religious policies through which (he claims) he won the allegiance of the population.[8]

The mention of Cyrus in Isaiah 44:28; 45:1; 45:13 reveals the high expectations associated with him among the exilic Jewish community. Although the Cyrus Cylinder does not mention the exiled Jewish people in particular, it details the kind of policies reflected in Jewish writings of this period, especially in the proclamation of Cyrus in Ezra 1:1–4 (cf. 2 Chron. 36:22–23) and decree of Cyrus in Ezra 6:1–5.[9] Ezra 1 describes an early response to Cyrus's policies as a group of Jews returned to Palestine under the leadership of Sheshbazzar (539–537 B.C.). These Jews transported temple utensils that had been confiscated by Nebuchadnezzar in 587 B.C. and had been stored in a temple in Babylon (Ezra 1:9–11; 5:13–14) and "laid the foundations of the house of God" (Ezra 5:15–16).

Cyrus did not rule for long over his expansive realm. He was killed in 530 B.C. on a military expedition on the eastern frontier of the empire and with his

7. *ANET*, 315–16, with minor revisions.

8. On the veracity of this claim see M. J. Boda, "Terrifying the Horns: Persia and Babylon in Zechariah 1:7–6:15," *CBQ* 67 (2005): forthcoming.

9. The first is written in Hebrew, the second in Aramaic. The first is more like a modern press release, while the second is the legal memorandum in the Persian archives; H. G. M. Williamson, *Ezra, Nehemiah* (WBC 16; Waco, Tex.: Word, 1985), 6–7; also more recently, idem, "Exile and After: Historical Study," in *The Face of Old Testament Studies: A Survey of Contemporary Approaches*, ed. D. W. Baker and B. T. Arnold (Grand Rapids: Baker, 1999), 236–65.

death rule was transferred to his son Cambyses. The transition was relatively smooth and enabled Cambyses to carry out his father's dream to invade Egypt, incorporating it into the empire in 525. While in Egypt, however, Cambyses' hold on the home front was challenged when in March 522, one of the Magi in the court (Bardiya/Gaumata) rebelled and claimed he was Smerdis, the brother Cambyses had quietly killed before embarking for Egypt. Enticed by a promise of relaxed tax policies, the core of the empire supported this rebellion, forcing Cambyses to return to Mesopotamia. Unfortunately, he would never reach his destination, accidentally wounding himself with his knife en route.

One of Cambyses' generals who was related to the royal family, Darius, assumed control of the Persian army. He returned to Media and, along with "the Seven" (representatives from the seven leading Persian families), conspired against Bardiya/Gaumata and killed him in September 522 B.C.[10] This action set off further rebellions across the empire that consumed much of Darius's energies in the first few years as he consolidated his power.

Rebellions in two areas of the empire are relevant to the study of Haggai and Zechariah. Babylon rebelled immediately under Nidintu-Bel (Nebuchadnezzar III), but this was crushed in December 522 B.C. by Darius himself, who subsequently remained in Babylon until June 521 in order to establish his control. Egypt revolted in 519, prompting Darius's military expedition in 519–518 B.C., which returned Egypt to his dominion. After this Darius moved eastward and took the Indus valley, placing the three major river valleys of the ancient Near East (Nile, Tigris-Euphrates, Indus) under one ruler for the first time in history.

During this period Jews continued to return to Palestine, and in the early years of Darius built an altar, reintroduced sacrificial rites, restored the foundation of the temple, and completed the structure by 515 B.C. (Ezra 2–6). This was accomplished through the benevolent intervention of Darius amidst hostility from others in Palestine (Ezra 5–6).

The temple building activity described in Ezra is clearly in the background of the books of Haggai and Zechariah, which are dated early in Darius's reign (520, 518 B.C.). During this period Zerubbabel, a descendant of David, returned to the land along with the high priest Joshua, a descendant of Zadok. Inspired by the prophets Haggai and Zechariah, these leaders supervised the rebuilding of the temple and restoration of the worship of God in Jerusalem (Ezra 5:1–2).

The recent rebellions in the Persian empire can also be discerned behind the books of Haggai and Zechariah. Although the prophecies in Haggai are dated between the Babylonian and Egyptian revolts (520 B.C.), their vision of

10. T. C. Young, "The Consolidation of the Empire and Its Limits of Growth under Darius and Xerxes," in CAH, 4:54; A. Kuhrt, "Babylonia from Cyrus to Xerxes," in CAH, 4:129.

the reversal of worldly power before the Lord Almighty draws on recent experience that fueled Jewish expectation. The many allusions to Babylon in the visions of Zechariah (Zech. 1:15, 19, 21; 2:6, 7; 5:11; 6:8, 10) must be linked to Darius's repression of revolts in that region in the early years of his reign. Although Cyrus had seized control of Babylon, he did not bring the expected devastation on that city (Ps. 137:8; Isa. 13–14; 47–48; Jer. 25:12–16; 50–51).[11] But because of their rebellion after Cambyses' death, the Babylonians were punished severely by Darius, actions closer to the prophetic expectation. While the books of Chronicles and Ezra link the end of exile and fulfillment of restoration with Cyrus's reign, the visions of Zechariah (520) link them with Darius's actions in 522–521.[12]

The appearance of Zerubbabel and Joshua in the early years of Darius's reign must be related to the latter's concern for the integrity of the empire. The fact that the emperor moved against the Egyptians in 519–518 B.C. suggests that Zerubbabel (and possibly also Joshua) may have been commissioned to restore order in the province of Yehud. Zerubbabel apparently served as governor of Yehud,[13] which lay within the satrapy of Beyond the River. Once rebellions subsided in his empire, Darius restructured the empire politically and encouraged the development of local legal codes within the various provinces.

After 500 B.C. signs of trouble began to appear for Darius, mostly a result of his determination to extend Persian dominion into Europe. Typical of his problems was the famous battle of Marathon in 490, in which he was defeated by the Greeks. Immediately after this a rebellion arose in Egypt (486), but Darius died, passing the throne to his son Xerxes I.

The youthful Xerxes (486–465 B.C.) replicated the early reign of his father, returning Egypt to Persian control and suppressing two rebellions in

---

11. In the Cyrus Cylinder Cyrus declares: "Without any battle, he made him enter his own town Babylon, sparing Babylon any calamity."

12. See R. Albertz, "Darius in Place of Cyrus: The First Edition of Deutero-Isaiah (Isaiah 40.1–52.12) in 521 B.C.E.," *JSOT* 27 (2003): 371–88 on Darius and restoration; cf. Boda, "Horns."

13. Yehud is the name given to the Persian period province that comprised the core of the old kingdom of Judah (southern kingdom). The term "governor" (*peḥah*) is difficult to define in the Persian system, see Briant, *Cyrus*, 65–67, 484–85, 601–2. Drawing from biblical and archaeological sources recent research has demonstrated a continuous line of governors in Yehud from the outset of Persian hegemony; cf. C. L. Meyers and E. M. Meyers, *Haggai, Zechariah 1–8: A New Translation with Introduction and Commentary* (AB 25b; Garden City, N.Y.: Doubleday, 1987); H. G. M. Williamson, "The Governors of Judah under the Persians," *TynBul* 39 (1988): 59–82; D. S. Vanderhooft, "New Evidence Pertaining to the Transition from Neo-Babylonian to Achaemenid Administration in Palestine," in *Yahwism After the Exile: Perspectives on Israelite Religion in the Persian Era,* ed. B. Becking and R. Albertz (Studies in Theology and Religion 5; Assen: Royal Van Gorcum, 2003), 231–33.

Babylon. Also like his father, he had little success with the Greeks in his campaigns in Europe in 480–478. After his vast army defeated the handful of Spartans at the famous battle of Thermopylae, which opened the way for the sack of an empty Athens, his forces, under the direction of his general Mardonius, were defeated at Salamis, Plataea, and Mycale. After these losses Xerxes expended considerable energy on completing his showcase capital Persepolis. He was killed in his sleep by two of his closest officials in 465 and succeeded by his son Artaxerxes I (465–424).

Persian defeats in Europe and rebellions in Babylon and Egypt had an impact on Yehud. Ultimately the Persians established a series of fortresses in and around the province in order to solidify their European and Egyptian interests, but closer control of this key land link between Mesopotamia and Egypt was instituted from the beginning of the fifth century.[14] Zerubbabel's reign came to an end sometime in the last decade of the sixth century (ca. 510 B.C.). There are strong indications in Zechariah 11:4–16 that his tenure ended unsatisfactorily, but archaeological records reveal that he was succeeded by his son-in-law Elnathan, who had married Zerubbabel's daughter Shelomith, therefore extending a leadership role for the Davidic line until around 490.[15] After this point members of the Davidic line were present in Yehud but did not participate in provincial leadership (1 Chron. 3:17–24; Ezra 8:2).

Although the evidence is scanty, there are indications that the Jews who lived in Yehud during the reign of Xerxes and the early part of Artaxerxes' reign experienced much opposition (Ezra 4:6–23). Although they sought to rebuild the city and fortify its walls, all efforts were thwarted by their enemies. Hope, however, was soon on its way, first in the form of a priestly scribe named Ezra, commissioned in 458 B.C. by the emperor to promulgate and administrate a legal code within the province of Yehud (Ezra 7–10; esp. 7:14, 25), and then in the form of a former cupbearer to the emperor named Nehemiah, commissioned in 445 B.C. as governor and empowered to rebuild the wall of Jerusalem (Neh. 1–13).

B. Dating the Prophetic Books

THERE IS LITTLE DEBATE over the dating of Haggai and Zechariah 1–8, with most scholars placing the completion of these sections soon after the dates identified in the superscriptions: that is, the second year of Darius (520 B.C.:

14. K. G. Hoglund, *Achaemenid Imperial Administration in Syria-Palestine and the Mission of Ezra and Nehemiah* (Atlanta: Scholars Press, 1992).

15. Cf. Boda, "Reading," 277–91; E. M. Meyers, "The Shelomith Seal and Aspects of the Judean Restoration: Some Additional Reconsiderations," *ErIsr* 18 (1985): 33*–38*.

Hag. 1:1, 15; 2:1, 10, 23; Zech. 1:1, 7) and the fourth year of Darius (518 B.C.: Zech. 7:1).[16] Meyers and Meyers, for instance, have linked the publication of these books with the dedication of the temple (since the dedication is not mentioned in Hag. 1–2; Zech. 1–8).[17] This conclusion, however, is based on the conviction that these two prophetic sections were a unified body focused on the theme of temple rebuilding. Although most likely Haggai was completed for the foundation-laying ceremony, with a copy of the book encased in the foundation, this does not appear to be the case for Zechariah 1–8. The lack of mention of the completion of the temple in Zechariah 1–8 is most likely due to the fact that Zechariah's interests are far broader than the physical restoration of the temple edifice, including especially the renewal of city and people, physically and spiritually. Nevertheless, there is no reason to date Zechariah 1–8 too long after the completion of the temple.

Dating the various parts of Zechariah 9–14 has been a challenge. These chapters provide no historical superscriptions, and proposals have run from the eighth to the second century B.C.[18] The majority opinion has been that these texts arose in a period after Alexander's Hellenistic subjugation of the ancient Near East (i.e., after 333 B.C.). These arguments were based primarily on a view that the genre of this section arose at a later period (apocalyptic), that the tension lying behind the passage relates to a split between Jews and Samaritans, and that a few key passages reflect incidents from a later period: the picture of conquest in 9:1–8, the mention of Greece in 9:13, the reference to the disposal of three shepherds in one month in 11:8, and the reference to "the one whom they have pierced" in 12:10.

This consensus has been seriously challenged in recent decades, however. The evidence provided above in favor of a date in the Hellenistic period has been called into question. Apocalyptic features in texts need not indicate a late date, nor is the Jew/Samaritan split the first sign of sociological tension in the Persian/Greek period. The evidence from the various passages is not helpful for ascertaining a specific context, as the picture of conquest in 9:1–8 does not fit Alexander's conquest (or any other one we know of). The reference to Greece in 9:13 may be either a later gloss or a metaphorical reference to Phoenicians; even if it is Greece, note that Persia interacted with Greece early in Darius's reign.

---

16. M. J. Boda, "From Fasts to Feasts: The Literary Function of Zechariah 7–8," *CBQ* 65 (2003): 403–4.

17. Meyers and Meyers, *Haggai*, xlv.

18. See the review of literature in A. E. Hill, "Dating Second Zechariah: A Linguistic Reexamination," *HAR* 6 (1982): 105–34, and P. L. Redditt, "Nehemiah's First Mission and the Date of Zechariah 9–14," *CBQ* 56 (1994): 664–78.

In a positive vein, three key works have provided strong reasons to date Zechariah 9–14 in the early Persian period. (1) Hanson's analysis of apocalyptic style concludes that these chapters range from the mid–sixth to the late fourth centuries B.C.[19] (2) Hill's analysis of the language of Zechariah 10–14 shows that the various passages should be dated between 515 and 475 B.C.[20] (3) Redditt's socio-literary arguments that the conflicts described in chapters 9–14 fit the experience of the Jewish community in the province of Yehud in the early Persian period (i.e., from 515 B.C. [Zerubbabel] until 445 B.C. [Nehemiah]) are helpful.

These arguments provide a foundation for my own conclusion that chapters 9–14 arose during the early Persian period (post-515 B.C.). Recently I have argued for the close association between chapters 1–8 and 9–14, noting that chapters 7–8 function as an appropriate segue between chapters 1–6 and chapters 9–14.[21] This confirms that chapters 9–14 originated after the redaction of chapters 7–8, which occurred no sooner than 518 B.C. (cf. 7:1). Zechariah 11:4–16, however, most likely depicts the end of the tenure of Zerubbabel as governor (ca. 510 B.C.) in Yehud and marks the end of a period of increased royal hope for the Davidic house (9:9–10) and of national hope for the reunification of the tribes (chs. 9–10).[22]

The positive prospects for the reunification of north and south (now found in two different Persian provinces, Samaria and Yehud) and for the renewal of the Davidic throne (through Zerubbabel) suggest that the oracles in chapters 9–10 arose in the period between 515 B.C. and the end of Zerubbabel's tenure (ca. 510 B.C.). References to drought in 10:1–3a would fit this early period, as attested in passages like Haggai 1:6, 11; 2:15–19; Zechariah 8:12 (see comments on these passages). Furthermore, allusions to idolatry in Zechariah 10:1–3a (cf. 13:2–3) fit into the earliest part of the Persian period, since idolatry is ultimately eradicated in the Persian period (see comments on 10:1–2).

Crossing into chapters 12–14, there remains hope for the renewal of the Davidic house (12:7–8, 12–13; 13:1), although such renewal will result in

19. Paul D. Hanson, *The Dawn of Apocalyptic* (Philadelphia: Fortress, 1979), 280–401 (esp. 291).

20. Hill, "Dating," 105–34. The statistical research found in Y. T. Radday and D. Wickmann, "Unity of Zechariah Examined in the Light of Statistical Linguistics," *ZAW* 87 (1975): 30–55, suggests that at least part of Zech. 9–14 (at least chs. 9–11) could have arisen from the same source as chs. 1–8. However, this was seriously challenged in S. L. Portnoy and D. L. Petersen, "Biblical Texts and Statistical Analysis: Zechariah and Beyond," *JBL* 103 (1984): 11–21, who concluded that chs. 1–8, 9–11, and 12–14 all evidence different literary styles.

21. Boda, "Fasts to Feasts," 390–407.

22. Boda, "Reading," 277–91.

leadership that empowers the community (12:7–8) and may be related to a non-Zadokite line of priesthood (12:13). Additionally, the world of these two oracles (chs. 12–14) is one in which Jerusalem and its surrounding province are distinguishable and possibly in conflict. Such a distinction would fit a period when Jerusalem's status had become a threat to that of the surrounding province.

Evidence for the elevation of the status of Jerusalem can be culled from two key eras in the early Persian period with the present literary evidence. (1) There is the period between 520 and 510 B.C. as new energy, personnel, and resources were being poured into the temple restoration in Jerusalem, sanctioned by the Persian crown. (2) There is the period following 445 B.C. during Nehemiah's tenure as governor as the city was restored.

Although the earlier period is possible, evidence from Nehemiah suggests that even at this later date the city had not prospered demographically (Neh. 7:4–5), most likely because of the lack of protection around the city and the abundance of destruction. The initiative of the governor to import people into the city from the surrounding province (11:1–2) had the potential of causing tension within this struggling province. Therefore, while Zechariah 9–10 can be placed in 515–510 and chapter 11 along with the shepherd pieces (10:1–3a; 11:1–3, 17; possibly also 13:7–9) in post-510, chapters 12–14 arose sometime after 510, maybe even as late as 445. In such a context the prophet encouraged the community through visions of restoration and renewal while exhorting them to faithfulness and warning against abusive and idolatrous leadership.

C. The Prophets

HAGGAI. LITTLE IS known of this prophet who was so instrumental in the restoration of the Jewish community in the wake of the Babylonian exile. The book of Ezra honors him alongside Zechariah as instrumental in encouraging the community to rebuild the temple (Ezra 5:1–2; 6:14). The book of Haggai also bears witness to this role. Each of his messages is linked in some way to the rebuilding project, whether urging the initiation of building (Hag. 1:1–15), encouraging its continuation (2:1–9), or affirming the completion of a key stage (2:10–23).

Although his name is unique in the Hebrew Bible, the archaeological record reveals its widespread use in the Babylonian period.[23] The name is derived from the Semitic word for "feast" (*ḥag*), an appropriate name for a prophet focused on rebuilding the temple, the context for the main feasts in

23. Meyers and Meyers, *Haggai*, 8–9.

the Jewish calendar. Moreover, each of his messages is delivered on a day associated with a festal or liturgical event (see commentary). The book ends on an eschatological note with great hope for the future as is typical of several prophetic books in the Hebrew Bible (Isa. 66; Hos. 14; Joel 3; Amos 9; Mic. 7; Zeph. 3; Zech. 14).

Zechariah. Ezra 5:1–2; 6:14 presents Zechariah as a prophetic champion of the temple project. The intimate connection between this prophet and the restoration of the temple is discernible within his book. He promises the rebuilding of the temple (Zech. 1:16; 6:12–15), announces the return of God's presence (1:16; 2:5, 10, 13), supports the reinstatement of priestly service (3:1–7; 6:13), envisions temple furnishings (4:1–14; 6:14), and prophesies at the refoundation ceremony with Haggai (4:6b–10a; 8:9–13).[24]

This connection to the temple is not surprising because Zechariah apparently came from priestly stock, heading up an important clan in a later period (Neh. 12:16). His grandfather Iddo returned with Zerubbabel and Joshua around 520 B.C. (12:4), and he himself is linked to the generation of Joshua's son, Joiakim. If this is correct, Zechariah would have been young in 520 B.C. as he began his prophetic career.

For a prophetic voice to arise from a priestly context is not odd (see Jer. 1:1; Ezek. 1:3), for prophets and priests are closely associated in the Babylonian and Persian periods.[25] The role of prophets in the temple context is difficult to delineate in detail, but it appears that one crucial function was to deliver the response of God to the requests of his people (see the books of Joel and Jeremiah; Zech. 7 fills a similar role, where the people come to the temple and make a request of the priests and prophets and Zechariah delivers an oracle).

The overall flow of Zechariah suggests an increasing tension between Zechariah's prophetic community and the leadership in Jerusalem. Although 3:1–10 and 6:9–15 affirm Zadokite priests, affording them significant responsibility in the restoration community, these pericopes carefully circumscribe their role by championing the cause of the royal *ṣemaḥ* (Branch) figure.[26] Concerns over the priesthood come to the fore in chapters 7–8 as Zechariah attacks the present generation, including the priests, for replicating the sins of the past (7:5).[27]

---

24. For this last aspect see B. Halpern, "The Ritual Background of Zechariah's Temple Song," *CBQ* 40 (1978): 167–90.

25. See, e.g., A. R. Johnson, *The Cultic Prophet in Ancient Israel* (Cardiff: Univ. of Wales Press, 1962); cf. M. J. Boda, "From Complaint to Contrition: Peering Through the Liturgical Window of Jer 14,1–15,4," *ZAW* 113 (2001): 186–97.

26. See M. J. Boda, "Oil, Crowns and Thrones: Prophet, Priest and King in Zechariah 1:7—6:15," *JHS* 3 (2001): Art.10.

27. See Boda, "Fasts to Feasts," 390–407.

In Zechariah 9–14 the tension continues as prophecies attack the shepherds of the flock, a reference to leadership closely connected with the Persians.[28] The key prophetic sign-acts in 11:4–16 indicate the community's inappropriate rejection of Davidic leadership and the subsequent appointment of another leader. Zechariah 12:1–13:6 anticipates spiritual renewal not only within the house of David but also within a family of priests from a different line from that of Joshua, the high priest. Joshua arose from the family that traced its roots to the priest Zadok (chief priest of David and Solomon), Aaron (brother of Moses), and ultimately Levi's son Kohath (1 Chron. 6:1–15). The family mentioned in Zechariah 12:13 (Shimei) traced its roots to Levi's other son, Gershom (1 Chron. 6:17; cf. Ex. 6:16–17; Num. 3:17–18).

Interestingly, Zechariah is identified as a descendant of a man named Iddo (Zech. 1:1, 7) and as one who led the priestly family of Iddo (Neh. 12:16). The name "Iddo" is associated with a family of Levites in the line of Gershom (1 Chron. 6:21), the same family as that of Shimei (see Zech. 12:12–13). Thus, Zechariah 9–14 seems to proclaim the rejection of Zadokite priestly leadership in the wake of the absence of leadership from the Davidic line in Yehud in the early Persian period. Another line of priests, one possibly related to Zechariah, is associated with future Davidic hopes.

Zechariah 9–14 represents an important stage in the history of prophecy. Here we find a rich variety of forms as well as a large number of allusions drawn from earlier prophets. This section is witness to the important role that the later prophetic tradition played within the Jewish community, namely, as interpreter of the earlier prophets, bringing these ancient words to life within a new context.

D. The Community

HAGGAI AND ZECHARIAH were involved in the community of Yehud, a province on the western fringe of the Persian empire. Through their books and other Jewish documents and remains from this period we can reconstruct the basic contours of this society.

Leaders. The community was led by two key figures who returned from Babylonian exile in the first phase of Persian rule after the fall of Babylon in 539 B.C.: Zerubbabel and Joshua.

Zerubbabel. There has been much discussion over the identity and ancestry of Zerubbabel. A comparison of the genealogy of the Davidic line in 1 Chronicles 3:17–24 with the patrynomic of Zerubbabel provided in Haggai (as well as in Ezra and Nehemiah) reveals a point of tension. In 1 Chronicles 3:19,

28. Boda, "Reading," 277–91.

Pedaiah is named as the father of Zerubbabel while, according to Haggai, Shealtiel is his father. Suggested solutions range from the postulation of a Levirate marriage between Shealtiel's widow and Pedaiah,[29] to textual changes,[30] to conjecturing the presence of two different Zerubbabels,[31] to the suggestion of a difference between his father's personal and throne names.[32] None of these suggestions is satisfactory. No sons are ever listed for Shealtiel (1 Chron. 3:17–24); thus if he was childless, a substitute heir was necessary. Most likely Zerubbabel was identified as the proper heir, adopted into the line of Shealtiel.

This connection to the Davidic line is probably what qualified Zerubbabel to serve as governor of Yehud.[33] Ezra and Nehemiah indicate that a man named Sheshbazzar served as governor in an earlier phase of the Persian period (Ezra 5:14) and that Nehemiah filled the same role in the middle of the following century (Neh. 5:14–18). This second passage alludes to "earlier governors," evidence for which has been provided by archaeological finds.[34]

Joshua. The book of Haggai also highlights Joshua, son of the high priest Jehozadak. His genealogy reveals that he is part of the line of Zadokite priests. The origin of the Zadokite line of priests in Israel's religious structure is linked to the political intrigue of the united kingdom under David and Solomon. In David's reign Zadok served as priest with Abiathar (from the line of Eli, 1 Sam. 1). However, when Adonijah rebelled against David and sought the throne over Solomon, Abiathar fell from grace by supporting Adonijah while Zadok was faithful to Solomon. Solomon removed Abiathar from office (1 Kings 2:26–27) and replaced him with Zadok (2:35). During the Exile, Ezekiel affirms the Zadokites for their purity. The future temple building and its services are linked to this line (Ezek. 44).[35]

People. The community that these figures led and to whom these prophets spoke was a diverse group. In simplistic terms one can identify two

---

29. E.g., L. H. Brockington, *Ezra, Nehemiah, and Esther* (NCB; Greenwood, S.C.: Attic, 1969), 53; J. Bright, *A History of Israel*, 4th ed. (Louisville: Westminister John Knox, 2000), 366 n. 360.

30. H. G. T. Mitchell, J. M. P. Smith, and J. A. Brewer, *A Critical and Exegetical Commentary on Haggai, Zechariah, Malachi and Jonah* (ICC; Edinburgh: T. & T. Clark, 1912), 43.

31. S. Talmon, "Ezra and Nehemiah," in *IDBSup*, 391.

32. Meyers and Meyers, *Haggai*, 10.

33. There is evidence that the Persians did appoint leadership from among the ancient ruling houses of subjugated nations, e.g., Cicilia, Cyprus, Phoenicia; see Briant, *Cyrus*, 64, 488–90, 952.

34. Williamson, "Governors," 59–82; Meyers and Meyers, *Haggai*, 14.

35. Cf. R. DeVaux, *Ancient Israel*, 2 vols. (New York: Darton, Longman, & Todd, 1961), 2:372–76; D. I. Block, *The Book of Ezekiel: Chapters 25–48* (NICOT; Grand Rapids: Eerdmans, 1998), 633–48. Koch explains the absence of the title "high priest" in Ezra-Nehemiah on sociological grounds: "vehement quarrels among the priesthood of the Second Temple

types of people. (1) There were those who had returned from the Diaspora (mostly in Mesopotamia, but also Egypt), a long list of whom is provided in Ezra 2 and Nehemiah 7. (2) There were those who had remained in or moved into the land following the demise of the kingdom of Judah by the Babylonians in 587 B.C. Such distinctions appear to underlie the description of the celebration of the Passover in Ezra 6:19–22, which states: "So the Israelites who had returned from the exile ate it, together with all who had separated themselves from the unclean practices of their Gentile neighbors in order to seek the LORD, the God of Israel" (Ezra 6:21).

The province in which this community lived was smaller than its preexilic monarchical counterpart, covering only the central hills of Judah and excluding the Shephelah and the coastal plain to the west, with Jericho/Bethel at the northern, En-Gedi/Tekoa/Beth-Zur/Keilah at the southern, and the rift valley (Jordan/Dead Sea) at the eastern extremes. The population was only one-third of its preexilic size, estimated between 13,350 and 20,650, while the capital city Jerusalem was reduced to one-fifth of its preexilic size. Its economy was largely dependent on the traditional mix of agrarian and animal husbandry, with taxation received through a combination of an emerging money system alongside an "in-kind" system.[36]

E. Literary History and Structure of Haggai and Zechariah

PROPHECY AND LITERATURE. Typically prophecy is associated with people who reveal words or visions from God to his people. This is why prophetic books are often linked to a specific individual such as Isaiah (Isa. 1:1; 2:1; 13:1), Jeremiah (Jer. 1:1–3), or Ezekiel (Ezek. 1:1). But prophecy is not merely an oral phenomenon; it is also a written text. Prophetic figures and their entourage were concerned to preserve a literary record of the oral declarations of the prophet.

The process from oral message to written text is difficult to trace. Jeremiah used the services of his scribe Baruch, who was charged with writing on a

---

about the time of Ezra"; K. Koch, "Ezra and Meremoth: Remarks on the History of the High Priesthood," in *'Shaarei Talmon': Studies in the Bible, Qumran, and the Ancient Near East Presented to Shemaryahu Talmon*, ed. M. Fishbane, E. Tov, and W. W. Fields (Winona Lake, Ind.: Eisenbrauns, 1992), 109. Eskenazi explains this on literary grounds, claiming that the book of Ezra "promotes the centrality of the community by persistently subsuming leaders to the community"; T. C. Eskenazi, *In an Age of Prose: A Literary Approach to Ezra-Nehemiah* (Atlanta: Scholars Press, 1988), 48–53, 136.

36. For these figures see C. E. Carter, *The Emergence of Yehud in the Persian Period* (JSOTSup; Sheffield: Sheffield Academic Press, 1999).

scroll words dictated by the prophet (Jer. 45:1; cf. Jer. 36). This suggests that disciples gathered around prophetic figures (see 2 Kings 6:1) and were instrumental in transferring prophecy from its original oral form into its present literary state. The use of third-person superscriptions to introduce prophetic books (e.g., Isa. 1:1; Jer. 1:1–3) as opposed to first-person superscriptions (e.g., Isa. 6:1; 8:1; Jer. 2:1), suggests that people other than the prophets were involved in the writing and editorial process. Although the prophets themselves may have been involved in this process, it is not necessary.

Often examination of editorial processes is disparaged among some biblical scholars, so it is essential to highlight the importance of studying this process for our interpretation of the prophetic message.[37] (1) The study of the editorial content of a biblical book is as important to exegesis as the study of the original prophetic declarations. The editorial pieces within prophetic books provide an important context for reading prophecies by placing them in a particular historical context (identifying the period of the writing down of the message as well as that of the original speaker and audience), in a particular literary context (drawing together a body of prophecies into a single collection with an overall structure), and in a particular revelatory context (reminding the audience that these words found their origin in the divine). These shape our reading strategy for the interpretation of the prophecies and thus demand our attention.

(2) Investigation of the development of a book through time contributes to our understanding of the final form of that book by offering reasons for the particular structure and by isolating the various units of the completed text. Once these various units are isolated and their background investigated, it is important to ask why the final editor of the book placed them in their present position. Prophetic books are not merely anthologies of prophetic material but rhetorical masterpieces that use the earlier oral materials of the prophets.

A close look at the books of Haggai and Zechariah highlights the important role played by editors in the publication of the oral pronouncements of these two prophets. It is consistent with an evangelical view of Scripture that close associates of the prophets took the words revealed to the prophets by God and shaped them into a powerful message for later generations to read and profit from. The following section will focus on the editorial processes that produced these ancient books.

---

37. See the recent work of Randall Tan, who advocates "composition criticism" instead of "redaction criticism"; R. K. J. Tan, "Recent Developments in Redaction Criticism: From Investigation of Textual Prehistory Back to Historical-Grammatical Exegesis?" *JETS* 44 (2001): 599–614.

Haggai. The superscriptions in 1:1, 15; 2:1, 10, 20 offer initial clues on the history of the editorial process. Haggai 1:1 and 2:1 both tell us that "the word of the LORD came *through* [*beyad*] the prophet Haggai," while 2:10, 20 introduce their sections with the claim that "the word of the LORD came *to* [*ʾel*] the prophet Haggai." The first two sections (1:1–2:9) are addressed to the same three audiences: Zerubbabel, Joshua, people/remnant. The second two sections (2:10–23), however, do not mention Joshua but only the "priests" (2:11), people/nation (2:14), and Zerubbabel (2:21, 23). This evidence suggests either that the book underwent multiple editions (1:1–2:9 and then 2:10–23) or that the final editor drew from sources that used diverse methods of recording the prophet's witness.

These various pieces place Haggai in a particular community in history, addressing their needs and concerns and calling them to faithfulness to Yahweh's purposes. The structure of the book is shaped by the phases expected for a rebuilding project, guiding the reader from a call to initiate the project to an encouragement to continue the project to a celebration of the completion of its initial phase. In the first section (1:1–15), Haggai is calling the people to rebuild the temple by focusing on present difficulties. The section ends by depicting their initial response. In the second section (2:1–9), the prophet encourages the people in their work by pointing to a bright eschatological future for the community. The third section (2:10–23) draws together these various motifs from 1:1–2:9 into a final message of the prophet, focusing on past, present, and future. In this section Joshua recedes to the sideline while Zerubbabel comes to the fore.

Although focused on a limited portion of the rebuilding project (the foundation laying), Haggai has great theological significance. It masterfully intertwines the already and the not-yet, the present and the eschatological, showing the future significance of present faithfulness.

Zechariah 1–8. Like Haggai, Zechariah 1–8 also contains clear evidence of editorial activity. On three occasions (1:1, 7; 7:1) superscriptions similar to those of Haggai introduce a block of material that has its own integrity. On the level of genre and rhetoric 1:1–6 and 7:1–8:23 are clearly distinguished from 1:7–6:15. Both 1:1–6 and 7:1–8:23 contain significant oral material written in prose style accompanied by narrative. Furthermore, these two sections use similar vocabulary and allude to similar traditions.[38] By contrast, 1:7–6:15 consists of a series of reports of visions interspersed with oracles and sign-acts. Each of these sections has its own history of compilation, which we will investigate more closely.

38. See M. J. Boda, "Zechariah: Master Mason or Penitential Prophet?" in *Yahwism After the Exile: Perspectives on Israelite Religion in the Persian Era*, ed. B. Becking and R. Albertz (Studies in Theology and Religion 5; Assen: Royal Van Gorcum, 2003), 49–69.

The core of the central vision-oracle section consists of a series of visions received by Zechariah. Although the entire section is linked to a particular day (1:7), this only indicates the date on which this material was delivered to the people and says nothing about when the prophet received it. That this process may have extended over a period of time is suggested by a comparison of 1:8 with 4:1. In 1:8 Zechariah reports that "during the night I had a vision" and then in 4:1 that "the angel who talked with me returned and wakened me." This suggests that the visionary experience had at least two phases.

The first three visions (1:8–2:5) as well as the final vision (6:1–8) are closely related by the theme of the punishment of Babylon and restoration of a community in Jerusalem. The initial vision sets the agenda, the second and third visions fill out the details, and the final vision announces its inauguration. Attached to these two visions are the two nonvisionary pieces in 2:6–13 and 6:9–15, both of which bring the visions "down to the earth"; that is, they show the implications of this vision for the Persian period community. Following the visionary promises of 1:8–2:5, the prophet exhorts the community to flee Babylon and return to the land because of God's imminent return (2:6–13). Following the visionary announcement of 6:1–8, the prophet reminds the returning exilic priests of the priority of this community and the expected return of a royal figure (6:9–15). The vision in chapter 3 stands out from the other visions in 1:8–6:8.[39] It displays close affinities with 6:9–15 and addresses Persian period figures directly.

The three visions that occur after 4:1 all focus attention on initial issues in a Jerusalem and Judah being rebuilt and repopulated: the empowerment of the building project (ch. 4) and the purification of the community (ch. 5). Zechariah 4 is interrupted halfway through by two oracles concerning Zerubbabel. These oracles have been placed in the middle of this vision on purpose to highlight the importance of prophecy for the rebuilding project.[40]

This assortment of prophetic pieces reflecting a variety of genres, messages, and contexts has been drawn together into one section by the editor responsible for 1:7. This person obviously was seeking to communicate an overall message by bringing these various pericopes together in this particular sequence. This section announces the comforting news of the long-awaited restoration. God was disciplining Babylon, releasing his people, and rebuilding his city and temple. This good news was designed to motivate the people to return from Babylon and rebuild the temple (2:6–13; 6:9–15) and

39. Cf. Meyers and Meyers, *Haggai*, 179–80; T. Pola, "Form and Meaning in Zechariah 3," in *Yahwism After the Exile: Perspectives on Israelite Religion in the Persian Era*, ed. B. Becking and R. Albertz (Studies in Theology and Religion 5; Assen: Royal Van Gorcum, 2003), 156–67.

40. Boda, "Oil," Article 10.

to encourage the priests to fulfill their responsibilities in the temple and cooperate with the royal figure in the rebuilding project (3:1–10; 6:9–15). Prophetic endorsement of royal participation in the rebuilding project is encouraged in chapter 4 and the importance of adherence to the law is highlighted in chapter 5.

The final form of 1:8–6:15 reveals a breadth of concern. Although the temple is mentioned in the visions and oracles (1:16; 2:10, 13; 3:7; 4:9; 6:12–15), they also expand restoration to include the return and renewal of the people (physically, socially, spiritually), the transformation of the entire city and province, and the inclusion of "many nations" among God's people.

This broader agenda in Zechariah can also be discerned in the prose pieces that surround the vision-oracle section in 1:7–6:15. At the core of 1:1–6 is Zechariah's speech to the community in which he draws their attention to the obstinacy of past generations and the need for the present generation to repent (1:2–6a). This speech is introduced by a superscription (1:1) and concluded by a description of the positive response of his audience (1:6b).

Zechariah 7:1–8:23, however, poses a greater challenge.[41] The superscription in 7:1 introduces a short narrative account in which a group of people approach the priests and prophets at the temple for clarification on a liturgical matter (7:2–3). This elicits a response from Zechariah that continues until 8:23. That this material has been drawn from earlier sources written by Zechariah himself is suggested by the regular appearance of the formula, "the word of the LORD Almighty came to me" (7:4; 8:1, 18). But the role of an editor is also implied by the appearance of the formula, "the word of the LORD Almighty came to Zechariah" (7:1, 8).

To identify the foundational level of 7:1–8:23 it is important to return to the original question of the group of people. In 7:3 they ask whether they should continue their practice of fasting at the appointed times during the year. Zechariah appears to begin to answer this question in 7:5 as he confronts the priests and people on the authenticity of their fasting and then links their behavior with that of the generation sent into exile.

Clearly by 8:18–19 the original question is answered, but the material starting at the beginning of chapter 8 does not seem to fit the flow of the answer. It appears that the original account of Zechariah's interaction with the people and priests consisted of 7:2–14 . . . 8:14–23. Zechariah 8:14 introduces the contrast motif ("just as I had . . . so now I have"), providing the appropriate transition from the disaster at the end of chapter 7 to the anticipated blessing of 8:18–23. The key to this blessing both for the former generation (7:9–10) as well as the present generation (8:16–17) is justice.

---

41. For details see Boda, "Fasts to Feasts," 390–407.

Into the midst of this original speech the editor has brought two prophecies (8:1–8, 9–13)[42] delivered by Zechariah that anticipate future blessing. Although these "interruptions" appear awkward to us, interrupting the flow of the original account, such "interruptions" are a rhetorical technique used elsewhere in this corpus, in particular in the vision of chapter 4. These two prophetic insertions foreshadow and anticipate the conclusion of the original speech.

Zechariah 1:1–6 and 7:1–8:23 draw attention to the message of the earlier prophets in order to emphasize that repentance is essential for the realization of restoration. Zechariah 1:1–6 presents a model of the appropriate response of the community to the ancient message of the prophets as the prophet summarizes their message (1:2–6a) and the people respond through repentance and admission of guilt (1:6b). This short pericope shapes our reading of 1:7–6:15, reminding the reader that the comforting message of restoration that follows is given to a penitent community. After this comforting message with its broader agenda of restoration, 7:1–8:23 returns the reader to the initial message and tone of 1:1–6 and reveals that restoration will not be realized unless the entire community renounces the patterns of the past and lives in faithfulness to covenant. The final picture is one of glorious hope, but this will not be realized until there is a transformation in the behavioral patterns of the community.

The setting in which the editor responsible for the final shape of Zechariah 1–8 completed this work is difficult to discern. All we know is that this reached its final form sometime after 518 B.C. (see 7:1), but its message is clearly one that challenges the community to reflect deeply on the definition of restoration and not equate it with the completion of the temple, but rather broaden such a definition to include spiritual and social renewal.

Zechariah 9–14. The historical superscriptions that appeared throughout chapters 1–8 at key seams in the text are not used in chapters 9–14. This has led many scholars to separate these chapters off from the rest of the book as a distinct corpus, even though there is no ancient textual evidence for this approach.

Two superscriptions do appear in these chapters, both beginning with the phrase "An Oracle. The word of the LORD . . ." (9:1; 12:1). This simple marker divides the six chapters into two sections of three each: 9–11 and 12–14.[43] This word is used as a superscription elsewhere in prophetic literature,

42. The first may be a collection of prophecies.

43. See Boda, "Reading," 282–97. Floyd, building on the earlier work of Weis, argues that this phrase is a genre marker that designates this material as an interpretation of an earlier section of prophecy (i.e., chs. 1–8 for chs. 9–11 and chs. 1–11 for chs. 12–14); cf. R. Weis, "A Definition of the Genre *Maśśa'*, in the Hebrew Bible" (Ph.D., Claremont Graduate School, 1986); M. H. Floyd, *Minor Prophets*, Part 2 (FOTL 22; Grand Rapids: Eerdmans, 2000); esp. idem, "The *Maśśa'*, As a Type of Prophetic Book," *JBL* 121 (2002): 401–22.

notably in the oracles against the nations in Isaiah 13–23. Jeremiah's attack on the false prophets shows that by his time this term was synonymous with a prophetic message (Jer. 23:33–40). Although the term may have been used for a negative prophetic message, in Zechariah 9–14 and Malachi it functions as a general term to signify a prophetic collection.

Internal evidence confirms that this term introduces a prophetic collection. (1) Chapters 9–11 focus attention on issues related to Judah and Joseph, the northern and southern tribal entities. In contrast, there is no mention of the Joseph tribes in chapters 12–14, for these focus on the house of David, the inhabitants of Jerusalem, and the house of Judah (12:2, 4–5, 7–8, 10; 13:1; 14:14, 21). (2) Throughout chapters 12–14 one finds the regular repetition of the key phrase "on that day" (*beyom-hahuʾ*), sometimes preceded by the untranslated construction *wehayah* ("and it will be"; 12:3, 4, 6, 8, 9, 11, 13:1, 4; 14:4, 6, 8, 9, 13, 20, 21). This phrase occurs only once in chapters 9–11 with the same eschatological sense (9:16; cf. 11:11).

While these characteristics clearly distinguish chapters 9–11 from 12–14, there are also points of contact that show that these two sections have been woven together as a unified whole.[44] (1) Zechariah 13:7–9 shares similar rhetorical (vocative introduction) and thematic (shepherd, sheep) characteristics with the transitional pieces in chapters 9–11: 10:1–3; 11:1–3; 11:17. (2) Chapters 12 and 14 use strong divine warrior imagery with a global dimension, a characteristic of chapters 9–10. (3) One finds the same linkage between idolatry and prophecy/divination in 13:1–6 as in 10:1–3.

Therefore, one can discern continuity and discontinuity between chapters 9–11 and 12–14. The two collections may have distinct roots (see further below), but they share a common tradition and prophetic community. They have been gathered together into a final collection and need to be interpreted in this larger context.

The first two pericopes (9:1–17 and 10:3b–12) show affinity through their positive tone, concern for Judah and Ephraim, and focus on the return from exile. The first one (9:1–17) has two basic levels: (1) a depiction of God as divine warrior recapturing his palace/sanctuary and then defending, saving, and prospering his people (9:1–8, 14–17),[45] and (2) an address to Zion (placed strategically between verses 8 and 14, in the transition between God's return to the sanctuary and his salvation of the people) that celebrates the

---

44. Also see the superb work of Redditt, "Nehemiah's First Mission and the Date of Zechariah 9–14," 664–78, the influence of which will be seen in my reflection on the development of this part of Zechariah.

45. The switch between first and third person in 9:1–8, 14–17 is not odd; one can see this in 9:1–8, where there is a move from third person (9:1–4) to first person (9:6–8) and then in 9:14–17 back to third person.

arrival of the king and the return of the exiles from Judah and Ephraim, who will become God's weapons (9:9–13).

The second pericope (10:3b–12) shows affinity with the qualities of chapter 9: on a stylistic level it has the cadence of the first level of chapter 9 (switching between first and third person), while on a thematic level it is connected to the second level of chapter 9 (with reference to Judah, Ephraim, restoration). There are several key themes. (1) Restoration is inaugurated by God, who breaks into Israel's history to instigate and complete redemption (9:1–8, 14–17; 10:3b, 6, 8–10, 12). (2) Restoration is envisioned for both Judah and Ephraim as they are rescued from foreign bondage, although Judah has the leading role to play (9:11–13, 16–17; 10:6–11). (3) The people are described as God's flock, a term emphasizing God's personal and caring leadership with the people (9:16; 10:3b).

These two sections in chapters 9–10 contrast the two pieces found in chapters 12–14. Each of these units (12:2–13:6; 14:1–21) is introduced by the Hebrew interjection *hinneh* (12:2; 14:1)[46] and contains the recurring rhetorical phrase "on that day" (12:3, 4, 6, 8, 9, 11; 13:1, 4; 14:4, 6, 8, 9, 13, 20, 21). Rather than Judah-Ephraim, chapters 12–14 focus on a different pair: Judah-Jerusalem, with no mention of Ephraim. Whereas chapters 9–10 depict God's return to his sanctuary-city and subsequent rescue of his people from the nations, chapters 12–14 picture the attack of Jerusalem by all the nations of the earth, a battle in which God intervenes on Jerusalem's behalf, defeats the nations, and makes Jerusalem a sanctified space (cleansed, holy).[47] Chapters 12–14 also share similar lexical stock (12:2b/14:14a; 12:2, 6/14:14b; 12:6/14:10; 12:9/14:16; 12:12–14/14:17–18).[48]

Although each of these four major pericopes in chapters 9–14 has its unique internal logic and message, our study so far has highlighted clear affinities within 9–10 and 12–14. But to this point we have not discussed one other elongated prophetic portion here: 11:4–16.

Zechariah 11:4–16 clearly stands out from the other four sections already described with its unique genre form of sign-act allegory. The shepherd motif is prominent in this section as it describes the community's rejection of God's shepherd and the subsequent appointment of a bad shepherd. There is great focus on the breaking of two staffs. The precise meaning of the names of these staffs is a matter of great debate (see commentary), but the significance of these staffs is clear. The breaking of the first staff signifies

46. Often translated "behold," but untranslated in the NIV.

47. See further D. R. Jones, "Fresh Interpretation of Zechariah 9–11," *VT* 12 (1962): 241–59.

48. E. J. C. Tigchelaar, *Prophets of Old and the Day of the End: Zechariah, the Book of Watchers and Apocalyptic* (OtSt 35 Leiden: Brill, 1996), 220.

the "revoking the covenant I had made with all the nations" (11:10). The breaking of the second staff signifies "breaking the brotherhood between Judah and Israel" (11:14). These two actions of breaking correspond to two key discontinuities between the oracles in chapters 9–10 and 12–14, especially seen in the focus on God's destruction of "all the nations" and the absence of reference to Israel in chapters 12–14.

The key role that the shepherd allegory plays in transitioning the reader from chapters 9–11 to 12–14 explains four other short units that have not been accounted for to this point: 10:1–3a, 11:1–3, 17; 13:7–9. Each of these stands out from the surrounding text by using imperatival/attention vocabulary, a negative tone, and the shepherd motif. In this they show close affinity with the shepherd allegory of 11:4–16 and appear to be part of the redactional structure. These shorter shepherd units all describe the poor leadership that replaced the rejected Davidic leadership of 11:4–16. There is a progression between the various pieces: from the Lord's anger (10:1–3a), to the prophecy of destruction (11:1–3), to a curse (11:17), to the execution of judgment (13:7–9).

This analysis reveals three major levels to chapters 9–14: two oracles on return from captivity historically focused (9:1–17; 10:3b–12), two oracles on God's defeat of the nations eschatologically focused (12:1–13:6; 14:1–21), and shepherd motif pieces denoting the discipline of the leadership in Israel distributed throughout the text (10:1–3a, 11:1–3, 4–16, 17; 13:7–9).

Our work so far has sought to note the various components of this fascinating section of Zechariah, but we must ask finally the question of the meaning of that final form. The message of Zechariah 9–14 is one of expectation and reality. The prophet highlights the great work of God in the redemptive-historical events surrounding the restoration of his people in the Persian period. Although many exiles have already returned, more from both Judah and Israel will return to a land ruled by God and his king. God will use Judah to rescue Israel from their exile.

But this is not the reality of the Persian period community. Although exiles return, this does not happen en masse, nor does it include exiles from Israel (the northern kingdom). This incongruity leads to a further word from God that explains the lack of fulfillment. This lack is traced to a problem connected with leadership within the community. Having rejected God's appointed Davidic leader (Zerubbabel), the community is given over to uncaring and oppressive leaders in Yehud and in the nations. God attacks such leadership, linking them to the patterns of preexilic Judah that were judged by God (10:1–3a; 11:1–3).

The community's rejection of God's leadership has serious implications for the future, annulling both God's agreement with the nations to care for his people and jeopardizing hope of the reunion of Israel and Judah. The vision in 12:1–13:6 shows God rescuing his people from the threat of the nations, but then turns the focus internally to deal with the sin of the leadership within the province. The vision in chapter 14 again shows God's rescue of Jerusalem, but this time the vision is externally oriented as the defeat of the nations leads to the attraction of the defeated nations to Jerusalem in worship (Feast of Tabernacles).

Zechariah 9–14 thus reveals a community in tension. It does not, however, abandon Jerusalem and its Davidic house as the focus of hope, although it ignores the priestly leadership at the temple. It reflects the final phase of the trajectory established in chapters 1–8. In chapters 7–8 we see the prophet attack the leadership and the people highlight a replication of preexilic patterns, even though the prophet has great hope for the future centered around Jerusalem, which will be a holy city as well as a place that attracts the nations.[49]

One can sense a growing concern in Zechariah 1–14 over the issue of leadership: from the absence of concern or focus in 1:1–6, to an affirmation with clear delimitation of priestly prerogatives in 1:7–6:15, to the beginning of criticism in 7:1–8:23, to a serious critique in chapters 9–14. There is also a growth in the Zecharian tradition in eschatological orientation: from the prophetic-historical message of 1:1–6 focused on immediate repentance; to the visions and oracles of immediate future return, restoration, and renewal in 1:7–6:15; to the distant future restoration ideals internally and externally in Zech. 7:1–8:23; to the eschatological focus of chapters 9–14. Finally, while 1:1–6 says nothing of oppression of the poor in the community, one of the visions in 1:7–6:15 (5:1–4) alludes to manipulation of the legal system and then 7:1–8:23 focuses attention on such oppression as evidence of a lack of true penitence. This appears to come to a climax in the shepherd allegory at the center of chapters 9–14, which speaks much of the helpless in the flock.

Although it is difficult to ascertain the authorship and date of Zechariah 9–14, it has a legitimate place in this book. It represents the enduring legacy of the prophet Zechariah, some sections possibly arising from the prophet himself and others perhaps through a community that preserved and echoed his message after his death. This message of repentance ultimately distanced this prophet from the temple he supported in the earlier phases of his ministry. The absence of any reference to the completion of this temple in Zechariah is not surprising in light of Zechariah's insistence that spiritual renewal must accompany physical rebuilding.

---

49. For details of this argument see Boda, "Fasts to Feasts," 390–407.

F. Theological Themes

God. The key role of the prophet in ancient Israel was to orient the people theologically (cf. Isa. 30:10–11). First and foremost the prophets offered their generation a vision of God. What vision of God, then, do the books of Haggai and Zechariah offer to their readers?

The God of Haggai and Zechariah is clearly the God of grace and mercy. He is a God who loves his people and proclaims his passion to save them from the nations and renew their lives in the Promised Land. He offers them words of mercy and comfort (Zech. 1:13, 16), encouraging them to "be strong" and "not fear" (Hag. 2:4–5). He declares his intention to have compassion on them (Zech. 10:6). Consistently, the prophets depict God at work for his people: restoring their people and land (1:7–17), breaking the power of the nations (1:18–21; 6:1–8), protecting them from external threats (2:1–5), delivering them from the nations (2:6–13), defending them from accusations and cleansing them from the stain of sin (ch. 3), enabling them through his Spirit to accomplish their work (ch. 4), and promising them a glorious future as a remnant saved from the nations (8:1–13).

God's mercy is closely linked with his electing choice of his people; that is, it is an act of his sovereign will (Zech. 1:17; 2:12; 3:2). But God does not restrict his salvific actions to his chosen people. He displays his deep interest in the nations, for whom there is a place in his kingdom (2:11; 8:13, 20–23; 9:7; 14:16–19).

These portraits of God's mercy, however, do not contradict another aspect of the prophetic revelation of God in these books, namely, that he is a God of discipline and justice. God disciplines his people who do not follow his priorities (Hag. 1:9–11; 2:14–19). His anger is displayed in his past discipline of the preexilic generation, which ignored the prophetic witness (Zech. 1:1–6, 12; 7:7–14; 8:11). God takes sin seriously and will bring severe discipline on those who do not share his attitude (ch. 5). As with his mercy, so with his justice, God's anger is also directed against the nations (1:15), whom he promises to judge (1:18–21; 6:1–8; chs. 9–14).

God's ability to enact both mercy and justice is linked throughout these books to his status as Creator of the universe and Lord of history. The opening and closing visions in Zechariah 1–6 show that he is in control of the universe, is aware of its status, and is able to act with sovereign power (chs. 9–14). His ability to shake the cosmos and manipulate history enables him to bring salvation (Hag. 2:6–9, 20–23; Zech. 12:1). He uses his creation not only to bless his people (Hag. 1:19; Zech. 1:17; 3:10; 8:12) but also to bring discipline (Hag. 1:1–11; 2:10–19).

God is also presented as a God of relationship and presence. He is a God who presences himself with his people, consistently declaring, "I am with you" (Hag. 1:13; 2:4–5; Zech. 2:5, 10–13; 4:6; cf. 8:23; 10:5). This presencing of God with his people is closely related to his passion for covenant intimacy, as expressed in Zechariah 8:8, "They will be my people, and I will be faithful and righteous to them as their God," and in 13:9, "I will say, 'They are my people,' and they will say, 'The LORD is our God.'"

Community. This vision of God provides a foundation for a second key theological witness of these prophets: their vision of the community of God. Haggai and Zechariah speak to a community living in and emerging out of the darkness of the exilic experience. During this period the community clung to God's promises declared in the Law and the Prophets, namely, that after a period of exile God would deliver his disciplined people.

For Haggai and Zechariah the restoration was multidimensional. Fundamentally, it involved the return of God's presence (Hag. 1:13; 2:4–5; Zech. 1:16–17; 2:1–5, 10–13; 8:23; 9:8) to a rebuilt temple (Hag. 1:8; Zech. 1:16; 2:1–5; 6:9–15) in the chosen city of Jerusalem (Zech. 1:14–17; 2:12; 3:2; 8:3). Accompanying this presence would be blessing, often expressed in terms of material bounty from the land (Hag. 1:1–11; 2:6–9, 15–19; Zech. 2:1–5; 3:10; 8:4–5, 9–13; 9:17; 10:1), and protection, often expressed in terms of military conquest of the world (Hag. 2:22; Zech. 1:15, 18–21; 2:7–9; 9:1–8, 13–16; 10:3–7; 12:2–9; 14:1–15).

The reinstatement of the Davidic line is linked to this vision of restoration (Hag. 2:20–23; Zech. 3:8–9; 6:9–15; 9:9–10; 12:10, 12), but so also is the return of the community to the land (Zech. 2:4, 6, 7; 8:3, 7–8; 9:11–13, 16–17; 10:6–12). This remnant will experience a renewal of covenant relationship with God (Hag. 2:5; Zech. 8:8; 13:9) and purification by God's grace (Hag. 2:10–14; Zech. 3:1–5, 9; 13:1; 14:20–21) as they celebrate with joy (Zech. 8:18–19). The restoration will have a clear global dimension as the nations are not only conquered (Hag. 2:22; Zech. 1:15, 18–21; 2:7–9; 9:1–8, 13–16; 10:3–7, 11; 12:2–9; 14:1–15) but also integrated into the covenant community (Zech. 2:11; 8:20–23; 9:7, 10; 14:16–21).

In both prophets this vision of restoration is clearly linked to the sovereign actions of the God of promise, yet each prophet calls for human response. Haggai's focus is clearly on the need for physically rebuilding the temple complex as the realization of the promised restoration. Whether provoking them to begin the project (Hag. 1), encouraging them to persevere (2:1–9), or celebrating their accomplishments (2:10–23), Haggai intertwines restoration and the temple reconstruction. He identifies the rebuilding project as the key initial step that will transform the past of curse to the future of blessing flowing from God's renewed presence. By assuming this responsibility, the people are clearly turning to God (2:17).

Zechariah builds on Haggai's message by calling for the community to renew its covenant relationship with God (Zech. 1:3).[50] This renewal will mean loving one's neighbor as oneself, exemplified in just relationships (5:1–4; 7:8–10; 8:16–17, 19), and loving the Lord God with all one's heart, soul, and mind, exemplified in pure worship (5:5–11). This need for penitence is an issue for both the community as a whole (11:4–16) and for its leadership (7:5; 10:1–3; 11:1–17; 12:10–13:6; 13:7–9).

These two prophets complement each other. Both announce an imminent restoration inaugurated by the return of God dependent on repentance of the people. For Haggai repentance means rebuilding the temple, for Zechariah purity in covenant relationships. While Haggai's message is summarized in his words, "Build the house, so that I may take pleasure in it and be honored" (Hag. 1:8), Zechariah's message is encapsulated in his cry, "Return to me ... and I will return to you" (Zech. 1:3). For both the ultimate goal is the return of the presence and blessing of God to his people in order to transform the cosmos.

Bridging Contexts

OUR CONSIDERATION OF the original context of Haggai and Zechariah has exposed the deep roots these books have in the history of an ancient community, a feature these books share with all biblical books. On the one hand this feature is to be celebrated, for it reminds us of the relevance of revelation. This is something highlighted by the writer of Hebrews, who addresses the issue of ancient prophecy: "In the past God spoke to our forefathers through the prophets at many times and in various ways" (Heb. 1:1). This statement affirms that God used the prophets to communicate his will to his people. It also reminds us that this happened "at many times" and "in various ways"; that is, such revelation was delivered in relevant ways to people in their own cultural and historical contexts. It is this feature, however, that often intimidates present-day interpreters who desire to connect these ancient texts to contemporary contexts.

In light of this, this section of our introduction addresses key issues of interpretation that will lay a foundation for the commentary that follows. In particular it focuses on familiarizing the reader with hermeneutical strategies related to literature and theology that are essential in order to understand these ancient works and interpret them in light of redemptive history.

50. See Boda, "Penitential Prophet," 49–69.

A. The Character of Prophetic Literature and Its Use in the New Testament

A FEW YEARS AGO one of my former professors turned on the television and came across a news report of recent events in the Middle East. With the help of maps the news anchor was describing the movements of troops with detailed precision. It soon became clear that a coalition of Arab nations was poised to strike at Israel. As the camera moved back and brought the news anchor into view, my professor recognized him as a Christian leader well known for his interpretation of biblical prophecy. Rather than describing events that had already happened, this man was projecting a possible future for the troubled region, based on evidence drawn from ancient prophecies in the Bible and recent events in the Middle East.

For many this approach to Old Testament prophetic material is not exceptional. Most Christians approach the prophets as sages whose primary activity was peering through a spiritual keyhole into the dimly lit room of the future. This approach is based on the words of passages like 1 Peter 1:10–12, in which the prophets are depicted as those who searched for more light on the future messianic figure. Such a search is confirmed by the many references in the New Testament to the fulfillment of prophetic expectation in Christ and the early church.

Although this aspect of prophetic ministry must be celebrated, a perusal of the prophetic books as well as the New Testament provides a fuller picture. The prophets do, it is true, speak of future events, the "foretelling" aspect of prophetic ministry, but the majority of their prophecies were focused on the values and actions of their contemporaries, the "forthtelling" aspect of prophetic ministry. Even when they spoke of future events, in nearly every case they did so with an eye on the present generation. The prophets were also concerned with the past. They often recited the story of Israel (both its positive and negative elements) in order to challenge the present generation to obedience (see Jer. 2; Ezek. 16, 18, 20; Hos. 11).

New Testament use of the ancient prophets reveals sensitivity to both the foretelling and the forthtelling aspects of prophetic ministry.[51] Although

51. Barton has traced approaches to ancient prophecy current in Judaism and Christianity in the Second Temple period (from the Exile to the end of the New Testament period). He isolates four basic "modes" of reading the prophets: as ethical instruction, as foreknowledge of the present day, as revelation of the divine plan of history, and as theologian and mystic. His second and third categories are similar to my "foretelling" mode, while his first and fourth are similar to "forthtelling"; J. Barton, *Oracles of God: Perceptions of Ancient Prophecy in Israel After the Exile* (London: Darton Longman, & Todd, 1986).

New Testament speakers and writers often show how Christ and the church fulfilled the expectations of ancient Hebrew prophecy (e.g., Matt. 1:23; Isa. 7:14; Matt. 2:6; Mic. 5:2; Matt. 2:18; Jer. 31:15), they regularly draw on these ancient books as the foundation of their exhortations to the Christian community.

Not only did Christ say that he did not come to abolish the Law and the Prophets, forbidding breaking their commands (Matt. 5:17–20), but he also claimed that his commands were simply a summary of the prophet's moral teaching (7:12; 22:40). The early church used prophetic calls to repentance (Acts 13:40; Hab. 1:5) and to faith (Rom. 1:17; Hab. 2:4; Rom. 10:11; Isa. 28:16; Rom. 10:13; Joel 2:32; 2 Cor. 6:2; Isa. 49:8; Heb. 10:37–38; Hab. 2:3–4) as invitations to experience God's forgiveness in Christ.

New Testament theology is founded on prophetic material, laying the foundation for reflection on sin (Rom. 3:15–17; Isa. 59:7–8), sovereignty (Rom. 9:19–21; Isa. 29:16; 45:9; Rom. 9:13; Mal. 1:2–3), omniscience (Rom. 11:34; 1 Cor. 2:16; Isa. 40:13), divine wisdom (1 Cor. 1:19; Isa. 29:14), grace (1 Cor. 2:9; Isa. 64:4), resurrection (1 Cor. 15:54–55; Isa. 25:8; Hos. 13:14), and revelation (1 Peter 1:23–25; Isa. 40:6–8). The New Testament calls the people to a life of faithfulness by citing the prophets (2 Cor. 6:17; Isa. 52:11; Ezek. 20:34, 41; 1 Cor. 1:29–30; Jer. 9:24) while also encouraging hope and confidence in faith (1 Peter 3:13–16; Isa. 8:12).

This evidence of the New Testament's use of the Hebrew prophets is reflected in Paul's description of the Old Testament to Timothy as "able to make you wise for salvation through faith in Christ Jesus" (2 Tim. 3:15) as well as "useful for teaching, rebuking, correcting and training in righteousness" (3:16). The first aspect highlights the role of prophecy to illuminate the great redemptive story both past and future, which culminates in the advent of Christ. The second aspect, which must be rooted in the first aspect, encourages the use of the Old Testament to shape faithful living in the present age.

This evidence highlights the passion of the prophets to speak to the present and future and reveals the interpretive sensitivity of the New Testament to these two aspects of prophetic ministry. This stresses the "how," that is, how the New Testament uses these ancient texts within the Christian community. But we must search for the "why"; that is, why did the New Testament use these texts in this way? What biblical-theological rationale did the early Christian community use that enabled them to access the prophets (and the Old Testament in general) as texts relevant to the church? In doing so we will discover that the "foretelling" aspects of ancient prophecy actually enhance the "forthtelling" aspects.

B. The Biblical-Theological Relationship Between the Prophets and the Church

RETURNING TO MY former professor's "news report" introduced above, the Christian leader he encountered used ancient prophecies to predict military events in the contemporary Middle East. This kind of connection between ancient and modern contexts is not exceptional. Many Christians assume that the creation of the state of Israel in 1948 is confirmation of their approach to Old and New Testament prophecies. For these interpreters the Bible anticipates a future age in which God will establish a Jewish kingdom in Jerusalem. The nations of the earth, incited by wicked leadership, will arise against this kingdom in rebellion against God and march to Jerusalem for a fight to the finish. God will defeat these forces, judge the wicked, and establish a new heaven and earth.

Other Christians, however, have argued strongly against this strain of interpretation. In their view Israel in the Bible is not first of all an ethnic entity but a spiritual one. Jesus fulfilled the role of Israel and established a new Israel, the church. He prophesied the destruction of the temple as God's judgment on unbelieving Israel and offered himself as the new temple through whom humanity has access to God. The destruction of Jerusalem and its temple in A.D. 70 not only vindicated Jesus but also signaled the assumption of the promises of Israel by the church.

This brief introduction to these two approaches to Israel exposes major hermeneutical conflict in the church's interpretation of the Old Testament in general and prophecy in particular. Obviously the resolution of this conflict will have enormous implications on how one appropriates the message of Haggai and Zechariah for the church today.

Israel in redemptive history. In order to clarify the biblical-theological relationship between Israel and the church, we must move back in redemptive history to a key event that defines Israel as a nation, the call of Abraham in Genesis 12. Genesis 1–11 relates the creation of the world, the fall of humanity, and the subsequent struggle between righteousness and sin. Through the Flood God "recreates" the earth in order to establish a covenant with humanity represented now in Noah.[52] The subsequent chapters reveal the enduring (Tower of Babel) and universal (Table of Nations) character of sin.

52. Compare Gen. 1 with 7:11–8:5. In Gen. 1 God creates "form," fills this form, and commissions humanity. In 7:11–24 God removes the form that destroys the life and then after sending a "wind" (8:1; same Heb. word as "spirit" of 1:2), reestablishes the form (8:2–14) before refilling that form (8:15–22), and then recommissions humanity (9:1–7).

With this larger stage of creation and culture in view, Genesis follows one particular line from Noah's family: the descendants of Shem (Gen. 11:10–32). To this line God gives a special promise: "I will make your name great, and you will be a blessing. I will bless those who bless you, and whoever curses you I will curse; and all peoples on earth will be blessed through you" (12:2b–3). This promise highlights the impact that Abraham will have on "all peoples on earth." At the foundation of Israel's faith, therefore, is the assertion that they have been called into existence to bring blessing to the entire world. Genesis then provides several stories that foreshadow the redemptive fulfillment of this family's role of universal blessing—such as Abram's rescue of Lot (ch. 14), his intercession for Sodom (ch. 18), and Joseph's rise to power in Egypt at a time of universal crisis (chs. 37–50).

The Old Testament relates the story of God's rescuing Israel from Egypt (Exodus), establishing a covenant with them as a nation (Exodus–Numbers), sustaining them through the desert (Exodus–Deuteronomy), giving them a land (Joshua), and establishing a united kingdom under Davidic kingship (Samuel–Kings). The purpose of these great acts of salvation, however, remains global: the blessing of the nations. Israel was called out from the nations of the earth to serve as a "kingdom of priests" (Ex. 19:4–6), that is, a nation with a priestly duty for the world. Their obedience was designed to make an impact on the nations of the world (Deut. 4:6–8).

God promised to extend his rule over the nations through the Davidic kingdom (Ps. 2) and through this rule to bring God's blessing to the nations (72:15). Even the prophets, who knew well the faults of their nation, never lost sight of God's global purposes, consistently holding out the hope of the restoration of Israel, the universal rule of Yahweh, and the blessing of the nations (Jer. 4:2; Zech. 8:13; cf. Isa. 19:24–25).

Jesus. The New Testament clearly situates Jesus within this larger Old Testament story. He fulfills the promises given to Abraham (see Gal. 3:16; cf. Gen. 12:7; 13:15; 24:7) and David (see Acts 13:33; Heb. 1:5; cf. 2 Sam. 7:12–16; Ps. 2). He assumes the role of Israel and David as the source of blessing to the entire earth (Acts 3:25; Gal. 3:8).

> In other words, the New Testament writers were convinced that Jesus Christ was not some mysterious figure suddenly dropped from the blue, with no connection to the almost two thousand years of God's activity in history that had preceded him. Rather, Jesus Christ was the completion and fulfillment and final reinterpretation of that lively history, and so he can only be fully understood in terms of it.[53]

53. E. R. Achtemeier, *Preaching from the Old Testament* (Louisville: Westminster John Knox, 1989), 25; cf. D. L. Baker, *Two Testaments, One Bible: A Study of the Theological Relationship*

Recent research on Jesus has bolstered this connection between him and the Old Testament story. His message focused on the restoration of Israel as a nation, the fulfillment of the hopes of the Old Testament.[54] By gathering around himself a group of "twelve," Jesus was suggesting the establishment of a new Israel (Matt. 10:2–4; Mark 3:16–19; Luke 6:14–16). By linking the death-resurrection of his body with the destruction-restoration of the temple, Jesus was signaling the appearance of a new temple (Matt. 26:61; 27:40; Mark 14:58; 15:29; John 2:18–22). Near the end of his ministry, as his message was rejected by the Jewish leadership, he pronounced judgment on Israel and its key institution, the temple (Matt. 24; Mark 13; Luke 21; cf. Luke 19:39–44). This prophetic message was fulfilled in A.D. 70 as the Romans destroyed Jerusalem, confirming the creation of a new Israel through Jesus' followers. Jesus came to restore Israel, but in ways not always consistent with the expectations of his generation.[55]

Church. This message informs the message and mission of the early church. Acts begins with a key conversation between Christ and his disciples in which they ask him whether the kingdom will be restored to Israel (Acts 1:6). Although he replies that the Father alone knows the precise answer (1:7), he suggests the first step toward the establishment of God's universal kingdom: "But you will receive power when the Holy Spirit comes on you; and you will be my witnesses in Jerusalem, and in all Judea and Samaria, and to the ends of the earth" (1:8).

Acts 1:12–26 then relates the story of the apostolic replacement for Judas. The significance of this story lies in the symbolism of an apostolic foundation of twelve Jewish men. As with Jesus, the appointment of the Twelve can only be linked to the twelve tribes of Israel.

Acts 1 sets the scene for the story of the day of Pentecost in Acts 2. In his sermon Peter, standing "up with the Eleven" (emphasizing the symbolism of new Israel), announces that the coming of the Holy Spirit is the fulfillment

---

Between the Old and New Testaments, rev. ed. (Leicester: Apollos, 1991); C. J. H. Wright, *Knowing Jesus Through the Old Testament* (Downers Grove, Ill.: InterVarsity Press, 1995).

54. See esp. E. P. Sanders, *Jesus and Judaism* (London: SCM, 1985), 61–119; G. R. Beasley-Murray, *Jesus and the Kingdom of God* (Grand Rapids: Eerdmans, 1986); N. T. Wright, Victory; S. McKnight, *A New Vision for Israel: The Teaching of Jesus in National Context* (Grand Rapids: Eerdmans, 1999). Sanders concludes: "Jesus intended Jewish restoration" (p. 116).

55. As Sanders notes, "Jesus shared the world-view that I have called 'Jewish restoration eschatology.' The key facts are his start under John the Baptist, the call of the twelve, his expectation of a new (or at least renewed) temple, and the eschatological setting of the work of the apostles (Gal. 1.2; Rom. 11.11–13, 25–32; 15.15–19)," but also that "neither he nor his disciples thought that the kingdom would be established by force of arms. They looked for an eschatological miracle"; Sanders, *Jesus and Judaism,* 326.

of the ancient prophecy of Joel (Joel 2:28–32). By citing this ancient prophecy, Peter reveals that the outpouring of the Spirit on Pentecost and the calling on God by this remnant returned from the nations to Jerusalem is the fulfillment of the prophetic hope for the restoration of Israel. The "three thousand" who repented, were baptized (Acts 2:38–41), and entered into this community (2:42–47) were the new Israel. This community will move out from Jerusalem and spread the kingdom to the ends of the earth.

This understanding of the church as the new Israel is echoed throughout the New Testament. In Galatians 6:16 the church is identified as the "Israel of God," in Philippians 3:3 as the "[true] circumcision." Gentiles who enter the church enter the commonwealth of Israel (Eph. 2:12). In describing the bride of the Lamb as the new Jerusalem, Revelation 21:12 reveals that the names of the twelve tribes of Israel are written on her gates. First Peter 2:9–10 takes titles formerly used of Israel in the Old Testament and applies them to the church community (cf. Ex. 19:6; Hos. 2:16–23). Likewise Hebrews 8:8–12 reveals that the Israelite new covenant promise (Jer. 31:31–34) has now been established through Jesus for the church.

The church is thus identified as the promised restoration community of Israel. In and through Christ and founded on the new Twelve, this community extends to Gentiles as well, drawing them in as legitimate members to the new Israel (Eph. 2:11–22; 3:6; cf. Rom. 10:12; Gal. 3:28; Col. 3:11) and finally fulfilling that ancient promise to Abraham in Genesis 12 (Gal. 3:14). But although the church is identified as the community restored through Christ's work, there are indications that the exile is an ongoing reality for God's people and that the motif is used for the experience of the church as they await Christ's return.[56]

Thus, the church is described as Israel "scattered" (James 1:1; 1 Peter 1:1; cf. Deut. 30:4; Neh. 1:9; Ps. 147:2; Isa. 49:6), as "strangers" and "aliens" in this world (1 Peter 1:1; 2:11; cf. Ezra 8:35; Ps. 119:5; Ezek. 20:38; Heb. 11:13). We are encouraged, then, to "stand firm" (Phil. 4:1) because "our citizenship is in heaven," from which "we eagerly await a Savior," that is, the "Lord Jesus

56. Cf. L. Ryken, J. C. Wilhoit, and T. Longman, "Restoration," in *Dictionary of Biblical Imagery* (Downers Grove, Ill.: InterVarsity Press, 1997), 250–51; I. M. Duguid, "Exile," in *New Dictionary of Biblical Theology*, ed. T. D. Alexander and B. S. Rosner (Downers Grove, Ill.: InterVarsity Press, 2000), 477–78; see W. J. Webb, *Returning Home: New Covenant and Second Exodus As the Context for 2 Corinthians 6:14–7:1* (JSNTSup 85; Sheffield: Sheffield Academic Press, 1993); D. L. Bock, "The Trial and Death of Jesus in N. T. Wright's Jesus and the Victory of God," in *Jesus and the Restoration of Israel: A Critical Assessment of N. T. Wright's Jesus and the Victory of God*, ed. C. Newman (Downers Grove, Ill.: InterVarsity Press, 1999), 101–25; S. Hafemann, "Paul and the Exile of Israel in Galatians 3–4," in *Exile: Old Testament, Jewish and Christian Conceptions*, ed. J. M. Scott (JSJSup 56; Leiden: Brill, 1997), 329–71.

Christ" (Phil. 3:20).[57] The apostle Peter declares that Christ's return will be the time when God will "restore everything" (Acts 3:21). When the disciples, prior to his ascension, ask Jesus when he is going to "restore the kingdom to Israel," he discourages them from speculating on the precise time and encourages them to preach the gospel to all nations, implying that restoration is still future and is connected with the spread of the gospel (1:6–8).

This "already–not yet" aspect of the exile–restoration theological complex is a regular feature of New Testament theology. Christ has come and is coming, Christians are sanctified and being sanctified, this world is redeemed and being redeemed. Rather than disappointing us as members of this new covenant community, this aspect is a comfort and encouragement to live faithfully in this world as we await the consummation of all things. It also brings alive Old Testament texts that depict God's people awaiting his deliverance, something not lost on the writer of Hebrews 11 (esp. 11:8–10, 13–16).

Jews. If the church is identified as the new Israel, restored and being restored, what then of the Jews as an enduring ethnic and religious community? There are some who find no space in New Testament theology for a future for Israel as a special nation or community, now that the church has fulfilled Israel's role in redemptive history.[58] The destruction of Jerusalem in A.D. 70 was God's judgment against a disobedient community, bringing an end to the national hopes of Israel. The remnant of Israel has been preserved in the apostolic community of the church. Others, however, propose a biblical theology with parallel redemptive tracks for Israel and the church.[59] These theologians distinguish between the present dispensation of the church with its mission to the Gentiles and God's plan for Israel, which will reach fulfillment in a future millennial kingdom. For many of these, the reestablishment of Israel as a nation in 1948 presages this coming Jewish kingdom.

---

57. Paul uses similar language and motifs to describe the movement of Gentiles from outside Israel into the new Israel of God in Eph. 2:12, 19, but this should not be confused with the enduring exilic motif for the church in relationship to the world.

58. E.g., D. E. Holwerda, *Jesus and Israel: One Covenant or Two?* (Leicester: Inter-Varsity Press, 1995); M. H. Woudstra, "Israel and the Church: A Case for Continuity," in *Continuity and Discontinuity: Perspectives on the Relationship Between the Old and New Testaments,* ed. J. S. Feinberg (Westchester, Ill.: Crossway, 1988), 221–38.

59. E.g., H. Lindsey, *The Late Great Planet Earth* (Grand Rapids: Zondervan, 1970); J. S. Feinberg, "Hermeneutics of Discontinuity," in *Continuity and Discontinuity: Perspectives on the Relationship Between the Old and New Testaments,* ed. J. S. Feinberg (Westchester, Ill.: Crossway, 1988), 109–28; J. E. Walvoord, *Armageddon, Oil and the Middle East Crisis* (Grand Rapids: Zondervan, 1990). Blaising represents new trends in dispensational theology, although his use of the work of Sanders, Wright, and McKnight to bolster his arguments is not appropriate; C. A. Blaising, "The Future of Israel as a Theological Question," *JETS* 44 (2001): 435–50.

Both of these views, however, are extremes that fail to do justice to the New Testament witness.[60] On the one hand, any attempt to create parallel redemptive tracks for Israel and the Church fails to recognize the unique and climactic work of Christ on the cross. This sacrifice was for Jew and Gentile alike, and any suggestion of a return to temple sacrifice does not take seriously the New Testament message of the atonement. On the other hand, the New Testament witness reserves special attention for the Jewish community through whom God's revelation and redemption has come to humanity. Key to understanding this is the argument of Romans 9–11.

After reviewing the foundations of Christian theology in Romans 1–8 and before laying out the implications of this theology for our life in this world (chs. 12–16), Paul grapples with the issue of Israel's rejection of Christ. Clearly he refers here to the physical descendants of Abraham, that is, ethnic Israel (9:2–5). Paul struggles with the implications of Israel's rejection for one's view of God: If Israel has rejected God's Messiah, has God's Word failed (9:6)? Paul provides a perspective on the future of the Jewish community within redemptive history.

(1) He asserts that physical descent does not constitute membership in Israel; rather, only those to whom God has extended mercy are included in Israel (Rom. 9:6–18).[61] (2) He argues that God's desire is to include the Gentiles in his covenant people, an inclusion made possible through the hardening of Israel's heart (9:19–33). (3) He reminds his readers that God has offered the message of Jesus to the Israelites, some of whom accepted it while others rejected it (ch. 10). The message has now gone out to the nations to evoke jealousy in Israel (10:19–20). (4) He declares that God has not rejected his people but has saved a remnant, of which Paul is representative (11:1–10). (5) Paul sees the expansion of the gospel among the Gentiles as a means to make Israel envious (11:11–32).

Two points are clear in these chapters. (1) Paul does not construct parallel redemptive tracks for Israel and the church. It is one olive tree, from which branches are cut out (Jews) and into which branches are grafted (Gentiles). That olive tree is the community of God established through the sacrifice of Christ on the cross. (2) For Paul, Israel (even "all Israel," 11:26) is not a matter of ethnicity alone but also of the heart (9:6).

---

60. For similar approaches to this issue see H. K. LaRondelle, *The Israel of God in Prophecy: Principles of Prophetic Interpretation* (AUMSR 13; Berrien Springs, Mich.: Andrews Univ. Press, 1983); S. Motyer, *Israel in the Plan of God* (Leicester: Inter-Varsity Press, 1989); Holwerda, *Jesus and Israel*; and G. E. Ladd, *A Theology of the New Testament*, rev. ed. (Grand Rapids: Eerdmans, 1993), 103–9, 200–201.

61. Earlier in the letter (Rom. 2:28–29) Paul has used similar language to speak of true Israel. Being a true Israelite is a matter of the heart, not lineage.

Therefore, Romans 9–11 argues that there is a future for the Jewish community, but not apart from Jesus and his gospel. While the gospel of the kingdom extended out from Israel to the nations through the community of the Twelve, the apostle Paul envisions an interesting twist in redemptive history: God has now hardened Israel as the nations are saved and will use these redeemed nations to bring salvation to the Jews. True Israel will assume its place *within* Christ's redeemed community. Through Israel the blessing of God extended to the nations and to Israel is the same blessing as all enter into the bride of Christ.[62]

C. Haggai-Zechariah and the New Testament

THIS PERSPECTIVE ON ISRAEL and the church helps us see how the original message of Haggai and Zechariah was taken up in the New Testament witness.

1. Haggai and Zechariah 1–8. The prophet Haggai calls his generation to pursue the priority of temple reconstruction. Although this message was focused on the present generation and their responsibility, an eschatological tone is evident in Haggai 2:1–9 and 2:20–23. For him present obedience is intricately linked with the inauguration of the new age in which Yahweh will rule the world through his Davidic vice-regent. The participation of both Zerubbabel (a descendant of David) and Joshua (the priestly line commissioned by David) in this rebuilding project is important to this eschatological vision. Zechariah continues this trend of linking the rebuilding of the temple and city with the inauguration of the new age and the restoration of the Davidic line. For him the key figure is Zerubbabel, with Joshua playing a supporting role (cf. Zech. 4:6b–10a; 6:9–15).

This emphasis within Haggai and Zechariah 1–8 lays the foundation for New Testament messianic claims for Jesus. The genealogies of Jesus in Matthew and Luke, although tracing different lines after King David, intersect prior to Christ in the person of Zerubbabel (Matt. 1:12–13; Luke 3:27). The early church saw Jesus not only as arising from Zerubbabel but ultimately fulfilling the hopes attached to him. The language of Matthew 27:28–29 and John 19:5, both of which describe the crowning of Jesus (with thorns), appears to be influenced by the description of the crowning of *ṣemaḥ* ("the Branch") in Zechariah 6:11.[63]

62. However, Scripture does not tell us the specific timing and means of this renewal among ethnic Israel.

63. B. Lindars, *New Testament Apologetic: The Doctrinal Significance of the Old Testament Quotations* (London: SCM, 1961), 70.

This connection is bolstered by the fact that the Gospel writer includes Pilate's declaration "Behold the man," an allusion to the declaration of Zechariah in 6:12. As the ultimate *ṣemaḥ*/Zerubbabel Jesus has the proper authority not only to destroy his temple but also to rebuild it, even if this does not match the expectations of his generation. As N. T. Wright has argued, "Jesus is to be the reality towards which the figure of Zerubbabel was pointing. Judgment will be followed by a strange new rebuilding."[64]

Both Haggai and Zechariah 1–8 speak of the return of God as the key sign of this eschatological age. This, however, is not fulfilled in their generation, and throughout the coming era many within the Jewish community will continue to long for this return.[65] According to the early Christian witness this return has been realized in the coming of Jesus (Luke 1:68, 78; 7:16; 15:14; cf. Luke 19:44; 1 Peter 2:12).[66]

Christ's discussion of fasting and feasting in the Gospels (Matt. 9:15–16/Mark 2:19–22/Luke 5:34–37) must be interpreted against the background of Zechariah's promised transformation in 7:1–8:23. When Christ discourages fasting, he is insinuating that the restoration has now begun.[67] So also Christ's inclusion of the Gentiles in this feasting in Matthew 8:11–12 is based on Zechariah 1–8 (2:11; 8:8, 18–23), where not only are fasts turned into feasts but also Gentiles join Jews in the festal community of God.[68] Furthermore, Christ's expectation of the gathering of the elect from the four winds of heaven at the eschaton (Matt. 24:31; Mark 13:27) draws from the restoration vision of Zechariah 2:6; 6:1–8.[69]

The influence of Haggai and Zechariah 1–8 is also found in the New Testament outside the Gospel accounts in contexts that set the fulfillment of their vision of restoration into the eschatological future of the church.[70] For

---

64. Wright, *Victory*, 500; cf. 483–84 (esp. n. 94), 499–500, 520–21.

65. See ibid., 615–24, esp. 622, where Wright cites the intertestamental evidence of *1 En.* 1:3–4, 9; *T. Mos.* 10:1, 3, 7; 12:13; *Jub* 1:26–28; 11Q19 (11Q Temple[a]) 29:3–9; cf. R. L. Webb, *John the Baptizer and Prophet: A Socio-Historical Study* (JSNTSup 62; Sheffield: Sheffield Academic Press, 1991), ch. 7. This is not true of all Jews in this period, as has been argued by G. I. Davies, "The Presence of God in the Second Temple and Rabbinic Doctrine," in *Templum Amicitiae: Essays on the Second Temple Presented to Ernst Bammel*, ed. W. Horbury (JSNTSup 48; Sheffield: Sheffield Academic Press, 1991), 32–36; see esp. the evidence of Matt. 23:21.

66. For Zechariah a key human response to God's promised restoration is the call to flee from Babylon, which is being judged (Zech. 2:6–8). Wright (*Victory*, 358) has argued that this language is picked up in Christ's message of Mark 13 and applied to the Jerusalem of his day.

67. Ibid., 433–34.

68. Cf. Beasley-Murray, *Jesus*, 170–71, 332.

69. Lindars, *New Testament Apologetic*, 111; Beasley-Murray, *Jesus*, 332.

70. For these see Lindars, *New Testament Apologetic*, 111.

instance, Hebrews 12:26 draws on Haggai 2:6 to describe God's cataclysmic shaking of the cosmos in the renewal of all things. Revelation 21:3 appears to be drawing on Zechariah 2:14, when the new Jerusalem appears as a bride and God dwells with humanity in covenant relationship. This suggests that ultimate fulfillment of Zechariah's vision of restoration is seen in the future.[71]

These various passages reveal the importance of Haggai and Zechariah to the eschatological vision of Jesus and the early church. For them the eschaton is already breaking in through Christ's earthly ministry, even as there is expectation of much more to come (compare Hag. 2:6 with Heb. 12:26).

Zechariah 9–14. Zechariah 9–14 develops a future expectation for Israel in two successive waves. In the first wave (chs. 9–10) one finds a message of expectation in which God returns in triumph, introduces his king, and saves his people from exile, uniting all twelve tribes. In the second wave, God cleanses this community and defeats the nations, establishing his rule on earth. Jerusalem appears at the center of these expectations as the seat of God's rule, the destination of the restoration community, the site of the battle against the nations, and the home of God's holy community.

This expectation, however, is declared to a community in turmoil. The prophetic voices of Zechariah 9–14 speak against a leadership in Jerusalem that cares little for God's people and in some way is associated with idolatry/divination (10:1–3; 11:1–17; 13:1–9). It is uncertain as to who this leadership is. Most likely no one from Davidic lineage is in view; rather, Zadokite priests seem to be in liaison with Persian officials because of the following evidence:

1. There is a positive role to be played by the Davidic house (12:1–13:6), through the line of Nathan.
2. The Davidic house is linked to a priestly family, but it is the Levitical line through Shimei, so that the Zadokite priestly line, presently ruling in Jerusalem, is left out.
3. Although there is a positive view of Jerusalem, problems are apparent in the city at the moment, related to ritual issues (priestly) as well as some form of idolatry/divination. It is difficult to imagine that Zadokite priests would be involved in idolatry/divination, so it is

71. The book of Revelation draws heavily on Zech. 1–6, but in some cases this appears to be nothing more than just using the images to express a future vision (e.g., Zech. 4:10/Rev. 5:6: the lamb on the throne had seven horns and seven eyes, which are the seven spirits of God sent out into all the earth; Zech. 6:1–3/Rev. 6:2: white, red, black, pale horses sent out to bring God's judgment; Zech. 6:5/Rev. 7:1–4: angels at four corners of world, preventing wind from blowing until the 144,000 could be sealed on their foreheads for protection—all tribes; Zech. 4:11–14/Rev. 11:4: two olive trees as prophets; Zech. 3:1/Rev. 12:9/20:2: Satan).

most likely that this is related to a Persian-endorsed governor after the Davidic line, who may have used Persian methods and religion and thus brought ritual impurity to the city.

4. The shepherds are seen as intimately linked to "owners," who are the nations (Persians). Perhaps the shepherds are to be equated with the priests, and the owners with the Persians and their officials. Alternatively, perhaps the shepherds represent the Persian governors, and the owners represent the emperor. It is impossible to be certain about this.

Thus, Zechariah 9–14 envisions a great work of God that will be accomplished for, among, and through his people and have a global impact. This will be accomplished by God's intervention in their history, his cleansing and provision of leadership (royal and priestly), and his restoration of a holy community.

It is not surprising, then, that the New Testament alludes explicitly and implicitly to Zechariah 9–14 in its portrayal of Jesus.[72]

- His entry into Jerusalem is patterned after 9:9 (Matt. 21:5; Mark 11:1–11; Luke 19; John 12:15).
- His promise of "living water" to those gathered for the Feast of Tabernacles declares the fulfillment in his ministry of Zechariah 14:8, 16–19 (John 7:38).[73]
- His cleansing of the temple with a refusal to allow people to carry or sell vessels in it is probably a play on Zechariah 14:20–21 (Matt. 21; Mark 11:16; Luke 19; John 2:16).

---

72. This fact has been documented in great detail by many scholars sources: esp. by C. H. Dodd, *According to the Scriptures: The Sub-Structure of New Testament Theology* (London: Nisbet, 1952), 64–67, 72–74; Lindars, *New Testament Apologetic*, 110–37; F. F. Bruce, "The Book of Zechariah and the Passion Narrative," BJRL 43 (1960–1961); F. F. Bruce, *This Is That: The New Testament Development of Some Old Testament Themes* (Exeter: Paternoster, 1968), 100–14; R. T. France, *Jesus and the Old Testament: His Application of Old Testament Passages to Himself and His Mission* (London: Tyndale, 1971); J. Marcus, *The Way of the Lord: Christological Exegesis of the Old Testament in the Gospel of Mark* (Louisville: Westminster John Knox, 1992), 154–64, 196–98, 207–13; Wright, *Victory*, 344–45, 358; and C. Evans, "Aspects of Exile and Restoration in the Proclamation of Jesus and the Gospels," in *Exile: Old Testament, Jewish and Christian Conceptions*, ed. J. M. Scott (SJSJ 56; Leiden: Brill, 1997), 327; idem, "Jesus and Zechariah's Messianic Hope," in *Authenticating the Activities of Jesus*, ed. C. A. Evans and B. D. Chilton (NTTS 28.2; Leiden: Brill, 1998), 373–88. See further lists in M. J. Boda, *Haggai-Zechariah Research: A Bibliographic Survey* (Tools for Biblical Studies; Leiden: DEO Publishing, 2003).

73. Black also suggests an allusion in John 19:34 in the flow of blood and "water" from Jesus' pierced side; M. C. Black, "The Rejected and Slain Messiah Who Is Coming with His Angels: The Messianic Exegesis of Zechariah 9–14 in the Passion Narratives" (Ph.D., Emory University, 1990), 238.

- His judgment of the temple, delivered on the Mount of Olives, speaks of a great battle of the nations against Jerusalem, and the flight of his disciples contains strong links to Zechariah 14 (esp. 14:1–3, 4–5, 9; cf. Mark 13; Matt. 27).[74]
- His arrest and death, followed by the fearful flight of his disciples, are linked to Zechariah 13:7 (Mark 14:27; John 16).
- His betrayal by Judas to the Jewish leadership is linked to Zechariah 11:13 (Matt. 26:14–16; 27:3–10).[75]
- The reference to his "little flock" is likely a play on the pastoral language of Zechariah 11:11; 13:7 (Luke 12:32); similarly, his depiction of Israel as a "sheep without a shepherd" alludes to Zechariah 10:2 (Matt. 9:36; Mark 6:34).[76]
- The piercing of Jesus' side is linked to Zechariah 12:10 (John 19:37), as is the mourning of women at the crucifixion (Luke 23:27).
- The earthquake and appearance of holy ones alludes to Zechariah 14:3–5 (Matt. 27:51–53).

In the most detailed analysis of connections between Zechariah 9–14 and the Gospels, Mark Black concludes that these six chapters are "the most-quoted portion of the OT in the gospel accounts of the final days of Jesus . . . the number of events and details in the gospels which are *integrally* related to Zech. 9–14 is staggering."[77] The reason for this is linked by Black to the way in which Zechariah 9–14 envisions the future:

> What the early church discovered after being led to Zech. 9–14 is a whole eschatological schema which involved the sending of the messiah; his subsequent rejection, suffering, and death; the repentance, cleansing, and restoration which would follow the death; and the resurrection of the saints which would follow in the messianic kingdom.[78]

The general correspondence is clear: (1) The events in Zechariah 9–14 and Christ's Passion occur in the vicinity of Jerusalem; (2) the primary actors

74. See Wright: "The force of the setting then seems to be that this was Jesus' paradoxical retelling of the great story found in Zechariah 14: in predicting Jerusalem's last great struggle, the 'coming' of YHWH, and the final arrival of the divine kingdom, he was acting to fulfil, in his own reinterpreted fashion, the prophecy of Zechariah"; Wright, *Victory*, 345.

75. On the attribution of this prophecy in Matthew to Jeremiah see Bruce, "Passion Narrative," 341.

76. See other possible connections: Zech. 14:4 and Matt. 17:20; Mark 11:23; Zech. 11:6 and Mark 9:31; Zech. 9:11 and Mark 14:24; Zech. 9:14 and Matt. 24:31; Zech. 12:3 and Luke 21:24.

77. Black, "Rejected and Slain Messiah," 234, 237.

78. Ibid., 239.

in both are indifferent Jewish leaders who oppose and reject God's representative; (3) a representative of God is shepherd and king and by the will of God suffers and dies; and (4) nations who were formerly enemies of Israel are brought to worship God.[79] The sequence of events is also similar. Even if Zechariah 9–14 was originally only a collection of oracles,[80] there is a general correspondence between the Passion narratives and these chapters from Zechariah, as Black has shown: [81]

Event	Zechariah	Gospels
Messiah enters	9:9–10	Mark 11:1–11 & par.
Covenant established	9:11	Mark 14:24 & par.
Messiah rejected	11:4–17	Matt. 27:51–53; Mark 12:1–12 etc.
Messiah betrayed	11:12–13	Mark 14:10–11; Matt. 27:3–10
Messiah deserted	13:7	Mark 14:26–31, 50, 66–72 & par.
Death of Messiah	12:10; 13:7	Mark 15 & par.; John 19:28–37
Mourning of people	12:11–14	Luke 23:27; Mark 15:39–45 & par.
Cleansing of people	13:1, 8–9	John 7:38; Mark 14:24 et al.
Resurrection	14:3–5	Matt. 27:51–53; Mark 16 & par.

Like Zechariah, Jesus stood against the leadership of his day and came to realize the eschatological hopes of Israel. Thus, Zechariah 9–14 is first and foremost "fulfilled" and enacted by Jesus through his earthly ministry. As C. H. Dodd has concluded:

> The employment of these scriptures as testimonies to the *kerygma* indicates that the crisis out of which the Christian movement arose is regarded as the realization of the prophetic vision of judgment and redemption ... the prophets seriously believed that what they spoke of (in however cryptic terms) would happen. The early Christians believed it had happened, or at least was in process of happening.[82]

Dodd's final sentence reveals another aspect of the New Testament witness, namely, that the fulfillment of Zechariah 9–14 was viewed as past as well as future.[83] These prophecies, therefore, were "declaring that which had happened, was happening and would happen, indistinguishably."[84]

---

79. See esp. Wright, *Victory*, 586–87.

80. Black, "Rejected and Slain Messiah," 243. As Black notes: "The reader is nonetheless encouraged to form in his/her mind a picture of the eschatological drama by which Yahweh will restore his people and bring the nations to himself" (p. 240).

81. Ibid., 245.

82. Dodd, *According to the Scriptures*, 72–73.

83. Notice, e.g., how in his depiction of future judgment, Jesus uses language similar to Zech. 14:5 (Matt. 25:31; cf. 1 Thess. 3:13).

84. Dodd, *According to the Scriptures*, 74.

This "not yet" approach to Zechariah 9–14 can also be discerned in Revelation. Revelation 1:7 clearly alludes to Zechariah 12:10: "Look, he is coming with the clouds, and every eye will see him, even those who pierced him; and all the peoples of the earth will mourn because of him. So shall it be! Amen." This continues the belief that Christ indeed came to fulfill the expectations of Zechariah 9–14, but in doing so it pushes the realization of this fulfillment in the future and expands the fulfillment to include not only Israel but also the nations.[85]

A similar trend is also discernible in the complex of events described in Revelation 20–22, which Sweet calls "a creative reinterpretation of scripture in the light of the cross":

> Zechariah 14 takes up the same motifs, which are all echoed in Revelation 20–2: the nations gathered against Jerusalem (14:2); the fountain (14:8); removal of the curse (14:11); the survivors come up to keep the feast of Tabernacles, or ingathering (14:16); Jerusalem is all holy (14:20).[86]

These links reveal that Zechariah 9–14 was influential for early Christian interpretation of the first phase of Christ's ministry (up to his resurrection), but also for the expected final phase (at the eschaton). As his ministry initiated a much larger complex of events, one must not confine the fulfillment of these chapters to this first phase of Christ's ministry, but see how it is being fulfilled in and through the church in history and will reach its climax in the return of Christ.

D. Implications

IN THIS BRIDGING CONTEXTS section we have noted that prophecy in general originated as messages focused on both present and future; that is, it had both a forthtelling as well as a foretelling aspect. The "foretelling" aspects of these ancient prophecies connect the Christian community to these texts and invite the Christian interpreter to heed their "forthtelling" aspects. (1) Haggai and

---

85. One may see in the destruction of Jerusalem the fulfillment of Rev. 1:7, but this can hardly be the case for Rev. 20–22.

86. J. P. Sweet, "Maintaining the Testimony of Jesus: The Suffering of Christians in the Revelation of John (and Use of Zech 12–14 in the NT)," in *Suffering and Martyrdom in the New Testament: Studies Presented to G. M. Styler*, ed. W. Horbury (Cambridge: Cambridge Univ. Press, 1981), 112; see the more general comments of W. Harrelson, "Messianic Expectations at the Time of Jesus," *SLJT* 32 (1988): 40: "As to specific content, the books of Revelation and Hebrews show the closest connections with the eschatology of Ezekiel and Zechariah."

Zechariah point to Christ as the One through whom the ancient hopes were and will be fulfilled, inviting us to celebrate God's redemptive actions and situate ourselves within this larger story. (2) In light of this connection, Haggai and Zechariah espouse essential values for the church as the new Israel, established and being established by Jesus.

These two aspects of prophetic literature are evident in the approach of the New Testament to the ancient prophecy. As an essential part of the Old Testament witness, writes Paul in his paradigmatic statement, the prophets are "able to make you wise for salvation through faith in Christ Jesus" (2 Tim. 3:15) and are "useful for teaching, rebuking, correcting and training in righteousness" (2 Tim. 3:16).

In many circles the prophets are used merely as sign posts pointing to redemption in Christ. In others the prophets are moral agents who shape the ethical agenda of the church.[87] Taking our lead from the character of the prophetic literature and from the New Testament interpretation, our interpretation must strike a balance between these two aspects.

I can remember well a course on preaching Christ from the Old Testament that I took with Edmund Clowney.[88] Dr. Clowney repeatedly stressed the need to preach Old Testament texts with the great story of redemption in mind, to demonstrate how the Old Testament anticipates the gospel. When a student raised a concern over the relevance of such preaching for his church ministry, Dr. Clowney gently reminded us that there was nothing more relevant than witness to the death and resurrection of Jesus Christ, more practical than the transforming message of the gospel. In a pragmatic culture filled with how-to books, it is easy to miss the powerful witness of the Scriptures to God's redemptive plan. The prophets make us "wise for salvation through faith in Christ Jesus," and this salvation needs to be proclaimed and celebrated within the Christian community.

This, however, need not be separated from the ethical dimension of the prophetic message, as Paul makes clear in 2 Timothy 3:16–17. The prophets too are useful in rebuking, correcting, and training us in righteousness. Deeply rooted in the story of salvation we must proclaim the message of the prophets, which shape our view of God as well as our walk with him.

---

87. Notice the vigorous debate over the use of the Old Testament in the Dutch (*Gereformeerde*) church between "redemptive historical" and "example" preaching; cf. S. Greidanus, *Sola Scriptura: Problems and Principles in Preaching Historical Texts* (Toronto: Wedge, 1970).

88. See E. P. Clowney, *Preaching and Biblical Theology* (Grand Rapids: Eerdmans, 1961); idem, "Preaching Christ from All the Scriptures," in The Preacher and Preaching, ed. S. T. Logan (Phillipsburg, N.J.: Presbyterian and Reformed, 1986), 163–91; idem, The *Unfolding Mystery: Discovering Christ in the Old Testament* (Leicester: Inter-Varsity Press, 1988).

This orientation to the biblical-theological relationship between prophecy and the New Testament needs to shape our hermeneutical approach to Haggai and Zechariah. Understanding Haggai and Zechariah demands sensitivity to the various contexts of these passages. (1) It requires exegesis of the message of this corpus, determining the meaning of the various messages in their original contexts and the way these texts spoke to their original communities. (2) It requires sensitivity to the way in which this message was appropriated by Jesus and his community. (3) Based on this foundation, this ancient text continues to speak to the community of faith today, identifying Jesus and his followers as the focus of eschatological hope while shaping our vision of the present and future of the church.

Contemporary Significance

BY PLACING HAGGAI AND ZECHARIAH in their historical and literary as well as canonical and redemptive-historical contexts, this introduction has laid the foundation for wise and creative interpretation in our present context. As the remnant community longing for full restoration, the church today is comforted by the proclamation of the character and action of God in these prophets, while at the same time it is challenged by their exhortation to respond to this God through faith and obedience. Throughout the commentary we will discuss issues relevant to contemporary life, but some points of contact are provided below to show you the potential of this book to inform and transform Christian experience.

Passion and presence. These books grant us vivid glimpses of God. We discover that God is passionate for his people, reflected not only in his disciplinary actions of the Exile but also in his extension of grace in this new phase of redemptive history. This passionate God consistently expresses his desire to presence himself among his people, a desire that will be realized through the rebuilding of the temple and repentance of the people.

This immanent presence, however, should not be taken lightly, for God is still the transcendent God of the cosmos, who rules as king and will enact punishment on the rebellious. This message is relevant to a generation far more open to the spiritual dimension of human existence than in the past. It reminds us that "church" is ultimately about a relationship with a God who has passionately pursued us in grace. However, to this same generation these glimpses of God challenge present patterns of creating God in our own image.

Salvation and judgment. Haggai and Zechariah offer us a balanced view of God's character. These prophets reveal a God who extends his grace in the present and future, but also who disciplines and judges the impenitent. These are not seen as contradictory but as reflections of the holy character of the Lord Almighty. The prophets announce a new era of grace and restoration, but this does not ignore human sinfulness. God's desire is to purify a remnant for his name's sake. These books, therefore, are books of comfort for God's people today. However, at many points in the prophetic witness the message is a challenge to holiness and faithfulness.

Priorities and discipline. Both Haggai and Zechariah challenge the community of God to consider carefully their actions in light of his priorities. They teach the church today that God sometimes shouts to his people through the difficult circumstances of their lives, reminding them of his priorities. The way is not always easy, however, for those who follow these priorities, but God encourages those whose lives are consumed by his call that participation in kingdom work is essential to the ultimate fulfillment of his sovereign plans.

This message has great potential for shaping the agenda of the church today. It motivates God's people to participate in kingdom work in whatever form that may take, whether in church, society, or family. These prophets have a significant message for those undergoing suffering in their lives. For some people and communities God's message may be to rearrange behavior according to his priorities, while for others his message may be one of comfort, offering hope and encouragement to persevere in their calling.

Worship and word. These prophets have much to say about our practice of worship and treatment of God's Word today within our communities of faith. Worship is relational activity; that is, it has as its goal the relational encounter between God and his people expressed through the phrase: "They will be my people, and I will be their God." The message of these prophets is relevant to the church today living in a period of heightened spiritual sensitivity.

In such a world the church is called to discern carefully the spiritual patterns of a society that often creates religion in its own image rather than submitting before the personal covenant Creator of the universe. Consistently throughout these books the Word of God is placed at the center of community life—either the oral prophetic word proclaimed by Haggai and Zechariah or the written Word of ages past. These prophets call the community to bend their knees, open their ears, fix their eyes, and attune their hearts to this life-giving Word from the Lord Almighty.

Purity and justice. These prophets call their communities to a holiness that reflects that of the Lord God, who calls them to be holy as he is holy. Such purity, based on restored covenant relationship through divine grace, is encouraged in various areas of life, including the issues of priorities and worship (see above), but also in terms of our relationship with our fellow human beings. Among a community experiencing financial crises, Zechariah calls the community to avoid the unjust patterns of the past that caused the Exile and to display the covenant faithfulness and love that God outlined in the Law and the Prophets. It is this social injustice that is singled out in Zechariah 7–8 as the reason why the community went into exile and why their exilic hardship extends into the indefinite future. The church today cannot ignore this aspect of these books. Believers must be a catalyst for social justice as we proclaim the gospel in word and deed.

Nations and kingdom. These prophets clearly manifest a cosmic vision of God's kingdom. They see that the ultimate destination of redemptive history is nothing less than God's global dominion over the nations. At times this vision is negative as the prophets describe the subjugation of the power of rebellious and abusive nations. At other times this vision is positive as the prophets picture the nations' entrance into the community of faith. These themes relate to us today as we seek to extend God's kingdom to the ends of the earth. They remind us of God's intentions for the nations—to rule, but also to save.

Messiah and kingdom. Both prophets anticipate the arrival of a royal figure through whom God will rule these nations (Hag. 2:20–23; Zech. 3:8–10; 6:9–15; 9:9–10; 12:10–14). Zerubbabel's participation in leadership is a sign of God's faithful design on the Davidic line, a line that will continue unabated through the next four centuries and ultimately produce Jesus the Christ, who will usher in God's kingdom. However, the methods of his subjugation of the nations are surprising in light of some aspects of Haggai and Zechariah, for it is through suffering that Christ reveals the powerful arm of the Lord. According to the early church, this suffering is foreshadowed in Zechariah 9–14 (9:9–10; 11:4–17; 13:7–9).

Unity and leadership. Haggai and Zechariah both speak of the importance of unity and leadership to the accomplishment of God's kingdom purposes. They envision a community in which king, priest, and prophet cooperate to bring God's rule on earth. They see a future in which northern and southern tribes and urban and rural populations will live in unity once again. Key to this unity is leadership purified in their motives and practices, replicating the example of God as the ultimate Shepherd of the sheep. It was leadership that led the people astray in the preexilic generations, and God's displeasure with any restoration of such leadership is evident throughout Zechariah (esp. chs. 9–14). God commits himself to lead his dear flock, but he accomplishes this through providing leaders for his community. These books, thus, challenge us as we lead and follow in his covenant community today.

This introduction has sought to shape a hermeneutical framework for our interpretation of these prophetic books. It makes clear that in this commentary we will strive for a balanced multidimensional reading of these books with attention to both the ancient historical and literary aspects, as well as the biblical-theological and contemporary potential of these books for the church today. That such is possible is witness to the grace of the revelatory God of Israel, who not only spoke in the past but continues to speak today to us by his Spirit through this Word.

Outline of Haggai

A. Exhortation to Rebuild the Temple (1:1–15)
   1. Superscription (1:1)
   2. Prophetic Message (1:2–11)
   3. People's Response (1:12–14)
   4. Subscription (1:15)

B. Encouragement for Restoring the Former Glory (2:1–9)
   1. Superscription (2:1)
   2. Identifying the Issue (2:2–3)
   3. Prophetic Encouragement (2:4–5)
   4. Promise of Future Glory (2:6–9)

C. Prophetic Message on the Day the Foundation Was Laid (2:10–23)
   1. Superscription (2:10)
   2. Past Defilement (2:11–14)
   3. Present As Transformation from Past Curse to Future Blessing (2:15–19)
   4. Superscription (2:20)
   5. Future Triumph (2:21–23)

Outline of Zechariah

A. Sermon and Narrative: God's Call and Promise to Return (1:1–6)
   1. Superscription (1:1)
   2. Sermon (1:2–6a)
   3. Narrative (1:6b)

B. Vision of Horses, Oracles of Comfort (1:7–17)
   1. Superscription (1:7)
   2. Visionary Scene (1:8–13)
   3. Oracles (1:14–17)

- **C. Vision of the Horns and Plowmen (1:18–21)**
  1. Vision of the Horns (1:18–19)
  2. Vision of the Plowmen (1:20–21)
- **D. Vision and Oracle: Jerusalem's Walls and God's Presence (2:1–5)**
  1. Vision (2:1–4)
  2. Oracle (2:5)
- **E. Oracle of Return of People and God (2:6–13)**
  1. Call to Escape (2:6–9)
  2. Call to Rejoice (2:10–13)
- **F. Vision, Sign-Act and Oracle: Joshua, *ṣemaḥ*, and Blessing (3:1–10)**
  1. Court/Investiture Scene (3:1–5)
  2. Angelic Oracular Interpretation (3:6–10)
- **G. Vision and Oracle: The Lampstand, the Olive Trees, and Prophecy (4:1–14)**
  1. Vision of the Lampstand: Observation (Part 1) (4:1–6a)
  2. Oracles of Encouragement to Zerubbabel (4:6b–10a)
  3. Vision of the Lampstand: Interpretation (Part 2) (4:10b–14)
- **H. Vision and Oracle: The Flying Scroll and God's Judgment (5:1–4)**
  1. Description of Scene (5:1–2)
  2. Interpretation of Scene (5:3)
  3. Oracle of Judgment (5:4)
- **I. Vision of the Flying Ephah (5:5–11)**
  1. Description and Interpretation of Scene 1: Measuring Basket (5:5–6)
  2. Description and Interpretation of Scene 2: Woman (5:7–8)
  3. Description and Interpretation of Scene 3: Winged Women and Flight (5:9–11)
- **J. Vision of the Four Chariots (6:1–8)**
  1. Description of Scene (Part 1) (6:1–3)
  2. Interpretation of Scene (Part 1) (6:4–6)
  3. Description of Scene (Part 2) (6:7)
  4. Interpretation of Scene (Part 2) (6:8)
- **K. Sign-Act of the Two Crowns (6:9–15)**
  1. Exhortation (6:9–14)
  2. Explanation (6:15)
- **L. Sermon, Narrative, and Oracles: From Fasts to Feasts (7:1–8:23)**
  1. Superscription (7:1)

2. Narrative Introduction and Question of Delegation: Entreating Yahweh (7:2–3)
3. Zechariah's Challenge of Fasting Ritual (7:4–6)
4. Review of God's Word and Discipline in the Past (7:7–14)
5. God's Salvation of the Remnant: Oracles (8:1–8)
6. God's Salvation of the Remnant: Sermon (8:9–13)
7. God's New Determination (8:14–15)
8. God's Ethical Demand (8:16–17)
9. Transformation of Fasts to Feasts (8:18–19)
10. Impact on the Nations: Entreating Yahweh (8:20–23)

M. Return of God, King, and People (9:1–17)

1. God Returns in Triumph (9:1–8)
2. The King Receives His Kingdom (9:9–11)
3. The People Return to the Kingdom (9:12–17)

N. The Restoration of the Tribes (10:1–12)

1. Transforming Judah (10:1–5)
2. Restoring Joseph (10:6–12)

O. The Crisis and Cleansing of Leadership (11:1–17)

1. Announcing Judgment (11:1–3)
2. Prophetic Sign-Act of Shepherd and Sheep (11:4–16)
3. Judgment on a Leader (11:17)

P. Future Victory and Cleansing of God's People (12:1–13:6)

1. Introducing the God of the Oracle (12:1)
2. Victory for Jerusalem and Judah Against the Nations (12:2–8)
3. Repentance and Cleansing for Victorious Jerusalem (12:9–13:1)
4. Judgment on Idolatry and False Prophecy (13:2–3)
5. Enduring Eradication of False Prophecy (13:4–6)

Q. The Shepherd Struck, the Flock Scattered (13:7–9)

R. Future Victory and Submission of the Nations (14:1–21)

1. Judgment on Jerusalem (14:1–2)
2. Appearance of Yahweh (14:3–5)
3. Transforming the Cosmos, Assuming His Rule (14:6–11)
4. Defeating the Nations (14:12–15)
5. Worshiping Yahweh (14:16–21)

Bibliography on Haggai and Zechariah

The bibliography below is a select group of influential and helpful resources written in the English language over the past few decades. For a full list of works in various languages over the past century along with a review of the past two decades see the following resources:

Boda, M. J. "Majoring on the Minors: Recent Research on Haggai and Zechariah." *Currents in Biblical Research* 2 (2003): 33–68.

______. *Haggai-Zechariah Research: A Bibliographic Survey*. Tools for Biblical Studies. Leiden: DEO Publishing, 2003.

Haggai

Influential and Helpful Commentaries

Achtemeier, Elizabeth Rice. *Nahum–Malachi*. IBC. Atlanta: John Knox, 1986.

Brown, William P. *Obadiah Through Malachi*. Westminster Bible Companion. Louisville: Westminster John Knox, 1996.

Coggins, R. J. *Haggai, Zechariah, Malachi*. OTG. Sheffield: Sheffield Academic Press, 1987.

Floyd, Michael H. *Minor Prophets, Part 2*. FOTL 22. Grand Rapids: Eerdmans, 2000.

Glazier-McDonald, Beth. "Haggai." Pages 228–29 in *The Women's Bible Commentary*. Ed. Carol A. Newsom. London: SPCK, 1992.

Mason, R. A. *The Books of Haggai, Zechariah and Malachi*. CBC. Cambridge: Cambridge Univ. Press, 1977.

Merrill, Eugene H. *Haggai, Zechariah, Malachi: An Exegetical Commentary*. Chicago: Moody Press, 1994.

Meyers, Carol L., and Eric M. Meyers. *Haggai, Zechariah 1–8: A New Translation with Introduction and Commentary*. AB 25b. Garden City, N.Y.: Doubleday, 1987.

Ollenburger, Ben C. "Haggai, Zechariah and Malachi." Pages 405–14 in *The Books of the Bible*. Volume I: *The Old Testament/The Hebrew Bible*. Ed. Bernhard W. Anderson. New York: Scribners, 1989.

Petersen, David L. *Haggai and Zechariah 1–8: A Commentary*. OTL. London: SCM, 1984.

Redditt, Paul L. *Haggai, Zechariah and Malachi*. NCB. London: M. Pickering/Harper Collins, 1995.

Smith, Ralph L. *Micah-Malachi*. WBC 32. Dallas: Word, 1990.

Stuhlmueller, C. "Haggai-Zechariah-Malachi." Pages 387–401 in *The Jerome Biblical Commentary*. Ed. R. E. Brown, J. A. Fitzmyer, and R. E. Murphy. London: Geoffrey Chapman, 1970.

Sweeney, Marvin A. *The Twelve Prophets*. 2 vols. Berit Olam. Collegeville, Minn.: Liturgical, 2000.

Verhoef, Pieter A. *The Books of Haggai and Malachi*. NICOT. Grand Rapids: Eerdmans, 1987.

Helpful and Influential Monographs and Articles

Ackroyd, Peter R. "Some Interpretive Glosses in the Book of Haggai." *JJS* 7 (1956): 163–67.

_____. "Two Old Testament Historical Problems of the Early Persian Period." *JNES* 17 (1958): 13–27.

_____. *Exile and Restoration: A Study of Hebrew Thought of the Sixth Century B.C.* OTL. Philadelphia: Westminster, 1968.

Bedford, P. R. "Discerning the Time: Haggai, Zechariah and the Delay in the Rebuilding of the Jerusalem Temple." Pages 71–94 in *The Pitcher Is Broken: Memorial Essays for Gösta W. Ahlström*. Ed. Steven W. Holloway and Lowell K. Handy. Sheffield: Sheffield Academic Press, 1995.

_____. *Temple Restoration in Early Achaemenid Judah*. SJSJ. Leiden: Brill, 2001.

Berquist, J. L. *Judaism in Persia's Shadow: A Social and Cultural Approach*. Philadelphia: Fortress, 1995.

Boda, Mark J. "Haggai: Master Rhetorician." *TynBul* 51 (2000): 295–304.

Christensen, Duane L. "Impulse and Design in the Book of Haggai." *JETS* 35 (1992): 445–56.

Clark, David J. "Problems in Haggai 2:15–19." *BT* 34 (1983): 432–39.

_____. "Discourse Structure in Haggai." *Journal of Translation and Textlinguistics* 5 (1992): 13–24.

Clines, D. J. A. "Haggai's Temple, Constructed, Deconstructed and Reconstructed." Pages 60–87 in *Second Temple Studies: 2. Temple and Community in the Persian Period*. Ed. T. C. Eskenazi and K. H. Richards. Sheffield: Sheffield Academic Press, 1994.

Craig, Kenneth M. "Interrogatives in Haggai-Zechariah: A Literary Thread?" Pages 224–44 in *Forming Prophetic Literature: Essays on Isaiah and the Twelve in Honor of John D. W. Watts*. Ed. James W. Watts and Paul R. House. Sheffield: Sheffield Academic Press, 1996.

Dumbrell, W. J. "Kingship and Temple in the Post-Exilic Period." *RTR* 37 (1978): 33–42.

Floyd, Michael H. "The Nature of the Narrative and the Evidence of Redaction in Haggai." *VT* 45 (1995): 470–90.

Hildebrand, David R. "Temple Ritual: A Paradigm for Moral Holiness in Haggai II 10–19." *VT* 39 (1989): 154–68.

Holbrook, David J. "Narrowing Down Haggai: Examining Style in Light of Discourse and Content." *Journal of Translation and Textlinguistics* 7 (1995): 1–12.

Hurowitz, Victor. *I Have Built You an Exalted House: Temple Building in the Bible in Light of Mesopotamian and North West Semitic Writings*. JSOTSup 115. Sheffield: Sheffield Academic Press, 1992.

Kessler, John. "The Shaking of the Nations: An Eschatological View." *JETS* 30 (1987): 159–66.

_____. "The Second Year of Darius and the Prophet Haggai." *Transeuphratene* 5 (1992): 63–84.

_____. *The Book of Haggai: Prophecy and Society in Early Persian Yehud*. VTSup 91. Leiden: Brill, 2002.

Mason, Rex. "Haggai, Theology of." *NIDOTTE*, 4:691–93.

_____. "Prophets of the Restoration." Pages 137–54 in *Israel's Prophetic Tradition*. Ed. R. Coggins, A. Phillips, and M. Knibb. Cambridge: Cambridge Univ. Press, 1982.

May, H. G. "'This People' and 'This Nation' in Haggai." *VT* 18 (1968): 190–97.

Pfeil, Rüdiger. "When Is a Gôy a Goy"? The Interpretation of Haggai 2:10–19." Pages 261–78 in *A Tribute to Gleason Archer*. Ed. Walter C. Kaiser Jr. and Ronald F. Youngblood. Chicago: Moody Press, 1986.

Pierce, Ronald W. "Literary Connectors and a Haggai–Zechariah–Malachi Corpus." *JETS* 27 (1984): 277–89.

_____. "A Thematic Development of the Haggai–Zechariah–Malachi Corpus." *JETS* 27 (1984): 401–11.

Prinsloo, W. S. "The Cohesion of Haggai 1:4–11." Pages 337–43 in *'Wünschet Jerusalem Frieden': Collected Communications to the XIIth Congress of the International Organization for the Study of the Old Testament (Jerusalem 1986)*. Ed. Matthias Augustin and Klaus-Dietrich Schunck. Frankfurt am Main: Peter Lang, 1988.

Rose, W. H. *Zemah and Zerubbabel: Messianic Expectations in the Early Postexilic Period*. JSOTSup 304. Sheffield: Sheffield Academic Press, 2000.

Siebeneck, Robert T. "Messianism of Aggeus and Proto-Zacharias." *CBQ* 19 (1957): 312–28.

Sim, Ronald J. "Notes on Haggai 2:10–21." *Journal of Translation and Textlinguistics* 5 (1992): 25–36.

Smith, Daniel L. *The Religion of the Landless: The Social Context of the Babylonian Exile*. Bloomington, Ind.: Meyer-Stone Books, 1989.

Sykes, Seth. *Time and Space in Haggai-Zechariah 1–8: A Bakhtinian Analysis of a Prophetic Chronicle*. Studies in Biblical Literature 24. New York: Peter Lang, 2002.

Tadmor, Hayim. "'The Appointed Time Has Not Yet Arrived': The Historical Background of Haggai 1:2." Pages 401–8 in *Ki Baruch hu: Ancient Near Eastern, Biblical, and Judaic Studies in Honor of Baruch A. Levine*. Ed. Robert Chazan, William W. Hallo, and Lawrence H. Schiffman. Winona Lake, Ind.: Eisenbrauns, 1999.

Tollington, Janet. *Tradition and Innovation in Haggai and Zechariah 1–8*. JSOTSup 150. Sheffield: Sheffield Academic Press, 1993.

_____. "Readings in Haggai: From the Prophet to the Completed Book, a Changing Message in Changing Times." Pages 194–208 in *The Crisis of Israelite Religion: Transformation of Religious Tradition in Exilic and Post-Exilic Times*. Ed. Bob Becking and Marjo C. A. Korpel. Leiden: Brill, 1999.

Townsend, T. N. "Additional Comments on Haggai II 10–19." *VT* 18 (1968): 559–60.

Van Amerongen, Marianne. "Structuring Division Markers in Haggai." Pages 51–79 in *Delimitation Criticism: A New Tool in Biblical Scholarship*. Ed. Marjo Korpel and Josef Oesch. Assen: Van Gorcum, 2000.

Van Rooy, H. F. "Eschatology and Audience: The Eschatology of Haggai." *OTE* 1 (1988): 49–63.

Verhoef, P. A. "Notes on the Dates in the Book of Haggai." Pages 259–67 in *Text and Context: Old Testament and Semitic Studies for F. C. Fensham*. Ed. W. Claassen. Sheffield: Sheffield Academic Press, 1988.

Whedbee, J. William. "A Question-Answer Schema in Haggai 1: The Form and Function of Haggai 1:9–11." Pages 184–94 in *Biblical and Near Eastern Studies: Essays in Honor of William Sanford LaSor*. Ed. G. A. Tuttle. Grand Rapids: Eerdmans, 1978.

Wolf, Herbert. "'The Desire of All Nations' in Haggai 2:7: Messianic or Not?" *JETS* 19 (1976): 97–102.

Zechariah

Influential and Helpful Commentaries

Achtemeier, Elizabeth Rice. *Nahum–Malachi*. IBC. Atlanta: John Knox, 1986.

Baldwin, Joyce G. *Haggai, Zechariah, Malachi: An Introduction and Commentary*. TOTC. Downers Grove, Ill.: InterVarsity, 1972.

Brown, William P. *Obadiah Through Malachi*. Westminster Bible Companion. Louisville: Westminster John Knox, 1996.

Coggins, R. J. *Haggai, Zechariah, Malachi*. OTG. Sheffield: Sheffield Academic Press, 1987.

Conrad, Edgar W. *Zechariah*. Readings. Sheffield: Sheffield Academic Press, 1999.

Floyd, Michael H. *Minor Prophets, Part 2*. FOTL 22 . Grand Rapids: Eerdmans, 2000.

Mason, R. A. *The Books of Haggai, Zechariah and Malachi*. CBC. Cambridge: Cambridge Univ. Press, 1977.

Merrill, Eugene H. *Haggai, Zechariah, Malachi: An Exegetical Commentary*. Chicago: Moody Press, 1994.

Meyers, Carol L., and Eric M. Meyers. *Haggai, Zechariah 1–8: A New Translation with Introduction and Commentary*. AB 25b. Garden City, N.Y.: Doubleday, 1987.

______. *Zechariah 9–14: A New Translation with Introduction and Commentary* AB 25c. New York: Doubleday, 1993.

Ollenburger, Ben C. "Haggai, Zechariah and Malachi." Pages 405–14 in *The Books of the Bible*. Volume I: *The Old Testament/The Hebrew Bible*. Ed. Bernhard W. Anderson. New York: Scribners, 1989.

______. "The Book of Zechariah." Pages 733–840 in vol. 7, *The New Interpreter's Bible*. Ed. Leander E. Keck. Nashville: Abingdon, 1996.

Petersen, David L. *Haggai and Zechariah 1–8: A Commentary*. OTL. London: SCM, 1984.

______. *Zechariah 9–14 and Malachi: A Commentary*. OTL. Louisville: Westminster John Knox, 1995.

Redditt, Paul L. *Haggai, Zechariah and Malachi*. NCB. London: M. Pickering/Harper Collins, 1995.

Smith, Ralph L. *Micah-Malachi*. WBC 32. Dallas: Word, 1990.

Stuhlmueller, Carroll. *Rebuilding with Hope: A Commentary on the Books of Haggai and Zechariah*. ITC. Grand Rapids: Eerdmans, 1988.

Sweeney, Marvin A. *The Twelve Prophets*. 2 vols. Berit Olam. Collegeville, Minn.: Liturgical, 2000.

Influential and Helpful Monographs and Articles: Zechariah 1–8

Barker, Margaret. "The Two Figures in Zechariah." *HeyJ* 18 (1977): 33–46.

Beatty, Bernard. "Who Wears the Crown(s)? A Rationale for Editing Forwards." *Downside Review* 113 (1995): 1–19.

Bedford, P. R. *Temple Restoration in Early Achaemenid Judah*. SJSJ. Leiden: Brill, 2001.

Berquist, J. L. *Judaism in Persia's Shadow: A Social and Cultural Approach*. Philadelphia: Fortress, 1995.

Boda, Mark J. "Oil, Crowns and Thrones: Prophet, Priest and King in Zechariah 1:7–6:15." *JHS* 3 (2001): Article 10.

______. "From Fasts to Feasts: The Literary Function of Zechariah 7–8." *CBQ* 65 (2003): 390–407.

______. "Zechariah: Master Mason or Penitential Prophet?" Pages 49–69 in *Yahwism After the Exile: Perspectives on Israelite Religion in the Persian Era*. Ed. Bob Becking and Rainer Albertz. Assen: Royal Van Gorcum, 2003.

______. "Terrifying the Horns: Persia and Babylon in Zechariah 1:7–6:15." *CBQ* 76 (2005): forthcoming.

Butterworth, Mike. *Structure and the Book of Zechariah*. JSOTSup 130. Sheffield: Sheffield Academic Press, 1992.

Clark, David J. "Discourse Structure in Zechariah 7:1–8:23." *BT* 36 (1985): 328–35.

______. "Vision and Oracle in Zechariah 1–6." Pages 529–60 in *Biblical Hebrew and Discourse Linguistics*. Ed. Robert D. Bergen. Winona Lake, Ind.: Eisenbrauns, 1994.

Collins, John J. "The Eschatology of Zechariah." Pages 74–84 in *Knowing the End from the Beginning*. Ed. Lester Grabbe. Sheffield: Sheffield Academic Press, 2003.

Cook, Stephen L. *Prophecy and Apocalypticism: The Postexilic Social Setting*. Minneapolis: Fortress, 1995.

Craig, Kenneth M. "Interrogatives in Haggai-Zechariah: A Literary Thread?" Pages 224–44 in *Forming Prophetic Literature: Essays on Isaiah and the Twelve in Honor of John D. W. Watts*. Ed. James W. Watts and Paul R. House. Sheffield: Sheffield Academic Press, 1996.

Evans, Craig. A. "Jesus and Zechariah's Messianic Hope." Pages 373–88 in *Authenticating the Activities of Jesus*. Ed. C. A. Evans and B. D. Chilton. Leiden: Brill, 1998.

______. "'The Two Sons of Oil': Early Evidence of Messianic Interpretation of Zechariah 4:14 in 4Q254 4 2." Pages 566–75 in *The Provo International Conference on the Dead Sea Scrolls: Technological Innovations, New Texts, and Reformulated Issues*. Ed. Donald W. Parry and Eugene Ulrich. Leiden: Brill, 1999.

Floyd, Michael H. "The Nature of the Narrative and the Evidence of Redaction in Haggai." *VT* 45 (1995): 470–90.

______. "The Evil in the Ephah: Reading Zechariah 5:5–11 in Its Literary Context." *CBQ* 58 (1996): 51–68.

______. "Cosmos and History in Zechariah's View of the Restoration (Zechariah 1:7–6:15)." Pages 125–44 in *Problems in Biblical Theology: Essays in Honor of Rolf Knierim*. Ed. Henry T. C. Sun and Keith L. Eades. Grand Rapids: Eerdmans, 1997.

Freedman, David Noel. "The Flying Scroll in Zechariah 5:1–4." Pages 42–48 in *Studies in Near Eastern Culture and History*. Ed. J. Bellamy. Ann Arbor: University of Michigan Center for Near Eastern and North African Studies, 1990.

Halpern, Baruch. "The Ritual Background of Zechariah's Temple Song." *CBQ* 40 (1978): 167–90.

Hartle, James A. "The Literary Unity of Zechariah." *JETS* 35 (1992): 145–57.

Kessler, John. "Diaspora and Homeland in the Early Achaemenid Period: Community, Geography and Demography in Zech. 1–8." In *New Approaches to the Persian Period.* Ed. Jon L. Berquist (Semeia Studies; Atlanta: Society of Biblical Literature; Leiden: Brill, 2005), forthcoming.

Laato, Antti. "Zachariah 4,6b–10a and the Akkadian Royal Building Inscriptions." *ZAW* 106 (1994): 53–69.

Love, Mark Cameron. *The Evasive Text: Zechariah 1–8 and the Frustrated Reader.* JSOTSup 296. Sheffield: Sheffield Academic Press, 1999.

Luria, Ben Zion. "Zechariah Is One Book." *Beth Mikra* 36 124 (1990): 74–79.

Marinkovic, P. "What Does Zechariah 1–8 Tell Us About the Second Temple?" Pages 88–103 in *Second Temple Studies.* Volume 2: *Temple and Community in the Persian Period.* Ed. T. C. Eskenazi and K. H. Richards. Sheffield: Sheffield Academic Press, 1994.

Mason, Rex A. "The Relation of Zech 9–14 to Proto-Zechariah." *ZAW* 88 (1976): 227–39.

______. *Preaching the Tradition: Homily and Hermeneutics After the Exile.* Cambridge: Cambridge Univ. Press, 1990.

______. "The Messiah in the Postexilic Old Testament Literature." Pages 338–64 in *King and Messiah in Israel and the Ancient Near East: Proceedings of the Oxford Old Testament Seminar.* Ed. John Day. Sheffield: Sheffield Academic Press, 1998.

Meyers, Carol L., and Eric M. Meyers. "Jerusalem and Zion After the Exile: The Evidence of First Zechariah." Pages 121–35 in *Shaarei Talmon: Studies in the Bible, Qumran, and the Ancient Near East Presented to Shemaryahu Talmon.* Ed. M. Fishbane and E. Tov. Winona Lake, Ind.: Eisenbrauns, 1992.

Meyers, Eric M. "Messianism in First and Second Zechariah and the End of Biblical Prophecy." Pages 127–42 in *Go to the Land I Will Show You: Studies in Honor of Dwight W. Young.* Ed. Joseph E. Coleson and Victor H. Matthews. Winona Lake, Ind.: Eisenbrauns, 1996.

Nurmela, Risto. *Prophets in Dialogue: Inner-Biblical Allusions in Zechariah 1–8 and 9–14.* Åbo: Åbo Akademi University, 1996.

Petersen, David L. "Zechariah's Visions: A Theological Perspective." *VT* 34 (1984): 195–206.

Pola, Thomas. "Form and Meaning in Zechariah 3." Pages 156–67 in *Yahwism After the Exile: Perspectives on Israelite Religion in the Persian Era.* Ed. B. Becking and R. Albertz. Assen: Royal Van Gorcum, 2003.

Redditt, Paul L. "Zerubbabel, Joshua, and the Night Visions of Zechariah." *CBQ* 54 (1992): 249–59.

Rooke, D. W. *Zadok's Heirs: The Role and Development of the High Priesthood in Ancient Israel*. OTM. Oxford: Oxford Univ. Press, 2000.

Rose, Wolter H. *Zemah and Zerubbabel: Messianic Expectations in the Early Postexilic Period*. JSOTSup 304. Sheffield: Sheffield Academic Press, 2000.

______. "Messianic Expectations in the Early Postexilic Period." Pages 168–85 in *Yahwism After the Exile: Perspectives on Israelite Religion in the Persian Era*. Ed. B. Becking and R. Albertz. Assen: Royal Van Gorcum, 2003.

Rudman, Dominic. "Zechariah 5 and the Priestly Law." *SJOT* 14 (2000): 194–206.

Schmid, Konrad, and Odil Hannes Steck. "Restoration Expectations in the Prophetic Tradition of the Old Testament." Pages 41–82 in *Restoration: Old Testament, Jewish and Christian Conceptions*. Ed. James M. Scott. Leiden: Brill, 2000.

Sinclair, Lawrence A. "Redaction of Zechariah 1–8." *BR* 20 (1975): 36–47.

Strand, Kenneth A. "The Two Olive Trees of Zechariah 4 and Revelation 11." *AUSS* 20 (1982): 257–61.

Sykes, Seth. "Time and Space in Haggai-Zechariah 1–8: A Bakhtinian Analysis of a Prophetic Chronicle." *JSOT* 76 (1997): 97–124.

______. *Time and Space in Haggai-Zechariah 1–8: A Bakhtinian Analysis of a Prophetic Chronicle*. Studies in Biblical Literature 24. New York: Peter Lang, 2002.

Tidwell, N. L. A. "*Waʾomar* (Zech 3:5) and the Genre of Zechariah's Fourth Vision." *JBL* 94 (1975): 343–55.

Tiemeyer, Lena. "The Guilty Priesthood (Zech. 3)." Pages 1–20 in *The Book of Zechariah and Its Influence*. Ed. C. M. Tuckett. Aldershot: Ashgate, 2003.

Tigchelaar, Eibert J. C. *Prophets of Old and the Day of the End: Zechariah, the Book of Watchers and Apocalyptic*. *OtSt* 35. Leiden: Brill, 1996.

Tollington, Janet E. *Tradition and Innovation in Haggai and Zechariah 1–8*. JSOTSup 150. Sheffield: Sheffield Academic Press, 1993.

Tuckett, C. M., ed. *The Book of Zechariah and Its Influence*. Aldershot: Ashgate, 2003.

Van der Woude, Adam S. "Zion as Primeval Stone in Zechariah 3 and 4." Pages 237–48 in *Text and Context: Old Testament and Semitic Studies for F. C. Fensham*. Ed. W. Claassen. Sheffield: Sheffield Academic Press, 1988.

VanderKam, James C. "Joshua the High Priest and the Interpretation of Zechariah 3." *CBQ* 53 (1991): 553–70.

______. "Joshua the High Priest and the Interpretation of Zechariah 3." Pages 157–76 in *From Revelation to Canon. Studies in the Hebrew Bible and Second Temple Literature*. Ed. James C. Vanderkam. Leiden: Brill, 2000.

Wolters, Al. "Confessional Criticism and the Night Visions of Zechariah." Pages 90–117 in *Renewing Biblical Interpretation*. Ed. Craig Bartholomew et al. Grand Rapids: Zondervan, 2000.

Influential and Helpful Monographs and Articles: Zechariah 9–14

Berquist, J. L. *Judaism in Persia's Shadow: A Social and Cultural Approach*. Philadelphia: Fortress, 1995.

Black, Mark C. "The Rejected and Slain Messiah Who Is Coming with His Angels: The Messianic Exegesis of Zechariah 9–14 in the Passion Narratives." Ph.D. diss., Emory University, 1990.

Boda, Mark J. "From Fasts to Feasts: The Literary Function of Zechariah 7–8." *CBQ* 65 (2003): 390–407.

_____. "Reading Between the Lines: Zechariah 11:4–16 in Its Literary Contexts." Pages 277–91 in *Bringing Out the Treasure: Inner Biblical Allusion and Zechariah 9–14*. Ed. Mark J. Boda and Michael H. Floyd. Sheffield: Sheffield Academic Press, 2003.

Boda, Mark J., and Michael H. Floyd, eds. *Bringing Out the Treasure: Inner Biblical Allusion and Zechariah 9–14*. JSOTSup 370. Sheffield: Sheffield Academic Press, 2003.

Butterworth, Mike. *Structure and the Book of Zechariah*. JSOTSup 130. Sheffield: Sheffield Academic Press, 1992.

Clark, David J. "Discourse Structure in Zechariah 9–14: Skeleton or Phantom." Pages 64–80 in *Issues in Bible Translation*. Ed. P. C. Stine. London: United Bible Societies, 1988.

Cook, Stephen L. *Prophecy & Apocalypticism: The Postexilic Social Setting*. Minneapolis: Fortress, 1995.

Craig, Kenneth M. "Interrogatives in Haggai-Zechariah: A Literary Thread?" Pages 224–44 in *Forming Prophetic Literature: Essays on Isaiah and the Twelve in Honor of John D. W. Watts*. James W. Watts and Paul R. House. Sheffield: Sheffield Academic Press, 1996.

Crotty, Robert B. "The Suffering Moses of Deutero-Zechariah." *Colloquium* 14 (1982): 43–50.

Duguid, Iain. "Messianic Themes in Zechariah 9–14." Pages 265–80 in *The Lord's Anointed: Interpretation of Old Testament Messianic Texts*. Ed. Philip E. Satterthwaite. Carlisle: Paternoster, 1995.

Finley, Thomas J. "The Sheep Merchants of Zechariah 11." *GTJ* 3 (1982): 51–65.

Floyd, Michael H. "The *Maśśā*ʾ As a Type of Prophetic Book." *JBL* 121 (2002): 401–22.

Good, Robert M. "Zechariah 14:13 and Related Texts: Brother Against Brother in War." *Maarav* 8 (1992): 39–47.

Gordon, Robert P. "Inscribed Pots and Zechariah XIV 20–1." *VT* 42 (1992): 120–23.

Hanson, Paul D. *The Dawn of Apocalyptic: The Historical and Sociological Roots of Jewish Apocalyptic Eschatology*. Rev. ed. Philadelphia: Fortress, 1979.

Hartle, James A. "The Literary Unity of Zechariah." *JETS* 35 (1992): 145–57.

Hill, Andrew E. "Dating Second Zechariah: A Linguistic Reexamination." *HAR* 6 (1982): 105–34.

Hobbs, T. R. "The Language of Warfare in Zechariah 9–14." Pages 103–28 in *After the Exile: Essays in Honour of Rex Mason*. Ed. J. Barton and D. J. Reimer. Macon, Ga.: Mercer Univ. Press, 1996.

Janzen, J. Gerald. "On the Most Important Word in the Shema." *VT* 37 (1987): 280–300.

Larkin, Katrina J. *The Eschatology of Second Zechariah: A Study of the Formation of a Mantological Wisdom Anthology*. CBET 6. Kampen: Kok, 1994.

Laubscher, F. du T. "Epiphany and Sun Mythology in Zechariah 14." *JNSL* 20 (1994): 125–38.

Leske, Adrian. "Context and Meaning of Zechariah 9:9." *CBQ* 62 (2000): 663–78.

Luria, Ben Zion. "Zechariah Is One Book." *Beth Mikra* 36 (1990): 74–79.

Mason, R. A. "The Relation of Zech 9–14 to Proto-Zechariah." *ZAW* 88 (1976): 227–39.

______. "Inner Biblical Exegesis in Zech. 9–14." *GTJ* 3 (1982): 51–65.

______. "Some Examples of Inner Biblical Exegesis in Zech. IX–XIV." Pages 343–54 in *Studia Evangelica. Vol. VII: Papers Presented to the 5th International Congress on Biblical Studies Held at Oxford, 1973*. Ed. Elizabeth A. Livingstone. Berlin: Akademie Verlag, 1982.

______. "The Messiah in the Postexilic Old Testament Literature." Pages 338–64 in *King and Messiah in Israel and the Ancient Near East: Proceedings of the Oxford Old Testament Seminar*. Ed. John Day. Sheffield: *Sheffield Academic Press*, 1998.

______. "The Use of Earlier Biblical Material in Zechariah 9–14: A Study in Inner Biblical Exegesis." Pages 1–208 in *Bringing out the Treasure: Inner Biblical Allusion and Zechariah 9–14*. JSOTSup 304. Ed. Mark J. Boda and Michael H. Floyd. Sheffield: Sheffield Academic Press, 2003.

Meyer, Lester V. "An Allegory Concerning the Monarchy: Zech 11:4–17; 13:7–9." Pages 225–40 in *Scripture in History and Theology*. Ed. A. L. Merrill and T. W. Overholt. Pittsburgh: Pickwick, 1977.

Meyers, Carol L., and Eric M. Meyers. "Demography and Diatribes: Yehud's Population and the Prophecy of Second Zechariah." Pages 268–85 in *Scripture and Other Artifacts: Essays in Honor of Philip J. King*. Ed. Michael D. Coogan, J. Cheryl Exum, and Lawrence E. Stager. Louisville: Westminster John Knox, 1994.

_____. "The Future Fortunes of the House of David: The Evidence of Second Zechariah." Pages 207–22 in *Fortunate the Eyes That See: Essays in Honor of David Noel Freedman in Celebration of His Seventieth Birthday*. Ed. Astrid Beck. Grand Rapids: Eerdmans, 1995.

Meyers, Eric M. "The Crisis of the Mid-Fifth Century BCE: Second Zechariah and the 'End' of Prophecy." Pages 713–72 in *Pomegranates and Golden Bells: Studies in Biblical, Jewish, and Near Eastern Ritual, Law, and Literature in Honor of Jacob Milgrom*. Ed. David P. Wright, David Noel Freedman, and Avi Hurvitz. Winona Lake, Ind.: Eisenbrauns, 1995.

_____. "Messianism in First and Second Zechariah and the End of Biblical Prophecy." Pages 127–42 in *Go to the Land I Will Show You: Studies in Honor of Dwight W. Young*. Ed. Joseph E. Coleson and Victor H. Matthews. Winona Lake, Ind.: Eisenbrauns, 1996.

Miller, John H. "Haggai–Zechariah: Prophets of the Now and Future." *Currents in Theology and Mission* 6 (1979): 99–104.

Mitchell, David C. *The Message of the Psalter: An Eschatological Programme in the Book of Psalms*. JSNTSup 252. Sheffield: Sheffield Academic Press, 1997.

Moseman, R. David. "Reading the Two Zechariah's As One." *RevEx* 97 (2000): 487–98.

Nielsen, Eduard. "A Note on Zechariah 14,4–5." Pages 33–37 in *In the Last Days: On Jewish and Christian Apocalyptic and Its Period*. Ed. Knud Jeppesen. Aarhus: Aarhus Univ. Press, 1994.

Nogalski, James D. *Redactional Processes in the Book of the Twelve*. BZAW 218. Berlin: de Gruyter, 1993.

North, Robert. "Prophecy to Apocalyptic Via Zechariah." Pages 47–74 in *Congress Volume: Uppsala, 1971*. Ed. H. Nyberg. Leiden: Brill, 1972.

Nurmela, Risto. *Prophets in Dialogue: Inner-Biblical Allusions in Zechariah 1–8 and 9–14*. Åbo: Åbo Akademi University, 1996.

Parunak, H. Van Dyke. *Linguistic Density Plots in Zechariah*. The Computer Bible 20. Wooster, Ohio: Biblical Research Associates, 1979.

Person, Raymond F. *Second Zechariah and the Deuteronomic School*. JSOTSup 167. Sheffield: Sheffield Academic Press, 1993.

Petersen, David L. *Late Israelite Prophecy: Studies in Deutero-Prophetic Literature and in Chronicles*. SBLMS 23. Missoula, Mont.: Scholars Press, 1977.

_____. "Israelite Prophecy: Change Versus Continuity." Pages 190–203 in *Congress Volume, Leuven, 1989*. Ed. J. Emerton. Leiden: Brill, 1989.

Pierce, Ronald W. "Literary Connectors and a Haggai–Zechariah–Malachi Corpus." *JETS* 27 (1984): 277–89.

_____. "A Thematic Development of the Haggai–Zechariah–Malachi Corpus." *JETS* 27 (1984): 401–11.

Radday, Yehuda T., and Dieter Wickmann. "Unity of Zechariah Examined in the Light of Statistical Linguistics." *ZAW* 87 (1975): 30–55.

Redditt, Paul L. "Israel's Shepherds: Hope and Pessimism in Zechariah 9–14." *CBQ* 51(1989): 631–42.

______. "The Two Shepherds in Zechariah 11:4–17." *CBQ* 55 (1993): 676–86.

______. "Nehemiah's First Mission and the Date of Zechariah 9–14." *CBQ* 56 (1994): 664–78.

______. "Zechariah 9–14, Malachi, and the Redaction of the Book of the Twelve." Pages 245–68 in *Forming Prophetic Literature: Essays on Isaiah and the Twelve in Honor of John D. W. Watts*. Ed. James W. Watts and Paul R. House. Sheffield: Sheffield Academic Press, 1996.

Rhea, Robert. "Attack on Prophecy: Zechariah 13,1–6." *ZAW* 107 (1995): 288–93.

Rubenstein, Jeffrey L. "Sukkot, Eschatology and Zechariah 14." *RB* 103 (1996): 161–95.

Schaefer, Konrad R. "The Ending of the Book of Zechariah: A Commentary." *RB* 100 (1993): 165–238.

______. "Zechariah 14 and the Composition of the Book of Zechariah." *RB* 100 (1993): 368–98.

______. "Zechariah 14: A Study in Allusion." *CBQ* 57 (1995): 66–91.

Schellenberg, Angeline Falk. "One in the Bond of War: The Unity of Deutero-Zechariah." *Didaskalia* (2001): 101–15.

Schniedewind, William M. *The Word of God in Transition: From Prophet to Exegete in the Second Temple Period*. JSOTSup 197. Sheffield: Sheffield Academic Press, 1995.

Tigchelaar, Eibert J. C. *Prophets of Old and the Day of the End: Zechariah, the Book of Watchers and Apocalyptic*. OtSt 35. Leiden: Brill, 1996.

Tuckett, C. M., ed. *The Book of Zechariah and Its Influence*. Aldershot: Ashgate, 2003.

Wolters, Al. "Zechariah 14: A Dialogue with the History of Interpretation." *Mid-America Journal of Theology* 13 (2002): 1–18.

Haggai 1:1–11

IN THE SECOND year of King Darius, on the first day of the sixth month, the word of the LORD came through the prophet Haggai to Zerubbabel son of Shealtiel, governor of Judah, and to Joshua son of Jehozadak, the high priest:

2This is what the LORD Almighty says: "These people say, 'The time has not yet come for the LORD's house to be built.'"

3Then the word of the LORD came through the prophet Haggai: 4"Is it a time for you yourselves to be living in your paneled houses, while this house remains a ruin?"

5Now this is what the LORD Almighty says: "Give careful thought to your ways. 6You have planted much, but have harvested little. You eat, but never have enough. You drink, but never have your fill. You put on clothes, but are not warm. You earn wages, only to put them in a purse with holes in it."

7This is what the LORD Almighty says: "Give careful thought to your ways. 8Go up into the mountains and bring down timber and build the house, so that I may take pleasure in it and be honored," says the LORD. 9"You expected much, but see, it turned out to be little. What you brought home, I blew away. Why?" declares the LORD Almighty. "Because of my house, which remains a ruin, while each of you is busy with his own house. 10Therefore, because of you the heavens have withheld their dew and the earth its crops. 11I called for a drought on the fields and the mountains, on the grain, the new wine, the oil and whatever the ground produces, on men and cattle, and on the labor of your hands."

Original Meaning

HAGGAI SPEAKS INTO a community still feeling the aftershocks of a recent Persian political earthquake, which involved the mysterious death of the Persian emperor Cambyses and the ensuing rise of the new emperor, Darius, to the throne (522 B.C.). The prophetic work of Haggai, the political work of Zerubbabel, and the priestly work of Joshua must be seen against the backdrop of these recent events as the new emperor moved to restore peace to the edges of his empire. Although there is no evidence of rebellion in Egypt when Haggai's first message is dated

(520), by the next year Egypt would revolt and Darius would have to move to quell the rebellion.

There are signs of economic hardship during Darius's early years as emperor because of economic "reforms" (i.e., taxation resulting in inflation). Any financial resources of those who returned from exile in the waves of people accompanying Zerubbabel and Joshua would have been rendered worthless in the early years of Darius.[1]

Haggai's message comes at a significant time not only in the history of the Persian empire, but also in the yearly and monthly rhythm of the Jewish people. Although it is August 520 B.C., on the eve of the season of the grape, fig, and pomegranate harvests, there is clearly concern that the harvest is not as plentiful as would be expected. It is also the first day of the month, the time of the New Moon offering. On the day when this offering should be sacrificed, Haggai (whose name is derived from the Heb. word "feast") receives a message from God for the people to rebuild the structure that will make the monthly ritual of the New Moon offering possible (cf. Ezra 3:1).

Haggai's call to rebuild the temple does not represent the first initiative to restore this structure; according to Ezra 5:13–16 the project had begun immediately following the decree of Cyrus in 539–537 (cf. Ezra 1). This initial activity, however, did not find success, and as Haggai emerges in 520 the work must begin from scratch. If Ezra 3:1 describes activity during the second year of Darius's reign (see the introduction), at the beginning of the seventh month Zerubbabel and Joshua began to rebuild the altar and offer sacrifices to God. Haggai's initial message, then, precedes this activity by one month.

Two background elements are important here. (1) Haggai is a participant in a new period of prophecy that draws on older forms of prophetic speech, using them in new ways while also devising new forms and styles.[2] (2) Haggai's message assumes an understanding of the representational nature of the leadership of this community. Approaches to this pericope that rightly see a distinction between the audiences of the statement in Haggai 1:2 and those in 1:4–11 do not take into account the fact that Zerubbabel and Joshua are being addressed as representatives of the people. The address begins by telling the recently arrived leaders about the attitude of the people toward rebuilding the temple and then addressing the issue directly to the people.

There is evidence of unity in the prophetic message in 1:1–11, which can be seen on the level of form and content. Some have identified this section

---

1. See Ezra 2:64–69; Neh. 7:66–72; cf. debate between J. Blenkinsopp, *Ezra-Nehemiah: A Commentary* (OTL; Philadelphia: Westminster, 1988), 95, and H. G. M. Williamson, *Ezra, Nehemiah* (WBC 16; Waco, Tex.: Word, 1985), 38, on the financial resources of this early Persian period community.

2. See M. J. Boda, "Haggai: Master Rhetorician," *TynBul* 51 (2000): 295–304.

as a "prophetic disputation," which includes the following three elements: description of the people's present attitude, challenge of this attitude through question, and pronouncement of Yahweh.[3] There are also significant links in terms of content between 1:2–7 and 1:9–11.[4] Thus, this initial section constitutes a prophetic message delivered to the people either through or in the presence of Zerubbabel and Joshua. The narrative response to this message in 1:12–14 is inseparable from the prophetic message not only because it displays the effect of the message on the leaders and people, but also because 1:1 joins 1:15 to close off the literary unit (see Original Meaning on 1:12–15).

At the center of the prophetic message is the call for the people to action, followed by two responses by Yahweh (1:8). On each side is the dialogue, and, although in this dialogue one does not hear the voice of the people, God's speeches anticipate and voice the people's thoughts and hearts. This is seen in verses 2–7 when God says: "These people say ..." (v. 2) and in verses 9–11 when the Lord declares: "Why?" (v. 9). In both dialogues there is a connection between two basic issues: the house of the Lord and the poverty of the people. At first the connection is made subtly: through the use of the interrogative: "Is it time for you yourselves ..." and the reflective verb: "Give careful thought to your ways...." But as we move into verses 9–11, the connection is made directly and abrasively: "Why? ... Because...." God makes this clear in verse 11.

There is much in this initial prophetic encounter that addresses the predicament of the people. They are experiencing curses at the hand of Yahweh, who is displeased with their lack of attention to rebuilding the temple. The prophet is calling them to action and warning that inaction will mean further curses. However, this human action is linked to God's purposes and activity. The ultimate purpose of this project is the pleasure and glory of God. Ultimately they are not to do it for relief from curse but for the pleasure and glory of God.

Detailed Analysis

HAGGAI'S MESSAGE INITIALLY engages the leadership of the community: Zerubbabel and Joshua (1:1). These two men form the leadership team of the early Persian community in the book of Ezra (Ezra 3:2, 8; 5:2, 10), who led groups

3. R. A. Mason, *Preaching the Tradition: Homily and Hermeneutics After the Exile* (Cambridge: Cambridge Univ. Press, 1990), 286 n. 6; cf. J. W. Whedbee, "A Question-Answer Schema in Haggai 1: The Form and Function of Haggai 1:9–11," in *Biblical and Near Eastern Studies: Essays in Honor of William Sanford LaSor*, ed. G. A. Tuttle (Grand Rapids: Eerdmans, 1978), 184–94.

4. So Whedbee, "Question-Answer," 192; cf. E. H. Merrill, *Haggai, Zechariah, Malachi: An Exegetical Commentary* (Chicago: Moody Press, 1994), 25.

of returning exiles at the beginning of Darius's reign. Zerubbabel's name and lineage reveal his representative role. As son of Shealtiel and grandson of Jehoiachin, the second to last king of Judah (1 Chron. 3:17–19), and as political ruler over the Persian province of Yehud ("governor of Judah"), he represents the Davidic line. At the same time his name, which means "seed of Babylon," highlights his role as representative of the community that had experienced the exile in Mesopotamia.

Joshua is "the high priest" and traces his line through Jehozadak, who is linked through Zadok to Aaron (1 Chron. 6:1–5, 14–15). By highlighting the descendants of the leaders of the first temple building (David/Solomon, Zadok), Haggai legitimates the temple rebuilding project. This view of the Davidic and Zadokite descendants in partnership in rebuilding the temple is akin to the view of the restoration of the temple in Ezekiel and, especially, Jeremiah (Ezek. 34:23–24; 37:24–25; Ezek. 40–48; cf. Jer. 33:14–22; see comments on Zech. 6:9–15).

The editor of Haggai introduces the prophetic words of Haggai with the phrase "the word of the LORD came through the prophet Haggai." The Hebrew prepositional phrase represented by "through" in the NIV is one associated with prophetic speech in the Deuteronomic history and some prophets (e.g., 2 Kings 14:25; Jer. 37:2; Ezek. 38:17) and may be a subtle reminder that Haggai stands in the long line established by the classical prophets.[5]

The prophetic message begins in 1:2 as Haggai establishes his authority by linking the message to "the LORD Almighty." This name for God will appear consistently in both Haggai and Zechariah. "LORD" (Heb. *yhwh*) is the name of God revealed to the Israelites through Moses as he entered into covenant with this people (Ex. 3:14–15; 6:2–3; 33:19; 34:6–7). "Almighty" (or "of hosts"; Heb. *ṣebaʾot*) is a name suggesting war, since it is used to speak of an organized army unit (Judg. 8:6; 9:29) as well as of a group of heavenly beings as God's armies (Josh. 5:14–15; 1 Kings 22:19). However, the consistent use of this word in prophetic material in general and the Persian period prophetic books in particular reveals that this name for God has lost all connection with the context of war and is a name that speaks mainly of the might and power of God.[6]

Haggai's declaration begins with a saying circulating among the populace at that time: "The time has not yet come for the LORD's house to be built."[7]

5. Cf. Mason, *Preaching*, 192; M. J. Boda, *Praying the Tradition: The Origin and Use of Tradition in Nehemiah 9* (BZAW 277; Berlin: de Gruyter, 1999), 137–39.

6. Contra P. L. Redditt, *Haggai, Zechariah and Malachi* (NCB; London: M. Pickering/HarperCollins, 1995), 18; J. G. Baldwin, *Haggai, Zechariah, Malachi: An Introduction and Commentary* (TOTC; Downers Grove, Ill.: InterVarsity Press, 1972), 44–45; cf. P. A. Verhoef, *The Books of Haggai and Malachi* (NICOT; Grand Rapids: Eerdmans, 1987), 52.

7. See Ezek. 12:21–25, 26–28; 18:1–4 for similar prophetic rhetoric.

The use of "these people" shows Yahweh's displeasure with his covenant people (cf. Isa. 7:16; 8:11).[8] They claim that the time has not come to rebuild the temple. The reason behind this lack of action may lie on the theological level, with the people waiting for the appearance of a messianic figure in order to begin the project[9] or for the completion of the seventy years prophesied by Jeremiah.[10] Or perhaps the reason is a lack of commitment to the rebuilding project because of their Persian overlords (see the political intrigue in Ezra 1–6) or a realization that they have insufficient financial and material resources.

It is this final consideration that appears uppermost on the people's mind as Haggai addresses this issue directly in 1:3–4. Having informed the newly arrived leadership of the sentiment of the people, the prophet now directs his attention to the people, which is signaled through the repetition of the same phrase just used to introduce the speech to Zerubbabel and Joshua ("Then the word of the LORD came through the prophet Haggai").

Haggai uses three rhetorical techniques that place great emphasis on his message.[11] (1) He plays on the quotation of the people he has just cited to the leaders of the community: "Is it a time...?" (2) Rather than delivering a direct attack, a rhetorical question forces the people to think through the issue at hand. (3) The building up of redundant terms ("you yourselves") accentuates the contrast between their treatment of themselves and their treatment of God.[12]

These techniques bolster the power of the message. Haggai contrasts the houses in which the people are living with the house of God. Defining the precise nature of this contrast is difficult because the word translated "paneled" in the NIV can also be rendered "roofed."[13] If the word is "roofed," the contrast is between completion and incompletion. If the word is "paneled," the contrast is between luxury and austerity. Considering that Haggai describes them living in these houses while also referring to financial matters in the following message, the NIV is most appropriate. While the temple lies in ruins, the people are living in nicely decorated homes.

---

8. Cf. Verhoef, *Haggai*, 56; D. L. Petersen, *Haggai and Zechariah 1–8: A Commentary* (OTL; London: SCM, 1984), 47.

9. R. G. Hammerton-Kelly, based on Ezek. 37:24–28; 40–43, concludes: "Rebuilding was a betrayal of the eschatological hope" ("The Temple and the Origins of Jewish Apocalyptic," *VT* 20 [1970]: 12).

10. See comments on Zech. 1:7–17 and 7:1–14.

11. See Boda, "Haggai," 295–304.

12. Cf. GKC §135d, g.

13. The nominal form is used for a roof in 1 Kings 6:15; so O. H. Steck, "Zu Haggai 1 2–11," *ZAW* 83 (1971): 362; Meyers and Meyers, *Haggai, Zechariah 1–8*. However, in 1 Kings 7:7 the interior paneling of a building is the referent (paneled with cedar), so Petersen, *Haggai*, 48.

This contrast provides another allusion back to the Davidic-Solomonic origins of the temple building project. The use of the word "house" to contrast the temple of God with the homes of the people is also used in 2 Samuel 7 as David desires to build a temple for the Lord.[14] Living in his completed and luxurious house, David feels guilty over the lack of such a house for God. Ultimately the house (temple) that David commissions his son to build contains such paneling (cedar, 1 Kings 6:9), and ironically (for Haggai's purpose) so also does Solomon's palace (1 Kings 7:3, 7).[15] Haggai is subtly calling the people to share the priorities of David and Solomon. If David felt guilty about living in a "house" before God's "house" was completed and if Solomon provided a "paneled" house for God before himself, how can they live in paneled homes before the temple was rebuilt?

With this rhetorical question still ringing in their ears, the people are now called to consider deeply another issue. The phrase "give careful thought to your ways" is unique to Haggai (1:5, 7; 2:15, 18) and calls for deep reflection over past behavior and experience. This identical phrase is repeated in 1:7 and creates an envelope around the exposure of past experience.[16]

Verse 6 outlines what the prophet calls the people to consider deeply. The cadence of this verse in the Hebrew text produces a powerful effect beginning with the main verb "you have planted much" and then followed by staccato bursts of infinitives that are captured by the translation: "eaten, but there is no satiety; drunk, but there is no quenching; dressed, but there is no warmth." The initial scenario refers to the foundation of the economy, which then has an impact on all else in life materially: hunger, thirst, clothing, wages.[17] The reference to "drink" is not a reference to drunkenness but rather

14. The use of this leitmotif "house" is masterful in 2 Sam. 7, where "house" is used to refer to palace (7:1, 2), to temple (7:5, 7, 13), and to dynasty (7:11, 16).

15. The use of this term "paneled" (with cedar) comes to represent the decadence of the Davidic dynasty (cf. Jer. 22:14).

16. Following Whedbee ("Question-Answer," 184–94), who correctly sees the word "ways" as referring to past activity, not future activity. This view is bolstered by recognizing that when the phrase "consider" ("set your hearts on") is used later in Haggai (2:15–19) and takes into account past and future, the word "ways" is dropped; contra Redditt, *Haggai*, 20; Petersen, *Haggai*, 51; H. G. T. Mitchell, J. M. P. Smith, and J. A. Brewer, *A Critical and Exegetical Commentary on Haggai, Zechariah, Malachi and Jonah* (ICC; Edinburgh: T. & T. Clark, 1912), 47. They see the second appearance as introducing the imperatives in 1:8 (future action), based on the view that the clause "This is what the LORD Almighty says" is an introductory phrase, not a concluding one. But this view fails to take into account that 1:7a is introducing a declaration: "Give careful thought to your ways."

17. This list reflects C. E. Carter's conclusion from the material evidence of the Persian period that "a monied economy" existed "alongside of a traditional in-kind, taxation system"; see his *The Emergence of Yehud in the Persian Period* (JSOTSup; Sheffield: Sheffield Academic Press, 1999), 283.

to quenching of thirst.[18] The final scenario picks up on an economy in which coinage is utilized. The word for "purse" is used elsewhere in the Hebrew Bible to refer to a carrying pouch;[19] here it is followed by the participle usually translated "pierced" or "bored," thus, "with a hole in it" (2 Kings 12:10).

Through these words, Haggai expects the people to notice that their experience parallels the kinds of curses outlined in the Torah when the covenant relationship between Yahweh and his people was strained (see Lev. 26; Deut. 28–30, esp. Deut. 28:38–40).[20] Haggai builds on the foundation of classical prophets, whom Yahweh used as covenant prosecutors,[21] calling the people to the covenant and using its provisions of both blessing and curse to encourage response.

Up until this point Haggai's message has used indirect rhetorical techniques.[22] He has asked a question (1:4) and called for deep contemplation (1:5–7). The weight of interpretation has been placed on the shoulders of the recipients of the message, and even the two issues introduced—the timing of the building of the temple and the poor material conditions of the people—have not yet been directly linked. Beginning in verse 8, the message becomes more forceful and direct, and subtle techniques will be abandoned. The prophet calls for three actions: "go up," "bring down," and "build." Each action builds on the previous one, and the ultimate destination is the rebuilding of the temple, utilizing vocabulary plucked from the mouth of the people in 1:2 ("house to be rebuilt").

Most commentators are puzzled as to why Haggai refers only to "timber" or wood in this call to rebuild the temple when stones are needed as well. Most likely stones were in plenteous supply from the destruction of the temple, but new wood is needed to replace the timbers burned by the Babylonians (2 Kings 25:9).[23] This solution, however, should not obscure an

18. With H. W. Wolff, *Haggai: A Commentary* (CC; Minneapolis: Augsburg, 1988), 30; contra R. Alden, "Haggai," in *EBC,* ed. F. E. Gaebelein (Grand Rapids: Zondervan, 1985), 7:581, who says: "These people were unable to drown their sorrows because of the inadequate vintage."

19. It can carry silver (Gen. 42:35), money (Prov. 7:20), myrrh (Song 1:13), a life (1 Sam. 25:29), or even sins (Job 14:17).

20. Cf. E. R. Achtemeier, *Nahum–Malachi* (IBC; Atlanta: John Knox, 1986), 99; M. Weinfeld, *Deuteronomy and the Deuteronomic School* (Oxford: Clarendon, 1972), 122 n. 6; D. R. Hillers, *Treaty Curses and the Old Testament Prophets* (BibOr 16; Rome: Pontifical Biblical Institute, 1964), 28. They consider these "futility curses."

21. See D. R. Hillers, *Covenant: The History of a Biblical Idea* (Baltimore: Johns Hopkins Univ. Press, 1969), 120–42; E. W. Nicholson, *God and His People: Covenant and Theology in the Old Testament* (Oxford: Clarendon, 1986); R. E. Clements, *Old Testament Prophecy: From Oracles to Canon* (Louisville: Westminster John Knox, 1996).

22. See Boda, "Haggai," 295–304.

23. Merrill, *Haggai,* 26.

important allusion Haggai makes in this command, in that the people have finished their wood "paneled" houses (as David and Solomon) and yet have no motivation to rebuild God's house. Haggai is calling the people again to follow the lead of Solomon, who built the first temple and had to go up into the mountains to retrieve wood for the temple (1 Kings 5).[24]

Next the prophet offers the purpose of this activity. (1) God will "take pleasure" in it, a Hebrew verb (*rṣh*) regularly used in ritual contexts to refer to God's acceptance of a sacrifice or a priestly service (e.g., 2 Sam. 24:23; Ps. 51:19). (2) God will "be honored" or glorified, that is, gain prestige and be praised through this house.[25] These two verbs provide the ultimate context of building the temple. Although it will soon be related directly to the predicament in which the community finds itself, the purpose of the rebuilding transcends the mere removal of covenant curses and relates ultimately to the pleasure and glory of God. The predicament of the community to which Haggai returns in 1:9–11 will be explained as action by God himself, prompted by inattention to his priorities of pleasure and glory in favor of the priorities of human needs.

Once the core imperatives and purposes are disclosed in 1:8, the prophet returns to the issues of 1:6 by utilizing similar vocabulary, themes, and forms. Verse 9 begins with an unusual form in Hebrew (infinitive absolute), picking up on the string of infinitives in 1:6 and creating again a choppy cadence (lit., expecting much, beholding little). The same Hebrew vocabulary begins this verse as 1:6 ("much . . . little") and the same play on "house" is used here as in 1:4.[26]

The contrast, however, is that now the two issues mentioned in 1:2–7 are linked directly. Taking up first the issue of the material conditions of the people (the second issue identified in 1:2–7), the prophet leads the people directly back to the issue of the timing for building the temple (the first issue identified in 1:2–7). These issues are linked directly by the question "Why?"

---

24. Cf. Ezra 3:7, which refers to the same event.

25. Some commentators make connections from this reference to the glorification of Yahweh to the glory of God that indwelt the temple (Ezek. 11:23), based on the shared root *kbd* in Hebrew; see Merrill, *Haggai*, 27; Verhoef, *Haggai*, 68; C. Stuhlmueller, *Rebuilding with Hope: A Commentary on the Books of Haggai and Zechariah* (ITC; Grand Rapids: Eerdmans, 1988), 20–21. However, in this particular context the glory is not the spiritual presence of Yahweh in the temple, but the praise of Yahweh; cf. Petersen, *Haggai*, 51. Petersen (ibid.) appropriately comments: "None of the Niphʾal uses of this verb which refer to Yahweh entail his cultic presence. Instead, they signify Yahweh's gaining prestige or revenge. Haggai is therefore speaking of glory, Yahweh's having greater prestige now that the house is finished and not of the sanctification of his house."

26. Note that there are three references to "house" in verse 9.

and then the answer "because": God (as the subject of the verb "blew away") now reveals through Haggai that he is the reason for their deplorable conditions.[27] The verb "blew away" is associated with destruction in prophetic literature where it is used in connection with fire (Isa. 54:16; Ezek. 22:20–21). However, its use here may be paralleling the image found in Isaiah 40:7, 24, where God blows and humanity and its endeavors wither, especially in light of the following verse (Hag. 1:10) and its focus on drought.[28]

With harvest approaching, Haggai reminds the people of their expectation for past harvests and reveals that the disappointing yields can be directly linked to the discipline of God. This discipline is then connected directly to the misplaced priorities of the community. The phrase "busy with his own house" (lit., "you are running, each to his house") expresses figuratively the passion of the people, while the "house" is representative of their own interests. While God's house lies in ruins, they are passionately pursuing their own agenda.

Verses 10–11 return to the predicament of the people. The initial phrase represented by "therefore" (*ʿal-ken*) usually signals a transition in prophetic speech to the warning of future judgment (e.g., Amos 5:11, 16–17), a strong motivating force for obedience to the message. Haggai, however, uses this signal to help the people interpret past circumstances.[29] This reinforces the direct link between the two issues now clearly articulated in a way that leaves no question in the minds of the people that the reason they are experiencing such difficult times is because they are not rebuilding the temple.

Haggai describes God's judgment on the people with a series of merisms to encompass all of creation and all of human activity within creation. In 1:10 the fundamental cause is that both "the heavens" and "the earth" (cf. Gen. 1:1) are not cooperating with humanity to produce sustenance. The heavens are not providing the essential precipitation for life, nor is the earth providing the nutrients. The use of the "dew" is not surprising, especially considering the time of year (August).[30] The period between the "latter" (spring) and "early" (fall) rains is a time in which little to no rain falls in Israel. In a land

---

27. See R. P. Carroll, "Eschatological Delay in the Prophetic Tradition," *ZAW* 94 (1982): 47–58, esp. 56, who shows that Haggai explains the delay in prophetic fulfillment by pointing to the behavior of the people.

28. Using the verbs *nšp* and *nšb*, rather than *npḥ* as in Hag. 1:9. Cf. Verhoef, *Haggai,* 70–71.

29. Wolff, *Haggai,* 48; W. A. M. Beuken, *Haggai-Sacharja 1–8* (Assen: van Gorcum, 1967), 188; Steck, "Zu Haggai 1 2–11," 371.

30. Cf. esp. J. I. Packer, M. C. Tenney, and W. White, eds. *The Bible Almanac* (Nashville: Thomas Nelson, 1980), 195–96, 265; see "Dew" in M. C. Tenney, ed. *The Zondervan Pictorial Encyclopedia of the Bible* (Grand Rapids: Zondervan, 1976), 2:118; Alden, "Haggai," 582; Redditt, *Haggai,* 22.

almost exclusively reliant on water from precipitation, the presence of dew can mean the difference between life and death for vegetation. The image of dew is not as common as that of rain for the blessing or curse of God but is found on several occasions (Gen. 27:28, 39; Deut. 33:13, 28; 2 Sam. 1:21; 1 Kings 17:1; Prov. 19:12).

In Haggai 1:11 creation's lack of cooperation with humanity in the production of crops is traced to the Creator, who has "called for a drought." Lest the people forget the ultimate cause behind these circumstances, once again Yahweh is the subject of the verb. This is consistent with the covenant foundation of Israel's faith, and 1:10–11 may be drawn from a list of curses outlined in Deuteronomy 28 (esp. 28:22–24). The word "drought" here, however, has more than covenantal overtones; it is used for rhetorical effect. On two occasions in this passage Haggai has referred to the state of the temple as "ruins" (Hag. 1:4, 9). This Hebrew word (*ḥareb*) shares the same Hebrew consonants as the word for "drought" (*ḥoreb*), implying that as long as the temple's condition is "ruins" (*ḥareb*), the people's condition will be "drought" (*ḥoreb*).

Yahweh's call for a drought is followed by a series of adverbial phrases arranged in couplets and triplets to express the totality of the drought. It is on "the fields" and "the mountains," encompassing both types of land, including the more expansive cultivated fields (e.g., the Shephelah) as well as the mountain terraces (e.g., the Judean hill country). The latter is surprising for the mountain region gets significant rain. The drought extends to the fruit of these different land types, which are harvested at various times in the agricultural year: the grain of the cultivated fields in the spring and the olive oil and new wine of the mountain region in the fall.

These three products are chosen because they succinctly describe the crops available in the land, so that the list is followed by the statement: "whatever the ground produces." This identical list of products is found in the covenant promises and threats in the Torah (e.g., Deut. 11:13–17). Finally, Haggai mentions humans and cattle, who together rely on and seek to cultivate these various crops, ending off with the summary statement: "on the labor of your hands." Here they see the futility of their labors on the land because of Yahweh's curse occasioned by their disobedience. As their labors on their houses at the expense of God's house has caused the curse, so God's curse falls upon their agricultural labors (their fields).

This curse has made its way from the created order, to the basic land types, to the cultivated vegetation that grows on these soils, to the humans who attempt to produce their sustenance from these crops.[31] This progression of

31. The same progression is evident in the creation account of Gen. 1: heavens/earth, inhabitable land, vegetation, animal/human life.

thought in 1:10–11 reminds the people that although the curse is coming through natural means, the ultimate source is supernatural: Yahweh, their covenant partner.

Bridging Contexts

HAGGAI SEEKS TO AWAKEN the people of God to the link between their behavior and their circumstances. He calls them to consider their care for their own homes at the expense of the temple (their behavior) and then their experience of drought and hardship (their circumstances). He wants them to reverse their behavior and thus bring pleasure and glory to God.

We have laid a foundation for the contemporary significance of this prophetic material in Haggai in the Bridging Contexts section of our introduction, where we noted the two modes of prophetic speech: foretelling and forthtelling. This initial prophecy by Haggai is pure forthtelling; that is, the prophet declares this message to his contemporaries in order that they may respond to the priorities of Yahweh in their generation—in this case, the rebuilding of the temple. Christian readers of this passage can appropriate this message on the basis of its status as God-breathed Scripture that is useful for teaching—that is, useful for shaping our own priorities today in a vastly different world (2 Tim. 3:16–17). However, before turning to the contemporary implications of this passage, a closer look at two biblical-theological themes will help us see the importance and applicability of the priorities espoused in Haggai 1:1–11.

The role of the temple. The first theme is that of the temple, which controls so much of this initial passage in Haggai. How can the Christian community appropriate texts that relate to the rebuilding of a temple when Jesus himself, in his earthly ministry, ultimately rejected and judged the temple? A closer look at the role of the temple will help us grasp Haggai's passion for its rebuilding and provide a link to our application of his message for the church today.

The temple was a symbol of God's manifest presence among his people. Its roots can be traced to the building of the tabernacle in the desert, an exercise essential for the experience of the manifest presence of God in the community of Israel. Exodus 25–40 is concerned with providing a dwelling place for Yahweh in Israel's camp. The sheer size of this narrative reveals that the construction of the tabernacle was an important priority for this covenant God. Thus, although ethical demands were important components of the people's response in covenant relationship, so also the building of the tabernacle was essential.

The structure of Exodus 25–40 reveals the purpose of the building of the tabernacle, a purpose that parallels the building of the temple in later times. Exodus 25:9 makes this purpose clear when Yahweh says: "Then have them make a sanctuary for me, and I will dwell among them." The remainder of Exodus is a meticulous record of the instructions for this building (Ex. 25–31) and the account of its construction (Ex. 35–40), interrupted only by the rebellion with the golden calf. The final scene reveals the success of this grand project as Yahweh descends from the mountain and fills the tabernacle with his glory (40:34–35).

The tabernacle represented God's presence for a people on the move in the desert, but once David ascended the throne, he saw the need for a more permanent dwelling for God. God's speech to David in 2 Samuel 7 reveals the close link between tabernacle and temple (2 Sam. 7:5–7). At first God's speech does not appear positive toward David's vision of a temple, but we soon learn that God will commission David's son to build the temple (7:13). Solomon constructs this temple and identifies this structure as a special place of God's manifest presence (1 Kings 8:27–30), which fills the Holy Place as in the tabernacle (8:10–13).

God's abandonment of the temple in Ezekiel is seen as the utmost judgment and is but a precursor of the Babylonian destruction of the temple (2 Kings 25). The literature of the exilic period reveals the people's incredible shock at the destruction of their place of God's manifest presence (Ps. 74; 79; Lam. 1:10). Yet there remained a hope among the exiles that the temple would one day be rebuilt (Ezek. 40–48). That rebuilding became synonymous during this period with restoration of the people and thus lies at the core of God's purposes among his people.[32]

The importance of the temple does not end with the Persian period community. This community served an important purpose in redemptive history as they established a community gathered around temple and law. This temple sustained them through the dark days of oppression under the Persians, Greeks, and eventually Romans. It is not surprising that the early chapters of Luke highlight members of the faithful community gathered around the temple: Zechariah (Luke 1:5–25), Joseph and Mary (2:21–24), Simeon (2:25–35), Anna (2:36–39), and even Jesus (2:41–50). From this community would come not only the Messiah but also an entire new covenant community. During this period God's people were being prepared for the next phase in

32. Notice how Ackroyd intertwines these themes of temple and community in his review of the presentation of the restoration in Haggai and Zechariah; P. R. Ackroyd, *Exile and Restoration: A Study of Hebrew Thought of the Sixth Century B.C.* (OTL; Philadelphia: Westminster, 1968), 153–217.

redemptive history, one in which the community would no longer be defined by political borders as the kingdom was extended to the entire world.

Temple theology is an essential part of New Testament theology as well. Christ is the One in whom the manifest presence of God now dwells (John 1:14; 2:18–22). It is not surprising that the apostolic community pictures the church (which is "the body of Christ") as also the arena of God's manifest presence and thus as the temple of God and Christ (1 Cor. 3:16–17; 6:19; 2 Cor. 6:16; Eph. 2:21; 1 Peter 2:4–10).

The temple is thus an important point of theological contact for those of us in the Christian community. It traces its roots to the tabernacle of old, the building of which lay at the core of the covenant relationship between God and his people. Provision for God's presence among his people was so important because from this place God's rule emanates throughout the earth. It is thus representative of his kingdom, and the call to build is seen as a high priority because it lies at the core of God's kingdom and redemptive work on earth.

Blessings and curses. The second biblical-theological theme is that of blessing and curse. The origins of retribution theology can be traced to the Sinai covenant described in the Pentateuch.[33] There we find several instances in which response to the demands of the covenant is placed against the backdrop of a God who is able to bring blessing or curse according to the people's response to the law (Lev. 26; Deut. 28–30): blessing as a reward for obedience, and curses not viewed as rejection but as discipline to lead the people back to a covenant relationship. The prophets will pick up on this important covenant feature as they prosecute the nation for their disobedience and encourage them to bring their lives into conformity with the covenant.

Similarly, the two main traditions of historical writing in Israel (the Deuteronomic history and the Chronicler's history) view the life of the nation from the perspective of blessing and cursing (the former to explain the demise of the nation, the latter to engender hope for obedience). Although the influence of this retribution theology can also be identified within wisdom literature and the Psalms (cf. Ps. 1), this literature has helped to define more clearly the boundaries and limits of retribution theology: Blessing is not always the reward for obedience (Ps. 73; Job 21:7), and curse cannot always be traced to disobedience (Job). The experience of hardship and suffering in

33. Clearly Haggai has in mind the Sinaitic form of blessing/cursing. Mitchell confirms this by showing that while the content of the Abrahamic blessing was descendants, fame, dominion, God's presence, the content of the Sinai blessing was fertility of domesticated animals and crops; see C. W. Mitchell, *The Meaning of BRK "to bless" in the Old Testament* (SBLDS 95; Atlanta: Scholars Press, 1987), 29, 36 (though Mitchell does not do justice to this theme in Haggai).

the life of the believer may be linked to covenant disobedience, but there are other reasons as well.[34]

The kind of blessing and cursing described above is founded on the covenant relationship established at Sinai. It stands in contrast, however, to another strain of blessing and cursing that is linked to the covenant relationship established between Abraham and Yahweh in Genesis.[35] Whereas blessing is conditional in the Sinaitic covenant, blessing is unconditional in the Abrahamic covenant.[36] The promises of blessing to the patriarchs are intended to motivate them to enter relationship with Yahweh, while promises of blessing to the Israelites at Sinai were to motivate them to observe the demands of the covenant already made.[37] Intimately linked to the kind of blessing in the patriarchal narratives is the promise of blessing offered to living creatures in Genesis 1:22, 28, both of which refer to a multiplication of living beings on earth.

The New Testament appropriation of the theology of blessing from the Old Testament is first of all from the patriarchal model of unconditional blessing. Peter in Acts 3:25–26 and Paul in Galatians 3:8–9, 14 appropriate the Abrahamic covenantal blessing for Christians, associating it with the redemptive work of Christ.[38] In Ephesians 1:3, blessings are again equated with the spiritual benefits of Christ's redemptive work for his people.

There is, however, some evidence of the use of blessing in a way similar to its use in the Sinaitic covenant. Christ grants blessing to those who portray the qualities of the kingdom (Matt. 5:1–12//Luke 6:20–23). This reward is future (5:12) and largely spiritual (Matt. 25:31–36). In addition, Christ offers curses to those who do not portray the qualities of the kingdom (Luke

---

34. These other reasons are summarized by W. C. Kaiser, *A Biblical Approach to Personal Suffering* (Chicago: Moody, 1982). The list includes retributive suffering (Deut. 30:19), educational or disciplinary suffering (Job 36:10, 15; 33:16; Prov. 3:11; 13:24; 15:5; Heb. 12:7), vicarious suffering (Isa. 53:5; 42:1–4; 49:4; 50:6; 52:13–53:12), empathetic suffering (Gen. 6:5–6; Ex. 32:14; Judg. 2:15; 1 Sam. 15:11; Isa. 63:9; Hos. 11:8; Rom. 12:15; 2 Cor. 2:4), doxological suffering (Gen. 45:4, 5, 7; 50:20; John 9:3), evidential or testimonial suffering (Job 1–2), revelational suffering (Hosea; Jeremiah); eschatological or apocalyptic suffering (Daniel, Revelation).

35. Cf. I. Nowell, "The Narrative Context of Blessing in the Old Testament," in *Blessing and Power*, ed. M. Collins and D. Power (Concilium; Edinburgh: T. & T. Clark, 1985), 3–12.

36. C. C. Westermann, *Blessing in the Bible and the Life of the Church*, trans. K. Crim, (OBT; Philadelphia: Fortress, 1978), 47–49.

37. Mitchell, *The Meaning of BRK*, 28–36.

38. Westermann (*Blessing*, 77) comments on Gal. 3: "Here we have a conscious and emphatic transformation of the Old Testament concept of blessing. In the fulfillment of the promise, the blessing of God was transformed into God's saving deeds in Christ."

6:24–26; cf. Matt. 25:41). Truly Christ did look to a future spiritual blessing in heaven, but this did not exclude blessing in the present age (Mark 10:29–30). Thus, for those in the kingdom, there is the promise of blessing both in the present and future, both in terms of spiritual experience and in terms of physical provision.

Although there is not an extensive use of the terms blessing and cursing in the New Testament, the concept of retribution theology is evident throughout. The reality is that God does bring blessing on his people (James 1:17) and cares for our needs as we seek his kingdom (Matt. 6:33–34). He also continues to bring discipline into our lives because he loves us as a father (Heb. 12:1–13). Once one understands the Old Testament view of blessing and cursing as discipline rather than merely punishment, the connection to the New Testament context is much easier. Although we do not find in the New Testament as much emphasis on this biblical theme as we find in the Old Testament, it continues to have relevance for the church.

Many in the church are tempted to react to the exploitation of this biblical theological theme by those called "health and wealth preachers."[39] Such a reaction has led to a distancing of many within the church from this important theological theme.[40] Of course, the error of the health and wealth gospel is that it absolutizes a truth in the Bible at the expense of other truths, a trend corrected by the wisdom tradition in the Old Testament. Note the words of Kaiser: "Thus it would appear that a legitimate concept of wealth and possessions has been taken and hyped up to an exaggerated position without retaining the balance that it receives in its biblical context."[41]

These two key themes in Haggai's opening message, temple and retribution, invite Christian readers to embrace the message of 1:1–11.

Contemporary Significance

ALTHOUGH THE MINOR PROPHETS rarely find their way into the preaching schedule of churches, most Christians will encounter Haggai 1 at some point in their life, since it is often dusted off when a church initiates a building project. There is, of course, an easy link between building the temple and building a church. Often that hermeneutical swing

39. See Kaiser's excellent critique of this movement and review of this biblical-theological theme in his "The Old Testament Promise of Material Blessings and the Contemporary Believer," *TrinJ* 9 n.s. (1988): 151–70.

40. Achtemeier plays this down considerably; Achtemeier, *Nahum–Malachi*, 99; idem, *Preaching from the Minor Prophets: Texts and Sermon Suggestions* (Grand Rapids: Eerdmans, 1998), 107–11.

41. Kaiser, "Material Blessings," 162.

does not take seriously the core values of this passage and makes the connection in a simplistic manner. Although this connection may be appropriate, it is important to keep the larger context in mind as the connection is made.

Discipline. Haggai 1 teaches us about the experience of discipline in our lives. The prophet uses the experience of covenant curse in the lives of the people as an opportunity to consider God's priorities in their generation. He traces the hand of God in the suffering they have experienced in the recent past and shows how this is connected to their lack of passion for rebuilding the temple.

The heavy emphasis on the agricultural world does not resonate with the majority of the world today, who live in burgeoning cities cut off from the land. In an effort to control our own destiny as human beings, the world has moved increasingly to urban centers, where the environment can be controlled by our modern technology. Our hope is that we can eradicate the uncertainties of life and achieve a utopian existence. Interestingly, there is at present a movement back to rural settings from North America's largest cities.[42] The city has not been a panacea, for hardships now come in the form of business failures, disintegrating families, and financial crises rather than in drought.

As we have already noted, the prophet is not suggesting that every experience of suffering or hardship is automatically a sign of God's discipline in our lives. However, many within the church today have moved to the opposite extreme, where there is little sense or expectation of the intrusion of God into their everyday affairs. In their desire to remain true to the biblical portrayal of the Lord as the redemptive-historical God, they have relegated God to the "historical" and ignored his ongoing work in everyday life.

This is a new twist on the deistic heresy of the modern era. Whereas Deists believe that God created the world and then set it in motion with internal laws without ongoing intrusion, the new deists send the message that God has saved his people and set in motion the principles and forces to sustain this community without personal intrusion. But New Testament descriptions of the death of Ananias and Sapphira (Acts 5) and sickness within the Corinthian church (1 Cor. 11:29–30) show a God who continues to interact with the circumstances of his people.

In light of this, experiences of hardship should always become opportunities for spiritual reflection in our lives, turning us heavenward to ask hard questions. The various psalms of disorientation in the Psalter encourage us

42. See *Time* (December 8, 1997).

to ask God about the hardships that enter our lives.[43] These questions are not expressions of rebellion but rather the honest voice of a child reliant on a parent. Such questions, however, should be accompanied by questions directed inward as we ask God to search us for those areas that do not reflect the priorities of the kingdom (Ps. 139).[44] If under the searchlight of God's Word we have need of repentance, we should turn from our sins and walk in a way consistent with this penitence.

This final step is important. In Haggai we are not told anything about the *words* of repentance, only the *acts* of repentance as they "obeyed the voice of the LORD their God" and "came and began to work" (1:14). God desires more than just empty words; he wants deeds—a truth echoed in the words of James 1:22: "Do not merely listen to the word, and so deceive yourselves. Do what it says."

Misplaced priorities. Haggai links Judah's hardship to misplaced priorities in their lives. This is displayed poignantly in the contrast between concern for their own homes and concern for God's house. The issue here is not the amount of resources available but rather the priorities of the people. They are concerned first with themselves and their own comfort and extravagance. This message is not saying that one cannot enjoy the blessings of a home, but after two decades of inactivity at the temple site while homes were being built and beautified, the prophet identifies deficiencies in the priorities of the community.

Haggai speaks this message to a people struggling financially rather than to a wealthy class. We often associate the fixation on materialism with the wealthy classes of our society, but money and its attainment and disbursement may be in reality a greater priority for the vast middle class in the West than for any other class. Its grip on our consciousness often strips us of passion for the priorities of the kingdom. Since the majority of the church in North America is made up of middle class members, the message of Haggai is a powerful corrective to our generation.[45]

---

43. See W. Brueggemann, "The Costly Loss of Lament," *JSOT* 36 (1986): 57–71; idem, "The Formfulness of Grief," *Int* 31 (1977): 267–74; idem, *The Message of the Psalms: A Theological Commentary* (Augsburg Old Testament Studies; Minneapolis: Augsburg, 1984); W. Brueggemann and P. D. Miller, *The Psalms and the Life of Faith* (Minneapolis: Fortress, 1995).

44. M. J. Boda, "The Priceless Gain of Penitence: From Communal Lament to Penitential Prayer in the 'Exilic' Liturgy of Israel," *HBT* 25 (2003): 51–75.

45. See Packer for the grip of hedonism in our lives and the influence it has on our spirituality; J. I. Packer, *Hot Tub Religion* (Wheaton: Tyndale, 1987), 67–101. Similarly, Foster identifies the hold of money on our evangelical culture; R. Foster, *Money, Sex and Power* (New York: Harper and Row, 1985), 19–87.

It may be tempting for church leaders to limit this financial connection to building programs, but the message of 1:1–11 relates to our use of our financial resources for all aspects of kingdom work. That may mean redirecting our financial resources to broaden the ministry of the church to care for the poor and needy within the community or to reach youth within the neighborhood high school. It may mean designating a fixed percentage of church income for extending the gospel to unreached people groups whether at home or abroad.

Haggai 1:1–11 should not only be related to individual members within the church, but should shape the agenda of the church community as a whole. It is easy for churches to become cesspools of narcissism, placing priority on their paneled houses of worship with little care for the community around them. This passage, read in light of the New Testament's redefinition of the temple as the Christian community, challenges it to release their resources for God's kingdom work beyond the physical structures of a building and to reconsider funds invested in such structures.

Haggai's message, however, extends far beyond the issue of financial resources and materialism. It speaks to our priorities in general. These are displayed vividly in our financial priorities but are also seen in our time management, goal setting, and family expectations. In a world filled with increasing activities and opportunities, individuals and families need to ask serious questions about their priorities in light of God's kingdom. What values do we bring to modern life and society that reflect the priorities of God? Will we establish individual and family rhythms of rest that release us from the tyranny of the urgent? Will we clear space in our schedules to hear the voice of God and rejuvenate our souls?

When I was a pastor in Toronto, Ontario, one of our members was an executive with a major bank in Canada. Because of superb job performance he was offered a promotion to a higher paying job. To the surprise of the officers of the bank, he rejected the offer. His reason: He was not willing to jeopardize the well-being of his family and faith to fulfill the unrealistic expectations of the company. Assuredly, it had consequences for this man's career and financial security, but he made this decision in light of God's kingdom purposes.

The church also has a role to play within our societies. We should get God's kingdom values onto the agenda of our communities and nations, not only through participation in government but also through involvement in community life. In a recent visit to a large city in North America, I was told of a Christian couple who were key members of a community association that had a vision to help troubled teens within their area of the city. As a leader within this association, this couple was able to offer facilities and personnel from their local church in order to facilitate an athletic program for the community.

In our stewardship of the various resources God has given us, we must be directed by the priorities of God and his kingdom. Christ's call in Matthew 6:33 echoes Haggai's call in chapter 1 to seek first God's kingdom and interests for they lie at the center of all human history and activity. As we do so, God has promised to provide our needs.

Priority of the glory of God. Haggai also moves us to see our world from God's perspective, to make his priorities our priorities and see the consequences of not sharing these priorities. It places, then, at its center not the human predicament (that is only a means to an end) but rather divine desire, a desire defined as God's pleasure and glorification.

Down the street from my home is a seventy-year-old church whose cornerstone proclaims: "To the glory of God," a phrase commonly used to dress such stones throughout North America. Today this same phrase often appears in the preamble of church vision statements printed in church bulletins or displayed prominently in the church foyer. Hopefully, these cornerstones and vision statements truly reflect the passion of God's people to make his glory the ultimate purpose of the church. Building projects—indeed, all kingdom work—must be for God's pleasure and glory.

This approach to the work of the kingdom is radically theocentric. A church that is anthropocentric in its approach will place as the primary concern the meeting of human needs. This, however, is inadequate in the economy of God's kingdom work. The meeting of human needs is but a means to an end, and that end is the pleasure and glory of God. As A. W. Tozer once wrote:

> The purpose of God in sending His Son to die and rise and live and be at the right hand of God the Father was that He might restore to us the missing jewel, the jewel of worship; that we might come back and learn to do again that which we were created to do in the first place—worship the Lord in the beauty of holiness, to spend our time in awesome wonder and adoration of God, feeling and expressing it, and letting it get into our labors and doing nothing except as an act of worship to Almighty God through His Son Jesus Christ.[46]

The church should be theocentric, placing God at the center of all activity and passionately preserving this priority. As believers evaluate their participation in the work of the kingdom, the first question must be: Are we

46. A. W. Tozer, *Worship: The Missing Jewel in the Evangelical Church* (Harrisburg, Pa.: Christian Publications, 1961), 12.

bringing pleasure and glory to God through this work? If such is not the case, the work is irrelevant to God's priorities for the kingdom.[47]

This is not to say that the meeting of human need is unrelated to the work of the kingdom. In the preceding paragraphs I have sought to expand our vision of the kingdom beyond bricks and mortar to the human concerns that surround us locally and globally. However, human need is met for a greater purpose than the betterment of the human race; it finds its purpose in the greater pleasure and glory offered to God as a result.[48] Note these conclusions of John Piper:

> The ultimate goal of God in all of history is to uphold and display his glory for the enjoyment of the redeemed from every tribe and tongue and people and nation. His goal is the gladness of his people because God is most glorified in us when we are most satisfied in him. Delight is a higher tribute than duty. The chief end of God is to glorify God and enjoy his glory for ever. Since his glory is magnified most in the God-centered passions of his joyful people, God's self-exultation and our jubilation are one. The greatest news in all the world is that God's ultimate aim to be glorified and man's aim to be satisfied are not at odds.[49]

In his exposition of the life and words of the prophet Jeremiah, Eugene Petersen shares his observations of the behavior of tree swallows near his retreat in Montana one summer. For several weeks he had observed the swallows gathering food for their mates and chicks and finally was delighted to see three babies perched on an old branch four feet above the surface of the lake. He was about to watch the three chicks learn how to fly.

One adult swallow got alongside the chicks and started shoving them out toward the end of the branch—pushing, pushing, pushing. The end one fell off. Somewhere between the branch and the water four feet below, the wings started working, and the fledgling was off on his own. Then the second one. The third was not to be bullied. At the last possible moment his grip

47. This emphasis on the pleasure and glory of God is the focus of John Piper's splendid book, *The Pleasures of God* (Portland: Multnomah, 1991). Surprisingly, he does not touch on Hag. 1.

48. See J. Piper's work on missions and his work on preaching, *Let the Nations Be Glad: The Supremacy of God in Missions* (Grand Rapids: Baker, 1993); idem, *The Supremacy of God in Preaching* (Grand Rapids: Baker, 1990). In the first he argues that the ultimate goal of missions is not the salvation of human souls but the glorification of God. In the second he urges preachers to preach about God and his glory, a practice that is intensely practical insofar as it offers the only hope for the intense problems of our people today.

49. Piper, *Nations*, 219.

on the branch loosened just enough so that he swung downward, then tightened again, bulldog tenacious. The parent was persistent. He pecked at the desperately clinging talons until it was more painful for the chick to hang on than risk the insecurities of flying. He released his grip, and the inexperienced wings began pumping. The mature swallow knew what the chick did not—that it would fly and that there was no danger in making it do what it was perfectly designed to do.[50]

With this Petersen concludes: "Birds have feet and can walk. Birds have talons and can grasp a branch securely. They can walk; they can cling. But *flying* is their characteristic action, and not until they fly are they living at their best, gracefully and beautifully." There are many things that we can pursue in life as human beings, but ultimately it is the pursuit of the pleasure and glory of God that lies at the core of our being as those created in his image. This chapter has shown us God's passion of this purpose in our lives and communities, a passion that may involve even experiences of suffering to propel us from self-absorbed hedonism to God focused activity.

50. E. H. Peterson, *Run with the Horses: The Question for Life at its Best* (Downers Grove, Ill.: InterVarsity Press, 1983), 42–43.

Haggai 1:12–15

THEN ZERUBBABEL SON of Shealtiel, Joshua son of Jehozadak, the high priest, and the whole remnant of the people obeyed the voice of the LORD their God and the message of the prophet Haggai, because the LORD their God had sent him. And the people feared the LORD.

13Then Haggai, the LORD's messenger, gave this message of
the LORD to the people: "I am with you," declares the LORD.
14So the LORD stirred up the spirit of Zerubbabel son of
Shealtiel, governor of Judah, and the spirit of Joshua son of
Jehozadak, the high priest, and the spirit of the whole remnant
of the people. They came and began to work on the house of
the LORD Almighty, their God, 15on the twenty-fourth day of
the sixth month in the second year of King Darius.

Original Meaning

UNLIKE THE FIRST SECTION of Haggai (see 1:1), the date for 1:12–15 is provided at the end of the section: the twenty-fourth day of the sixth month in the second year of Darius, twenty-three days after the first message. This date places the commencement of work in the midst of the grape, fig, and pomegranate harvests. Although the people may have responded positively immediately to the message (1:12), the work on the temple would have started after proper preparations had been made and the harvest was complete.

This section describes the people's response to Haggai's message in 1:1–11, which is given both from the divine and human perspective. At the center is the core promise: "I am with you." This response represents a massive step of faith. Nearly two decades prior to this, an earlier group of Jews under their governor Sheshbazzar had responded to the invitation of Cyrus and began to work on the same temple site, yet with little success (see Ezra 1; 5:15–16). Now amidst threats from those in adjoining Persian provinces (see 3:3; 4:1–5; 5:1–6:15), a new generation begins the temple project anew. The message of God's promised presence is essential to bolster the faith of these underdogs.

As already noted in the comments on 1:1–11, verses 12–15 need to be interpreted in light of verses 1–11. This is suggested by the inversion of the date formulae that appear in 1:1 and 1:15, a rhetorical technique that forges the two sections together,[1] as well as by the close similarity between the lists of people in 1:1 and 1:12. This section thus functions as a narrative description of the people's response to the message of the prophet in 1:1–11.

Detailed Analysis

THIS PASSAGE DESCRIBES the people's reaction to the message of the prophet Haggai. As in 1:1, Zerubbabel and Joshua are listed, but the people are mentioned as well: "whole remnant of the people."[2] When the people were mentioned at 1:2, they were referred to as "these people" (1:2), a somewhat derogatory appellation that revealed a distance in the relationship between God and the covenant people. Now, however, they are identified as the "remnant," a term drawn from the prophetic tradition. Mason sees the importance of this move: "May the editor be expressing the opinion that it was the prophetic word of Yahweh and their response to it which constituted them as the true Israel, the genuine 'remnant'?"[3] The notion of a remnant among the people is important for the classical prophets. God does not reject but rather disciplines his people. The remnant is the group that emerges from this discipline sanctified and purified for service.[4]

The initial response of the people with their leaders is twofold: obedience and fear. The phrase "obey the voice" (*šamaᶜ beqol*) of God is a regular expression in Hebrew literature denoting a positive response to God's covenant demands.

The second response is that of "fear." Although it may be tempting to see here the typical covenant response in Deuteronomy and elsewhere (i.e., the posture of reverent submission and trust in Yahweh; e.g., Deut. 10:12, 20),[5] the Hebrew phrase used here (*yaraᵓ mippeney*, "to fear in the presence of") is one used

---

1. There has been much discussion over the origin of what I have identified as the "subscription" in 1:15b. Many see here the date for a "misplaced" oracle in 2:15–19, but there is no textual support for this. I agree with Redditt that 1:15 is an inclusion device, bracketing the entire section; Redditt, *Haggai*, 23. However, I disagree with his attempt to lop off the end of 1:15b and use it for 2:1. This would disrupt the inclusion pattern used here in which 1:1 uses the order Year-Month-Day and then 1:15 uses the order Day-Month-Year.

2. R. Mason (*Preaching*, 192) notes this emergence of the people and explains it this way: "Perhaps the reason the people are not so described in 1:1 is that it was only by their disobedience to God's word through his 'messenger,' described in 1:12–14, that they proved themselves to be truly the remnant of prophetic promise"; see also his "The Purpose of the 'Editorial Framework' of the Book of Haggai," *VT* 27 (1977): 418.

3. Mason, "Purpose," 418.

4. Hasel traces this remnant theme through the prophets: Isa. 10:20–22; 11:11, 16; 28:5; 37:4, 31, 32; 46:3; Jer. 23:3; 31:7; Mic. 2:12; 5:6, 7; 7:18; Zeph. 2:7, 9; 3:13; but also in the expectation of the Persian period community (Ezra 9:14; Zech. 8:11); G. F. Hasel, *The Remnant: The History and Theology of the Remnant Idea from Genesis to Isaiah*, 3d ed. (AUMSR 5; Berrien Springs, Mich.: Andrews Univ. Press, 1980).

5. See Weinfeld, *Deuteronomy*, 332–33.

elsewhere for humanity's response to judgment or to the awesome presence of God (Deut. 5:5; 13:11; 17:13; 19:20; 21:21).[6] Both are appropriate here. Haggai has identified the presence of God in judgment in their recent past, and their response is one of trembling fear as they willingly receive the word.

Haggai's message is equated with the voice of God by placing them in apposition. "The voice of the LORD their God" is not somehow distinct from the message of the prophet Haggai. Rather, the only message they have heard is the one that came through the prophet, and this is the voice of the Lord. Their response, therefore, echoes the response of the nation that first heard the covenant at Sinai, for it was the voice of God that they feared, and they begged Moses to become the prophetic mediator of the message of God (Ex. 20; Deut. 5). Haggai is thus cast into the role of Moses, delivering the message of God, his voice to a new generation.

The people's response elicits a short but important response from the Lord: "I am with you" (1:13). This phrase draws from a legacy of assurance by God to those who assume a task from his hand (see Ex. 3:12; Judg. 6:12; Jer. 1:8, 19). Interestingly, when David desires to build the first temple, Nathan the prophet said "for the LORD is with you" (2 Sam. 7:3). The same assurance is now given to another generation seeking to fulfill the passion of David.

Verse 13 provides an excellent transition from the initial response of the people to the revelation of the work of God in verse 14. The core promise comprises two words in Hebrew, identifying the two partners in this new project: the people ("you") and Yahweh ("I"). It begins the movement toward God as the source of this great project that climaxes in the following verse. A people, obedient yet filled with fear, are comforted by God, who reassures them by this simple promise that he accepts them and will accompany them in this great enterprise.

This reassurance of his presence flows into the divine perspective on the response of the people. The same participants are noted in verse 14 as in verse 12, but now instead of being the subjects of the verbs, the people are the objects and Yahweh the actor: Yahweh "stirs up" (Hiphil of *ʿwr*) their "spirits." Elsewhere this verb refers to God's action to set in motion the restoration of the people in the Persian period and is connected to his work through the Persian emperor Cyrus (2 Chron. 36:22–23; Ezra 1:1; Isa. 41:2, 25; 45:13). However, as Ezra 1:5 shows, this action also extended to God's people. This verb emphasizes God's active role in moving the affections of his people to respond to the message. It reflects the vision of the new covenant seen in Jeremiah (Jer. 31–33), in which God not only writes the law on the hearts of the people (31:33) but even moves their affections (32:40).

---

6. Cf. Verhoef, *Haggai*, 83.

In light of the fact that Haggai is pictured as a second Moses who delivers the word of God to a responsive (obeying and fearing) generation, paralleling the Sinaitic covenant community, it is interesting that a similar verbal idea is used in the context of the building of the tabernacle (Ex. 35:29; 36:2) to refer to the willingness of the people to give and to work on the tabernacle.[7] In that context, however, the people are the subjects of this verb, while in Haggai Yahweh is the subject, evidence of a shift toward the new covenant ethos proclaimed by Jeremiah.

As the text ends the description of the people's response and closes the first section of the book, the author announces that the people begin to work on the temple. Note the repetition of the name "LORD Almighty" here, whose word began this section (1:2), and the subscription of the date, arranged in reverse order to that found in verse 1.

Bridging Contexts

IN THIS BRIEF DESCRIPTION of the people's response to Haggai's message, this passage emphasizes the qualities of human covenant faithfulness, the provision of God's presence, and the authority of the prophetic word. The example and experience of this ancient community are instructive for us as Christians today who follow in their footsteps as we seek to fulfill God's kingdom priorities for our generation. The precedent for Christian appropriation of a story like this is established by Paul in 1 Corinthians 10:1–13, where the apostle uses the experience of the desert community to encourage faithfulness among the Corinthian believers. This is appropriate, he says, because we are the ones "on whom the fulfillment of the ages has come." As the ultimate expression of the community of God, the church can learn from these ancient examples and, in even greater ways because of Christ's sacrifice and the Spirit's endowment, walk faithfully.

Remnant. In 1:12 the community that displays the qualities of covenant faithfulness is called the "remnant." This word, as noted above, is a theological term connected to the rich Old Testament prophetic tradition. The concept of the remnant assumes both continuity and discontinuity with the community of old. A remnant is a portion that remains and assumes that formerly there was a community from which the portion was taken. A remnant, however, is only a portion, and although bearing similarities with the whole it becomes a new entity. As the prophets develop the theme of the remnant in the Old Testament, they show that God's promises remain intact, but that they will be fulfilled through a purified community, the remnant.

7. See Mason, *Preaching*, 193.

The use of the remnant motif in Haggai is not surprising for it is intimately linked to the important themes of covenant discipline and the presence of God. The remnant represents those who have experienced the covenant discipline of God and have emerged purified. At the same time the remnant is pictured as a community who will experience the presence of God; in particular, they will have God's Spirit within them (Ezek. 37:1–14; Joel 2:28–32).

The remnant is also offered a new covenant experience in the writings of both Jeremiah and Ezekiel. There we learn that God envisions a new covenant, which, although utilizing the same law base of the old covenant, will rely on God's internal work in the hearts of the people (Jer. 31:31–34; cf. Ezek. 16:59–63). The focus in covenant references in Jeremiah is on the work of God to accomplish covenant fidelity (Jer. 32:36–41, esp. 40). Ezekiel echoes this emphasis by linking this work to the Spirit in the context of rebuilding the temple (Ezek. 36:24–38). Interestingly, Ezekiel speaks of an everlasting covenant that combines the themes of the Davidic line, the sanctuary, and the remnant, also seen in Haggai 1 (Ezek. 37:15–28).

This remnant theme carries over into the New Testament and sets the stage for the advance of the church in Acts. One can hardly miss the allusions in Acts 2 to the returning of the remnant to the land of Israel (see the list of nations in Acts 2:9–11). Jews stream into Jerusalem from all over the ancient world, and as they do, they hear the wonders of God in their own languages. Peter explains these phenomena by quoting from Joel 2, a passage that refers to the remnant (the survivors) returning and receiving the Spirit of God (see Joel 2:32). This sermon results in the salvation of three thousand on that day, the foundation layer of the church.

As the church is born in Acts 2, it is described as the remnant community that has been purified and on whom rests God's Spirit. Elsewhere in the New Testament, the church is pictured as the recipients of the new covenant through Christ (Luke 22:20; 1 Cor. 11:25; 2 Cor. 3:6; Heb. 8:6; 9:15). As the "remnant," the community of Christ needs to replicate the qualities of covenant faithfulness depicted in Haggai 1:12–15, that is, to stand in awe before God and respond in obedience to his Word as they pursue Christ's kingdom.

Presence. To such a community God promises his presence: "I am with you." The use of this phrase in a passage speaking of the building of the place of God's manifest presence (temple) is important. Note how the event that breaks up the account of the tabernacle construction in Exodus 25–40 is the story of the golden calf rebellion and the subsequent interaction between Yahweh and Moses (chs. 32–34). The focus of that interaction is a fierce dialogue between Yahweh and Moses over the provision of his presence (ch. 33). God agrees to provide his presence with Moses as they build the tabernacle and continue their journey to the Promised Land. Likewise,

Solomon is aware of the blessing of God's presence with him and his people as he dedicates the temple (1 Kings 8:57).[8]

It is not surprising, then, that as Christ sends forth his disciples in Matthew 28:18–20, his parting promise is the provision of his presence. This presence is clearly outlined in John 14:15–31 as the Holy Spirit sent by Christ to his people. Acts pictures a community who experiences Christ's presence through the Spirit as they take the gospel to the world (Acts 1:8; 2).

As Haggai promised Yahweh's presence for those involved in the kingdom work of the temple in the Persian period, so Christ promises his presence for his disciples. That promise far transcends that of Haggai's as the presence of Yahweh comes to fill each believer permanently. However, the link is unmistakable and provides an important connection to our life in Christ.

Revelation. Not only does this narrative emphasize the covenant partners, God and his community, but also the prophetic mediator who faithfully delivers God's message to his people. The authority of the word of this mediator is stressed by equating the voice of God with the prophet's message ("voice of the LORD their God and message of the prophet Haggai") and by the declaration of the calling of the prophet ("the LORD their God had sent him ... the LORD's messenger ... the message of the LORD to the people"). To hear the prophet was to hear God.

Such a respect for God's message is displayed in the words the Israelites heard thundering from Sinai in Exodus 20:1–17. Significantly, the response of the Exodus generation to God's word on Mount Sinai was identical to the reaction of Haggai's generation: They "feared" (20:18). It is this experience that prompted Moses' appointment as mediator of God's word to his generation (Ex. 20:19–21), a model that shaped the prophetic movement throughout the history of Israel. The narrator here is emphasizing that Haggai shares a legitimate place in the long line of prophets, beginning with Moses, who mediated God's word to his people. The response of the people emphasizes the authority of this Word.

---

8. Westermann (*Blessing,* 34) has noted the intimate connection between blessing and temple, drawing these two important themes in our passage together beautifully: "The temple is properly the place for bestowal of blessing (1 Kings 8). Blessing flows forth from the cultic acts in the temple upon the people and the land. Groups of pilgrims and processions go to the temple in order to obtain blessing for themselves and their families, for their cattle and their fields. If the temple should be destroyed and the worship there be ended, then the source of blessing for the land is cut off. This is shown by Solomon's prayer at the dedication of the temple (1 Kings 8), by the proclamations of the prophet Haggai, and above all by the psalms of blessing and the psalms of pilgrimage (Ps. 65; 115:12–15; 128:5; 129:8; 132, etc.)." See also Ps. 84, a psalm of pilgrimage to the temple that repeats the word blessing three times, connecting blessing with life in and journey toward the temple.

Contemporary Significance

HUMAN RESPONSE. By depicting the response of the people and designating this group as the "remnant," Haggai 1:12–15 affirms this response as normative—that is, the proper response of God's people is always obedience to his voice. This response is only possible because of a depth of covenant relationship with God, a relationship in which the people hear his word. Haggai's message was accepted by a remnant that had open ears to hear. This obedience has two aspects: "fear" and "work." The first is the internal quality of submissive reverence for the word of God, while the second is the external quality of committed action.

Our response to God's Word today is no different. Based on the depth of covenant relationship with God through Christ's sacrifice on the cross and through the Spirit's empowerment in our lives, we are called to listen attentively to God's Word and to respond in obedience. Such obedience will arise from an internal depth of reverence for the God who speaks to us and will result in active obedience. James 1:22–25 echoes this concern:

> Do not merely listen to the word, and so deceive yourselves. Do what it says. Anyone who listens to the word but does not do what it says is like a man who looks at his face in a mirror and, after looking at himself, goes away and immediately forgets what he looks like. But the man who looks intently into the perfect law that gives freedom, and continues to do this, not forgetting what he has heard, but doing it—he will be blessed in what he does.

James's instruction is not to discontinue listening to God's Word, but rather to look "intently" and continue to "do this." Notice how he reflects the message of Haggai by linking such obedience to blessings from God.

This teaching of James is especially appropriate for those who have been Christians for an extended period of time. One of the core values of the church is the preaching and teaching of God's Word (e.g., Acts 2:41; Eph. 4:11–16; 1 Tim. 4:11–16). However, it is easy for regular parishioners' (let alone pastors') knowledge of that Word to exceed the appropriation of that Word in their life. This should affect our patterns as individuals and churches. It may be better for us to focus on fewer experiences in the Word followed by longer reflection on its implications for lives and godliness than to quickly move ahead to the next passage in our journey through the Bible. The danger is to become used to listening to the Word without responding in actions, to feed the intellect without moving the affections and impacting the will.

Prophetic word. The reverent response of the people cannot be separated from their conviction of the divine origin of Haggai's prophetic word. However, several trends in contemporary Christian culture have led to a loss of this emphasis within the church. (1) With Bibles translated into our native tongues and multiple copies residing in many homes, it is easy to lose sight of the wonder of the revelation that we hold in our hands today. These words, now reproduced in written form, were delivered throughout the history of God's people by his chosen servants, the prophets.

(2) Attacks on the veracity of the Scriptures have led to a lack of confidence in God's Word as authoritative. For some the Bible contains God's word but is not his word in totality.

(3) Recent hermeneutical reflection has called into question the ability of God's people to interpret the biblical text, suggesting that interpretation is nothing more than the reflection of one's own mind. Such factors have led to a devaluing of the ancient Scriptures in the life of the church.

With such factors a reality today, how can we recover appropriate reverence and respect for God's Word? Surely one must meet theological challenges to the doctrine of Scripture through careful study of the biblical text, theological history, and philosophy. But this is not enough. Recovering reverence and respect for the Word of God will mean reshaping our approach to that Word.

(1) This needs to happen on the *individual level*. A friend of mine was asked to deliver a seminar on the authority of Scripture in preaching at a national meeting of his denomination. Surprising to some, he focused his seminar not on the latest theological debates over the authority of Scripture. Instead, he taught them how to pray through Scripture, seeking to guide the pastors into a conversation with God over the passages they had studied so faithfully. Without minimizing the importance of theological debate over authority, I believe that this was an important strategy for recovering the practical authority of Scripture within the church today. People must approach God's Word as revelation and respond to him in the depth of their affections through prayer as a pathway to response, that is, to act out their presumed beliefs.

Such an approach to Scripture is reflected in prayers in the Bible. For instance, Ezra 9, Nehemiah 1 and 9, and Daniel 9 are filled with allusions to and quotations from the books of the Law. These texts show how exegesis became prayer.[9]

---

9. Boda, *Praying*; J. H. Newman, "Nehemiah 9 and the Scripturalization of Prayer in the Second Temple Period," in *The Function of Scripture in Early Jewish and Christian Tradition*, ed. C. A. Evans and J. A. Sanders (JSNTSup 154; Sheffield: Sheffield Academic Press, 1998), 112–23; idem, *Praying by the Book: The Scripturalization of Prayer in Second Temple Judaism* (SBLEJL 14; Atlanta: Scholars Press, 1999).

(2) This advice must also be appropriated on the *communal level*. The use and treatment of Scripture in our contexts of worship and fellowship both reflect and shape our view of God's Word. A few years ago I attended a church in Glasgow, Scotland on a Sunday morning. The first item in that service was not the invocation or the procession of the pastor. Instead, an elderly man appeared from behind the platform with a gargantuan Bible in his hand. He gingerly climbed the steps up to the raised pulpit of the church, carefully set the Bible on the pulpit, and descended. This ritual, practiced weekly at that church, reminded the people of the importance and authority of God's Word for that community of faith. Other churches I have attended communicate this reverence in other ways, whether through standing as the Bible is read aloud or by declaring "thus far God's Word." These rituals subtly shape a community's view of the Word.

We find evidence of these kinds of rituals in Nehemiah 8. There we see that when Ezra opens the book of the Law, the people stand up and then bow down and worship the Lord. So reverent are these people for the words of this book that when they hear them, they begin to weep because of their lack of obedience to its demands. This example shows us a community whose respect for God's Word leads to a depth of response that grips their affections.

The "remnant" in Haggai's day had a deep respect for the Word of God delivered to them through the Lord's prophet. Such respect had deep roots within this community. How do we nourish that kind of respect? Clearly it will mean a deep stirring in the hearts of our people and community, something accomplished by the Spirit's work but also by human response. It also means recovering the kind of rituals that remind us of the importance of this Word—that is, rhythms that create an ethos of respect for the Word in which the Spirit can do a new work. May we find creative ways to foster this within our individual and corporate lives today.

Divine provision. Haggai 1:12–15 reminds us that God graciously grants us the resources to fulfill his priorities, making it clear that even the human response is a work of the Almighty God as he stirs his people to action and then promises his presence to sustain the work. This does not preclude human involvement; rather, it assumes it. However, in the new covenant, God accompanies the call with his empowerment (see Jer. 31:31–34). He provides the spiritual resources, especially through the Spirit, to fulfill his mandate within our generation. This is the great mystery of Philippians 2:12–13, in which Paul calls the people to "continue to work out your salvation with fear and trembling for it is God who works in you to will and to act according to his good purpose." The resources are provided by the sovereign God as we respond to his call.

There is also an implicit warning to the church in the description of the response in Haggai 1:12–14. Once the response is described in verse 12, the focus of attention quickly moves to God's promised presence ("I am with you") and the revelation that even this response found its source in God's prompting. In fulfilling the work of the kingdom, it is surprising how often the church focuses on the human level and thus robs God of the glory due him. The first order of business in building projects or evangelistic campaigns is often the hiring of a slick advertising or fundraising organization rather than securing the presence of the Lord Almighty and asking him to stir up a community empowered by the Spirit to accomplish the great task ahead. By this I am not suggesting that God cannot work in and through the human participants; rather, I am pointing out the speed by which we move to the human at the expense, I believe, of the divine.

Christ has promised his presence with us through his Spirit today. The church today needs to live in recognition of the Spirit's work in our lives and communities and cry to God for the work of the Spirit in our midst (Luke 11:13).

Martin Lloyd-Jones ends his study of revival by commenting on the prayer of Isaiah in Isaiah 64:1–2 ("Oh that you would rend the heavens and come down, that the mountains would tremble before you! As when fire sets twigs ablaze and causes water to boil, come down to make your name known to your enemies and cause the nations to quake before you!"). He calls the church to cry to God for the presence of God's Spirit among us in order to fulfill their mission:

> The reason why men and women are outside the Church is that they do not know God, they do not know his name. . . . And they will never know it until they see a manifestation of it, and, so we pray, descend, come down, rend the heavens that these adversaries may know thy name. Nothing will make them listen but that. We have tried everything else, have we not? The church has never been so brilliant in her organisations as she is at the present time and as she has been during the whole of this century, she is using every means that the world can use and can give her, but the statistics go on repeating their miserable tale. . . .
>
> What is the matter? These people do not know the name of the Lord, and there is only one thing that we can do, we must pray to him to rend the heavens and to make his name known, so that not only may they know it, but further, so that the nations may "tremble at thy

> presence," that knowing the name of the Lord, they may begin to fear him, and to desist from sin.[10]

May this prayer be the prayer of our churches today as we return to God in obedience and cry for the renewal that only his presence through his Spirit can bring.

10. D. M. Lloyd-Jones, *Revival* (Westchester, Ill.: Crossway, 1987), 310.

Haggai 2:1–9

ON THE TWENTY-FIRST day of the seventh month, the word of the LORD came through the prophet Haggai: 2"Speak to Zerubbabel son of Shealtiel, governor of Judah, to Joshua son of Jehozadak, the high priest, and to the remnant of the people. Ask them, 3'Who of you is left who saw this house in its former glory? How does it look to you now? Does it not seem to you like nothing? 4But now be strong, O Zerubbabel,' declares the LORD. 'Be strong, O Joshua son of Jehozadak, the high priest. Be strong, all you people of the land,' declares the LORD, 'and work. For I am with you,' declares the LORD Almighty. 5'This is what I covenanted with you when you came out of Egypt. And my Spirit remains among you. Do not fear.'

6"This is what the LORD Almighty says: 'In a little while I will once more shake the heavens and the earth, the sea and the dry land. 7I will shake all nations, and the desired of all nations will come, and I will fill this house with glory,' says the LORD Almighty. 8'The silver is mine and the gold is mine,' declares the LORD Almighty. 9'The glory of this present house will be greater than the glory of the former house,' says the LORD Almighty. 'And in this place I will grant peace,' declares the LORD Almighty."

Original Meaning

THE EVENTS IN HAGGAI 1 took place in the sixth month with the initial prophetic message coming on the first day and the response on the twenty-fourth day. The message of 2:1–9 is thus delivered almost a month after the beginning of the work.[1] The date in our calendar is October 17, 520 B.C. It is not surprising that after a month of rebuilding the people are discouraged, especially since the initial phase of clearing rubble would be extremely arduous. But there are further reasons why on this particular day the frustration of the people reaches a crescendo.

1. Although the year is not mentioned in 2:1, the assumption is that the events are still in the second year of Darius's reign (cf. 2:10).

Ezra 3:1–6 suggests that by the first day of the seventh month, the sacrificial and festal system had been reinstituted on the rebuilt altar on the temple site.[2] Haggai 2:1–9 places this oracle on day 21 of this seventh month, which was the busiest month in the Israelite festal calendar (Feast of Trumpets, day 1 [Lev. 23:23–25; Num. 29:1–6]; Day of Atonement, day 10 [Lev. 16:2–34; 23:26–32; Num. 29:7–11]; Feast of Tabernacles, days 15–22 [Lev. 23:33–43; Num. 29:12–39; Deut. 16:13–17]). By day 21 of this month (cf. Hag. 2:1), the penultimate day of the Feast of Tabernacles, which celebrated the harvest (Ex. 23:16; 34:22), the lack of progress on the project coupled with the enormity of the task yet to come may have been accentuated by the frustration of celebrating a third festal event in the unsightly ruins.

This feast has two names in the Pentateuch, both of which have significance for Haggai's message. As the Feast of Ingathering (Ex. 23:16; 34:22), it was one of the three opportunities for tithing in the Israelite festal calendar (cf. Lev. 23:39; Deut. 16:13–17). This function adds to the frustration of the people, who are reminded of their lack of resources because of bad harvests (Hag. 1). As the Feast of Tabernacles, this feast was a yearly reminder to the people of the desert experience, of the period of longing for settled life in the Promised Land (Lev. 23:43). In many ways the people are reliving the experience of those who left Egypt and journeyed to a new land.

The date of this prophetic message corresponds to another important event in the history of Israel. It was during this festival over four centuries earlier that Solomon dedicated the temple (1 Kings 8:2).[3] The many allusions to this great Solomonic temple in this prophetic message show clearly that Haggai and his people have this event in mind, so that comparisons with the earlier project may have led to discouragement. In other words, as God's people are overwhelmed by their external circumstances and their internal expectations, Haggai is moved to deliver his second oracle.

This oracle is also influenced by movements on the world stage. Haggai declares this message in a period in Persian history when Darius was beginning to firmly grasp the reins of power in the Persian heartland.[4] To a people who had observed the vulnerability of the great Persian empire, Haggai points this discouraged people to the sovereignty of Yahweh over the affairs and resources of the nations. They will soon experience the firstfruits of this

---

2. See the Original Meaning section of the introduction for the argument that the events of Ezra 3 are contemporaneous with the events of Haggai.

3. Merrill identifies the year of this event as 960 B.C., 440 years earlier (Merrill, *Haggai*, 36).

4. Cf. P. R. Ackroyd, "Two Old Testament Historical Problems of the Early Persian Period," *JNES* 17 (1958): 13–27.

prophecy as Darius grants to them the resources of the Persian empire for the rebuilding of the temple.[5]

As in chapter 1, so now in 2:1–9 the prophet is a master of combining divergent vocabulary and styles from older prophetic speech into a rhetorical unity.[6] He begins with that dialogical style we first observed in 1:4 and uses a series of questions to win a hearing among his audience. Then he launches into a speech form that some consider as containing the elements of the priestly oracle of salvation ("I am with you," "do not fear"; e.g., Isa. 35:4)[7] and others as the elements of the encouragement for a task (e.g., Josh. 1:6–9).[8] Haggai appears to be combining both forms here into a new entity. He stretches this form by expanding the assurance with an extended promise of God's cataclysmic action, echoing the oracles of salvation found in the classical prophets in general and Isaiah 40–48 in particular.[9]

This creative amalgamation of prophetic forms creates a literary masterpiece. After the introduction in verse 1, Yahweh identifies the audience who will receive the message (v. 2). This is followed immediately by identifying the issue that precipitates the prophetic message (v. 3). Discouragement has set in among the people because of comparisons to the former glory of the temple prior to the Babylonian destruction in 587 B.C. The message then

---

5. Ezra 5:1–6:15, esp. 6:8, 13–14. By this point Darius has firm control of the empire, although there are some rebellions yet to come in the following years (Egypt); for past and present research see J. Kessler, "The Second Year of Darius and the Prophet Haggai," *Transeuphratene* 5 (1992): 63–84. The vision of upheaval in Haggai is one linked to God's initiative rather than to a popular uprising. This does not deny that the upheavals of the recent past would have been on the minds of the original audience and thus important to understanding the imagery in this passage (see Smith, *Micah-Malachi,* 158).

6. See my criticism of the atomizing approach of Wolff, *Haggai,* 72, in Boda, "Haggai," 296 n. 292.

7. Petersen, *Haggai,* 64–66. Merrill (*Haggai,* 37) identifies the strong links to the language of Isaiah but sees Haggai as drawing on Isaiah rather than on the priestly oracle tradition.

8. This genre has often been called "Installation to Office," but because of its use in different contexts than an installation, Mason rightly makes it more general by entitling it "Encouragement for a Task" (see his *Preaching,* 193–94). Cf. R. B. Dillard, *2 Chronicles* (WBC 15; Waco, Tex.: Word, 1987), 4–5; H. G. M. Williamson, "The Accession of Solomon in the Book of Chronicles," *VT* 26 (1976): 351–61; R. Braun, "Solomon, the Chosen Temple Builder: The Significance of 1 Chronicles 22, 28, and 29 for the Theology of Chronicles," *JBL* 95 (1976): 581–90, esp. 586–88; D. J. McCarthy, "An Installation Genre?" *JBL* 90 (1971): 31–41; cf. Petersen, *Haggai,* 66.

9. Cf. W. VanGemeren, "Oracles of Salvation," in *Cracking Old Testament Codes: A Guide to Interpreting the Literary Genres of the Old Testament,* ed. D. B. Sandy and J. R. L. Giese (Nashville: Broadman & Holman, 1995), 139–55.

addresses the people forcefully through a series of imperatives: "Be strong [3x] ... and work ... do not fear" (2:4–5).

The controlling imperative is "work," drawing on the description of the response of the same people to Haggai's first message in 1:14. This central command focusing on the external action of the people, however, is flanked by two commands focusing on internal motivational issues. In order to work they will need both the positive motivation to "be strong" and the negative motivation to avoid "fear." Each is linked subsequently to a particular promise of Yahweh through the causal particle *ki* ("for"), providing motivations for this human activity and attitude in Yahweh himself.

The first motivation focuses on God's presence (vv. 4–5) and is linked to Haggai's encouragement "be strong." The second motivation focuses on God's action (vv. 6–9) and is linked to Haggai's encouragement "do not fear." By verse 9 Yahweh has addressed the concern of the people picking up on the vocabulary of the rhetorical questions in verse 3. There is a sense of closure as he promises to exceed the former glory of the temple, but also a sense of comfort that this glory will overflow into prosperity for the community who obeys.

Identification of the Issue (2:1–3)

IN VERSE 2, Yahweh instructs Haggai to speak to those who have responded positively to the initial prophetic call to rebuild the temple: Zerubbabel (the royal figure in David's line), Joshua (the priestly figure in Aaron's and Zadok's line), and the remnant of the people (cf. 1:12, 14). By addressing the remnant, Haggai is speaking to that portion of the people who have responded to the call and assumed the role of the anticipated "remnant," an important theological evaluation identifying them as the purified community that had survived the Exile (see Original Meaning section of 1:12–15).

Haggai begins with a series of rhetorical questions (2:3).[10] In style similar to 1:1–11, he addresses the people and their leaders directly by emphasizing "you" in each line. He identifies a portion of the community who had seen the temple before the Babylonian destruction of 587 B.C. Here we find a wordplay as Haggai picks up on the root for "remnant" found in 2:2 (*š*ʾ*r*) and immediately turns to those who are "left" (i.e., the remnant) who saw the temple in its former glory. Those who are the source of greatest skepticism are the remnant of the remnant, those truly purified through the Exile and still among the

10. The NIV is slightly misleading at this point by using the phrase "Ask them." This translates *leʾmor* (lit., saying), which is just a marker picking up the main verb "speak" (ʾ*amar*) at the beginning of 2:2. Therefore, this word is introducing the entire prophetic message, not just the questions of 2:3.

community.[11] It is not entirely impossible that there were people in their seventies who had seen the temple prior to its destruction in 587.

There is a progression of thought in the questions, moving the hearers from the past to the present and then demanding a comparison between the two. Notably Haggai does not allow the audience to distinguish the present temple structure from the past structure; rather, he makes a comparison between the glory of the two houses instead of the structures themselves.[12] This is a subtle reminder that this temple is the same structure as Solomon's; the only difference is the "glory," and, as we will discover, God will soon remedy that difference. This "glory" is not the glory of Yahweh's presence but rather the material elegance of the building (cf. 2:6–9). This understanding, however, does not preclude the use of double entendre here to subtly remind the hearers of the glory of God's presence as in the temple of old (see further below).

The third rhetorical question creates a climax, for in it Haggai joins the opinion of the skeptics within the remnant who are the focus of his message. Petersen highlights this technique: "Such a formulation elicits their response and in so doing establishes rapport with that sector of the community which is dissatisfied."[13] Haggai has identified a significant source of discouragement for those rebuilding the temple and in so doing has empathized with them. He will now challenge the community to rise above such discouragement, based on the resources of their God.[14]

Encouragement for the Task (2:4–9)

TO OFFER HIS ENCOURAGEMENT, Haggai begins with a phrase often used to mark a transition from the past to the present in Hebrew compositions: *weʿattah* ("but now").[15] This transition marker is followed by a threefold use of the verb *ḥazaq* ("be strong") addressing each of the parties identified in 2:2. The term *ḥazaq* is an important element in other instances where encouragement

---

11. Haggai's question does not offer us a clue to whether he was an exile or remained in Palestine during the Babylonian period (Redditt, *Haggai*, 24; contra Baldwin, *Haggai*, 28). His rhetoric suggests that he had not seen the temple (Merrill, *Haggai*, 20).

12. See Verhoef, *Haggai*, 96, 105.

13. Petersen, *Haggai*, 64. Mitchell notes this rhetorical device as well; H. G. T. Mitchell, J. M. P. Smith, and J. A. Brewer, *A Critical and Exegetical Commentary on Haggai, Zechariah, Malachi and Jonah* (ICC; Edinburgh: T. & T. Clark, 1912), 60.

14. See Boda, "Haggai," 295–304.

15. See Hag. 1:5; 2:15, especially after Haggai's dialogical style. This serves as a transition marker in prayers (e.g., Neh. 9:32) and prophetic speeches (e.g., Jer. 26:12–13; 27:4–7). See Boda, *Praying*, 29–30.

for a task is needed.[16] The call to "be strong" is followed by a plural imperative "and work," addressed to all three parties together. The opposition is originating among the people, but the message is directed both to the leadership and the people to encourage them to work together as strengthened parties.[17] The final imperative is found at the end of 2:5 ("do not fear"), a phrase often associated with the verb *ḥazaq* in the encouragement for a task.

In summary, the central imperative is "to work," with the assumption that this work is on the temple project. It is surrounded by two imperatives often used to motivate God's people to a great task expressed in the positive ("be strong") and the negative ("do not fear").

Haggai's imperatives are coupled with two reasons why the leaders and people should work, both introduced by the Hebrew word *ki* ("for"): in 2:4b, "for I am with you"; in 2:6, "for this is what the LORD Almighty says."[18] (1) The first reason is directly related to the imperative "be strong" and entails God's promise of his presence. In order to accomplish the core imperative "work," the people will need to be strong, but this strength is linked to God's presence with them, a point already emphasized in the prophet's message to this remnant in 1:12. Now a month later Haggai fills out this promise further by alluding to the promise of God's presence to the Israelites who were rescued from Egypt.

Haggai here is drawing from the account of the golden calf rebellion in Exodus 32–34. In these crucial chapters at the foot of Mount Sinai, God threatened to withdraw from the Israelites because of their rebellion. Moses begged Yahweh to remain and, after receiving a glimpse of Yahweh's glory, cries to him: "If I have found favor in your eyes ... then let the LORD go with us." Yahweh's response is odd: "I am making a covenant with you...." From this we can conclude that assurance that Yahweh's presence will remain with the people is essential to the making of the covenant.

The reference to the Spirit in the context of the Exodus generation is a feature of two later interpretations of the Exodus and desert experiences (Neh. 9:20, 30; Isa. 63:10, 11, 14). In both these passages, Yahweh's presence among the people is interpreted as the "good/holy Spirit" who resided among

16. Note its use in contexts where Israelites are entering battle (Josh. 1:7, 9; 10:25; 2 Sam. 10:12).

17. There is no object for the verb *ʿaśah* ("and work"). Meyers and Meyers see the object as the initial phrase in 2:5, but Verhoef's suggestion that the implied object is *melaʾkah* ("work," as in 1:14) is superior; Meyers and Meyers, *Haggai*, 98; Verhoef, *Haggai*, 98.

18. Petersen, *Haggai*, 67; on 2:6, *ki* is untranslated in the NIV.

them.[19] The allusion to the covenant in Haggai 2:5 coupled with a reference to the Spirit remaining indicates that Haggai intends to remind the people of God's promise after the golden calf rebellion. It is important to remember that the golden calf narrative interrupts the account of the tabernacle construction (Ex. 25–40). Now in the rebuilding of the place of God's manifest presence, Haggai comforts the people by reminding them of God's promised presence after rebellion in the desert, a presence that enabled that community to build the tabernacle.

(2) The second motivation is linked directly to a second element often associated with the genre "encouragement to a task": "Do not fear" (2:5c). In order to do their "work," the people must avoid fear. Their greatest fear is of the mighty nations that surround them. This struggling province on the edge of the great Persian empire was dwarfed by the empire and the stronger provinces around them. Fear was evident in the early days of the leadership of Zerubbabel and Joshua (cf. Ezra 3:3; 4:4–5), but the prophet is commissioned to dissuade the people from such fear and to back this up with God's promise of direct action on their behalf. Yahweh will cause a cosmic upheaval that will not only allay their fears but rectify their original discouragement caused by comparison of the glory of the former temple with that of the present project.

The initial phrase "in a little while once more" accentuates both the imminence of and the precedence for the activity of Yahweh. In the Hebrew text the phrase "once more" comes first and alludes to an earlier event in which such activity of Yahweh took place. There is a precedent for the activity referred to in this passage, and with the many allusions in this passage to the Exodus and desert traditions, this earlier "shaking" is that which took place at Mount Sinai (Ex. 19:16–19). Hebrews 12:27 makes this connection as well. The phrase "in a little while," using similar (though not identical) vocabulary to other prophetic promises to signify an event in the future, identifies the imminence of this activity.

---

19. Contra Wolff, who interprets this Spirit as the prophetic spirit residing in Haggai; Wolff, *Haggai*, 80. Petersen is stretching things to connect this reference to God's work of stirring up the spirit of the leaders and community in 1:14, for the spirit in that context is human, not divine; Petersen, *Haggai*, 65. Verhoef, Stuhlmueller, Mason, and Baldwin all identify a link here between 2:5 and the cloud in the desert; cf. Verhoef, *Haggai*, 100–101; Stuhlmueller, *Rebuilding*, 26; Mason, *Preaching*, 193; Baldwin, *Haggai*, 47. Mason demonstrates how the Heb. participle used here (NIV "remains") is also used of the pillar of cloud in Exodus (e.g., Ex. 33:10); R. A. Mason, *The Books of Haggai, Zechariah and Malachi* (CBC; Cambridge: Cambridge Univ. Press, 1977), 20; cf. L. Sabourin, "The Biblical Cloud: Terminology and Traditions," *BTB* 4 (1974): 290–311; R. J. Sklba, " 'Until the Spirit from on High is Poured Out on Us' (Isa 32:15): Reflections on the Role of the Spirit in the Exile," *CBQ* 46 (1984): 1–17.

Yahweh's activity is identified as "shaking" (Hiphil of *rʿš*), a verb elsewhere associated with the appearance of Yahweh either in revelation (as on Sinai) or in battle (as in the Exodus).[20] When Yahweh appears, the cosmos responds with earthquake and storm. In time it becomes associated with future eschatological events, when the cosmos will be renewed. Haggai appears to be drawing all of these connotations into his view of the future. Yahweh, the divine warrior, will appear as he did at Sinai, shaking both cosmos and the nations.

The list ("the heavens and the earth, the sea and the dry land") associated with the first use of *rʿš* (2:6) is a merism speaking of the entirety of the cosmos. The first two members ("the heavens and the earth") refer to all of creation (cf. Gen. 1:1), the second two ("the sea and the dry land") divide up the earth (cf. Hag. 1:9–10). God's cataclysmic action first affects creation, but then finds its goal in the context of human affairs when it causes a secondary shaking affecting "all nations."[21] It is this second shaking that supports the call to "not fear" in 2:5 and eventually answers the concern over the lack of glory in the temple.

When God shakes the nations, the result is that the "desired of all nations will come," an action identified in the following phrase as fulfilling God's intention to fill the temple with glory. There has been much debate over the meaning of the word "desired" in 2:7.[22] The ancient Latin translation (Vulgate) translates this word with strong messianic overtones, an interpretation that finds its way even into the hymnology of the church ("Come, thou long-expected Jesus, dear desire of every nation"). However, in this passage these precious things ("desired") appear to be material resources given for the temple rebuilding project, either the "precious vessels" absconded by

---

20. B. S. Childs, "The Enemy from the North and the Chaos Tradition," *JBL* 78 (1959): 187–98; Mason, *Haggai*, 20; H. F. van Rooy, "Eschatology and Audience: The Eschatology of Haggai," *OTE* 1 (1988): 59. Most would not make a distinction between revelation and battle, but I do not want to impose the holy war concept onto Yahweh's appearance at Sinai. Childs notes that "very early in Israel's history the verb became associated with the theophany of Yahweh, when he revealed his power over the creation in a quaking or shaking of the earth (Judg. 5:4; Ps. 18:8). In both these instances the reference to the Sinai theophany is apparent"; Childs, "Enemy," 189.

21. Kessler notes the flow of the Hebrew grammar at this point ("Shaking," 159–66). The second use of *rʿš* is a waw consecutive perfect, denoting a second sequence dependent either logically or temporally on the first.

22. Heb. *ḥemdat* is a feminine singular noun, but the verb "will come" is plural. Because the LXX translates this with *ta eklekta* ("choice things"), some interpreters have changed *ḥemdat* to *ḥamudot*, the plural form of this noun. There is no need, however, for this emendation, for it is common to combine a feminine singular with a plural verb when speaking of abstract concepts (GKC §145b; §145e, although GKC is inconsistent here and seeks to revocalize this word in Hag. 2:7).

Nebuchadnezzar (2 Chron. 36:10),[23] spoils from a victorious battle,[24] or tribute from a submissive people.[25] In any case, the nations display their submission by bringing these precious things into the temple, an action paralleled in the latter part of Isaiah (60:5; 61:6; 66:20), where the rebuilding of the temple is envisioned as the work of the Gentiles who return with the Israelites and contribute to the rebuilding of the temple.

The following phrase appears to strengthen this approach to the "desired of all nations," for God promises to "fill this house with glory." In verse 3 the focus was on the material "glory" (splendor) of the temple, not the glory of God's manifest presence. It is material glory that appears also to be the sense here in verse 7, especially with the reference to silver and gold in verse 8. However, the combination of the verb "fill," the concept of God's dwelling place ("this house"), and the word "glory" is only found elsewhere in the Hebrew Bible in connection with God's glory filling the tabernacle/temple (Ex. 40:34, 35; 1 Kings 8:11; 2 Chron. 5:14; 7:1, 2; Ezek. 10:3, 4; 43:5).[26] Interestingly, one finds references to God's glory in connection with the rebuilding of the temple with Gentile resources in Isaiah 60–66 (60:1, 2, 13; 66:18–20).[27]

Taking a step further than the latter part of Isaiah, Haggai uses a wordplay to allude to the filling of the temple with God's glory, but he identifies this glory with the material beautification of the temple caused by God's shaking of the nations. This wordplay is strengthened by the semantic range of the Hebrew word *kabod*, which can also be used to refer to wealth (cf. Isa. 10:3

---

23. Wolff, *Haggai*, 81; Petersen, *Haggai*, 68.

24. Verhoef, *Haggai*, 103.

25. Meyers and Meyers, *Haggai*, 53; Mason, *Preaching*, 188. Stuhlmueller and Merrill see in this an allusion to the temple of Solomon that was furnished by tribute (2 Sam. 8:7–8, 10–11; 2 Kings 7:51; 1 Chron. 29:3–5); see Stuhlmueller, *Rebuilding*, 30; Merrill, *Haggai*, 40.

26. H. Wolf, " 'The Desire of All Nations' in Haggai 2:7: Messianic or Not?" *JETS* 19 (1976): 101: "the only glory said to 'fill the temple' in Scripture is the shekinah cloud itself."

27. Many have seen here only the material definition of glory: e.g., Verhoef, *Haggai*, 104; R. T. Siebeneck, "Messianism of Aggeus and Proto-Zacharias," *CBQ* 19 (1957): 315; Petersen, *Haggai*, 68; Stuhlmueller, *Rebuilding*, 30; or only the spiritual definition of glory: e.g., Merrill, *Haggai*, 41; Meyers and Meyers, *Haggai*, 54. This latter aspect has also been construed as the presence of the Messiah; see C. Feinberg, "Haggai," in *The Wycliffe Bible Commentary*, ed. C. F. Pfeiffer and E. F. Harrison (Chicago: Moody, 1962), 893. We have identified here a wordplay connoting *both* material and spiritual definitions; cf. Merrill, *Haggai*, 40–41; Mason, *Preaching*, 188; Mason, *Haggai*, 21; D. A. Smith, "Haggai," in *The Broadman Bible Commentary*, Volume 7: *Hosea-Malachi*, ed. C. J. Allen (London: Marshall, Morgan & Scott, 1972), 302. The emphasis, however, is on the material as an expression of the spiritual with no messianic overtones in the text itself; contra Wolf, "Desire," 101.

and esp. 61:4–6; 66:12). This is a significant contribution to the understanding of God's glory in this period of rebuilding. The sign of God's glory and presence will be his sovereign shaking of the nations and the subsequent material adornment of the temple.

God's right to shake the nations and extract their treasures for his temple is backed up by the claims of verse 8, in which the ownership of the silver and gold—that is, the material resources of the world—is ultimately traced to the Lord. This is particularly relevant to a people who have recently seen Darius obtain the wealth and tribute of the nations.

Verse 9 serves two purposes. It reveals the final goal of the shaking of the cosmos/nations and brings closure to the entire passage, addressing the people's concern introduced in verse 3 by repeating the same vocabulary ("glory," "this," "house," "former"). One should not miss in the English translation that this does not refer to two different houses (former and present houses), but rather to two different glories of the same house: "The latter glory of this house shall be greater than the former."[28] To a people discouraged by the intimidating goal of matching the Solomonic temple, this promise would engender hope.

Nevertheless, Haggai is not finished with his comfort. He offers them a final word of encouragement in the latter half of verse 9: "And in this place I will grant peace." Many see here a broadening of the prophetic message to include Jerusalem as a whole,[29] but the reference is most likely to the temple discussed in the first half of the verse.[30] Haggai is identifying the temple as the source of peace (*šalom*), a term that can be translated as "prosperity," the blessed state of an abundant life, as Wolff puts it: "salvation in a comprehensive sense:

---

28. Similar to Baldwin, *Haggai,* 48; see Mitchell, Smith, and Brewer, *Haggai,* 63. Verhoef makes this point in the commentary but translates similar to NIV; Verhoef, *Haggai,* 91–109.

29. Merrill, *Haggai,* 41 n. 16; Baldwin, *Haggai,* 49. Some appeal to a wordplay between Jerusalem and the Heb. word *šalom* ("peace"; cf. also Deut. 12:5; 2 Kings 22:16–20; Jer. 7:3, 7, 20). Moreover, Haggai describes the temple as "the LORD's house" (1:2, 9, 14), "this house" (2:3, 7, 9a); "the house" (1:8); "the LORD's temple" (2:15, 18), and not "this place." But the most natural referent for "this place" in 2:9b is the place that precedes it in 2:9a, which also uses the demonstrative "this" ("this present house"). Furthermore, "this place" is used as a synonym for the temple in 1 Kings 8:29–30; 2 Chron. 6:20–21, 38, 40; 7:12; cf. Wolff, *Haggai,* 83.

30. Many recent scholars have shown connections between the focus on the temple in the Persian period community and a similar focus seen in Mesopotamian communities in which temples served an important economic function; cf. M. J. Boda, "Majoring on the Minors: Recent Research on Haggai and Zechariah," *Currents in Biblical Research* 2 (2003): 33–68. This may have influenced Haggai's preaching and produced sociological conditions conducive to the rebuilding of the temple.

the absence of both hunger and sword, life without privation and without enmity."[31]

Such a promise would be even more attractive to this people, for their discouragement over the progress on the project would be fostered by the fear of famine and oppression still fresh in their memories. It instills hope that the future glory of the house will have an effect on the people. The prosperity that God will bring to the temple will spill over into the community of God. Although the focus is on God and his glory (1:8), Yahweh's glory affects the community as well and brings prosperity.

This final word of comfort creates a strong link with the promise of glory, for as Durham has aptly argued, there is a close relationship between *šalom* in the Hebrew Bible and the presence of God.[32] The priestly blessing of Numbers 6:22–27 associates God's intimate presence with the reception of blessings, in particular the blessing of *šalom*. This connection between *šalom* and presence is reflected in Haggai 2:1–9 from the initial motivation in 2:5 ("for I am with you ... and my Spirit remains among you") to the second motivation in 2:7, 9, which alludes to the presence of God ("I will fill this house with glory").

In sum, Haggai calls a disgruntled and discouraged community to work with renewed strength and without paralyzing fear. But the promise of the presence and action of the Lord Almighty consumes the majority of the passage and provides them the hope to finish the project. His message speaks with sensitivity to the immediate generation, promising God's presence with them as they face the greatest challenge of their lives. At the same time, he calls them to trace God's hand in their present, seeing how he remains in sovereign charge of the affairs of the nations and is already beginning to place the treasures of the nations at their disposal.

Bridging Contexts

HAGGAI 1 ASSUMES that God's people are in an overwhelming predicament. The source of this predicament, however, is identified as the disobedience of a people who have refused to rebuild the temple. Their willingness portrayed in 1:12–14 shows that there has been repentance, and the people are immediately identified as the

31. Wolff, *Haggai*, 83. The LXX adds a phrase here: "and peace of soul for the strengthening of all who help to build this temple," displaying an attempt to reinterpret this in terms of spiritual rather than material blessing. Cf. P. R. Ackroyd, "Some Interpretive Glosses in the Book of Haggai," *JJS* 7 (1956): 164–65.

32. J. I. Durham, "Shalom and the Presence of God," in *Proclamation and Presence: Old Testament Essays in Honor of Gwynne Henton Davies*, ed. J. I. Durham and J. R. Porter (Richmond, Va.: Knox, 1970), 272–93.

remnant community. Chapter 2 begins where chapter 1 left off. The people are again identified as the remnant community, but they are once again in an overwhelming predicament. This time, however, the people are not chastised for disobedience; rather, they are encouraged by the prophet who identifies with their need.

The greatest source of the people's discouragement is revealed as the comparison between the preexilic glory of the temple and its present inglorious state. As with the issue of priorities in Haggai 1, most modern readers resonate with this reaction of the people in chapter 2. It draws us into the prophetic message because we have all thought or encountered reminiscing over "the good old days." This notwithstanding, there is much in this passage that distances the modern reader from appropriating its truth; to those issues we now turn.

The presence of God and the Spirit. Haggai 2:1–9 assumes the importance of the rebuilding of the temple. This great project was essential to this Persian period community, for it was the place of God's manifest presence. Rebuilding the temple was key to the reinstitution of the community of God, a priority made clear during the Babylonian period by the prophet Ezekiel (Ezek. 40–48).

Although the temple was the designated place of God's manifest presence on earth, those who rise to the challenge of building the temple are immediately promised God's presence through the words: "I am with you." It is this promise that becomes a springboard for encouraging the people to continue rebuilding.

The presence of God is promised to many within the Old Testament, running, in the words of Achtemeier, as "the silver thread throughout the whole story of the Bible."[33] It was this personal presence that drew the ancestors of Israel to Yahweh in covenant and sustained them along their journey (Gen. 26:3, 24; 28:15; 39:2, 21, 23). Throughout Old Testament redemptive history this same promise is echoed not only to those whom God raised up to lead his people—Moses/Joshua (Ex. 3:12; Deut. 31:6, 8; Josh. 1:5); the judges (Judg. 6:12); the kings (1 Sam. 10:6–7; 1 Kings 8:57); the prophets (Jer. 1:8, 19; 20:11)—but also to the people as a whole (Ex. 34:9; Isa. 41:10; 43:2, 5; Jer. 30:11; 46:28).

As New Testament redemptive history begins, we hear in God's promise of presence to Mary (Luke 1:28) confirmation that such promises are relevant to the new age.[34] Christ is keenly aware of Yahweh's presence with him

---

33. Achtemeier, *Preaching from the Minor Prophets,* 110.

34. There has been some disagreement over whether the presence of God was recognized by Second Temple Judaism as having returned to the temple. On one side of this issue are researchers like N. T. Wright, *Jesus and the Victory of God* (Christian Origins and the

in his ministry (John 8:29; 16:32). When he is leaving this earth, his final promise is cast in similar language to that of Haggai: "I will be with you always" (Matt. 28:20). It is not surprising, then, that Paul describes an experience in which he was comforted by God through words similar to our passage in Haggai (cf. Acts 18:9–10). Individuals and communities involved in kingdom activity are promised the presence of God.

This presence is specifically identified in Haggai 2 as God's Spirit who remains among them. This is an important development in the history of revelation, as Haggai demonstrates that God's presence is experienced through his Spirit (see above, Isa. 63:10, 11, 14). This link between the Spirit and God's presence is alluded to in the experience of Joshua (cf. Deut. 34:9; Josh. 1:5), but is made more clear in the account of the installation of kings. In 1 Samuel 10:6–7 the signs accompanying the Spirit's endowment of the king for service become evidence that Yahweh is with that king. Once Saul is rejected and David is anointed, the sign that God's presence and authority have passed to David is the transfer of the Spirit (16:13–14).[35]

Old Testament believers, however, did not experience the Spirit on an individual level; rather, it was a gift to the community in their covenant leaders. Moses expressed a wish in Numbers 11:29 that all God's people would experience the Spirit as he did. This passing wish became prophetic expectation in Joel 2 when the prophet envisioned a day when the entire community would experience the Spirit. Christ foreshadowed this era in his discourses on the Spirit in John 14 and 16, in which he spoke of the Spirit who would bring his presence to his people forever (14:16). The promise to be with his disciples in their kingdom work (Matt. 28:20; Acts 1:8) intersects with the climactic moment in redemptive history when God's Spirit was poured out upon the early church (Acts 2), turning prophetic expectation to reality.

Haggai's promise of the presence of God and the Spirit of God take on even greater significance for those of us living in this later phase of redemptive history. The church has been promised an even greater and more intimate, and thus, more comforting experience of the Spirit of God and his presence than those to whom the prophet Haggai spoke.

Question of God 2; Minneapolis: Fortress, 1996), 615–24, esp. 622, and R. L. Webb, John the Baptizer and Prophet: A Socio-Historical Study (JSNTSup 62; Sheffield: Sheffield Academic, 1991), ch. 7, who see longing for the return of God's presence in texts like 1 *En.* 1:3–4, 9; *T. Mos.* 10:1, 3, 7; 12:13; *Jub.* 1:26–28; 11Q19 (11Q Temple[a]) 29:3–9. On the other side are researchers like G. I. Davies, "The Presence of God in the Second Temple and Rabbinic Doctrine," in *Templum Amicitiae: Essays on the Second Temple Presented to Ernst Bammel,* ed. W. Horbury (*JSNT*Sup 48; Sheffield: Sheffield Academic, 1991), 32–36, who has highlighted evidence in favor of a perceived return. Note esp. the testimony of Matt. 23:21.

35. D. M. Howard, "The Transfer of Power from Saul to David in 1 Sam 16:13–14," *JETS* 32 (1989): 473, 483.

Material adornment of the temple and prosperity for the people. The second foundation for Haggai's encouragement of the people, which focuses on God's promised action on behalf of his people, proves far more challenging for those who seek to appropriate this passage for the community of faith today. Several elements cause concern for Christian interpreters of Haggai, ranging from the sense of imminence in the message of Haggai (2:6), to the heavy emphasis on the material adornment of the temple (2:7–8) and the resulting prosperity of the people (2:9). The level of uncomfortability with these themes within the Christian and even Jewish communities is reflected in the early precedent of the church to identify the "desired" in 2:7 as a messianic reference (see Vulgate) or to add material at the end of 2:9 to speak of a spiritual prosperity (see LXX).

In contrast to these interpretative conclusions, Haggai envisions an action of God that will happen in the near future and will result in the material adornment of the temple and prosperity for the people. This, indeed, happened during Haggai's generation. The material glory of the nations did flow into Darius's coffers, and these were directed to the work on the temple (Ezra 5–6; see esp. 6:6–8, 13–14).[36] Haggai's description of this event does not portray the specific means by which this event will take place, but it does identify Yahweh as the ultimate cause as he controls the affairs of the nations.

This beautification of the temple will continue until the time of Herod, who diverts the resources of the Roman empire to expand this temple and overshadow the glory of Solomon's temple.[37] This causes great concern for those aware of New Testament developments, for this Herodian temple is treated negatively by Christ's cleansing of it and evaluation of it as a "den of robbers" (Matt. 21:12–13; Mark 11:15–18; Luke 19:45–48). Moreover, in John 2:13–22, Jesus presents himself as the alternative for the temple. The rejection of the temple and its material glory appears confirmed by Christ's prophetic treatment of the temple in Matthew 24, the apparent reverse of the

---

36. See E. M. Yamauchi, *Persia and the Bible* (Grand Rapids: Baker, 1990), 129–85, esp. 155–59; T. C. Young, "The Consolidation of the Empire and Its Limits of Growth under Darius and Xerxes," in *Persia, Greece and the Western Mediterranean c. 525 to 479 B.C.*, ed. J. Boardman et al. (CAH 4: Cambridge: Cambridge Univ. Press, 1988), 53–66; T. M. Bolin, "The Temple of YHWH at Elephantine and Persian Religious Policy," in *The Triumph of Elohim: From Yahwisms to Judaisms*, ed. D. Edelman (Grand Rapids: Eerdmans, 1995), 127–42; P. R. Bedford, "Early Achaemenid Monarchs and Indigenous Cults: Towards the Definition of Imperial Policy," in *Religion in the Ancient World: New Themes and Approaches*, ed. M. Dillon (Amsterdam: Hakkert, 1996), 17–39.

37. Cf. M. Haran, *Temples and Temple-Service in Ancient Israel: An Inquiry into Biblical Cult Phenomena and the Historical Setting of the Priestly School* (Winona Lake, Ind.: Eisenbrauns, 1985), 44–45.

prophecy of Haggai, for a convulsing of the nations (24:4–8) will result in the destruction of the temple. Such destruction became reality in A.D. 70 when the Romans put down the Jewish rebellion.

When one combines this negative treatment of the temple structure with the spiritual transformation of the temple theme in the New Testament (see Bridging Contexts section of 1:1–11), it is understandable why many have been tempted to soften the material aspect of Haggai's message. Although there is no question that the New Testament does transform the temple theme in significant ways, this does not mean that previous experiences with the temple are to be denigrated. Note that when Christ attacks the second temple as a "den of robbers," he is merely reusing the words of Jeremiah uttered in describing the first temple (Jer. 7:11). By attacking temple use in his day, Jeremiah was not disqualifying the first temple as a place of interaction with God. Similarly, Christ's attack does not make Haggai's temple illegitimate, especially in light of the fact that he considered it the place of God's manifest presence (Matt. 23:21).

It is significant that two of the earliest testimonies to the fulfillment of the messianic hope in Jesus come from the lips of individuals linked to the temple and its services (Simeon and Anna; Luke 2:25–38). This reveals that the temple was essential for the preservation of the remnant community, through whom the Incarnation became a reality. Note too that the early church used this same temple for worship (Acts 2:42–47, esp. v. 46; 3:1, 11), showing that it continued to function as a place for enriching the remnant community.

In other words, Christian interpreters do not need to discard the material aspects of the temple, for they were important to God's redemptive purposes to bring the Messiah into this world. In this we see a sovereign God at work, controlling the nations' resources for his purposes.

Haggai's vision of the centripetal attraction of the temple and Jerusalem for the nations is not a novel idea. This theme can be traced throughout the book of Isaiah. It is first broached in Isaiah 2:1–4, in which the nations stream to the temple, and in Isaiah 60–66 one finds these nations bringing their wealth to enrich the temple. It is not surprising, then, that Paul taps into Isaiah in Romans 15 to justify his work among the Gentiles (cf. Rom. 15:12 with Isa. 11:10; Rom. 15:21 with Isa. 52:15). Haggai's vision of the participation of the nations in the building of the temple is a foreshadowing of their participation in the gospel in the New Testament.

This should not lead us to merely spiritualize the material elements of Haggai's prophecy. Yahweh promised his people that he would provide the material resources to accomplish the building of the kingdom and to make it reflect his glory. This can be traced to his sovereignty over these resources as Creator and Sustainer of the cosmos. The same is true for the church. This same sovereign God promises to provide the resources for kingdom work on the spiritual as well as material planes. The church as the place of God's manifest presence (i.e., "God's temple," 1 Cor. 3:16–17) needs material resources to carry out the Great Commission, and God promises to provide those resources (see 2 Cor. 11:7–10; Phil. 4:10–20; 1 Tim. 5:17–18).

The temptation to spiritualize the material aspects of this passage can be traced into the LXX addition to Hag. 2:9. This addition makes the "peace" (*šalom*) an inner, spiritual peace. As noted in the discussion of this word above, *šalom* is far more holistic in its meaning and is used to describe a state of abundance and prosperity on both spiritual and material planes. God's promise to us as his community is one that includes our physical well-being, although one needs to be careful to avoid the extremes represented by the health and wealth propagators (see Bridging Contexts section of 1:1–11).

One more shaking. As noted above, the writer of Hebrews draws on Haggai 2:6 in Hebrews 12:26.[38] One should be careful not to allow this passage to shape one's entire interpretation of the passage (as if the writer of Hebrews is exhausting the meaning of the entire passage). Nevertheless, there has been a tendency to ignore this later use as incorrect. The writer of Hebrews notes the significance of the phrase "once more," especially as it relates to the experience of Israel at Sinai. In this passage, which contrasts the two mountains of Sinai and Zion, he reminds Christians that they have come to the latter mountain.[39] However, lest they think that the God of Zion will

---

38. Commentators are generally agreed that the writer of Hebrews is relying on the LXX form of Hag. 2:6; see H. W. Attridge, *The Epistle to the Hebrews* (Hermeneia; Philadelphia: Fortress, 1989), 380; P. Ellingworth, *The Epistle to the Hebrews: A Commentary on the Greek Text* (NIGTC; Grand Rapids: Eerdmans, 1992), 686, although three modifications are made to this text through which the writer seeks to stress that in "contrast to Sinai, where the earth alone was shaken, the future shaking will extend to heaven as well"; W. L. Lane, *Hebrews 9–13* (WBC 47B; Dallas: Word, 1991), 478–80; cf. R. M. Wilson, *Hebrews* (NCB; Grand Rapids: Eerdmans, 1987), 233. Some also recognize that the writer of Hebrews also has Hag. 2:20–23 in mind with the reference to "kingdom" in Heb. 12:29; cf. F. F. Bruce, *The Epistle to the Hebrews* (NICNT; Grand Rapids: Eerdmans, 1990), 364; Lane, *Hebrews 9–13*, 484.

39. On this contrast in Heb. 12:18–29, see esp. T. Long, *Hebrews* (IBC; Louisville: Westminster John Knox, 1997), 136–41. Buchanan makes the interesting observation that Heb. 1:1–12:29 is "a unified homily centered around the one text of Ps 110, which the author quoted from time to time. He never quoted the whole Psalm, but, by alluding to one verse, he presumed that the reader understood the rest of the Psalm," an intertextual technique I have noted elsewhere; see M. J. Boda, "Reading Between the Lines: Zechariah 11:4–16 in Its Literary Contexts," in *Bringing Out the Treasure: Inner Biblical Allusion and Zechariah 9–14*, ed. M. J. Boda and M. H. Floyd (JSOTSup 304; Sheffield: Sheffield Academic Press, 2003),

overlook disobedience, he reminds them of the prophecy in Haggai that applied the Sinai traditions (note above) to a people rebuilding the temple on Mount Zion and anticipated a future shaking of the entire cosmos (not just earth) as was experienced by those at the foot of Sinai.

This eschatological shaking will be the ultimate expression of the sovereignty of God.[40] The application of the writer of Hebrews is a call to faithfulness, thankfulness, and worship of this awesome God because we are receiving an unshakable kingdom. Those who lived under the threat of the nations in the early church (Heb. 12:4–11) were challenged by the message of Haggai in the same way that his original hearers were challenged, that is, to continue in faithful service in light of God's promised intervention in history.[41] Such a vision of God was also intended to instill in them a reverence for God and a passion for his kingdom even in the midst of trying circumstances.

Contemporary Significance

THE VALUE OF 2:1–9 lies in its function to describe the resources God offered to these people who have obeyed his call in Haggai 1. The response of the people in 1:12–14 to Yahweh's call through Haggai was immediately greeted with the promise of Yahweh's presence ("I am with you"). Haggai 2:1–9 fills out in detail the significance of this promise for the people.

Back to the future. We resonate in significant ways with this passage because we have all experienced similar emotions as we approach the task of the kingdom. We compare the present with the past and become dissatisfied and even disillusioned with our present experience. For those who are older, it comes with reflection on earlier experiences with God either personal or

277–91. It is interesting that Ps. 110 is clearly drawn from the Zion tradition (Davidic-Melchizedekian) and refers to the defeat of the nations by a royal figure. The contrast in Hebrews, therefore, may be between Sinai and its priesthood, on the one side, and Zion and its royal priesthood, on the other. In Heb. 12 this argument comes to its conclusion.

40. The precise referent of this shaking is a matter of great debate, ranging from the destruction of Jerusalem, to the events of Christ's passion, to a future eschatological event; Attridge, *Hebrews*, 382. The latter appears to be in view here, as Bruce, *Hebrews*, 364.

41. Although the message in Haggai largely focused on encouragement to continue the monumental task of rebuilding, the message in Hebrews shifts to a warning that believers must continue lest they be judged: "The promise expressed through the citation of the biblical text is that those who reject the new covenant revelation will receive the same summary judgment as those who disregarded the revelation given at Sinai. The citation of the text expresses the pastoral concern for the threat of apostasy within the community in 12:14–29" (see Lane, *Hebrews 9–13*, 480–81).

communal, experiences in which there was a sense of God's manifest presence and action.

Several years ago I attended a family camp that had its roots in the late nineteenth century. Every day the bell rang before 6 A.M. to call people to the early morning prayer meeting and thereafter every couple of hours for the daily rhythm of Bible teachers, worship services, and evangelistic meetings. One day I sauntered down to the bell tower and awaited the advent of the "ringer." He arrived at the prescribed hour and rang the bell with the passion of a child. As I engaged him in conversation and asked him about the camp, he began his speech with the words: "It just isn't like the old days . . ." before listing evidence of the way in which the present generation was not living up to the experience of past generations.

Later a friend of mine was speaking to another older camper a day after camp had finished. This older gent had just returned from the auditorium where the youth meetings had been held and noticed that there was dust on the kneeling bar at the front of the hall, evidence that called into question the depth of spiritual encounter among the teens the previous week. However, as I walked about the camp and listened to the various speakers among youth and adults alike, I was impressed with the depth of biblical teaching and the response to the Word of God. It is easy to become trapped into evaluating the present experience of the church with past paradigms of spirituality rather than remaining open to the ways in which God is impacting the present generation in culturally relevant ways.

Lest this be perceived as an attack on the elderly, let me say that those who are younger in the faith are not exempt. I have found that as younger Christians read or hear redemptive and church history, they can easily become dissatisfied with the present state of the church and what is perceived as lack. It is possible to focus so intently on the experiences of past giants of the faith that one begins to live vicariously through these stories and examples and squelch one's own immediate experience with God.

Such reflection on the past is not entirely illegitimate. Haggai himself agrees with the older members of his community that the present lacks the glory of the past. There is something good in this longing to experience afresh the glory of the past. Such honest evaluation forces us out of our complacency and drives us to our knees. J. Edwin Orr has offered a great service to the church by highlighting the revivals of the past.[42] Teaching on church

42. J. E. Orr, *The Second Evangelical Awakening: An Account of the Second Worldwide Evangelical Revival Beginning in the Mid-nineteenth Century* (London: Marshall, Morgan & Scott, 1955); J. E. Orr, *Evangelical Awakenings in Africa* (Minneapolis: Bethany Fellowship, 1975).

history is desperately needed in our seminaries and churches today to offer the past as a corrective for the present: pitfalls to avoid and patterns to emulate. Indeed, I have found that reading the classics of preachers from the past has profoundly affected me and my students in our preparation and communication of sermons.

However, when such reflection on the past leads to inaction, we need to hear the message of Haggai 2:1–9. In dwelling on the past, some are tempted to say: "Why even try, we can't match such great tasks in the past." These reactions are inappropriate within the kingdom, and to this Haggai addresses his message.

Inside out. It is important to note that Haggai immediately moves behind the symptom (lack of work) to the internal motivations of the people: "Be strong and do not fear." Haggai's message moves beyond external duty to the kingdom to the inner core attitudes essential for sustained commitment to the kingdom. He does not command duty for the sake of duty; rather, he moves to the heart where passion for the kingdom is fostered.

The cry of duty that proved so effective for many within the church a generation ago has lost its hold on a new generation. For many within the older generation this is a sign of the weakening of the church. However, there is an important lesson to be learned at this juncture in church history, that when duty is performed without passionate engagement, duty will ultimately lose its hold on the church. Haggai demands commitment to the task of the kingdom, but he is aware that such commitment is nurtured only by fostering the passion of heart religion. Haggai's message matches that of the earlier prophets—attention to the heart before action (Jer. 9:23–24)—and can be discerned in Christ's attack on the pharisaic attention to duty over relationship (Matt. 23) and his revelation that eternal life is found in intimate relationship with Yahweh (John 17:3).

This is often missed in the preaching and teaching of the church. In the present shift towards "how to" sermons and books, it is easy to put our focus on the lists of duties to perform or actions to avoid that are identified as necessary for godliness. Without losing sight of God's call to obedience, we must put greater focus on the Spirit's shaping of our human affections, that is, on God's vision to transform his people from the inside out.

Missio Dei. Haggai's message offers the community of God encouragement. He is not a moralist. He is not calling his people to pull themselves up by their own bootstraps, nor is he insisting people do kingdom work apart from the resources of God. The majority of this prophetic passage focuses attention on God—on his action on their behalf.

Much energy is being expended within the church today on the issue of renewal. Such introspection, associated in decades past with waning mainline denominations, is now common among evangelical fellowships.[43] There is a sense that evangelicalism as a movement has lost some of its momentum and that this is reflected in the lack of passion for missions and/or denominational distinctives.

In his evaluation of this trend among Protestant denominations both in North America and in the Two-Thirds World, Wilbert Shenk notes four strategies that have been employed for renewal in the past before advocating his own view as the answer.[44] He claims that some have sought for renewal by reaffirming their own tradition, some by returning to the model of the primitive, apostolic church, others by restructuring the denomination, and still others by adapting the church to the cultural trends of the day. Shenk believes the answer lies in recovering the *missio Dei*, the mission of God given to the church, which he describes as "intensified witness to the reign of God."

At first sight, it appears that Haggai agrees with Shenk's answer as the ancient prophet cries "work." But this command addressed to the human participants in this great project of the kingdom recedes into the background as Yahweh comes to the fore. By this we are not suggesting that human work is unimportant or in opposition to the kingdom. However, as the "work" becomes bogged down in discouragement, the focus of the passage moves from the human partners to the divine Sustainer and to the ultimate source of renewal: Yahweh.

Through this Haggai identifies *missio Dei* as the key to the discouragement, but in a different sense than Shenk. This *missio Dei* is the mission of God—the presence and action of God on behalf of the people. With Shenk, Haggai's message ignores those who look exclusively to traditionalism, restructuring, or enculturation for the answer. Instead, Haggai calls the community to work with renewed strength and without fear as they rediscover God's resources experienced in the community in yet new and transcendent ways for the present generation, and they seek to know where and what God is doing in our present world to build his kingdom.

Renewed vigor is discovered as our focus becomes God. Haggai makes it clear as he calls his generation to this project in chapter 1, that the purpose of this work was theocentric: the pleasure and glory of God (1:8). Often we begin with this purpose in mind, but we do not allow this focus to inform the human effort to accomplish it. Haggai reveals that a project with God as its purpose must also have God as the resource on the way to completion.

---

43. See, e.g., W. R. Shenk, "The Southern Baptists Restructure to Reach the Unreached Peoples," *Missions Frontiers Bulletin* (July-October, 1997), 15–18.

44. W. R. Shenk, "Mission, Renewal and the Future of the Church," *International Bulletin for Missionary Research* (October, 1997), 154–59.

Haggai's message needs to permeate the depth of our beings as the people of God, both individually and corporately. It is tempting to live in step with the prevailing culture of our time, a culture that has insulated itself from all threats of defeat or failure. But to live in step with the God of Haggai is to place oneself in the dangerous position of trusting in God, to grasp the hand of the Creator and Redeemer of the universe.

Presence of God. Not only does this passage focus on God's action on behalf of his people but also on his presence in their midst. This shows us the importance of nurturing the presence of God in our lives both individually and corporately, not only in the focused rhythms of individual and corporate disciplines of worship, but also through a sustained consciousness of God's abiding presence with us throughout our days and weeks. Leadership manuals often stress the importance of communication within organizations that are undergoing transition, and thus Christian leaders have become adept at taking considerable time in their corporate gatherings to highlight progress and stress vision. Although this is a wise principle, it is important that Christian leaders not jeopardize the community's need to experience God's presence in their corporate celebrations, to retain a vertical as well as horizontal orientation.

This is also true on the individual level as individuals and families experience transition. It is tempting in the midst of trying circumstances to forego our spiritual rhythms, but these are when we need them more than ever. This may be as simple as prayer with our children or spouse at a regular slot each day or a faith community gathering for a period of prayer at a regular time each year or week. I can remember serving on a church staff and board for whom the experience of the presence of God was so important that they set aside a significant period (thirty to sixty minutes) at the *beginning* of each board and staff meeting to seek God's presence and pray for their people and ministry.

Transcending the past. As God is presented in this prophetic message, the community is drawn to the past. As the discouragement was occasioned by comparing the past with the present, so the encouragement uses the same strategy to show that the God of the past is the God of the present. This message, therefore, does not consign God to the past but produces expectation for God in the present. The same God who accompanied the first community of Israelites through the desert is the same God who accompanies this community. The same God who shook the earth at Sinai before the first community of Israelites is the same God who continues to shake the earth today. This is not, then, an attempt to re-create the primitive community, but to experience the divine resources of that community in our contemporary context.

While I have been writing this commentary, my wife and I have renovated a three-story 1913 house. This involved gutting the home down to the studs by removing lathe and plaster before reconstructing the house to match the style of 1913 complete with hard wood floors and trim, vintage paint colors, and oval tub and shower curtain. Indeed, we longed for the elegance of the past. But let me assure you that we were not willing (or allowed by building code) to match this ancient style completely: the knob-and-tube electrical wiring had to be upgraded to sustain computers and microwaves. The early twentieth-century metal plumbing had to be removed and replaced by PVC pipes. The walls and roofs had to be filled with insulation and the windows upgraded. We wanted certain aspects of the past, but we also wanted to transcend this past: to avoid wind drafts, water leaks, and electrical fires.

God uses Haggai to call a generation to experience God in the present, not only in similar ways to the past but in ways that would dwarf the past. This is what Christ meant by "you will do even greater things than these"—a promise linked inextricably with the sending of the Spirit into the midst of the Christian church (John 14:12; cf. 14:1–31). We often see the past as setting up patterns that are insurmountable. Haggai sees the past as setting precedents that provide a springboard to even greater miracles.

What does this mean for us today? It encourages us to ask God to expand our vision, to help us to think, believe, and act beyond our present expectations (Eph. 3:20–21). For Christian leadership teams this often means taking time apart to dream. When teams are doing long-range planning, there should be sustained time devoted to dreaming of what could be in light of a God of miracle. Often in planning sessions we spend far too much time transferring events from one year to the next that we are unable to think outside the confined box of our present experience.

When I was in the Philippines, I encountered a national university ministry group that started each year by discarding last year's program and beginning afresh. Although this may be too radical for many ministry situations, it does encourage us to loosen our grip on the past and ask God to do immeasurably more than we could ever ask or imagine in the present.

This is an important rhythm for individuals and families as well. Recently, a friend of mine, visiting a town in the Canadian Rockies, met the president of a college riding his motorcycle down the main street. When asked what he was doing, the president said that each year after graduation he set out for a long motorcycle ride to reflect over the past year and consider his future. Although there are possibly safer rhythms for such reflection available, this individual created an important space in his life to reflect on his experience and to look to God for direction and blessing as he contemplated the future.

Blessings untold. After the prophetic message answers the disillusionment of a discouraged community, God offers one final ray of hope. He promises to the church today that he intends to bless them beyond measure and grant peace and prosperity to them as a community. This will come as they experience God's presence and action through kingdom work. Although the purpose of kingdom work is the glory of God, this does not mean that our satisfaction is completely irrelevant. As we fulfill the purpose of bringing glory to God, we will experience the blessedness of the prosperity that accompanies his presence and rule.

Ultimately, the church longs to experience prosperity as a community. We are promised such prosperity in heaven, but Christ's vision for prosperity is to break into our experience now. Such prosperity becomes reality as we entrust ourselves to the God of presence and action, who will fill us with strength and dissuade all fears and thus enable us to work in the kingdom with passionate abandon.

Haggai 2:10–19

ON THE TWENTY-FOURTH day of the ninth month, in
the second year of Darius, the word of the LORD
came to the prophet Haggai: 11"This is what the
LORD Almighty says: 'Ask the priests what the law says: 12If a
person carries consecrated meat in the fold of his garment,
and that fold touches some bread or stew, some wine, oil or
other food, does it become consecrated?'"

The priests answered, "No."

13Then Haggai said, "If a person defiled by contact with a
dead body touches one of these things, does it become
defiled?"

"Yes," the priests replied, "it becomes defiled."

14Then Haggai said, "'So it is with this people and this
nation in my sight,' declares the LORD. 'Whatever they do and
whatever they offer there is defiled.

15"'Now give careful thought to this from this day on—
consider how things were before one stone was laid on
another in the LORD's temple. 16When anyone came to a heap
of twenty measures, there were only ten. When anyone went
to a wine vat to draw fifty measures, there were only twenty.
17I struck all the work of your hands with blight, mildew and
hail, yet you did not turn to me,' declares the LORD. 18'From
this day on, from this twenty-fourth day of the ninth month,
give careful thought to the day when the foundation of the
LORD's temple was laid. Give careful thought: 19Is there yet
any seed left in the barn? Until now, the vine and the fig tree,
the pomegranate and the olive tree have not borne fruit.

"'From this day on I will bless you.'"

Original Meaning

THE BOOK OF HAGGAI records the date of the prophet's prophecies in order to provide a historical backdrop for the reading of the text. To this point the dates have been linked to the feasts of the Jews—not surprising from a prophet whose name means "feast" and whose message is focused on the temple, the destination, and physical context of the feasts. Although at first sight this third pericope does not seem to follow this pattern, a closer look will reveal that it is connected to a significant celebration related to the temple rebuilding.

Its date coincides with the third month anniversary of the beginning of the rebuilding project (see Hag. 1:12–15) and, more importantly, with "the day when the foundation of the LORD's temple was laid" (2:18). This day also appears to provide the background for three other passages from the early Persian period (Ezra 3:10–13, Zech. 4:6b–10a; 8:9–13). The importance of this day in the rebuilding project is evidenced in extrabiblical documents describing temple rebuilding rituals in the ancient Near East.[1]

Such rituals accompanied the rebuilding of ancient Near Eastern temples—from the decision to build until the dedication of the completed building. An initial ceremony typical in the Mesopotamian rebuilding work was the *kalu* ceremony, in which a professional sang laments as a brick from the old temple was removed. This brick was then laid in the new structure by a royal representative and priests purified the site. Moreover, references to blessing and abundance accompanied the laying of the foundation and rebuilding of the temple.

These elements help us understand various components in 2:10–23. On this day, Haggai addresses not only the people as a whole on the topic of blessing (vv. 15–19), but the priestly caste on the topic of purity (vv. 10–14) and Zerubbabel on the topic of royal power (vv. 20–23).[2] Thus, it preserves the trend established in previous pericopes. Haggai's message is once again linked to a ritual celebration, but this time with a ceremony connected with the rebuilding of the temple. This is an important signal to the Persian authorities as well as to the Jewish people that substantial progress has been made on the temple structure.

In past research, the extent of Haggai's message has been determined by highlighting the superscriptions at 2:10 and 2:20. Some students of 2:10–19 have observed, however, that even this section does not have integrity as a

---

1. See my review of this research in Boda, "Majoring," 33–68. These links to ancient Near Eastern customs are not surprising because it was the Persian emperor who commissioned the rebuilding of the temple in the first place. By this I am not suggesting that Israelite religion is syncretistic; only that there were certain generic customs that accompanied the rebuilding of temples, which were used by the Israelites in their project; see B. Halpern, "The Ritual Background of Zechariah's Temple Song," *CBQ* 40 (1978): 180–81: "The complex is distinctively monotheistic in its nuance. There is no hint of the pagan Mesopotamian worldview."

2. See esp. Zech. 4:6–10, in which Zerubbabel is involved in a ceremony connected with the foundation laying in which allusion is made to a special stone. This is an important corrective to Dumbrell, "Kingship," 33–42, who ignores the importance of royal hope in the later Babylonian and Persian Period; see H. G. M. Williamson, "Eschatology in Chronicles," *TynBul* (1977): 115–54.

unit but consists of two unrelated prophetic messages: 2:10–14 and 2:15–19. Furthermore, close affinities between 2:15–19 and chapter 1 led to the view that 2:15–19 originally followed 1:15 but was separated due to scribal error.[3]

Several recent studies have overturned this faulty consensus, showing on textual, formal, and rhetorical grounds that this section belongs together.[4] Not only is there an absence of textual evidence for scribal error, but the structure of this passage follows that of earlier pericopes (superscription, messenger formula, naming of addressees, questions, and exhortation/ admonition). In 2:15 the word "now" (*weᶜattah*; cf. 1:5; 2:4) represents an important link in Hebrew speech that always appears, not at the outset of a speech, but rather midway, identifying the point of movement to the present.[5] Those who displace this passage to Haggai 1 force *weᶜattah* into a position unique in all Hebrew literature.[6]

Haggai 2:10–19 manifests an integral unity. The prophet begins in 2:10–14 by engaging the priests in a Torah ruling (2:10–13) as a prelude for his initial message that sacrifices are defiled because of contact with an altar defiled by the people (2:14). However, what begins on a negative note is soon transformed into a positive encouragement in 2:15–19. Although God's rejection of the sacrifices as a result of this defilement is now coupled with God's curse of their agricultural endeavors, these negative reactions by God

---

3. Pfeill has written what is unquestionably the best review of the issue, demonstrating how this theory of Rothstein became a working assumption among scholars of Haggai until reexamination revealed its bankruptcy; R. Pfeil, "When Is a Gôy a 'Goy'? The Interpretation of Haggai 2:10–19," in *A Tribute to Gleason Archer*, ed. J. Walter C. Kaiser Jr. and R. F. Youngblood (Chicago: Moody, 1986), 261–78; J. W. Rothstein, *Die Nachtgesichte des Sacharja: Studien zur Sacharja-prophetie und zur jüdischen geschichte im ersten nachexilischen Jahrhundert* (BWAT 8; Leipzig: J. C. Hinrichs'sche Buchhandlung, 1910). The influence of Rothstein's theory is displayed in Wolff's commentary on Haggai, which places the interpretation of 2:15–19 after that of 1:1–14; Wolff, *Haggai*, 57–68.

4. A turning point was K. Koch, "Haggais unreines Volk," *ZAW* 79 (1967): 52–66, followed by H. G. May, " 'This People' and 'This Nation' in Haggai," *VT* 18 (1968): 190–97, and T. N. Townsend, "Additional Comments on Haggai II 10–19," *VT* 18 (1968): 559–60. More recent work has been offered by Pfeil, "Gôy," 261–78; D. R. Hildebrand, "Temple Ritual: A Paradigm for Moral Holiness in Haggai II 10–19," *VT* 39 (1989): 154–68; E. R. Wendland, "Temple Site or Cemetery?—A Question of Perspective," *Journal of Translation and Textlinguistics* 5 (1992): 37–85.

5. See bibliography in Boda, *Praying*, 29–30.

6. Rothstein's displacement of 2:10–14 from 2:15–19 led him to the conclusion that the terms "this people" and "this nation" in 2:14 were referring to the enemies of the project (for him, Samaritans) depicted in Ezra 4:1–5, rather than the people themselves. Besides the arguments already noted for the unity of the passage above, there is ample support from the rest of the Heb. canon that Jews could be referred to as "this people" and "this nation" (see comments on 2:14).

are now placed in the past tense because of the significance of the day on which this oracle is delivered. This day is that on which the foundation of the temple will be laid. This activity, done by a people committed to finishing it, will result in the blessing of God: his acceptance of their offerings and grant of plenteous harvest.

This second section uses the repeated phrases "give careful thought" (3x) and "from this day on" (3x) to create a movement forward to the climactic declaration: "I will bless you" (2:19). The sense is that the prophet is interrupting the thought of the future-oriented main theme—"I will bless you"—with a regular reflection back that creates anticipation in the hearer/reader for the content of the future main theme.[7]

Past Defilement: Addressing the Priests (2:10–14)

HAGGAI'S FIRST SPEECH approaches the problems of the past using imagery associated with Israel's sacrificial and legal system. Following his pattern of rhetoric from earlier prophecies, Haggai avoids disclosure of his main theme (v. 14) until his audience is engaged (vv. 10–13).

The prophet begins with an instruction to make an inquiry of the priests. Although the priests in the Old Testament facilitated sacrifice for the Israelites (Lev. 1–8), they also represented them before God (Lev. 16) and communicated the law and its interpretation to the people.[8] The priest was expected to deliver decisions in any matter of law (e.g., Lev. 10:11; Deut. 17:8–13), especially in cases related to cultic ritual (e.g., Lev. 10:10–11; Ezek. 44:23–34).[9] The priests in Haggai 2:11–13 are functioning, then, as teachers of the law, ruling on a matter of cultic ritual for Haggai, a role bolstered by the presence of the same vocabulary as used here in Leviticus 10:10–11.[10] This vocabulary (esp. the terms "consecrated" [*qodeš*] and "defiled" [*ṭameʾ*]) demonstrates that these inquiries are concerned with ritual purity and in particular the transmission of purity and impurity.[11]

---

7. See Boda, "Haggai," 295–304.

8. For more on this see R. DeVaux, *Ancient Israel*, 2 vols. (New York: Darton-Longman-Todd, 1961), 1:154, 2:354.

9. The prophets cite abuse of this priestly duty in their indictments (Mic. 3:11; Jer. 18:18; Ezek. 7:26; 22:26; Zeph. 3:4), linking it to the profanation of God's name.

10. See E. M. Meyers, "The Use of Tôrâ in Haggai 2:11 and the Role of the Prophet in the Restoration Community," in *The Word of the Lord Shall Go Forth: Essays in Honor of David Noel Freedman in Celebration of His Sixtieth Birthday*, ed. C. L. Meyers and M. O'Connor (Winona Lake, Ind.: Eisenbrauns, 1983), 69–76; also M. A. Fishbane, *Biblical Interpretation in Ancient Israel* (Oxford: Clarendon, 1985), 297.

11. Petersen (*Haggai*, 74) notes that the common lexical opposites are holy/profane (*qodeš/ḥol*) and clean/unclean (*ṭahor/ṭameʾ*; cf. Lev. 10:10–11), but he justifies the word pair

The two scenarios in these verses contrast the ability of that which is consecrated or defiled to communicate that quality to another object. In each case three levels of contact are established: in the first (v. 12), meat–fold of garment–food; in the second (v. 13), dead body–person–food. (1) The first scenario concerns the contagious nature of holiness by drawing on the vocabulary of Leviticus 6:27, which concerns the sin offering. Interestingly, the setting assumed by the scenario is that of the peace offering (7:11–21) which, in contrast to the sin and guilt offerings (6:26; 7:6), could be taken home for consumption and explains why foods associated with normal domestic life appear in Haggai 2:12.[12]

Fishbane gets to the core meaning of this scenario when he contends that the concern here is the ability of holiness to be transferred to the third level.[13] The texts in question speak of the transfer of holiness from a consecrated object to a person or object, but the law is silent on the ability of that person or object to transfer that holiness to a third person or object. The priests are thus correct in their ruling: "No."

(2) The second scenario is concerned with the contagious nature of defilement (2:13), drawing on Leviticus 22:1–9 and Numbers 19:22. In this situation the first level of defilement is a corpse,[14] contact with which defiled a person for seven days—a defilement only terminated by the cleansing process described in Numbers 19:11–13.[15] In this case, however, there is ample evidence that one so defiled also had the ability to defile a third person or thing (Lev. 22:4; Num. 19:22). This contrasts the first scenario, as Hildebrand has observed: "The two questions contrast holiness with uncleanness, both concerning contact to the third degree. Uncleanness is passed on to the third degree; holiness is not. In a word, uncleanness is more contagious than holiness."[16]

---

used in Hag. 2 on the basis of a typology in which holy and unclean are the two opposite extremes: "Of these notions, *qōdeš* (holiness) and *ṭāmēʾ* (impurity) are the truly powerful forces. The middle terms do not entail such power and represent something akin to neutral states. Neither cleanness or profaneness per se are typically capable of passing on their qualities." This appears a bit too rigid, especially when the contrast holiness/uncleanness (*qōdeš/ṭumʾah*) is found in a passage connected with the second scenario in 2:13.

12. See Petersen, *Haggai*, 76; Petersen (p. 71) highlights especially the word "stew" (*nazid*, found elsewhere only in Gen. 25:29; 2 Kings 4:38).

13. Fishbane, *Biblical Interpretation*, 297; cf. D. R. Hildebrand, "Temple Ritual: A Paradigm for Moral Holiness in Haggai II 10-19," *VT* 39 (1989): 160; Merrill, *Haggai*, 46.

14. Here expressed euphemistically by the Hebrew word *nepeš* (body; also Num. 5:2; 9:6, 7, 10), a shortened form of *nepeš met* (dead body, Num. 6:6).

15. D. P. Wright, "Unclean and Clean (OT)," *ABD*, 6:730: "The most severe of all the permitted impurities is the human corpse, called the 'father of the fathers of uncleanness' in later rabbinic tradition"; cf. idem, *The Disposal of Impurity: Elimination Rites in the Bible and in Hittite and Mesopotamian Literature* (Atlanta: Scholars Press, 1987).

16. Hildebrand, "Temple Ritual," 161; Fishbane agrees in *Biblical Interpretation*, 297.

Once again the priests' answer consists of one word in Hebrew ("defiled"), which represents the starting point for the prophet's main thrust.[17] God is drawing an analogy between the defilement in the scenario and the defilement of the people. Note the repetition of the Hebrew word *ken* ("so," which looks back to the priests' answer) three times in verse 14 before repeating the priests' answer again at the end of the verse: (lit.) "So this people, and so this nation before me, declares the LORD, and so all the works of their hands, and [as a result] that which they offer there is defiled." The rhetoric builds towards a climax in the final phrase, which returns to the cultic sphere, which was the concern of many of the texts providing the legal background for this passage. The people's offerings were defiled because the people were defiled. Both in the second scenario and the community's experience, defilement is contagious and disqualifies worship.

Scholars have clearly demonstrated from the rest of the Hebrew canon that the terms "this people" and "this nation" refer to the Jewish community.[18] Earlier prophets used the phrase "this people" almost exclusively to refer to the people of God rather than to foreigners,[19] while "this nation" occurs only five other times in the Hebrew canon and each time has the Jewish community in mind (Ex. 33:12–13; Jer. 5:9, 29; 7:28; 9:9). In addition, when the prophets use these phrases, they are predominantly negative in focus, a trend evidenced here in Haggai 2:14.[20] It is interesting, however, that the same two titles also appear in Exodus 33:12–13,[21] in a passage following the famous golden calf incident in Exodus 32, which has influenced Haggai's message in Haggai 2:4–5. As the tabernacle of old, so also the temple would

---

17. Fishbane wisely noted this: "In effect, the prophet is only concerned with the second of these two questions. He depends on a negative reply to the first question in order to set up a positive answer to the second"; Fishbane, *Biblical Interpretation*, 297; contra Sim who wants both scenarios to impact on the final message; R. J. Sim, "Notes on Haggai 2:10-21," *Journal of Translation and Textlinguistics* 5 (1992): 29–33.

18. See A. Cody, "When Is the Chosen People Called a gôy?" VT 14 (1964): 1–6; K. Koch, "Haggais unreines Volk," *ZAW* 79 (1967): 52–66; H. G. May, "'This People' and 'This Nation' in Haggai," *VT* 18 (1968): 190–97; R. J. Coggins, *Samaritans and Jews: The Origins of Samaritanism Reconsidered* (Atlanta: John Knox, 1975), 46–52; and esp. Hildebrand, "Temple Ritual," 154–68, whose article provides the statistics for the following remarks.

19. The only reference to a foreign people comes in Isa. 23:13 (Babylon).

20. The ratio of negative to positive reveals this trend both for "this people" (10 vs. 2 in Isaiah, e.g., Isa. 6:9–10; 8:6–12; 25:4 in Jeremiah, e.g., 14:10–11) and for "this nation" (6 vs. 0 in the Old Testament).

21. Although the word pair "people/nation" does appear elsewhere for Israel (Deut. 4:6; Ps. 33:12; Isa. 1:4; 9:2–3; Jer. 33:24; Zeph. 2:9), only in Ex. 33:12–13 and Hag. 2:14 does it appear together with the demonstrative "this."

be constructed by a community cleansed from defilement, forgiven for disobedience.

Defilement has been transferred from "this people and this nation" to "whatever they do" (lit., "all the works of their hands"). Although some treat this phrase as referring to work on the temple site[22] and others as an allusion to agricultural produce,[23] it most likely refers to sacrificial activity on the altar. First, the verb in the following phrase ("offer") is a sacrificial term used only for animal sacrifices. Moreover, the antecedent of the word "there" at the end of verse 14 must be the first phrase, and since it is connected with offering sacrifice, it must refer to the altar. Similar to the preceding scenarios, this application sets up three levels of contact as a defiled people have defiled the altar and in turn defiled the sacrifices they offer there.

The text does not explicitly state the cause of this defilement; as a result, many views have filled this gap, ranging from moral and ritual failure to contact with the temple ruins.[24] Most likely, however, this defilement finds its source in the neglect in rebuilding the temple,[25] not only because it suits Haggai's message here but also because of the reference to the altar rather than the entire temple complex. The point is that the project needs to progress beyond the "altar" stage; God demands an entire temple structure and not merely an altar on a cleared site.

From Past Curse to Future Blessing through Present Obedience (2:15–19)

HAGGAI NOW MOVES to the present through the structural marker *weʿattah* ("now"), which highlights the function of the initial address to the priests to encourage reflection on the reason for past problems that will be left behind after the ceremonies of the present day. Three times in this speech Haggai says "give careful thought" (2:15, 18), echoing Haggai's initial speech to the

22. E.g., Beuken, *Haggai,* 73; R. A. Mason, "Prophets of the Restoration," in *Israel's Prophetic Tradition,* ed. R. Coggins, A. Phillips, and M. Knibb (Cambridge: Cambridge Univ. Press, 1982), 144; Verhoef, *Haggai,* 120.

23. E.g., Redditt, *Haggai,* 28; Petersen, *Haggai,* 83.

24. See LXX for the moral view. Wolff, *Haggai,* 88: "Because of their morning profits (?). They will suffer pains because of their wickedness. And you 'hate in the gates those who reprove'"; cf. Ackroyd, who concludes that the intention of the glossator is to argue that "the rebuilding must be accompanied by moral reformation"; Ackroyd, "Glosses," 165–66. The ritual failure view is based either on Ex. 29:36–37 or Ezek. 43:18–25; cf. Petersen, *Haggai,* 84. The temple ruin view reveals an allegorizing tendency in that the temple ruin is compared to a "corpse." This is obviously an overzealous attempt to connect the second legal scenario to the final speech; Sim, "Notes," 33.

25. Verhoef, *Haggai,* 120; May, "This People," 190–97.

people in 1:5, 7 (which also reflected on past agricultural curses). Here, however, "to your ways" is missing after "give careful thought" because the reflection is not exclusively on the past (as in Hag. 1) but on the future as well.

Another repeated phrase is "from this day on" (Heb. *maᶜelah*, 2:15, 18, 19), a phrase translated in various ways because of what has been perceived as the awkward flow of this section.[26] To understand this phrase and the passage means to discern the creative rhetoric of a prophet who introduces multiple thoughts simultaneously,[27] forcing the people to think of past (before one stone was laid on another), present (this day), and future (this day on) at the same time. Although most words are linked to the description of the frustrating past, great emphasis falls on the expected future by beginning and ending with this time reference and constantly interrupting the declaration of the future dimension. Most emphasis, however, is placed on the significance of the present day, which represents the segue from a cursed past to blessed future.

The first movement to the past is signaled by the Hebrew phrase *miṭṭerem* ("before" in 2:15).[28] Standing in juxtaposition to the immediately preceding phrase ("from this day on"), which begins in the present and moves to the future, this phrase begins in the present before moving to the past. The day on which "one stone was laid on another in the LORD's temple" is the present day, the day of foundational laying, and probably refers to the royal ceremony of laying the "first stone" (see comments above and on Zech. 4:6b–10a).[29]

Through this time reference Haggai calls his audience to consider their past experience in language reminiscent of chapter 1. In contrast, however, this prophetic message comes later in the year after the harvests are completed, and there is a sense of reflection back on this experience. The word "heap" (*ᶜaremah* in 2:16) refers to a pile of harvested grain (e.g., Ruth 3:7; Neh. 13:15), while the vocabulary in the following line is used in connection with wine production.[30] Although Petersen argues that this verse refers to

---

26. Usually the LXX translates this phrase as "from this day backward" (e.g., 1 Sam. 16:13; 30:25). Clark links it to "give careful thought" rather than "I will bless you"; D. J. Clark, "Problems in Haggai 2:15–19," *BT* 34 (1983): 432.

27. See Boda, "Haggai," 295–304.

28. The phrase in the NIV "consider how things were" in 2:15 is not represented in the Heb. text, but is an attempt to smooth over the rhetorical swing from future to past. Some have repointed the MT at the beginning of 2:16 (*mihyotam*: "from being to them") to *mah-heyitem* ("how was it to you" = "how did you fare?"); Petersen, *Haggai*, 86; Hildebrand, "Temple Ritual," 157; Merrill, *Haggai*, 49. Note that the LXX does indicate a question here and may have mistranslated it, "What sort of people were you?"

29. See Petersen, *Haggai*, 90.

30. There is some speculation over what each term refers to in v. 16 (cf. Isa. 63:3). The text has first *yeqeb* (NIV "wine vat") and then *purah* (NIV possibly "measures"). There is general

mysterious disappearance of food,[31] the use of the infinitive "to draw" (*laḥśop*) suggests expectation ("in order to draw") as in Haggai 1:9. The yields of this harvest are far below expectation: expecting twenty measures of grain they find only ten; expecting fifty measures of wine they find only twenty.[32]

The similarity to Haggai 1 continues as the prophet now identifies the reason for these unmet expectations: Yahweh has struck them with covenant curses.[33] The Hebrew text makes the attack from Yahweh even more personal by first identifying the object of Yahweh's striking as "you" before clarifying it as the people's agricultural endeavors: (lit.) "I struck you with blight, mildew and hail, that is, all the works of your hands." This verse is nearly identical to the words of Amos 4:9[34] and shows how Haggai creatively uses the tradition of the classical prophets by drawing on Amos's indictment of the people but using it to force reflection on the past rather than to introduce judgment in the future.

The phrase "all the work of your hands" must refer to the agricultural endeavors of the people because of the covenant curses that follow. God's discipline has come through "blight, mildew and hail." Amos's original list of "blight and mildew" is a common lexical pair in the Hebrew Bible, denoting opposite conditions of covenant curse (Deut. 28:22; 1 Kings 8:37; 2 Chron. 6:28). "Blight" refers to the result of scorching hot easterly winds from the desert, while "mildew" refers to a condition caused by the damp westerly winds from the Mediterranean. The contrast is thus east versus west, dry versus damp.[35] Haggai expands this pair to a triad of conditions, including also "hail," thus adding the dimensions of height and temperature to those of space and humidity.

---

consensus that the word *yeqeb* refers to the vat that collects the wine; cf. Petersen, *Haggai*, 86. The word *purah*, however, is interpreted as a kind of measurement in many of the versions (e.g., LXX, Vulgate). This, however, is not the sense suggested in Isa. 63:3 (NIV "winepress"); thus it is commonly identified as a word describing either the entire area of winemaking or the pressing chamber; cf. Petersen, *Haggai*, 86; Merrill, *Haggai*, 50; Verhoef, *Haggai*, 126. In this case either a preposition (*mem*) has dropped out (a result of assimilation with the end of the Heb. word for fifty, *ḥamiššim*) or the word functions as an adverbial accusative. In either case the translation should be: "When anyone went to a wine vat to draw fifty (measures) from the winepress, there were only twenty."

31. Petersen, *Haggai*, 90.

32. Hildebrand, "Temple Ritual," 165, sees here an expectation.

33. Petersen's approach to 2:16 leads him to the view that 2:17 does not refer to cause but rather to further experience of difficulty; Petersen, *Haggai*, 90–93.

34. Clark, "Haggai 2:15–19," 434; Hildebrand, "Temple Ritual," 165; Petersen, *Haggai*, 91.

35. J. Nogalski incorrectly sees in blight, mildew, hail the problem of "too much water, not of a drought" and thus identifies 2:17 as an insertion which enhances Haggai's connection to the Book of the Twelve; Nogalski, *Literary Precursors*, 227.

Both in Amos's time and in Haggai's time, the people did not respond to God's discipline. Verse 17 thus reveals both the source of the frustration described in verse 16 as well as the purpose of that frustration, which was not merely to punish wrongdoing but also to lead the community back to God in relationship and obedience. This confirms the connection, already established in verse 16, to the covenant tradition of ancient Israel (Deut. 28:22; 1 Kings 8:37; 2 Chron. 6:28; Amos 4:9), which approaches covenant curse as God's means to draw his people back to himself, not to reject them as covenant partner (cf. Lev. 26: 40–45; Deut. 30:1–10).

In verse 18 Haggai momentarily leaves the past to continue his future-oriented rhetoric. As he guides the audience from past back to the future, the prophet again cries "give careful thought." He then looks to the future by resuming where he broke off in verse 15 before identifying the specific day to which he has been referring: "from this twenty-fourth day of the ninth month." This again links this message both to the previous interchange with the priests (v. 10) and the subsequent oracle to Zerubbabel (v. 20). He then fills out the ceremonial significance of this day in the phrase "the day when the foundation of the LORD's temple was laid" (see above).[36] This ceremony is an official signal from the people that they will carry through on the building project.

As Haggai makes his final transition from future to past, he calls one final time for deep reflection ("Give careful thought") to introduce two frustrations in the past: (1) the low stock of seed in the barns, an issue that fits this particular time of year (the completion of seeding in mid-December leaves the people little on which to survive until the next harvest);[37] (2) lack of grapes, figs, pomegranates, and olives—the other major category of produce in Palestine. These four crops were essential to Palestine's economy (Num. 13:23; Deut. 8:7–8), providing food and drink to the population (grapes, figs, pomegranates) as well as fuel (olive) and dye (pomegranate). The first three crops were harvested in the early fall (August/September), while olive trees bore

---

36. This phrase begins with the preposition *lemin*, which has been variously interpreted. The lamed is probably just introducing this phrase as a further delineation of the previous phrase: "namely"; Wolff, *Haggai*, 59; Verhoef, *Haggai*, 111; KB 465; BDB 483. Merrill, however, sees this lamed as "to" completing "from . . . to" in this verse; Merrill, *Haggai*, 53.

37. Clark outlines the basic options for this initial question and argues for the one we have here. However, in contrast to us, he thinks this question functions as a positive encouragement ("Consider the present, since you started to rebuild the temple, the Lord has given enough rain to soften the earth and allow you to plant the seed for next year's harvest"); Clark, 0"Haggai 2:15–19," 432–39. See Hildebrand, who notes how appropriate this message is for mid-December rather than three months earlier; Hildebrand, "Temple Ritual," 168.

fruit in the later fall (September–December). Now from the vantage point of mid-December, the prophet reminds them that the harvest is over and there is no fruit.

Haggai finally returns to consider the future and to finish the sentence he began in verse 15 (repeating "from this day"). He declares climactically: "I will bless."[38] Until this point in his messages, the prophet has not mentioned the word "bless" directly. He has spoken of curse as the result of the people's disobedience in the past and alluded to future blessing. Now he makes this explicit. God's blessing will accompany this community, which has displayed its obedience by laying the foundation of the temple.[39] This declaration of God's blessing builds on the negative background of verse 17, which alludes to the curses so foundational to the covenant relationship between God and his people. It shows that God's desire is that his people will experience blessing and that the curse is intended as prelude to repentance and blessing. This is why after the strong warnings of covenant curse in Deuteronomy 27–29, God declares that when the people experience such curses, if they "return" to him (30:2), they will experience blessing once again.

Bridging Contexts

TEMPLE AND SACRIFICE. The event that occasions these oracles at the end of Haggai is the ceremony accompanying the laying of the foundation of the temple. The importance of this event is often lost on modern readers who look at the Old Testament through the lens of the New Testament theology of a community that needs no temple. However, for God's people here (to whom we are related through Christ), this event is highly significant for it emphasizes their link to their glorious past, the temple foundation created by Solomon, and signals the dawning of a new day for their community. The rebuilding of the temple is an act of obedience to God's call and is key to the return of God's presence and blessing.

As Christians we may also celebrate this refoundation event as one of the many glorious redemptive-historical events that are recorded in the Bible.

---

38. The NIV inserts the understood "you" which does not appear in the Heb. text. This final statement is extremely abrupt and stands out as an oddity for it does not have the expected accusative. Merrill (*Haggai*, 56) argues that this abrupt style prepares the way for the speech to Zerubbabel in 2:20–23. I propose that it functions as creative rhetoric, driving home the main point of the section after building towards it in 2:15–19a.

39. Laato has noted the importance of pronouncements of blessing in Mesopotamian rebuilding ceremonies and in Hag. 2:19; A. Laato, "Zachariah 4,6b–10a and the Akkadian Royal Building Inscriptions," *ZAW* 106 (1994): 60, 64–65. G. A. Anderson (*Sacrifices*, 91–126) notes a link between temple building and fertility, although I disagree with his conclusion of a Canaanite background to Hag. 2.

The rebuilt temple would sustain the faith of the community of God, and in its courts Jesus and his disciples would inaugurate a new era of redemptive history. Well after this physical temple was destroyed by the Romans (in A.D. 70), the temple endured as an important symbol for the church, providing a theological image for describing its character as the place of the manifest and holy presence of God.

It appears from Ezra 3 that one of the first acts of the community that returned in the early days of Darius was the rebuilding of the altar amongst the temple rubble. This passion for sacrifices—what Tremper Longman III has called "the strangest aspect of Israel's worship to us living in the twenty-first century"[40]—does not immediately connect with us as New Testament believers living in the shadow of the cross. But for our ancient predecessors in the Old Testament community, it was essential to experience covenant relationship with a holy God at the temple.

The various sacrifices presented in Leviticus enabled and fostered the covenant relationship between God and his people. Some of the sacrifices (Lev. 1: *ʿolah*; Lev. 5: *ḥaṭṭaʾt*; Lev. 5–7: *ʾašam*) made the relationship possible by providing atonement for the sins of the people, restoring relationship broken by sinful acts and motives. Such sacrifices were clearly foundational to this covenant relationship, but they opened the way for other sacrifices that fostered this relationship either through offering a gift to God (Lev. 2: *minḥah*) or providing an opportunity for fellowship or thanksgiving (Lev. 3, 7: *šelamim*).[41]

New Testament fulfillment of sacrifice follows the trajectory set by these two Old Testament aspects. On the one side, the sacrifice of Jesus is seen as the once-for-all atoning sacrifice that enables a relationship with God (Heb. 9–10). On the other side, we are encouraged to offer our lives (Rom. 12:1–2; Phil. 2:17; 2 Tim. 4:6; 1 Peter 2:5; Rev. 6:9), our gifts (Phil. 4:18), our worship (Heb. 13:15; Rev. 5:8; 8:3), our acts of kindness (Heb. 13:16), and our faith (Phil. 2:17) as sacrifices that foster this covenant relationship founded on Christ's sacrifice.[42]

While the Old Testament has verbal modes for offering praise, fellowship, and thanksgiving to God (psalms and prayers), sacrifice was essential for restoring relationship between a holy God and a sinful people. In light of this,

---

40. T. Longman, *Immanuel in Our Place: Seeing Christ in Israel's Worship* (Phillipsburg, N.J.: Presbyterian & Reformed, 2001), 75.

41. For these various sacrifices and their fulfillment in the New Testament in and through Christ and the church, see V. Poythress, *The Shadow of Christ in the Law of Moses* (Brentwood, Tenn.: Wolgemuth & Hyatt, 1991), 41–49; A. E. Hill, *Enter His Courts with Praise: Old Testament Worship for the New Testament Church* (Grand Rapids: Baker, 1993), 119–20; R. T. Beckwith, "Sacrifice," in *New Dictionary of Biblical Theology*, ed. T. D. Alexander and B. S. Rosner (Downers Grove, Ill.: InterVarsity Press, 2000), 754–62; Longman, *Immanuel*, 77–115.

42. See esp. Beckwith, "Sacrifice," 759–61.

one can appreciate the passion of this people for the rebuilding of the altar as well as the deep concern they would have felt when the prophet Haggai questioned the legitimacy of their sacrificial acts. It equates to our Christian passion for the rehearsal and celebration of the sacrifice of Christ and the deep concern we would feel if someone questioned the legitimacy of Christ's sacrificial act.

The ceremonies of temple refoundation and sacrifice, then, provide the backdrop for the presentation of the prophet Haggai. In his message he speaks negatively of past defilement and yet positively of future blessing. These two further themes have enduring relevance to us in the church today as we consider them in light of the cross.

Past defilement. Modern readers of this ancient text do not appreciate the rhetoric of Haggai 2:10–14, mostly because of the obscure nature of the initial dialogue between Haggai and the priests. But Haggai was extremely relevant in his speech forms, accommodating them to his audience with sensitivity.[43] In order to comprehend this introductory paragraph, the modern reader must gain an appreciation for the symbolic nature of the law in ancient Israel.

One major aspect in the law is the careful delineation of holiness. Underlying this consistent aspect and foundational to its interpretation is the holiness of God. God is holy; he is wholly other, distinct from his creation and perfect in his being (cf. Isa. 6). For this holy God to be present with his people meant a careful delineation of what among created things would be allowed to be in his presence. Only those elements of fallen creation that had been consecrated or separated to him alone were acceptable. God defined these carefully through the law, and they included only a limited number of created things, whether people, sacrifices, or utensils. Such careful attention to the code of holiness in the law is occasioned by the curse that accompanies sin in our world. Inattention to these codes resulted in a break in relationship with God and was a constant reminder of the need for redemption from sin and imperfection caused by the Fall.

But ceremonial holiness is not the only kind of holiness in the law. It is balanced by demands for ethical holiness, the basis of which is the holy character of God, who makes his people holy (Lev. 20:7). This is the same phrase used for ceremonial holiness (21:8; cf. 20:25–26). These two types of holiness are not so easily differentiated in the law, even though Christ makes a clear distinction between the two in the Gospels (Matt. 23:23–25). Haggai connects the one to the other without difficulty, showing how ethical dis-

43. See Boda, "Haggai," 295–304.

obedience has resulted in ceremonial defilement and rendered the people's sacrifices unacceptable in the past. In the New Testament the ceremonial law is declared fulfilled in Christ through his death, while the ethical law has continuing validity. Haggai's accent on the ethical resonates with this Christian understanding of the law as articulated by Christ in Matt. 23:23–25.

Future blessing. While Haggai 2:10–14 uses the terminology of holiness to typify this break in relationship with God, 2:15–19, functioning as transition from past to future, uses the terminology of curse and blessing to reflect on the consequences of breaking the covenant relationship. Herein lies another distancing feature of this final section of Haggai, an issue that we have already treated in detail in our discussion of 1:1–11 (see Bridging Contexts). There we concluded that the Old Testament theology of retribution (i.e., that God blesses the obedient and disciplines the disobedient) is a principle that is carefully defined in the Old Testament itself and balanced with the theology of God's sovereign freedom to allow suffering in the lives of the obedient and to delay disciplining the disobedient.

The New Testament echoes these two theological aspects as Christ promises material and spiritual blessing to his followers and yet also expects suffering as a key feature of the life of discipleship. Both Old and New Testament believers, then, could and can expect that their acts of obedience will result in blessing either in this life or the next, while remaining aware that such acts may be greeted with suffering.[44]

Contemporary Significance

FILTHY TOUCH. In Greek mythology Midas was the king of Phrygia to whom the god Dionysus gave the power to turn all he touched into gold as a reward for assisting Dionysus's teacher Silenus. Midas soon realizes that this miraculous power is not a reward but a curse, for even his food turns to gold. The greedy king is only freed after crying to Dionysus, who instructs him to bathe in the river Pactolus.

Haggai 2:10–14 presents a people with a powerful touch, a touch that also has disastrous consequences. Their disobedience has rendered their sacrifices defiled before their God. According to Ezra 3:1–6, when the people returned to the land early in the reign of Darius, one of their first priorities was to rebuild the altar and reinstitute the rhythm of sacrifice in the Holy Land. This revealed the importance they placed on atonement and worship as a people.

44. Such suffering may be a result of fallenness (whether physical diseases or opposition to Christ's claims), but also may be related to God's greater purposes; see Bridging Contexts section of 1:1–11.

Unfortunately, these people did not continue their reconstruction efforts and instead focused attention on their own homes at the expense of the temple (Hag. 1), disobeying God's call to reconstruct his sanctuary. This disobedience rendered their sacrifices unacceptable before their holy God and created the crisis of curse evident in the book of Haggai.

As the prophet begins a speech that will ultimately describe the positive future of the people, he reminds them of their past predicament and links this disaster to their disobedience. This section, therefore, begins by helping God's people recognize the power of sin in their lives. Their sin disqualifies the very acts designed to cover sin and enhance relationship with the Lord. This first part of the prophet's oracle on the day of the foundation laying echoes the message of the prophet Samuel to Saul:

> Does the LORD delight in burnt offerings and sacrifices
> as much as in obeying the voice of the LORD?
> To obey is better than sacrifice,
> and to heed is better than the fat of rams.
> For rebellion is like the sin of divination,
> and arrogance like the evil of idolatry. (1 Sam. 15:22–23)

This message is a consistent theme elsewhere in the Old Testament, echoed by psalmist (Ps. 40:6–8; 51:16–17), sage (Prov. 21:3), and prophet alike (Isa. 1:10–20; Jer. 7:21–26; Hos. 6:6; Amos 5:21–27; Mic. 6:6–8). Although God has provided sacrifice to atone for sin and facilitate worship, he desires an obedient people who will live out covenant faithfulness from the heart. This divine design is showcased in the words of the psalmist who said: "I desire to do your will, O my God; your law is within my heart" (Ps. 40:8), or the prophet who cried: "Let justice roll like a river, righteousness like a never-failing stream!" (Amos 5:24). Through Jesus God has instituted the new covenant, which places the law within the hearts of his people by his Spirit (Jer. 31:33; Ezek. 36:27) and invites them to walk now in obedience before him.

Haggai 2:10–14 reminds God's people of the seriousness of disobedience, something that is not lessened in light of Christ's ultimate sacrifice. If anything, as Hebrews 6 has warned us, it is heightened. This echoes the concern of Paul in Romans 6:1–2 when he wrote: "What shall we say then? Shall we go on sinning so that grace may increase? By no means!"

As human beings our acts of sacrifice and worship are defiled by the touch of our fallen hands. Only through Jesus, the One who transforms our fallenness through his death and resurrection, can our sacrifices be acceptable before God. Those who are redeemed by Jesus can now walk in obedience by the Holy Spirit. However, even this new covenant community can become trapped in the meaningless practice of sacrifice without obedience by persisting in disobedience both as we celebrate the forgiveness we have received through Christ's sacrifice and also as we offer spiritual sacrifices in word and deed to the Lord.

Haggai 2:10–14 is a humbling reminder of our fallenness and a vivid depiction of the insidious nature of sin that threatens our relationship with God. On the one hand, Jesus' sacrifice resolves the dilemma of this passage as he atones for our sin, purifies us, and enables us to walk in obedience. On the other hand, as we struggle to walk in a manner worthy of the calling of Christ (Eph. 4:1), we realize how much we need the empowerment of the Spirit to avoid repeating the failure of Haggai's community (Eph. 3:14–21).

It is easy within the church today to bring our sacrifice, whether our verbal worship, our material contributions, or our gifts and abilities, and yet be walking in disobedience either because of a heart that is disengaged from the God of covenant or because of a pattern of life contrary to God's standards. It is easy to become the "whitewashed tombs" of the Pharisees of Jesus' day—looking beautiful on the outside (by bringing all the right sacrifices) and yet on the inside being "full of dead men's bones and everything unclean" (Matt. 23:27).

This is a great danger, for instance, for those who lead God's people in their corporate "sacrifice" of praise (worship services) on a weekly basis or for all who offer "sacrifices" of service through preaching, teaching, caring, giving (and a host of others) on a daily basis. It is easy to become so proficient in the mechanics of these activities that we give little consideration to the importance and impact of individual and corporate obedience, thus offering defiled "sacrifices" to our holy God.

The importance of an obedient walk to our corporate and individual worship (in word and deed) is highlighted at the outset of that great book of worship in the Old Testament, the Psalms. Psalm 1 is clear as it pictures two paths in life, the way of the wicked and the way of the righteous. Its perspective is also transparent as it promotes the rejection of the way of the wicked and the adoption of the way of the righteous. This latter way is closely related to one's "delight in the law of the LORD," the law on which this one "meditates day and night." These truths are not unique to this psalm. However, one should notice the key placement of Psalm 1 at the beginning of the Psalter, for which it serves as an introduction to the book as a whole.[45]

---

45. For this see recent literature on Psalms as a book: James Luther Mays, "The Place of Torah Psalms in the Psalter," *JBL* 106 (1987): 3–12; W. Brueggemann, "Bounded by Obedience and Praise: The Psalms as Canon," *JSOT* 50 (1991): 63–92; J. C. McCann and N. R. McCann, *A Theological Introduction to the Book of Psalms: The Psalms As Torah* (Nashville, Tenn.: Abingdon, 1993); G. H. Wilson, *The Editing of the Hebrew Psalter* (Chico, Calif.: Scholars Press, 1985); idem, *Psalms* (NIVAC; Grand Rapids: Zondervan, 2002).

Serving as the gateway into this book that prompts the worship of and fellowship with the God of Israel and Creation, Psalm 1 reminds us of the importance of our walk to all our acts of sacrifice.

Marking the seasons. When I stumbled across an old picture of my school recently, what caught my attention was my father-in-law at the center of the old black-and-white photograph. In the scene he stands with several other men and women dressed in suits and dresses, standing in the middle of a field. He is holding a shovel in his hands, and the photograph catches the group in what appears to be the act of digging a hole. If you have not grown up in Western culture, this photograph makes no sense for it is filled with oddities: people fancily dressed about to engage in menial labor. But most of us in the West have seen such a ceremony, the groundbreaking ceremony for a new building—in this case, for a new seminary addition to a college. These ceremonies often bring together an odd assortment of people, including the architect, contractor, owner, and bank manager. A shovel is painted gold, and the participants gather together to dig the first hole together, marking the beginning of the construction process. In Christian contexts this ceremony will include a prayer of dedication.

The foundation-laying ceremony in Haggai 2:10–19 is one practiced throughout the ancient Near East in the dedication of temples. Just as groundbreaking ceremonies are not essentially "Christian" activities yet have been appropriated and sanctified by Christian organizations as a way of marking an important juncture in the life of the Christian community, so the Israelites incorporated ceremonies into the rhythm of their community. As we have already noted, several times in 2:15–19 the prophet emphasizes "from this day on," a day that we have identified as the day the foundation was laid for the house of God. This day signaled far more than just a key phase in the rebuilding project. For Haggai it designated a new phase in the redemptive story of this community, for it marked the transition from cursing to blessing.

During the past month I have been involved in three different ceremonies marking a major transition in the lives of my students: a graduation, a wedding, and an ordination. These events have reminded me of the importance of marking the seasons of our lives through ritual and worship. However, many Christian traditions reject the ceremonial in spiritual communal life. Such rejection does not hold true for physical life, as they typically celebrate yearly rhythms of birth, marriage, and death. But when it comes to spiritual rhythms, they rarely celebrate these, distancing themselves from high church traditions.

The reason given for such rejection is usually linked to Paul's statement that there are no special days, that all days are redeemed by Christ (Col. 2:16–17). Paul, however, directs this statement to those who used observance of special Jewish holy days as the foundation for their acceptance before God. He did not intend to suggest that celebrating special moments in the life of the individual and community is inappropriate.

As individuals and communities of faith we celebrate the new phase in our redemptive stories on a regular basis through the celebration of the Lord's Supper. This is a reminder that from the day of Christ's death and resurrection, God's curse was turned away from us. It is no wonder that such an experience of remembrance (1 Cor. 11:24) is also to be an experience of renewing grace and sustenance (John 6:48–58).

Another important redemptive marker in the life of the Christian community is the day of one's baptism or confirmation. On this day the individual within the community marks the transition from curse to blessing through faith in Christ.

Not only does Haggai 2:15–19 stress the importance of celebrating key moments of salvation, it also encourages us to celebrate key times of transition in the life of the community, such as moving to a new location, receiving new members, submitting to new leadership, or experiencing spiritual renewal. As Haggai's community of old did, we must approach God with penitent and expectant hearts, reaffirming our commitment to him in order that we may hear his voice of promise afresh: "From this day on I will bless you."

Blessing. This passage traces the transition from cursing to blessing, a transition linked to the day of the foundation laying of the Second Temple. As God's people we also trace the same transition to the day of the foundation laying of another temple, the temple of Christ, a day that involved his sacrifice and inaugurated a new phase of redemptive history (John 2:19–22). The apostle Paul echoes this message in his citation of Deuteronomy 27:26 in Galatians 3:10–14 when he traces the transformation from curse ("Cursed is everyone who does not continue to do everything written in the Book of the Law") to blessing (the blessing given to Abraham) to the work of Christ: "Christ redeemed us from the curse of the law by becoming a curse for us."[46]

Because of this we now have received a multitude of blessings in Jesus. In fact, Ephesians 1:3 says that the Father has "blessed us in the heavenly realms with every spiritual blessing in Christ," including such blessings as adoption as his children (1:5), redemption through his blood (1:7), forgiveness of sins (1:7), knowledge of his will (1:9), and sealing by the Holy Spirit (1:13). These foundational blessings that mark us as the people of the new covenant, however, are just the beginning of the kind of blessing that God promises us.

---

46. See M. J. Evans, "Blessing/Curse," in *New Dictionary of Biblical Theology*, ed. T. D. Alexander and B. S. Rosner (Downers Grove, Ill.: InterVarsity Press, 2000), 401.

At its core, blessing is the communication of the life of the Creator to us (cf. Gen. 1:28–30 with 3:14–19). This helps us to understand Christ's promise that he has come to give us life—life in abundance. Through Jesus the Father now breathes life into his people (John 20:22; cf. Gen. 2:7), re-creating them to fully experience all that he intended for them in the garden at the beginning of history. For Christians, then, such blessing is not limited to the "spiritual" realm, but rather impacts the "physical" realm as God promises to grant fullness of life.

As Christians we must live in light of this truth. We must hear the voice of the prophet that assures us of God's blessing in this life and the next, assurance that sustains us even when we do not see its reality in our present circumstances. We must take opportunities to celebrate the blessing of the fullness of life we have received in and through Jesus Christ, both corporately and individually. When we do not see evidence of such blessing in our lives, we must be open to the fact that God may be crying for our attention, while not losing sight of the fact that he may have other reasons for withholding blessing from us (see Bridging Contexts section of 1:1–11).

Haggai 2:20–23

THE WORD OF the LORD came to Haggai a second time
on the twenty-fourth day of the month: [21]"Tell Zerub-
babel governor of Judah that I will shake the heavens
and the earth. [22]I will overturn royal thrones and shatter the
power of the foreign kingdoms. I will overthrow chariots and
their drivers; horses and their riders will fall, each by the
sword of his brother.
[23]"'On that day,' declares the LORD Almighty, 'I will take
you, my servant Zerubbabel son of Shealtiel,' declares the
LORD, 'and I will make you like my signet ring, for I have cho-
sen you,' declares the LORD Almighty."

Original Meaning

AS NOTED IN our discussion of the previous section, 2:10–23 represents prophetic oracles delivered by Haggai at the ceremony celebrating the foundation laying of the Second Temple.[1] Each section addresses a different group important on such ceremonial days in the ancient Near East: the priests (2:10–14), the people (2:15–19) and the royal house (2:20–23). Moreover, we argued that 2:10–19 is a unity, delivered orally on the same occasion. The final four verses of Haggai is another speech delivered on the same day, so that 2:10–23 forms a literary unity.

(1) The affinity between 2:10–19 and 2:20–23 is highlighted in distinctions between their superscriptions and those found in 1:1–2:9 (compare "through the prophet" in 1:1; 2:1 with "to the prophet" in 2:10, 20) and between their description of the audience (in 1:1–2:9, inclusive lists; in 2:10–23, each addressed in turn). (2) The rhetorical shape of the two superscriptions in 2:10, 20 are arranged in reverse order (2:10—date formula, messenger formula; 2:20—messenger formula, date formula). (3) This argument for unity is bolstered by attention to the audiences addressed, for only 2:10–23 taken together address the three main participants at an ancient foundation-laying ceremony (priest, people, king). (4) The temporal referents of the three messages provide a structural flow that enhances unity: the address to the priests reflects on the past (2:10–14), the address to the king looks to the

1. See Original Meaning section for 2:10–19.

future (2:20–23), and the address to the people bridges these two sections by moving from past to future (2:15–19).[2]

Haggai 2:10–23 functions as a positive encouragement for the people, affirming their decision to move forward in the rebuilding project and to lay the foundation of the temple. This encouragement is offered by comparing the dismal past with the promised future, linking blessing to the obedient response of the people. This future blessing is ultimately linked to the reestablishment of the royal house represented by Zerubbabel, who becomes a symbol of hope for the community of God. For the purposes of this commentary we are studying 2:20–23 in a separate section, but we must stress its close relationship with 2:10–19.

The upheavals described in the message to Zerubbabel in 2:20–23 can be seen more vividly against the backdrop of recent events in the Persian empire. As we noted in 2:10–19, Darius was beginning to exercise his unquestioned control of the vast Persian empire after the rebellions that preceded and followed the former emperor Cambyses' death. The references to political upheaval in 2:21–22 would have been received by a community that had witnessed the recent vulnerability of the Persian hegemony. This, however, does not mean that Haggai is advocating rebellion among the Jews against their Persian overlords.[3] Rather, Haggai envisions God's action on behalf of his people and, in particular, his Davidic ruler.

The phrase "I will bless you" (2:19) completes the message spoken directly to the people on the important day of laying the temple's foundation. The flow of the messages in 2:10–19 has moved the audience from the past to the future through the present. To this point, however, this blessed future is close at hand, linked to the anticipated harvests within a few months. The final message on "the twenty-fourth day of the [ninth] month" (2:20–23) will carry the chronology a step further, looking to the breaking in of the eschaton. Although these verses focus attention on Zerubbabel, the prophetic word begins with the appearance of Yahweh, which provides the foundation for the blessing to Zerubbabel.

The weaving together of the theme of subjugation of the nations with that of royal investment is vividly displayed in Psalm 2, where the nations are in rebellion against Yahweh and his anointed one, and Yahweh affirms his adoption of the Davidic royal.[4] This installation is linked to "Zion, my holy

---

2. Merrill (*Haggai*, 56) explains the abruptness of the declaration in 2:19, "I will bless you," by saying that this blessing is expressed in the eschatological hope of 2:20–23. Although he may have a point in the flow of the passage, this abruptness can be explained in terms of creative rhetoric of 2:10–23 (see comments on 2:10–19).

3. Kessler, "Darius," 63–84.

4. See G. Sauer, "Serubbabel in der Sicht Haggais und Sacharjas," in *Das ferne und nahe Wort: Festschrift Leonhard Rost*, ed. F. Maass (Berlin: Töpelmann, 1967), 202–3, who notes this connection to Ps. 2 as well as to Ps. 110.

hill," from where Yahweh exercises his rule on earth through his vice-regent, the Davidic king. As Zerubbabel leads the people in rebuilding the place of God's presence on earth from which he exercises rule through the Davidic king, we are reminded of God's authority and power over the nations.[5] Theophany (i.e., the appearance of Yahweh), subjugation of the nations, and the Davidic dynasty are compatible themes that display unity.

Detailed Analysis

THE FINAL SECTION begins in 2:20 with a superscription dated to the same day as 2:10–19. That this repetition is intentional is clear from the phrase "a second time." The order of this superscription in the Hebrew text is the reverse of the superscription in 2:10, creating a chiastic structure that may have been designed to bind these two oracles together.

The audience of this message is clearly defined from the outset as Zerubbabel, the political ruler of the province (see the introduction, Original Meaning section). As the message progresses, however, this designation will be left to the side as Haggai unfolds the significance of this character to the future of God's people in 2:23 (see further below).

The message begins with similar vocabulary and structure as in 2:6. The phrase "I will ... shake the heavens and the earth" signals the appearing of God, and the word *goyim* (in 2:22, "foreign"; in 2:6, "nations") speaks of the nations. In other words, the flow of words is from cosmos to nations in both sections. The ultimate goal of each unit, however, is different. Whereas in 2:6–9 the disruption of the cosmos began a process that ultimately resulted in the wealth of the nations streaming into the temple, in 2:21–22 the same disruption ultimately leads to the subjugation of the nations. Observe Wolff's comments on the relationship between these two sections: "Verse 22 can be understood as an elucidation of what this upheaval means, since it talks about the overthrow of national power and destruction of military potential."[6]

In our interpretation of 2:6–8 we noted the use of vocabulary associated with the theme of divine warrior in the Old Testament and the subsequent tribute the conquering king expected. Now the "shaking of the nations" alluded to in 2:7 is filled out in more detail in 2:22. These two prophetic visions are compatible and accentuate a different aspect of this future event. Haggai 2:6–9 focuses attention on the result of God's intervention, while 2:21–23 reveals aspects of the intervention itself.

---

5. Note the similar connection between theophany, temple, and subjugation of the nations in Ps. 48 and 68.

6. Wolff, *Haggai*, 104.

Verse 22 develops the military aspect of Haggai's future vision through the use of battle imagery drawn from Israel's heritage. The term "overturn" (*hpk*) connotes total and instantaneous destruction by God's unlimited power and is used most regularly to describe God's annihilation of Sodom and Gomorrah (e.g., Gen. 19:21, 25, 29; Deut. 29:23; Lam. 4:6; Amos 4:11; cf. Isa. 1:7–9; Jer. 20:16).[7] In Deuteronomy and the prophets it refers to the judgment of God on his people, but Haggai is called to reverse this trend and use it for foreign nations (as Gen. 19) alongside the term "shatter" (*šmd*), a more common term for divine judgment of the nations (e.g., Deut. 2:20–23; 9:1–6). The general character of the object of this divine action ("royal thrones,"[8] "power of the foreign kingdoms") also expresses the totality of this defeat: It topples thrones and powers, kingdoms and nations.

In the second part of verse 22 the focus moves from general political to specific military vocabulary as the prophet continues to draw from stock Israelite images. The "overthrow" of "chariots and their drivers" and the "fall" of "horses and their riders" draws on the Exodus tradition in which Pharaoh is defeated (e.g., Ex. 14:23–25).[9] Even the most potent military resources available to ancient rulers will "fall." This last word is a euphemism for death,[10] the cause of which is identified in the final phrase ("each by the sword of his brother"). While many have seen here an allusion to Gideon's defeat of Midian in Judges 7:22,[11] the vocabulary is closer to Ezekiel's description of the defeat of Gog in Ezekiel 38:21,[12] a defeat that also speaks of the subjugation of the nations for the sake of Israel.[13] In the end God causes such confusion

7. Because this gloss for this verb is not exclusively related to Sodom and Gomorrah, Petersen may be correct when he argues that this verb is drawn from the tradition of oracles against nations rather than that of Sodom and Gomorrah; Petersen, *Haggai,* 98.

8. The phrase represented by "royal thrones" in Heb. is lit. "the throne of kingdoms." Some have argued that the use of the singular "throne" with the plural "kingdoms" is a veiled reference to the Persian hegemony over the many kingdoms of the world at this point in history; Meyers and Meyers, *Haggai,* 67; cf. Wolff, *Haggai,* 103, for others. This, however, is probably an example of a Heb. idiom in which a singular is used with the plural to express a compound idea; Verhoef, *Haggai,* 144; Wolff, *Haggai,* 103; Petersen, *Haggai,* 100; GKC 124§p-r.

9. In Jer. 51:20–21 this vocabulary is used to represent the power of a nation.

10. Cf. Beuken, who lists Isa. 32:19; Jer. 13:18; 48:15; Lam. 1:9; Ezek. 26:16; 30:6 to show that "fall" (*yarad*) means "go down to the underworld," a sense seen in the Exodus tradition as well (Ex. 15:5); Beuken, *Haggai,* 80 n. 1. Verhoef notes Isa. 34:7 and Jer. 48:15 as examples where *yarad* is used to refer to the death of animals and humans in battle contexts; Verhoef, *Haggai,* 145.

11. Petersen, *Haggai,* 101; Wolff, *Haggai,* 103; Verhoef, *Haggai,* 145.

12. Petersen, *Haggai,* 101.

13. There are surprising connections between this section and the end of Ezekiel, which envisions the return of God's people after exile (Ezek. 36–37) in a scenario where "my servant David" (37:24) plays a key role and is intimately linked to "my sanctuary" (37:26–28). The defeat

in his enemies that ironically they are the ones who enact judgment on themselves, confirming the ineptitude of human political power and military prowess. Such ineptitude has been demonstrated to this Jewish community in the recent Persian upheaval at the accession of Darius.[14]

God's destruction of power structures of humanity serves as the foundation for the final theme of this prophetic message in 2:23. The phrase "on that day" serves, first, as a transitional phrase to link the two parts of the message in a cause-effect relationship. It looks back to the events of 2:21b–22 that provide the details of "that day," and then link the actions in 2:23 to the events. This phrase also serves to delineate the time reference for the actions described in 2:21–23. It is used regularly in prophetic literature as the prophets look to a future time of fulfillment (e.g., Isa. 2:11–20; Jer. 25:33; Amos 8:3, 9) and is intimately linked to the eschatological time called the "Day of Yahweh."[15] Thus, Haggai is not given a specific timetable for the actions described here but peers into the indefinite future.

The message now focuses on Zerubbabel. Yahweh declares that he will "take" (*lqḥ*) Zerubbabel, a common verb in Hebrew often found in contexts in which God changes the status of an individual.[16] In particular *lqḥ* is found in contexts in which Davidic kings are anointed for kingship (2 Sam. 7:8; 2 Kings 14:21; 23:30) and represents the first of a series of allusions to Davidic kingship in this final verse.[17]

---

of the nations in chs. 38–39 is followed then by a vision of a new temple (chs. 40–48). Haggai 2:20–23 combines these same elements: defeat of the nations, appointment of a Davidic ruler, rebuilding of a sanctuary.

14. Petersen with Beyse and Wolff argue correctly that one need not set up an either-or choice between ancient Israelite tradition and contemporary Persian history. Although the former provided the vocabulary, the latter would have an effect on the audience who heard this message. By this, however, we are not saying that Haggai's message is meant as a call to rebellion, contra L. Waterman, "The Camouflaged Purge of Three Messianic Conspirators," *JNES* 13 (1954): 73–78; cf. Petersen, *Haggai,* 101; K.-M. Beyse, *Serubbabel und die Königserwartungen der Propheten Haggai und Sacharja: Eine historische und traditionsgeschichtliche Untersuchung* (Arbeiten zur Theologie 1/48; Stuttgart: Calwer, 1972), 55–56; Wolff, *Haggai,* 103.

15. The "Day of Yahweh" is developed throughout prophetic literature as that time when God will defeat his foes; cf. G. von Rad, *Old Testament Theology* (Edinburgh: Oliver and Boyd, 1962), 2:119–23.

16. Gen. 24:7 and Josh. 24:3 (Abraham); Ex. 6:7 and Deut. 4:20 (Israelites); Num. 3:12 (Levites); 2 Sam. 7:8 (David); 2 Kings 2:3 (Elijah's death); 14:21 (Azariah); 23:30 (Jehoahaz); Amos 7:15 (Amos).

17. Contra W. H. Rose, *Zemah and Zerubbabel: Messianic Expectations in the Early Postexilic Period* (JSOTSup 304; Sheffield: Sheffield Academic, 2000). Rose argues that the terminology used here is not restricted to Davidic tradition. Although this is true for each term isolated from the other, it is the combination of these terms that restricts the allusion to the Davidic tradition.

Zerubbabel is identified as "son of Shealtiel" in contrast to the original address in 2:21, which called him "governor of Judah." Once Haggai has described the overthrow of human power in 2:22, it is inappropriate to continue to refer to Zerubbabel by his title as a small political player in the bureaucracy of the Persian empire. By calling him "son of Shealtiel" Haggai is alluding to his genealogical connection to the royal line of David. The phrase "my servant" continues this emphasis, for this is a term often associated with the Davidic kings.[18] In the role as "servant" of the divine King, the Davidic ruler was the "favorite confidant of the King, one who remains in the vicinity of the king, who knows the mind and wishes of the king, and who executes the confidential assignments of his master."[19] This title accentuates the intimate relationship between Yahweh and the Davidic ruler.

The second action of Yahweh in relationship to Zerubbabel is that he will "make" him "like my signet ring." The combination of the verb *śwm* ("make") and the preposition *k* ("like") produces the connotation of "make the equivalent of" or "make into."[20] This verb thus completes the progression from one state to another begun by "take" in the first half of the verse.

Yahweh appoints Zerubbabel as "my signet ring" (*ḥotam*). This image is a common one in the royal vocabulary of the ancient Near East, designating a piece of metal jewelry on which was etched an impression of the seal of the king. It symbolized his authority because of its use to authenticate legal documents and royal pronouncements (Est. 8:10; Ezek. 28:12; 1 Macc. 6:15) and by extension was regarded as a precious possession (Song 8:6).

Haggai is alluding here to an earlier prophetic message to the Davidic line. In Jeremiah 22:24 the prophet Jeremiah attacked the Davidic king Jehoiachin with a message of judgment: "Even if you, Jehoiachin son of Jehoiakim king of Judah, were a signet ring on my right hand, I would still pull you off." The ensuing message in Jeremiah 22 speaks of Yahweh's rejection of Jehoiachin and his exile to Babylon, and it ends by prophesying that "none of his offspring will sit on the throne of David or rule anymore in Judah" (22:30). This "offspring" (*zeraᶜ*) is defined in 22:28 as his "children" (*zeraᶜ*) who went into exile with him. As Haggai now addresses one of those who was born in the Exile (Zerubbabel, meaning "seed of Babel") prophesied by Jeremiah for the Davidic line, he revisits the message to the Davidic line.

This message is carefully phrased in terms that define the appropriate role for the Davidic line in Yahweh's kingdom. Both images used ("servant"

---

18. 2 Sam. 3:18; 7:5, 8; 1 Kings 11:32, 34, 36; 1 Chron. 17:4; 2 Chron. 32:16; Ps. 78:70; 89:3; 132:10.

19. Verhoef, *Haggai,* 146.

20. So Wolff, *Haggai,* 105: Gen. 13:16; 1 Kings 19:2; Hos. 2:3. Thus it is not a simile but a construction of appointment.

and "signet ring") are passive images of instrument, for the "servant" is one who responds to the commands of his master and has no authority apart from his relationship to this lord, and a "signet ring" has no value apart from its connection to the king who wears it. The Davidic king was expected to fill the role of vice-regent on earth, executing Yahweh's authority and representing Yahweh's interests in this world (see Ps. 2). The downfall of the preexilic Davidic kings was their penchant for exercising authority beyond these carefully defined boundaries. The future of the Davidic line is based on a return to the original intention of the royal office in Israel.

Haggai is not contradicting Jeremiah's prophecy but rather making a creative play on the prophecy and revealing a future for the Davidic line. This may explain why Haggai refers to Zerubbabel as "son of Shealtiel" throughout this book. The genealogy of the Davidic line in 1 Chronicles 3:10–24 consistently uses the term "his son" to refer to the chosen individual to rule in the Davidic dynasty. Following Jehoiachin's name in 3:17, Shealtiel is designated "his son." No descendants are listed for "Shealtiel"; only Pedaiah's sons are given, one of whom is Zerubbabel. This implies that the line was to pass through Shealtiel, but that it was Pedaiah who provided the needed child. Zerubbabel is thus explicitly placed in the Davidic line by associating him with Shealtiel but is clearly of the generation that did not go into exile, the generation Jeremiah promised would not reign in Judah. Two generations removed and having been cleansed through exilic suffering, the Davidic line is now addressed by Haggai and granted hope of a future reinstatement to their unique position as "signet ring" for Yahweh.

The reason for Yahweh's action is given in the final phrase of the announcement: "for I have chosen you"—another phrase drawn from the pool of vocabulary associated with the appointment of the Davidic dynasty.[21] Although "chosen" (*baḥar*) is used to refer to God's election of Israel as a nation (e.g., Deut. 4:37),[22] it can also refer to God's choice of David, especially when combined with "my servant" (e.g., 1 Sam. 16:8–10; 2 Sam. 6:21; Ps. 78:70).

In sum, 2:20–23 concludes the larger pericope that began in 2:10. In 2:10–14 the prophet reflects on past defilement that had produced the destitution. With the obedience of the people represented by their completion of the foundation of the temple, the prophet then anticipates a bright future, focusing the people's attention on promises of blessing that will reverse the predicaments of the past (2:15–19). But 2:20–23 shows us that this promise

21. Meyers and Meyers (*Haggai*, 70) may have a point when they claim that this word is used when referring to the choice of a dynasty, esp. because it is used at the choice of Saul (1 Sam. 10:24) and David (2 Sam. 6:21).

22. Cf. Weinfeld, *Deuteronomy*, 327.

of blessing in the immediate future is but the firstfruits of a far greater blessing. Yahweh will shake the universe, overthrow human power, and appoint the Davidic line to its rightful place as vice-regent over the world.

Bridging Contexts

AS IN 2:1–9, so here at the conclusion of this book we see the transition from forthtelling to foretelling and the intimate relationship between the two (see the introduction, Bridging Contexts section). The exhortation to Haggai's community clearly has a future dimension as the prophet expects nothing less than the breaking in of God's universal kingdom and rule. In doing this the prophet is not only offering a vision of the future but also displaying the intimate connection between present and future. This hope is clearly centered on God, who will create the conditions conducive for the future rule of his prince and people. But this divine work ultimately focuses on the reestablishment of the Davidic line; thus, a quick orientation to this line and its relevance to us is useful for ascertaining the contemporary significance of this passage.

Zerubbabel. By the time we come to 2:20–23, we have left the accursed past behind and find ourselves in the future. Haggai's final message is one of hope for the future of the Davidic line. It addresses Zerubbabel as a symbol of the enduring nature of God's promises to David. But this promise is carefully couched in terms that reveal that the ultimate purpose of this reinstatement is the rule of God on earth through Davidic rulers.

It is not surprising to find this promise to the Davidic descendant in the context of the ceremony for the foundation laying of the temple. The temple project was a core accomplishment of the Davidic dynasty at its inception (see esp. 2 Sam. 5–7; 1 Kings 6–9; 1 Chron. 13–17; 22; 28–29; 2 Chron. 1–7), and the care of the temple was to be an ongoing priority (2 Kings 12; 23). The temple was the place of God's manifest presence, the place from which he ruled the earth in relationship with the Davidic king (Ps. 2; 84). By rebuilding the temple, the people in Haggai's day are fulfilling the priorities of the Davidic line, providing a palace for the Great King, Yahweh. The ultimate purpose of this rebuilding project is now revealed: It is the first step in the program of God to bring his rule to the nations of the world.

Haggai focuses attention on the hope represented in the person of Zerubbabel. Some see here an optimistic prophet who oversteps his boundaries and places far too much focus on the historical figure of Zerubbabel.[23] There is,

---

23. E.g., Waterman, "Purge," 73–78; see recent review of this in Kessler, "Darius," 63–84.

however, precedent for speaking about an individual while having his descendants in mind in the Hebrew Bible. Hosea 3:4–5, in speaking about the future when the Israelites will repent, speaks of David while meaning his descendants:

> For the Israelites will live many days without king or prince, without sacrifice or sacred stones, without ephod or idol. Afterward the Israelites will return and seek the LORD their God and David their king. They will come trembling to the LORD and to his blessings in the last days.

Similarly, Ezekiel 34:23–24; 37:24–25 anticipates the coming of David:

> I will place over them one shepherd, my servant David, and he will tend them; he will tend them and be their shepherd. I the LORD will be their God, and my servant David will be prince among them. I the LORD have spoken.
>
> My servant David will be king over them, and they will all have one shepherd. They will follow my laws and be careful to keep my decrees. They will live in the land I gave to my servant Jacob, the land where your fathers lived. They and their children and their children's children will live there forever, and David my servant will be their prince forever.

Haggai is declaring that God is doing a new thing in their day, and Zerubbabel is a symbol of the future of the Davidic line. This is not lost on the writers of both Matthew and Luke, who include Zerubbabel in their list of Jesus' lineage. These two genealogies agree verbatim in their tracing of Christ's line from Abraham to Solomon and then diverge until they get to the figures of Zerubbabel and Shealtiel after the Exile. They then diverge again until Joseph. It is not our intention to discuss these genealogies and their differences in detail, but this evidence shows that Zerubbabel is an important figure in the history of the Davidic line. The New Testament makes clear that the hope of the Davidic line finds its fulfillment in Jesus who is called Christ, or Messiah.

Messiah. Jesus came to establish God's rule on earth as the Davidic king. The genealogy in Matthew's Gospel makes this clear from the outset as it identifies Jesus as the "Christ" (*Christos*, Gk. for Heb. word meaning Messiah), who was the "son of David" (Matt. 1:1). Later in that same chapter Matthew links this same Jesus with the "Immanuel" promised to the Davidic king Ahaz by the prophet Isaiah (Isa. 7:14), and then again in the following chapter he cites the promise of Micah that a ruler will come out of Bethlehem (Mic. 5:2), the hometown of David.

The opening sermon of the early church, which Peter preached on Pentecost, emphasizes Jesus' fulfillment of the Davidic hope that God would place one of his descendants on his throne (Acts 2:30). The apostle Paul echoes the Davidic link when describing Jesus' human lineage at the outset of his theological treatise to the Romans: "who as to his human nature was a descendant of David" (Rom. 1:3). It is not surprising that Psalm 2, a psalm celebrating the installation of the Davidic king to the royal throne, is one of the most oft cited Old Testament passages in the New Testament (Acts 4:25–26; 13:33; Heb. 1:5; Rev. 2:27).

The first installment of this fulfillment was accomplished through Jesus' death on the cross and subsequent resurrection from the dead. The mystery of the cross event is that through this act God exercised his rule over the earth. This is made clear in Isaiah's prophecy in Isaiah 52–53, which speaks of the victory of God, announced to his people by the messengers who bring good news: "Our God reigns" (52:7). God reigns by laying bare his holy arm (52:10). It is then with shock that Isaiah gazes on this "arm of the LORD" and declares with astonishment: "Who has believed our message and to whom has the arm of the LORD been revealed" (53:1). This astonishment arises from his incredulity at seeing a man dying in agony at the hands of wicked men (53:2–12). God accomplishes his powerful victory through Christ's death on a cross, after which he ascends to heaven to sit at his right hand as God's vice-regent over the earth.

Community of the Messiah. There is, however, a "not yet" to the "already" of this first installment. We long for the full exercise of God's dominion on earth, that God's will in heaven will be done on earth. This is accomplished through those on whom has come the promise of David—that is, the church, through whom God desires to exercise his rule on earth. This is why the apostle Paul can transform the promise originally directed to the Davidic line into a promise for the new community of Christ, the church (2 Cor. 6:18; cf. 2 Sam. 7:8, 14). In Christ we now are called to be his vice-regents on earth, to exercise his rule, for all authority has been given to us (Matt. 28:18–20). The proclamation in word and deed of the gospel through an oft-times suffering church is God's surprising strategy to exercise his rule on earth. The church longs for the day when God will shake the earth and its power structures in the final days even as we experience the firstfruits of such shaking as we proclaim the gospel in the world.

Contemporary Significance

I PICKED UP a newspaper the other day, it read something like this:

> The world is too big for us. Too much going on, too many crimes, too much violence and excitement. Try as you will you get behind in the race.... It's an incessant strain, to keep pace ... and still you lose ground. Science empties its discoveries in you so fast that you stagger beneath them in hopeless bewilderment. The political world is news seen so rapidly you're out of breath trying to keep pace with who's in and who's out. Everything is high pressure. Human nature can't endure much more!

This newspaper: *The Atlantic Journal*. The date: June 16, 1833—over 170 years ago.

My world is too big! Douglas Coupland has become a spokesman for the cross-section of society now called Generation X.[24] In his two books *Generation X* and *Life after God*, Coupland shares vignettes from the lives of this younger generation. He defines a condition among Generation X termed *optional paralysis*: "the tendency, when given unlimited choices, to make none."[25]

This is not limited to Generation X, for we all are bombarded by more and more choices these days. And not only more choices, but more and more information. Why? Because in an ironic twist our big world is shrinking. As the world shrinks, we all think that will mean that the world will become more manageable, that we will feel more significant in this shrinking world. Instead, the opposite happens: As the world shrinks, we feel ourselves shrinking with it. We feel more and more insignificant in our global village.

Danish theologian Søren Kierkegaard accurately captures the frustration we all feel in trying to communicate the gospel while feeling that not only ourselves but our message itself is irrelevant and insignificant in this global village. Kierkegaard begins with the scene of a fire backstage of a theater on the opening night of a new comedy production. A clown realized the danger and pushed through the curtains to alert the audience. They applauded. The clown repeated his warning more urgently. By now he was center stage, flailing his arms, his eyes wide in panic. The crowd went wild. Whistles. Cheers. Raucous laughter. Never had they seen such a routine! Kierkegaard concludes: "I think the world will come to an end in the same way. The human race will stand in thunderous ovation, calling for an encore,

24. D. Coupland, *Generation X: Tales for an Accelerated Culture* (New York: St. Martin's, 1991); idem, *Life After God* (New York: Pocket, 1995).

25. Coupland, *Generation X*, 139.

convinced it's just another happy joke. And so, what if you try to warn the world?"[26]

Over 2,500 years ago a prophet stumbled onto the world stage into a situation much like ours today. It was a world witnessing one of the first attempts at a global village achieved through advances in technology, control of commerce, and alignment of political forces. In his shrinking world that appeared to sideline God's people, to cast this prophet as a clown crying "fire," Haggai was called to faithfully proclaim an eternal message, a message of hope, a message of triumph.

Comforting the saints. There is a climactic and triumphant tone to this final prophetic message in Haggai. There has been a progressive movement in the book as a whole from its initial message, which called the people out of their complacency to begin the project, to this final message, which celebrates the obedience of the people in the first stage of the temple rebuilding. Although they are still far from completing this temple structure, Haggai's message is finished. Through this message, however, we learn that he sees implications for this project far beyond the mere reversal of the dire human situation of the Jews in 520 B.C. Haggai sees it as the first step in the establishment of God's rule on earth. He looks to the future establishment of the Davidic line to its rightful place as vice-regent on earth. Zerubbabel's participation in the present project is a powerful symbol of that future reality.

Haggai began his message on the day of the foundation laying with a healthy assessment of the condition of his people (2:10–14). These people were unqualified to be in the presence of the holy God because of their disobedience in the matter of building his temple. This defilement was the source of the curses they experienced as a people. Cut off from the presence of their King, they had not received the blessing that accompanies his rule; instead, they had experienced his wrath and curse. Obedience brought renewal of relationship and consecration of the people, and with that, blessing. But ultimately this blessing will be eclipsed by the brilliance of the appearance of God. Such temporal blessing connected with the harvest is only the beginning. God promises to affirm his choice of the Davidic line and people and reign on earth.

In one sense this passage has been fulfilled in the arrival of Christ in the line of David and his ascension to his heavenly throne. In another sense it remains unfulfilled as we await the final arrival of this Davidic ruler in the last days. We must, of course, admit that we live in a radically different era from that of God's people in Haggai's day; at the same time, however, our posture is similar as we await the final consummation of God's rule through Jesus.

---

26. S. Kierkegaard, *Either/Or: A Fragment of Life* (New York: Penguin, 1992), 49.

The coming of Christ means that we can live with far more hope than those who lived in Haggai's time. Jesus has come, fulfilling the prophetic hope of the Old Testament. This grants to us far more closure and certainty than those who longed for the coming messianic age (Heb. 12:39–40; 1 Peter 1:10–12). We continue to live, though, in faith as Haggai's audience of old, awaiting the ultimate shaking of the cosmos, the overthrow of all earthly power through the arrival of the divine warrior in the last days (Rev. 19).

Global warning. Although this passage functions as comfort for God's people, offering hope to a people dwarfed by great imperial forces, one should not miss its function as a warning to human authorities, that is, to "royal thrones" and the "power of the foreign kingdoms" propped up by "chariots and their drivers; horses and their riders." It is easy to spiritualize such references and limit application to forces of spiritual evil, the devil, and his minions. However, the prophet speaks here of literal political powers that will be overthrown by God's "shaking."

We cannot escape from the society in which we live. For the majority of Christians in our world today (most of whom live in the Two-Thirds World), following Christ's call and expanding his kingdom means suffering at the hands of dictators and their military forces. Such suffering is not evidence of the lack of fulfillment of Haggai 2:20–23, but rather marks the beginning of the end for oppressive political systems. Just as God established his kingdom through the suffering Christ, so he will do so through the suffering community of Christ.

It is easy for Christians who live in democracies to equate their political system with "the kingdom of God and of his Christ." However, even this human system must ultimately give way to the kingdom of God. This means that Christians who live within democratic nations must consider carefully the role of their governments within the global community and understand that this kind of political system leaves us accountable for the actions of our representatives, whether they are in Ottawa, Washington, or London. Such evaluation of our role within the global community must be followed by response in word and deed. Christians must have the courage within their nations not only to call their governments to account but also to function as salt and light throughout our culture, whether through political protest, social action, courageous proclamation, or faithful service.

The church worldwide must take seriously its role in proclaiming and enacting the anticipated and already-realized kingdom of Jesus. Haggai 2:20–23 gives us confidence to fulfill our calling as we entrust ourselves to the One who created and will one day shake the heavens and earth.

Local faithfulness with global implications. Haggai 2:10–23 as a whole, therefore, has ongoing relevance for those of us who live in anticipation of the coming age. It reminds us that God is concerned about our welfare and that he desires to bless us as we obey his kingdom demands. These verses focus attention especially on the perseverance of this community through the difficult and discouraging early moments of rebuilding. Such perseverance is exemplified in the foundation-laying ceremony of this passage. God promises blessing to this community that has persevered and in a similar way to those of us who persevere in kingdom activity today.

We often live our lives as Christians as though our everyday activities have no significance in the overall redemptive plan of God for our world. In our postmodern world of short attention spans and split-second communication we have lost patience with perseverance. To a community in the initial steps of rebuilding the temple, God declares his blessing for their perseverance and reveals that such perseverance will ultimately bear fruit in the transformation of the cosmos. Do we as the church realize this? Have we grasped the truth that God's plan is to work through us as his people to bring his rule and justice on earth? Do we live life with this confidence that as those who are the redeemed community in Christ we are invested with the authority of Christ to make disciples of all nations, bringing them into line with the demands of the sovereign Lord of the universe?

May God strengthen us to place kingdom activity in its proper perspective. The Israelite community in the Persian period was a community dwarfed by the power of the Persian empire, and today as we live in an increasingly secularized world, we may be tempted as the church to cower in submission, to live in fear. But we have even greater reasons to expect the cataclysmic upheaval of the cosmos, for the Zerubbabel who was to come has come and through his resurrection confirms the promise of old. Haggai calls us to embrace that cataclysm as our hope and to live faithfully until Zerubbabel's greatest son, our Lord Jesus Christ, returns.

Zechariah 1:1–6

IN THE EIGHTH month of the second year of Darius, the
word of the LORD came to the prophet Zechariah son of
Berekiah, the son of Iddo:
2"The LORD was very angry with your forefathers. 3There-
fore tell the people: This is what the LORD Almighty says:
'Return to me,' declares the LORD Almighty, 'and I will return
to you,' says the LORD Almighty. 4Do not be like your forefa-
thers, to whom the earlier prophets proclaimed: This is what
the LORD Almighty says: 'Turn from your evil ways and your
evil practices.' But they would not listen or pay attention to
me, declares the LORD. 5Where are your forefathers now? And
the prophets, do they live forever? 6But did not my words and
my decrees, which I commanded my servants the prophets,
overtake your forefathers?
"Then they repented and said, 'The LORD Almighty has
done to us what our ways and practices deserve, just as he
determined to do.'"

Original Meaning

THE BOOK OF Zechariah begins in similar fashion to Haggai by providing the date of the prophetic utterance and the identity of the prophetic voice. This date, with the day of the month omitted, is not as specific as one finds in either Haggai (Hag. 1:1, 15; 2:1, 10, 18, 20) or the rest of Zechariah 1–8 (cf. Zech. 1:7; 7:1).[1] This ambiguity makes it more difficult to identify a specific date for the prophetic utterance for it could be sometime in October-November 520 B.C.

This period follows an upheaval in the Persian empire. It was the time of transition from the reign of Cambyses (Cyrus's son) to Darius I, which may have raised hopes among the Jews that now Israel might be able to take its place as the seat of God's universal rule of the nations. But as the powerful Darius quelled rebellions across the empire, any such hopes were dashed. Into

1. Meyers and Meyers read too much into this omission by positing a rhetorical intention, linking it to the desire of an editor to join Haggai and Zechariah 1–8 together as a literary whole and to its central position in all the dates of the combined corpus; C. L. Meyers and E. M. Meyers, *Haggai, Zechariah 1–8: A New Translation with Introduction and Commentary* (AB 25b; Garden City, N.Y.: Doubleday, 1987), 90.

this context steps the prophet Zechariah, building on the work of Haggai, who had encouraged the people by revealing God's plan to establish his rule (Hag. 2:6–7, 20–23) and identified rebuilding the temple as the initial phase of this plan.[2] Zechariah takes restoration to another level by calling the people to covenant renewal alongside their rebuilding project.

The prophetic voice is not only placed in a temporal context, but also in a genealogical and sociological one. Zechariah is identified as the son of Berekiah, the son of Iddo. As indicated in our introduction (see Original Meaning section), Zechariah apparently comes from a priestly family and functions as temple prophet. His lineage opens a window into the setting of this initial pericope. Whereas some have linked this book, along with that of Haggai, to the dedication of the temple in 515 B.C., this does not do justice to its content.[3] Although Zechariah's message is connected to the rebuilding of the temple, this is not his main focus. He expands his message beyond the temple to the city as a whole and beyond physical rebuilding to moral renewal. He sets this tone from the outset in this initial section.

Rather than the dedication of the rebuilt temple, Zechariah 1–8 displays links to a tradition of prayer that arises out of the ashes of the exilic experience in response to the agenda of both Moses and Solomon.[4] This kind of prayer, which exerts its influence on Jewish liturgical practice throughout the intertestamental period, has been tagged *penitential prayer*, defined in the following way: "a direct address to God in which an individual or group confesses sins and petitions for forgiveness. Frequently, the petitioner hopes that the prayer will also be the first step toward removing the problems facing the community or the petitioner."[5]

Penitential prayer arises from the agenda for renewal presented in the blessings and curses of the Torah (Lev. 26; Deut. 28–30) and Solomon's prayer of dedication for the temple (1 Kings 8). Deuteronomy 30 anticipates life for Israel after disobedience has resulted in the curse of exile. Moses presents a return to God as essential to begin the process of restoration. However, it is

---

2. All of the dates in Haggai precede those in Zechariah, except for those in Hag. 2:10–23, which occur in the month after the first date in Zec. 1:1, but two months prior to the second date in Zec 1:7.

3. See M. J. Boda, "Zechariah: Master Mason or Penitential Prophet," in *Yahwism After the Exile: Perspectives on Israelite Religion in the Persian Era*, ed. B. Becking and R. Albertz (Studies in Theology and Religion 5; Assen: Royal Van Gorcum, 2002), 49–69.

4. See ibid.; see also R. A. Werline, *Penitential Prayer in Second Temple Judaism: The Development of a Religious Institution* (SBLEJL 13; Atlanta: Scholars Press, 1998); M. J. Boda, *Praying the Tradition: The Origin and Use of Tradition in Nehemiah 9* (BZAW 277; Berlin: de Gruyter, 1999); R. J. Bautch, *Developments in Genre Between Post-Exilic Penitential Prayers and the Psalms of Communal Lament* (SBLABS; Atlanta: Society of Biblical Literature, 2003).

5. Werline, *Penitential Prayer*, 2.

Leviticus 26 that provides the specific way in which one displays such a return to Yahweh: confession of one's sin along with the sins of previous generations. Moreover, as Solomon anticipates life for future generations in exile, he sets an agenda for renewal that begins with confession (1 Kings 8:46–51).

This agenda for renewal is evident in the biblical penitential prayers of Ezra 9; Nehemiah 1 and 9; Psalm 6; and Daniel 9. Here one finds a group of prayers with similar vocabulary, motifs, and attendant actions (signs of lament and contrition like fasting, sackcloth, dust on the head, weeping).[6] These prayers were seen as essential to bring an end to the Exile and to begin the restoration. This is particularly noticeable in Daniel 9, when Daniel realizes that the time is nearing for the end of the exilic seventy-year period. His penitential prayer is evidence that the community felt this was the first step in inaugurating the new age.

It is interesting that these prayers display a close affinity with the prophetic message presented in Zechariah 1:1–6; 7–8. In penitential prayers, one finds that the former generation ("fathers"; Ezra 9:7; Neh. 1:6; 9:2, 9, 16, 23, 32, 34, 36; Ps. 106:6, 7; Dan. 9:6, 8, 16), who did not listen to the prophets ("my servants"; Ezra 9:11; Neh. 9:26–30; Dan. 9:6, 10), are attacked, and the present generation responds by confessing their culpability (Ezra 9:6, 7, 13; Neh. 1:6 [2x]; 9:2, 29, 33, 37; Ps. 106:6, 43; Dan. 9:5, 8, 11, 13, 15, 16, 20) while affirming Yahweh's justice (Ezra 9:15; Neh. 9:33; Dan. 9:7, 9, 15). In particular, phrases found in one of these prayers (Neh. 9) are limited almost exclusively to Zechariah 1:1–6; 7–8.[7] In addition, Zechariah 7–8 comments on the exilic liturgical cycle of fasting, seeking to shape the agenda for this cycle. Fasting is also a common feature in the penitential prayer tradition.

By the time of Ezra and Nehemiah the penitential prayer tradition is clearly associated with the priests. Zechariah, arising out of the priestly context as a prophetic voice, is a good candidate to set the agenda for true repentance to accompany such liturgical acts of penitence. As a cultic prophet his messages may constitute God's response to such acts of contrition and function as shapers of appropriate penitence to bring restoration for God's people.[8]

---

6. H. Gunkel and J. Begrich (*Introduction to Psalms: The Genres of the Religious Lyric of Israel* [Mercer Library of Biblical Studies; Macon, Ga.: Mercer Univ. Press, 1998], 82–85) and E. Lipinski (*La liturgie pénitentielle dans la Bible*; vol. 52, *Lectio divina* [Paris: Les éditions du Cerf, 1969], 27–35) linked these to days of fasting and lament in the preexilic times.

7. Neh. 9:29 = Zech. 7:11 (stubbornly they turned their backs); Neh. 9:30 = Zech. 7:12 (by his Spirit through the earlier prophets); Neh. 9:34 = Zech. 1:4; 7:11 (refused to pay attention); Neh. 9:35 = Zech. 1:4, 6 (turn from your evil ways).

8. Applegate also notes the similarity between the question of the angel of the Lord in Zech. 1:12 and "the sort of lament an individual or community might bring to a prophet to seek the Lord's answer"; J. Applegate, "Jeremiah and the Seventy Years in the Hebrew Bible," in *The Book of Jeremiah and Its Reception; Le livre de Jérémie et sa réception*, ed. A. H. W. Curtis and T. Römer (BETL 128; Leuven: University, 1997), 103; cf. M. J. Boda, "From Complaint to Contrition: Peering Through the Liturgical Window of Jer 14,1–15,4," *ZAW* 113 (2001): 186–97.

An initial read through 1:2–6 may cause some confusion. In the short space of five verses, one finds multiple layers of quoted material: God speaks to Zechariah, telling him to declare to the present generation a message that includes a quotation of former prophets who were relaying a message from God to a former generation. Although difficult at points to follow, it reflects a rhetorical trend in later prophecy in which Yahweh is emphasized as the source of the prophetic speech, even if that is at the expense of flow.[9]

Verse 6b has presented some confusion. The NIV has placed this section in quotation marks, reflecting a common opinion that it refers to the former generation's response to the prophets' message. This is based on the fact that the section immediately preceding this phrase (1:6a) refers to the "forefathers" and the content of the speech is "our ways and practices."[10] In this view 1:6b is a continuation of the speech of Yahweh. Others see 1:6b as referring to the generation in Zechariah's time, an interpretation produced by either emending the text in 1:6a to read "you" instead of "your fathers" or by reading the verbs in 1:6b as commands ("repent and say") instead of statements ("they repented and said").[11]

But one does not need to introduce emendations in the Hebrew text to identify 1:6b with Zechariah's generation, for on rhetorical and form-critical grounds this is most certainly the case. (1) The point of the argument in 1:4–6a is that the former generation has been punished according to God's righteous judgment delivered to them by the former prophets. To suggest that this generation "repented" moves in an opposite direction to the assertion of the message. The words of God "overtook" the rebellious generation, and that generation is now dead.

(2) The Hebrew penitential prayer tradition in the Babylonian and Persian periods reveals a view of sin that is intergenerational. Later generations regularly confess the sins of former generations (Ezra 9:7; Neh. 1:6; 9:2; Dan. 9:16).[12] Zechariah 1:6b is thus a report of the reaction of the people to Zechariah's initial message and picks up the narrative thread that begins in 1:1. It is similar to the flow of Haggai 1:1–15, which describes the prophetic message followed by a narrative overview of the response of the people.

Zechariah 1:2 sets the context for the prophetic message with a look to the past, expressing God's anger (*qaṣap*) towards the former generation. This

9. Cf. M. J. Boda, "Haggai: Master Rhetorician," *TynBul* 51 (2000): 295–304. In contrast to Haggai, Zechariah is deeply conscious of his link to the prophetic tradition of old (compare Zech. 1:4–6 with 7:7, 12).

10. D. L. Petersen, *Haggai and Zechariah 1–8: A Commentary* (OTL; London: SCM, 1984), 110.

11. For the first view see *BHS*; for the second see W. Rudolph, *Haggai, Sacharja 1–8, Sacharja 9–14, Maleachi* (KAT 13; Gütersloh: Mohn, 1976).

12. See Boda (*Praying the Tradition*, 47–54) for this feature and its theological foundation.

is explained in more detail in 1:4–6a and is a negative example for Zechariah's contemporaries to avoid. Verse 3 then looks to the future, identifying the goal of this prophetic message, which has both a human (1:6b) and divine (1:7–2:13) element, using the same verb for both.

Detailed Analysis

GOD BEGINS HIS MESSAGE for the present generation by looking to the past. The text builds up Hebrew words to express the intensity of his anger toward the former generation.[13] Yahweh's anger is found at many points in the Old Testament.[14] Its connection to God reveals that anger is not evil in and of itself. At its core, God's anger reveals his passion that arises out of and protects his holy character. It is not surprising that the majority of references to that anger are found in the context of the covenant—in particular, the breaking of the covenant. The covenant is the vehicle of relationship between a holy God and his people. Its demands express his holy character and denote the standard required of the community who would relate to this holy God.

Expressions of God's anger in the biblical text nearly always lead to consequences in the lives of humans, usually some form of disciplinary action. Closely related to the covenant relationship between God and his people, his anger often expresses his care for that relationship, whether that lies in disciplining his people or protecting them from foreign nations. In some cases it is used as a vehicle of divine disclosure to encourage the people or to warn those opposed to his purposes.

This use of an emotive relational term (*qaṣap*) to speak of his punitive destruction of the land and exile of the people reminds Zechariah's generation of the core values that define the Exile and ultimately the restoration for which they long. God is a covenantal God, that is, a relational God, and he desires exclusivity and devotion in his relationship with his people. The past generation disregarded this relationship, even when Yahweh sent his messengers to remind them, as we will soon hear in 1:4–6a.

One does not usually expect such a statement at the outset of a speech. It appears on the surface to be overtly negative. However, the great paradox of the revelation of God's wrath in the Old Testament is that it is often juxtaposed with and an opportunity for an expression of grace: ". . . the working out of God's wrath is tempered by his grace and mercy. In fact, it is in the midst of wrath that God may reveal his mercy (Hab. 3:2), manifesting and

---

13. In Heb. one way of expressing intensity is to repeat a finite verb with the same root in the infinitive or a nominal version of that root.

14. B. E. Baloian, *Anger in the Old Testament* (American University Studies Series VII, Theology and Religion 99; New York: Lang, 1992).

bestowing his grace upon guilty sinners (Gen. 3:15)."[15] It is significant that when the prophets use God's anger, they often do so in the context of the shortness of that anger, promising mercy and assistance (Isa. 57:16; 64:4, 8; Zech. 1:15).[16] Beginning with a reference to God's anger with the former generation thus produces in the original readers the expectation that there will be a turn to something new, that the mercy of God is imminent.

This opportunity for a transformation in the relationship occurs as God calls Zechariah's generation to turn to him, so that he may turn to them. Although this turning surely has moral implications as seen in 1:4 ("turn from your evil ways"), at the outset it is defined primarily in relational terms: "Return to me."[17] This reflects the agenda for renewal after exile laid out in Deuteronomy 30:2. Key to restoration after the discipline of the Exile is a return to Yahweh.

God promises to reciprocate by returning to them. Although Deuteronomy 30 does use the same verb (*šwb*, "return") to describe God's response to the people's turning, it is used to speak of restoration of one's fortunes rather than a return of God to his people as in Zechariah 1. With God as subject, this verb can refer to the restoration of something (as Deut. 30), to God's turning from an intended purpose (usually relenting from anger; Num. 25:4; Deut. 13:17; Josh. 7:26; 2 Kings 23:26; Isa. 5:25; Jonah 3:9), to rewarding someone (2 Sam. 22:21, 25), or to returning with his presence to his people (Num. 10:36; Isa. 52:8; 63:17). It is this latter sense that Zechariah has in mind in chapter 1, as is typical elsewhere in this book (Zech. 1:16; 8:3). God offers to return with his presence to his people, the presence and glory that abandoned them in Ezekiel 10 and was promised to return in Ezekiel 43.

Having identified the expected goal of this prophetic message through the imperative "return," the prophet fills out further the negative example of the former generations, which is to be avoided (1:4–6a). The phrase "earlier prophets" refers to the prophets of the preexilic period in general but draws from Jeremiah in particular (cf. Jer. 7:3, 5; 11:8; 23:22; 25:5; 35:15).[18] This summary of Jeremiah's message places Zechariah securely in the same line as the earlier prophets, stressing continuity in Yahweh's message to his people. At the same time it reminds the people that they must heed this message because the prophetic word had dire consequences.

This quotation defines further the nature of the "return" introduced in 1:3. This return, which is relational at its core, has an important ethical

---

15. Gerard Van Groningen, "קָצַף," *TWOT*, § 2058, 2:808.

16. See *TLOT*, 3:1158.

17. See also Mal. 3:7, where there is no disjuncture between the personal, relational, and the ethical.

18. See Boda, "Penitential Prophet," 49–69.

dimension. The actions of the people, described by using a regular word pair in Hebrew prophetic literature ("ways . . . practices [deeds]") denotes their entire way of life (Jer. 4:18; 17:10; 32:19; Hos. 4:9; 12:3). These actions are not divorced from internal motivations of the heart as can be seen in Jeremiah's combination of internal and external in Jeremiah 17:10: "I the LORD search the heart and examine the mind, to reward a man according to his conduct, according to what his deeds deserve."

In the end, however, this call to ethical purity is kept in relational terms in Zechariah 1:4 as God sadly reports: "They would not listen or pay attention to me." Additionally, the preposition accompanying the term "turn/return" (both *šwb*) is different. In 1:3 it was "to"; now in 1:4 it is "from." This identifies a dual nature to the kind of "turning" that God is describing: It involves a turning *from* one thing and a turning *to* something else. In this case, the people are turning from their lifestyle of evil to their God in covenant relationship.

In 1:5 Zechariah uses a series of rhetorical questions to outline the result of ignoring the prophetic message. This technique forces the original audience to reflect deeply on the negative example of the former generation and on how they will respond to the same message of the prophets in their generation.

The point of the rhetorical questions is to contrast the nature of human existence with the nature of God's word. The first two questions remind the people that human existence is ephemeral, for the disobedient generation had died, many punished with the curses brought on by their rebellion. Even the prophets who spoke God's word display the passing nature of human existence. The one constant throughout the ages is God's word, which must be heeded when it is delivered by the prophets. The word "overtake" (Hiphil of *nśg*) is used often in contexts describing a battle in which one army or person pursues another (1 Sam. 30:8; 2 Kings 25:5; Ps. 7:5; 18:37). This is drawn into the covenant context in Deuteronomy 28:2, 15, 45, where Yahweh defines the blessings and curses that are essential to the covenant relationship (cf. Jer. 42:16).

The nouns "words" and "decrees" (*dabar/ḥoq*) join a range of terms that refer in general to the requirements of the covenant made with Israel on Sinai (also *miṣwah, torah, mišpaṭ*). This range includes not only the specific requirements of individual commands but also the blessings and curses that provide accountability for the relationship. It is the covenant at Sinai that is picked up by the prophetic movement and used as the standard for God's people (2 Kings 17:13).

Zechariah's reflection on the past with the subtle yet powerful depiction of the consequences of disobedience has its desired effect on his generation in 1:6b. The translation "repented" in the NIV obscures the connection with the previous verses, for the Hebrew word underlying this translation (*šwb*) is the same one used in the imperatives in 1:3–4 ("return"). The prophet's immediate audience reflects the agenda for renewal spelled out in Deuteronomy 30 in order to bring restoration.

The specifics of this "turning to God" in 1:6b are not revealed. Many have concluded that it refers to rebuilding the temple and is thus linked to the work of Haggai. But this does not appear to be the case.[19] Zechariah's view of "turning" is first of all relational (see 1:3), and when this is fleshed out further, it is ethical in nature (1:5; 7:9–10). Although his ministry is intimately related to the temple, it seems to build on the foundation of Haggai and move the agenda a step further, focusing more attention on the core covenant values of relationship and ethics.

The narrative description of the people's response is followed by the declaration of the people. At first sight this may seem inappropriate as an expression of one's "turning" to God. However, an important feature in the penitential prayer tradition so influential in this period is the affirmation that the hardship that has entered their lives is a result of the discipline of God and that this discipline is just. Note, for example, Nehemiah 9:33: "In all that has happened to us, you have been just; you have acted faithfully, while we did wrong" (cf. Dan. 9:7, 14; Ezra 9:15).

The people, in other words, agree that the covenant curses did overtake the people and that this was Yahweh's purpose. This purpose is described by the Hebrew verb *zmm* ("determined"), which occurs elsewhere in the Hebrew Bible with God as its subject, usually with the negative connotation of punishment (Jer. 4:28; 51:12; Lam. 2:17). However, Zechariah 8:14–15 reveals that Zechariah will proclaim the other side of God's purpose. For a penitent people, God's purposes are positive.

The people reflect another feature of the penitential prayer tradition when they refer to the sins of the past generations as their own sins (cf. Ezra 9; Neh. 1; 9; Dan. 9). They understand that their lives are intimately connected to this former generation that rebelled against God's word and received his discipline. Renewal begins by turning away from the rebellious heritage that has preceded them. The agenda for this feature in the penitential prayer tradition can be traced to the words of Moses reflecting on the future rebellion of God's people (Lev. 26:39–40), where he tells them that they will experience discipline because of their sins and those of former generations and that renewal begins with confessing their sins and those of former generations. Verse 6b, then, represents a response to this agenda of Moses

19. Ibid.

in Leviticus 26, along with Deuteronomy 30, which emphasizes the need to return to God.

Zechariah 1:1–6 introduces us to the book of Zechariah as a whole. As with Haggai, it begins with a people who need renewal, and in like manner the people respond to the message. This does not mean that there are not issues remaining to be dealt with, but it does offer, at the outset, a positive picture of a community displaying attitudes and actions contrasting those of rebellious former generations. This fulfills the human side of the equation introduced in 1:3; the people display a return to relationship with Yahweh. Zechariah's visions will introduce the divine dimension of this equation as we move from the earthly context with its classical prophetic forms into the otherworldly context of night visions.

Bridging Contexts

THE PROPHETIC MESSAGE of these six verses is a message for the church today. Assuredly it speaks to a specific generation at a particular period in the long history of the community of God. But this community has found its fulfillment in the church (see the introduction, Bridging Contexts section), a fact that makes this passage applicable to Christians today.

Repentance. The book of Zechariah begins with an invitation to the Persian period community to return to God. They are also reminded of the dire consequences that followed the rejection of this message in past generations. Zechariah's generation takes the first step toward the resolution of the covenant crisis through a repentance characterized by confession of sin and affirmation of God's justice.[20]

This same message of repentance will reverberate throughout the ongoing "exile" of God's people in the centuries that follow as they long for the completion of the restoration program initiated in the early Persian period.[21] It is not surprising, then, to find that this message of repentance launches the redemptive program of God in the Gospels, where it appears on the lips of the prophetic figure John the Baptist (Matt. 3:2, 8, 11; Mark 1:4, 5; Luke 3:3). He was the voice preparing the way for the return of Yahweh and the release of his people from exile. John's baptism was a baptism of repentance (Matt. 3:11; Mark 1:4; Acts 13:24; 19:4). When Jesus underwent this baptism, he was not admitting sin but rather functioning as representative Israelite, symbolically confessing the sins of the nation and being cleansed by the waters.

20. See ibid.; also M. J. Boda, "The Priceless Gain of Penitence: From Communal Lament to Penitential Prayer in the 'Exilic' Liturgy of Israel," *HBT* 25 (2003): 51–75.

21. See Werline's *Penitential Prayer* for the use of penitential prayer in this period.

This theme of repentance was also a feature in the preaching of Jesus (Matt. 4:17; 11:20–21; Luke 5:32; 13:3, 5; 15:7, 10). When he sent his disciples out to preach and teach, the Gospel writer tells us that repentance was also their theme (Mark 6:12). This explains why the message of repentance was an essential component in the proclamation of the gospel by the early church (Acts 2:38; 3:19; 5:31; 8:22; 11:18; 17:30; 20:21; 26:20; Rom. 2:4; 2 Cor. 7:9–10; 12:21; 2 Tim. 2:25; Heb. 6:1, 6; 2 Peter 3:9; Rev. 2:5, 16, 21, 22; 3:3, 19; 9:20, 21; 16:9, 11).

Zechariah's call to repentance is thus applicable to Christians today. It is a call to all humanity to return to the One who created us. It also reminds those who have entered into covenant relationship that they should live a life of repentance, turning to God in relationship and forsaking all affections and actions that threaten that relationship.

Generational issues. For Zechariah's generation repentance was not an individual issue; it was corporate and generational. The Persian period community lived with the consequences of the disobedience of early generations, including loss of political independence, payment of taxes to a foreign overlord, and a significant decrease in population. Their repentance not only expresses their desire not to continue in the sinful tradition of past generations, but it is also on behalf of the offenses of a generation now long dead.

As already noted, this view of intergenerational guilt is founded on the instruction of Moses in connection with the discipline of the people through exile (see Lev. 26:39–42):[22]

> Those of you who are left will waste away in the lands of their enemies because of their sins; also because of their fathers' sins they will waste away.
>
> But if they will confess their sins and the sins of their fathers—their treachery against me and their hostility towards me, which made me hostile toward them so that I sent them into the land of their enemies—then when their uncircumcised hearts are humbled and they pay for their sin, I will remember my covenant with Jacob and my covenant with Isaac and my covenant with Abraham, and I will remember the land.

This same approach to guilt appears in 2 Kings 21:10–16, where Manasseh's violation of God's covenant through idolatry and injustice incites God's judgment of his people, promising to destroy Jerusalem and exile his

22. Also note the repeated description of God as One who punishes to the third and fourth generation (Ex. 20:5; 34:7; Num. 14:18; Deut. 5:9); on this see esp. J. S. Kaminsky, *Corporate Responsibility in the Hebrew Bible* (JSOTSup 196; Sheffield: Sheffield Academic Press, 1995).

people. Even after Josiah's national renewal, the writer of Kings reminds us: "Nevertheless, the LORD did not turn away from the heat of his fierce anger, which burned against Judah because of all that Manasseh had done to provoke him to anger" (2 Kings 23:26). Moreover, when Jehoiakim's kingdom is attacked by raiders, the writer of Kings again comments: "Surely these things happened to Judah according to the LORD's command, in order to remove them from his presence because of the sins of Manasseh and all he had done" (24:3).

This approach to sin and guilt, with its cumulative and intergenerational character, seems to be at odds with another stream of Old Testament theology represented in Jeremiah, Ezekiel, and Chronicles. Ezekiel and Jeremiah both cite a proverb circulating among the people:

> The fathers have eaten sour grapes,
> and the children's teeth are set on edge. (Jer. 31:29; cf. Ezek. 18:2)

Simply put, the exiles are blaming a past generation for their present predicament.

Ezekiel counters this theological position first by stating that "the soul who sins is the one who will die" (Ezek. 18:4), and then by providing three scenarios that support this statement. These scenarios trace three generations of a family—the first righteous, the second wicked, and the third righteous. The righteous generations will live while the wicked one will die. Furthermore, he claims, "the son will not share the guilt of the father, nor will the father share the guilt of the son. The righteousness of the righteous man will be credited to him, and the wickedness of the wicked will be charged against him" (18:20). Although Jeremiah's response is not as elaborate as Ezekiel's, the message is the same: "Everyone will die for his own sin; whoever eats sour grapes—his own teeth will be set on edge" (Jer. 31:30).

The books of Chronicles build on this view of sin and guilt and show how it was operative throughout the history of Judah. The principle is displayed most vividly in the Chronicler's rendition of God's word to Solomon at the dedication of the temple: "If my people, who are called by my name, will humble themselves and pray and seek my face and turn from their wicked ways, then will I hear from heaven and will forgive their sin and will heal their land" (2 Chron. 7:14). In Chronicles those who humbly pray, seek, and turn are those who prosper and are blessed; those who do not are cursed. These books show both the potential of each generation to start afresh and the role that penitence plays in this new beginning.[23]

---

23. See esp. the example of Manasseh in 2 Chron. 33.

How do we reconcile these two streams of Old Testament theology? One way of resolving them is to see in Jeremiah, Ezekiel, and Chronicles the foundation of a New Testament theology of individual responsibility and faith that transcends the approach of Leviticus and Kings. But is this the case?

A careful look at Leviticus 26 reveals how Moses declares that the people will waste away not only, yet not primarily, because of the sins of their fathers, but because of *their own sins* (26:39). It is obvious that they are in the position of exile because of the sins of a former generation (this is merely cause and effect), but the fact that they are remaining in exile is due to their own sins. Furthermore, he calls them to confess *their sins* before he calls them to confess the sins of their fathers (26:40).

Similarly, in 1–2 Kings the generations that were actually punished were never innocent themselves but rather culpable. Most likely the proverbial saying circulating among the people was actually a twisting of the kind of theology underlying Leviticus 26 and 1–2 Kings in order to divert attention from the disobedience of the present generation. In the end, then, we are still left with a view of sin and guilt that has intergenerational implications. But the cycle of guilt and sin can be broken within a generation through repentance and obedience.

This is a difficult concept for those of us who have grown up in the West to grasp, with our individualistic approach to life and spirituality. The penitential prayer tradition in the Old Testament suggests that we are situated within a broader community and that our repentance is not merely the exercise of isolated individuals, but rather of people positioned within a community with a heritage.

Anger of God. One cannot hide the emphasis on God's anger in this passage. Clearly Yahweh is "very angry," and this anger led to severe discipline of an earlier generation because they refused to respond. For many Christians this focus on God's wrath is evidence of a serious disjuncture between the Old and New Testaments. In the former God is presented as a God of wrath and judgment, while in the latter he is a God of love and forgiveness. If this presupposition is left unchallenged, it will be difficult to appropriate Zechariah 1:1–6 for the church today.

One cannot, of course, avoid many passages in the Old Testament that highlight God's wrath in the face of sin both inside and outside of Israel. But this is not the focus of the Old Testament witness. Interestingly, in the Old Testament the two main theological creedal traditions focus greatest attention on the gracious acts of God rather than his discipline.[24]

The majority of the instances of the narrative creed of Israel rehearse the redemptive acts of God (e.g., Deut. 6; 26; Josh. 24; 1 Sam. 12:8; Ps. 78; 105;

24. See Boda, "Priceless Gain," 51–75.

106; 135; 136; Neh. 9; Jer. 32; Ezek. 20), and the consistent element among these is the declaration of God's grace in the Exodus and Conquest. And in the other theological creedal tradition in the Old Testament, the character creed of Israel (e.g., Ex. 34; Num. 14; Neh. 9; Ps. 86; 103; 111; 145; Joel 2; Jonah 4; Nah. 1), the main focus is on the grace of God—the One who is merciful, gracious, slow to anger and abounding in steadfast love and faithfulness. Thus, it is a caricature to designate the Old Testament as the testament of wrath or judgment, for in it we find a revelation of God's grace that lays the foundation for the New Testament theology of salvation.

Likewise, the New Testament is not bereft of wrath and judgment. A quick look at Christ's teaching on the sheep and the goats in Matthew 25, his seven woes against the teachers of the law and the Pharisees in Matthew 23, the revelation of the wrath of God in Romans 1, or the expectation of final judgement in Revelation reminds us of the great continuity between the two testaments.

The same God lies behind both Old and New Testaments, and this means that we must take seriously his revelation through Zechariah in 1:1–6. Indeed, the Incarnation has brought this teaching to a new level, but not to a level where it can be set aside. Rather, the response to this prophetic message is more attractive today because God has come in human flesh, and it is possible because of the coming of the Spirit to indwell the community of God.

Contemporary Significance

REPENTANCE AS RELATIONSHIP. There is little question that within my family Christmas was the most anticipated season of the year. With seven children the opening of gifts was a monumental enterprise and took a good portion of Christmas morning. Each year there was one gift that arrived from my grandparents who lived far away in New Jersey: a large box of salt water taffy. I'm sure it produced pleasant childhood memories for my mother who had grown up on the Jersey shore, but for her Canadian children, each with a sweet tooth, it was the gift that kept on giving well into the new year.

Of course, there was a rule associated with the consumption of this delicacy: We could only take one each day. By mid-January the box was empty of its contents, and soon everyone had forgotten about taffy. That was until one day I returned from grade school and was invited into my mother's bedroom for a little chat. On her bed was a plastic bag filled with a multitude of wrappings that had once encased salt water taffy, obviously well beyond one child's allotment.

I knew where mom had found the bag. Over the Christmas holidays I had eaten well beyond my ration, and in order to conceal my deceit I had stuffed them in a bag behind the drawer in my dresser. My mother, who was extremely tidy, had taken out that drawer to clean the dust and discovered my little hiding place.

As I raised my surprised eyes from the bag on the bed, they met the sad eyes of my mother. She asked me to sit down on the bed and then sadly told me that it wasn't the salt water taffy that bothered her, but rather the fact that I had deceived her. My sensitive heart broke; I wept and asked her forgiveness. I have never forgotten this moment, because in it I think I came to the realization that sin is far more an issue of relationship than one of behavior. Surely my sinful actions could not be ignored, but they threatened my relationship with my mother, which was a far greater concern.

Biblical repentance is a matter of turning *to* as well as turning *from*, an abandonment into the arms of a God passionate for relationship. Biblical repentance is not just focused on behavioral patterns, but more importantly, more fundamentally on relational patterns: someone to love, not just some way to act. By reorienting our perspective on sin and repentance, we do not reduce but enhance the call to purity and holiness. Set in this covenantal context we are encouraged to live faithfully before God in all areas of life, not just in areas prescribed in our limited list of vices and virtues.

Repentance as entrance to and way of life. Its prominence in the message of the early church reveals that repentance is key at the outset of our Christian experience. As we declare the gospel, we must echo the message of Christ and the disciples, calling people to turn from their sin and turn to their Creator in faithful relationship. During the 1980s and continuing until today, a debate has raged within evangelicalism between those who accentuate the passive character of the faith relationship and those who emphasize the active character of this relationship.[25] For the former, faith alone is required of the believer. The Christian life is initiated by a response to Christ as our Savior, through whom we receive forgiveness of our sin and an invitation to live in relationship with our Creator. Advocates of the active character of this relationship, by contrast, emphasize that Christ cannot be discovered as Savior without also being acknowledged as Lord, for Christ's own call to his generation always emphasized the cost of discipleship.

This debate, however, polarized two essential themes in Christian theology that cannot and should not be treated as separate. Prophecies of the new covenant in Jeremiah and Ezekiel reveal to us the important principle

25. The two key figures were originally J. F. MacArthur, *The Gospel According to Jesus* (Grand Rapids: Zondervan, 1988), and Z. C. Hodges, *Absolutely Free! A Biblical Reply to Lordship Salvation* (Grand Rapids: Zondervan, 1989). However, see more recently C. C. Bing, *Lordship Salvation: A Biblical Evaluation and Response* (Burleson, Tex.: Grace Life, 1992), and M. Horton, ed., *Christ the Lord: The Reformation and Lordship Salvation* (Grand Rapids: Baker, 1992).

that God did not abandon his purpose to create a holy nation who would walk in obedience. However, it is clear that this purpose would be realized through a renewed covenant by a great divine work that would transform his people (Jer. 31:31–34; Ezek. 36:24–32; 37:1–14, 24). In this way, the enduring message is a call to penitence and holiness, but this is accomplished only through the miraculous work of the Spirit of God made possible by the passion of Christ. Such a balance is expressed so beautifully by the apostle Paul: "Therefore, my dear friends, as you have always obeyed—not only in my presence, but now much more in my absence—continue to work out your salvation with fear and trembling, for it is God who works in you to will and to act according to his good purpose" (Phil. 2:12–13).

The apostle Paul makes clear that the message of repentance is not restricted to the initial phase in our Christian walk. As Gordon Smith has written, "true conversion leads us to be always conscious of sin and our need to turn from it. Repentance is a strand in our conversion that remains a continuing and vital element of the spiritual life. For without its abiding presence, there is no transformation."[26] With the proclivity to turn away from our Creator and to follow other gods, repentance is the constant turning to God in faithful relationship.

In light of this, Christian communities can encourage repentance among their adherents through communal rhythms of repentance. In reaction to medieval abuses in the penance system of the Roman Catholic church, Protestant traditions have generally rejected communal rites of penitence. Yet there seems to be evidence of the confession of sin to fellow believers in the New Testament (Acts 19:18; James 5:16; 1 John 1:8–10). This can happen in private settings with fellow believers, but also in public contexts as the community gathers together for worship. It means opportunity for oral expressions of penitence, but also time for private confession. An opportune time is prior to the reception of the Lord's Supper.

Confession. The sin described in Zechariah 1:1–6 is linked to God's discipline of his rebellious nation in 587 B.C. This context is important as we consider the action and declaration of the people in 1:6b. An important step in the life of the nation was the realization that the destruction of Jerusalem was justified in light of their rebellion against God.[27] This justification of God here is an admission that the people's behavior was indeed sinful and that God's response was appropriate in light of the covenant.

Such a response to God's discipline in our lives is an appropriate model for Christians today. Although not all trials and tribulations that we experience

---

26. G. T. Smith, *Beginning Well: Christian Conversion and Authentic Transformation* (Downers Grove, Ill.: InterVarsity Press, 2001), 167.

27. See Boda, "Priceless Gain," 51–75.

can be linked to sinful patterns in our lives, there are times when God disciplines us in order to purify our motives and actions.[28] He does this because of his intense love for us—as the writer of Hebrews says, as a father loves his children (Heb. 12:1–17). When we become conscious of sin in our lives, the doorway to repentance is thus the admission that we have sinned and that God has been justified in his discipline in our lives. This may seem like a small step, but repentance is often thwarted by proud refusal to admit our rebellion—the key to the justification of God's discipline. The prayer of Psalm 51:3–4 echoes the theme of Zechariah 1:6b:

> For I know my transgressions,
>   and my sin is always before me.
> Against you, you only, have I sinned
>   and done what is evil in your sight,
> so that you are proved right when you speak
>   and justified when you judge.

One can hardly miss the intimate link between the admission of sin and the justification of God through the words "so that" in Psalm 51:4.

In similar fashion the thanksgiving for forgiveness in Psalm 32:3–5 encourages acknowledgment of sin as essential to forgiveness:

> When I kept silent,
>   my bones wasted away
>   through my groaning all day long.
> For day and night
>   your hand was heavy upon me;
> my strength was sapped
>   as in the heat of summer.
> Then I acknowledged my sin to you
>   and did not cover up my iniquity.
> I said, "I will confess
>   my transgressions to the LORD"—
> and you forgave
>   the guilt of my sin.

A similar expression on the communal level can be found in the book of Lamentations.[29] In the central composition in chapter 3, the speaker considers

---

28. See the summary of Walter Kaiser's survey of the biblical theology of suffering in the Bridging Contexts Section of Hag. 1:1–11. Here we are speaking only of educational/disciplinary suffering.

29. Boda, "Priceless Gain," 51–75.

suffering as a result of sin and invites the community to examination, repentance, and confession:

> Why should any living man complain
> when punished for his sins?
> Let us examine our ways and test them,
> and let us return to the LORD.
> Let us lift up our hearts and our hands
> to God in heaven, and say:
> "We have sinned and rebelled. . . ." (Lam. 3:39–42)

This is an important theological step forward in Israel's liturgical responses to the Exile, which finds full expression in the many penitential prayers of the Persian period (Ezra 9; Neh. 1 and 9; Dan. 9). They provide patterns for communal expression of penitence for the church today (see Zech. 12:1–13:6).

Communal dimensions. Zechariah 1:1–6 highlights the communal dimension of repentance; that is, repentance is not just a matter between individuals and God but also between communities and God. The sin of his chosen community was far more than the accumulated rebellion of individuals; it had a sociological dimension that he sought to cleanse through exile. The community had strayed far from God, transgressing the call to love the Lord their God with all their hearts, souls, and minds and to love their neighbors as themselves. This was reflected in the social institutions of their community: the family and home, the priesthood and temple, and the monarchy and palace. Repentance and confession were thus not only for the individual members of this community but also for the community as a corporate and historical entity.

The response of the people encourages the church today to provide opportunity for repentance and confession for the community as a whole. Churches should build into their worship calendars not only times of celebration, but also seasons of reflection and repentance. I know one church that sets aside a week each year for sacred assembly in which they gather as a community for deep reflection, honest repentance, and vibrant celebration (using the model of Neh. 9). This creates a rhythm within the community that has an impact on the individual members, while forcing the community to deal with corporate issues.

Church leadership should take time to reflect on the ways the corporate ethos and practice of the church fall short of God's ideal and may have damaged people or groups of people under their care. When a friend of mine assumed the leadership of a church, he soon discovered, when attempting to hire a new staff member, that there was serious dysfunction in the relationship between the pastors and elders of the church. Rather than forging ahead with the process, he wisely ceased the search and commenced prayerful reflection with the elders and staff on the causes of the dysfunction. This period of reflection led them to recognize key corporate issues that had developed in the church. The end result was public teaching on these issues and their resolution, thus providing a foundation for the church to grow and prosper.

Purpose of God. An important theme throughout 1:1–6 is the unyielding purpose of God. In the history of Israel God expressed this purpose initially through his prophetic words to his community and ultimately through his sovereign actions in history in the destruction and exile of Judah. The haunting questions of verse 6 remind us of God's pursuit of his purposes as his words "overtake" the earlier generation. So also the confession of the people later in this verse is a reminder of his determination ("just as he determined to do").

God's words are true and faithful. When all human institutions fail, God's words will not. His will cannot be thwarted. On the one side this is extremely comforting as we reflect on the many promises that God has given to his children. But there is another side as well. God will faithfully discipline his children as part of his program of grace in their lives. Grasping this theological truth encourages us to pursue him passionately.

Word of God. In this passage the message of God's enduring word is key to repentance. The prophets were sent by God to call the people back to faithful relationship, and it is the words of the prophets that are rehearsed here for those people. Although the fathers and even the prophets themselves were not eternal, these words are not only eternal, according to Zechariah, but they are potent ("did not my words ... overtake your forefathers?"). This reminds us of the importance of the Word of God to the rhythms of repentance.

The centrality of God's Word for penitence is evident in the penitential prayer tradition in the Old Testament. In Nehemiah 9 the people read from "the Book of the Law of the LORD their God for a quarter of the day" before confessing their sins to God (Neh. 9:3). Their prayer is an anthology of quotations from this law book (9:5–37). Both Ezra and Nehemiah cry to God in penitence (Ezra 9; Neh. 1), and each cite God's law in their prayer (Ezra 9:10–12; Neh. 1:8–9). Daniel's penitential prayer results from his reading of "the word of the LORD given to Jeremiah the prophet" (Dan. 9:2).[30]

30. On the importance and use of Scripture in prayers of this period, see Boda, *Praying the Tradition*; J. H. Newman, "Nehemiah 9 and the Scripturalization of Prayer in the Second Temple Period," in *The Function of Scripture in Early Jewish and Christian Tradition*, ed. C. A. Evans and J. A. Sanders (JSNTSup 154 Sheffield: Sheffield Academic Press, 1998), 112–23; idem, *Praying by the Book: The Scripturalization of Prayer in Second Temple Judaism* (SBLEJL 14; Atlanta: Scholars Press, 1999).

These examples show us the key role played by God's Word in the rhythms of penitence within his community. They show us that repentance occurs as communities and individuals consistently encounter that Word in their lives. They also encourage us to provide opportunity for penitential response (among other responses, such as praise and thanksgiving) in our times of teaching and learning from the Word of God.

Zechariah 1:7–17

ON THE TWENTY-FOURTH day of the eleventh month,
the month of Shebat, in the second year of Darius,
the word of the LORD came to the prophet
Zechariah son of Berekiah, the son of Iddo.
8During the night I had a vision—and there before me was
a man riding a red horse! He was standing among the myrtle
trees in a ravine. Behind him were red, brown and white
horses.
9I asked, "What are these, my lord?"
The angel who was talking with me answered, "I will show
you what they are."
10Then the man standing among the myrtle trees explained,
"They are the ones the LORD has sent to go throughout the
earth."
11And they reported to the angel of the LORD, who was
standing among the myrtle trees, "We have gone throughout
the earth and found the whole world at rest and in peace."
12Then the angel of the LORD said, "LORD Almighty, how
long will you withhold mercy from Jerusalem and from the
towns of Judah, which you have been angry with these sev-
enty years?" 13So the LORD spoke kind and comforting words
to the angel who talked with me.
14Then the angel who was speaking to me said, "Proclaim
this word: This is what the LORD Almighty says: 'I am very
jealous for Jerusalem and Zion, 15but I am very angry with the
nations that feel secure. I was only a little angry, but they
added to the calamity.'
16"Therefore, this is what the LORD says: 'I will return to
Jerusalem with mercy, and there my house will be rebuilt. And
the measuring line will be stretched out over Jerusalem,'
declares the LORD Almighty.
17"Proclaim further: This is what the LORD Almighty says:
'My towns will again overflow with prosperity, and the LORD
will again comfort Zion and choose Jerusalem.'"

Original Meaning

IN THE OVERALL SCHEME of Zechariah 1–8, 1:7 is the doorway into the visionary world of the prophet. We can see this entrance not merely by the presence of genre elements distinct from 1:1–6 but also by the occurrence of the second of three superscriptions (cf. 1:1, 7; 7:1), identifying the date as the twenty-fourth day of the eleventh month (Shebat) in the second year of Darius—that is, February 15, 519 B.C.

The Setting (1:8a)

THIS SERIES OF VISIONS in 1:7–6:15 is often referred to as the "night visions." This first vision comes "during the night" (1:8). Later in 4:1, Zechariah informs us that the angel "wakened me, as a man is wakened from his sleep," repeating the nocturnal motif. No other historical superscription is provided until the reader leaves the night vision series in 7:1, suggesting that all these visions and their accompanying oracles were delivered to the people on that twenty-fourth day of the eleventh month in the second year of Darius. However, the superscription only informs us when Zechariah proclaims these visions to the people, not when he experienced them.

The historical context suggested by several of the night visions appears to be earlier than the superscription in 1:7. The first vision gives no evidence that there has been a break in the Exile since the beginning of deportations in the early part of the sixth century. The second vision identifies that the nations who were at peace and feeling secure in the first vision are the same nations who scattered Judah (1:21). This nation is clearly identified in 2:6–13 as Babylon, the land of the north, the same nation on which God pours out wrath in 6:1–8 and to which idolatry is sent in 5:5–11. These pieces of evidence suggest that these visions reflect the final days of the Babylonian empire (545–539 B.C.), nearly twenty years prior to the date given in 1:7.

It is possible that Zechariah first delivered these visions to the exiles in Babylon prior to the Persian conquest of the ancient Near East and now reuses them (either in oral or written form) for those who have returned to the land. It is also possible that these visions are merely retrospective, reviewing what God has already done and taking the people on a journey into the heavenly realms to the time when power transferred from Babylonia to Persia. But is there a simpler option?[1]

Both Persian and Greek historical sources depict a relatively smooth transition from Babylonian to Persian rule for the city of Babylon and its

1. For details of the argument to follow see M. J. Boda, "Terrifying the Horns: Persia and Babylon in Zechariah 1:7–6:15," *CBQ* 67 (2005): forthcoming.

immediately surrounding territories. The powerful priestly faction in Babylon had grown dissatisfied with the final Babylonian emperor (Nabonidus), and the people readily accepted Cyrus's rule. Cyrus secured continuity in this transition by favoring the priests and their temples and by retaining high ranking bureaucrats who had served Nabonidus. This kind of treatment of foreign populations helps explain why the Jews were allowed to return to Palestine and rebuild their temple, ensuring that Cyrus would be celebrated within Jewish tradition as a great liberator.

Cyrus did not, however, fulfill the prophetic expectation that the Babylonians would be judged by God for their mistreatment of the Jews (e.g., Jer. 50–51). It was Darius who fulfilled this expectation, after the Babylonians revolted three times in the transition from Cambyses to Darius, rebellions that were met with significant force and brutality by the new king.

These visions, therefore, fit the historical context of the Jewish community living in the wake of recent upheavals in the Persian empire associated with Cambyses and Darius. The period of Babylon's "rest" has ended and the enemy of the Jews is finally receiving punishment for their abuse of Israel. This punishment is a key component of the restoration hope in the exilic period and serves as a catalyst for the fuller restoration that will occur during Darius's reign, the miracle that includes rebuilding the city and temple and restoring the rhythms of spiritual renewal.

The Scene (1:8b)

IN THE FIRST night vision Zechariah records a scene drawn from the military context. A "man" is riding a red horse, standing among the myrtle trees with a group of horses behind him. The translation of the NIV, with its use of the word "red" and the insertion of an exclamation mark, implies that there is something odd about the scene.[2] In reality this is not odd at all.[3]

The colors identified for the horses are the normal range of colors found in nature. The Hebrew term for "red" (*ʾadom*) can be used for a deep brown

---

2. Clark expresses this well: "if we say that the first horse was 'red', we immediately make him sound strange and improbable"; D. J. Clark, "The Case of the Vanishing Angel," *BT* 33 (1982): 216.

3. Horses were important to the Persians, who used them extensively; see M. A. Littauer and J. H. Crouwel, *Wheeled Vehicles and Ridden Animals in the Ancient Near East* (Leiden: Brill, 1979), 144–60, and Herodotus, who wrote that Persians were taught three things: to use the bow, to ride a horse, and to speak the truth (*The Histories* 1.136). The Jews of this time saw horses used in war, but also in the messenger service of Darius; see Littauer and Crouwel, *Wheeled Vehicles*, 158, and Herodotus, *The Histories* 8.98. Horses reappear at the end of this vision series (6:1–8) and ultimately feature prominently in apocalyptic literature (cf. Rev. 6:1–8; 19:11–21). In full-blown apocalyptic (e.g., Revelation) the colors take on symbolic character, but this should not be assumed here.

horse or a chestnut horse, for the chromatic range of this word includes brown (animals), yellowish-brown (lentils), deep red (blood), wine color (wine), and pink (flesh).[4] The Hebrew term behind "brown" (*śaroq*) should be translated "sorrel," a color combining red and white that produces a pinkish tone and is found among horses.[5] The final color, "white" (*laban*), regularly occurs among horses. There is no need then to attach symbolic meanings to the colors of the horses in this scene. Moreoever, these colors may have been used to provide camouflage for the riders at this particular time of year.[6]

There is no indication as to the number of horses behind the "man riding a red horse." Literally the Hebrew reads: "Behind him there were horses, chestnut ones, sorrel ones, and white ones," which may mean that there are three troops grouped according to color.[7] While there is no indication as to whether there are mounts on these horses, most likely there are since in 1:11 "they" report to the angel of the Lord, filling the role of military spies who report on the conditions of the world.[8] The reader is tipped off to this by the use of the verb "go throughout/have gone throughout" (1:10–11). This verb speaks about a journey over an extensive territory. In Joshua 18:4 men are appointed to survey the land, and in 1 Chronicles 21:4 Joab goes throughout Israel to count David's troops. Those mounted on the horses have been surveying military conditions in the world and now report back to their commanding officer.

Horses will reappear in the final vision in 6:1–8. But there is a different color scheme there, and the horses will be pulling chariots. This is an important contrast. The horses in our first vision are chosen for speed, not strength. Their mission is different from that in the later vision (see Original Meaning section of 6:1–8).

The position of the horses "among the myrtle trees in a ravine" is the natural setting for a secret reconnaissance rendezvous. The myrtle tree, an evergreen bush growing between six and eight feet, provides an ideal cover in the barren Palestine winter landscape. The word "ravine" (*meṣulah*) is more difficult

---

4. See A. Brenner, *Colour Terms in the Old Testament* (JSOTSup 21; Sheffield: Sheffield Academic Press, 1982), 80.

5. Brenner identifies this as a secondary term, related to the primary color denoted by *ʾadom* (ibid., 114–15). Its presence here in a list alongside *ʾadom* shows that it cannot be subsumed under it but is distinct from it. See R. P. Gordon, "An Inner-Targum Corruption (Zech I 8)," *VT* 25 (1975): 216–21, for a review of the approaches of the ancient versions to this difficult word. Also W. D. McHardy, "The Horses in Zechariah," in *In Memoriam: Paul Kahle*, ed. M. Black and G. Fohrer (BZAW 103; Berlin: Töpelmann, 1968), 174–79.

6. Meyers and Meyers (*Haggai*, 113) describe the terrain of this month in Palestine as red-white.

7. So Clark, "Case," 217.

8. Ibid.

to interpret. Every other occurrence of this morpheme refers to the watery deep,[9] but Zechariah 1 contains no water imagery. It is probably related to the Hebrew root *ṣll* ("to grow dark, shadow") and the noun *ṣel* ("shadow, shade"). This root is connected with trees in Ezekiel 31:3, in which the branches of a cedar overshadow the forest (cf. also Neh. 13:19). With this in mind, the Hebrew word for "in a ravine" perhaps should be translated "in the shadows," referring metaphorically to the secret position of the horses in the shadows of the trees, where a debriefing after a reconnaissance mission can occur.

There has been some confusion over the identity of the different characters encountered in the night vision.[10] The man "standing among the myrtle trees" (1:8, 10) is apparently the angel of the Lord, who also is "standing among the myrtle trees" (1:11). The use of the term "man" (*ʾîš*) does not mean this individual is human (see Gen. 32:24). The angel of the Lord is here pictured in human form receiving the reports from his spies. Some identify this as a Christophany (a preincarnate appearance of Christ),[11] but there is no need to do so even when in Zechariah 3:1–2 (and elsewhere in the Hebrew Bible) the angel of the Lord appears to speak as if he were the Lord. The angel of the Lord is the Lord's special messenger, sent to act and communicate on God's behalf. He carries with him the authority of the One who sent him.

One may be tempted to identify the angel of the Lord with "the angel who was talking with me" because, although in 1:9–10 Zechariah's question is directed to "the angel who was talking with me," it is the "angel of the LORD" who provides the answer. So also in 1:13, in response to the question of the angel of the Lord in 1:12, the Lord offers comfort to the "angel who talked with me." However, these angels should probably be kept separate. They are working in tandem to provide revelation. In the first exchange Zechariah asks the subordinate angel a question and that angel takes him to his commanding officer to provide the answer. In the second exchange, it is appropriate that the highest commanding officer speak directly to the Lord, but it is equally appropriate that the Lord bypass the commanding officer and provide the answer to the one who must comfort Zechariah.

What we find in this first vision, then, is a scene drawn from a military context. A group returning from a worldwide reconnaissance mission is reporting back to the commanding officer in a secret location. Such a military scene

---

9. Thus Petersen (*Haggai*, 136) sees here the cosmic deep over which the angel is hovering; cf. Ex. 15:5; Neh. 9:11; Job 41:31; Ps. 68:22; 69:2, 15; 88:6; 107:24; Jonah 2:4; Mic. 7:19; Zech. 10:11.

10. See Clark, "Case," 213–18, for the many options, which range from one to three angels. My conclusion on this matter is similar to Clark's, although I propose other reasons.

11. W. C. Kaiser, *Zechariah* (ComC 21; Dallas: Word, 1992), 305.

reminds the readers that the Lord is in control of their history, even if it is not always evident in the experience of those under foreign hegemony.

The Dialogue (1:9–17)

THE REPORT of the reconnaissance mission appears at first to be positive, for the angels have found "the whole world at rest and peace." This, however, is hardly comforting to the angel of the Lord, who appears to be looking for evidence of an upheaval that will usher in a new day for God's people. He takes on the intermediary role of the prophet and cries out to Yahweh: "How long?" This question, a borderline accusation implying that God is ultimately in charge of their suffering, is familiar to the Hebrew reader from its use in the classic laments of the Psalter (cf. Ps. 6:4; 74:10; 80:5; 90:13).[12] In this genre of psalm God's people cry to him to transform their difficult circumstances. The angel of the Lord voices the cry of the people awaiting the end of their exile. Here the prophet sees that the concern of the people on the earthly plane (see Zech. 7:1–5) is a major theme in the heavenly court.

The angel of the Lord identifies Yahweh as the sovereign judge who remains in control of the discipline of his covenant people (1:12). "Jerusalem" and "the towns of Judah" refer to these people, subtly alluding to the physical aspect of the restoration in the Persian period. Yahweh has been withholding mercy from his people, which is traced back to his "angry" disposition toward them. The word for God's anger in 1:12 (*zaᶜam*) is different from that used in 1:2 (*qaṣap*), but it speaks to Yahweh's just disposition towards his disobedient people.

The allusion to the "seventy years" clearly refers to the Exile, the purpose of which was to discipline God's people. This motif of seventy years is well known from the prophet Jeremiah (see Jer. 25:11–12; 29:10; see also 2 Chron. 36:21; Dan. 9:2). Jeremiah is cited as the source in both 2 Chronicles 36:21 and Daniel 9:2, but not in Zechariah 1:12 or 7:5.[13]

Jeremiah uses the seventy-year motif for the period of Jewish servitude to the king of Babylon, after which God will punish the Babylonians and provide salvation for the Jews. Ascertaining the precise starting and ending

---

12. For this connection see both Janet E. Tollington, *Tradition and Innovation in Haggai and Zechariah 1–8* (JSOTSup 150; Sheffield: Sheffield Academic Press, 1993), 184, and Applegate, "Jeremiah and the Seventy Years," 103. Tollington also notes similarity to the prophetic oracles of Jeremiah (Jer. 4:14, 21; 23:26; 31:22; 47:5; cf. 1 Kings 18:21; Ex. 10:3; Num. 14:27; 1 Sam. 16:1; Hos. 8:5) and Isa. 6:11. See discussion of penitential prayer in the Original Meaning section of 1:1–6; cf. Boda, "Complaint," 186–97; idem, "Penitential Prophet," 49–69.

13. See M. A. Fishbane, *Biblical Interpretation in Ancient Israel* (Oxford: Clarendon, 1985), 479–85.

dates of this time period, however, has been a point of debate in the history of interpretation.[14] The use of this motif in 2 Chronicles 36:21, where the rise of Cyrus is seen as evidence of the end of the Exile, appears to link the ending date with the events surrounding 539 B.C. This may be the case in Daniel 9:2, although there is considerable confusion over the identity of Darius the Mede.[15]

The references in Zechariah show connection and yet divergence from the previous evidence. The seventy years in 1:12 speaks of a period prior to the visionary experience. This vision, along with the ones in 1:18–21 and 6:1–8, make it clear that God's punishment of the Babylonians lies in the near future and will bring an end to the seventy years. Additionally, the reference in 7:5 reveals that the seventy-year period is still continuing in 518 B.C. This suggests that for Zechariah the seventy years of exile endured until the reign of Darius; in other words, either Zechariah disagrees with the Chronicler on the literal fulfillment of the seventy years of exile or the seventy-year image is figurative in nature. In order to answer this we need to look at the use of this image elsewhere in the ancient Near East and the Bible.

The image of seventy years as a motif connected with the destruction of a city by divine wrath is found on the Black Stone of Esarhaddon. There seventy years is the period of desolation of the city of Babylon, an interval later reduced to only eleven years.[16] But why seventy years? The answer to this remains a mystery, but the strongest clues comes from two passages in the Old Testament. First of all, seventy years is used as a motif for the punishment of the city of Tyre in Isaiah 23:15–18, where it is referred to as "the span of a king's life." Furthermore, Psalm 90:10 uses "seventy" to refer generally to the life span of a human being. Most likely seventy years for exile functions in the same way as forty years functioned for the desert generation. It was a period of time that ensured that the disobedient were cleansed from the community.

This evidence helps us to resolve the debate over whether the seventy-year motif is symbolic or literal. As noted in Psalm 90, this motif is a general term for the human life span (both seventy and eighty are given, though

---

14. For an argument for a precise seventy years from 609–539 B.C., see R. E. Winkle, "Jeremiah's Seventy Years for Babylon: A Re-assessment (Part I: The Scriptural Data)," *AUSS* 25 (1987): 201–14; idem, "Jeremiah's Seventy Years for Babylon: A Re-assessment (Part II: The Historical Data)," *AUSS* 25 (1987): 289–99.

15. L. L. Grabbe, "Another Look at the Gestalt of 'Darius the Mede,'" *CBQ* 50 (1988): 198–213; W. H. Shea, "Darius the Mede in His Persian-Babylonian Setting," *AUSS* 29 (1991): 235–57; B. E. Colless, "Cyrus the Persian as Darius the Mede in the Book of Daniel," *JSOT* 56 (1992): 113–26; Boda, "Horns."

16. Cf. E. Lipinski, "Recherches sur le livre de Zacharie," *VT* 20 (1970): 39.

seventy is the normal life span), but this is an approximate period. Thus, the number functions in one way symbolically, but in another it is intended to refer to a literal span of life, not some completely undefined period.

Applying this argument to the issue of the seventy years of exile, a via media approach emerges. Seventy years is a symbol that refers to the span of human life, an appropriate time for the desolation of a land to ensure that the guilty generation has passed away. At the same time, it does refer to a literal period, even if the community and prophet are not timing this period down to the very second.[17]

As we said earlier, the "How long?" cry of the angel of the Lord reflects on the divine plane the human longing of this period. Here we encounter a cry for the end of the Exile using the genre of communal lament. As we listen in on God's response to the angel's cry, we hear echoed the themes of penitential prayer, which we first encountered in 1:1–6: God was justifiably angry, but now it is time for restoration.

Even before we hear God's message, we are prepared for a positive response for he speaks "kind and comforting words" to the angel. "Kind" words are "pleasant" words, words that are positive (using an adjective often translated as "good"). The word "comforting" speaks to the nature of these pleasant words and sets them against the context of the hardship of the Exile alluded to in the previous verse. These words, however, are not meant for the subordinate angel alone. He is to act as an intermediary, passing on the message to the prophet, who in turn is God's agent for communicating to his people.

The message proper is given in 1:14–17. Zechariah is to announce salvation to the people of God. As in 1:12, so now throughout the announcement, the people are symbolized in urban terms like "Jerusalem," "towns," and "Zion." The content of the message merges the physical and social aspects of the restoration.

The Lord expresses his message again in highly emotive terms. His promise flows out of his character and is secured by his intense loyalty to his people. He proclaims that he is "very jealous" for Jerusalem and Zion. This term (*qanaʾ*) reveals the intense passion of God for his people and his city and can be translated as either "zealous" or "jealous." God's passion for his people is reflected at times in his zealous care for them, but when they do not display exclusive devotion to him, he is passionately jealous, demanding such devotion.

---

17. Winkle has convincingly shown that the intention of Jeremiah, Chronicles, and Daniel is to define an exact period with a precise ending date; Winkle, "Jeremiah's Seventy Years: Part I," 201–14, and "Jeremiah's Seventy Years: Part II," 289–99.

The zeal of God for his people is then linked with the anger of God toward the nations (1:15). This is accomplished grammatically by the juxtaposition of the two concepts in chiastic ordering in Hebrew: "I am zealous for Jerusalem and for Zion with great zeal, and with great anger I am angry with the nations." God's passionate zeal for his people is expressed through his passionate anger with the nations who abused them. The degree of his anger toward his people is far below the level of abuse inflicted on them by the nations.[18]

This revelation that God's anger is "little" does not contradict the message of 1:2 that God is very angry with his people.[19] At issue in 1:15 is a comparison between God's design for judgment and the nations' expression of that judgment. This does not then let the Israelites off the hook for their disobedience. Yahweh reminds them he was justifiably angry with Israel for breaking covenant, but the nations have taken this beyond God's desired discipline.

After describing the present situation, the prophetic message makes a transition to the announcement of salvation with the word "therefore" (1:16). Yahweh promises to "return to Jerusalem with mercy." This declaration plays off of two previous statements in this chapter. In the near context, it is a direct response to the cry of the angel of the Lord (1:12) as the Hebrew root (*rḥm*) is expressed in nominal form, "mercy" (*raḥamim*). In the larger context of chapter 1, it brings closure to the promise expressed in 1:3, for now that the people have "returned" (1:6; NIV "repented"; cf. 1:3), Yahweh responds and promises his return.

Earlier we noted that the return of Yahweh to his people refers to the return of his glorious presence to the temple (see comments on 1:3). This is further bolstered in 1:16 by the immediately following statement—"there my house will be rebuilt"—and the reference to the measuring line stretched out over Jerusalem. The "house" is obviously the temple, a necessity if God's presence is to reside once again in Jerusalem. The "measuring line" (*qaw*) refers to a string used by builders to ascertain the line of the city walls, one of the first acts in construction. Although the term "measuring" (*middah*) is not included here, this is implied by the context. The word functions as a metonymy for the whole process of rebuilding. By speaking of the initial step, the prophet refers to the entire project.

---

18. The NIV "I was only a little angry" is to be preferred. Some have translated "little" in terms of duration (thus related to the question "how long?"), but this should be seen as an adverb of degree, contrasting God's "great" anger toward the nations ("I am very angry").

19. For various approaches to the contrast between 1:1–6 and 1:7–21 see Applegate, "Jeremiah and the Seventy Years," 104–5. I do not agree with Applegate's approach that we have here a theodicy that shifts responsibility for the severity of the Exile from Yahweh to the nations.

Zechariah's message will not avoid the rebuilding project. In this way he echoes the message of Haggai, who spoke of the reconstruction of the temple and of the expected prosperity in the rebuilt city. But Zechariah's message moves in new directions, building on the foundation of Haggai's revelation. He places more emphasis on the divine and human inhabitants of the temple structure. He is more concerned to speak of God's return to fill the temple and the sign of his new disposition of mercy and of the people's renewal of covenant duties and standards.

One can see here the influence of the great prophet Ezekiel.[20] Zechariah's words echo two motifs found in Ezekiel: the return of Yahweh to his temple as the sign of restoration (Ezek. 43:4) and the measuring line as symbol of rebuilding (40:1–3). Zechariah's vision, however, expands beyond the temple by speaking of God's attention to the city as a whole.

Zechariah 1:17 takes the prophet's announcement a final crucial step. Not only will God rebuild his house and his city, but he will also make them prosperous as he comforts and chooses them. This again links the oracle back to the initial message offered to the subordinate angel in 1:13. The same Hebrew roots are picked up here in 1:17 ("kind and comforting words"; "prosperity . . . comfort"). But even more important is the subtle link here to the preexilic experience of the nation by the repetition of "again." Those times of prosperity in the past, namely, the period of David and Solomon, will once again be realized.

The verb "choose" (*bḥr*), not found in the initial message to the subordinate angel in 1:13, is important for the Persian period community. Other references to the "choosing" of Jerusalem in the Old Testament are exclusively linked to the function of the first temple as the place of God's presence (1 Kings 11:13, 32, 36; 14:21; 2 Kings 21:7; 23:27; Ps. 78:68; 132:13). Second Kings 23:27 speaks of God's rejection of the city he had chosen, a move that leads to its destruction and the exile of its people. When Zechariah is instructed to speak of God's choice of Jerusalem again, this is a sign to the community that God again has great designs for this city, this rebuilding project,

20. There has been much debate over the connections between Ezekiel and Zechariah. Hanson, MacKay, and Hamerton-Kelly identify Zechariah closely with Ezekiel; P. D. Hanson, *The Dawn of Apocalyptic: The Historical and Sociological Roots of Jewish Apocalyptic Eschatology*, rev. ed. (Philadelphia: Fortress, 1979), 249; C. Mackay, "Zechariah in Relation to Ezekiel 40–48," *EvQ* 40 (1968): 197–210; R. G. Hammerton-Kelly, "The Temple and the Origins of Jewish Apocalyptic," *VT* 20 (1970): 14; see recently S. S. Tuell, "Haggai-Zechariah: Prophecy after the Manner of Ezekiel," in *SBLSP* 2000 (Atlanta: Society of Biblical Literature, 2000), 263–86. Petersen presents eight contrasts between the corpora; Petersen, *Haggai*, 116–20. Cook treads the via media by listing the long list of connections while remaining sensitive to the differences; S. L. Cook, *Prophecy and Apocalypticism: The Postexilic Social Setting* (Minneapolis: Fortress, 1995), 148–53.

and ultimately his people. This theme will be repeated two more times (2:12; 3:2). God's return is the key sign that he has chosen Jerusalem once again.

In summary, in this initial night vision our eyes are opened to a spiritual scene. Moving from the prophetic message of 1:1–6 with evidence of a penitent people in Judah, we see what is happening on the spiritual plane. Angels fresh from a reconnaissance mission throughout the earth report that all is peaceful. This prompts the angel of the Lord to intercede for Israel and to ask why God is not turning toward his people to save them. God answers with comfort and mercy; his passion is turned toward his people to rescue them and bring judgment on the nations. He will return to his temple and city, rebuilding and filling them with prosperity.

Bridging Contexts

Form and interpretation. The literary form of Zechariah's night visions both attracts and frustrates the modern reader. The use of visionary experience cast within a story framework engages the imagination, enticing us to consider the message by experiencing the vision. In the first vision the prophet could have merely related the message in verses 14–17, but by receiving glimpses into his visionary world the audience is prepared intellectually and emotionally for the message. Unfortunately, however, as the modern reader pursues the precise message intended by the prophet, frustration sets in.

We often associate prophets with verbal communication, individuals who spoke God's word with authority. There is, however, another aspect to prophetic ministry that is overlooked. The prophets are also visualizers of revelation. This is suggested by two of the most common words for a prophet in the Old Testament: *ḥozeh* and *roʾeh*, often translated as "seer" (1 Sam. 9:9; Isa. 30:9, 10; Amos 7:12–16).[21] Yahweh defines this visual aspect of the prophetic ministry in Numbers 12:6–8 by describing prophets as those to whom he reveals through dreams and visions.

We have few windows into this visionary aspect of prophetic ministry throughout much of the history of prophetism. Although many of the oracles may have been revealed in this form, all we possess now is the final verbal product in oracular form. But at several places the visionary aspects can be observed. In 1 Kings 22:19–22, the prophet Micaiah relates a visionary experience he had as a preface to his condemnation of King Ahab. The last three chapters of Amos slip into the visionary mode as God dialogues with the prophet, showing him various objects (Amos 7–8) or declaring his word (Amos 9). Jeremiah had similar visionary experiences both at the time of his calling (1:11–19) and

21. Cf. W. VanGemeren, *Interpreting the Prophetic Word* (Grand Rapids: Zondervan, 1990).

during Jehoiachin's reign (Jer. 24; 25:15–33). In Ezekiel the visionary mode becomes a regular feature in prophetic revelation (e.g., Ezek. 1–3; 8; 10; 37; 40–48); also in Daniel visions are clearly dominant (Dan. 7–12).

A comparison of these various books, however, reveals some differences in the character of the visions.[22] In Amos and Jeremiah the imagery consists of objects drawn from the normal life of the people: locusts, fire, walls, plumb line, basket of ripe fruit, almond tree branch, boiling pot, two baskets of figs, and cup of wine. In Ezekiel, however, the imagery becomes unusual, such as the living creatures with four faces and four wings connected with wheels (Ezek. 1). Similarly, Daniel speaks of a beast that is like a lion with wings of an eagle. When these wings are torn off, the beast stands like a human on two feet and is given a heart (Dan. 7).

In Amos and Jeremiah the visions are static; that is, there is little motion. In Ezekiel, however, the prophet is on the move and can be whisked from place to place via the heavenly realm (Ezek. 8). So also in Daniel, although the prophet has visions within his head (Dan. 7:15), he sees himself in transit (8:2).

In Amos and Jeremiah the visions are concerned with contemporary issues—in particular, the impending judgment of God's people because of their disobedience. Likewise in Ezekiel, the issues are contemporary concerns (e.g., his calling or the detestable practices in the temple) or issues in the near future (e.g., the return of Israel or the rebuilding of the temple). With Daniel, however, the visions presage an eschatological era, seeing successions of kingdoms in history (Dan. 7) and periods of seventy times seven years (Dan. 9).

This diversity suggests a development in the genre of prophetic vision, a transformation that ultimately ends in the genre represented by the book of Revelation: apocalyptic. This term is drawn from the Greek word for "revelation" (*apocalypsis*) and refers to any literature that bears similarity to the book of Revelation. Apocalyptic appears to find its roots in prophetic visionary literature but soon takes on its own character. For many apocalyptic in its full-fledged form is found in Daniel 7–12 and in Revelation, but Ezekiel and even portions of Isaiah (24–27; 56–66) have similarities. These latter examples are often tagged as proto-apocalyptic.[23]

---

22. Niditch is esp. sensitive to the historical transformation of the vision form in Israelite history; S. Niditch, *The Symbolic Vision in Biblical Tradition* (Chico, Calif.: Scholars Press, 1983); cf. B. O. Long, "Reports of Visions Among the Prophets," *JBL* 95 (1976): 353–65.

23. For further discussion of the context and form of apocalyptic, see Hanson, *The Dawn of Apocalyptic*; J. J. Collins, ed., *Apocalypse: The Morphology of a Genre* (Semeia 14; Missoula, Mont.: Scholars Press, 1979); Cook, *Prophecy and Apocalypticism*; for bibliography see F. J. Murphy, "Apocalypses and Apocalypticism: The State of the Question," *CurBS* 2 (1994): 147–180; M. J. Boda, "Majoring on the Minors: Recent Research on Haggai and Zechariah," *CurBR* 2 (2003): 33–68.

Gottwald defines apocalyptic as "a type of revelatory literature with a narrative framework in which a revelation about end-time judgment and salvation and/or about the heavenly realms is given to a human being by an otherworldly messenger."[24] It is usually recognizable by the surface features of mediated revelation and bizarre imagery. In it God employs a mediator (Dan. 12:5–13) and/or an otherwordly journey to communicate his message (Ezekiel). Although there is plenty of imagery in prophetic literature, in apocalyptic the imagery is often bizarre and sometimes even grotesque.

Underlying these surface features are several fundamental characteristics. (1) In its fully mature form, apocalyptic asserts a deterministic historiography—that is, that God is sovereign over history and that judgment or salvation is certain. (2) It displays a strong dualism with a sharp division between right and wrong. This feature may appear close to many features in New Age spirituality or even some strains of science fiction, but it is distinct in that God is clearly in control and there is no question of his triumph. (3) As to human involvement, apocalyptic is highly pessimistic, with a rejection of human involvement and belief that God alone can usher in a new era of salvation. (4) Finally, apocalyptic is futuristic in orientation. The events described are in the future and thus one lives for and with the vision of the splendor of the new age with little regard to the impact of the vision on present realities.

These features cannot be divorced from the sociological setting in which apocalyptic arose. In most cases apocalyptic is the product of oppressed societies or classes. The book of Revelation is traditionally placed in the context of John's imprisonment (Rev. 1:9); Ezekiel (Ezek. 1:1) and Daniel (Dan. 1) are set in the Exile. Such oppression explains why symbolic imagery is a regular feature in apocalyptic. It is useful to veil the true intention or meaning from the oppressors. Such oppression gives rise to the ideological features identified above.

With this review in mind we now turn to the night visions in Zechariah 1–6. In some ways they bear close resemblance to visions of Amos and Jeremiah with their focus on ordinary objects, such as the horse, chariot, measuring line, priestly clothing, olive tree, lampstand, scroll, and measuring basket. Nevertheless, the presentation of these objects is far from ordinary as they are placed in an otherworldly scene and explained by angelic intermediaries. Zechariah 1–6 concerns contemporary issues and thus is closer to Amos, Jeremiah, and Ezekiel than to Daniel and Revelation. Zechariah's visions are somewhere between the static presentations of Amos and Jeremiah

24. N. K. Gottwald, *The Hebrew Bible: A Socio-Literary Introduction* (Philadelphia: Fortress, 1985), 584.

and the mobile experiences of Daniel and Revelation. Thus, the night visions represent prophetic vision in transformation to apocalyptic and can be described as proto-apocalyptic.

In order to understand the message of all visionary material, one needs to be comfortable with its unique method of expressing truth, methods drawn from the wells of narrative and poetry. (1) The interpreter needs to be comfortable with narrative literature and should begin by identifying the setting and characters in the scene. One should not be surprised if these are not always as complete as in a full narrative passage. (2) Prophetic visions and apocalyptic use features drawn from the world of poetry, developing these characters and settings in order to communicate symbolic meaning. One must answer the following crucial question: What would these symbols have meant to the original readers?

Symbols are used in visionary literature for many reasons. In full-blown apocalyptic, as already noted, they may be used to protect the community or individual responsible for the material. But in addition, a symbol may be used for illustrative purposes to portray a message vividly or to capture the imagination and attention of the reader. Finally, a symbol may be used in order to express a message more accurately. Because of people's inability to understand a cosmic spiritual battle between good and evil, a symbol offers a window into this otherworldly reality.

In order to discern the meaning of the symbol to its original readers, one must first interpret the symbol as a symbol, grasping a clear picture of the image and then identifying what it represents. In doing this one should trace the sources of the symbol to discover its meaning in the community that received it. This will mean sensitivity to other earlier uses of the symbol within the biblical corpus and even within the ancient Near Eastern context. Yet one should be careful not to assume that every visionary/apocalyptic writer uses symbols the same way, although they may be cognizant of other writers, which may contribute to their use of the symbol. Having identified the symbol and its meaning, one can then consider the symbol within its immediate literature context. Symbols should not be abstracted from their respective passages but be placed within that context with sensitivity to how they contribute to the overall message of the passage. Especially note the relationship of the symbol to the main theme being treated.

Familiarity with the passage and its basic features will contribute to the discovery of its overall theme. This theme can be discerned by attention to the flow of the narrative (ultimate plot of the passage), to important dialogue (esp. the voice of God or an intermediary), or to the resulting prophetic message (the prophet may be called to speak in response to the scene).

Prophetic visions and apocalyptic often convey a message of hope or warning. To a people undergoing incredible hardship, God often sends a message of comfort, offering them hope in their deplorable circumstances, or a message of challenge, calling them to faithfulness. He may also send a message of warning, calling them to repent or avoid evil. Visionary scenes may even contain elements of both a negative and positive message.

History and theology. Not only does the literary form frustrate the modern reader, but so does the historical context. The images used in the visions are often lost on the modern and Western reader. We have attempted in the Original Meaning section to unpack these images to modern eyes, but it is difficult to recapture the emotion and impact of these images to the original audience. Beyond the images, the issues of this particular community in the early Persian period are often difficult to connect to our own experience. Most of us have not seen the destruction of our homeland, nor have we lived in bondage in a foreign land, so we cannot connect emotionally with the original audience.

One way of overcoming these frustrations is to tap into the resources of biblical theology (see comments in the introduction, Bridging Contexts section). The New Testament, written in a Greco-Roman-Jewish world, takes the imagery of exile and restoration and translates it into a new covenant context. We learn there that Christ came to bring the ultimate end to exile and restore his people to a kingdom defined by God, not Jewish expectations. The apostolic witness continues this theological transformation reminding us that we are strangers among the nations while we long for the new Jerusalem (Phil. 3:20). We have all felt that longing in our hearts as believers, and in that way the unique historical context of the early Persian period community echoes our own experience and reveals principles for living through these circumstances.

Therefore, with sensitivity to the images of this initial vision and the ones that follow and how they relate to the community to whom they were first addressed, and with the realization of the church's theological relationship to these ancient visions, we now turn to highlight their contemporary significance to us today.

Contemporary Significance

I REMEMBER A television commercial several years ago that began with a close-up view of a blade of grass in a field, on which was a little ant. After pausing for a moment on this scene, the camera then moved back, away from the blade of grass to the patch of ground, and from the patch of ground to the field, from the field to the province, to the country, to the continent, to the hemisphere, to the globe; then it suspended us as the audience for just a moment before returning at triple speed in reverse order until we were gazing at the ant on the blade of grass. In many ways the first night vision parallels the journey of the commercial. From the tiny Jewish community living in the insignificant province of Yehud, we are taken up into the first of several heavenly scenes, where we are offered a divine viewpoint. While 1:1–6 described the confession of this community as they responded to God's call to return to him, the first night vision takes us on a heavenly excursion to hear of God's intention for this community.

God's sovereign rule. The visionary scene accentuates the sovereignty of God over the affairs of the world. The reconnaissance mission symbolizes his omniscient awareness of the situation of his people. Similarly, the question "How long?" asked by the angel of the Lord in 1:12, expresses the assumption that God is superintending the experience of his people.

For those living in exile this was an important issue. In the wake of Jerusalem's destruction there were at least three responses.[25] (1) Some associated the fall of the state with an apparent offense of the Canaanite gods who had been honored before the Israelites' arrival and urged worship of these gods. (2) Others saw in the defeat of Judah and triumph of Babylon, the defeat of Yahweh and ascendancy of the Babylonian Marduk and advised the worship of the conquering god. (3) Some identified the people's infidelity against Yahweh as the key issue. As time wore on, however, the first two views became increasingly attractive to those in exile. Was Yahweh really the sovereign Lord? This glimpse into the heavenlies counters that the Lord is well aware of the situation of his people and that he is in charge of their destiny.

Our view of God's sovereignty is often challenged in the everyday experience of our lives. Such challenges often come from hardship or lack of answers to our prayers. They may also come from observing movements of history around us or the apparent success of the ungodly. In each case our theology of God's dominion over the universe is challenged, and with devastating results.

The Asaphite who wrote Psalm 73 also experienced these kinds of challenges. He questioned the sovereign love of God as he watched the successes of the ungodly. The more he watched them, the greater became their prosperity and the larger his own predicament. He shared what saved him from abandoning his faith in verse 17: "I entered the sanctuary of God, then I understood their final destiny." In God's sanctuary he discovered God's

25. P. R. Ackroyd, *Exile and Restoration: A Study of Hebrew Thought of the Sixth Century B.C.* (OTL; Philadelphia: Westminster, 1968), 39–

presence ("I am always with you, you hold me by my right hand," 73:23) and God's sovereignty ("You guide me with your counsel," 73:24), and he was able to declare: "But as for me, it is good to be near God. I have made the Sovereign LORD my refuge" (73:28).

In a sense Zechariah's initial vision is a journey into the sanctuary. The heavenly curtain is pulled back, and the prophet and people are reminded that the Lord is in full control even when they do not sense it. This reminds me of C. S. Lewis's famous *Screwtape Letters*. In one letter the nephew demon is rejoicing in the fact that his Christian charge has begun to have doubts in his prayers to God ("our Enemy"). Uncle Screwtape reprimands his foolish nephew, Wormwood, with these words:

> Do not be deceived, Wormwood. Our cause is never more in danger than when a human, no longer desiring, but still intending, to do our Enemy's will, looks round upon a universe from which every trace of Him seems to have vanished, and asks why he has been forsaken, and still obeys.[26]

Faith in God's sovereignty is essential to the walk of faithfulness as we await the return of Christ. The words of the apostles in Acts powerfully express such faith for us as Christians. Fresh from persecution they "raised their voices together in prayer to God" and began with the simple cry: "Sovereign Lord" (Acts 4:23–30). May that also be our cry as the people of God.

The people's access. With the curtain pulled back, some may be surprised at the candor of the dialogue. The question of the angel of the Lord gets directly to the point: "How long will you withhold mercy?" (Zech. 1:12). This is reminiscent of the laments in the Psalter, where we regularly hear such open declarations that almost sound like challenges to the sovereignty we have just finished highlighting. But the witness of the psalms shows us that God is open to hear our cries. Christ declared the appropriateness of such expressions with his cry on the cross, "My God, my God, why have you forsaken me?" (Mark 15:34), an act that is clearly not sinful or an evidence of faithlessness (Heb. 5:7–8; cf. 4:14–16).[27] We are invited as Christians not only to replicate Christ's example in his suffering (1 Peter 2:21–25) but also to express our suffering to God (James 5:13).

---

26. C. S. Lewis, *The Screwtape Letters* (Charlotte, N.C.: Commission, 1976), 51 (letter 8).

27. This does not mean that we can spend our lives in lament indefinitely, for God's desire is ultimately the expression of praise as he saves us from our predicaments and restores us to health. Note the repeating refrain in Ps. 42–43: "Why are you downcast, O my soul? Why so disturbed within me? Put your hope in God, for I will yet praise him, my Savior and my God" (42:5, 11; 43:5); see the introduction to W. Brueggemann, *The Message of the Psalms: A Theological Commentary* (Augsburg Old Testament Studies: Minneapolis: Augsburg, 1984).

Willem VanGemeren has expressed this in his statement: "True faith is not an apathetic acceptance of whatever comes to pass."[28] In similar fashion we are encouraged by the sensitive treatise of John Calvin:

> Now among the Christians there are also new Stoics, who count it depraved not only to groan and weep but also to be sad and care ridden. These paradoxes proceed, for the most part, from idle men, who, exercising themselves more in speculation than in action, can do nothing but invent such paradoxes for us. Yet we have nothing to do with this iron philosophy which our Lord and Master has condemned not only by his word, but also by his example. For he groaned and wept both over his own and others' misfortunes. And he taught his disciples in the same way: "The world," he says, "will rejoice; but you will be sorrowful and will weep" [John 16:20 p.]. And that no one might turn it into a vice, he openly proclaimed, "Blessed are those who mourn" [Matt. 5:4]. No wonder! For if all weeping is condemned, what shall we judge concerning the Lord himself, from whose body tears of blood trickled down [Luke 22:44]? If all fear is branded as unbelief, how shall we account for that dread with which, we read, he was heavily stricken [Matt. 26:37; Mark 14:33]? If all sadness displeases us, how will it please us that he confesses his soul "sorrowful even to death" [Matt. 26:38]?[29]

In more recent times, Walter Brueggemann has noted the "costly loss of lament" from the functioning canon of the church, that is, from our worship expressions.[30] Brueggemann voices his concern that by participating exclusively in "history-stifling praise," we can encourage psychological inauthenticity in our people's relationship with God. Such inauthenticity can foster conditions conducive to hypocrisy as we seek to praise with no recourse to lament.

The angelic mediator in Zechariah 1:7–17 presents the pained voice of the community awaiting God's redemption. The sovereign God listens to his people, hears them in their pain, and responds in grace. The first vision encourages us to speak to our God, especially in the midst of our suffering, crying for his grace.

God's zealous passion. The candor we have observed is the first surprise to the typical depiction of the "sovereign LORD." We have often viewed this

28. W. A. VanGemeren, "Psalms," *EBC*, 5:567.

29. J. Calvin, *Institutes of the Christian Religion*, trans. J. T. McNeill and F. L. Battles (LCC 20; Philadelphia: Westminster, 1960), 709.

30. W. Brueggemann, "The Costly Loss of Lament," *JSOT* 36 (1986): 57–71; repr. in *The Psalms and the Life of Faith*, ed. P. D. Miller (Minneapolis: Fortress, 1995), 98–111; note also my caution, however, in Boda, "Priceless Gain," 51–75.

doctrine via the image of the English schoolmaster stripped of emotion and do not expect such nonsense to be tolerated in the Lord's presence. But a second surprise is in store: The sovereign Lord is the God of passion. In response to the angel's question the Lord speaks "kind and comforting words." These words are then relayed to the prophet in 1:14–15, and they are words of passion: extreme anger with the nations and intense zeal for his people.

We are accustomed to the first emotion, anger, from the biblical witness. We remember well the wrath of God expressed throughout the prophets, warning the people to return to him in covenant fidelity. But we must not forget the passionate love of God for his people, a feature expressed vividly in the book of Hosea. He is the God who cared for Israel as a father cares for his son (Hos. 11:1–5) and as a husband for his wife (chs. 1–3). Listen to God's heart in 11:8:

> How can I give you up, Ephraim?
>   How can I hand you over, Israel?
> How can I treat you like Admah?
>   How can I make you like Zeboiim?
> My heart is changed within me;
>   all my compassion is aroused.

Zechariah 1:7–17 does not ignore the reality of past judgment brought on by the sin of the people ("I was only a little angry," v. 15), but it reveals that the Exile was designed as discipline and that God's passion for his people never abated. He loves them with an everlasting love.

On one level Jesus brought a full end to the discipline of the Exile as God poured out his zealous wrath for the sins of humanity on his own Son. God passionately pursues us in Christ with his love, mercy, and kindness. On another level, as we await the death of sin at Christ's second coming, God continues to bring discipline into our lives. It is not easy when God brings such difficulties into our lives, whether acts of discipline or not, to sustain confidence in his mercy. But such discipline is truly an expression of his love and mercy in our lives (Heb. 12:1–11), even if we cannot identify the reason for such experiences. Zechariah 1:7–17 reminds us of the ultimate goal of all discipline—deepened and purified relationship with our covenant Lord.

God's comforting and prosperous presence. This ultimate goal is identified in the final section of 1:7–17 where God promises his presence among his people. In the prophetic sermon that set up this night vision (1:1–6), God called his people into a reciprocal relationship of intimacy: "Return to me ... that I may return to you." The return he demands of his people is clearly a return to covenant faithfulness, following his "words" and "decrees" (1:5). Such a return will result in a mutual return of God to them.

The New Testament makes it clear that God's presence was ultimately communicated to his people in redemptive history through his Son, Jesus Christ, in whom "all his fullness" dwelt (Col. 1:19; 2:9). Near the end of his earthly ministry Jesus promised his continued presence with his people as they gathered together (Matt. 28:20) and as they made disciples among the nations (28:18–20; cf. Acts 18:10). This continued presence stands out more clearly in Christ's teaching in John 14–16. There he reveals that he has communicated the presence of the Father to them (14:8–14). But he also speaks of "another Counselor," who will continue the presence of Christ among them (14:16, 26; 15:26; 16:7). When Jesus tells them in 14:17, "you know him, for he lives with you and will be in you," he is referring to the Holy Spirit's role in their lives.

(1) The presence of God is, first of all, a comforting presence. Although it is true that many prophetic messages in the Old Testament warn of impending judgment and call for repentance (cf. Zech. 1:1–6), one should not miss the other "tone" of the prophetic voice: comfort and assurance. Isaiah 40:1–2 sets such a tone for the second part of the book of Isaiah:

> Comfort, comfort my people,
>   says your God.
> Speak tenderly to Jerusalem,
>   and proclaim to her
> that her hard service has been completed,
>   that her sin has been paid for,
> that she has received from the LORD's hand
>   double for all her sins.

Zechariah 1:7–17 links comfort and choice. As we have noted above, the election of Jerusalem is consistently linked to God's habitation of Zion. God's promised return with his presence is indeed comforting words for this community. Ezekiel observed the glory of God abandoning the city and people (Ezek. 10) and prophesied a return to a rebuilt temple (ch. 43). Zechariah now delivers the news from God that the time has now come for a return of his presence.

God offers comfort to us on this side of the cross in redemptive history. He has entered our world through Jesus, who communicates his presence to those who receive him and are called the children of God. The Spirit, that other Counselor, continues to communicate Christ's presence to the church. This is why we assemble together as a community, desirous to experience that presence and communicate it to one another. As we walk through difficulties communally and individually, God's presence in the community of faith, the new temple of God, offers us comfort.

One regular practice in the church that I attend offers a visible expression of such comfort for those walking through painful difficulties in their lives. My pastor asks for those who have a need or are facing a difficult situation to stand up in their place. They are assured that they will not have to go forward or say anything but merely stand there as those in the immediate area place a hand of comfort on their shoulder. The pastor then prays for these people and their needs. Although a simple and short exercise within the flow of our service, this is the kind of liturgical rhythm that communicates that this community gathers together for comfort.

So also as we walk through daily life as Christians, the communities in which we live need to see us as people of comfort. A young man whom I mentored as a teen now pastors in a small farming community in Saskatchewan, Canada. Recently I received a phone call from the local constable of the Royal Canadian Mounted Police in that community. The police officer was doing a background check on my friend so that he could function as a counselor within the victim impact program for the region. Of course, I vouched for my friend, giving him a glowing recommendation. The policeman, who was not a believer, shared that he was not surprised at my recommendation. He told me that the previous week a family had lost their teen in a tragic suicide and that my friend, having heard the news, had walked through this tragedy with this family, even though they were not members of his church. The talk in the coffee shops of that small town was all about the new pastor in town who had offered comfort to a hurting family.

(2) According to 1:7–17, the presence of God is also a prosperous presence, for where God's presence is, we are told, "my towns will again overflow with prosperity." As we argued in our discussion of Haggai's prophecies (see esp. Hag. 1:1–11; 2:10–19), this theme of prosperity need not be "spiritualized" as we come into the new covenant era of redemptive history. God does continue to promise to care for our physical needs and bless us in physical ways (cf. Matt. 6:28–34; 19:29; Mark 10:29–30). But certainly we can rejoice in the inner and relational prosperity we have received through the Spirit's presence in our lives and communities.

We are often reticent to ask God for his prosperous care of our needs. But as individuals and communities who live by faith, we are encouraged by God's promises of such care as we seek first his kingdom. Often we do not receive because we are too afraid to ask God.

Zechariah 1:18–21

THEN I LOOKED up—and there before me were four horns! [19]I asked the angel who was speaking to me, "What are these?"

He answered me, "These are the horns that scattered Judah, Israel and Jerusalem."

[20]Then the LORD showed me four craftsmen. [21]I asked, "What are these coming to do?"

He answered, "These are the horns that scattered Judah so that no one could raise his head, but the craftsmen have come to terrify them and throw down these horns of the nations who lifted up their horns against the land of Judah to scatter its people."

Original Meaning

WITH THE PROCLAMATION of Yahweh still ringing in their ears, one that offered hope to Israel and warning to her enemies, the reader now enters a second visionary scene. This vision is clearly distinguished from the former by the oracle of 1:14–17, yet it is closely related to the previous one as it describes the first stage in the fulfillment of the first vision.

The historical context that lies behind this vision is the same as the one identified for the first vision (see comments on 1:7). As we argued in our introduction to 1:7–17, it was in the early phase of Darius's reign that the Babylonians received significant punishment from the Persians for their support of Gaumata and rebellion against Darius. This is signified in the present vision by the horns (Babylonians) disciplined by the ploughmen (Persians).[1]

Detailed Analysis

THE VISION BEGINS with a phrase that marks the starting point of several of the other visions in Zechariah 1–6: "Then I looked up—and there before me were . . ." (cf. 2:1; 5:1; 6:1). As Zechariah moves into this new scene, he

1. For fuller argument and interaction with other views, see Boda, "Horns."

leaves behind the many characters from the first vision and finds himself alone with the "angel who was speaking to me." This angel will remain a constant companion in Zechariah's otherworldly journey, appearing in most of the eight visions and apparently acting as a tour guide for the bewildered prophet.

In this second vision, Zechariah sees four horns and what are often identified as four craftsmen. Although one of the shorter visions in the series, 1:18–21 has given rise to much controversy both as to its basic imagery and its meaning. The image of the horn is related to one of three contexts. (1) The most common context is that of the animal world, where an animal's horn is a source of offensive and defensive power. This is used consistently for the power of a nation, usually with a view to its military ability (cf. Deut. 33:17; 1 Sam. 2:10; Ps. 18:2; 75:10; Jer. 48:25; Mic. 4:13). In the apocalyptic material of the book of Daniel (Dan. 7–8), the horn represents the military power of the nations. For some interpreters these horns are independent of any animal, while for others animals are assumed in the vision.

(2) The second context is that of clothing, in which horns are attached to a helmet. In this view the image is similar to that of the animal context above, but the introduction of a helmet smoothes out the tension between the horns and the later reference to craftsmen. Craftsmen do not usually work with horns, but they could work with some kind of a helmet.

(3) The final context is the temple. Some interpreters associate the horns with the four-horned altars found within temples in Palestine. This fits well with the period in which parts of Zechariah are dated, during which temple construction was underway, while providing a link between the horns and the craftsmen who appear in the vision.

This third suggestion must be dismissed immediately. It is difficult to ascertain how "horns" that scatter Judah and are related to foreign nations can somehow be connected to the horns of an altar. The second suggestion (horned helmet) is a possibility, but it appears necessary only because there is confusion over how the "craftsmen" relate to the "horns" in the vision. The suggestion of animal horns is the most natural, though it does appear to create tension with the image of "craftsmen." In order to understand the horns, we must then examine "the craftsmen."

The Hebrew word underlying the term "craftsmen" (*ḥarašim*) is a general word for artisans who work with some kind of material, such as wood, metal, or stone (cf. Isa. 3:3; Hos. 13:2). It falls within the semantic range of the Hebrew verb that uses the same consonants (*ḥrš*) and means "to cut, engrave." These same consonants, however, are used for a second root in Hebrew (homonym), which appears elsewhere in its verbal form and means "to plow" (Ps. 129:3; Isa. 28:24; Amos 9:13). Using this second verb, we can translate the term used in Zechariah 1:20 as "plowmen." This meaning connects much better with the image of a horn and, of course, the animals (either goats or bulls) connected with these horns.

Furthermore, the term "to terrify" (*ḥrd*) in 1:21 is used elsewhere in the Hebrew Bible in connection with animals to speak of "driving off" a group of animals (see Isa. 17:2; cf. also Deut. 28:26; Jer. 7:33). Finally, the verb "throw down" (*ydh*) in 1:21 has often been difficult for translators, because there are only two other places where this Hebrew verb has the same sense. In Jeremiah 50:14 it refers to shooting arrows at an enemy (Babylon!), and in Lamentations 3:53 the object of the verb is "stones," which are obviously thrown.[2] Thus, the scene we find here in Zechariah 1:18–21 is one in which two large animals with four horns are being driven away.

The angel tells Zechariah that these horns are those that have "scattered Judah, Israel and Jerusalem." As already mentioned, the horn is a common image for the military might of a nation, and the connection to the nations is made explicit in the interpretation of 1:21. Because the list includes both Judah and Israel, it reviews the history of both northern and southern kingdoms, against whom two great empires, Assyria and Babylon, applied their military strength.[3] The use of the verb "scattered" is appropriate to the agricultural image of this vision (cf. Isa 30:24). It regularly refers to the exile of the Jews, both with explicit reference to agricultural imagery (e.g., Isa. 41:15; Jer. 15:7; 31:10) as well as without (Lev. 26:33; 1 Kings 14:15; cf. Jer. 49:32, 36).

The devastation of the exilic experience for both nations is summed up in 1:21 in the Hebrew idiom "a man could not raise his head" (*loʾ naśaʾ roʾšo*). In the negative form it is used for loss of freedom, and in the positive for regaining of independence. One can see the positive expression in Genesis 40:20–21 and Jeremiah 52:31, where officials are released from prison (Pharaoh's butler, King Jehoiachin). In military contexts it can be used in the positive form, meaning a person is able to engage in battle (Ps. 83:2), or in the negative, meaning a person is defeated (Judg. 8:28). Here in Zechariah 1:21 the verb "raise" (*nśʾ*) is used for the action of the nations (lit., "who raised a horn against the land of Judah to scatter it") and of the resulting condition of the Jews ("which scattered Judah so that no one could raise his head").

It is almost universally agreed that the plowmen must be representing Persia in this context. The significance of the number four is difficult to discern. "Four" is used to speak of completeness (the "four winds of heaven," 2:6; 6:5), related to the four directions (north, south, east, west). But in this case,

---

2. M. J. Dahood, *Psalms* (AB 16–17; Garden City, N.Y.: Doubleday, 1966), 2:354.

3. Although the animals are not mentioned, they are clearly in view. In the second explanation of the angel in 1:21, the angel refers to "the nations who lifted up their horns."

it may merely be matching the "four horns" with "four" plowmen, meaning that they are powerful enough to drive away the four horns.

In this second vision Zechariah sees a scene that offers hope to his community. The nations that have scattered Israel will be driven back to their places, powerless to abuse the Jewish community any longer. The Assyrians and Babylonians will no longer hold power over the Jews because the Persians have arisen as a benevolent servant in the hands of Yahweh.

This vision is closely related, then, with the first (1:7–17). In that initial vision the angel of the Lord lamented the peaceful conditions of the cosmos and the apparent lack of action by Yahweh to punish the nations who had abused the Jewish community beyond Yahweh's desire (1:12–15). Nothing was said there about the punishment of those nations. Instead, the message focused on God's first priority: to return to Jerusalem, rebuild her, and bring prosperity. This second vision, then, offers a revelation of what must precede this rebuilding project: the smashing of the power of the nations. Zechariah is also shown God's passion for his people, expressed in his punishment of Babylon. This provides both comfort and hope to a discouraged people.

Bridging Contexts

Image and reality. Our interpretation of 1:18–21 has demonstrated the skills that were encouraged in our introduction to Hebrew visionary literature in 1:7–17 (see Bridging Contexts section). We have examined each of the images in their ancient contexts as well as in their present literary context, identifying the role the images (including the numbers) play in the overall message of the vision as a whole. We did not put great focus on the number of horns and plowmen, but rather saw the number of horns as typifying the two kingdoms (two animals with two horns each) that had scattered Israel and Judah (Babylon and Assyria) and the number of plowmen as signifying nothing more than a force adequate for terrifying the animals.

This image would not have been odd to the prophet; rather, he would have understood it readily in an agrarian society. It also signifies important events in the contemporary experience of his community. As we transition now to application, we must ask how this image and its meaning within this ancient community has enduring significance for those of faith today.

Faith and response. Zechariah 1:18–21 must be interpreted in the larger context of the vision series to which it belongs. It continues God's response to the cry of the angel ("How long?") in the initial vision in the chapter, promising God's punishment of the nations that have mistreated his people.

It is difficult to put ourselves in the shoes of a generation that lived its entire life under foreign domination. For not ten, not twenty, but for fifty to seventy years Jews lived under foreign rule, whether they remained in their land or were in exile in Mesopotamia. For most people this was the only existence they had ever known, yet their religious traditions were a constant reminder that this was only temporary and that God had promised them peaceful existence in their own land.

This contrast between faith and reality would have elicited various responses. Some would have felt discouragement, awaiting salvation and yet never experiencing it. Some would have felt anger, anger at God for abandoning them and anger at their enemies for abusing them—an anger that may have tempted them to action in order to usher in a new kingdom. To these kinds of people comes Zechariah's vision of hope, encouraging a demoralized community to trust the God of redemptive history.

Such responses to the collision of faith and reality endured among the Jewish community in the centuries that followed as they read and reread the visions of Zechariah. The New Testament reflects these responses and proclaims Jesus as the One who will ultimately deliver his people from their dilemma, yet in ways that are not expected. But his renewed community, the church, also finds comfort in the ancient promises of Zechariah, as we live in hope of the full realization of restoration. In this way, we can appropriate the comfort of this ancient message as the penitent community of God.

Contemporary Significance

HELPLESSNESS—POSTURE FOR GRACE. As one who grew up in Canada, I know well the feeling of helplessness on the world stage. Although Canadians have enjoyed the many benefits of Western society, their population is but thirty million and their armed forces are among the smallest, used almost exclusively for peacekeeping across the globe. It is true that Canadian leaders are invited to Washington regularly and contribute at the G8 summits, but in the end their voice and economy are no match for those of larger members.

This feeling of helplessness, however, is shallow compared to the depth of helplessness felt by the Jews of old. This was a nation that had lost everything (freedom, land, temple, leadership) to the great Mesopotamian powers and their military and economic might. There is no question that such helplessness is not the ultimate goal in biblical expectation, but it is fascinating how often the condition of helplessness is preparatory for grace throughout redemptive history.

At the outset of Israel's history we watch Abraham and his family wandering around Canaan in weakness with the promise of God's provision of the land (Genesis). Joseph goes from the place of privilege as the favored son in Canaan to the depth of helplessness in Egypt (Gen. 37–50). The Israelites experience oppressive slavery in Egypt (Ex. 1–12), Naomi loses all in Moab (Ruth), and David flees from Saul in the desert of Judah (1 Sam. 19–31). Each of these stories in which God brings miraculous salvation begins with the main characters mired in hopeless circumstances.

On the flip side, it is interesting how those with great resources either are disqualified from service or lose them prior to success. Moses, with all the resources of Egypt, must go to the desert before he returns to lead his people (Ex. 2–4). Gideon, with a sizable military force, is stripped of all but three hundred men to fight the Midianites (Judg. 6–7). Saul has the physical stature of a great warrior but ultimately does not fulfill God's mandate (1 Sam. 8–16). Solomon has the wisdom of a great leader, but his great resources lead him into sin, resulting in the fracturing of the nation (1 Kings 1–11).

The ultimate symbol of this principle is the Incarnation. Christ came in a helpless state and conquers through the helplessness of the cross. This is not only the basis for our vulnerable walk of faith, but it is an example to those who take up their cross and follow him. The weak things of the world conquer, not because of their weakness but because of the necessity for faith. Helplessness forces the believer to trust in the only One who can rescue them from their predicament.

I remember how clearly my wife and I sensed that God had called us to go to England to pursue my doctoral studies. However, one year into the experience we were coming to the end of our financial resources. My wife began to search for work, and each night we cried to God to provide for our needs. There we were in a foreign land without the necessary resources. We felt a depth of helplessness that we had never experienced before, and it was in such a state that we cried to God to care for us, to provide for our needs. Finding no success for employment as a teacher (the field in which she had two degrees), she applied to do data entry for a dictionary project at the university press.

At first this did not seem to be the miracle we had prayed for as I cared for my beloved children while writing my dissertation and learning German. But within three months she became the first employee in the project to perform her work at home, a privilege that continued for the rest of our time in England (and even for five years after that while living in Canada). Such a condition of helplessness forced us into the hands of our sovereign God of grace.

Unthinkable—opportunity for miracle. We must put ourselves once again into the shoes of those who first heard this vision. Most of them had lived through the turmoil of the demise of the Babylonian and the rise of the Persian empire. They had heard the prophecies of hope in Isaiah, Jeremiah, and

Ezekiel, which reminded them that God would ultimately rescue them, but in the darkness of the Exile such promises would have seemed a fantasy.

In the waning days of their empire, the Babylonians still held ultimate power over their subject nations. Truly Babylon's fall and punishment would have been unthinkable from the perspective of those controlled by the oppressive regime. When Cyrus defeated the Babylonians and took the reins of power, the Babylonians seemed to have been spared the kind of punishment they deserved, and months turned into years and years into decades. Again it appeared as if they had escaped God's vengeance and that this prophetic warning would come to nought. Yet this vision challenges the faith of the believing community, reminding them that God is the God of the impossible, even the unthinkable.

When we face insurmountable odds in our lives, God challenges us to turn to him in faith, who is able to transcend anything and everything we could ask or imagine (Eph. 3:20–21). Church history is filled with stories of God surprising his people, confirming his enduring commitment to redeem his creation.

One powerful example of this principle is George Müller.[4] A former drunk and thief who had been saved by God's grace, Müller moved from his native Germany to England to prepare for missionary service. But he ended up pastoring a congregation in Bristol, England. While reading a biography of A. H. Francke, a leader among the German Pietists, he discovered that this godly man had spearheaded a ministry to orphans in Halle (where Müller had gone to university). What caught Müller's eye in this biography was Francke's trust in God for all his needs, and so Müller began an orphanage based on the same principles. He never asked anyone for funds, but looked to God to provide for the needs of the thousands of orphans he nurtured in his orphanages. God answered the prayers of this man and his staff. God was indeed the God of the unthinkable, the Lord of the impossible.

Judgment—vengeance is God's. While this passage does stimulate hope in the midst of helplessness, its message is a sober one for God's enemies. One cannot ignore the fact that this is a vision of judgment. God does hold humanity accountable for their abuse of his people. This was true of the nation exiled for their abuse of their fellow citizens (1:15, "little angry"), but it was also true of the exiling nations who "added to the calamity" (1:15). The judgment of 1:18–21 is the outward expression of God's passion articulated in the first vision. That passion spells comfort for his people (1:13) but anger for his enemies (1:15). The one cannot be realized without the other. Although only God has the right to enact such judgment on the nations, ultimately his judgment is necessary in order to redeem his creation from sin.

4. G. Müller, *Autobiography of George Müller* (New Kensington, Pa.: Whitaker House, 1984); R. Steer, *George Müller: Delighted in God* (London: Hodder and Stoughton, 1975).

It is easy in a culture of toleration to avoid discussions of God's judgment, to accentuate his love, and to hide his discipline. But this is irresponsible for a community commissioned with revealing God in this world. Certainly at times many within church history have focused more attention on God's wrath, but the response to this should not be to abandon this biblical theme; instead, we should foster a balance between his love and wrath as evidenced in Scripture, demonstrated on the cross, and expected in the eschaton.

God's judgment does offer comfort to those who live under the oppression of the nations, even in our world today. Each year my local church focuses attention on those Christians who are undergoing suffering around the globe. On the "International Day of Prayer for the Persecuted Church" we cannot escape the reality that the majority of our Christian sisters and brothers in this world follow Christ at the threat of their very lives.[5] Although we pray for the salvation of the wicked, God's promised justice does afford his people hope as they endure suffering and hardship at the hands of the wicked people even to this day. This theology of justice should inform our prayers for the persecuted church as we join in solidarity with them not only on one Sunday during the year, but also each time we gather together.

5. For up-to-date information, see www.idop.org.

Zechariah 2:1–5

THEN I LOOKED up—and there before me was a man
with a measuring line in his hand! [2]I asked, "Where are
you going?"

He answered me, "To measure Jerusalem, to find out how wide and how long it is."

[3]Then the angel who was speaking to me left, and another
angel came to meet him [4]and said to him: "Run, tell that
young man, 'Jerusalem will be a city without walls because of
the great number of men and livestock in it. [5]And I myself will
be a wall of fire around it,' declares the LORD, 'and I will be its
glory within.'"

Original Meaning

AS IN 1:18–21, this third vision begins with an introductory narrative sentence, distinguishing it from the previous revelation and yet continuing the visionary experience begun in 1:8. Both the second vision and this one unpack the promise of the initial vision to punish the nations (cf. 1:14–15 with 1:18–21) and restore the Lord's city (cf. 1:16–17 with 2:1–5).

This encounter with an individual holding surveying equipment in his hand fits the historical context in which the prophet Zechariah was living. The people had returned to the land and were in the midst of a major building project as they restored the temple in Jerusalem (Ezra 2–6; Hag. 1–2) and rebuilt some of the homes in the city (Hag. 1). With these projects underway, the thought of reconstructing a protective wall around the city would be natural in order to preserve their renewed urban assets.

The visionary narrative comes to an end in verse 5. God speaks to the young man about the building of a city and a wall in 2:4–5. But in 2:6–13 the focus moves in a different direction; this does not appear to be part of a speech to the young man, but rather a sermon speaking to those in exile, providing hope on the basis of the prophetic vision. The speaker is no longer the angel but the prophet. Although related to 2:4–5, the oracle in 2:6–13 expands beyond this vision to reflect on the first three visions. Therefore, we will deal with the oracle in a separate section.

Detailed Analysis

ZECHARIAH FIRST CATCHES SIGHT of a man with a measuring line in his hand. The Hebrew term *ḥebel middah* ("rope of measure") refers to a surveyor's line. It is a different term from the one found in either Zechariah 1:16 (*qaw*) or Ezekiel 40:3 (*qaneh*), but the same action is in mind. The objective is to define property and building lines.

Zechariah enters into the narrative by asking a question of the surveyor: "Where are you going?" The surveyor declares that he intends to measure the width and length of Jerusalem. The order of these words ("how wide and how long") is unusual in the Old Testament and only appears here and in Ezekiel 40–48. There, as here, one finds measuring for the rebuilding of the temple and the city (cf. Ezek. 45:1–8; 48:15–22).[1] This young man, therefore, appears to be proceeding to fulfill the exilic vision of Ezekiel. In the message that follows (Zech. 2:5), the reference to a "wall" implies that the measuring is in order to build a wall around Jerusalem.

There is some debate over the intention of the surveyor. Most interpreters have seen his intention in a negative way, that his measuring will limit the size of the city. Jerome, however, saw this act in a positive light, that his measuring was to show where God's fiery presence would be. There are several indications that the former interpretation is correct. In 2:3–4 one angel encounters another and sends him on an urgent mission. This sense of urgency is communicated by the presence of the disjunctive phrase in 2:3 "but another angel" (NIV, "and another angel"), the use of the terms "run, tell" in 2:4, and the reference to the surveyor as "a young man," a term that most likely indicates the authority of the speaker over the surveyor. The content of the message also bolsters the negative evaluation of the surveyor's action. In it the angel argues against limiting the size of the city because of the great number of people and animals.

By now Zechariah knows well the "angel who was speaking to me," an individual who has appeared in both visions so far and will be his constant companion throughout the night visions. The identity of the one called "another angel" is uncertain, although some have seen him as the angel of the Lord, which is a possibility because he appears to have authority over the "angel who was speaking to me."

There is some confusion over the identity of the "young man" to whom the angel must speak in 2:4. Some have linked this individual to the man with

1. Petersen, *Haggai*, 68.

the measuring line, while others link him to Zechariah himself.[2] It seems clear from the content of the message that it is directed to the man with the measuring line, not the prophet.

The message for the surveyor implies that his action of measuring is inappropriate because "Jerusalem will be a city without walls." The phrase "a city without walls" is a translation of the Hebrew word *perazot*, which occurs elsewhere in the Hebrew Bible only in Judges 5:7; Esther 9:19; Ezekiel 38:11. A similar word, drawn from the same Hebrew root, is used in 1 Samuel 6:18 to create a contrast between the fortified city and the unwalled village. To use this term for the former royal city of Jerusalem would be shocking. At the height of the monarchy in Israel, Jerusalem was not just any fortified city, it was *the* fortified city, the place of protection for the king, the ultimate stronghold for the nation.

A wall around a city served one main function: to protect it from enemies. This may appear odd to some; why would one fear enemies in a world under *Pax Persica*? The reality is that imperial structures did *not* ensure safety. The books of Ezra and Nehemiah expose inter- and intra-provincial vulnerability (Ezra 3:3; 4:1–6:13; Neh. 2:7–10, 19–20; 4:1–23; 6:1–7:3) as well as danger from bandits (Ezra 8:31).[3] There was, however, a trade-off for the protection created by a city wall, for a wall delimited the extent of the city.

For two reasons, then, Yahweh sees the measuring of the city, the first step in building a wall, as opposed to his agenda for this city. (1) Related to the restriction of a wall, Yahweh plans to fill Jerusalem with a multitude that no wall can contain. The term *perazot* would have been associated with smallness, for larger cities were fortified. However, the message immediately contradicts this impression by revealing that the reason for this status is the immense size of the city. Jerusalem will be filled with a "great number of men and livestock."

---

2. For the view that this is the man with the measuring line, see, e.g., H. G. T. Mitchell, J. M. P. Smith, and J. A. Brewer, *A Critical and Exegetical Commentary on Haggai, Zechariah, Malachi and Jonah* (ICC; Edinburgh: T. & T. Clark, 1912), 115. For the view that this is Zechariah, see, e.g., E. H. Merrill, *Haggai, Zechariah, Malachi: An Exegetical Commentary* (Chicago: Moody Press, 1994), 115. A third option is that the surveyor is the angel of the Lord; see F. D. Lindsey, "Zechariah," in *The Bible Knowledge Commentary: An Exposition of the Scriptures*, ed. J. F. Walvoord and R. B. Zuck (Wheaton: Victor Books, 1983–1985).

3. See T. C. Young, "The Consolidation of the Empire and Its Limits of Growth Under Darius and Xerxes," in *Persia, Greece and the Western Mediterranean c. 525 to 479 B.C.*, ed. J. Boardman et al. (CAH 4; Cambridge: Cambridge Univ. Press, 1988), 65. Young argues that Cyrus's "empire" was nothing "more than just regions collected and held together by military force" and that Darius transcended Cyrus through "the actual creation, for the first time, of a real empire: a governmental structure based on the army, on certain classes of the society whose loyalty was to the throne and not to some geographical region, and on the charisma, intelligence and moral fortitude of one man, Darius" (p. 63).

(2) Related to the protection afforded by a wall, Yahweh himself plans to shelter Jerusalem, just as he protected the Israelites in the desert. Such phrases as "a wall of fire around it" and "its glory within," reminiscent of Exodus 13:21–22; 24:17 and Numbers 9:15–23, remind the people that God's protecting presence remains with this community, who are living in circumstances parallel to the precarious context of the Exodus community. The promise of God's glory is also reminiscent of Ezekiel's vision of the return of God's glory in Ezekiel 43:1–5.[4]

Petersen draws an interesting parallel here to Pasargadae, the royal city of the early Achaemenid kings.[5] This showcase city was built without walls, surrounded instead by fire altars representing their god, Ahura Mazda.[6] Jerusalem is now identified as a city from which will emanate Yahweh's cosmic rule. The absence of walls reflects the confidence of its Ruler in his unlimited power and authority.

The two reasons cited for the absence of walls around Jerusalem are not mutually exclusive. The unlimited prosperity of this city is to be traced to the protective role of Yahweh around this city. Zechariah hears a message of hope in a time of extreme hardship.

The vision of Zechariah 2:1–5 unpacks the promises of the initial vision in 1:8–17, in particular, the promise that God will return (1:16), rebuild the temple and city (1:16), and restore prosperity (1:17). This continues the tone of comfort that began in 1:13 in response to the initial penitence of the people (1:1–6).

Bridging Contexts

HOPE VIA ASSURED PROSPERITY. While the second vision (1:18–21) offered hope to God's people through the negative message of a promised punishment of the nations, this third vision is the flip side of that same hope, now expressed through the positive message of assured prosperity for the nation. To grasp the significance of this ancient

---

4. Here is yet another connection to Ezekiel's vision of the rebuilt temple. However, this passage has a different focus: Zechariah expands the vision to the entire city, not merely the temple.

5. Cf. Petersen, *Haggai*, 171; Young, "Consolidation," 102; D. Stronach, *Pasargadae. A Report on the Excavations Conducted by the British Institute of Persian Studies from 1961 to 1963* (Oxford: Oxford Univ. Press, 1978). Although Darius did not abandon Pasargadae, he built his own special city, Persepolis; Young, "Consolidation," 46; M. Mallowan, "Cyrus the Great," in *The Cambridge History of Iran:* Volume 2—*The Median and Achaemenian Periods*, ed. I. Gershevitch (Cambridge: Cambridge Univ. Press, 1985), 396.

6. In addition Young notes that Pasargadae was "laid out much like an encampment . . . a 'tent city' translated into stone"; T. C. Young, "The Early History of the Medes and the Persians and

prophecy for contemporary audiences, it is important to set this message in its original context.

Although the downfall of Judah can be attributed to many historical factors over the first two decades of the sixth century, the events of the year 587–586 B.C. endured as symbols of the demise of the nation. The exile and abuse of the leadership, the incorporation of the territory into the Babylonian empire, and the destruction of the city and temple became the focus of attention in the prayers, speeches, and narratives of Jewish texts after this time. One cannot rate the importance of these symbols, but the physical destruction of the sacred capital of the Jews prompted strong reactions from God's people.

This is vividly displayed in various liturgical responses that arose in the Babylonian and Persian periods. Lamentations, for instance, voices the shock that the enemy entered, looted, and damaged the temple (Lam. 1:10; 2:6) while destroying strongholds (2:2, 5), ramparts (2:8), walls (2:8), gates (2:9), and foundations (4:11). Foreigners reacted to the destruction with shock (2:15) and disbelief (4:12), but for God's people the pain was almost beyond description.

Several psalms also preserve the reaction of the people:

> O God, the nations have invaded your inheritance;
> they have defiled your holy temple,
> they have reduced Jerusalem to rubble....
> How long, O LORD? Will you be angry forever?
> How long will your jealousy burn like fire? (Ps. 79:1, 5)

> Why have you rejected us forever, O God?
> Why does your anger smolder against the sheep of your pasture?
> Remember the people you purchased of old,
> the tribe of your inheritance, whom you redeemed—
> Mount Zion, where you dwelt.
> Turn your steps toward these everlasting ruins,
> all this destruction the enemy has brought on the sanctuary.
> Your foes roared in the place where you met with us;
> they set up their standards as signs.
> They behaved like men wielding axes
> to cut through a thicket of trees.
> They smashed all the carved paneling
> with their axes and hatchets.

the Achaemenid Empire to the Death of Cambyses," in *Persia, Greece and the Western Mediterranean c. 525 to 479 B.C.*, ed. J. Boardman et al. (CAH 4; Cambridge: Cambridge Univ. Press, 1988), 44. In light of the desert motifs in Zech. 2:1–5 this may explain the connection to Pasargadae.

> They burned your sanctuary to the ground;
> they defiled the dwelling place of your Name. (Ps. 74:1–7)

The depth of pain, highlighted by the searching questions of the classic psalms of lament ("how long ... why?"), reveals the importance of Jerusalem and the temple to the Jewish community living in the wake of the destruction of Judah.[7]

But why were these physical structures so important to this community? Why would the destruction of this city and sanctuary lead a people to sense that God had rejected them forever? To understand this, we must reflect on several passages in the foundational texts of the Jewish community. Deuteronomy 12 is part of a larger speech of Moses to the Israelites on the verge of occupation of the Promised Land, in which Moses sets out legislation to protect the exclusive worship of Yahweh in this new land. This legislation has negative and positive aspects. (1) The people are to eliminate all places of idolatrous worship strewn throughout the land (e.g., those on high mountains or hills, or under trees) and all objects that facilitate idolatry (e.g., altars, Asherah poles, or idols). (2) They are to centralize worship at the "place the LORD your God will choose from among all your tribes" (12:5). This place will be the place of God's presence ("put his Name there for his dwelling"). It will also be a place at which the people will "rejoice in everything you have put your hand to, because the LORD your God has blessed you" (12:7).

It is this legislation that explains the hope of kingship in Judges, which links the absence of a king with the fact that "everyone did as he saw fit" (Judg. 17:6; 21:25; cf. 18:1; 19:1), a clear allusion to the legislation of Deuteronomy 12. David is the one who fulfills this hope, for in the early part of his reign he centralized worship by transporting the ark and tabernacle to Jerusalem (2 Sam. 6; 1 Chron. 13–16; Ps. 122). His son Solomon completed David's centralization by constructing a permanent structure for the worship of the kingdom (1 Kings 5–8; 2 Chron. 2–7). During the dedication of the temple, God took up residence in this building, filling it with his manifest presence (1 Kings 8:10; 2 Chron. 5:13–14; 7:1–3).

From this temple God rules over all of Israel and receives tribute from his people (Ps. 84). But Israel's Zion tradition has more in view than just the land of Israel. From Zion God will extend his rule over the entire earth. It is the "joy of the whole earth" for the God whose "praise reaches to the ends of the earth" (Ps. 48:2, 10). This city will become the center of the earth as nations stream to the holy mountain (Isa. 2:1–4//Mic 4:1–3) and gladly trace their heritage to this city of God (Ps. 87).

---

7. Notice how the captors of Israel in exile demanded "songs of Zion" and how difficult it was to sing such happy songs (Ps. 137).

Such a strong theology of Zion explains why in the closing moments of the kingdom of Judah, the people pinned their hope of salvation on the temple:

> This is what the LORD Almighty, the God of Israel, says: Reform your ways and your actions, and I will let you live in this place. Do not trust in deceptive words and say, "This is the temple of the LORD, the temple of the LORD, the temple of the LORD!" (Jer. 7:3–4)

The temple became a place in which people trusted for salvation rather than responding to the prophetic call to repentance. Such trust, however, would not avert God's judgment (Jer. 7:14). In the end both city and temple would be destroyed. Nevertheless, the prophets did expect a renewal of the city and its sanctuary. God would one day look with compassion on her ruins (Isa. 51:3) and rebuild Jerusalem and her temple (Isa. 44:28; Ezek. 40–48). It is this hope that sustained the people throughout the coming centuries. Daniel longed for the restoration of the city, informed by his reading of Jeremiah and expressed through his penitential prayer (Dan. 9). Ezra pursued purity in his generation because of his desire to sustain the restoration of the city (Ezra 9:9). Nehemiah's mission was instigated by an inquiry about Jerusalem (Neh. 1).

Zechariah 2:1–5, therefore, declares the imminent fulfillment of the hopes of a people who have lost so much in 587 B.C., hopes based on a long theological tradition within Israel, beginning with Deuteronomy 12. Rebuilding the city is intricately linked with the return of God's presence and the experience of his blessing.

Underlying this message one can discern two key issues within this ancient community: a lack of vision and a lack of trust, both of which become evident in the prohibition to measure the city. (1) Decades of abuse under foreign oppression have dampened the hopes of the most optimistic among the Jewish community, both those living in exile and those remaining under foreign rule in the homeland. For many, the prophetic ideals of cosmic rule and unprecedented blessing have been tempered by present circumstances and reduced to realistic expectation. Zechariah's vision in 2:1–5 challenges the community to trust God's plan for his people.

(2) The other key issue is a lack of trust in God's protection for his people. Certainly this community has lived with many fears and experienced much abuse at the hands of foreigners. The vision encourages them through an allusion to their ancient exodus tradition. The journey from Egypt to Canaan was a precarious journey, which left them vulnerable and demanded trust in God. The Persian period community on a second exodus to reclaim their land would need similar trust in God, whose cloud of fire would protect

them from their enemies. This vision encourages trust in the same God who preserved his people through the dangers of the desert.

This vision speaks to the church today in similar ways. The symbol of Jerusalem and its temple is fulfilled ultimately in the church (1 Cor. 3:16–17; 6:19; 2 Cor. 6:16; Eph. 2:21; 1 Peter 2:4–5; Heb. 12:22) because of Christ (John 2:19–22). As we are involved in fulfilling Christ's commission to build his church, it is all too easy to live with limited and unbelieving vision.

Contemporary Significance

Presence of God. The promising vision of 2:1–5 provides a necessary perspective for a community emerging from exile. The New Testament echoes the themes of this vision as it encourages the nascent church community to view their world from God's perspective and as the early Christians live their new life of faith. Key to this encouragement is the promised presence of Christ through his Holy Spirit. Thus, in Acts 2 we find the disciples awaiting the arrival of the Spirit. When the Spirit comes on them in power, they are propelled forward into a life of precarious faith to accomplish feats greater than they could ever have imagined.

In Acts 4 Peter and John return from their meeting with the Sanhedrin to join with the voices of the community in prayer to God. Their initial words to God as a community reveal that they are viewing life from God's perspective ("Sovereign Lord"), and as they continue and ask for God to do great wonders through them in their generation, they reveal their willingness to live by faith in the midst of vulnerability. God graces this community with a powerful display of his presence, as their meeting place was shaken and they were filled with the Holy Spirit.

Fundamental to this message, both in Zechariah and Acts, is God's manifest presence in the midst of his people. Transformed vision and faithful living are possible only for the community that experiences God's personal presence in their midst. His presence is the glory within, consecrating and prospering God's people, and yet it is also the fire around, protecting the people. God's presence on the one side is terrible, for it strikes awe and fear in humanity (Ex. 19–20; Isa. 6); yet this presence is also necessary to the life of faith (Ex. 32–34).

The glorious message of the New Testament is that God has graced us with his presence through his Holy Spirit, who enlivens his faithful community (Rom. 8). Yet our churches and lives are often bereft of manifestations of his presence. As communities of faith we are often unaware of God's absence in our midst and need to cry to him to pour out his Spirit. Without that presence the challenges of this vision, to which we now turn, will never be realized.

Vision beyond—viewing the world from God's perspective. As already noted, the prohibition of measuring the city is related to two key issues that continue to challenge us today as Christians. The first is the temptation to limit our vision of the potential of the kingdom. It is easy to delimit the boundaries of God's city, to restrict our vision to human realities (past and present) rather than divine possibilities.

In our lives and communities of faith we must dream outside of our limited boxes. Sometimes these boxes are created by well-meaning people trying to protect God from losing face. These theological boxes with their careful limitations on what God actually does today can border on heresy or even blasphemy. Our theology must bear witness to the miraculous God of Scripture, who can and does do anything.

Sometimes these boxes are created by fearful people trying to preserve their community from change. As we will see in our consideration of 2:6–13, the "great number of men and livestock" envisioned in 2:5 is defined in 2:11–12 as those from outside the Jewish community. If built, the city walls that protected the Jews from hostile foreign nations would have limited these same nations from access to the community of God.

When I was a young boy, there was a special loft in the rafters of one of the garages on our block. My brother and two of his friends had established a secret club in this loft. One day my brother took me along to the club meeting. We ascended the ladder and I was ushered into the place of privilege. Almost immediately the two other boys, who along with my brother were a year older than I, began to whisper to themselves energetically. They then motioned to my brother to join them and informed him in no uncertain terms that I was banned from the loft because I was not part of the club. My brother turned to them and with indignation in his voice declared that if the club was not open to his little brother, then he was quitting the club. Taking my hand we both marched down the ladder and back to our house.

It is easy for the church to imitate such childish behavior. Zechariah 2:1–5, however, reminds us that the community of faith is not a private country club but rather a community center. The church is a city without walls, open to unprecedented and diverse growth.

Precarious life of faith—trusting in the God of the impossible. The prohibition of measuring the city not only challenges us to expand our vision in light of the character and acts of God in history and his vision for his people, but also to live by faith in this same God. To live without walls in a hostile environment will mean to live in vulnerability, to trust the God of the impossible. Zechariah's vision in 2:1–5 encouraged this community that had lived through much pain and disillusionment to entrust themselves to the God of the exodus community.

Such a precarious life of faith is not encouraged in churches in the West, especially in light of the many freedoms we enjoy. But a true life of faith may mean following a calling that is not expected or honored within our community—that is, counseling families in a needy urban context, planting a holistic church ministry within an inner-city neighborhood, caring for people suffering from AIDS, pursuing a life in the arts where few Christians can be found, receiving an orphan or abused child into our family, and the list could go on. The important point here is learning to trust God as we pursue the impossible.

Zechariah 2:1–5, therefore, encourages God's people to experience life in its fullness as they expand their vision of God, his purposes, and his people, and as they step out in new ventures of faith. This is only possible as God's presence is a reality in their midst individually and corporately.

Zechariah 2:6–13

"COME! COME! FLEE from the land of the north," declares the LORD, "for I have scattered you to the four winds of heaven," declares the LORD. 7"Come, O Zion! Escape, you who live in the Daughter of Babylon!" 8For this is what the LORD Almighty says: "After he has honored me and has sent me against the nations that have plundered you—for whoever touches you touches the apple of his eye—9I will surely raise my hand against them so that their slaves will plunder them. Then you will know that the LORD Almighty has sent me.

10"Shout and be glad, O Daughter of Zion. For I am coming, and I will live among you," declares the LORD. 11"Many nations will be joined with the LORD in that day and will become my people. I will live among you and you will know that the LORD Almighty has sent me to you. 12The LORD will inherit Judah as his portion in the holy land and will again choose Jerusalem. 13Be still before the LORD, all mankind, because he has roused himself from his holy dwelling."

Original Meaning

THE READER NOW MOVES from the world of vision to that of oracle. Although Zechariah incorporates oracles as integral elements into his visions (see 1:14–17; 2:4–5; 5:4),[1] the present section lies outside the vision of 2:1–5. Furthermore, the audience also has changed, for while in 2:4–5 the angel speaks to the "young man," 2:6–13 addresses the exilic community.[2]

The oracle continues emphases from 2:1–5, including expansion of the city (2:6, 7, 11; cf. 2:4) and the promise of God's presence (2:10–11; cf. 2:5). However, it also develops the theme of the scattering (2:6; cf. 1:19, 21) and abuse of God's people (2:8; cf. 1:15, 21)—key to the first two visions. This

1. See Long, "Reports," 353–65, for the use of oracles within visions.

2. See Petersen's comments (*Haggai*, 185): "They clearly breathe a spirit different from that of the visionary cycle." However, Petersen goes too far in seeing this section as "a disparate series of utterances," esp. considering vv. 6–9 and 10–13 both contain the formula "then you will know that the LORD Almighty has sent me to you" and the construction "Daughter of Babylon/Zion."

oracle builds on the previous visions and calls the people to respond to God's initial work and promise by returning to his land and city, where he promises his presence.

The oracle also reflects the same historical situation as the initial visions. The nations who "feel secure" and with whom the Lord is "very angry" in the first vision (1:15) are the "horns that scattered Judah," who will be terrified and thrown down in the second vision (1:21). This opens the way for rebuilding Jerusalem and the return of God's presence (2:4–5). This fits the historical context of the Jewish community during the transfer from Babylonian to Persian hegemony in the early Persian period (see comments on 1:7–17). The Babylonians are the ones who took Judah into exile ("scattered Judah"), and they were overthrown by the Persians, first as Cyrus broke their mastery of the ancient Near East in 539 B.C. and later as Darius exacted punishment on them for their rebellion against him (522–520 B.C.).

God's people are living within Babylon ("Daughter of Babylon," 2:7; "the nations that have plundered you," 2:8), which will be devastated by former slaves, that is, the Persians ("their slaves will plunder them," 2:9). The people are called to "escape" from Babylon (2:7) to "Judah/Jerusalem," the place where God's presence will again be found (2:12). The return of both people and God to the land suits the initiatives of the Persians in the early Persian period, who with political savvy allowed subjugated peoples to return and to rebuild their temples in the wake of a disastrous Babylonian religious policy.[3]

These thematic and historical connections between the three initial night visions and the oracle in 2:6–13 highlight the function of the oracle in the night vision complex.[4] At this crucial juncture, the oracle brings the message of the heavenly visions "down to earth"; that is, it calls the audience to respond, showing that these night visions have implications for their community (cf. 6:9–15). Whereas the apocalyptic tone of the visions and their accompanying messages emphasize the divine at the expense of the human, the prophetic oracle now invites human involvement in this great divine initiative. The people are to escape Babylon and return to Jerusalem, rejoicing in God's deliverance and expecting his return.

The present oracle consists of two sections of equal length, each distinguished by a series of imperatives: 2:6–9 (introduced by three uses of *hoy* [NIV "come"] and the imperatives "flee/escape") and 2:10–13 (introduced by

---

3. See the commentary introduction; Boda, "Horns." Notice how Darius seeks to follow in the footsteps of Cyrus by affirming his actions (see Ezra 5:1–6:15; cf. 1:1–11), something that fits Darius's drive for legitimacy; cf. M. M. Waters, "Darius and the Achaemenid Line," *Ancient History Bulletin* 10 (1996): 11–18.

4. There are also close verbal connections between this oracle and the last night vision in 6:1–8: "the four winds/spirits of heaven" (2:6; 6:5); "the land of the north" (2:6; 6:6, 8 [2x]).

the imperatives "shout/be glad"). The first section has an urgent tone as the people are called to escape the land of their captivity. The second calls them to rejoice as they return to their land, for God has promised his presence with them.

Call to Escape (2:6–9)

THE INITIAL ORACLE is the most urgent of the collection. It begins with the double exclamation "Come! Come!" (*hoy hoy*), a word that often appears at the beginning of the Woe Oracles of classic prophecy (e.g., Isa. 5), but here functions as a call for attention (as in Isa. 55:1).[5] The audience of this declaration is not clarified until Zechariah 2:7, where we are told that it is "you who live in the Daughter of Babylon," a reference to the exilic community in Mesopotamia. "Daughter of Babylon" functions as a synonym for Babylon and plays off the reference to "Daughter of Zion" in 2:10, juxtaposing the two cities and revealing that Zion will in the end be triumphant (see comments below).

The fact that Zion is living in Babylon is why they are called to flee/escape from the "land of the north," a common image representing the Mesopotamian lands—in this case, the Babylonians, who subjugated the people of Judah. Although Babylon is nearly due east of Jerusalem, the path of invading Mesopotamian armies was always from the north as they followed the ancient roads of the Fertile Crescent.

The reference to the "four winds of the heavens" does not create an allusion here to an "eschatological" return,[6] but rather to the returns that began at the end of the Babylonian era. Jeremiah uses the same language when speaking of Elam's destruction and exile:

> I will bring against Elam the four winds
>   from the four quarters of the heavens;
> I will scatter them to the four winds,
>   and there will not be a nation
>   where Elam's exiles do not go. (Jer. 49:36)

Although the Hebrew word for "scatter" here is different from the one in Zechariah 2:6, the reference to the "four winds" confirms that the same image is in mind. It is that of winnowing grain at harvest time, an agricultural process often performed on the tops of hills to utilize the natural breezes that carried

5. Possibly also Isa. 18:1; Jer. 47:6; cf. Petersen, *Haggai*, 173; J. G. Baldwin, *Haggai, Zechariah, Malachi: An Introduction and Commentary* (TOTC; Downers Grove, Ill.: InterVarsity Press, 1972), 108.

6. As does Merrill, *Haggai*, 119.

away the chaff. The four winds come from the four ends of the heavens (NIV "quarters" in Jer. 49:36) and thus symbolize the universal scattering of the people.[7] The universality of this expression does not contradict the first half of the verse that focuses on the "land of the north," for Jeremiah adopts similar rhetoric when he speaks of the direction of the Exile to and the return from both the land of the north and the ends of the earth (Jer. 3:18; 16:15; 23:8; 31:8).[8]

After calling the people to flee from their captivity in 2:6–7, Zechariah then explains why the people will escape from their captors. Echoing the message of the first two visions, Yahweh affirms that he will punish the nations who have plundered his people.

There has been much controversy over the meaning of 2:8–9 as a result of awkward Hebrew constructions. Verse 8 begins with an expression common in Zechariah: "For this is what the LORD Almighty says," a phrase that typically introduces a speech of Yahweh in the first person. The difficulty begins from this point on. For most commentators the majority of the Lord's quote that follows is to be attributed to the prophet Zechariah or one of his disciples, with the short central declaration ("I will surely raise my hand against them so that their slaves will plunder them") connected to Yahweh (so NIV text). Others have connected the first portion before this central declaration as a continuation of the messenger formula, functioning as an adverbial phrase modifying the verb "says" (answering the question "when?"; see NIV footnote).

To discern the flow of thought in this section, we should begin with the more common phrase that occurs at the end of verse 9: "Then you will know that the LORD Almighty has sent me," a phrase which also occurs at the end of 2:11. These declarations are unique to Zechariah and occur at two other points, 4:9 and 6:15, both in sections traditionally tagged as oracles lying outside the visions. In each of these occurrences the prophet refers to an action promised by Yahweh that will establish the legitimacy of his calling.[9] The action promised in both 4:9 and 6:15 is that of the rebuilding of the temple, both in reference to the exilic community's participation in that project with special attention to Zerubbabel's role. The action promised in 2:9 is God's release of his people, while the action in 2:11 is God's return among his people.

The first part of this declaration "then you will know" is used often in prophetic material (esp. Ezekiel), though it is normally connected to Yahweh

7. An allusion to the four winds will find its way into the vision series at 6:1–8 (see comments).

8. Petersen, *Haggai*, 175.

9. See B. Halpern, "The Ritual Background of Zechariah's Temple Song," *CBQ* 40 (1978): 168–69.

directly rather than to the prophet (e.g., Ezek. 6:7; 7:4, 9), drawing its origin from the experience of Moses (Ex. 6:7; 7:17; 8:22). The second part of the declaration ("the LORD has sent me to you") is rare elsewhere, appearing in Exodus 3:13, 14, 15; 7:16; Numbers 16:28, 29.[10] It is interesting that although the specific combination is unique to Zechariah ("then you will know that the LORD Almighty has sent me to you"), the calling of Moses in Exodus 3–6 is a common treasury for this phrase.[11] In most of these passages the formulas are used in connection with God's direct intervention in the affairs of his people, whether that is the Exodus (Ex. 10:2), provision in the desert (Ex. 16:12), victory in war (Deut. 9:3), discipline for disobedience (Ezek. 7:27), or salvation after judgment (16:62).

These other occurrences reveal the purpose of this particular formula in Zechariah. It is not primarily to remind the people of the oracle when it comes true. Rather, it is a rhetorical technique that bolsters the impact of the prophetic word, reminding the people that as a servant is sent with the authority of his master (2 Kings 5:22; 8:9; 18:27), so the prophet is sent with the authoritative words of God.[12]

Returning now to the initial phrase of the oracle begun in verse 8, we find there the use of the same verb "send" (*šlḥ*), which is the key to the legitimizing idiom. This suggests that, although unclear, it is to be interpreted in the same way. Yahweh's message does not begin until after the legitimizing idiom is introduced, bolstering the prophet's position as one through whom God brings his message of judgment to the nations.

The core of God's message is seen in the phrase, "I will surely raise my hand against them so that their slaves will plunder them." To raise one's hand against another is a Hebrew idiom usually referring to a violent action against an opponent. When Yahweh appears as the subject, it indicates a military action (Isa. 11:15; 19:16; cf. 10:32; 13:2). In both references in Isaiah Yahweh's action is directed against Egypt in a context containing allusions to the Exodus. So also here, the passage alludes to the Exodus in the phrase "their slaves will plunder them" (cf. Ex. 12:36),[13] indicating a reversal of the plundering activity of the Babylonians.

---

10. Cf. Isa. 48:16; 61:1; Jer. 25:17; 26:12, 15; 42:21. This term *šlḥ* ("send") is often associated with the calling of a prophet paralleling the paradigmatic calling of Moses (see Ex. 3:10; Isa. 6:8; Jer. 1:7; Ezek. 2:3–4).

11. Ezekiel uses the formula: "then they will know that a prophet has been among them" (Ezek. 2:5; 33:33), which is similar in theme but different in vocabulary.

12. This concern for the authority of prophecy may reflect a perception of crisis over the validity of the prophetic word in the early Persian period, a trend also seen in the book of Haggai, see Boda, "Haggai," 295–304.

13. Although a different word in Heb., the theme is synonymous.

This occurs "after he has honored me" (lit., "after glory"). This is the most hotly contested phrase in the oracle and is rendered as a description of the manner ("with insistence"),[14] the timing ("after glory," i.e., after his calling as a prophet or reception of visions),[15] or the purpose of the prophetic commission ("for glory"; cf. Ezek. 39:21).[16]

The link to Ezekiel 39 in this final suggestion provides a helpful clue for understanding this awkward phrase. Ezekiel 38–39 introduces us to the rise and fall of Gog and Magog, which is probably a coded reference to Babylon.[17] Ezekiel 39:21–29 clearly links this passage to the Exile and restoration of Israel, and there we read of God's displaying his "glory" among the nations, paralleled in the second half of the verse with a display of "the punishment I inflict and the hand I lay upon them" (39:21). Glory here is thus equated with God's judgment either on Israel (exile) or on their enemies (restoration). As Zechariah considers the restoration and the defeat of Babylon, he alludes to this prophecy of Ezekiel, saying that "after glory"—that is, after God's judgment—the prophet is sent to declare disaster for Babylon. Like Jeremiah (cf. Jer. 1:5, 10), Zechariah is to initiate disaster on the nations by announcing their fall.

The zeal of God that calls Zechariah to announce judgment is ignited by the character of the nations' actions. When they plundered Israel, they were touching "the apple of his eye." The idiom "daughter of the eye" is synonymous with another idiom, "the middle of the eye," appearing both independently and in conjunction with one another (Deut. 32:10; Ps. 17:8; Prov. 7:2; Lam. 2:18) and denoting vulnerability and by extension the inordinate care for something equated with it (Deut. 32:10; Ps. 17:8; Prov. 7:2). The verb "touch" when used in combination with the preposition *b* often denotes harmful touching (e.g., Gen. 26:11; 2 Sam. 14:10). God's statement is not merely that these nations harmed his people, but that when they harmed his people, they were in reality touching the dearest part of Yahweh himself.

---

14. Baldwin, *Haggai*, 109; T. Chary, *Aggeé-Zacharie, Malachie* (Paris: J. Gabalda, 1969), 70, cf. Ex. 11:5; Ps. 73:24; Eccl. 12:2.

15. Mitchell, Smith, and Brewer, *Haggai*, 141–42.

16. C. J. L. Kloos, "Zech. II 12: Really a Crux Interpretum?" *VT* 25 (1975): 729–36.

17. Clearly this point is debated as some see Magog as a reference to eschatological nations, others to nations north of Israel. Ezekiel is located in exile in the heartland of the Babylonian empire. Although he delivers oracles against many of the nations, the one exception is Babylon. Long ago, Boehmer saw in the word Magog a code for Babel, produced by shifting the Hebrew consonantal order by one letter and reversing the order: Thus "b-b" becomes "b-g" in the Hebrew alphabet and "l" becomes "m"; J. Boehmer, "Wer ist Gog von Magog? Ein Beitrag zur Auslegung des Buches Ezechiel," *ZWT* 40 (1897): 321–55. This is a modification of the well-known Atbash system used in Jeremiah, where Sheshach in Jer. 25:26; 51:41 and Leb Kamai in 51:1 are coded names for Babylon.

Call to Rejoice (2:10–13)

THE SECOND SECTION of the oracle opens with a new set of imperatives: "Shout . . . be glad." The mood changes from the harried cry to escape from a place of danger (2:6–9) to the exuberant call to rejoice. This section, therefore, represents the appropriate response of a community delivered from captivity (cf. Zeph. 3:14–18; also Jer. 31:7).

This community is identified as "Daughter of Zion," a phrase that creatively plays off of the earlier designation, "you who live in the Daughter of Babylon." The city of Jerusalem is often called "Zion" in the Old Testament, a name that predates David's conquest (2 Sam. 5:7) and becomes closely associated with God's presence, for on Mount Zion his presence dwells (Isa. 8:18) and there he is worshiped (Ps. 48:2). It becomes intimately linked with God's people, personifying the community of God mourning the fall of the state (Lam. 1:1–11)[18] and surviving through the Exile (Isa. 1:26–27; 49:14). As the people long for restoration, it is on Zion that their hopes are set (Ps. 69:35; 102:13) and to which they long to journey (Ps. 120–134).[19]

About 25 percent of the occurrences of the word "Zion" are in the phrase found here, "Daughter of Zion,"[20] half of which are positive, reflecting "dignity, joy, favor, and exaltation" (so Zech. 2:10), with the other half negative (cf. Lam. 2:13; Zeph. 3:14). The reason for the female image of "daughter" is difficult to discern. It appears to be a familiar idiom for cities (Ps. 45:12; 137:8; Isa. 23:10), not only because "city" (*ᶜir*) is a feminine noun in Hebrew, but also because "it is an image of the unity between place and people within which divine favor and civilization create a setting of stability and home."[21]

Ollenburger has noted that the "central theological notion evoked by the symbol of Zion is the kingship of Yahweh."[22] In many contexts as God

18. Cf. K. M. Heim, "The Personification of Jerusalem and the Drama of Her Bereavement in Lamentations," in *Zion, City of Our God*, ed. R. S. Hess and G. J. Wenham (Grand Rapids: Eerdmans, 1999), 129–69.

19. Although used in earlier eras, the final form of the Psalms of Ascent is most likely linked to the return to the land; cf. P. Satterthwaite, "Zion in the Songs of Ascents," in *Zion, City of Our God*, ed. R. S. Hess and G. J. Wenham (Grand Rapids: Eerdmans, 1999), 105–28.

20. See E. R. Follis, "Zion, Daughter of," *ABD*, 6:1103.

21. Ibid.; cf. L. Ryken, J. C. Wilhoit, and T. Longman, eds. *Dictionary of Biblical Imagery* (Downers Grove, Ill.: InterVarsity Press, 1998), 980–81; see esp. E. R. Follis, "The Holy City As Daughter," in *Directions in Biblical Hebrew Poetry*, ed. E. R. Follis (JSNTSup 40; Sheffield: Sheffield Academic Press, 1987), 173–84, who draws on the sociological position of women—"associated with stability, with the building up of society, with nurturing the community at its very heart and center."

22. B. C. Ollenburger, *Zion, the City of the Great King: A Theological Symbol of the Jerusalem Cult* (JSOTSup 41; Sheffield: Sheffield Academic Press, 1987), 146.

enters his royal city (Zion) and palace (temple), he is greeted with exuberant joy (e.g., Ps. 9:14).[23] This explains why the exhortation to rejoice in Zechariah 2:10 is based on the promise that God is "coming" to "live among" his people, a pledge repeated in verse 11 and found throughout the Old Testament to express God's presence in his sanctuaries (Ex. 25:8–9; Num. 35:34; 1 Kings 6:13; Ezek. 43:7; cf. 37:27).[24]

This reveals that those who respond to the exhortation to return to the land will be met there by the God who once abandoned the land (compare Ezek. 10 with Ezek. 37). This promise echoes the words of the first night vision in Zechariah 1:16, where God promised to return ("I will return to Jerusalem with mercy"), an assertion closely aligned with the promise to rebuild the temple ("there my house will be rebuilt"; 1:16) and that of the oracle in the third vision in 2:5: "I will be its glory within." The rebuilding of the temple will be useless if God does not bless the structure and community with his manifest presence.

Verse 11 introduces a surprise into the oracle by declaring that foreigners will enter the community of the Lord on the day when God's presence returns to Israel. That the expression "many nations" does not refer to the exilic community living among the nations but to the nations themselves is clear from other prophetic contexts that use this verb and imagery (Isa. 14:1; 56:3, 6; Jer. 50:5). The phrase "be joined" is clearly covenantal in nature (Isa. 56:6), a point made clear by the declaration "[they] will become my people," which is used throughout the Old Testament to typify the people's status in the God-Israel relationship (Jer. 31:33; 32:38). The fact that the oracle then repeats the phrase "I will live among you" after declaring the inclusion of these foreigners is an intentional technique to emphasize their participation in the covenant community and its privileged access to God's presence.

This reference to foreigners entering the community, coupled with the assertion of God's presence, connects this oracle to the third night vision (2:1–5), where the young man is forbidden to measure the city for its wall because of the potential size of the city (the great number of inhabitants) and protective role of Yahweh (a wall of fire). This oracle repeats the assertion of God's presence and explains the large size of the city.

If the inclusion of a great number of foreigners in the covenant community gives rise to questions about the special status of the land of Israel, verses 12–13 address any concerns. The universal vision will be realized through the particular reinstatement of Judah and Jerusalem as God's special possession. The verb "inherit" and the noun "portion" are well known from the

23. Ibid., 46–47.

24. Cf. A. Petitjean, *Les oracles du Proto-Zacharie: Un programme de restauration pour la communauté juive après l'exil* (Paris: Librairie Lecoffre, 1969), 133–35.

Conquest narratives, but there they refer to the Israelites' possession of the land (Josh. 19:9, 51; cf. Num. 18:20; 26:55).

Here in Zechariah 2:12 God is depicted as repossessing and reconquering the land of Judah, which he abandoned. "Judah" refers to the region rather than tribe because it is the object of "inherit" and identified as a subset of "the holy land." "Jerusalem" is a subset of Judah, and the phrase "his holy dwelling" in 2:13 anticipates the temple complex within Jerusalem. The particularistic tone of this verse shows that the universal impact of God's covenant will be accomplished through a return to his throne in the temple in Jerusalem in Judah in the holy land.[25] The land is still important to God's plans and is consecrated ("holy") for God's presence.

God's return to his land, city, and temple has implications for all humanity, who are called to silence with the interjection "be still" (*has*).[26] Silence is demanded because God is stirring and is about to appear among his subjects.[27] Most see "his holy dwelling" as denoting God's heavenly court, since the temple had not been rebuilt.[28] It therefore alludes to the temple rebuilding theme, which will restore Zion as the passageway to God's heavenly court. This signal to all humanity that God is entering his courtroom was the original reason for the joyous tone of this section of the oracle begun in verse 10 ("I will live among you"). The universal and particular emphases encountered throughout this section converge here.[29]

In summary, Zechariah 2:6–13 divides neatly into two sections each introduced by a series of imperatives. The first (2:6–9) focuses on God's salvation and the response expected of the people. Although the Lord has scattered the people in discipline, it is now time to restore the people he calls the "apple of his eye." The prophet calls them to respond by fleeing and escaping their captivity as God breaks the nations who subjugated them. The second section (2:10–13) emphasizes the presence of God and the response expected of the people. Although the Lord abandoned his temple, city, and land because of the disobedience of the people, he will now return to meet his escaping people. The prophet calls them to respond with shouts of joy as God returns to his temple. But there is a surprise in store. The prophet expands the scope of this community to include "many nations."

---

25. Cf. Ollenburger, *Zion*, who links Zion and kingship.

26. This is not an imperative and so does not designate a third section in the oracle.

27. Halpern, "Ritual Background," 167–90, argues that the verb ("roused himself") suggests divine warrior activity (Judg. 5:12; Isa. 14:8–10; 51:9; 52:1; Jer. 6:22; 25:32; 50:41; 51:11; cf. Isa. 42:10–13).

28. Cf. Merrill, *Haggai*, 128; Baldwin, *Haggai*, 112.

29. See Petersen, *Haggai*, 185.

Bridging Contexts

ALIENS JOURNEY HOME. For many, traveling in a 1970 Ford Ranch wagon packed with seven children and two parents is not their idea of a good time. But for my siblings and me it is one of our fondest childhood memories. My parents, raised in New York and New Jersey, would brave the dangers of the American Interstate system and set out from the Canadian prairies on a tour to their old haunts, complete with a trip to an upstate New York farm and a coastal New Jersey beach. But in those many summers I cannot remember a desire to move permanently to those faraway worlds. They were nice to visit, but I had my own life on the frozen tundra of Saskatchewan.

In the passionate cry of the prophet to return to the land, it is at first difficult to grasp the reason for such spirited zeal. The vast majority of North Americans have come from foreign contexts, immigrating to this continent over the past five centuries. The socio-psychological pattern for these immigrant groups is that the first generations typically have close associations with their homeland, but there is a subtle transformation in the succeeding generations as they assimilate into the dominant culture. This was driven home to me vividly when I was pastoring in a church in Toronto. One of the teens whose parents had emigrated from India before he was born asked his father concerning his grandparents: "When are those Indians going to go home?" At the second generation, the identity of this family had already shifted to the new country.

By Zechariah's time some families had lived in Mesopotamia for fifty, others up to seventy years. Surely they would have felt settled in this new country. Archaeological finds in Mesopotamia have revealed that some within the Jewish community were able to construct a comfortable life in their new land,[30] evidence displayed in Ezra as it catalogues considerable economic donations from the Mesopotamian Jewish community; Esther, Nehemiah, and Daniel also reveal traditions of successful Jews within the Persian aristocracy. Living in exile may have been difficult at first, but had they not grown accustomed to this new context? Is this merely a burst of nostalgia, a longing for the good old days in the Promised Land?

The prophet's passion can be linked to several factors. Sociologically, there is no question that there was considerable stigma attached to the alien within ancient Near Eastern cultures. We know this is true for immigrants today, especially for visible minorities, even within a North American milieu where immigration laid the foundation for the nations. This was even more

30. Ackroyd, *Exile*, 31–38; see the later evidence of the Murashu family, *ANET*, 221.

so in the ancient Near East, which explains why the Torah protected the rights of aliens and grouped them together with those most vulnerable within the society: fatherless and widows (see comments on 7:1–14).[31] Assimilation into the various Mesopotamian cultures would have been difficult because of the difference in language, traditions, and especially religious observance.

But there is something more going on here than sociology, for Zechariah's call is not merely an appeal to create a safe living space for the Jewish community; rather, it is based firmly on strong theological traditions within Old Testament revelation. In the covenant established with Abraham, God promised three things: people (Gen. 17:4–6), relationship (17:7), and land (17:8).[32] God's intention for Moses was that he would be the instrument to bring these three promises to fulfillment.

The book of Exodus begins with a numerous Jewish community threatening the Egyptians (Ex. 1–11). As this multitude is released from bondage, their immediate destination is Mount Sinai, where they meet with God and establish a national relationship with him through covenant (Ex. 12–39, esp. 20). As a result of this encounter, God comes to live in their midst (Ex. 40). With their sights on Canaan and the fulfillment of the third promise to Abraham, the people and their leader go astray and are forced to wander around the desert for forty years (Numbers). It is left to Joshua, not Moses, to finally storm the land of Canaan and realize the final promise of land. These redemptive events lie at the foundation of Jewish faith and Old Testament revelation (cf. Deut. 6:20–24; 26:1–11; Josh. 24; Neh. 9; Ps. 78; 104–106; 135–136).

At the Exile, however, all three of these promises were endangered. Violation of covenant through the infidelity of the people threatened the promise of relationship. The final blow is pictured in Ezekiel as the glory of God, representative of his presence, abandons the people and land through the east gate (Ezek. 10). Without God on their side, the promises of land and people are soon reversed. The land is handed over to enemies who subjugate the population and cart away numbers of people into exile (2 Kings 25).

Set in this theological context, the prophet's insistence on a flight from Babylon to return to the land is justified. Relationship with God is linked to a land, where he and his people will live together. Land ensured preservation of community and covenant for the people of God.

---

31. See, e.g., the ancient Code of Hammurabi, which sees the role of law "that the strong might not oppress the weak" (*ANET*, 164; see *ANET*, 164–98 for various ancient law codes).

32. See D. J. A. Clines, *The Theme of the Pentateuch* (JSOTSup 10; Sheffield: Sheffield Academic Press, 1978), for this tripartite structure and how it provides the shape of the Pentateuch as a whole.

Aliens find a home. As I mentioned at the outset, my identity as an "immigrant" child in Canada eventually was shaped by my new country and culture. For me home became Canada because I had adopted the values and traditions of the nation of my childhood rather than my birth.

Building on the prophetic vision of 2:1–5, a vision prohibiting a walled city that would limit urban growth, the oracle in 2:6–13 reveals the reason for the expansion potential of this city. The community released from bondage to experience afresh the presence of God is the community into whom God will bring "many nations." So also "all mankind" is hushed in the final verse as God rouses himself from his throne room. The restoration of the people to their land with a holy temple and city had implications for the whole world. In this we see the stark contrast between the two sections of the oracle in 2:6–13. Verses 6–9 view the nations in a negative light as those who plunder God's people and who will be plundered now by their former slaves. In verses 10–13, however, the nations are now invited into the community of God.

Such a perspective is not foreign to the Old Testament witness. From the outset of redemptive history, God has had such a global vision.[33] The promise to Abraham in Genesis 12, which is formalized through the covenant of land, relationship, and people in Genesis 15 and 17, envisions the blessing that God will bring to "all peoples on earth" through Abraham and his descendants (Gen. 12:2–3; cf. 18:18; 22:18; 26:4; 28:14). This blessing is fulfilled in the gospel (Rom. 4:13; Gal. 3:8, 29). Israel's call from God as a nation is understood as a priestly role as God declares in Exodus 19:4–6:

> You yourselves have seen what I did to Egypt, and how I carried you on eagles' wings and brought you to myself. Now if you obey me fully and keep my covenant, then out of all nations you will be my treasured possession. Although the whole earth is mine, you will be for me a kingdom of priests and a holy nation.

Israel is a "kingdom of priests and a holy nation" within the larger family of nations. As priests they will serve as mediators between God and the nations. This role is closely linked in Exodus 19:5 with their obedience to the covenant, which God laid before them and which is summarized in the following chapter, the Ten Commandments (Ex. 20).[34]

---

33. See J. H. Bavinck, *An Introduction to the Science of Missions*, trans. D. H. Freeman (Phillipsburg, N.J.: Presbyterian and Reformed, 1960); D. Senior and C. Stuhlmueller, *The Biblical Foundations for Mission* (London: SCM, 1983); W. C. Kaiser, *Mission in the Old Testament: Israel As a Light to the Nations* (Grand Rapids: Baker, 2000).

34. On this see C. J. H. Wright, *Living As the People of God: The Relevance of Old Testament Ethics* (Leicester: Inter-Varsity Press, 1983); idem, *Walking in the Ways of the Lord: The Ethical Authority of the Old Testament* (Downers Grove, Ill.: InterVarsity Press, 1995).

This vision for the nations is not restricted to revelation during the patriarchal and Exodus periods. God's covenant with David and his choice of Zion have a global dimension. Through the Davidic king Yahweh will exercise his rule over all the nations (Ps. 2) as well as communicate the blessing promised to Abraham (Ps. 72, esp. v. 17b). Zion, the Davidic capital in which Yahweh resides, is the place from which God exercises his rule over the whole earth (Ps. 48) and in which all the nations have a place (Ps. 87).

In light of this, the prophets envision a day when all the nations will be drawn to this city for teaching (Isa. 2:1–5//Mic. 4:1–5) and worship (Zech. 8:20–23). The prophet Jonah shows us that God's covenant compassion extends beyond the borders of Israel (Jonah 4). So also Isaiah introduces a servant figure who will be "a light for the Gentiles" (Isa. 42:6; 49:6).

Therefore, Zechariah 2:6–13 presents two aspects of Old Testament theology that must be kept in balance. God is intent on forming a people for himself, a redeemed community in which he dwells. This group, however, is not an exclusive group, but one into which God will bring others from among the nations. These two aspects are not unique to the Old Testament but can be traced throughout the New Testament as Jesus forms a community that is both transformed as well as transformative, not of the world and yet in the world. The New Testament speaks of the "world" as the system of rebellion against God and his people (John 7:7), yet at the same time as the object of God's love and redemption (John 3:16–17). We are saved out of this world by the grace of God into a relationship with him by his Spirit. This same Spirit propels us back into this world as instruments of God's grace to bring the "nations" into covenant relationship with him.

Contemporary Significance

ON ONE LEVEL the prophetic oracle in 2:6–13 is limited to its time and community. Through it we are escorted to front row seats in the arena of redemptive history to observe God's drama of salvation at one of its critical junctures: the return of God's presence and people to the temple, city, and land. This restoration will set in motion a complex of events that will eventually usher in the era of Christ and the church. This future era is intimated in the promise of the nations entering into covenant relationship with God.

We often forget that the church era was inaugurated in Jerusalem among a restoration community. The Feast of Pentecost brought Jews from far off countries. When God poured out his Spirit on that day, the apostle Peter stood up and cited Joel 2:28–32, a prophecy that speaks of the return of the remnant from exile: "On Mount Zion and in Jerusalem there will be deliverance, as the

LORD has said, among the survivors whom the LORD calls" (2:32). The church begins within a community returning from exile on whom the Spirit falls. This community that experienced God's presence through the filling of the Spirit is the community that is to be sent out empowered by that Spirit to bear witness to the gospel among the nations (Acts 1:8). In this way, then, this oracle shapes our behavior as the people of God.

Experiencing God's redemptive action. We cannot ignore the vigorous language at the outset of the oracle as the prophet calls his community to flee, to escape their land of captivity. The focus here is not on moral contamination; that is, the prophet is not saying come out and be separate from the evil Babylonians. Rather, the focus is on response to God's redemptive act; that is, God has broken the power of the oppressor and has thus freed them from captivity. They must now exercise that freedom. They have longed for this for seventy years (1:12), and God has now accomplished it; they must act on that.

Similarly, God in Christ has broken the power of the oppressor for his community and invites them to escape bondage. This freedom has many dimensions in the new covenant era, foundationally liberation from sin in all of its dimensions: personal, social, and spiritual. We who were born in our own "Babylon," a world of sin dominated by the prince of the power of the air, are saved by God's act of grace and called his "workmanship" (Eph. 2). We are invited to enter a new life in a new kingdom in Christ.

But the lives of many Christians and their communities do not always show evidence of the liberation God has provided for his people. There are many reasons for this. (1) There is the ongoing effect of sin. We live between the times, that is, between Christ's first and second coming. On the cross Christ defeated the power of sin, yet this does not mean that we no longer sin (1 John 1). When I say this, I am not capitulating to sin and saying that dealing with it is not important, only that we await ultimate restoration when Christ returns again. When I speak of sin, I do mean sin both on a personal level and on a corporate level. Sin does transcend the individual to the very systems and structures of our society, and these can keep God's people in bondage, whether that is due to economics, gender, race, or age.

(2) Related to this first reason is a more psychological one. For some, psychological and relational damage from their past has left scars that last a lifetime.[35] Others are even caught in a spiritual morass in which they are reliant on bondage for their sense of well-being.

(3) A third reason why liberation is not always evident is simply theological immaturity. I am not speaking here of whether a person has an academic

35. God redeems people, but this does not mean that the effects of their sin is eliminated: e.g., divorces, children, credit ratings, legal records.

theological degree, but whether a person has a solid grasp of the Bible's teaching on salvation in all of its dimensions. This is the problem that Paul addresses in the church at Rome, especially as he repeats the question: "Do you not know?" (Rom. 6:3, 17; 7:1).

Zechariah 2:6–13 offers hope to those who are still caught in bondage. God considers his people the "apple of his eye," a term of endearment, and has broken the forces that oppress them. He now urges them to experience this freedom as they enter his presence, to live in light of the freedom that God has accomplished through Christ as they walk in step with the Spirit. Such freedom will mean revisiting the reason for one's bondage and responding appropriately, whether that is confession of sin, godly counseling, or theological grounding (cf. comments above). All of these highlight the importance of a community of faith that has and is experiencing God's presence and power in their midst.

Celebrating God's redemptive presence. Experiencing God's redemption is one legitimate form of application for this passage of Scripture. The people are to respond to God's redemption by escaping from their bondage. The second half of 2:6–13 adds other responses to this initial one as the prophet calls the people to celebrate God's redemption. This celebration is based on the return of God into their midst.

God's presence, identified as the fulfillment of the promise of relationship to Abraham (Gen. 17) and the goal of the great act of redemption at the Red Sea (Ex. 40), is now the outcome of God's great act of restoration. The ultimate expression of this presence is seen in Christ who "tabernacled" among us (John 1:14). In him the Lord climactically "roused himself from his holy dwelling." This same Christ sent the Spirit of God to indwell his community (Acts 2; 1 Cor. 6:19; 2 Cor. 6:16; Eph. 2:21).

Because of this presence God's people are prompted to respond in two ways. (1) They are drawn to "shout and be glad," to rejoice in the presence of God. Today, the church rejoices because of God's expression of himself in the Incarnation and because of the ongoing presence of the Spirit in their midst. Worship as one expression of this joy is the natural response of a people redeemed from bondage and experiencing the presence of their God.

(2) But 2:13 accents another human response in worship: "Be still before the LORD," a response linked to God's holiness (cf. Hab. 2:20). Certainly we are encouraged to celebrate God's redemption with joyful shouts and songs, but sometimes it is easy to forget that we are worshiping the holy and awesome God of the universe and need to "worship God acceptably with reverence and awe, for our God is a consuming fire" (Heb. 12:28–29).

Our worship in the church today should be shaped by this prophetic oracle. We need an approach that balances the transcendence of God with his imminence, that is, the exaltedness of God above all his creation with the nearness of God within his creation. Furthermore, we need an approach that balances exuberant and expressive praise with quiet and reflective worship rather than juxtaposing these between traditions and even services within a single church.

Embracing God's redemptive plan. The church cannot ignore one final aspect in this passage. This oracle balances the call to God's community to "escape the corruption in the world caused by evil desires" (2 Peter 1:4), but also to embrace God's redemptive plan for the world. It is not difficult to appreciate the fear of a people, recently freed from the bondage of their exile in Babylon, to return to a state of subjection. This is this same fear that often has shaped the ministry of the church and limited its impact within its society and world.

This prompts several key questions. What is the goal of our church's ministry? In what ways do we limit the availability of our members to become active contributors to our society? Do our vision and preaching support those who live "among the nations," whether in the workplace or the neighborhood, in the university or the government? There is understandable fear that the church will lose its identity among the nations, but the call of Jesus is to go because he is with them always (Matt. 28:18–20).

The movie *The Legend of 1900* tells the story of a long-forgotten piano prodigy named "Danny Boodman T. D. Lemon 1900" (1900 for short). A poor family on their way to the United States as immigrants leaves their baby in the ballroom of the luxury liner *The Virginian*, on which they are traveling in third class, in the hope that a rich couple will find the baby and adopt him as their own. Instead, an engine room worker finds the baby, and the child grows up on the ship. This child possesses a remarkable ear for music and soon captivates audiences aboard *The Virginian* with music "that's never been heard before." His talents come to the attention of the great jazz artist Jelly Roll Morton, who challenges 1900 to a piano contest. Morton describes him this way: "I've been hearing a lot of talk about a guy ... he's supposed to have been born on this ship, and never been off it since." But even after 1900 humiliates Morton, he refuses to leave the ship.

The Virginian transports thousands of Italian immigrants from Italy to New York, who leave the ship to begin their new life in America—but not 1900, for he remains aboard. His good friend, the trumpet player Max, encourages him to "leave this ship, marry a nice woman, and have children ... all those things in life that are not immense, but are worth the effort," but to no avail. 1900 refused to leave.

In the closing encounter between 1900 and Max, the piano legend recounts the moment in his life when he stood on the gangplank of the ship and gazed out at the streets of New York, which appeared to spread out for infinity. He concludes: "I was born on this ship and the whole world passed me by . . . a thousand people at a time."

At times I wonder if we do not face a similar challenge in the church. Overwhelmed by the streets of our culture, the villages of our globe that seem to go on for infinity, we are content to allow the world to pass us by from the safe vantage point of our pew. Using the metaphor of the vision of Zechariah 2:1–5, we build walls around our city, providing safety for the community but shutting out the nations. These walls are often laudable activities in our churches. Many churches today are filled with programs that are exciting and relevant. But such internal programming can often stifle the involvement of our church (both on the individual and corporate level) in the life of our surrounding community, nation, and world.

As a pastor leading a ministry team, I was forced one summer to count the number of programs in our ministry area of the church. The number was astounding, and I had to admit that I was successfully capturing the attention of my parishioners but was simultaneously stripping them of any opportunity to reach out to their friends and family. Furthermore, as we sought to support these many ministries, we were starving funding and personnel for ministries that took place outside the walls of the church building, but also in more needy areas of our nation and world. Thus, we began the painful process of evaluating the many internal programs with an openness to reducing the number of ministries. At the same time, however, it remains important to encourage, empower, and enable God's people to live faithfully within their surrounding community in word and deed.

Another way that we build walls around our communities of faith is by focusing our attention on one target group at the exclusion of others. Although this can be helpful (and necessary) to reach an unreached group within our local communities, too much fixation on one particular group may set a tone of exclusion within the community of faith. Sometimes God surprises us as he brings an unexpected person (and often then group) into our lives or church.

One church I know noticed the emergence of several Cambodian families at their church, all of whom could be traced back to one or two families who had come a few years prior. This trend forced them to reflect deeply on what God was doing in their church, and as a result they were able to expand their vision and mission to support what they had discerned to be a new work of God in their midst. Such support led to great fruit not only within this church community but also within the larger body as they have been enriched by the presence of these believers.

Zechariah 2:6–13

Zechariah 2:6–13 reminds us of God's passion for the nations, a passion that informed his purposes for his people from the outset of redemptive history and climaxed in the revelation of his Son Jesus Christ and the community he established. Of course, this impact on the nations is possible only for the community that has been redeemed from the bondage of sin and cultivates God's presence in its midst through worship.

Zechariah 3

THEN HE SHOWED me Joshua the high priest standing
before the angel of the LORD, and Satan standing at
his right side to accuse him. 2 The LORD said to Satan,
"The LORD rebuke you, Satan! The LORD, who has chosen
Jerusalem, rebuke you! Is not this man a burning stick
snatched from the fire?"
3 Now Joshua was dressed in filthy clothes as he stood
before the angel. 4 The angel said to those who were standing
before him, "Take off his filthy clothes."
Then he said to Joshua, "See, I have taken away your sin,
and I will put rich garments on you."
5 Then I said, "Put a clean turban on his head." So they put
a clean turban on his head and clothed him, while the angel of
the LORD stood by.
6 The angel of the LORD gave this charge to Joshua: 7 "This
is what the LORD Almighty says: 'If you will walk in my ways
and keep my requirements, then you will govern my house
and have charge of my courts, and I will give you a place
among these standing here.
8 "'Listen, O high priest Joshua and your associates seated
before you, who are men symbolic of things to come: I am
going to bring my servant, the Branch. 9 See, the stone I have
set in front of Joshua! There are seven eyes on that one stone,
and I will engrave an inscription on it,' says the LORD
Almighty, 'and I will remove the sin of this land in a single day.
10 "'In that day each of you will invite his neighbor to sit
under his vine and fig tree,' declares the LORD Almighty."

Original Meaning

ZECHARIAH 3 BEGINS with court proceedings in the heavenly council. The high priest Joshua stands before this court in filthy clothes about to be prosecuted by "the Adversary" (NIV "Satan"). The Lord, however, discontinues the proceedings by rebuking the Adversary and explaining the condition of the high priest. With the Lord's backing, the angel of the Lord, who is overseeing the court, rectifies the high priest's condition by commanding his helpers to remove the filthy clothes and replace them with new vestments.

After the angel interprets this clothing act as a removal of guilt, the prophet interjects, requesting that a turban be placed on the priest's head. The angel then delivers a message to the high priest.[1] First he looks to the immediate present and gives him a solemn charge to fulfill his duties as high priest in the restored temple. Fulfillment of these duties will result in the provision of the prophetic word. Then the angel looks to the future, revealing that the establishment of the priests at the restored temple mount is a sign of a new era in redemptive history, one in which a Davidic ruler named *ṣemaḥ* (NIV "Branch") will come and remove the guilt of the land, ushering in a period of prosperity known before only in Solomon's reign.

This vision reflects a period in Zechariah's ministry after Joshua has returned to the land but prior to the arrival of Zerubbabel, the Davidic descendant.[2] The prophet affirms the role of the Zadokite priestly family, a family that has remained faithful during the Exile (see Ezek. 44:10–16), and installs their leader Joshua as high priest for the new temple and community. But the prophet also carefully delineates a role for the monarchy and argues that the reinstatement of the priestly house is a sign of the renewal of the royal house, which will usher in a new age of prosperity.

Court/Investiture Scene (3:1–5)

THE VISION OPENS with the ambiguous phrase "he showed me." Although the interpreting angel escorted the prophet in the earlier visions, he left the scene in 2:3. Most likely the subject here is the Lord himself, whose entrance was announced in 2:13.[3]

The Lord shows Zechariah a scene that features Joshua, a priestly figure, well known to us from the books of Ezra (see Ezra 3; 5:1–2) and Haggai (see Hag. 1:1–11). His lineage can be traced through his father Jehozadak to the great priest Zadok and ultimately to Aaron, brother of Moses and first high priest of Israel. Zadok served with Abiathar as priest under David (2 Sam. 15:24), and when Abiathar joined Adonijah's rebellion against David (1 Kings 2:26–27, 35), he assumed sole control of priestly duties in Jerusalem. Ezekiel lauds the Zadokite priests for their faithfulness during the Exile (Ezek. 44:10–16). According to Ezra and Haggai, Joshua emerges with Zerubbabel as the key leaders (one priestly, one royal) in the second phase of restoration.

---

1. On the unity of this passage, see M. J. Boda, "Oil, Crowns and Thrones: Prophet, Priest and King in Zechariah 1:7–6:15," *JHS* 3 (2001): Art. 10; also printed in *Currents in Biblical and Theological Dialogue* (2001), ed. J. K. Stafford (Winnipeg: St. John's College, Univ. of Manitoba, 2002), 89–106.

2. For details on this vision and its relationship to chs. 1–8 (esp. 6:9–15) and to history, see ibid.

3. Cf. 1:20, where the same verb ("showed") is used in reference to Yahweh.

Joshua is the focus of a meeting of the heavenly council in which the Lord is surrounded by his angelic messengers.[4] Zechariah's presence is not odd because prophets had access to the divine court (1 Kings 22:19–21; Isa. 6; Jer. 23:16–22; Ezek. 1–3; Amos 3:7). The prophet sees Joshua "standing before" the angel of the Lord. This phrase is used in the Old Testament to describe participants in a royal court (1 Sam. 16:21–22; Jer. 52:12) as well as a legal assembly (Num. 5:16, 18, 20; 27:2; 35:12; Deut. 19:17).[5] In Zechariah 3 these two contexts cannot be distinguished because the royal court functioned in the ancient Near East as a legal court.

On the right side of Joshua stands "Satan." Psalm 109, a psalm of someone accused who awaits trial,[6] also speaks of a *śaṭan* (NIV "accuser") on the right hand (109:6), who brings an accusation and seeks a guilty verdict (109:6–7; cf. vv. 4, 20, 29). In Zechariah 3, the *śaṭan* in the heavenly legal court is an angelic being who fills the role of prosecuting attorney for the purposes of the tribunal.[7] The content of these accusations is not delineated in the vision. However, the proceedings that follow strongly suggest that they focus on the unworthiness of the high priest to perform his duties.

Rather than deny the accusations, the Lord rebukes the accuser and declares his intention to change the deplorable condition of the high priest

---

4. See N. A. Tidwell, who traces a divine council genre defined as "a narrative event in the heavenly council on an occasion when that council is gathered to make some fateful decision concerning the affairs of men" (cf. 1 Kings 22:19–21; Isa. 6:1–13; Job 1–2); N. L. A. Tidwell, "*Waʾomar* (Zech 3:5) and the Genre of Zechariah's Fourth Vision," *JBL* 94 (1975): 343–55.

5. This combination is also used to depict priestly service before God (Deut. 10:8; 18:7), but other indications in Zech. 3 ultimately favor the legal context.

6. For a review of the process of sacral legal proceedings, see H.-J. Kraus, *Psalms 60–150: A Commentary* (Minneapolis: Augsburg, 1989), 1:53–54.

7. Some have suggested human enemies of Joshua within the Jewish community or the Persian administration, but the divine court is clearly in view (cf. Meyers and Meyers, *Haggai*, 184–85). Others see the enemies as both human and spiritual, that is, human enemies are in the background and the Adversary is the spiritual representation of their attacks to show God's rejection of the enemies (see P. L. Day, *An Adversary in Heaven: Satan in the Hebrew Bible* [HSM 43; Atlanta: Scholars Press, 1988], 149). Barker sees tension between Levitical priests who served in Jerusalem in exile, while Allan identifies it as tension between North and South priests; cf. M. Barker, "The Two Figures in Zechariah," *HeyJ* 18 (1977): 33–46; N. Allan, "The Identity of the Jerusalem Priesthood During the Exile," *HeyJ* 23 (1982): 268–69. These views, however, are based on a view of sociological fracture in the early Persian community. Others see here the devil of the New Testament, but there is no reason to infuse the New Testament theology of Satan into Zech. 3, as the expression used here (*haśśaṭan*) is a title ("the Adversary"), not a proper name ("Satan"). This may indicate that the Satan of New Testament theology began in this role in the heavenly court. The role is not in itself an "evil" role, any more than a prosecuting attorney in Western courts is "evil." See further Day, *Adversary*.

because of his election of Jerusalem, echoing early assertions of divine choice and renewed favor in the night visions (1:17; 2:12).[8] The condition of the high priest is explained by the fact that he is "a burning stick snatched from the fire," an allusion to the priest's recent release from exile in Babylon drawn from Amos 4:11, who condemned the impenitent nation prior to exile. This image is a reminder both of the past punishment as well as future grace.

Verse 3 slows down the vision narrative for a moment and signals a new phase in the legal proceedings: the verdict. Joshua's clothes are indeed filthy (*ṣoʾim*), a term unique to this verse in the Old Testament but closely related to two nouns (*ṣeʾah*, Deut. 23:14; Ezek. 4:12; *ṣoʾah*, 2 Kings 18:27; Isa. 28:8, both used for human excrement and the latter one also for vomit). Such uncleanness is obviously inappropriate for a high priest in the presence of deity.

The angel of the Lord addresses the verdict to "those who were standing before him" (i.e., other members of the heavenly court) and instructs them to remove the filthy clothes. Immediately the angel turns to Joshua and declares that he has removed his "sin," a term that appears in the high priestly clothing rituals described in Exodus 28:36–38 (NIV "guilt") and Numbers 18:1 (NIV "responsibility for offenses").[9] This connection between the removal of guilt and the high priestly clothes suggests that Joshua is not only portrayed a steward for God's temple palace but also represents the entire remnant community.[10]

Next the angel declares that he has clothed this priest with "pure garments" (NIV "rich garments"),[11] after which the prophet Zechariah commands the attendants to set a "clean turban" (*ṣanip*) on Joshua's head. Though this is a different term for headdress from that found in the Torah (*miṣnepeti*, cf. Ex. 29:6; Lev. 8:9; Num. 20:26–28),[12] the reader cannot help but think of the high priestly turban because it is modified by the adjective "clean"

---

8. This rhetoric of "choice" (*baḥar* + *b*) in connection with Jerusalem is unique to Zechariah. Elsewhere the expression is used of God's choice of David and Israel; cf. Petersen, *Haggai*, 191.

9. Cf. Petersen, *Haggai*, 194–96.

10. Suggested also by the references to God's choice of "Jerusalem" and the allusion to the Exile in v. 2.

11. See D. Winton Thomas, "A Note on מחלצות in Zechariah iii 4," *JTS* 33 (1931–32): 279–80; J. C. VanderKam, "Joshua the High Priest and the Interpretation of Zechariah 3," *CBQ* 53 (1991): 553–70. Most translations (including the NIV) place the final phrase in the future tense, but the infinitive absolute in this phrase relies on the previous verb for its sense, in this case a perfect ("I have taken away"; see LXX). The temptation to translate this in the future is because of the "clothed him" in v. 5. However, this reference may be a general statement bringing closure to the clothing process ("and so they clothed him"), or may serve literary purposes; so Meyers and Meyers, *Haggai*, 192.

12. It should be noted that these two words are both related to the same Heb. root, *ṣnp*.

(*ṭahor*), a term employed regularly in the priestly literature to speak of ritual purity (e.g., Lev. 10:10).

In the Torah the turban joins several other special items of clothing fabricated from the finest materials for the high priest upon his ordination (Ex. 28 and 39), and in the investiture ceremony it was the last piece of clothing to be donned before the anointing oil was applied (Ex. 29:6–7; cf. Lev. 8:9–12). The turban is also mentioned in another ritual context in the Torah, the Day of Atonement (Lev. 16:4). The priestly vestments worn on this day were made from a type of material called *bad* ("linen"), distinguishing them from the garments used on the day of consecration, which were made from several forms of *šeš* ("linen").[13] The Day of Atonement was the only day in the ritual calendar when the high priest was allowed to enter into the Most Holy Place, and on this day he made atonement for the sins of the Israelite community.

These two events in the Torah provide a backdrop for the imagery and rituals encountered in Zechariah 3. (1) Both highlighted the act of clothing the high priest and were concerned with the removal of "guilt" (Ex. 28:38; Lev. 16:21; Zech. 3:4, 9). (2) Both ceremonies made it possible for the Lord to dwell with his people through a consecrated mediator (Ex. 29:44–46) and sanctuary (Lev. 16:16 for the tabernacle; cf. 16:18 for the altar), an issue that prepares the way for this vision. Zechariah 3 announces a new day for Joshua as he is cleansed from the stain of the Exile and installed as priest of the temple, instrumental for removing guilt from the community.

This, however, is only half of the story, for although the imagery conjures up the high priestly garments of the Torah, the actual words used for Joshua's new clothing and turban can be traced to Isaiah 3:16–4:6. This passage begins by speaking of the proud "daughters of Zion" and promises judgment typified by the removal of their many luxuries (including pure garments and turbans). By the end of Isaiah 3 these women become indistinguishable from the personified city of Jerusalem (notice "her gates," 3:26), which mourns over the loss of inhabitants.

A reversal, however, occurs in Isaiah 4:2–6, which continues the imagery of the "daughters of Zion" (4:4), whose "filth" (*ṣoʾah*, cf. above) is removed by "the spirit of fire" (cf. imagery of fire in Zech. 3). In this period the "Branch [*ṣemaḥ*] of the LORD" will be beautiful and glorious, the same word used twice in the oracles in Zechariah 3 to speak of a coming figure who ushers in a period of blessing. In other words, this vision deliberately plays off Isaiah

---

13. For more on this, see M. Haran, *Temples and Temple Service in Ancient Israel: An Inquiry into Biblical Cult Phenomena and the Historical Setting of the Priestly School* (Winona Lake, Ind.: Eisenbrauns, 1985), 165–74.

3:16–4:6 as the God "who has chosen Jerusalem" promises a new day for his people.[14]

Angelic Oracular Interpretation (3:6–10)

UP TO THIS point in Zechariah 3 the focus has been on the scene and its action, with minimal interpretation (only 3:4). As in the other visions, this scene sets up an oracle that relates to the visionary scene. The angel's prophetic speech ("This is what the LORD Almighty says," 3:7; "declares the LORD Almighty," 3:10) is introduced by the verb "gave this charge" (Hiphil of *ʿwd*), a verb used elsewhere in connection with strong warnings delivered by a human (e.g., Gen. 43:3), by God (e.g., Ex. 19:21, 23), or by a prophet (e.g., Jer. 6:10).[15] The fact that the recipients of this action elsewhere are all being warned reveals a transition from a positive disposition in the interpretation in Zechariah 3:4, which declared God's removal of guilt, to a darker nuance, reminding the priest that this new status cannot be taken for granted.

This more negative tone becomes clear in 3:7. In contrast to the first speech to Joshua in 3:4, this second one begins with a series of conditional clauses, outlining expectations for the high priest. There are four conditional clauses, divided into two groups—the first two speaking in general and the second two in specific terms.

(1) The angel calls Joshua to "walk in my ways . . . keep my requirements." (a) The phrase "walk in my ways" is a general term for walking in covenantal fidelity to God expressed through obedience to Torah (e.g., Deut. 8:6). (b) "Keep my requirements" can also refer to general faithfulness to Torah (e.g., Lev. 18:30), but in priestly literature often refers to the service performed by a priest (e.g., Lev. 22:9). This phrase appears in two other contexts relevant to Zechariah 3. One of the last instructions on the day of the ordination of the high priest was the exhortation to remain at the Tent of Meeting for the seven days of the ritual and "do what the LORD requires" (Lev. 8:35; lit., "keep my requirements"). Moreover, Ezekiel uses this phrase to refer to the faithful ministry of the priestly line to which Joshua belonged (Zadokites; Ezek. 40:45, 46; 44:8, 14, 15, 16; 48:11), a line contrasted with other Levites who participated in idolatry (44:10). These priestly connections to the phrase "keep my requirements" strongly suggest that the angel is referring generally to faithful priestly service.

---

14. So Petersen, *Haggai*, 198.

15. This verb is found in legal contexts elsewhere in the Old Testament to refer to the testimony of witnesses (Deut. 4:26; 30:19; 31:28; 1 Kings 21:10, 13; Ps. 50:7; Jer. 32:10, 25, 44; Mal. 2:14). It is, however, difficult to see how the angel's speech could be interpreted as such testimony both in terms of its content as well as its place in the legal proceedings.

(2) From the more general call to covenantal and ritual faithfulness, the next two conditions focus on more specific actions ("govern ... have charge") within a prescribed area ("my house ... my courts"). The Hebrew verb *dyn* (NIV "govern") is usually translated as "judge" (Ps. 7:8), and the phrase "my house" refers to the location where this justice was dispensed, since legal proceedings in the sanctuary were included in priestly duties (Deut. 17:8–13) and anticipated by Ezekiel for the restored Zadokite priests (Ezek. 44:24). The subsequent reference to "courts" (*ḥaṣer*) refers to the courtyards within the sanctuary precincts (Ex. 27:9; Lev. 6:9, 19; 1 Kings 6:36; 7:12), where ritual activity took place, another responsibility suggested by Ezekiel's vision of the renewed Zadokite priestly service (Ezek. 44:17–23; cf. ch. 40).

If such conditions of faithfulness to the covenant in general and to priestly duties in particular are met, the angel promises the high priest "a place among these standing here." "These standing here" clearly refers to members of the heavenly council, but recent work on the Hebrew term that underlies the word "place" has demonstrated that the high priest is not being offered access to the heavenly council, but rather to individuals who already enjoy such access,[16] most likely prophets (cf. Zech. 7:3).[17]

With the completion of 3:7, the angel now returns to the unconditional tone, with the call to attention: "Listen." As in the previous verse, he is still addressing Joshua but now expands the discussion to include "your associates seated before you," a phrase that describes the relationship between a religious figure and his disciples (2 Kings 4:38; 6:1).[18] These are Joshua's priestly associates, who assist him with the temple justice and ritual (cf. Ezra 3:2; Zech. 6:9–15), a reference to the instatement of the Zadokite priesthood in the priestly service.

That the larger issue of Zadokite priesthood is in view here is bolstered by the following phrase, which links the "men symbolic of things to come" to "your associates" (Heb., "they") rather than to Joshua. But in what way can

16. See W. H. Rose, *Zemah and Zerubbabel: Messianic Expectations in the Early Postexilic Period* (JSOTSup 304; Sheffield: Sheffield Academic Press, 2000); idem, "Messianic Expectations in the Early Postexilic Period," in *Yahwism After the Exile: Perspectives on Israelite Religion in the Persian Era*, ed. B. Becking and R. Albertz (Studies in Theology and Religion 5; Assen: Royal Van Gorcum, 2003), 168–85; Boda, "Oil," Art. 10.

17. Thus, as VanderKam has suggested, it removes Joshua one step from the divine council, for he is "given individuals who have direct access to the divine presence" and intimates: "In fact, the promise may refer to the ongoing presence of people such as Zechariah" (VanderKam, "Joshua," 560).

18. The technical nature of this phrase in such contexts becomes clear in 2 Kings 6:1, where Elisha's disciples refer to their meeting place as "the place where we sit before you." So also in Ezek. 33:31 (cf. 8:1; 14:1; 20:1) it refers to the prophet declaring the word of the Lord to the elders of Israel in exile.

these be "men symbolic of things to come"? This phrase consists of only two words in the Hebrew text: *ʾanšê mopet*. Although *mopet* (NIV "symbolic of things to come") can denote God's visible signs before humanity (e.g., "wonders" in Ex. 7:3), the reference here is to prophetic revelation through object lessons or sign-acts.[19] Two prominent examples of sign-acts (*mopet*) are Ezekiel's acts of packing his belongings and digging through the wall (Ezek. 12:6, 11) and his silence at the death of his wife (24:24, 27).[20]

Sign-acts are "nonverbal behaviors ... whose primary purpose was communicative and interactive" in similar ways to verbal prophecy; that is, they "give advice, express conviction, indict" as well as "predict" (e.g., Jer. 13; Ezek. 3).[21] In what way, then, are the priests involved in a sign-act? There is no reason to deny the ceremony of clothing Joshua the status of sign-act, especially considering the involvement of the prophet in the procedure. Thus, the investiture of Joshua as a symbol of the installment of the Zadokite priesthood ("your associates") is the sign-act that expresses the conviction of God's approval of the priesthood. But there also appears to be a future aspect to this sign-act communicated in two phases in the section that follows.[22]

In the first phase, the angel speaks of someone called "my servant, the Branch [*ṣemaḥ*]"[23] Who is this individual and how does he relate to Joshua and

---

19. See K. G. Friebel, *Jeremiah's and Ezekiel's Sign-Acts* (JSOTSup 283; Sheffield: Sheffield Academic Press, 1999), 27–31.

20. So also Isa. 8:18 for Isaiah and his children.

21. Friebel, *Sign-Acts*, 14. Friebel identifies 6:9–15 as a sign-act (p. 14 n. 5); so also Meyers and Meyers, *Haggai*, 338; Hanson, *Dawn*, 256. For this form see esp. G. Fohrer, *Die symbolische Handlungen der Propheten*, 2d ed. (ATANT 54; Zurich: Zwingli Verlag, 1968), 18; K. Friebel, "A Hermeneutical Paradigm for Interpreting Prophetic Sign-Actions," *Didaskalia* 12/2 (2001): 25–45; M. J. Boda, "Reading Between the Lines: Zechariah 11:4–16 in Its Literary Contexts," in *Bringing Out the Treasure: Inner Biblical Allusion and Zechariah 9–14*, ed. M. J. Boda and M. H. Floyd (JSOTSup 304; Sheffield: Sheffield Academic Press, 2003), 277–91.

22. Verses 8–10 contain a series of clauses all beginning with the particle *ki*: "'Listen, O high priest Joshua and your associates seated before you, [*ki*] who are men symbolic of things to come: [*ki hinneh*] I am going to bring my servant, the Branch. See [*ki hinneh*], the stone I have set in front of Joshua! There are seven eyes on that one stone, and I will engrave an inscription on it,' says the LORD Almighty, 'and I will remove the sin of this land in a single day.'" This particle has a diverse semantic range and can be translated (among other ways) as causal ("because/for") or emphatic ("indeed"). The first instance with *ki* alone is most likely causal, providing the reason why Joshua should listen. The next two, however, with the adjoining Hebrew particle *hinneh* (often translated "behold"), are probably emphatic and structure the sign-act interpretation into two sections, one about the coming of *ṣemaḥ* and the other about the removal of sin.

23. The translation for *ṣemaḥ* is traditionally "Branch." This is inappropriate and represents an imposition of the imagery of Isa. 11:1 (where *neṣer*, "Branch," is used). See the thorough argument on this issue by Rose (*Zemah*, 91–120). The word *ṣemaḥ* refers to vegetation but will merely be transliterated in this commentary.

his priestly cohorts? In Isaiah 4:2–6 *ṣemaḥ* is used as a general image of prosperity, referring to rich vegetation and paralleled with "the fruit of the land" (4:2). This prosperity is experienced by "the survivors in Israel" (4:2) and "those who are left in Zion, who remain in Jerusalem" (4:3), phrases reflective of remnant and restoration theology. We have already noted the influence of Isaiah 3:16–4:6 on Zechariah 3 as the vision intertwines the clothing and condition of the "daughters of Zion" with the clothing and condition of the high priest. This reference to *ṣemaḥ* returns one final time to Isaiah 3:16–4:6 to speak of a coming age of prosperity typified by rich vegetation (cf. Zech. 3:10).

In Zechariah 3:8, however, there is a transformation of the image *ṣemaḥ*. Whereas in Isaiah 4 this word is a sign of prosperity, by linking it with "my servant" Zechariah 3:8 clearly identifies *ṣemaḥ* as a person. Outside of Zechariah 1–8, Jeremiah 23:5–6 and 33:15–16 are the only passages to use this image to refer to a human being—in both cases a Davidic descendant.[24]

If *ṣemaḥ* is a Davidic descendant, then in what way are these priests "symbolic of things to come"? Although some have suggested that the prophet is collapsing the royal house into the priestly office, this is not the case here.[25] A closer look at Jeremiah 33:15–22 reveals how Jeremiah links the hope of the endurance of David's royal line in Judah with the endurance of the priestly service in the temple. This is not lost on Zechariah, who reveals that the installment of Joshua as high priest foreshadows the coming age of *ṣemaḥ*.

The angel provides a second phase of his interpretation in 3:9–10 by drawing attention to "the stone I have set in front of Joshua." The phrase "I have set in front of" probably means "handed over to" (cf. Deut. 1:21; 2:36).[26] More controversial is the reference to "the stone." In recent years scholars have been split between several views,[27] interpreting the stone as the temple rebuilding project, the temple mount,[28] the desert rock spring (Num. 20),[29] the engraved metal plate on the turban (Ex. 28:38), or the engraved stones on the ephod of the high priest's vestments (Ex. 28:22–28). Of these views, the final two fit the context best because of connections to vocabulary in

---

24. This Davidic descendant is called "my servant" (Jer. 33:21), just as David was (2 Sam. 3:18; 7:5).

25. For detailed argument see Boda, "Oil," Art. 10.

26. Cf. van der Woude, "Zion," 245.

27. See Lipinski, "Recherches," 25–55; van der Woude, "Zion," 237–248; VanderKam, "Joshua," 553–70.

28. See VanderKam, "Joshua," 563–64.

29. To do this they translate the word "eyes" as "springs" (another legitimate gloss for the Heb. word) and see the "engraving" as an "opening" in the rock from which water pours forth.

texts describing the high priestly clothing ("stone, engraving") coupled with the mention of taking away "guilt" in "one day."

This stone has "seven eyes" on it, which may refer to facets of a gem,[30] to the letters engraved on the golden plate (Ex. 28:36–38),[31] or to the fourteen stones on the high priest's breastplate/ephod complex (Ex. 28:16–28).[32] In any of these cases, the stone is associated with the representative nature of the high priest for bearing the guilt of the nation, for the final phrase declares its significance: "I will remove the sin of this land in a single day."

This reference to the removal of sin in one day alludes to the high priest's role as representative of Israel who, through the rites of the Day of Atonement, made atonement for the sins of the people and for their defilement of the sanctuary. "Sin" (*ᶜawon*) is the same word used by the angel in verse 4 (for which we have suggested "guilt") and the same one used in the Day of Atonement legislation (Lev. 16:21–22).[33] The verb "remove" (*mwš*), however, is different from those found in the Day of Atonement rites (Lev. 16:30, 33). The use of this term in Zechariah 3:9 rather than those used in the Day of Atonement seems to distinguish this act from the high priestly ritual. Whereas the Day of Atonement was designed to "make atonement for" guilt and ritually "cleanse" the people and sanctuary, the day associated with Branch, to which and to whom the priestly investiture points, will be a day when "guilt" is removed permanently, making the Day of Atonement obsolete.[34]

Verse 10 concludes the angel's oracular interpretation. The idiom used here "each ... under his vine and fig tree" occurs elsewhere for the peace and prosperity experienced under a successful ruler, whether Solomon in the past (1 Kings 4:25) or the Lord in the future (Mic. 4:4).[35] The association of *ṣemaḥ*

---

30. A metaphorical use of "eye" similar to "sparkle of wine" (Prov. 23:31), "gleam of bronze" (Ezek. 1:4), or "face of the land" (Ex. 10:5; Num. 22:5); cf. Baldwin, *Haggai*, 117.

31. Petersen, *Haggai*, 211–12.

32. As VanderKam has argued ("Joshua," 553–70), there are seven "eyes," which is a dual in Heb., and thus it can be taken as seven pairs of eyes.

33. Interestingly the lead term in the high priestly confession is this word that appears to be a general term for the guilt, with the following two words, more specific terms, for the acts that led to the guilt (Lev. 16:21). This is confirmed in the following verse when the other two terms disappear and our term remains (16:22; NIV, "sins").

34. The intransitive occurrences of this Heb. verb express removal in strong terms, often in a negative way to refer to someone not leaving a place (Ex. 13:22; 33:11; Num. 14:44; Josh. 1:8; Judg. 6:18; Isa. 22:25; 46:7; 54:10; 59:21; Jer. 17:8; 31:36; etc.). For a superb discussion of the terms for bearing and removing sin in the priestly literature see B. J. Schwartz, "The Bearing of Sin in the Priestly Literature," in *Pomegranates and Golden Bells: Studies in Biblical, Jewish, and Near Eastern Ritual, Law, and Literature in Honor of Jacob Milgrom*, ed. D. P. Wright, D. N. Freedman, and A. Hurvitz (Winona Lake, Ind.: Eisenbrauns, 1995), 3–21.

35. Cf. also 2 Kings 18:31, where Sennacherib promises prosperity to those who will rebel against Hezekiah.

with the Davidic dynasty brings to mind the idyllic description in 1 Kings 4:25. But the Micah passage focuses on the role of the temple in the future universal rule of Yahweh (Mic. 4:1–5) and is followed by another prophetic piece that speaks of the return of the remnant, Mount Zion, and the Daughter of Zion. Whether or not the use of this idiom is linked to these specific passages, there is clearly a connection to rulership in a passage that speaks of *ṣemaḥ*, a future Davidic ruler.

The idiom, however, has a unique twist here in Zechariah 3, for its orientation is expressly communal: "Each of you will invite his neighbor." The future figure will usher in a new day of safety and prosperity, typified by the ability of each member of the community to offer hospitality. To those living in the wake of Babylonian hegemony, including destruction of their nation and, for many, captivity in a foreign land, this promise is comforting indeed.

In summary, Zechariah 3 completes a line of argument that began in 2:6. There the prophet exhorts the people, called "Zion" and "Daughter of Zion," to escape their captivity in Babylon and return to the land and city that God inherited, chose, and promised to indwell.[36] This prepares the way for the vision of chapter 3, which uses Joshua's investiture as high priest for two purposes. (1) It is an opportunity to speak to Joshua as high priest, assuring him of God's blessing and calling him to faithfulness in his duties. (2) It is also an opportunity to speak to Joshua as representative of his priestly line, which is a sign-act of something far greater—a new era in redemptive history that will culminate in the coming of a royal Davidic ruler. Key to this new era is the removal of guilt from the land and prosperity for its inhabitants.

Bridging Contexts

PRIEST, PROPHET, AND KING. "Monica Lewinsky ... Monica Lewinsky ... Monica Lewinksy." It did not matter whether the newscast was in English at Humphrey Airport in Minneapolis, in Dutch at Schiphol Airport in Amsterdam, or in Hebrew at Ben Gurion Airport near Tel Aviv, her name was recognizable across the globe on the same day I led a group of students from Saskatchewan, Canada, to the Israeli coastal city of

36. That the promise of God's indwelling in ch. 2 prepares the way for the focus on sin and rituals connected with its removal is confirmed in Schwartz's discussion of the vocabulary and rituals connected to the "bearing" and "removal" of sin in priestly texts. Schwartz has shown that dealing with sin was essential to accommodate God's presence with the people: "They must be driven away, so that the divine Presence will not be driven away. Maintaining the welfare of the community, ensuring the continued abiding Presence of the Lord, is paramount"; Schwartz, "Bearing of Sin," 21.

Jaffa. In a world on the brink of the Kosovo War, with El Niño devastating the globe and the Asian financial "flu" placing entire nations in the Far East in jeopardy, the lead story was Monica Lewinsky.

Growing up in Canada, I have always been fascinated by the American system of government, which always seemed so cumbersome to me in contrast to the simplicity of the British parliamentary system. What I call "cumbersome," however, my friends to the south call "balance of power." This system consists of three semi-independent branches, each with unique responsibilities, including a check on the others—the executive branch: the president of the United States; the legislative branch: the Congress (including the Senate and House of Representatives); and the judicial branch, the Supreme Court and its lesser courts and attorneys.

Enter, stage right: Monica Lewinsky, and what looked like a balance of power turned to all-out civil war: the judicial branch (aka Kenneth Starr), secretly taping conversations between Lewinsky and a girlfriend to get information on the president and handing out subpoenas to many of the President's closest aides; the executive branch (aka Bill Clinton), denying all; and the legislative branch, split down the middle with some supporting the executive and others the judicial branch, primarily along party lines. This balance of power was stretched to the limit in the lead-up to and in the aftermath of the impeachment proceedings of the president, at times leaving the nation disgusted, at other times undermining the ability of leaders to guide the nation with integrity.

Such disarray in the leadership of a nation, however, is not unique to late twentieth-century American life, but is evidenced in early sixth-century Judean life as well. The final days of the southern kingdom (Judah) were witness to tension and collusion between the three "branches" of leadership within Judean society: the royal, priestly, and prophetic branches (cf. Mic. 3:11). A quick look at Jeremiah 37:3 reveals the role played by all three of these branches: "King Zedekiah, however, sent Jehucal son of Shelemiah with the priest Zephaniah son of Maaseiah to Jeremiah the prophet with this message: 'Please pray to the LORD our God for us.'"

In this case king and priest were arrayed against prophet as the nation teetered on the brink of destruction. The balance of power that was to preserve the nation, however, was undermined by the refusal of two of the branches to heed the cry of the prophetic branch. Because of this refusal, the nation would ultimately end up in exile and the various branches dispersed and decimated by this devastation.

The vision in Zechariah 3 is a timely message for Zechariah's community as it proclaims the reemergence of these same branches of leadership within the restoration community. Although clearly priestly, prophetic, and royal figures lived in and through the Exile, an important sign that restoration arrived for the people was the reinstatement of these figures in official capacities in the temple and polity of the Persian period.

It is not surprising that the prophets were the first to emerge after the Exile, since their ministry continued throughout the exilic period (see Jeremiah and Ezekiel). Priestly and royal figures, however, were slow off the mark, considering they were restricted in the exercise of their role without temple (priest) or palace (king). A closer look at the priestly, prophetic, and royal figures in Zechariah 3 helps us identify the significance of the message of this passage for Zechariah's original audience and begin the process of identifying its significance for us today.

Joshua represents the priestly caste within Israel. Most of the priests were born in a land far distant from the holy ground of Israel and only heard of the priestly duties from the older generations. But as this passage shows with its reference to the cleansing of the entire land, Joshua also represents the entire exilic community as they return to the land. As the one who will serve in God's presence offering sacrifices and offerings on behalf of the people, the fate of Joshua is intertwined with that of the people. As a mediatorial figure positioned between God and his people, Joshua is essential for God to fulfill his promise of returning to the temple and for the people to have access to this presence.

The message from God through this vision is clear: Although filthy from the stain of the Exile, represented by the filthy clothing, God proclaims his grace for the high priest. The stain will be removed and new clothing provided in order to signal a new start for the priesthood and the people; it opens the way for the return of the Lord to his temple. There is little question that this reinstatement occurs in the early Persian period and that the rule of the Zadokite priests will endure for the next 350 years until the rise of the Hasmoneans.[37]

Essential to this new start for priesthood and people is the gift of prophets like Zechariah, who have access to the divine council. These mouthpieces of God's revelation arose throughout the history of God's people to guide the community in the ways of God. Haggai's queries of the priests in Haggai 2:10–14 and Zechariah's role alongside them in the temple in Zechariah 7:3 show the close relationship between priest and prophet in the early Persian period, a relationship evident in the preexilic era as well (Jer. 26:2, 7–8, 16; 23:16; 35:4; Lam. 2:20).[38] The books of Haggai, Zechariah, and Malachi

37. See D. W. Rooke, *Zadok's Heirs: The Role and Development of the High Priesthood in Ancient Israel* (OTM; Oxford: Oxford Univ. Press, 2000).

38. See Boda, "Complaint," 186–97.

trace the important role that such prophets play within the Persian period community as they encourage and warn the people. Similarly, Ezra 5–6 highlights the role of the prophetic word within this same community:

> Now Haggai the prophet and Zechariah the prophet, a descendant of Iddo, prophesied to the Jews in Judah and Jerusalem in the name of the God of Israel, who was over them. Then Zerubbabel son of Shealtiel and Jeshua son of Jozadak set to work to rebuild the house of God in Jerusalem. And the prophets of God were with them, helping them. (Ezra 5:1–2)

> So the elders of the Jews continued to build and prosper under the preaching of Haggai the prophet and Zechariah, a descendant of Iddo. They finished building the temple according to the command of the God of Israel and the decrees of Cyrus, Darius and Artaxerxes, kings of Persia. (Ezra 6:14)

In the first passage the prophets are placed alongside Zerubbabel and Joshua as instrumental in rebuilding the temple. In the second passage the preaching of the prophets is placed on the same level as the "decrees of Cyrus, Darius and Artaxerxes," the Persian emperors. Certainly nothing emphasizes more the key role that the prophets play in this formative period for the restoration. With access to the divine council, they are key conduits of discernment for this community as they seek God's word and encourage the people in their endeavors.

This vision finally focuses considerable attention on the reinstatement of the Davidic line. It represents a message to the priestly caste that their return to the temple courts foreshadows the coming of *ṣemaḥ* ("Branch"). Delivered in the period when Joshua and many priests have returned (see Zech. 6:9–15) but Zerubbabel, the Davidic scion, has not,[39] this reminds the priests of Jeremiah's promise that the fates of both priestly and royal lines are intertwined. They should anticipate a period of peace and prosperity with the two offices restored.

This hope in the reemergence of the Davidic line is a core element of Old Testament revelation and faith. God promised David an unending line of descendants to serve as vice-regent over his people and world (2 Sam. 7; Ps. 2). This was seriously threatened as the king was marched off into exile (2 Kings 24–25), but God's promises come true as he preserves his anointed one among the nations and ultimately returns his descendant to the Promised Land.

---

39. See Boda, "Oil," Art. 10.

A message for the church. Zechariah 3 thus speaks to a community long ago and far away. Its focus on the priestly order in Israel is a potential stumbling block for many Christian readers. Priests do not receive positive billing in the New Testament because of their opposition to Jesus' ministry. Moreover, the book of Hebrews clearly subordinates the Aaronic and Levitical priesthood to that of Christ's Melchizedekan priesthood, highlighting the way in which the Old Testament priesthood falls short of the ideal in Christ. It is this lack of fulfillment that provides an important segue for the Christian community to appropriate its message for the church today. The New Testament identifies Jesus as the ultimate fulfillment of the Davidic hope. In and through him the idyllic conditions of Zechariah 3 can be realized.

On the basis of this we cannot afford to miss the timely message of this chapter for us. It bears witness to God's continuing pursuit of his people. God reveals his persistent desire to be present with his community, a priority only possible through the priestly and sanctuary structure. He also reveals his continued gracious provision of salvation for his people, a provision that makes his presence possible. This passage reminds the church of Christ's grace, unmerited and yet available through God's faithfulness. The Adversary is accurate in his accusations: Joshua is a sorry sight and unworthy to be within the camp of Israel, let alone the divine council. But God declares a new start by his grace, on the basis of which we are called to faithfulness. As we hear the call to Joshua, we can hear a call to each of us as a community of priests within our world.

God's provision of the prophetic word in Joshua's time parallels his provision of the written Word today for the church. Although the New Testament is well aware that the written Word can spell death if it is only "tablets of stone" without the enlivening Spirit (2 Cor. 3:1–18; cf. John 5:37–40), it does describe that Word in dynamic terms. The Scriptures are "living and active" (Heb. 4:12), "living and enduring" (1 Peter 1:23), and therefore are "God-breathed and useful" (2 Tim. 3:16) and "at work in you who believe" (1 Thess. 2:13). In this way the Scriptures today grant us access to God's divine council.

The prophets, however, not only deliver God's word to his people, but also stand as mediatorial figures who bring the people's requests for discernment to the divine council.[40] In this way God's provision of the prophetic word in Zechariah 3 parallels provision of immediate access through Jesus Christ to the "throne of grace," that is, the divine council (Heb. 4:16).

40. See Boda, "Complaint," 186–97.

The arrival and rule of Zerubbabel on one level fulfill the anticipated reinstatement of the royal line.[41] One should not forget, however, that this does not exhaust the hopes of Jeremiah and Zechariah as Zerubbabel only functions as a governor in the Persian province of Yehud, not as king over an independent and prosperous state. After Zerubbabel the Davidic line continues its connection to civil rule only for a short period through the marriage of his daughter to his political successor. The frustrations accompanying and the reasons underlying the failure to realize the prophetic promises can be discerned in the prophetic sign-act of Zechariah 11 (see comments on 11:4–16).[42] These promises directed toward Zerubbabel are not realized in his time but await the coming of Someone greater in his family line. Thus, the divine pursuit to be present with his people, to provide cleansing, revelation, access, and prosperity, awaits the arrival of another: Jesus Christ. Zechariah 3 bears witness to God's great plan of redemption and through this engages us in our present context.

Contemporary Significance

GRACIOUS FOUNDATION. The vision of God's grace in Zechariah 3 foreshadows the work of Christ to provide cleansing for all and access to God's holy presence. We as Christians face the great danger of losing sight of the fundamental doctrine of grace in our walk with God. Often I have watched new Christians reveling in these doctrines alongside "mature" Christians who have lost the wonder and have been forced to evaluate my own definition of maturity in Christ.

This danger is particularly so within those traditions that emphasize the biblical principles of sanctification and the progressive work of the Holy Spirit in a believer. There is a tendency to create distance (both logically and temporally) between justification/regeneration/adoption and sanctification. Thus, some denominations speak of the "deeper life" and others of the "higher plane," expressions that reveal an honest passion for sanctification but which can lead to a loss of focus on the foundational doctrines of grace. This is usually not the intention of those who call the church to these holiness values.[43]

The wonder of the doctrine of grace should never be lost as we grow in the Christian life. Colossians 2:6–7 reminds us that we are to continue to live in Christ as we "received Christ Jesus as Lord." The grace of Christ is the foundation of our faith from first to last; we cannot somehow leave it behind as we mature in the faith.

---

41. The promises are placed on Zerubbabel, but Haggai speaks of him as a symbol of someone yet to come within his line (see comments on Hag. 2:20–23).

42. Also Boda, "Reading," 277–91.

43. See Smith's review of these issues, esp. in the Holiness movement in Smith, *Beginning Well*, 194–203.

The exhortations in Paul's various letters in the New Testament are always based securely on the theology of grace through Christ. For instance, the call to walk in holiness in Ephesians 4–6 ("live a life worthy of the calling you have received," 4:1) is based on all the blessings we have received "in Christ" in Ephesians 1–3 (e.g., 1:3). So also the exhortation to "offer your bodies as living sacrifices, holy and pleasing to God," which introduces a series of commands in Romans 12–15, is based securely on "God's mercy" (12:1), which is explicated in detail in Romans 1–11.

This pattern is not restricted to the New Testament; rather, it takes its lead from the foundational covenant document of the Old Testament: the Ten Commandments (Ex. 20; Deut. 5). Before delivering the Decalogue to his people, Yahweh reminds them of his gracious act of salvation: "I am the LORD your God, who brought you out of Egypt, out of the land of slavery" (Ex. 20:2; Deut. 5:6). All instruction in holiness, therefore, must be founded on an explanation of the grace we have received through Jesus' death, resurrection, and ascension. Anything short of this is dead moralism. As Clowney once noted, "the Scriptures are full of moral instruction and ethical exhortation, but the ground and motivation of all is found in the mercy of Jesus Christ."[44]

Churches can foster this tone of grace among their membership through regularly focusing on grace within their worship and teaching. This may sound surprising to some, but there are some traditions that focus so much on exhortations to purity that the evangelical message of grace has been silenced. This can create an inappropriate cloud of guilt that stunts spiritual growth. This may be why the regular spiritual rhythm that Christ instituted for us as the church is the Lord's Supper. By participating in this symbolic act of grace and remembrance, we are constantly reminded that our Christian lives are based on the gracious act of Jesus on the cross. Zechariah 3 served as an encouragement to the Persian period community that God had extended his grace to them through their high priest. This was but a foreshadowing of the kind of grace and cleansing he would one day communicate through Jesus.

Grace and the accuser. It is the sovereign choice and gracious provision of God in Zechariah 3 that ultimately undermine the arguments of the accuser (*śaṭan*). From what we can tell from this scene, most likely the angelic prosecutor in this scene is correct in his allegations against Joshua and the community he represents. Fresh from the Exile they are unqualified for the

44. See esp. E. P. Clowney, "Preaching Christ from All the Scriptures," in *The Preacher and Preaching*, ed. S. T. Logan (Phillipsburg, N.J.: Presbyterian and Reformed, 1986), 191. See esp. his chart on p. 179, in which he distinguishes clearly between allegorizing, moralizing, and redemptive-historical preaching.

presence of their holy God. The point in this chapter, however, is that God applies his sovereign grace to Joshua and that this alone dismisses the indictment against him.

Although it is difficult to know with certainty the identity of this accuser here, clearly he represents all attempts, whether from spiritual or human sources, to undermine our confidence in Christ's grace received through faith. This can be applied to our ultimate spiritual adversary, to whom is often attributed two great lies. Before we fall into sin, he whispers in our ear that such a sin is of no great consequence—only afterward to turn on us and remind us that the same sin has made us eternally unworthy for God's kingdom. Zechariah 3 reminds us of God's sovereign election and free grace, assuring revelation from God that silences both accuser and accusation.

Priestly calling. Having answered the accuser's charges by providing his grace and cleansing, God calls Joshua the high priest to fulfill his commission. This calling operates on two levels. (1) On the general level he is called to faithful living according to God's Word. (2) On a more particular plane, he is commanded to fulfill the specific duties of the high priest within the temple precincts.

The church functions in a similar way as God's priestly representatives on earth (1 Peter 2:5, 9). (1) In Revelation 1:6 it is this community, "freed ... from our sins by his blood," that is made into "priests to serve his God and Father" (cf. 5:10). We are called to faithfulness to the new covenant, to follow the commands of Christ and his apostles, which echo the themes of the Law and Prophets. This is the foundational calling of holiness and obedience.

(2) We are also called to fulfill our particular priestly duties. Individual believers and communities are called to specific tasks within their contexts. For individuals, that will be to discover, celebrate, refine, and exercise their God-given gifts in the church, family, or society. The church should be a place of encouragement and exploration for all those who seek to use their gifts. So also communities of faith are raised up within societies at particular junctures in history to speak or act as representatives of Christ. Church leadership should take this calling seriously and discern how this should play out in their unique ministry context. Exercising these particular callings, however, should flow out of the foundational faithfulness to God's core values of holiness, which is made possible by the grace of God in Christ.

Prophetic counsel. Joshua is promised prophetic voices that will provide access to God's will in the divine council. For Joshua that meant prophets like Haggai and Zechariah, who provided God's encouragement and exhortation throughout the rebuilding project.

All through the history of Israel God made clear that the prophetic word was one of the most crucial gifts to his community. He sent his word through these messengers in order to invite his people back to covenant intimacy (2 Kings 17:7–23; Neh. 9:26–32) and to warn them of the consequences of their disobedience.

So also God took seriously the sacredness of the prophetic word to his people. One of the severest prophecies of judgment is Micah's prophecy against the false prophets of his day (see Mic. 3). Although he speaks to all leadership in Israel (leader, priest, prophet) at the beginning and end of the message (3:1–4 and 9–12), Micah reserves the center admonition for one particular group: the prophets. He warns them that because they have used the prophetic office for their own ends, merely to feed themselves, their judgment will be "darkness," a symbol of silence from God: "There is no answer from God." God placed priority on the prophetic word throughout the history of his interaction with his people, and this will be no different among the restoration community. For Joshua access to the divine council through prophetic figures is key for the success of his priestly function as well as the spiritual vitality of his community.

So also for us, God has provided his voice through Scripture. This precious gift of revelation should never be taken for granted but be accepted as God's Word to our generation. But God has not left us on our own to interpret this Word. He guides us by his Spirit, who illuminates this Word for our minds and hearts.

This ministry of God's Spirit in illuminating his Word to us is necessary because of two important hermeneutical conditions we share as humans: our finitude and our fallenness. (1) A hermeneutic of finitude assesses properly the finite nature of our minds, namely, that we cannot grasp or understand everything in God's Word. These ancient texts are rich in history, imagery, and theology; thus, we are unable to fully grasp the complete dimensions of these texts because of the limitations of our minds and hearts. (2) A hermeneutic of fallenness takes seriously the fallen character of our minds, namely, that we refuse to grasp or understand everything in God's Word. In simplest terms, this means that there are some things we *can* not understand in God's Word and there are some things that we *will* not understand.

Fowl and Jones remind us of the importance of the life of the reader in interpreting Scripture.[45] They do highlight the great focus in our interpretations of Scripture on grasping the original context and intention of the author. But they also remind us that our greatest obstacle is not a historical one but a moral one; that is, scriptural interpretation "is also related to the character of the interpreters." A long-range view of such character development must be part of our communal vision:

45. S. E. Fowl and L. G. Jones, *Reading in Communion: Scripture and Ethics in Christian Life* (Grand Rapids: Eerdmans, 1991), 102.

> A Christ-like character, however, is not a commodity that can be purchased; neither can it be put on and taken off at will. It is formed over time through disciplined attention to our thoughts, words and practices. That is why in earlier chapters we have argued that Christian communities need to establish spaces in which believers can have their characters formed and informed by a true knowledge of God.

This is why the doctrine of the Holy Spirit is key to interpreting the Bible. God grants us his Spirit to illuminate our finite minds, opening them to his infinite truth and softening our fallen hearts to accept his authoritative truth. He grants his Spirit to communities of faith in which the Scriptures are read and interpreted. God continues to empower interpreters with his community to communicate his Word with relevance to contemporary generations and readers who live out this Word before one another and a watching world. God has granted us access to his divine court through the Scriptures, which are "living and active ... sharper than any double-edged sword ... penetrat[ing] even to dividing soul and spirit" (Heb. 4:12).

Royal prosperity. The vision of the high priestly clothing cannot be separated from the prophecy of the future removal of sin from the land. The prophet is shown a vision of a future when *ṣemaḥ* ("Branch") will usher in a new era in which sin will finally be removed. This era is the final stage of redemptive history, in which there will be prosperity within the community of God and peace among its members.

God's fulfillment of this prophecy came with the death and resurrection of Jesus Christ. This sacrificial act indeed did "remove the sin of this land in a single day" in a way that transcended the Old Testament Day of Atonement. Hebrews 10:11–13 develops this most thoroughly in the New Testament, when it states in relation to the daily sacrifices:

> Day after day every priest stands and performs his religious duties; again and again he offers the same sacrifices, which can never take away sins. But when this priest had offered for all time one sacrifice for sins, he sat down at the right hand of God. Since that time he waits for his enemies to be made his footstool, because by one sacrifice he has made perfect forever those who are being made holy.

The writer of Hebrews here combines the language of priesthood (priest) with that of the monarchy ("sat down at the right hand of God ... he waits for his enemies to be made his footstool"). The last phrase is a clue to the writer's intention. Jesus is being portrayed here as the priest-king in the order of Melchizedek, an order to which the Davidic line traces its roots (Ps. 110:1, 3; cf. Heb. 1:13; 7:1–8:13).

Christ as high priest fulfills once for all the ceremonies of the Day of Atonement. After describing the Day of Atonement ceremonies in Hebrews 9:1–10, the writer then introduces Christ: "He did not enter by means of the blood of goats and calves; but he entered the Most Holy Place once for all by his own blood, having obtained eternal redemption" (9:12).

This priest-king, the fulfillment of the *ṣemaḥ* hope of Zechariah 3, removes the sin of the land "once for all" through "one sacrifice." According to Hebrews this removal cleanses "our consciences from acts that lead to death, so that we may serve the living God" (Heb. 9:14b) and motivates us to "draw near to God with a sincere heart in full assurance of faith" and to "hold unswervingly to the hope we profess" (10:22–23).

This ultimate Day of Atonement inaugurated the final stage of redemptive history, in which we already are able to enjoy the prosperity and peace highlighted at the end of Zechariah 3. The Western church has often been too individualistic in its approach to the salvation accomplished through Christ. Zechariah 3 reminds us that the blessing of the gospel is communal in nature, propelling us outward to offer the blessing we have received to others within the covenant community and beyond. It also reminds us that God's salvation provides for our prosperity and physical as well as spiritual well-being.

This final idyllic picture of a community purified by God through Christ and sharing their prosperity with one another is one that should have a lasting impression on the readers of Zechariah 3. It encourages us to view the church as a place where God's blessing is shared with one another—whether that is sharing one's material, spiritual, emotional, or relational abundance. This may mean inviting a stranger at church into your home, offering a meal for a homeless person, providing hospice relief for a couple caring for a handicapped child or parent, and so on. Zechariah 3 shows us the power of grace within the church, for as people receive grace and prosperity from God, they in turn pour that into the lives of others.

Based on Catherine Ryan Hyde's book by the same name, the movie *Pay It Forward* captures the imagination of the audience by tracing the simple yet utopian scheme of an eleven-year-old boy, Trevor McKinney. When Mr. Simenot, his history teacher, challenges the class with an extra-credit assignment ("Think of an idea to change our world—and put it into action"), naive Trevor takes him seriously and conjures up the following plan: Instead of people paying others back for a good deed, they are to pay it forward to three other people. Similarly, Zechariah 3 encourages us to a utopian scheme that ultimately will transform the world—one taught by God, enabled by Jesus, empowered by the Holy Spirit, and carried out by the community of faith.

Zechariah 4

THEN THE ANGEL who talked with me returned and wak-
ened me, as a man is wakened from his sleep. 2He
asked me, "What do you see?"

I answered, "I see a solid gold lampstand with a bowl at the
top and seven lights on it, with seven channels to the lights.
3Also there are two olive trees by it, one on the right of the
bowl and the other on its left."

4I asked the angel who talked with me, "What are these, my
lord?"

5He answered, "Do you not know what these are?"

"No, my lord," I replied.

6So he said to me, "This is the word of the LORD to Zerub-
babel: 'Not by might nor by power, but by my Spirit,' says the
LORD Almighty.

7"What are you, O mighty mountain? Before Zerubbabel
you will become level ground. Then he will bring out the cap-
stone to shouts of 'God bless it! God bless it!'"

8Then the word of the LORD came to me: 9"The hands of
Zerubbabel have laid the foundation of this temple; his hands
will also complete it. Then you will know that the LORD
Almighty has sent me to you.

10"Who despises the day of small things? Men will rejoice
when they see the plumb line in the hand of Zerubbabel.

"(These seven are the eyes of the LORD, which range
throughout the earth.)"

11Then I asked the angel, "What are these two olive trees
on the right and the left of the lampstand?"

12Again I asked him, "What are these two olive branches
beside the two gold pipes that pour out golden oil?"

13He replied, "Do you not know what these are?"

"No, my lord," I said.

14So he said, "These are the two who are anointed to serve
the Lord of all the earth."

Original Meaning

OF ALL THE night visions, Zechariah 4 has attracted the most debate about the history of its redaction. Verses 6b–10a portrays the characteristics of prophetic oracular speech with its messenger formulas ("This is the word of the LORD to Zerubbabel ... says the LORD Almighty ... the word of the LORD came to me") and prophetic confirmation formula ("then you will know that the LORD Almighty has sent me to you"). It clearly interrupts the interchange between Zechariah and the interpreting angel.[1] Questions about the flow and meaning of this chapter have been compounded further by considerable debate over the meaning of the various images presented in the scene.

I maintain that in the original sequence of visions (without ch. 3), Zechariah 4 marked the center of the collection and was designed to elevate the role of prophecy within the restoration community. The lampstand (connected in the past to tabernacle and temple) represents the temple project, and its lamps (as the eyes of the Lord) identify it as the source of God's all-pervading presence throughout the earth. This project to restore God's presence and kingship on earth is fueled by the prophetic ministry of two key figures, Haggai and Zechariah. Into the middle of this vision are placed two oracles addressed to Zerubbabel, showcasing this prophetic role.[2]

The Vision (4:1–6a, 10b–14)

THE VISION BEGINS with the return of the "angel who talked with me." This figure is not mentioned in the previous chapter, having left the scene in 2:3. The angel "rouses" (*ʿwr*) the prophet from sleep as a man is "wakened" (also *ʿwr*) from his sleep (4:1). This form is rather odd within the conventions of normal language, for how can someone experience an action "as" one who experiences the same action? Some interpret this as arousal from "a state of lethargy" or from being "deep in thought, or in trance state."[3] However, a description of an otherworldly experience as one finds in Zechariah 1–6 stretches the limits of normal language: The prophet is awakened from sleep, but only "as" a normal awakening, for he does not awaken into the real world but into a visionary one.

The prophet, asked to describe the odd scene before him (4:2), answers: "I see a solid gold lampstand." Although the Hebrew term here (*menorah*) is used for a domestic lampstand (2 Kings 4:10), its appearance here is clearly

1. For this see Fishbane, *Biblical Interpretation*, 448–49.
2. For detailed argument see Boda, "Oil," Art. 10.
3. For the first, e.g., Merrill, *Haggai*, 146; the second, e.g., Petersen, *Haggai*, 216.

religious. The greatest concentration of this term in the Hebrew Bible is in the accounts of the tabernacle construction in the Torah (Ex. 24:33–40; 37:17–24; 40:4, 24; cf. Lev. 24:4; Num. 8:2–4).[4] Both here and in the tabernacle a lampstand made from "pure" (*ṭahor,* Ex. 25:31; here *kullah*) gold possesses seven lamps (*ner*).

Beyond these elements, however, the two articles have little in common. Whereas the lamps of the tabernacle lampstand are placed atop the main shaft in the six branches extending from that shaft, Zechariah's lamps are restricted to a bowl fitted at the top of the center shaft.[5] There is no mention of this term for "bowl" (*gullah*) in the tabernacle accounts, although there were cups (*gabiaᶜ*; Ex. 25:31, 33, 34; 37:17, 19, 20), but these were not reservoirs for lamp oil.

Bowl-shaped lampstands with seven lamps positioned on top of a center shaft, similar to the one described in this vision, have been uncovered in archaeological digs from the Middle Bronze period onward and were used at religious sites.[6] The seven "channels" (Heb. *muṣaqah*) to the lights are thus not to be interpreted as pipes but rather the spouts that held the wicks and directed the oil to the flame.

The difference between the tabernacle and visionary scene is accentuated by the presence of two olive trees situated by the lampstand on the left and the right. At this point the description of the scene ends, but we can discover further details of the olive trees from Zechariah's question in 4:12. There, following a question about the two olive trees, the prophet speaks of "two olive branches beside the two gold pipes that pour out golden oil." The Hebrew term *šibbolet* ("branches") is used elsewhere either of the fruit of grain crops (e.g., Ruth 2:2) or of flowing liquid (e.g., Isa. 27:12). Although it could be referring to the fruit of the olive tree (olives), the restriction elsewhere of this term to grain and the appearance of the terms "pipes" and "pour" in the phrases that follow tip the scale in favor of the second gloss. This would best be translated: "two olive streams that pour out golden oil through the two gold pipes."[7] The phrase "golden oil" translates *zahab,* normally "gold."

4. It also appears in the account of the temple construction in 1 Kings 7:49//2 Chron. 4:7, but there ten lampstands are created for the area outside the Most Holy Place (cf. 1 Chron. 28:15, although see 2 Chron. 13:11).

5. This is difficult to see in the NIV text, which does not translate the final phrase of 4:2. This final phrase repeats the phrase "at the top," which in turn modifies "the bowl" earlier in the verse. Thus, both the bowl and the lights are said to be "at/on the top" (lit., "on its head").

6. For other views of the shape of this article see R. North, "Zechariah's Seven-Spout Lampstand," *Bib* 51 (1970): 183–206, and Meyers and Meyers, *Haggai,* 227–77. Meyers and Meyers draw in archaeological evidence of *kernoi,* which were tubular vessels for pouring liquids; they equate these with the *gullah* ("bowl") of 4:2.

7. The preposition *beyad* ("beside") is here taken as instrumental, "through." See Hag. 1:1; 2:1; Zech. 7:7, 12; cf. Petersen, *Haggai,* 235–36.

The olive oil as it pours into the bowl looks like gold, an appropriate color considering it is flowing through golden pipes into a golden lampstand.

This evidence helps us to understand the connection between the lampstand and the olive trees. In contrast to the lampstand in the tabernacle, which was supplied with oil by the offerings of the Israelites and tended by the priests and Levites (Lev. 24:1–4; Num. 3:31; 4:9–10), this lampstand is connected to two olive trees by gold pipes that supplied the lampstand directly. The supply from these trees is plenteous as the oil gushes forth.

The use of numbers separates this vision into two major image complexes.[8] *Seven* is used for the various elements of the light-producing gold lampstand: seven lights with seven spouts. *Two* is used for the constituent parts of the source of the fuel for this lampstand: two olive trees with two streams through two gold pipes.

As in the other visions, the prophet searches for an explanation from the interpreting angel. It is uncertain whether in the ambiguous question, "What are these, my lord?" (4:4), the prophet has in mind the olive trees (the closest antecedent) or the lights on the lampstand. In any case, the angel chooses to reveal the significance of the vision in order of the appearance of elements and does so in two phases, each inaugurated by the question: "Do you not know what these are?" (4:5, 13). This question is a rhetorical technique intended to heighten the reader's expectation by prolonging the answer.

(1) The first phase focuses on the number *seven* and thus refers to the lampstand and, in particular, its seven lamps. Verse 10b (the continuation of the visionary experience after the oracular interlude) interprets them as the "eyes of the LORD, which range throughout the earth."

There are some who translate the Hebrew word for "eyes" (*ʿayin*) with a second legitimate gloss, "springs." These springs "flow over the whole earth."[9] However, the verb "range" (*šwṭ*) is one that often describes the movement of a person over a territory (Num. 11:8; Amos 8:12; Dan. 12:4), and the phrase "eyes of the LORD" appears elsewhere in the Old Testament to speak of God's observing the activities of his creation either to bring discipline or blessing (Deut. 11:12; Ps. 34:15; Prov. 5:21; 15:3; 22:12).

---

8. The two sections ultimately evince two interpretations. This approach contrasts that of van der Woude who sought for an interpretation for each part of the lampstand: lampstand (temple mountain), bowl (temple building), lamps (eyes of the Lord), olives (two sons of fresh oil); A. S. van der Woude, "Zion as Primeval Stone in Zechariah 3 and 4," in *Text and Context: Old Testament and Semitic Studies for F. C. Fensham*, ed. W. Claassen, (JSOTSup 48; Sheffield: Sheffield Academic Press, 1988), 239. This is wrapped up in his assumption that the oracle is part of the interpreting angel's response to the prophet. He, interestingly, does not find an interpretation of the elements in 4:12.

9. Baldwin, *Haggai*, 123.

Second Chronicles 16:9 contains the closest Hebrew idiom to Zechariah 4:10b when the prophet Hanani tells Asa that "the eyes of the LORD range throughout the earth to strengthen those whose hearts are fully committed to him." The same Hebrew word stock appears here: "eyes," "LORD," "range in all the earth." Although Hanani's message is one of doom for King Asa, the activity of God's eyes throughout the earth is pointedly a positive task: "to strengthen those whose hearts are fully committed to him." This text does, however, reveal the downside of this omniscient procedure. When the eyes fall on those who disobey, God may enact discipline. The interpretation is that this lampstand, with its obvious links to the ancient sanctuaries of Israel, is a reminder of God's omnipresence in the earth, mediated through this new temple. Through this renewed seat of his rule, he will exercise his reign on earth.[10]

(2) The second phase of the interpretation immediately follows in 4:11–12 as the prophet turns his attention to the olive trees and the pipe work that connects them to the lampstand. The angel reveals that "these are the two who are anointed to serve the LORD of all the earth." In other words, the olive trees symbolize two individuals. Olive tree imagery for humans is positive imagery that signifies a person "as beautiful, productive and important" (Judg. 9:9; Job 15:33; Ps. 128:3; Hos. 14:6; Jer. 11:16).[11] But who are these people?

Past interpretations have identified these two individuals with two prominent leaders in the early Persian period community, Zerubbabel and Joshua.[12] This has been based on the translation "anointed" (anointing practiced for royal and priestly figures) and the strong tradition of these two contemporaneous figures in Hebrew literature depicting the early Persian period (Ezra 2–6; Hag. 1–2; Zech. 1–8).[13] However, a closer look at the Hebrew text calls this consensus view into question and suggests a new direction.

---

10. For a list of the many scholars who have seen the menorah as symbolic of God's presence, as well as other options, including the worshiping community and the temple and cult, see W. H. Rose, *Zemah and Zerubbabel: Messianic Expectations in the Early Postexilic Period* (JSOTSup 304; Sheffield: Sheffield Academic Press, 2000)179; S. Niditch, *Symbolic Vision in the Biblical Tradition* (HSM 30; Chico, Calif.: Scholars Press, 1983), 104. Strand suggests Zerubbabel—in a wordplay on the "lamp" imagery associated with David's line (2 Sam. 21:17); K. A. Strand, "The Two Olive Trees of Zechariah 4 and Revelation 11," *AUSS* 20 (1982): 257–61.

11. Cf. Petersen, *Haggai*, 230. Strand ("Olive Trees," 259) links them to two pillars in Solomon's temple.

12. See R. T. Siebeneck, "Messianism of Aggeus and Proto-Zacharias," *CBQ* 19 (1957): 321. Van der Woude ("Zion," 239–40) modified the traditional view, identifying these two figures as the "expected messianic king and high priest of 6.13."

13. Thus, many have seen the mention of Joshua and Zerubbabel in Zech. 3–4 as evidence of the identity of these two individuals; see Merrill, *Haggai*, 155.

The phrase "the two who are anointed" (NIV) reads in the Hebrew text "the two sons of fresh oil." The term for oil here (*yiṣhar*) is never used elsewhere for anointing, a role reserved for the Hebrew word *šemen* (kings in 1 Sam. 16:13; 1 Kings 1:39; priests in Lev. 8:12; Ex. 30:23–33; the tabernacle in Lev. 8:10).[14] The term *yiṣhar* is reserved for unmanufactured oil from the olive tree, appropriate because it flows directly from tree to lampstand.

These two individuals "serve the Lord of all the earth." Again, this translation masks the Hebrew idiom "stand by the Lord of all the earth." This combination of the verb "stand" (*ᶜamad*) with the preposition "by" (*ᶜal*) followed by a reference to deity is found in 1 Kings 22:19. In this instance the prophet Micaiah observes God deliberating with the host of heaven, the divine council of angelic spirits who are "standing [*ᶜamad*] by [*ᶜal*]" God.[15] It is instructive that Micaiah has access to this scene, and the calls of other prophets reveal that the prophet was the one human allowed into this privileged position (Isa. 6; Ezek. 1–3; Jer. 23:16–22; Amos 3:7; cf. Ps. 89:6–7; Job 15:8).[16]

This evidence brings into question the traditional connection between Zechariah 4:14 and Zerubbabel and Joshua. If these two individuals are human beings in this passage, they are most likely prophetic figures.[17] The prominence of Haggai and Zechariah in the early Persian period and their crucial role in the rebuilding of the temple explains the presence of two prophetic figures in this vision (Ezra 5:1–2; 6:14; Hag. 1–2; Zech. 8:9–13).

Thus, the vision of the lampstand and olive trees emphasizes the role of the prophet in the restoration of the early Persian period. The lampstand, signifying the role of the temple as the location from which God's presence

---

14. Cf. Strand, "Olive Trees," 257–61; Petersen, *Haggai*, 230; contra Rudolph, *Haggai*, 107–8; R. A. Mason, *The Books of Haggai, Zechariah and Malachi* (CBC; Cambridge: Cambridge Univ. Press, 1977), 48; Baldwin, *Haggai*, 124; Merrill, *Haggai*, 155. Redditt has noted that *šemen* is used in a similar phrase (son of *šemen*, as here son of *yiṣhar*) in Isa. 5:1 and there designates "very fertile"; P. L. Redditt, "Zerubbabel, Joshua, and the Night Visions of Zechariah," *CBQ* 54 (1992): 251. He proposes that the image is of olive trees sated with oil. Even if this constituted an allusion to anointing rituals, Strand has wisely observed that the olive trees are "sons of oil" because they *furnish* oil, not because they have received or been anointed with oil; cf. Strand, "Olive Trees," 258.

15. This combination also occurs in 3:1, but there it is difficult to determine if the adversary is standing beside the angel of the Lord or beside Joshua. Notice also the similar construction in the prophetic call of Isaiah in Isa. 6:1–2: *ᶜamad* + *maᶜal* for the position of the seraphim.

16. See Rose for detailed evidence on these combinations; Rose, *Zemah*, 177–207.

17. Note that when elements of this vision are taken up in Rev. 11, these two individuals are clearly seen as prophetic, not royal or priestly, figures; cf. Strand, "Olive Trees," 257–61; M. G. Kline, "By My Spirit," *Kerux* 9/3 (1994): 27–29. Rose identifies them as angelic beings; Rose, *Zemah*, 177–207.

and sovereignty emanate throughout the earth, is fueled by oil supplied by the prophets. Therefore, at the center of the vision complex lies a strong reminder of the importance of the prophetic office and word within the restoration community.

The Oracles (4:6b–10a)

AS ALREADY NOTED, into this vision about the role of the prophetic word have been inserted two oracles addressed to Zerubbabel during the refounding of the temple. In its new context the author is driving home the point that the eyes of God ranging over the earth have discovered the faithfulness of Zerubbabel, and this prophetic word offers the strength needed for such an individual and the community he represents.

Zerubbabel's involvement in rebuilding the temple is well attested in the Old Testament. Haggai consistently refers to him as the governor of this province (Hag. 1:1, 14; 2:1, 21), and he is listed among those who returned to the land from captivity in Babylon (Ezra 2), rebuilt the altar (3:2), and relaid the foundation of the temple (3:8–13).

Zerubbabel's lineage is traced through Shealtiel to Jehoiachin and the Davidic royal line (1 Chron. 3:16–17). It is this royal connection that explains his role in the rituals accompanying the restoration of the temple foundation. When ancient Near Eastern temples were being rebuilt, the phases of the project were marked by certain rituals. One ritual occurred at the outset of work, in which a stone was chosen from the rubble of the former temple and carried out by a royal figure. Once the rubble was cleared, the foundation laying was begun with the royal figure laying the first stone of the new foundation.[18]

These two rituals provide the ritual background for the two oracles preserved in 4:6b–10a. (1) In the first, the prophet proclaims an oracle of confidence as Zerubbabel faces a mountain of rubble[19] and then brings out the

---

18. Haggai also bears witness to two phases in the work. The community begins work in Hag. 1:12–15 and is encouraged by the prophet to finish that preliminary work in 2:1–9. However, the foundation laying does not occur until a few months later (2:10–23; see esp. 2:18), revealing that the preliminary work involved clearing the rubble. Haggai, however, only records one ritual—the second one of foundation laying.

19. This view stands in contrast to those who interpret the mountain metaphorically either generally as the difficulties of this period or specifically as human adversaries: e.g., the high priest (with "mighty mountain" [*har-haggadol*] playing on high priest [*hakkohen haggadol*]), a Persian official, the Babylonians (cf. Jer. 51:25), other opposition (as Ezra 4:2, 4); cf. Petersen, *Haggai*, 239; E. Sellin, "Noch einmal der Stein des Sacharja," *ZAW* 48 (1942/43): 70; L. G. Rignell, *Die Nachtgesichte des Sacharja: Eine exegetische Studie* (Lund: Gleerup, 1950); Baldwin, *Haggai*, 121. Van der Woude ("Zion," 237–48), based on a Phoenician inscription, argues for any mythological mountain that competes with the glory of Mount Zion.

first stone (4:6b–7).[20] The ritual character of this oracle is confirmed by the reference to "shouts" of "God bless it! God bless it!" (lit., "Grace! Grace!"), indicating a response from a group of people.[21]

(2) In the second message (4:8–10a), the prophet addresses Zerubbabel at a later point in the project (after the clearing of the rubble) as the governor inaugurates the foundation laying. This message also alludes to another ritual when a "stone of tin" (NIV "plumb line") was handled by the royal figure. This "stone of tin" likely refers to a building deposit incorporated into the foundation, probably when the foundation phase was completed.[22]

Some have suggested that the "stone of tin" anticipates the completion of the temple project, but this is based on the translation of the first portion of 4:9: "The hands of Zerubbabel have laid the foundation of this temple; his hands will also complete it." The phrase "laid the foundation of this temple" refers to the inauguration of the foundation laying with the placing of the "first stone."[23] In the Hebrew text, the phrase "his hands will also complete it" is ambiguous, reading "his hands will complete." This could refer to either the temple structure as a whole or to the foundation-laying phase. The reference

---

20. The term here is *haʾeben haroʾšah* ("the stone, the head"). Some see this as a completion stone, such as a capstone; e.g., Baldwin, *Haggai*, 121; Merrill, *Haggai*, 160. However, here we adopt the view of those in the following footnote who see it as the first stone drawn from the rubble of the previous temple.

21. The theme of blessing and grace is found in the rituals surrounding Mesopotamian rebuilding rituals, and there are examples of liturgical shouts to the royal figure, cf. A. Laato, "Zachariah 4,6b–10a and the Akkadian Royal Building Inscriptions," *ZAW* 106 (1994): 60–61. Van der Woude ("Zion," 237–48) follows the ancient translations (LXX, Vulgate, Syriac), which see the Heb. word translated "shouts" here as "splendour" (from a different Heb. root).

22. Cf. R. S. Ellis, *Foundation Deposits in Ancient Mesopotamia* (Yale Near Eastern Researches; New Haven, Conn.: Yale Univ. Press, 1968), 101–2; Halpern, "Ritual Background," 167–90; D. L. Petersen, "Zerubbabel and Jerusalem Temple Reconstruction," *CBQ* 36 (1974): 366–72; Laato, "Zachariah 4,6b–10a," 53–69; see full bibliography in M. J. Boda, *Haggai-Zechariah Research: A Bibliographic Survey* (Tools for Biblical Studies; Leiden: DEO Publishing, 2003). The translation "plumb line" is based on early versions of the Old Testament, but the Heb. text does not use the word for "plumb line." Rather, it has "the stone of tin" (*haʾeben habbedil*), the second term of which is used for an alloy. Baldwin traces *bedil* to the Heb. root *badal*, which means "to separate" and thus sees the stone as the "separated stone" or the "chosen stone"; Baldwin, *Haggai*, 122. Van der Woude interprets this as an allusion to Zion (Temple Mount) as the primeval mountain, in this case called "'Separation,' because the primeval mountain separated cosmos from chaos for the first time"; van der Woude, "Zion," 243.

23. See Isa. 28:16, where the laying of the first stone is called "laying a foundation" (same verb as here). Obviously this involved more than one stone. Although the royal figure often was said to lay the foundation in ancient Near East rituals, this was only the beginning of the foundation laying process; see Ellis, *Foundation Deposits in Ancient Mesopotamia*, 31–32.

to a building deposit ("stone of tin") tips the interpretation in favor of the foundational-laying phase.[24]

These oracles are messages of encouragement and hope for Zerubbabel and the activity he commences. In both oracles there is evidence of a challenge that lies in the way of the leader. The first challenge is physical in nature, the great mountain of rubble that must be removed (4:7). The second challenge is communal in nature, the derision of those less than enthusiastic about the project (4:10). In both cases the prophet promises a reversal: The great mountain will become "level ground" and despising will become "rejoicing."

Although these oracles do contain the above similarities, they do have a slightly different message. The encouragement of Zerubbabel in the first oracle is linked to the message that God's Spirit will strengthen Zerubbabel for the monumental task that lies ahead. He must not rely on the "might" and "power" of humanity. These two words are used in the Old Testament to describe all aspects of human potency, whether physical (Eccl. 10:10; Judg. 16:5), military (2 Sam. 17:10), economic (Job 31:25; Deut. 8:18), or moral strength (1 Kings 1:52). The oracle focuses Zerubbabel's attention on God's Spirit as the source for the great task that lies ahead.

References to God's Spirit enabling his human instruments are associated with two offices in Israel: the prophet and the king. The sign of true prophecy is the presence of God's Spirit in the life of the prophet (Neh. 9:30; Joel 2:28–32; Mic. 3:8; Zech. 7:12; cf. Num. 24:2). When Micah attacks the false prophets of his day, he highlights the presence of the Spirit of the Lord as the source of his power (Mic. 3:8). The prophets transfer this power of the Spirit to the royal house at the beginning of the monarchy in Israel. The first two kings in Israel are commissioned to their tasks by physical anointing with oil by the prophet (1 Sam. 10:1; 16:13), but also by divine anointing with God's Spirit (1 Sam. 10:10; 16:13).[25] In Zechariah 4, one of the last prophets in Israel now reminds this royal figure of the need for the empowerment of the Spirit of God as the source of strength for the rebuilding project.

The second oracle again encourages Zerubbabel, but it focuses more on the credibility of his mission and on the reliability of the prophetic word. The prophet confronts those skeptical of the ability of Zerubbabel to complete

24. Metals are associated with foundation laying rituals, as Ellis pointed out (ibid., 31, 102–4, 140). These metals enhanced the value of the building and the validity of the ceremonies connected with its construction (cf. Isa. 54:11). Tin was used in tablets deposited in foundations. This practice is stopped in later Assyrian kings and not used by Neo-Babylonian rulers. However, in Persian times the practice revives.

25. Cf. D. M. Howard, "The Transfer of Power from Saul to David in 1 Sam 16:13–14," *JETS* 32 (1989): 473–83.

the foundation. Such skepticism can be discerned in several texts from this period. Haggai 2:1–9 links such skepticism to those who had seen the grandeur of the preexilic temple structure. Haggai's question "Does it not seem to you like nothing?" voices the feelings of many within the community.[26] So also Ezra 3:12–13 records the odd combination of rejoicing and weeping on the day of foundation laying. The prophet links his own credibility to the fact that Zerubbabel will surely complete the foundation phase.

The details of these two oracles bolster further the relationship between vision and oracle in Zechariah 4. In both the royal and prophetic offices are intertwined. The power of the Spirit well associated with the prophetic office and linked to the empowerment of the royal office is promised to Zerubbabel, who undertakes the temple building project in the first oracle. The promise of the prophet confronts the skepticism against Zerubbabel in the second oracle. Surely the "oil" of prophecy fueled the building project, bringing God's presence on earth.

Bridging Contexts

GIFT OF PROPHECY. One of the great privileges of a young father raising three boys is the opportunity to watch increasingly creative children's videos. *Toy Story* was certainly the "buzz" in our home when it arrived on the market and even more so within my family because my sister worked for the Manhattan toy company that produced and marketed toys for Disney movies. In *Toy Story* we first meet cowboy Woody, who is the beloved toy of Andy. Before long, however, the drama begins as a new toy enters into Andy's life and threatens to dethrone poor Woody from his place as most loved of the toys. This toy is Buzz Lightyear, a super space traveler with all the bells and whistles, whose trademark saying is: "To infinity and beyond."

Buzz, however, does not realize that he is a toy, and Woody sees it as his duty to teach Buzz the reality: You cannot fly, you are not a space traveler, you are a toy. Of course, he can't convince Buzz, who must come to this realization on his own. That moment occurs when Buzz is trapped in the evil neighborhood boy's house and happens upon a TV broadcasting a commercial about him. At first he thinks it is real, but the announcer makes it clear that Buzz Lightyear is only a toy. For Buzz, "to infinity and beyond" was nothing more than a fantasy.

In Israel, however, the prophets were the only ones who could claim what Buzz Lightyear had claimed. The long story of prophetism began with Moses

26. See Boda, "Haggai," 295–304, on the rhetorical technique of this speech in Haggai.

and extended through a multitude of personalities who faithfully revealed God's truth to his people, including Samuel, Nathan, Gad, Elijah, Elisha, Isaiah, Micah, Hosea, Amos, Nahum, Habakkuk, Jeremiah, Ezekiel, Haggai, and Zechariah.[27] God raised them up to be conduits of revelation to his people, often delivered through visions and dreams (Num. 12:6; 1 Sam. 3). The authority of this revelation is intimately linked to the prophetic claim that they had been "to infinity and beyond"; that is, they had privileged access to the council room, experiences that, according to Jeremiah's attack on the false prophets, enabled the true prophet to speak God's word:

> But which of them has stood in the council of the LORD
> to see or hear his word?
> Who has listened and heard his word? . . .
> But if they had stood in my council,
> they would have proclaimed my words to my people
> and would have turned them from their evil ways
> and from their evil deeds. (Jer. 23:18, 22)

Through Jeremiah's attack we are reminded of the dark backdrop of false prophecy against which we see the brilliance of this faithful line. We are given glimpses of this backdrop in the ministry of Elijah (1 Kings 18), Hosea (Hos. 4:5), Micah (Mic. 3:5–8), and Micaiah (1 Kings 22), but near the end of the monarchial period the backdrop becomes far darker. Jeremiah speaks often of prophets who prophesy falsely and bring condemnation on themselves (Jer. 2:8, 26; 5:13, 31; 6:13; 8:1, 10; 13:13; 14:13–15; 23:9–40; 37:19; 50:36). This tension is powerfully illustrated in the confrontation between Jeremiah and Hananiah in Jeremiah 27–28. So also Ezekiel focuses his attention on false prophets (Ezek. 13; cf. 22:28). The painful expressions of Lamentations reveal the disillusionment with the false prophets among the community living in the wake of the destruction of Jerusalem (Lam. 2:9, 14; 4:13).

This disillusionment may explain the character of the prophetic word in the early Persian period. Already in Ezekiel we see the constant use of prophetic formulas that are intended to bolster the divine origin of the message. Besides the typical "this is what the LORD says" (Ezek. 5:5) or "declares the LORD" (5:11), we find constant use of the phrases "then they/you will know that I am the LORD" (12:15; 13:9; 14:8; 15:7; 16:62; etc.), and "then they will know that a prophet has been among them" (2:5; 33:33). In Haggai, Zechariah, and Malachi, we see a marked elevation in the number of

27. See VanGemeren, *Interpreting*, 18–39.

prophetic formulas used to introduce the speeches of these prophets. This most likely reveals a crisis in the prophetic word, a greater popular skepticism toward prophecy in the wake of the Exile.[28]

This historical context reveals the timeliness of Zechariah's message within his community. This vision emphasizes the continuing role for the prophetic word in this crucial period of restoration. The community needed to see the prophet as a major source of God's power and presence in the rebuilding period. God was continuing to raise up his servants to speak to them and to encourage them in their pursuits.

Spirit of prophecy and royalty. There is no question that the Spirit of God is most often connected with the prophetic office in the Old Testament. When Moses cries out to God for assistance in leading the people from Egypt to Canaan, God promised to take of the Spirit that was on Moses and to distribute it to the various leaders of the tribes of Israel (Num. 11). The interesting feature of this act of God is that when this Spirit does fall on these leaders, the evidence of this empowerment is that they will prophesy (11:24–30). God's empowerment of Moses here is linked to his role as prophet for Israel (cf. Deut. 34:10–12).

In light of Numbers 11, throughout Israel's history the prophets are distinguished by their possession of the Spirit, who enables them to prophesy (2 Kings 2:9, 15, 16; 2 Chron. 15:1; Neh. 9:30). This relationship to the Spirit is confirmed in the testimony of the prophets themselves (Ezek. 2:2; 11:5; Dan. 4:18; Mic. 3:8). Furthermore, in scenes reminiscent of Numbers 11, the prophets are the source of the Spirit's endowment on the kings of Israel. Saul is anointed by the Spirit at the outset of his rule through an encounter with a procession of prophets (1 Sam. 10:6, 10). So also when David is anointed king as a young man by Samuel, the text emphasizes his reception of the Spirit alongside the removal of that Spirit from wayward Saul (16:13–14).[29]

Although the prophets are not the only ones who experience the presence of the Spirit in the Old Testament (e.g., Ex. 31:3; 35:31; Judg. 3:10; 6:34; Isa. 42:1; 61:1), they are a major conduit of the Spirit within the community and especially for the empowerment of the royal line. This connection to the royal line may explain why the prophecy to Zerubbabel has been inserted into the center of the vision report of Zechariah 4. As with David and Saul,

28. Boda, "Haggai," 295–304.

29. Cf. Howard, "Transfer," 473–83; W. Ma, "The Spirit (RUAH) of God in Isaiah 1–39," *Asian Journal of Theology* 3 (1989): 580–95; W. Hildebrandt, *An Old Testament Theology of the Spirit of God* (Peabody, Mass.: Hendrickson, 1995); L. J. Wood, *The Holy Spirit in the Old Testament* (Grand Rapids: Zondervan, 1976); R. J. Sklba, "'Until the Spirit from on High Is Poured Out on Us' (Isa 32:15): Reflections on the Role of the Spirit in the Exile," *CBQ* 46 (1984): 1–17.

the prophet endows the royal figure with the Spirit, the sign of his princely status and empowerment for the royal task that lay ahead.

Spirit, prophet, and the New Testament. How do we apply this to our new covenant community of faith? One of the main roles of the prophet in the Old Testament was to point the people back to God's revelation on Sinai, to remind them of God's covenant principles and demands (2 Kings 17:13). There is no question, then, that God's Word has been delivered to us through the canonical witness of Scripture and that this represents the continuing witness of God within his community. Anointed preachers and teachers of God's Word continue the prophetic tradition by declaring the canonical Word to God's people. This explains why the New Testament constantly refers the community and its leaders to this Word as the foundation for their truth, witness, and mission (2 Tim. 3:14–17; 1 Peter 1:22–25; cf. 1 Tim. 4:13).

But is there a continuing role for the prophet within the new covenant community? In recent years there has been considerable debate over the nature and function of prophecy in the church today.[30] Gaffin argues that the prophetic office has become obsolete with the coming of the canon and is no longer operative within the church today. Grudem has maintained, however, that there is a prophetic gift of the Spirit that involves revelation from God today, although carefully placing it on a lower level than Old Testament prophetic and New Testament apostolic speech. There is no room in this commentary to resolve this debate, but I think it is important to highlight one aspect of the New Testament theology of prophecy that is often overlooked and provides an opportunity to incorporate the theme of the Spirit's prophetic empowerment into the life of the church today.

In Acts 1:1–8 Christ instructs his disciples to go to Jerusalem and remain until the Holy Spirit is given to them. The coming of the Spirit on them will propel them forward as his "witnesses" to the ends of the earth, a statement programmatic for the book of Acts, which depicts the advance of gospel witness from Jerusalem to Rome.[31]

---

30. R. B. Gaffin, *Perspectives on Pentecost: New Testament Teaching on the Gifts of the Holy Spirit* (Grand Rapids: Baker, 1979); W. Grudem, *The Gift of Prophecy in the New Testament and Today* (Eastbourne: Kingsway, 1988); idem, ed. *Are Miraculous Gifts for Today? Four Views* (Grand Rapids: Zondervan, 1996).

31. The term "my witnesses" in Acts 1:8 has been linked to the words of Isa. 43:10, 12; 44:8, where it is used of the witness of Israel among the nations in opposition to idolatry. This may have prophetic overtones (Rev. 11:3) and may explain the paralleling of "servant" and "witness" in reference to Paul's ministry to the Gentiles in Acts 26:16. See Bruce, who notes links to Isa. 43:10; 44:28 and Luke 24:48, and Haenchen who notes the many uses of "witness" in Acts relating to the apostles (1:8, 22; 2:32; 3:15; 5:32; 10:39, 41; 13:31), Paul (22:15; 26:16), and Stephen (22:20). The subject, interestingly, of this witness is Jesus' resurrection and the context is Israel and the Gentiles. See F. F. Bruce, *The Acts of the Apostles* (Grand Rapids: Eerdmans, 1990), 103; E. Haenchen, *The Acts of the Apostles* (Oxford: Blackwell, 1971), 143 n. 8.

What is interesting is the fulfillment of Christ's promise in Acts 2. Peter interprets this coming of the Spirit on the community in Jerusalem as fulfillment of a prophecy in Joel that speaks of the coming of the Spirit and prophetic utterance. Peter declares the prophetic role of all Christians—a role defined by Acts 1:8 as a witness that will reach the ends of the earth.

The wonder of Acts 2 is that we encounter redemptive progression beyond Zechariah 4. Whereas the source of the Spirit is linked to the witness of the few prophets God raised up within the community, under new covenant administration the Spirit is given to all God's people (fulfilling Moses' wish in Num. 11), who form a prophetic community to the nations. The oil flows through all of us as God's prophetic community to bring his presence and rule on earth.

Contemporary Significance

THE MESSAGE OF ZECHARIAH 4 is greatly needed in the church today, calling us back to the primacy of Word and Spirit within the ministry of the church. For Zechariah these two were the essential components of the power needed to complete the God-given mission of the restoration community. For us in the new covenant community, these components have even greater potential, as Christ has poured out his Spirit on all members of the community and granted us the canon in its fullness.

Unlimited potential of the Spirit's power in the ministry of the church. The New Testament makes it clear that the impact of the gospel on the Roman world was not due to the leadership skills of great visionaries or oratorical abilities of gifted speakers, but rather to the power of the Spirit as he worked through the weakness of humanity (Acts 1:8; 2:1–41; 1 Thess. 1:4–6). Paul celebrated his weaknesses, for in them he saw an opportunity for God to display his glory and power (2 Cor. 12:1–10).

What a contrast to what we often find today in the church. As leaders today, too often we become more interested in the latest seminar on visionary leadership and public oratory than on experiencing the unction of God's Spirit in our lives and ministries. There is an increasing temptation to look to secular sources for guiding the church rather than to the One who has promised to build his church by storming the very gates of hell (Matt. 16:18).

Zechariah 4 calls the church back to the empowerment of God's Spirit for its life and mission. As already noted, the exciting possibility for the church, in contrast to the community of God in Zechariah's day, is that the conduit of the Spirit has been greatly expanded to involve the church as a whole. This calls us to empower the many within the church who have been gifted by God's Spirit to accomplish God's mission in this world.

The Spirit's empowerment provides us with the courage to overcome the incredible challenges that stand in our way. For Zerubbabel the challenge was represented by the pile of rubble that stood before his community as they commenced the rebuilding project. God's word through Zechariah came at the right time and reminded Zerubbabel of his need for the Spirit's empowerment to accomplish this task. So also today, as communities of faith we face formidable tasks that remind us of our desperate need for God's empowerment.

I think of the church in the inner city in the midst of communities with soaring crime rates, dissolving families, and with absent economic vitality, a formidable pile of rubble. Yet I have seen the power of God's Spirit work through communities of faith in these situations, performing miracles as they have impacted these communities in all the dimensions of life: physical, social, and spiritual. I think of the church in the suburbs facing the challenge of a community spellbound by all the comforts of our society, seeking to soothe their spiritual conscience through these pleasures and seeing their lives and families torn asunder by strife, again a formidable pile of rubble. Reaching these kinds of communities in all of their dimensions is a venture beyond human potential and requires the empowerment of God's Spirit.

The New Testament encourages God's people to seek the Spirit's empowerment in their lives. In John 20:21–22, Jesus, introduced in 1:3–4 as the One through whom "all things were made" and in whom "was life," performs a second decisive creative act. In one of his key post-resurrection appearances, Jesus says to his disciples: "'Peace be with you! As the Father has sent me, I am sending you.' With that he breathed on them and said, 'Receive the Holy Spirit.'" It is odd to see Jesus "breathing" on his disciples and linking that act with the reception of the Holy Spirit, but in doing so he is reenacting the original act of creation: "The LORD God formed the man from the dust of the ground and breathed into his nostrils the breath of life, and the man became a living being" (Gen. 2:7). The Spirit re-creates life, abundant and eternal in this new community.

This Spirit is thus essential to living as a new creation in this world, and so it is not surprising how much the early church spoke about the Spirit's role in their lives and ministry. Throughout Acts God's people were a people of the Spirit, who empowered them to be God's witnesses (Acts 1:8), to declare his praises (2:1–12), to proclaim truth with boldness (4:8–12, 31; 6:10; 7:55), and to serve (6:3). This focus on the Spirit's empowerment for service is evident in the close link between the gifts of service in the church and the Holy Spirit in New Testament teaching (1 Cor. 12; 14). These gifts, however, must be exercised in the context of a life that portrays the fruit of the Spirit—that is, a life of holiness, love, and peace (1 Cor. 13).

Paul emphasizes this aspect of the Spirit's work throughout his writings. Immediately prior to calling God's people to "live a life worthy of the calling you have received" (Eph. 4:1), he prayed for God to "strengthen you with power through his Spirit in your inner being" (3:16) and then encouraged these same people to "be filled with the Spirit" (5:18). Furthermore, he encouraged the Galatian church to "live by the Spirit," to be "led by the Spirit," to "keep in step with the Spirit" (Gal. 5:16, 18, 25). Thus, the life-giving Spirit truly empowers us for holy living and faithful service, both as individuals within our families, work, and churches, but also as communities of faith within our community, culture, and globe.

In light of the importance of the Spirit's work in our lives as Christians, as we participate in Christ's great plan to restore God's kingship on earth, we must follow the encouragement of Jesus himself, who invites us to ask for the Spirit's work in our lives: "If you then, though you are evil, know how to give good gifts to your children, how much more will your Father in heaven give the Holy Spirit to those who ask him" (Luke 11:13).[32] This invitation is often appropriated by holiness and Pentecostal streams of Christianity, but it should become the cry of all Christians who seriously desire the fullness of God's work in and through their lives.

But we must not forget that the Spirit is at work within those who are in "step with the Spirit" (Gal. 5:25), reminding us of the importance of walking in holiness and obedience as we courageously embrace God's work in this world. The biblical theology of the Spirit's work within his people is never exclusively passive or exclusively active; rather, as we are filled with God's Spirit, we are propelled forward to holiness and service, and as we obediently pursue God's work, we are promised the life-giving Spirit's empowerment.

Primacy of God's Word in the ministry of the church. Zechariah links the power of the Spirit to the revelation of God's word through the prophet in the restoration community. We often see the Spirit's work in terms of power and strength to perform a task, but here that power and strength are afforded through the words of encouragement and challenge relayed from God through the prophets.

As in the early church, so today the powerful combination of Spirit and Word is essential to advance the church's mission. One of our greatest needs is a return to Spirit-filled proclamation of God's Word in our churches. This message, first of all, is directed to those who have been charged with the regular proclamation of God's Word in the context of the church. In recent

32. For an elongated treatment of the issue of the Spirit's role in the Christian's life at conversion and beyond with discussion of differences between traditions, see Smith, *Beginning Well*, 190–203.

years we have witnessed a shift in the content and style of preaching in our pulpits from a didactic edification model (edifying the saved) to an experiential evangelistic model (reaching the unsaved). On one level this transformation is to be applauded and has resulted in much numerical growth. On another level, however, there is cause for concern as there has been a tendency to sideline God's Word in the process.

In recent years I have been invited to speak at several churches on weekend modular format courses, experiences that I always find enriching and invigorating. One pastoral staff member in a church that has witnessed phenomenal growth in the past decade admitted to me that they were bringing me in because of a perceived need within the congregation. Their people were coming to them asking for the pastors to go deeper in their sermons. The pastoral staff responded that this was as deep as they could go, but they would bring someone else in who could go deeper. This attitude, of course, secures employment for me in the near future, but it should be a signal to all that something is wrong.

This is true also for lay leadership within the church. I recently spoke with a pastor providing leadership for Christian education in a large affluent and well-educated church. This individual was lamenting the lack of laypeople who could or would teach the Bible in their church. One person agreed to teach a study but, after attending a seminar on evangelism in an American megachurch, pulled out of the responsibility so that he could evangelize. I am not trying to pit edification against evangelism and want to strongly endorse both as essential to the restoration of God's kingdom in our world. But my recent experiences reveal the challenge we now face in our generation of the church.

The New Testament makes it clear that the leadership of the church was called to the ministry of the Word of God. The apostles set the trajectory for us from the outset as they focused their attention on the ministry of the Word and prayer (Acts 6:3). Paul reminds the church in Ephesians 4 that God has given leaders to the church to prepare God's people for ministry so that they may attain maturity. A key characteristic of that maturity is doctrinal and theological (Eph. 4:14–16). This matches Paul's exhortations to Timothy and Titus. Well over one-third of Paul's letters to these two young leaders concerns doctrine, truth, and teaching. In our rush to create large churches relevant to our generation, we have redefined church leadership in ways more like the business world and less like the biblical witness.

For Zechariah the great work of restoration was fueled by the Spirit's gift of revelation through his Word. This is certainly true for those leading the church today as we face a culture increasingly hostile to the gospel, whether through hyper-secular or pantheistic influences. This will mean continued emphasis on the skills necessary for interpreting Scripture in its original context. But equally important is enhanced reflection on the application of biblical truth into our postmodern culture. Expertise in both of these areas is essential. If we attain maturity in exegesis without developing skills in application, we risk irrelevance. If we attain maturity in application without developing exegetical aptitude, we risk severing our link to the source of authority, the Word of God. We desperately need a generation of teachers and preachers on vocational and lay levels who display sensitivity to both Word and culture.

All members of the church need to hear this message, whether they are involved in public leadership and teaching or not. The gifts of both God's Word and Spirit are available to each one of us in Christ. God has given us these gifts that we might grow to maturity in the faith.

In the early 1980s on a short-term mission trip to the Philippines, I had the privilege of hearing Stephen Olford speak to a large group of believers in Manila. Olford compared two New Testament passages, Ephesians 5:18–20 and Colossians 3:16–17, most likely written during the same period in Paul's ministry. Olford observed that the two passages end in a similar way, highlighting the worship and gratitude of the church (Eph. 5:19–20; Col. 3:16–17) before teaching on submission within the church (Eph. 5:21–6:9; Col. 3:18–4:1). However, the introductory clause is different in each case. In Ephesians 5:18 Paul speaks of the filling of the Holy Spirit while in Colossians 3:16 he speaks of the Word of Christ dwelling within us through wise teaching. Olford used this fascinating parallel to reveal the essential connection between Word and Spirit for the growth of the church. His aphorism on the necessity of both Spirit and Word for Christian growth was unforgettable:

> Word without Spirit we dry up.
> Spirit without Word we blow up.
> *Word and Spirit we grow up.*

God grants us his Spirit as the Spirit of truth, who guides us into deeper spiritual insight and knowledge (Eph. 1:15–23; 3:14–21). This guidance is true for each one of us as individuals, but also for the church as a whole. We must return to Spirit-filled interpretations of God's Word on every level of the church as we face a cultural context hostile to the claims of this Word.

This means that we must recover the rhythms of exegesis as leaders in the church on the vocational and lay level. There is no replacement for the example of godly leadership working with the text before the community of faith, whether in Bible studies, formal growth classes, or sermons. This also should be supplemented with regular opportunities for God's people to learn how to interpret the Scriptures on their own.[33] However, it is not merely a matter of teaching interpretive methodology, for we cannot lose sight of the Spirit's role in interpretation.

When I began teaching courses on preaching, I searched for appropriate textbooks for the course. I found many books available on the market, written by authors who approached the Scriptures as authoritative for contemporary faith and life. But as I perused many of these books, I found little emphasis on the ministry of the Holy Spirit in the preparation and delivery of sermons. One of the most popular books for preaching in North America, which has influenced preachers studying at evangelical colleges and seminaries for the past twenty-five years, provided a systematic approach for studying the Scriptures and preparing a clear and concise message for contemporary audiences, but there was no mention of the ministry of the Holy Spirit and only a passing reference to the importance of prayer.

As I began to search for elongated treatments on the ministry of the Spirit and prayer for preaching, I found a section in John Stott's *Between Two Worlds* and a chapter in Martin Lloyd-Jones' classic *Preaching and Preachers*. Then I had to mine the works of earlier centuries, in which I found rich resources for preaching that guided earlier generations in the preparation of sermons for God's people.[34] These older giants of the faith knew the importance of cultivating the life of the Spirit in order that it might produce a rich harvest of deep, sensitive, and relevant preaching and teaching for their people. They consistently called leaders in the church to a life of prayer, especially but not exclusively in relation to the ministry of preaching and teaching. They remind us of the need to pray as we prepare to preach and teach this Word, a principle taught so clearly and passionately by James Flavel:

> Thus laying our foundations in the knowledge of principles, choosing our subjects by the people's necessities; handling them in apt language; working them first upon your own affections, enforcing them by strict conversation, and steeping this holy seed in prayer; we shall approve ourselves the prudent ministers of Christ.[35]

---

33. See J. R. McQuilkin, *Understanding and Applying the Bible*, rev. ed. (Chicago: Moody Press, 1992), or G. D. Fee and D. Stuart, *How to Read the Bible for All Its Worth*, 3d ed. (Grand Rapids: Zondervan, 2003).

34. I am thankful to my friend Philip Ryken (Tenth Presbyterian, Philadelphia) for suggestions on this great stream in the Protestant preaching tradition. Among the many I have read, see esp.: C. Bridges, *The Christian Ministry, with an Inquiry into the Causes of its Inefficiency* (Carlisle: Banner of Truth, 1830), 50–63; C. H. Spurgeon, *Lectures to My Students* (Lynchburg, Va.: Old Time Gospel Hour, 1875), 2–22; D. M. Lloyd-Jones, *Preaching and Preachers* (Grand Rapids: Zondervan, 1971), 304–25; A. W. Tozer, *The Divine Conquest* (Harrisburg, Pa.: Christian Publications, 1950), 64–93; E. M. Bounds, *Preacher and Prayer* (Grand Rapids: Zondervan, 1952).

35. James Flavel, *The Works of James Flavel* (London: The Banner of Truth Trust, 1968), 6:573–74.

As we look for passages to preach, as we interpret the Scriptures during the week, as we create sermons relevant to this generation, as we rise to preach and teach, we must seek God in prayer. Furthermore, we should not overlook the importance of prayer as our people seek to live out the truth of this Word in their daily lives, as John Owen so aptly wrote: "To preach the word, and not to follow it with prayer constantly and frequently, is to believe its use, neglect its end, and cast away all the seed of the gospel at random."[36]

Preachers and teachers of the Word must ask for wisdom and clarity, sensitivity and compassion, but above all they should cry to the heavenly Father for the unction of the Spirit of truth. The paucity of emphasis on the Spirit in the present generation has been addressed in Arturo Azurdia's book *Spirit Empowered Preaching,* in which he reminds us:

> In the final analysis, we take up our privilege as proclaimers of the gospel, not because we are more intelligent or creative than the world, nor because our powers of rhetorical and logistical techniques are greater than those of other religious spokesmen. None of these powers will ever serve to win one person to Jesus Christ. We must never forget that the Christian Church always advances from a position of human weakness, not human strength. . . . Instead, we step out to accomplish the greater works because the Spirit of God, on the merits of our Savior's death, has been given to us. According to His own good pleasure He will be pleased to take our feeble and flawed presentations of the gospel and fill them with His irresistible power, consequently overcoming the hearts of sinful people that, otherwise speaking, will prove to be impenetrable.[37]

The interpretation and declaration of God's Word today, through preaching and teaching, must take center stage in the ministry of the church. It must, however, be interpretation and declaration directed by the Holy Spirit, who sensitizes our hearts and minds to the intention of Scripture and to the real needs of the present generation. This is not to play down the importance of honing interpretive skills, becoming sensitive to the original context into which Scriptures were first transmitted, but it does mean cultivating the life of the Spirit within as we seek to declare God's truth relevantly and powerfully to our needy world and people.

---

36. Cited in Bridges, *Christian Ministry*, 21.

37. A. G. Azurdia III, *Spirit Empowered Preaching: The Vitality of the Holy Spirit in Preaching* (Ross-Shire, UK: Mentor, 1998), 27.

Zechariah 5:1–4

I LOOKED AGAIN—and there before me was a flying scroll!
[2]He asked me, "What do you see?" I answered, "I see a fly-
ing scroll, thirty feet long and fifteen feet wide."
[3]And he said to me, "This is the curse that is going out
over the whole land; for according to what it says on one side,
every thief will be banished, and according to what it says on
the other, everyone who swears falsely will be banished. [4]The
LORD Almighty declares, 'I will send it out, and it will enter
the house of the thief and the house of him who swears falsely
by my name. It will remain in his house and destroy it, both its
timbers and its stones.'"

Original Meaning

THE VISION OF the flying scroll continues the trend established in the vision of the olive trees (ch. 4) of addressing issues within the community in the Persian province of Yehud. But in contrast to the previous vision, this vision along with the one that follows (5:5–11) moves from the issue of leadership to that of purity within the community.[1]

This call to purity highlights two fundamental aspects of loyalty in the covenant tradition of Israel: the command to love the Lord with all one's heart, soul, and mind, represented by the first set of commandments (Ex. 20:1–11; Deut. 5:6–15), and to love one's neighbor as oneself, represented by the second set of commandments (Ex. 20:8–17; Deut. 5:12–21).[2] In the visions of Zechariah 5, these two foundational relationships are covered in reverse order.[3]

1. That these two visions are to be read together as a unit is suggested by the appearance of the verb *šwb* (NIV "again") at 5:1 and 6:1, but not in 5:5.

2. Notice how the Sabbath commandment functions as a linchpin between the two realms of relationship, instructing the people to keep it "holy" as a "Sabbath to the LORD your God," but also as a day to keep one from oppressing one's family, servants, or animals.

3. Some interpret the first vision (vv. 1–4) as a general call to both of these relationships (each side of the scroll covering one of the two relationships), while others interpret the second vision (vv. 5–11) as a continuation of the focus of the first on injustice. See further below.

This focus on the covenant base of Israel reflects influences both inside and outside the Jewish community. (1) It is known that Darius encouraged the documenting of legal traditions among the various people groups of his empire.[4] Zechariah's vision of a scroll hovering over the land with its allusions to Israel's ancient covenant documents identifies the Torah as the legal corpus of Yehud.[5] This reflects the great concern in the Persian period for religious education.[6] (2) Severe economic conditions in Yehud in the early Persian period contributed to social injustice as people, desperate for subsistence, took extreme, even illicit measures to survive.[7]

The vision begins with the description of the scene by the prophet (5:1–2) before the angel provides an interpretation (5:3) and Yahweh, an oracle (5:4). In contrast to previous visions, this one has a negative thrust, warning the inhabitants of the land of God's continuing commitment to the covenant principles outlined in the Mosaic law. Although the vision differs in form from the sermon recorded in chapters 7–8, it presents a similar theme.

Detailed Analysis

THE VISION OPENS with the autobiographical style typical of the night visions and utilizes the same expressions as in 1:18; 2:1: "I looked again—and there before me was ..." (lit., "I lifted my eyes and I looked and behold ..."; see also 5:9; 6:1). But then it follows the rhetoric of the vision in chapter 4 as an unnamed voice (most likely the angel of 4:1) asks, "What do you see?"—a question that provides an opportunity for the prophet to describe the flying scroll.

The scroll has several unusual features.[8] (1) Its position is suspended above the earth (i.e., "flying"); a prophet would normally encounter a scroll in the hand of a reader or writer (cf. Jer. 36; Ezek. 2:9; 3:1–3). (2) This scroll is

---

4. On this see J. Blenkinsopp, "The Mission of Udjahorresnet and Those of Ezra and Nehemiah," *JBL* 106 (1987): 409–21; J. L. Berquist, *Judaism in Persia's Shadow: A Social and Cultural Approach* (Philadelphia: Fortress, 1995), 137–39; and vigorous debate on this issue in J. W. Watts, ed. *Persia and Torah: The Theory of Imperial Authorization of the Pentateuch* (SBLSymS 17; Atlanta: Society of Biblical Literature, 2001).

5. Cf. V. H. Matthews, "The Social Context of Law in the Second Temple Period," *BTB* 28 (1998): 7–15.

6. Baldwin, *Haggai*, 126.

7. The difficulty of these economic conditions is reflected at many points in Haggai (Hag. 1:5–6, 9–11; 2:15–19). Zech. 8:9–13 reveals the socially fracturing effect of economic stress in this period. This focus on social injustice is the main thrust of Zechariah's sermon on the fasting tradition in Zech. 7–8 (cf. 7:8–10; 8:16–17, 19b).

8. So unusual is this image that the Septuagint translates this term as *drepanon* ("sickle").

written on both sides.[9] (3) Even more shocking are the proportions of this scroll: it is thirty by fifteen feet. Although scrolls in ancient times could approach thirty feet in length, they would never exceed one foot in width.

The first peculiarity (suspended above the earth) grants the scroll the ability to fulfill its purpose of judgment with swiftness while providing access to a large territory. The second oddity (double-sided) links this scroll to the foundational covenant document delivered to Moses on Mount Sinai, described in Exodus 32:15 as being written on both sides (employing the same Heb. idiom as in Zech. 5:3).[10] The significance of the third irregularity (large size), however, has been more difficult to ascertain.

(1) Some see here the dimensions of a holy space or item. Leading candidates include the portico of Solomon's temple (*ʾulam*; 1 Kings 6:3), the two cherubim on the ark of the covenant (6:23–26), the Holy Place in the tabernacle (Ex. 26), and the bronze altar of the temple (2 Chron. 4:2).[11] Of these the first two are the strongest for they can be linked to the administration of justice: The portico was likely the place where priestly justice was administered (cf. Zech. 3:7; Joel 2:17),[12] and the cherubim were the "winged guardians of the Mosaic tablets."[13] The fact that Solomon mentions a "curse" in the administration of justice in his dedication prayer for the first temple (1 Kings 8:31–32) makes the portico interpretation the most attractive of these options.[14]

---

9. The Hebrew idiom *mizzeh . . . mizzeh* is a spatial idiom for describing two sides or ends (Ex. 25:19; 26:13; 32:15 [tablets of the testimony]; 37:8; 38:15; Num. 22:24; Josh. 8:22, 33; 1 Sam. 14:4; 17:3; 23:26; 2 Sam. 2:13; 1 Kings 10:19, 20; Ezek. 45:7; 47:7, 12; 48:21; 2 Chron. 9:18, 19; 25), not a logical connector (on the one hand, on the other hand), as some have claimed.

10. So also Merrill, *Haggai*, 168; Chary, *Aggeé-Zacharie, Malachie*, 1000; Rignell, *Nachtgesichte*, 185; contra Mason, *Haggai*, 57, who links to Ezekiel's scroll (Ezek. 2:10). Note that a scroll is important to Jeremiah's prophetic revelation in Jer. 36, a passage clearly in mind in the prose sermon of Zech. 7–8, which also confronts social injustice in the Persian period.

11. On the various views, see esp. Mitchell, Smith, and Brewer, *Haggai*, 169; Mason, *Haggai*, 57; Halpern, "Ritual Background," 178–79; Jeremias, *Nachgesichte*, 189; Merrill, *Haggai*, 166; Meyers and Meyers, *Haggai*, 281; J. D. Douglas, "Tabernacle," in *New Bible Dictionary*, ed. J. D. Douglas (Wheaton: Tyndale, 1982). Baldwin, *Haggai*, 126, raises some questions about these dimensions.

12. Halpern, "Ritual Background," 179.

13. Meyers and Meyers, *Haggai*, 281.

14. This connection to the dimensions of the temple are important for those who see the rebuilding project as the driving force behind the night visions. The most ardent supporters of this interpretation recently have been Halpern, "Ritual Background," 178–79, and Meyers and Meyers, *Haggai*, 280. Chary notes that since ch. 4 was concerned with the temple, so also must ch. 5; Chary, *Aggeé-Zacharie, Malachie*, 99. Cf. my critique of these attempts in Boda, "Penitential Prophet," 49–69.

(2) A second approach[15] is that the dimensions signify the immensity of something associated with the scroll, either the "vast number of transgressions"[16] of the people or the large territory over which it is dispatched.

(3) A third approach does not see significance in the large size but only in the relative size of the dimensions, arguing that the scroll was still rolled up and the 2:1 ratio (30 by 15 feet) signifies either the dimensions of the text that is showing (1–3 columns)[17] or the length of scroll when unrolled and its diameter when rolled.[18] The large size would make it possible for someone to read the text from a distance.[19]

The difficulty with approaches that link the scroll to a holy space or item is that there are no indications in this context that the scroll is to be connected to the temple.[20] This attempt to read the night visions in light of the rebuilding project consistently distracts attention from the unique direction Zechariah takes in his message.[21] The significance of the size is most likely a combination of the latter two approaches, signifying a scroll that displays a section of the law and is commensurate with the size of transgression and territory.

Therefore, the double-sided nature of the scroll identifies this image with the covenant law of Israel while the flight and dimensions of the scroll emphasize the efficacy and universality of these covenant demands. No one can plead ignorance as it hovers imposingly above the earth,[22] and no one can escape its censure if its stipulations are disregarded.

---

15. Meyers and Meyers, *Haggai*, 280–81, and Merrill, *Haggai*, 166–67, argue that this approach is not mutually exclusive from the first.

16. Redditt, *Haggai*, 72.

17. Meyers and Meyers, *Haggai*, 281.

18. Merrill, *Haggai*, 167.

19. See D. N. Freedman, "The Flying Scroll in Zechariah 5:1–4," in *Studies in Near Eastern Culture and History*, ed. J. Bellamy (Ann Arbor: Univ. of Michigan Center for Near Eastern and North African Studies, 1990), 42–48, and his calculations.

20. So also Petersen, *Haggai*, 247: "It is equally difficult to explain what meaning that might have for the vision, the more so since the temple plays virtually no role in Zechariah's vision"; cf. Baldwin, *Haggai*, 126.

21. See Boda, "Penitential Prophet," 49–69. Meyers and Meyers reflect this distraction when they use this vision to claim that "concomitant with the idea of abundance is the notion that temple rebuilding promotes social order," and "the temple restoration, as inaugurated by a refoundation ceremony, will affect all facets of life"; Meyers and Meyers, *Haggai*, 284, 293.

22. There is some debate over whether the phrase "over the whole land" refers particularly to the province of Yehud or universally to the entire earth. Elsewhere in the Hebrew Bible it is used in both ways (more limited regions in Deut. 11:25; 1 Sam. 30:16; 2 Sam. 18:8; the cosmos in Gen. 1:29; 7:3; 8:9; 11:4, 8, 9). Elsewhere in the night visions "the whole land" is used in the more universal sense (1:11; 4:14; 6:5); if this is true here in 5:3, it means that Zechariah sees implications for the Jewish community wherever they may be.

The connection to the covenant base and its attendant legal demands is made clear in the explanation of the angel in 5:3. The angel identifies this scroll as "the curse" (*ha'alah*).[23] This term is used in two ways in the Hebrew Bible.[24] (1) It appears in covenant-making contexts and represents the consequence of violating covenant stipulations (Gen. 26:28; Deut. 29:11–20; Ezek. 16:59; 17:13). As God's people enter into relationship, they pronounce a curse (oath) on themselves if they breach this relationship. (2) It is used in covenant-enforcement contexts, where an infraction has been committed but cannot be proven (Lev. 5:1; Num. 5:16–28; Judg. 17:2; 1 Kings 8:3; 2 Chron. 6:22; Prov. 29:24). The last resort to determine guilt or innocence was to put the one accused (whether known or not) under a curse. It is inappropriate to drive a wedge between these two uses in the Persian period context because the former provides a foundation for the latter, but it appears that the imagery used here reflects the more individualized sense because of the cases presented in verses 3–4.

The argument for a more individualized legal context is bolstered by the use of the Hebrew verb *naqah* (NIV "will be banished") in 5:3. This term appears with *ha'alah* in Numbers 5:16–28 (cf. v. 19, 21).[25] The sense of the word there is that the individual will be cleared or freed from the consequences of the violation. This is most likely the meaning of the word here and results in the following translation: "This is the curse that is going out over the face of all the earth, for everyone who steals, according to what is written on the one side, has been cleared, and everyone who swears, according to what is written on the other side, has been cleared" (trans. mine).[26] The curse is going out because the guilty are going unpunished. The angel is declaring that the curse recited against the accused as the final step in the legal process will fulfill its purpose and bring destruction on those who are guilty. Although the scroll represents the entire law, for those who are disobedient it becomes the source of curse.

---

23. There may be a play on words here between the scroll (*megillah*) and the curse (*ha'alah*); cf. Petersen, *Haggai*, 246; C. Stuhlmueller, *Rebuilding with Hope: A Commentary on the Books of Haggai and Zechariah* (ITC; Grand Rapids: Eerdmans, 1988), 91.

24. See H. C. Brichto, *The Problem of "Curse" in the Hebrew Bible* (SBLMS 13; Philadelphia: Society of Biblical Literature, 1968).

25. The only other context in which these two terms appear is Gen. 24:41, in the context of a covenant oath between Abraham and his servant.

26. So similarly Petersen, *Haggai*, 245; Meyers and Meyers, *Haggai*, 286. The NIV, along with Baldwin and Merrill, takes this term in a figurative way as "to be cleaned out" ("banished"), similar to Isa. 3:26; Baldwin, *Haggai*, 127; Merrill, *Haggai*, 170. However, the connections to Num. 5:19 prohibit this translation.

The two infractions highlighted in 5:3–4 (stealing and perjury) are closely related and probably represent two successive acts by the same individual who not only stole, but then perverted justice by swearing falsely in a legal trial.[27] Although many have linked these infractions to the Decalogue (Ex. 20:7, 16; Deut. 5:11, 19), the source of this language is assuredly Leviticus 19:11–18 (esp. vv. 11–12),[28] which concludes with the general call to "love your neighbor as yourself" (19:18) and confronts the issue of oppression of the poor and the needy (19:9–10, 15).[29]

As noted above, socioeconomic evidence from this period suggests economic conditions that were leaving the poor and needy vulnerable (see comments on 7:1–14; 8:14–23). Brazen violation of the legal corpus with crafty manipulation of the legal system are a destructive combination. The fact that the punishment involves the destruction of one's house (5:4) suggests that the infractions are linked to the stealing of property, a key issue in the early Persian period as Jews returned to land once owned by their ancestors in the former kingdom of Judah.[30]

At the end of the vision and following the explanation of its elements, God's voice breaks in through the speech style typical of a Hebrew prophet ("declares the LORD Almighty").[31] If there is any question about the source of this flying scroll, this is clarified in verse 4 when God announces: "I will send it out." The efficacy of this curse is seen in the four verbs used in this verse: "send out," "enter," "remain," "destroy." The first two verbs are often used for opposite actions: What goes out eventually comes back in (cf. English, what goes up must come down).[32]

This "entering" is described as "remain," a verb often translated as "spending the night" and associated with hospitality (e.g., Gen. 19:2; 24:23, 25). This verb is followed here by the preposition *betok* ("in the midst of"), a preposition

27. Notice how elsewhere when "swearing" and "falsely" appear together, one also finds references to someone cheating and/or oppressing another (Gen. 21:23; Lev. 5:22, 24; 19:12; Jer. 5:2; 7:9; Mal. 3:5).

28. Cf. Petersen, *Haggai*, 250 n. 259. The language of "swearing" in Ex. 20:7//Deut. 5:11 is different from that in Lev. 19:12 and Zech. 5:4. See Huffmon's work on vocabulary connected with the third and ninth commandment: H. B. Huffmon, "The Fundamental Code Illustrated: The Third Commandment," in *Pomegranates and Golden Bells: Studies in Biblical, Jewish, and Near Eastern Ritual, Law, and Literature in Honor of Jacob Milgrom*, ed. D. P. Wright, D. N. Freedman, and A. Hurvitz (Winona Lake, Ind.: Eisenbrauns, 1995), 363–71. Zech. 5 and Lev. 19 show that one cannot draw firm lines between the third and ninth commandments as he does for they combine vocabulary from both commands.

29. There may be an allusion here to Jer. 7:9, where stealing and perjury are also paralleled in a sermon connected to the critique of temple practices.

30. Cf. Redditt, *Haggai*, 72.

31. See also 1:14–17; 2:9; 3:6–10.

32. These two verbs are used in the Heb. idiom for the regular activity of humanity: "going out ... coming in" (see Ps. 121:8; Zech. 8:10; cf. 2 Sam. 3:25; 1 Kings 15:17).

that emphasizes location in the center of the object.[33] This highlights the ability of this curse to enter into the private center of the violator's home. The irony of this association is that this "guest," allowed into the privacy of the home, will "destroy" (*kalah*). This final verb is often used for completing or finishing a project or activity (a temple, 2 Chron. 8:16; a speech, Gen. 17:22; a meal, 1 Kings 1:41) and, similar to the English idioms "finish someone off" or "bring an end to," can be used for the totality of destruction.

These verbs denote God's judgment directed at the "house" of the violator. "House" should be interpreted, at least on the first level, in literal terms, particularly because the sense of total destruction is emphasized by the reference to "timbers" and "stones," the basic building materials for Jewish houses.[34] However, it is possible that "house" here is functioning as a synecdoche,[35] in which it represents the entire lifestyle of the violator.[36]

In sum, after a series of visions proclaiming promise to the Persian period community, this passage delivers a warning. It reminds those within the covenant community that they cannot ignore or abuse God's covenant law and expect to escape discipline. Although granted a new start by Yahweh in this new phase of redemptive history, he continues to take sin seriously and demands covenant loyalty with one's neighbor. This vision raises the profile of the law as the guide to life in covenant relationship. It especially reminds the Jewish community of their need to protect the weak and vulnerable by obeying the law and exercising justice in the courts.

Bridging Contexts

THE ROLE OF THE LAW. This vision of the flying scroll emphasizes the role of the law in the life of the early Persian period community. This is just the beginning of the struggle to place the law at the center of this community, a struggle reflected in the work of Ezra and Nehemiah (Ezra 7–10; Neh. 5, 8–10, 13). Such stress, however, on the law has often distanced Christian readers from these texts.

This alienation from the law within the Christian community has often been linked to Luther's contrast of law and gospel in the Reformation period. In this theological configuration, Romans and Galatians are used to argue that

33. Elsewhere only used of Joshua (Josh. 8:9), when he remained for the night at the center of the military camp of Israel (the place of greatest protection for the commander).

34. Cf. Lev. 14:45 for combination of timbers and stones as the totality of a house in context of destruction.

35. A poetic image in which the part stands for the whole.

36. So also Merrill, *Haggai*, 170. Notice the use of "house" as the focus of punishment and judgment by Mesopotamian kings in Ezra 6:11; Dan. 2:5; 3:29. It is also found in ancient Near Eastern treaties; cf. Petersen, *Haggai*, 251.

the law stands in opposition to the gospel by encouraging an earlier generation to obtain salvation through obedience to its demands, which it cannot do. Thus, the law is relegated to the role of "schoolmaster" to reveal the need for Christ (Gal. 3:24).

Several references to the law in these New Testament letters, however, stand in contrast to this simplistic conclusion. The law is declared "good" in Romans 7:16, 22, 25 (cf. 7:7). Those who live by faith fulfill the law (3:31; 8:4), and the law Paul has in mind is clearly the Torah (7:7; 13:9). One must carefully differentiate between Paul's use of *law* "to denote the status of the person who looks to the law, and therefore to works of law, as the way of justification and acceptance with God" and *law* as Torah or teaching.[37] A closer look at several aspects of the Old Testament theology of law is instructive for interpreting the law in our contemporary context.

(1) A discussion of law must begin with orientation in covenant theology. The law was not an abstract list of behavioral patterns but rather core values defining a relationship. The foundation of this covenant relationship was clearly the redemptive work and character of Yahweh, who delivered Israel from slavery in Egypt (Ex. 20:1; Deut. 5:6; cf. Deut. 7:7–11). The people were invited to respond to this God of grace through relationships of fidelity, both with God (Ex. 20:3–11; Deut. 5:7–11) as well as with one's neighbor (Ex. 20:12–17; Deut. 5:12–21). The blessings and curses found near the end of the law (Lev. 26; Deut. 27–28; cf. 30:1) are to be viewed not as rewards and punishments but as provision and discipline. Blessings represent the "life" (Deut. 4:1; 5:16, 33; 8:3; 32:46–47; Lev. 18:5; Neh. 9:29; Ezek. 20:11) that this relationship is to foster, and "curses" are signs of death that lie outside the relationship and function as signals for the people to return to God, who grants life. At the foundation of the law, therefore, is a covenant relationship of grace.

(2) The Old Testament theology of law is not only relational in orientation but also internal. The law was not merely to be an external code to be followed; rather, it was to become part of the inner fabric of one's affections, as reflected in the following exhortations: "observe with all your heart" (Deut. 26:16); "take to heart" (32:46); "do not . . . let them slip from your heart" (4:9); "be on your hearts" (6:6).

(3) A third aspect of the Old Testament theology of law was that it was exemplary in character. The law provided guidance for a people living in a particular context at a particular time. Because of this, interpretation of law formed an important function for the leadership of Israel (see comments on Hag. 2:10–14), as they dispensed guidance for faithful worship and relationships: whether

37. J. Murray, "Law in the New Testament," in *The New Bible Dictionary*, ed. J. D. Douglas (Grand Rapids: Eerdmans, 1962), 721–23.

priest (Jer. 2:8; Hos. 4:6; Hag. 2:10–14), king (Deut. 17:18–20), prophet (Isa. 1:10; 5:24; Hos. 8:1), or sage (Jer. 8:8, 9; cf. Prov. 28:4, 7, 9; 29:18; 31:5).[38]

With these three theological principles in mind, it is not surprising that the prophets envision a future for the law in redemptive history. Prophets depict the law going forth from Jerusalem to the entire world, drawing humanity to its source (Isa. 2:1–5//Mic. 4:1–5; Isa. 42:4, 21; 51:4). They also describe a new covenant in which the law will finally reach its original destination as it is written on hearts renewed by the Spirit of God (Jer. 31:31–34; Ezek. 11:19–20; 36:26–27).

The New Testament bears witness to the fulfillment of this prophetic expectation as it celebrates the institution of the new covenant through Jesus Christ's death on the cross. Paul speaks of letters written by the Spirit on hearts rather than on stone (2 Cor. 3:2–7) and of a circumcision of the heart by the Spirit, not by a written code (Rom. 2:29). The writer of Hebrews, citing Jeremiah 31, says that the new covenant means the old will become obsolete (Heb. 8:7–13; 10:15–18). These references, however, do not mean that the law will be disqualified; rather, the means by which the law will become a reality in the lives of the believers will be through the Spirit because of Christ's mediation (Heb. 9:15).[39]

Zechariah 5:1–4 is an appropriate passage for believers today as they follow Christ, who asserted that he did not "come to abolish the Law or the Prophets" but "to fulfill them" (Matt. 5:17). Through his act of sacrifice, he fulfills the law for us and provides the resource for his community to express the law's values in every generation. Empowered by the Spirit, we must replicate those values in our lives and communities so that "the true purpose of the law, namely, to lead man into a fruitful, abundant life of fellowship with God, will be fully realized."[40]

Contemporary Significance

Word of God. The vision of the flying scroll communicated an important message to the Jewish community in Zechariah's day, advocating the centrality of God's law for them to seek covenant

38. See Fee and Stuart, *Read*, 135–47, esp. 147.

39. Considerable work has been done recently on the approach of Second Temple Judaism to the law. In particular, Sanders's "covenant nomism" stresses the main themes we have identified in our reading of the Old Testament theology of law; cf. S. McKnight, *A New Vision for Israel: The Teaching of Jesus in National Context* (Grand Rapids: Eerdmans, 1999), 197–237. Similar appreciation of law is well documented in the work of Reformed theologians (e.g., see Murray, "Law," 721–23).

40. J. E. Hartley, "*Tôrâ*," in *Theological Wordbook of the Old Testament*, ed. R. L. Harris, G. L. Archer, and B. K. Waltke (Chicago: Moody Press, 1980), 1:405.

renewal. This message has enduring significance for the Christian community as we seek to embody individually and corporately the values of this ancient law. With the confidence that Christians now live in the new era of the Spirit, we must be a community transfixed by the law of Christ, which is being written on our hearts.

Communities that take seriously this message are those who hold the written Word of God in high regard within their corporate rhythms of fellowship and worship. This means regular preaching and teaching from the Scriptures, as was the practice of the ancient church, but also consistent reading from Old and New Testaments.

There are some who regard such respect for the Word as bibliolatry (worship of the written Word), but such need not be the case. The written Word was important to the Persian period community. When Ezra opened "the book" in Nehemiah 8:5–6, the community stood in reverence and gave praise to God. This is not worship of the written Word but praise of the God who revealed it to humanity. The Word was precious to this community because of its origin in God. So also in the New Testament Paul reminds young Timothy of the supremacy of the Scriptures in the practice of his ministry: "All Scripture is God-breathed and is useful for teaching, rebuking, correcting and training in righteousness" (2 Tim. 3:16).

Zechariah 5:1–4, therefore, encourages Christian communities today to place the teaching and reading of Scriptures at the center of their communal life. It challenges several trends in contemporary church life. (1) There is a constant temptation today to build communities of faith without a strong foundation in the preaching, teaching, and reading of the Scriptures. Some of this can be attributed to a sincere passion to evangelize the unchurched by providing nonthreatening environments. There is a danger, however, in such ministry models to remove the scriptural underpinnings of a Christian community and to minimize the role of the written Word in young believers' lives. It is important, therefore, for all ministry models to create appropriate venues for the community to encounter the Scriptures.

(2) Many evangelical traditions have not exploited the power of reading Scripture in the context of community. With the priority on preaching and teaching the written Word, communal reading of Scripture has been marginalized. Many contemporary Christian traditions regularly incorporate the reading of the Scriptures in their communal worship experiences. These traditions take their lead from the ancient tradition of the church, which has likely been influenced by Jewish tradition established at least by the Persian period.

For instance, Nehemiah 9 provides a model of Jewish worship in which the people "read from the Book of the Law of the LORD their God for a quarter of the day" (Neh. 9:3).[41] The prayer that follows is filled with allusions to the early Scriptures of Israel, revealing the impact of these writings on the vocabulary of the community.[42] Furthermore, the central feature of the Jewish festivals to this day is the reading of entire books of the Old Testament: at Passover (Song of Songs); Pentecost (Ruth); Ninth of Ab, that is, the destruction of Jerusalem (Lamentations); Tabernacles (Ecclesiastes); and Purim (Esther).[43]

In my ministry among college and seminary students I have tried to encourage the reading of large sections of Scripture as part of the regular rhythm of our life as a learning community. We have read such sections as Lamentations, Esther, Psalms 120–134 (Psalms of Ascent), Revelation, and the Gospel Passion narrative. My hope is that churches will set aside times throughout the year for special services of Scripture reading. This is one way to ensure that a Christian community remains a community of the Word.

(3) A third trend within the church today that presents a challenge to the priority of the Scriptures lies in the area of hermeneutics. Criticism of modern approaches to reality and truth by post-foundational figures has led to considerable hermeneutical suspicion and epistemological confusion. The admission that all human interpretation is ultimately perspectival has led to the conclusion that all truth is relative to the perception of the interpreter.[44] The impact on the life of the church has been considerable, with loss of confidence in the Scriptures since they are often presented to Christians through interpreters (preachers and teachers).

These challenges, however, need not lead to a crisis of confidence in or a lack of attention to the Scriptures. The biblical record of God's community consistently shows the importance of the written Word to God's people during a premodern era. Rather, important perspectives can be gained from recent reflection on the present crisis in hermeneutics, which can provide a way ahead for interpreters and communities alike.

There has been much value in this epistemological shift as Christian preachers have been forced to face their limited perspective. This reevaluation of Christian hermeneutics has encouraged greater humility and care in interpreting Scripture. Christian interpreters must approach the text with far

---

41. See M. Duggan, *The Covenant Renewal in Ezra-Nehemiah (Neh 7:72b–10:40): An Exegetical, Literary, and Theological Study* (SBLDS 164; Atlanta: Society of Biblical Literature, 2001).

42. See Boda, *Praying*; Newman, "Nehemiah 9," 112–23.

43. H. E. Clem, "Megilloth," *ABD*, 4:680. Notice also how much of the New Testament functioned originally as letters that were read to congregations.

44. See D. A. Carson, *The Gagging of God: Christianity Confronts Pluralism* (Grand Rapids: Zondervan, 1992); K. J. Vanhoozer, *Is There a Meaning in This Text? The Bible, The Reader, and the Morality of Literary Knowledge* (Grand Rapids: Zondervan, 1998).

more humility, recognizing their dependence on God to grasp its ancient meaning and discover creative significance for contemporary audiences. Because of the role of the interpreter in interpretation, Christian students of the Bible must place great priority on what they bring to the text, not only retaining a healthy suspicion of their presuppositions but also attending to their experience with God and humanity. Finally, since all interpreters are situated within community, it is important to draw on the resources of that community and to be informed by the breadth of perspective that only a community can bring to the text.[45]

Discipline of God. Zechariah 5:1–4 takes the prophet in a new direction. Here we see the flip side of God's covenant zeal: his zealous protection of his righteous standards and the people they were designed to protect. Hebrews 12:4–11 makes it clear that in the life of faith, God continues to discipline his people in order to purify them. Sometimes he must shout to us through the circumstances of our lives in order to awaken us from our rebellious slumber.

This does not mean that every difficulty that enters into our lives is necessarily God's discipline. Suffering and pain can have many causes and serve many purposes, only one of which is discipline of sin. But when we do experience difficulty, we must take this time to reflect on our walk with God. James encourages this while instructing on how to deal with sickness within the church. Those who are sick are to confess their sins to one another when requesting anointing from the elders (James 5:14–20). This shows the importance of the community in the discipline of God; a community of accountability is a means of God's grace.

The Psalter provides excellent models of prayers appropriate for reflection on sin in our lives. Psalm 139 is a cry to God to search the believer for "any offensive way." Psalm 51 moves to the next step when sin has been identified, providing a model for confessing sin to God. Finally, Psalm 32 is a model for giving thanksgiving for the forgiveness of sin. Such a progression of expressions to God should become a regular rhythm within the community of faith as a whole, not only for sin within individual lives but also within whole communities.

Sin of the community. Zechariah 5:1–4 is addressed to the specific issue of disobedience to the second part of Israel's covenant foundation, that is, love of one's neighbor. The key issue is not merely the violation of a specific sin (stealing) but also the perversion of justice in order to escape punishment for that sin (swearing falsely).

---

45. For this see Fowl and Jones, *Reading in Communion*.

Today we encounter this vision afresh through Christ's call to "love your neighbor as yourself." We must resist the temptation to "spiritualize" away this vision; instead, we must examine the ways in which we have "stolen" from our fellow human beings and then perverted justice to escape punishment. This could be through active exploitation of the economic system (avoiding taxes, abusing welfare, underpaying employees, fudging expense accounts) or through passive perversion (ignoring poverty, silencing minorities). The gospel has implications for our economic life as well as for our prayer life; it has both a sociological and an individual dimension.

In a recent address to the American Academy of Religion, a famous African-American theologian identified what he dubbed "the great sin of theology."[46] That sin he named as "silence": silence at the various forms of oppression and evil in society. The risks for those who speak out are always high, whether they be Dietrich Bonhoeffer or Martin Luther King, but theologians must take seriously their call to confront the sin of their generation.

For many Christians, the first step towards responding to 5:1–4 is a deep reflection on the ways in which our communities have manipulated the economic systems of society for their own benefit. Such reflection must lead to confession of those sins individually and corporately. But there is another step, as the forgiven psalmist says in Psalm 32:8: "I will instruct you and teach you in *the way you should go*" (italics added). Believers need to step out in faith and become agents of transformation within their communities—not only speaking for those who have lost hope but also acting in Christ's name to alleviate their suffering.

46. James H. Cone, "Theology's Great Sin," paper given at American Academy of Religion, Denver, Colo. (Nov. 19, 2001).

Zechariah 5:5–11

THEN THE ANGEL who was speaking to me came forward
and said to me, "Look up and see what this is that is
appearing."
6I asked, "What is it?"
He replied, "It is a measuring basket." And he added, "This
is the iniquity of the people throughout the land."
7Then the cover of lead was raised, and there in the basket
sat a woman! 8He said, "This is wickedness," and he pushed
her back into the basket and pushed the lead cover down over
its mouth.
9Then I looked up—and there before me were two women,
with the wind in their wings! They had wings like those of a
stork, and they lifted up the basket between heaven and earth.
10"Where are they taking the basket?" I asked the angel
who was speaking to me.
11He replied, "To the country of Babylonia to build a house
for it. When it is ready, the basket will be set there in its
place."

Original Meaning

INTERPRETATIONS OF THIS vision can be classified into two basic groups. (1) Some see the vision as continuing the emphasis on social injustice begun in 5:1–4.[1] This view relies heavily on the presence of several Hebrew words in this vision: *ʾepah* ("measuring basket," vv. 6, 7, 9, 10), *kikkar* ("cover," v. 7), and *ʾeben* ("cover," v. 8), all connected to a standard measuring unit (cf. Lev. 19:36; Deut. 25:14, 15; Prov. 20:10; Ezek. 45:10–11; Amos 8:5; and esp. Mic. 6:11).[2]

(2) Others see this vision as taking the concern over sin introduced by the previous vision (5:1–4) in a new direction by confronting illicit worship

1. For this see Petersen, *Haggai*, 255–59; M. Barker, "The Evil in Zechariah," *HeyJ* 19 (1978): 23; Stuhlmueller, *Rebuilding*, 92; Merrill, *Haggai*, 174; Baldwin, *Haggai*, 128 (although she also embraces the second approach on p. 129); recently D. Rudman, "Zechariah 5 and the Priestly Law," *SJOT* 14 (2000): 194–206.

2. In Mic. 6:10–11 the words *rašaʿ* and *rešaʿ* are also present, possibly the source of the word *rišʿah* ("wickedness") in Zech. 5:8.

practices.[3] The strongest evidence for this view lies in the latter half of the vision as the basket is transported to Babylon to a "house" where it rests "in its place." Elsewhere in the Hebrew Bible the word "place" (*mekunah*) refers exclusively to the base of a holy object in a sanctuary (e.g., 1 Kings 7:28; Ezra 3:3). This usage suggests that the "house" in Babylon is a "temple" (the word for both is the same, *bayit*) and that the basket is destined for sacred use.[4]

Earlier features in the vision also suit this approach. The "woman" in the basket is connected via other Scripture passages to idolatry—for example, as the idol of a goddess seated on a throne (Asherah, Ishtar/Astarte), as Queen Athaliah the idolatrous monarch, who is called "wicked" (2 Chron. 24:7), or as foreign wives from exile who had introduced idolatry into the Judean community (Ezra 9–10; Neh. 13:23–27). "Wickedness" (*rišʿah*), a term used to identify this woman, is connected to the idolatry of surrounding nations in Deuteronomy 9:4–5 (cf. 8:19–20) and Ezekiel 5:6–7 (cf. 5:9, 11).[5] Finally, *ʾepah*, so important to the first approach, can refer to a basket used to transport an offering of grain (Lev. 5:11; cf. 6:13).[6]

The accumulated evidence for the second approach tips the argument in its favor. Whereas the vision in 5:1–4 confronted covenant infidelity in human relationships, the second vision confronts covenant infidelity in the people's relationship with God. Yahweh is a jealous God, who will not tolerate any rival.

This vision does portray some uniqueness in structure. It proceeds through stages rather than being a single revelation of a scene at the outset, which is then discussed by the angel and the recipient. In the first stage the prophet sees a measuring basket, which is then interpreted (5:5–6). In the second stage the lead cover is raised to reveal a woman, who is then identified (5:7–8). Finally, two winged women appear, and their significance is revealed (5:9–11).

This vision brings attention back to an important theme of the first half of the vision series. The focus there was to offer comfort to the Jewish community through declaring God's punishment of Babylon (1:18–21) and the release of exiles (2:6–13). Just prior to the launch of God's punishment on

---

3. For this see Mitchell, Smith, and Brewer, *Haggai*, 173–74; S. Marenof, "Note Concerning the Meaning of the Word 'Ephah,' Zechariah 5:5–11," *AJSL* 48 (1931–32): 264–67; Meyers and Meyers, *Haggai*, 296–316; Mason, *Haggai*, 58; Redditt, *Haggai*, 75; Floyd, "Evil," 51–68.

4. Even the proponents of the social injustice approach see the ultimate function of this basket as sacred; e.g., Petersen, *Haggai*, 262. Notice Rudman, "Zechariah 5," 205: "While there may not be any explicit connection with idolatry in the contents of the ephah, it would seem that there certainly is a cultic flavour to the 'house' which is built for it."

5. Elsewhere this word is used in very general terms (Deut. 25:2; Isa. 9:17; Mal. 1:4; 3:15, 19). In Ezek. 18:20, 27 the meaning is general but is linked more specifically to idolatry and injustice (18:1–17; cf. 33:12, 19).

6. Meyers and Meyers, *Haggai*, 296.

Babylon and release of the exiles in the final vision of 6:1–8, the present vision reminds the audience that those who return must not bring Babylonian idolatry with them.

A Measuring Basket (5:5–6)

THE MAIN CHARACTERS in the vision are the "angel who was speaking with me" and "me" (presumably Zechariah)—the same characters interacting in the previous vision. Although it is difficult to discern why this angel is "going out" (*yaṣaʾ*; NIV "came forward"), it most likely is related to the fact that the vision of chapter 4 (also of ch. 3) took place inside the sanctuary and now the "going out" signals a move to an outside venue.[7] The prophet follows the angel and is commanded to observe a new scene: "a measuring basket" exiting the sanctuary.

As in the other visions, this one takes an ordinary object to create an extraordinary scene. The word for "measuring basket" (*ʾepah*) denotes a commonly accepted measurement ("ephah") that in time came to denote a container that holds this amount.[8] The presence of such a basket in a temple context is not odd, for such containers were used to weigh grain offerings.[9]

The angel identifies this container as "the iniquity of the people in all the land." Scholars have hotly debated this phrase because of considerable divergence between the Hebrew text and the ancient versions. The Hebrew text, followed by the Latin Vulgate, reads here: "This is their eye"; the LXX and Syriac versions read: "This is their iniquity." This variety can be traced to the difference of a single consonant in Hebrew (*ʿynm* versus *ʿwnm*). The Hebrew/Latin reading must be interpreted figuratively—as a reference to omniscience (like the eye of God in 4:10, so here evil has an eye),[10] to a hostile attitude (their hostile eye),[11] to appearance (Lev. 13:5; Num. 11:7),[12]

7. Although the flying scroll of 5:1–4 seems to fit better in an outdoors context, it is perhaps appropriate to the sanctuary, where the covenant document was stored in the ark. Notice how in 5:3 the scroll is "going out" and in 5:4 God promises to "send it out" (same verb in Hiphil, "cause to go out"). This seems to be future action, and the source of this scroll would be God's sanctuary.

8. The preexilic ephah was about ten litres, but the Persian period ephah, influenced by the Babylonian metrological system, was much larger, about thirty-six litres; cf. R. Fuller, "אֵיפָה," *NIDOTTE*, 1:385.

9. They were also used to carry grain offerings into the sanctuary (Meyers and Meyers, *Haggai*, 296), but the presence of a "weight" on top of the container shows it has been borrowed from the scale area.

10. Cf. Floyd, "Evil," 51–68; Merrill, *Haggai*, 172–73. Merrill says "their eye" is an abbreviation for the longer phrase in 4:10.

11. Barker, "Evil," 22.

12. See, e.g., Meyers and Meyers, *Haggai*, 297. This is similar to the KJV's "resemblance"; cf. M. Bic, *Die Nachtgeschichte des Sacharja: Eine Auslegung von Sacharja 1–6* (Neukirchen-Vluyn: Neukirchener, 1964), 56.

or to visibility,[13] all of which stretch this Hebrew word beyond its usual semantic range. The LXX and Syriac reading ("their iniquity") fits the context and explains best the use of the possessive ending "their," a reference to the inhabitants of the earth.[14]

Although it is difficult to determine whether the Hebrew word *ᶜawon* means sinful acts ("iniquity") or their consequences ("guilt" or "punishment"), here it likely refers to "guilt." This distinguishes clearly the basket (guilt) and its content (a woman called wickedness, *rišᶜah*),[15] a distinction seen in the only other passage that uses these two words (Ezek. 18:20, 27). This guilt is cosmic in scope, for it is "in all the land," or better, "throughout all the earth" (cf. 1:10, 11; 4:10, 14; 5:3; 6:5, 7). The idolatrous practices of Babylon that have spread throughout the world by their military might have stained God's people, land, and sanctuary.

A Woman in the Basket (5:7–8)

THE SECOND PHASE of the vision reveals the contents of the basket. The prophet sees a "talent weight of lead" (NIV, "cover of lead"), described in verse 8 as a "stone of lead" (NIV, "lead cover"), perched atop the basket. While this object might denote the regular lid of a container,[16] it most likely denotes a weight taken from the temple scales, a helpful object to keep the woman from escaping.[17] The raising of the weight allows the prophet to peer inside the basket to see a woman in a sitting position.

The angel identifies her as "wickedness" (*rišᶜah*), a term used elsewhere of the idolatry of the nations around Israel (see above). The use of this term along with a female image in a sitting position destined for a pedestal in a sanctuary (see below) indicates that this woman is a goddess or her idol, representing the idolatrous worship of the people.[18] As noted already, the woman is distinguished from the basket, just as the guilt of sin is distinguished from the act of sin. Both the guilt and its act must be sent to Babylon, which explains

13. Rignell, *Nachtgesichte*, 191; D. R. Jones, *Haggai, Zechariah, and Malachi: Introduction and Commentary* (Torch Bible Commentaries; London: SCM, 1962), 83.

14. So Petersen, *Haggai*, 256; Baldwin, *Haggai*, 128; Redditt, *Haggai*, 73.

15. So Petersen, *Haggai*, 256.

16. See Gen. 29:2–3, where a stone covered a well. In this scenario one has to take "talent weight" back to its supposed root of "round" and argue that it means "a round thing."

17. Note the use of the term "stone" here with the word "lead" (which is a metal) and parallel to the term "talent weight" (which is never used elsewhere of a lid). This means that "stone" is being used here in its technical sense of "weight."

18. For the connection to idolatry see M. Delcor, "La vision de la femme dans l'Epha de Zach, 5:5–11 à la lumière de la littérature hittite," *RHR* 187 (1975): 137–45.

the angel's cautious treatment of this woman, lest she (the activity) escape and incur further guilt.[19]

Two Winged Women (5:9–11)

THE "ONE" WOMAN in the basket is clearly distinguished from the "two women" who now enter the vision. These women possess wings, a feature that matches the iconography of the ancient Near East, where therioanthropic beings (part human, part animal) are featured in depictions of deity.[20]

Two features of these wings are noted. (1) There is "wind in their wings" (cf. 2 Sam. 22:11; Ps. 18:10; Hos. 4:19). The first two references are interesting because they occur parallel to God's mounting cherubim for a ride, suggesting that this idiom may have been connected to the flight of heavenly beings. Another option is that this idiom pictures the women being carried along effortlessly by wind currents. The association between "wind" and God occurs throughout the Old Testament, suggesting that God endorses this action (cf. Gen. 8:1; Ex. 15:10).[21]

(2) These wings are like the wings "of a stork." The choice of the stork is appropriate for several reasons. The stork possessed large and powerful wings, able to propel her to great heights—a necessary prerequisite for beings intent on transporting this basket to a far off land. For the Israelites, the stork manifested a migratory pattern north (Jer. 8:7), a route matching the intended flight of the basket to Babylon (see comments on Zech. 2:6).[22] Moreover, the stork's designation as unclean in Israelite law (Lev. 11:19; Deut. 14:18) qualifies this bird's wings for the unseemly task of conveying "guilt" and "wickedness" to their appropriate site.[23]

Such wings enable the women to elevate the measuring basket "between earth and heaven." "The heavens and the earth" is a common word pair in Hebrew, an idiom that normally denotes the cosmos as a whole (e.g., Gen. 1:1). Here we find the preposition "between" (*ben*) and the word order "earth . . . heaven" (see also 1 Chron. 21:16; Ezek. 8:3). In all three cases this region appears to designate a neutral zone where heavenly beings are able to carry out their mission unimpeded by earth's inhabitants. The use of this idiom in Zechariah 5:9 may allude intentionally to Ezekiel's experience in Ezekiel 8,

19. Notice the double use of the word "pushed" (*šalak*, "to throw, shove"). The lead stone is placed "over its mouth," that is, the opening of the measuring basket that is closest the referent, not the mouth of the woman.

20. These match depictions of angelic beings in the Bible (cf. Isa. 6). Floyd ("Evil," 51–68) sees these beings as contrasting the cherubim that form God's throne in the temple.

21. This is sometimes a challenge in Heb., in which the word for "spirit" and "wind" is the same (*ruʾaḥ*), and some say expresses double entendre, see Merrill, *Haggai*, 175.

22. See Meyers and Meyers, *Haggai*, 307.

23. So, e.g., Rudman, "Zechariah 5," 204.

where he is transported from Babylon (Ezek. 1:3) to the temple in Jerusalem. There he observes the worship of many gods, with particular mention of the Babylonian god Tammuz (8:14).[24] God declares that such acts "will drive me far from my sanctuary" (8:6). For Yahweh to return to this temple, as Zechariah's vision complex promises (Zech. 1:16), such abominations must be removed from the temple.

Zechariah finally asks the obvious question: "Where are they taking the measuring basket?" The angel replies that the destination is (lit.) "the land of Shinar" (NIV, "the country of Babylonia"). This is the ancient name for the Mesopotamian plain, which included the cities of Babel, Erech, Akkad, and Calneh (Gen. 10:10). The allusion to this region here must be connected to the role of Babylon in the destruction and exile of Jerusalem and Judah (see Zech. 1:18–21; 2:6–13).[25]

But the particular phrase "land of Shinar" has another connotation as well. It was in Shinar that the infamous episode of the "tower of Babel" was set (Gen. 11), a story that expresses the aspiration of humanity to invade God's heavenly abode and overthrow his rule.[26] The people hoped that by building their city and their tower they would prevent their dispersion over the earth, a scheme in direct violation of God's creation mandate (Gen. 1:28). The "tower" in this city was most likely a temple structure, akin to the ziggurats that dotted the landscape of Mesopotamia. Zechariah 5:11 appears to be playing off the tower of Babel tradition. As in Genesis 11, it refers to the land of Shinar and to a temple structure ("a house") that will be built. In contrast, God, who once spread the rebellious inhabitants of Shinar out to fill the earth, now sends back to this center of wickedness the practices that had infested God's holy temple.

The resting place of the measuring basket with its dangerous contents is a temple built specially for it. As mentioned at the outset, the word used for "its place" is a term used elsewhere only when describing religious objects in the temple in Jerusalem, whether it stands for the bronze basins in Solomon's temple (1 Kings 7:27, 29) that were transported off to Babylon by Nebuchadnezzar (2 Kings 25:13, 16//Jer. 52:17, 20; Jer. 27:19) or the refounded altar in the Second Temple (Ezra 3:3).[27] Because it contains an idol, we can assume that this new structure will function as a shrine for the worship of the goddess contained therein.

---

24. Tammuz was a Mesopotamian god whose death was commemorated by mourning and possibly the source of seasonal change. One of the goddesses with which he was associated was Ishtar, which may explain why Ezek. 8 was influential on Zechariah's vision.

25. Boda, "Horns," forthcoming.

26. It is interesting that the folk etymology of "Babylon" was that it meant "the gate of the gods," even if this is rejected as the true etymology by Assyriologists; Merrill, *Haggai*, 176.

27. The identical construction is used in both Zech. 5:11 and Ezra 3:3.

Bridging Contexts

REJECTION OF IDOLATRY. As in chapter 5, Zechariah confronts the issue of sin within the returned Jewish community. The focus now moves to the foundational relationship in Old Testament faith: the relationship between God and his people, protected by the first three commandments in the Decalogue and summarized splendidly by Moses in Deuteronomy 6:4–5: "Hear, O Israel: The LORD our God, the LORD is one. Love the LORD your God with all your heart and with all your soul and with all your strength." Idolatry threatens the love relationship between God and his people and is thus rejected by Moses and all who follow his lead.

The worship of other gods is not a new development in the tradition of Israel. A review of Israel's redemptive story in Joshua 24 discloses that the two great migrations in Israel's tradition (Abraham, Exodus) were preceded by idol worship (24:3, 14) and anticipates that the nation would face constant temptation to such worship (24:14–27).

This is, indeed, true in the story of the nation. Idols and the gods and goddesses they represent become distractions for the people from the earliest days of life in Canaan (e.g., Judg. 8:22–27; 17–18) through the periods of the united (1 Kings 11:1–8) and divided kingdoms (12:28–33). In 2 Kings 17 idolatry is listed as the major reason for God's judgment on the kingdoms, a point confirmed by the prophets (e.g., Hos. 3:1, 4; 4:12; Amos 2:4; Mic. 1:6–7). These concerns are clear as well from the archaeological record. Although Yahweh is preeminent in the worship of Israel, other gods and goddesses are mentioned.[28] In particular, Yahweh is linked with Asherah, who functions as his divine consort.[29]

The fall of the northern kingdom to the Assyrians resulted in an exchange of peoples between Palestine and Mesopotamia. The narrator in 2 Kings

---

28. Millard has noted this in his review of names on ostraca and seals of the Assyrian period: Out of 1200 names, 557 are combined with *yhwh* (Yahweh), 77 with *ʾel* (God), 35 with other deities; A. Millard, "The History of Israel Against the Background of Ancient Near Eastern Religious History," in *From Ancient Sites of Israel: Essays on Archaeology, History and Theology in Memory of A. Saarisalo*, ed. T. Eskola and E. Junkkaala (Helsinki: Theological Institute of Finland, 1998), 101–17. Cf. J. H. Tigay, *You Shall Have No Other Gods: Israelite Religion in the Light of Hebrew Inscriptions* (HSS 31; Atlanta: Scholars Press, 1986); M. S. Smith, *The Early History of God: Yahweh and the Other Deities in Ancient Israel* (San Francisco: Harper & Row, 1990); S. Ackerman, *Under Every Green Tree: Popular Religion in Sixth-Century Judah* (HSM 46; Atlanta: Scholars Press, 1992); J. Day, *Yahweh and the Gods and Goddesses of Canaan* (JSOTSup 265; Sheffield: Sheffield Academic Press, 2000).

29. E. Stern, "Religion in Palestine in the Assyrian and Persian Periods," in *The Crisis of Israelite Religion: Transformation of Religious Tradition in Exilic and Post-Exilic Times*, ed. B. Becking and M. C. A. Korpel (Leiden: Brill, 1999), 244–53, esp. 247–48.

17:24–41 emphasizes that the worship of other gods accompanied these new immigrants, resulting in a syncretistic fusion of Mesopotamian and Yahwistic religion. In the closing days of the southern kingdom, Jeremiah regularly confronted idolatrous practices drawn from both Canaanite (Jer. 7:9; 11:13, 17; 32:29, 35) and Mesopotamian sources (7:18; 44:17–25).[30]

Jeremiah reflects on the crisis in Israelite religion that accompanied the fall of Jerusalem and destruction of its sanctuary. That event produced three major religious reactions.[31] Some related this disaster to an offense of the god(s) of Canaan and thus sought to remedy this by worshiping them (Jer. 44; Ezek. 8). Others accepted the religion of the conquering Babylonians, acknowledging that their gods were victorious over Yahweh (Ezek. 8; 20:32; Dan. 3; 7). Finally, a number interpreted the disaster as divine judgment from Yahweh and encouraged faithful worship of him alone (Lam. 3:40; cf. 2 Kings 17).

None of these strategies gained the upper hand across the Jewish communities. The archaeological record shows that at least the exilic community in Egypt incorporated gods from the Egyptian and Canaanite pantheon into their worship practices.[32] However, the record in Palestine suggests that in the Persian period the Jews in Yehud were successful in eradicating idolatry from their ranks. How long this took is a point of great debate,[33] but it appears that the exiles returning from Babylonia championed a policy against idolatry.

Against this background Zechariah's vision signals a transition to a new phase in the history of the Jews. In the literary context of Zechariah 1–8 and the historical context of the early Persian period, the reason for an idol being returned to Mesopotamia is because this is the place from which many of the exiles were now returning. However, in the history of Israel, Mesopotamia was often a key source of idolatry, insofar as it was the idolatrous center from

---

30. Queen of Heaven is probably Ishtar, Babylonian goddess of love and fertility (cf. 2 Kings 21; 23:4–14).

31. See Ackroyd, *Exile*, 39–49. For Isaiah's reaction to idolatry see Isa. 40:18–20; 41:6–7; 46:5–7.

32. See Stern, "Religion," 255; H. Niehr, "Religio-Historical Aspects of the 'Early Post-Exilic' Period," in *The Crisis of Israelite Religion: Transformation of Religious Tradition in Exilic and Post-Exilic Times*, ed. B. Becking and M. C. A. Korpel (Leiden: Brill, 1999), 240.

33. M. Smith, "Jewish Religious Life in the Persian Period," in *The Cambridge History of Judaism:* Volume One: *Introduction: The Persian Period*, ed. W. Davies and L. Finkelstein (Cambridge: Cambridge Univ. Press, 1984), 219–78; Ackerman, *Green Tree*; and Niehr, "Aspects," 228–44, argue for enduring idolatrous practices into the Persian period. E. J. Bickerman, "The Diaspora: The Babylonian Captivity," in *The Cambridge History of Judaism:* Volume One: *Introduction: The Persian Period*, 162–88, suggests a transitional period until 480 B.C. Stern, "Religion," 245–55, argues for radical discontinuity between Babylonian and Persian period practices.

which Abraham was called (Josh. 24:2–3) and from where idolatry flooded the Promised Land after the falls of the northern and southern kingdoms (2 Kings 17:24–41; Ezek. 8).

Idolatry was an abomination to God because it represented infidelity in the covenant relationship established between him and his people. Yahweh is a jealous God, who passionately disallowed any rival (Ex. 20:4–6). The covenantal and relational nature of idolatry is illustrated by a consistent use of the image of adultery to explain the offense of idolatry (Jer. 3; Ezek. 16; 23; Hosea). Although the idols were nothing and had no power on their own (Isa. 41:22; 42:8, 17; 44:9; 45:16, 20; 46:1; 48:5, 14; 57:6, 13), they were connected with gods (Deut. 32:17; Ps. 107:37). The key is that, whether or not they actually represented a spiritual force (demon, god, goddess), the focus is on the violation of the exclusive relationship between God and his people.

Rejection of idolatry is also a feature in New Testament revelation. Paul sees the idol as "nothing" (1 Cor. 8:4), yet he does identify it with the worship of "gods" and "demons" (1 Cor. 8:5–6; 10:18–21). Idolatry is connected to the most hideous sins, such as debauchery, lust, drunkenness, orgies, carousing, magic arts, sexual immorality, murder, falsehood, covetousness, greed, slander, and swindling (1 Cor. 5:10; 6:9; 1 Peter 4:3; Rev. 22:15). Although these passages refer to the actual worship of idols, idolatry takes on a more general meaning for sin (Eph. 5:5; Col. 3:5; 1 John 5:21). Its consistent association with sins such as lust, greed, and drunkenness suggests that it has come to mean anything that distracts our devotion to God and fosters values that are the opposite of those Christ seeks to cultivate in us.

This more general sense is vividly displayed in Romans 1:18–25, where Paul identifies the essence of idolatry. At its core, worshiping and serving created things rather than the Creator represent the refusal to acknowledge God and the exchange of truth for a lie. This foundational rejection of God leads to the spread of sin in the world as a result of God's judgment.

Understanding idolatry within Zechariah's community and its broader biblical-theological context helps us to see the significance of Zechariah 5:5–11 for our community of faith today. Zechariah must address the sin of idolatry. As the people return to the land to rebuild the temple, they cannot afford to repeat the preexilic pattern of infidelity through idolatry that ultimately resulted in the Exile. As the Second Temple rises before the community, Zechariah looks beyond the physical project to the spiritual renewal needed to ensure God's presence with his people. We have already seen in 1:1–6 how repentance was essential to this renewal—that is, a turning from the wicked practices and ways that will be defined more specifically in chapters 7–8 as social injustice.[34] Here, however, the prophet rejects idolatrous practices within his community because they undermine the spiritual vitality of the people by enticing them to trust foreign gods created by human hands rather than the Creator, the Lord God.

In the same way as we seek to fulfill God's commission to extend his kingdom through the living temple of the church, we must reject idolatry and set our affections on God alone.

Contemporary Significance

RECOVERING WORSHIP IN THE CHURCH. One of the exciting features of the past decade within the church has been the recovery of worship within our corporate life. Gone are the days when the worship section of our services was considered the "preliminaries"—that is, those elements that preceded the main event, the sermon. Today considerable time and resources are devoted to facilitating creative worship experiences, allowing God's people to use gifts in worship through the performing and fine arts. Even the sermon itself is increasingly defined under the rubric of worship. Through it God speaks to his people and draws them by his Spirit to offer their lives as living sacrifices to him.

One of our present challenges, however, is a proper definition of worship. It is easy to focus attention on the external practice of worship (song, dance, instruments, art) and ignore the internal affections of the heart. Focusing on the internal explains the equation of idolatry with covenant relationship in the Old Testament and the close association between idolatry and sin in the New Testament. God calls us to purity in both affections and practice as we walk with him.

Purity in affections lies at the core of true worship. Anything that competes with God for our affections falls in that category. With the influx of Eastern religions into Western culture, it may be a carved idol. But it could just as easily be another person or a pursuit that lures our affections away from our God and Lord. Zechariah 5:6–11 encourages us as God's people to take stock of our affections, for "where your treasure is, there your heart will be also" (Matt. 6:21).

This kind of reflection must take place on the level of individual and family as we consider our life goals and weekly activities. It does not mean that we abandon all our pursuits and retreat to a monastery to ensure that our hearts are focused on God alone. Rather, it means initiating and maintaining

34. Boda, "Penitential Prophet", 49–69.

an orientation to life that has Christ as the center and God as the goal. In this way we will be able to fulfill Paul's call to us in Colossians 3:17: "And whatever you do, whether in word or deed, do it all in the name of the Lord Jesus, giving thanks to God the Father through him."

Practicing this text may simply mean setting time aside each day, week, and year to reflect on our lives. For my wife and I, our wedding anniversary is an important moment to take stock of our lives both as individuals and as a family. In my ministry as pastor and teacher, I have always valued weekly and yearly rhythms to reflect on my personal vision and mission, while also seeking to encourage such reflection among my leaders not only individually but also corporately. The unexamined life, family, and ministry are doomed to mediocrity.

But God is also concerned with purity in practice. This means that it is possible for our practice of worship to lead us away from rather than toward God. We can see this within the contemporary worship experience of the church on several levels.

(1) It is easy for "worship" to become an occasion for fulfilling our need for entertainment, producing an emotional experience that has nothing to do with divine devotion but rather with human gratification. A worship leader who also travels as a Christian performer once related his own struggle with determining this line between devotion and gratification. He attended his church and was caught up in an experience of worship. But later that day he attended a concert performed by a secular band and realized that he experienced the same response. This forced him to reflect on the main goal of worship and the definition of true worship. By this I am not saying that our worship should avoid emotions, for an intellectualized worship can be just as dangerous as an emotional one. However, the fact that we are moved in and through a worship experience does not necessarily mean that we have worshiped.

(2) It is easy for "worship" to be placed into the hands of performing artists who have little theological training or spiritual depth. I was impressed recently by a pastor of a large urban church whose son approached him, wanting to lead a worship team at his church. The pastor encouraged his son to first take a course on Old Testament theology at a local seminary. Of course, I was thrilled with this fatherly advice because of my vocational interest in Old Testament studies, but what thrilled me more was the fact that this pastor took seriously the role that worship leaders play in the theological formation of his congregation.

With worship leaders designing at least a half hour of worship at weekly services (if not more), it is obvious that they will have at least as much, if not more, influence on the theological formation of local congregations as pastors do when they preach the Scriptures. Charged with such a task, they need to pay careful attention to Paul's word to Timothy: "Watch your life and doctrine closely. Persevere in them, because if you do, you will save both yourself and your hearers" (1 Tim. 4:16). To be a worship leader today demands a high level of theological and spiritual training. Worship teams should be trained in more than just key changes and PowerPoint productions. They desperately need to be mentored in their study and experience of God.

Recovering worship in our culture. We must also live lives of practice because of the cultural milieu in which we live. In his recent acclaimed review of experiential religion, Harvey Cox cites lyrics from British rock singer Sting's song "If I Ever Lose My Faith in You":

> You could say I lost my faith in science and progress.
> You could say I lost my belief in the holy church.
> You could say I lost my sense of direction.

Cox interprets these lyrics by writing:

> . . . many have now lost faith *both* in "science and progress" *and* in "the holy church." People are still willing to rely on science for the limited things it has proven it can do, but they no longer believe it will answer their deepest questions. They remain vaguely intrigued with the traditional religions, but not with conventional churches. They want to pick and choose and are less willing to accept religions either as systems of truth or as institutions.[35]

Cox highlights the restoration of spirituality onto the agenda of our culture, a restoration that is reflected well in a recent book I spied at my local coffee shop.[36] In this book I found photographs depicting shrines in various private homes in North America. Most of them revealed an eclectic blend of objects from various religions, combined to create a syncretistic display in the privacy of a person's home. Unquestionably this book reflects the tenor of our times in which religion is a blend of various traditions assembled according to individual taste.

Cox places my experience in the local coffee shop into socio-religious perspective in his paraphrase of Danièle Hervieu-Léger's description of religion today as "spiritual bricolage":

---

35. H. Cox, *Fire from Heaven: The Rise of Pentecostal Spirituality and the Reshaping of Religion in the Twenty-First Century* (Reading, Mass.: Perseus, 1995), 299.

36. Unfortunately I could not find the bibliographical details of this book.

> It is a radically personal style of piety in which, as it were, each person is constantly compiling his or her own collage of symbols and practices in the light of what coheres with their own changing experiences in the tortuous passage through life in a world where the old, allegedly comprehensive charts no longer command confidence.[37]

I discovered this contemporary openness to spirituality on a recent flight from Calgary to Edmonton. I sat next to an older woman sporting a beautiful tan, and in the course of our conversation she told me she was returning from a six-week trip to Mexico. She explained that each year she traveled to the coast of Mexico to help lead six week-long "environmental retreats." Facilitators at these events included leading scientists from around the world who led the participants to discover various aspects of nature during the day. In the evening this woman, who had a degree from a seminary in eastern Canada, led the group in yoga with the express purpose of becoming one with the environment.

Curiosity got the better of me, so I asked another question: "Who come to these retreats?" I anticipated she would describe an eccentric lot. Instead, she informed me that the participants were top corporate, governmental, and educational leaders from across the globe. The six weeks were fully booked each year as their various institutions paid exorbitant fees for the retreats. Probing further I discovered that one of the leading banks in Canada employs two "spiritual directors" within one province to facilitate spiritual discovery for their executives. This encounter opened my eyes again to a new spiritual mood in Western culture.

Our challenge in this milieu is to capitalize on this new openness to spirituality while not compromising our Christian values.[38] On the one side, we need discernment from the Scriptures as to what is appropriate spiritual practice and what is idolatrous. Many Western converts entering the church in the coming decades will need wise counsel from Christian leaders and mentors to separate truth from error in their spiritual practices. On the other side, there is an active role that the church can play in shaping the spiritual agenda of a generation. This begins with the first issue considered above, the ongoing renewal of worship within the church. As people encounter vibrant communities of faith that passionately pursue the presence of God through proper worship, they are drawn to the witness of the gospel.

---

37. Cox, *Fire from Heaven*, 305.

38. By expressing this concern I risk Cox's label of "fundamentalism," which he sees as the other major response to the collapse of modernity and the institutional church (ibid., 300–304).

But this agenda for the renewal of worship should also spill out into the surrounding community. The church should take the initiative and provide guidance for spiritual discovery within the broader communities in which they serve. This may mean providing classes in Christian spiritual disciplines at a local community center or facilitating a Christian environmental retreat that invites people to discover creation and their Creator. It may mean that we need to provide opportunities for unbelievers to join us as a community in our corporate worship experiences in order to model worship in spirit and truth.[39] At times we can also find ways to involve our local community in our worship experiences, even if it is as simple as an annual singing of Handel's *Messiah* or a Christmas pageant experience during Advent.

Jesus describes his mission in terms of the Father seeking a worshiping community: "Yet a time is coming and has now come, when the true worshipers will worship the Father in spirit and truth, for they are the kind of worshipers the Father seeks" (John 4:23). It is not surprising, then, that when the church was founded through the outpouring of the Holy Spirit by the ascended Christ in Acts 2, their initial activity was worship as they began "declaring the wonders of God" in the languages of the many people gathered in Jerusalem. From this kind of worshiping community came the proclamation of the gospel of Jesus Christ (Acts 2:14–40) and the conversion of the multitudes (2:41).

Zechariah 5:5–11 challenges the church today to faithfulness in affection and action as we worship our God: to love the Lord our God with all our heart, soul, mind, and strength. The Persian period Jewish community facing the temptations and influence of pagan religion were called to purity and fidelity. This message is equally important today as we seek to live faithfully before our God in our eclectic religious milieu.

---

39. See also M. Dawn, *Reaching Out Without Dumbing Down: A Theology of Worship for the Turn-of-the-Century Culture* (Grand Rapids: Eerdmans, 1995), and S. Morgenthaler, *Worship Evangelism: Inviting Unbelievers into the Presence of God* (Grand Rapids: Zondervan, 1999).

Zechariah 6:1–8

I LOOKED UP again—and there before me were four chariots
coming out from between two mountains—mountains of
bronze! [2]The first chariot had red horses, the second black,
[3]the third white, and the fourth dappled—all of them power-
ful. [4]I asked the angel who was speaking to me, "What are
these, my lord?"

[5]The angel answered me, "These are the four spirits of
heaven, going out from standing in the presence of the Lord
of the whole world. [6]The one with the black horses is going
toward the north country, the one with the white horses
toward the west, and the one with the dappled horses toward
the south."

[7]When the powerful horses went out, they were straining
to go throughout the earth. And he said, "Go throughout the
earth!" So they went throughout the earth. [8]Then he called to
me, "Look, those going toward the north country have given
my Spirit rest in the land of the north."

Original Meaning

THE FINAL VISION functions as both climax and closure for the string of night visions. Clearly this vision is intended to remind the audience of the initial vision in 1:8–17 since it uses various colored horses (1:8; 6:2, 6) whose role is to patrol the earth (1:10–11; 6:7). But this allusion to the initial vision is designed more for contrast than for comparison, for here the horses pull chariots and are beginning rather than completing their mission. This contrast reveals the relationship between the first and last visions: the promise of divine liberation is now becoming reality. Reconnaissance teams have become military forces ready for battle.

The prophet encounters a scene at the entrance to the divine council.[1] Exiting it are the four winds of heaven, God's agents for judgment, depicted as four chariots each drawn by different colored horses. Three of the chariots are used for military action, with a fourth retained for defensive purposes.

1. Tidwell and Halpern both note divine council connections in visions 1, 4, 5, 8, thus the envelope (1, 8) and central (4, 5) visions; Tidwell, "*Waʾomar*," 343–55; Halpern, "Ritual Background," 167–90.

Two teams are to head to the north (black, white) with the third to head south (dappled). These powerful beasts are ready for war, pawing the ground, straining to go forth, yet awaiting their master's permission. When they are finally released, the Lord turns to the prophet and highlights the actions of the two chariots headed north. They bring judgment on "the land of the north," venting God's wrath on the nation who exiled his people.

This vision depicts in broad terms God's punishment of Babylon and his release of Jews in the early Persian period. This complex of events began in 539 B.C. as the empire of the Babylonian Nabonidus and his son Belshazzar (Dan. 5) was conquered by Cyrus (see the introduction). These events were presaged in Isaiah 44:28; 45:1; 45:13, which link the feats of Cyrus to the sovereign operations of the Lord, a connection echoed in the interpretations of this period in 2 Chronicles 36:22–23 and Ezra 1:1–4; 6:14. Zechariah announces the final installment of this complex of events at the beginning of Darius's reign as the new emperor exacts punishment on the rebellious Babylonians.[2] He sees this punishment and release as an act of divine initiative but makes no explicit mention of the Persian involvement.[3]

The core theme of this vision is the sovereignty of the God of grace. In bringing closure to the series of visions, it depicts the fulfillment of God's promise to break the ruling power of the oppressive Babylonians. God's comforting words have become reality as he unleashes his might on the helpless Babylonians. This has tremendous implications for his people, who will be freed to return to their land and rebuild their society. These human responses to God's initiative are highlighted in the prophetic sign act that follows in 6:9–15.

Detailed Analysis

THE FINAL VISION opens with the formula used in the vision in 5:1, a formula closely allied with those in 1:18 and 2:1. As in most visions, the image is presented before any dialogue takes place, a technique that brings the scene into the foreground of the prophetic revelation. Here the prophet sees four chariots each pulled by a different set of colored horses coming out from between two mountains of bronze.

Use of mountain imagery to speak of God's residence is something shared by both the Israelites and their neighbors in Canaan (Ps. 3:4; 48:1–3).[4] That

2. See Boda, "Horns."

3. This is typical of apocalyptic literature, where the human is played down at the expense of the divine, a feature that may be related to political savvy in a volatile international environment.

4. Mountain imagery is connected with El, Baal, Anat, and Mot in the Ugaritic texts; see R. J. Clifford, *The Cosmic Mountain in Canaan and the Old Testament* (HSM 4; Cambridge, Mass.: Harvard Univ. Press, 1972), 132. The most prominent is Mount Zaphon, which is clearly

the mountains are somehow connected to God's dwelling place is seen in the angel's interpretation in 6:5, where the prophet is told that the chariots are "going out from ... the presence of the LORD." But the difficulty of linking this imagery to the Canaanite context is the specific reference to "two mountains." The imagery is more likely drawn from Mesopotamian imagery.[5] There, because of geography, deity was rarely connected to mountains. The one exception was the sun god, Shamash, who is depicted between two mountains situated within two open doors to the heavenly domain.

The composition of the mountains in Zechariah 6 is "bronze" (or copper), a color that fits with that of the rising sun.[6] This connection also explains the reference to chariots and horses, for when Josiah cleanses the temple of the sun cult in 2 Kings 23:11, he also removes "the horses ... the chariots dedicated to the sun" (cf. Ezek. 8:16–18).

Zechariah's depiction focuses on these chariots and horses in 6:2–3. In his first vision, the prophet saw horses of various colors, but chariots were not involved. The presence of chariots here highlights a key difference in assignment. Whereas the first vision depicted horses fresh from a reconnaissance mission for which speed was essential, this final vision pictures horses embarking on a retribution campaign for which power is crucial. Thus, these horses pull chariots, symbolic of military strength (Ex. 14:25–26; Josh. 11:6; Judg. 4:15–16; 1 Sam. 13:5; 1 Kings 10:26–29)[7] and associated in ancient Near Eastern religious imagery with the divine warrior and his hosts (Deut. 33:26; Ps. 68:17; 104:3–4; Isa. 19:1; Hab. 3:8).[8]

---

linked to Baal and appears in connection with Jerusalem in Ps. 48:2 (57–79). In one Ugaritic text the Mount of El is identified as "the meeting of the (divine) council" (42).

5. By this we are not suggesting syncretism, something about which Zechariah is extremely vexed in the preceding vision (5:5–11). Rather, the Israelites used common religious imagery sometimes as we do in the West when we speak of heaven as "up" and hell as "down," or with a specific polemic in mind, that is, to show Yahweh's sovereignty. Thus, Ps. 29 has many links to Canaanite poems honoring Baal, but these terms are used of Yahweh for polemical as well as liturgical ends. See F. M. Cross, *Canaanite Myth and Hebrew Epic: Essays in the History of the Religion of Israel* (Cambridge, Mass.: Harvard Univ. Press, 1973), 151–56.

6. "Bronze" is used regularly in the Old Testament as an image of strength (Deut. 28:23; Judg. 16:21; 2 Chron. 33:11; 36:6; Jer. 1:18; 52:11; Lam. 3:7).

7. For the use of horses and chariots in Persian battles see Littauer and Crouwel, *Wheeled Vehicles*, 144–60.

8. For an excellent review of research on divine warrior imagery see T. Longman and D. G. Reid, *God Is a Warrior* (SOTBT; Grand Rapids: Zondervan, 1995); P. D. Miller, *The Divine Warrior in Early Israel* (Cambridge, Mass.: Harvard Univ. Press, 1973), 105; also G. von Rad, *Holy War in Ancient Israel*, trans. M. J. Dawn (Grand Rapids: Eerdmans, 1990). Interestingly God is pictured in the Old Testament utilizing chariots/horses (2 Kings 6:17) and also wind (Ex. 14:21), cf. Longman and Reid, *Warrior*, 42–43; Ryken, Wilhoit, and Longman, *DBI*, 210–13.

Colors are associated with each of the four chariots. As we argued on 1:7–17, there is nothing odd about any of these colors, all of which can be found in the various species of horses. In this vision they seem to function only to distinguish the chariots.[9] Their order is given: red, black, white, and spotted. At the end of the list is the adjective "powerful," which not only describes the strength of all the horses, necessary to pull heavy chariots quickly and efficiently into battle, but also captures their disposition in "straining to go throughout the earth."

As in the first three visions, Zechariah is the first to speak, turning to the interpreting angel and asking, "What are these, my lord?" (6:4). The angel identifies the horse-drawn chariots as "the four spirits of heaven." The Hebrew word for "spirit" (*ruaḥ*) can also be translated as "wind" or "breath." We have already encountered the "four winds of heaven" in the oracle that follows the first three night visions (2:6–13). There God tells the Babylonian exilic community to return home from "the land of the north" because God had scattered them to "the four winds of heaven" (there *ruaḥ* cannot mean "four spirits").

A similar use of this expression occurs in Jeremiah 49:36, where the prophet calls the "four winds" from the "four ends of the heavens" against Elam to scatter them to all these winds. The image there is that of winnowing grain with the chaff blowing away. These four winds appear to symbolize the four "ends" or extremities of the heavens, that is, the directions of the compass.[10] In Ezekiel 37:9 the prophet is instructed to command the "wind" (NIV "breath") to come from the "four winds" and blow (NIV "breathe") life into the dry bones, which represent exilic Israel. Here we have the imagery of the infusion of life (as in Gen. 2). Finally, Daniel 8:8; 11:4 refer to these "four winds," where they refer to directions or areas of the world.

On the basis of these passages, it appears that the "four winds" are found in the north, south, east, and west, which are depicted as being the extremities of the world and are the source of wind (for winnowing) and air (for breathing). Those who translate "winds" as "spirits" in Zechariah 6:5 are reading it in relationship to the verb "standing," an odd association for "winds."[11]

---

9. One may be tempted to relate color with function because of Rev. 6:1–8, but Zech. 6:1–8 does not offer the same guidance as Revelation, even though Revelation may have drawn on the night visions; cf. Strand, "Olive Trees," 257–61; idem, "An Overlooked Old Testament Background to Revelation 11:1," *AUSS* 22 (1984): 317–32.

10. Ps. 19:7 says the sun makes a circuit from one "end" of the heavens to the other; this seems analogous to the "ends of the earth" in Isa. 40:28; 41:5, 9; Job 28:24; cf. Ryken, Wilhoit, and Longman, eds. *DBI*, 952: "to picture all winds together emphasizes the totality of God's sovereign dominion."

11. Note how 1 Kings 22:19–23 depicts spirits standing before God to accomplish his will (cf. Job 1:6; 2:1).

However, Psalm 104:4 makes it clear that God makes winds his "messengers," utilizing the wind to accomplish his will, either to destroy (Jer. 49:36) or save (Ezek. 37:9).[12]

These "winds" are going out from "standing in the presence of the Lord of the whole world" (6:5). This term "standing" is used of someone stationed at a post, whether that is Miriam watching out for Moses (Ex. 2:4) or a prophet awaiting God's voice (Hab. 2:1). It can be used of someone standing against another, especially in military contexts (1 Sam. 17:16; Ps. 2:2; Jer. 46:4). But the use in Zechariah 6:5 is the same in construction and meaning as in Job 1:6 and 2:1, where angels present themselves before God. It appears, then, that the winds of heaven are depicted as leaving the divine council where they have received their orders. God is "the Lord of the whole world," a title reinforced by his command over the four winds of heaven.

Verse 6 describes the destinations of the various chariots. This verse has caused considerable debate in the history of interpretation. The list of chariots with horses in 6:2 contained four colors (red, black, white, dappled) followed by the adjective "powerful," but in 6:6 there is no mention of the chariot with red horses, yet 6:7 begins with a reference to the "powerful horses." So where are the powerful red horses? Added to this difficulty is what some have described as evidence of textual corruption in the awkward syntax at the beginning of verse 6 in the Hebrew text.

There have been two common approaches to rectify this absence of the chariot with red horses. (1) Some scholars emend the word "powerful" (*haʾamuṣṣim*) in verse 7 to "red" (*ʾadummim*). However, besides the lack of manuscript support for this change, the remainder of this verse seems to refer to the activity of all the horses, describing God's unleashing their power. (2) Other scholars insert a reference to the chariot with red horses at the beginning of verse 6, thereby clearing up the awkward syntax.[13] But this awkwardness has been overplayed, for there are other places in the Old Testament where a similar kind of syntax occurs.[14]

These attempts have been motivated by the desire to insert a reference to red horses into the text. Is there perhaps a reason why the red horses are not sent out? (1) One possibility is that the red horses are pulling the chariot of

12. See further Ryken, Wilhoit, and Longman, eds. *DBI*, 951–52, on the positive and negative role for wind. As Creator, Yahweh uses wind according to his pleasure (Ps. 135:7; 148:8; Jer. 10:13; 51:16). To describe the outpouring of God's wrath in 587 B.C. the prophets use wind imagery (Jer. 4:11–13; 18:17; Ezek. 13:13).

13. Cf. Baldwin, *Haggai*, 131; Petersen, *Haggai*, 263–64; Meyers and Meyers, *Haggai*, 326.

14. This "so-called 'independent relative' clause" can be used in a verbal or verbless clause. See Gen. 7:23, "those with him," Num. 22:6, "the one whom you bless," and esp. 2 Kings 6:16, "More are they who are with us"; cf. *IBHS*, §19.13c.

the commanding officer.[15] In the first vision (1:8, 11), the angel of the Lord is mounted on a red horse and is the one receiving the reports. Perhaps the vision assumes that this chariot is to remain behind to await the results of the campaign or to protect the divine portal. (2) Another option is that the red horses are stationed in the east, the only direction not mentioned in verse 6. Since we have already argued that the imagery of this vision is drawn from the Mesopotamian view of the sun rising from behind the mountains in the east, it is possible that the eastern "wind" does not have to travel anywhere.

This second option is based on the assumption that the vision refers to three of the four directions in verse 6. This, however, is far from certain. There is no question about the destinations of the first and last chariots in verse 6: The chariot with the black horses is heading to the north and the one with dappled horses to the south. As the Hebrew text stands, the chariot with the white horses follows the one with the black horses to the north country (*ʾel-ʾaḥarehem*, lit., "to behind them"; cf. 2 Sam. 5:23; esp. 2 Kings 9:18–19).[16] Some, however, have seen here a reference to the direction west, drawing on one of two Hebrew idioms.[17]

The combined weight of the Hebrew and Greek textual tradition is difficult to ignore. It appears that originally the text spoke only of two directions: north and south. Although the "four winds" do originate in the four compass points of the earth, this does not mean that their work is restricted to these four directions. It is true that Jeremiah 49:36 depicts these winds as originating in and bound for the four compass points, a sense also found in Zechariah 2. But Ezekiel 37:9 speaks of the wind as originating in the four compass points but then accomplishing something in a single locale, bringing life to exilic Israel.

It is significant that in both Ezekiel 37 and Zechariah 6, the word "wind" is used in the plural to refer to "four" winds but also in the singular to refer to "the wind" (Ezek. 37:9–10) and "my wind/spirit" (Ezek. 37:14; Zech. 6:8). It appears that the "four winds" refers to the source of all wind, but this should not presuppose a return to these four directions. The chariots head in two directions, north and south, with both black and white heading to the north, highlighting the greater force needed to subdue the "land of the north."[18]

---

15. Cf. Merrill, *Haggai*, 186.

16. The LXX matches the Hebrew MT, while the Vulgate has "behind the east."

17. Both involve slight emendations; Petersen, *Haggai*, 264. West is sometimes represented by the preposition "behind." It reveals a Semitic mindset about establishing directions as one faces east. Thus, east is represented by *qedem*, from *qadam* ("to come or be in front of"); south is represented by *teman*, from *yamin* ("right, right hand"); and west by *yam* ("sea") or *negeb* ("Negev," for south).

18. Merrill suggests that in the end north and south covers the four compass points, since one must go north in Palestine to head east and south to head west; Merrill, *Haggai*, 185–86.

Verse 7 emphasizes the eagerness of the chariot teams to accomplish their mission. Again we read the term "powerful" to emphasize the energy of these horses. They are "chomping at the bit," seeking permission from their commander, the Lord before whom they are standing, to patrol the earth. The scene in the first vision also mentioned a military patrol, but there the vision is filled with images of secrecy, an accent absent in this final vision. By using the same word for patrolling (going throughout the earth; cf. 1:10–11), the two visions are clearly related and, simultaneously, contrasted. The comforting promise of the Lord in the first vision is becoming a reality in this final vision.

The fulfillment of the promise is made more specific in verse 8, the climax of this vision and of the vision complex as a whole. The Lord "cries" (Hiphil of *zʿq*; NIV "called") to the prophet, a verb used elsewhere with the sense of urgency of summoning to war (Judg. 4:10, 13; 2 Sam. 20:4, 5), calling for repentance (Jonah 3:7), or crying for help (Job 35:9).

Although chariots are going to the south and north, it is the northbound teams that are highlighted. This focus on the "land of the north" is an important statement in the context of the early Persian period. (1) It reminds the audience that the collapse of the Babylonian empire before the Persian Cyrus and its subsequent punishment by Darius was the work of the Lord.[19] It was an expression of the Lord's grace and mercy as he was inaugurating a new phase in redemptive history. (2) Although the restoration is viewed as global (north and south), emphasis is placed on the exiled community in Babylon. This emphasis may be linked to Jeremiah's negative evaluation of the Egyptian exiled community (see Jer. 42). But certainly Zechariah focuses most attention on the community returning from Babylon, affirming their role and leadership in the restoration project (Zech. 2:6–3:10; 4:6–10; 6:9–15).

The Lord says that they "have given my Spirit rest." We find here the final appearance of *ruaḥ* ("wind/breath/spirit") already encountered in the vision, but what is the referent here? A clue is offered by another passage that speaks of the four winds: Jeremiah 49:36–37. There too God uses the four winds to enact judgment. In 49:37, this mission is linked to "my fierce anger." It is interesting that *ruaḥ* can be used to signify anger (Judg. 8:3; Prov. 16:32; 29:11).[20] Ezekiel uses a consistent expression that conveys the completion of God's anger (Hiphil of *nuaḥ*, "to cause to rest, subside; e.g., Ezek. 16:42; 24:13) against the object of his wrath (in Ezekiel's case, Israel), and this same verb is used here except that the Hebrew for "anger" is replaced with the *ruaḥ*.

19. So also Ezra 1:1–4 (cf. 2 Chron. 36) emphasizes the divine superintendence of Cyrus's ascendancy. See also Ezra 6:14b, where the command of God is paralleled with the decrees of the Persian emperors.

20. See Petersen, *Haggai*, 271; cf. Rudolph, *Haggai*, 125.

The reason for this replacement is the symbolism of the vision: The wind is the agent of God's wrath, and the same word can be used for anger, an instance of double entendre.

Thus the wind of God as an expression of his wrath has been spent against the land of the north, the Babylonians. The first and second visions have come to fulfillment: God has enacted punishment on the "nations that feel secure," who "added to the calamity" and "scattered Judah, Israel and Jerusalem" (1:15, 19). Zechariah 6:8 bolsters the intimate connection between the first and final visions, bringing climactic closure to the series of visions. The series as a whole reminds the returned community that the initial signs of the return of God, promised at the outset, are being played out in the world stage in their generation. This reminder of God's grace is to encourage the people to continue in their initiatives of both reconstruction and (even more important) repentance, while stimulating hope for their future.

Bridging Contexts

THERE IS NO QUESTION that visionary literature is enticing. Its ability to engage the imagination and surprise the reader explains our fascination with prophetic and apocalyptic books. However, there is a flip side here. Such language can frustrate the reader who asks, "What does this mean?" If even the prophet asks "What are these?" (1:9, 19, 21; 4:4, 11, 13; 5:6; 6:4), what chance does the modern reader have to understand, let alone apply these odd revelations?

An example of this frustration can be highlighted through this vision in 6:1–8. We have already noted that "wind," "chariots," and "horses" are identified as agents of God's wrath in the Old Testament. The imagery of wind at times reflects God's use of natural forces to accomplish his means (Ex. 14), but there is also evidence that chariots and horses are linked to a divine army of spiritual beings who bring victory (Josh. 5:13–15; 2 Kings 2:11–12; 6:17).

The interpretation in Zechariah 6:1–8 makes it clear that these chariots and horses are representative of the "winds" of God and thus should not be confused with the divine armies. However, unless one argues for the destruction of Babylon by a tornado or hurricane (unattested in any tradition), these "winds" appear to play a symbolic role in the vision, representing God's invisible shaping of history, which is evidenced by the overthrow and punishment of Babylonian hegemony by the Persians. Thus, we have here an image (horse-drawn chariots) piled upon symbol (winds), reflecting reality (God's use of Persia). This reminds us of the need for a sensitive reading of the vision, which reads images and symbols in the way they were intended, that is, as images and symbols without jumping prematurely to "reality."

One may be tempted, for instance, to use Zechariah 6:1–8 as the basis for delineating the structure of the heavenly realms. In some Christian writing, passages like this one contribute to the foundation of systems seeking to elaborate the composition and activities of beings in the heavenly realms. This may seem to some as innocent conjectures, but this has been used in recent years as the basis for everything from counseling (techniques for casting out spirits), to discipleship (Neil Anderson), to missions and prayer (the 10/40 window).[21] One must be careful to focus on the clear referent intended by the images and symbols and not press the evidence beyond the intention of the Bible.

We will now identify those themes that lie at the core of this passage and how we can understand them in the larger context of redemptive history. This will provide a transitional platform from which we can complete the journey to our contemporary culture.

Exile and restoration—redemptive-pedagogical/redemptive-historical. In Zechariah 6:1–8 we see the completion of an important theological strand introduced at the outset of the night visions: God's merciful passion for his people expressed in breaking Babylonian power. This return from exile is a key feature in the theology of the Old Testament. Moses in the Torah (Lev. 26; Deut. 28–30), Solomon (1 Kings 8; 2 Chron. 6), and the prophets (Isa. 35; Jer. 30; Ezek. 37) all express God's desire to bring an end to exile through a sovereign act in which he releases them from captivity and restores them to their own land. The Torah links this sovereign act to God's gracious character, his compassion for and delight in his people (Deut. 30:3, 9), as well as his commitment to the classic covenants (Lev. 26:42, 45).

These texts, however, also delineate the human aspect of restoration. Exile-restoration is defined as a redemptive-pedagogical tool, designed to reset the patterns of purity and faith in the lives of God's community. It is easy to fall into the trap of seeing exile as the judgment of an offended God delivering a sentence with no intention for rehabilitation. However, exile was designed as a redemptive tool to turn the people to God in covenant relationship, to return to him and restore relationship. Zechariah does not ignore the demand on the human partner, for he has already linked the repentance of the people in 1:1–6 with the promises of 1:7–17, which in turn foreshadow the divine action of 6:1–8.

The exile-restoration of God's community is, however, not only redemptive-pedagogical; it is also redemptive-historical. It is a marker in the history of

21. See K. N. Foster, *Binding and Loosing: Exercising Authority over the Dark Powers* (Harrisburg, Pa.: Christian Publications, 1998), 249–67; T. Longman, *Daniel* (NIVAC; Grand Rapids, Mich.: Zondervan, 1999), 249–51.

God's people that signals a fundamental change in the character of his community. Never again will they attain national identity; rather, the kingdom will be defined and realized through an identity that transcends political categories (Acts 1). The Exile will have a lasting impact on the patterns of life for the community of God and shape the message of the New Testament.

Babylon. Although global in scope, Zechariah 6:1–8 does place considerable emphasis on the return of the Babylonian exilic community. Certainly there were many living in exile in other regions (Egypt, Moab, Ammon, Edom; Jer. 40–41) or who had never left the land (2 Kings 25:12). Why is Zechariah so focused on the Jewish community in Babylon? Part of this may have to do with the fact that he began his life and ministry among this exilic community (whom he consistently addresses: Zech. 2:6–13; 6:9–15).

But one also must take into account several other factors. (1) Among the Babylonian community were two key families: the royal family of David through Jehoiachin, on whom the Deuteronomic History places much hope (2 Kings 25:27–30),[22] and the priestly family of Zadok, a line highlighted and affirmed by Ezekiel (Ezek. 40:46; 43:19; 44:15). The presence of these key figures among the Babylonian exilic community led to their identification with the remnant. (2) The experience of the Babylonian community closely paralleled that of the patriarchal and Exodus generations described in the Torah, a correspondence exploited in the prophetic tradition.[23] (3) The returns of the early Persian period were precipitated by the shattering of Babylonian control, the power responsible for dealing the final blows to the southern kingdom and parading its leaders into exile.

The image of Babylon, therefore, is important to those interpreting the exilic and restoration periods. Although Isaiah exploits Babylon as representative of the nations and their power (Isa. 13; 21) as he warns the Davidic kings not to rely on this power, Isaiah 39 represents a transition in that prophetic witness to Babylon's role as instrument of God's discipline. Such a role is also highlighted in the Deuteronomic History's account of the closing days of the kingdom of Judah (2 Kings 24:1–4), Jeremiah's interpretation of the Babylonian advance against Judah (e.g., Jer. 20:4–6; 21:1–10; 27:1–22), and Ezekiel's interpretation of the Babylonian attack on Tyre and Egypt (Ezek. 26; 30; 32).

The second part of Isaiah (Isa. 43:14; 47:1; 48:14, 20), however, turns the rhetoric back against Babylon. Such a change is also discernible in Habakkuk's struggle with the continuing rule of the Babylonians (Hab. 1–2)

---

22. Something confirmed by archaeological discoveries in Babylon; cf. *ANET*, 308.

23. R. W. Klein, *Israel in Exile: A Theological Interpretation* (OBT; Philadelphia: Fortress, 1979), 38–39, 111–12.

and in Jeremiah's interpretation of the Exile (Jer. 25:1–14; cf. chs. 50–51). After a brief period as instrument of God's wrath, Babylon returns to its status as symbol of rebellion against God. Zechariah 1:7–17 has already highlighted the reason for God's discipline of Babylon. God admits that he used Babylon to correct his people, but that Babylon exceeded her role. Babylon's punishment at the outset of Darius's rule (the time when these visions are delivered) is a sign for the community that God is at work fulfilling his promises to them, one of which was the punishment of their captors. In light of this, the fulfillment of the other promises should be expected as they continue to turn to God in faithful obedience.

As the historical Babylon lies defeated in the early Persian period, it endures as an image in the Biblical witness. It is not surprising that in the New Testament Babylon becomes equated either with Rome or all worldly power and evil (1 Peter 5:13; Rev. 14:8: 16:19; 17:5; 18:2, 10, 21).[24] Thus, the defeat of Babylon described in Zechariah 6:8 foreshadows the ultimate defeat of evil at the cross and through the triumph of Christ at his second coming.

Divine warrior-king. The defeat of Babylon in 6:1–8 is traced to the divine council of the sovereign Lord rather than to the war council of the Persians. This is an important feature of Zechariah's message as he interprets history to comfort and motivate a generation discouraged from living under the oppressive realities of foreign kings. Although there is considerable emphasis on the divine at the expense of the human in apocalyptic literature, this is generally the case when one encounters divine warrior imagery throughout the biblical corpus.

The use of chariot and horse imagery in 6:1–8 clearly links this action to divine warrior imagery. God's role in fighting on Israel's behalf is not merely a benevolent overture on his part but rather a divine prerogative. This is vividly displayed in the Exodus experience, where God fought on behalf of Israel by using spiritual and natural forces (Ex. 14). Israel stood by helplessly, not lifting a finger, even though armed for war (Ex. 13:18).

The song commemorating the miracle of the Exodus (Ex. 15) reveals why God must be the one who brings victory. The song begins by celebrating the great military feat of the Lord whose name is "warrior" (Ex. 15:3). In the following section there are royal allusions ("majestic ... greatness of

---

24. Note C. S. Keener, *Revelation* (NIVAC; Grand Rapids: Zondervan, 2000), 406; and D. E. Johnson, *Triumph of the Lamb: A Commentary on Revelation* (Phillipsburg, N.J.: Presbyterian and Reformed, 2001), 243–44, who link the image of Babylon to Rome and yet see more. However, Gentry links it to Jerusalem; K. L. Gentry, *Before Jerusalem Fell: Dating the Book of Revelation*, 2d ed. (Bethesda, Md.: International Scholars Publications, 1996); idem, *He Shall Have Dominion: A Postmillenial Eschatology*, 2d ed. (Tyler, Tex.: Institute for Christian Economics, 1997), 391–96.

your majesty . . . majestic in holiness"; 15:6, 7, 11), which reach a climax at the conclusion of the song: "The LORD will reign forever and ever" (15:18). This military victory wrought by the Lord and his instruments has confirmed his kingship in Israel and the world.[25]

This intertwining of military and royal privilege helps us to see God's concern over the kind of royal figure that the Israelites request in 1 Samuel 8 and 12. God's concern is not with a royal house (see Gen. 17:6; 49:8–12; Deut. 17:14–20) but rather with the Israelites' desire for a king like the other nations, who will lead them into battle (1 Sam. 8:19–20; 12:12). David is seen as a great royal figure because he does not rely on his own strength but rather inquires of God and entrusts the victory into his hands (1 Sam. 17; 2 Sam. 5:17–25).

Such divine warrior theology and imagery would have resonated with those who lived through the helpless and oppressive conditions of the Exile. Separated into small communities and demoralized by alien status, they saw little hope of freedom. But Zechariah reveals that God is working on behalf of his people, breaking the back of the Babylonian overlord.

This divine warrior theology continues unabated through the biblical witness.[26] As we are helplessly oppressed by "Babylon," God promises to act on our behalf. Thus Christ is presented as a divine warrior figure in the New Testament, serving as God's arm to break the powers of darkness foreshadowed by aspects of his earthly ministry and completed through his death on the cross (Col. 2:13–15). There is, however, one future aspect to Christ's work: The church, Christ's representative, continues to battle against the powers of darkness with strength provided by the Lord (Eph. 6:10–20) as it awaits the ultimate vanquishing at the end of redemptive history (Mark 13; Rev. 19:11–19).

As Zechariah 6:1–8 reminds its original audience of God's grace expressed through his role as divine warrior on their behalf, so it reminds those of us living in a later period of redemptive history that God continues to demand this as an expression of his kingship in our lives. To take this on ourselves—that is, to do battle by our own strength and power rather than rely on his power—is to deny him royal prerogative.

Although the human dimension is muted in divine warrior theology and imagery, two human elements should not be forgotten. (1) Those who benefit from God's intervention are those who trust and wait on God. Thus, in contrast to Saul, who did not wait for God's priest-prophet for fear of losing

25. Notice the pattern of divine warfare in the Bible and ancient Near East highlighted by Longman and Reid: 1. Warfare; 2. Victory; 3. Kingship; 4. House building; 5. Celebration. Following victory in war comes kingship; Longman and Reid, *Warrior*, 83–88.

26. See esp. Longman and Reid, *Warrior*; and C. Sherlock, *The God Who Fights: The War Tradition in the Holy Scripture* (Rutherford Studies in Contemporary Theology 6; Lewiston, N.Y.: Mellen, 1993).

his army and the battle (1 Sam. 13), David inquires of God and grants the heavenly army priority of battle position (2 Sam. 5:17–22). Furthermore, in contrast to Saul, the "giant" of Israel who cowers before the mighty Goliath, the pint-sized David approaches the giant without aid of military armor "in the name of the LORD Almighty, the God of the armies of Israel" (1 Sam. 17:45).

(2) Those who benefit from God's intervention are those who walk in covenant faithfulness before him. The covenant blessings and curses in Leviticus 26 and Deuteronomy 28 emphasize that God will bring victory for those who follow the covenant demands but defeat for those who abandon the covenant (see esp. Deut. 28:7, 25). The prophets echo this but extend it even further by warning that God will turn on his people and treat them as an enemy (e.g., Jer. 21:3–7; cf. Lam. 2:5). This clarifies the meaning of the angel of the Lord's statement in Joshua 5:13 as he surprises Joshua on the eve of the battle against Jericho. When asked by Joshua whether he was on Israel's side or their enemies, the angel answers: "Neither ... but as commander of the army of the LORD I have now come." Assistance from God is not assumed but rather conditioned on human fidelity. He does not serve us, but we serve him.[27]

The second of these human postures is more prominent in the larger context of Zechariah 1–8. In its final form, the promise of restoration is linked intimately to the community's response to the covenant demands of 1:1–6, an emphasis echoed in the visions of chapter 5. But one cannot ignore the aspect of trust demanded of those called to return to the land.

These twin human responses to God's promises to act on behalf of his people weave their way into the New Testament witness as well. Experiencing the victory of the divine warrior on the cross involves repentance and faith (Matt. 21:32; Acts 20:21). Donning the "armor of God" against evil powers involves faith ("shield of faith"; Eph. 6:16) and righteousness ("breastplate of righteousness," 6:14). These postures are crucial to sustained fidelity to our divine warrior as we await his second coming (Heb. 11:1–12:2; Rev. 2:5, 16, 21, 22; 3:3, 19).

Contemporary Significance

PAST. ZECHARIAH 6:1–8 declared to believers living in the early Persian period that God had fulfilled his commitment to break the oppression of Babylon. For those still in exile, this was an incentive to return to the land (cf. Zech. 2), signaling a new phase in redemptive history. For those who had returned it was a reminder of God's grace, especially important as they pursued the rebuilding of the temple in a volatile and hostile environment (Ezra 2–6).

27. This is the concern of Jeremiah in his day. Based on a false conclusion from Isaiah's teaching (Isa. 1:8), the people had assumed that Jerusalem was inviolable; that is, no one would or could take it because of the Lord's presence and promise (Jer. 7:4; cf. Ps. 48).

But this message continued to speak throughout the history of redemption as God consistently rescued his people. This redemption came to a climax in the work of God in Christ, who is represented as both the community longing for release from exile and the God waging divine war on their behalf. These two lines intersect in Christ on the cross: He suffered as the ultimate child of the Exile under the Babylon of his day (Rome), but then rose from the grave to victory. This victory is the turning point in the history of redemption, and we also look back to this event as foundational for our faith.

Through Zechariah 6:1–8 the Christian community revels in God's grace displayed in this era of redemptive history: the rescue from Babylonian exile and the elimination of an age-old threat, one that could curb or control the return and restoration. It is interesting that the New Testament identifies the event of the Exile as an important marker in the story of redemption, placing it on par with Abraham, David, and Christ (Matt. 1:17). One key response to Zechariah 6:1–8 is to thank God for his grace extended to his community throughout the ages. It prompts praise for the story of restoration that began in the Persian period and culminated at the cross.

Future. Based on this "already" foundation, the New Testament encourages us to expect the "not yet," that Christ will ultimately give us victory at the end of time as he gathers his people from the four winds (Mark 13:27) who are living in exile (see the introduction, Bridging Contexts section).[28] One day our divine warrior will appear and enact justice on the earth (Rev. 19), and "there will be no more death or mourning or crying or pain" (Rev. 21:4).

This future aspect stimulates not only praise for God's great purposes but also hope, a distinguishing mark of Christian belief (e.g., Rom. 12:12; 1 Cor. 13:13; Col. 1:4, 23; 1 Thess. 4:13; Titus 2:13; 1 Peter 1:3, 13). God's redemptive actions, highlighted by his prophet Zechariah, stimulate hope within his people who long for the completion of redemptive history.

The story is often told of the young Christian convert who was given a Bible to read. Not knowing where to begin, she followed her poor reading habit of turning to the final chapter of the book to find out the end of the story. Of course, there she found the book of Revelation, a book often avoided by Christians today because of its alien imagery and symbols. Attending church the next week she told the pastor that she had been reading her new Bible throughout the week. At first delighted by her vibrant testimony of newfound faith, he was soon concerned when he discovered she had been reading Revelation. As she spoke with him, it was obvious that she had enjoyed her reading of the Bible, so he asked her to share her impressions of this obscure book. She proceeded to inform him that the book showed her that in the end, "we win." This young convert had ascertained the fundamental posture of Revelation for Christian living: hope.

---

28. See Ryken, Wilhoit, and Longman, eds. *DBI*, 250–51.

Present. For those of us living between the past "already" and the future "not yet," Zechariah 6:1–8 serves as comforting revelation of God's intentions. It not only prompts praise and stimulates hope, but it also encourages faith, that is, to entrust ourselves into the hands of this kind of God, full of grace and yet sovereignly acting for his people.

Sometimes it is difficult to see God at work in our times of darkness. The Jews in Zechariah's time were longing for the completion of God's promises of old, but God's times and means do not always align with human expectations. Nevertheless, Zechariah reveals that recent events in Babylon were indeed part of God's redemptive work for his people.

We live in similar circumstances today as God's people. In a world of uncertainty, whether because of the global issues of war, terrorism, disease, or poverty or because of personal issues of family strife, personal health, or economic instability, we seek to live faithfully as disciples of Christ. Such faithful living involves both trust and theology.

On the one hand, we desperately need the sensibilities of faith and trust to lean on our God and not our own human initiatives and strength. This is taught implicitly through 6:1–8 with its focus on God and his activity rather than on the people and their activity. For the Jews living under the powerful thumb of the nations and powerless to change the course of their history, they had to learn trust in this sovereign Lord, who alone could bring redemption and justice for his people. For those of us living in the West, however, we must not forget that we can easily be tagged with the name Babylon and must be conscious of ways in which we contribute to the abuse of even those with whom we share the name of Christ in nations around the world.

On the other hand, we also need a theology shaped by the biblical revelation of God. By lifting the eyes of his contemporaries to this vision of God, Zechariah was expanding the theology of a generation, reminding them that God is sovereign in the affairs of humanity.

As a young pastor ministering to the needs of youth in Toronto, I came to a place of exhaustion after a year. In a crisis of faith I realized how important my theology was to the practice of ministry. Prompted by a close pastoral colleague who reminded me of the doctrine of the sovereignty of God, I was able to entrust that ministry into the hands of the sovereign One, who alone could transform the lives of these young people. Although intellectually I would have defended the doctrine of God's sovereignty, in practice I denied it. I needed a vision of God such as Zechariah experienced to inform and provoke faith in my sovereign God.

In a world of uncertainty we need to recapture the doctrine of the sovereignty of God in the affairs of humanity. Zechariah 6:1–8 expresses this sovereignty in two ways. (1) It speaks of the strength of that sovereignty symbolized in the "powerful" horses he sends forth into the world. God as sovereign Lord of the universe is mighty enough to accomplish his work. (2) It speaks of the extent of that sovereignty symbolized by the "four winds" and expressed in the phrase "the Lord of the whole world." These elements emphasize that the global range of his sovereignty is not restricted to a single locale but encompasses the entire cosmos.

Faithful living thus involves a combination of trust and theology. These two aspects of faithful living are inseparable and together enable us to grow in faith and faithfulness. We must grow in faith in the sovereign One as we release ourselves in increasing ways into his trustworthy hands. But we must also grow in our knowledge of the sovereign One by studying the story of his people in canon and history and by tracing his care in our own experience.

Not only does this passage prompt faithful living as we trust in a sovereign God, but it also reminds us that vengeance lies in God's hands, not our own. God's people had been abused by the Babylonians. There is no question that this abuse originally stemmed from God's discipline on his people as a result of their disobedience. But as the initial vision of 1:7–17 announced from God: "I was only a little angry, but they added to the calamity" (1:15). Zechariah 6:1–8, the depiction of the fulfillment of the intentions of 1:7–17, traces the exacting of God's wrath on Babylon. This wrath, expressed through the Persian Darius, is ultimately linked to God's purposes. The weak and insignificant Jews of this period, powerless to induce this fulfillment of prophecy, were forced to place vengeance into the hands of their sovereign God.

So also in our time as we experience persecution in our world, we can rest assured that vengeance ultimately lies in the hands of our sovereign God. This releases us to forgive those who wrong us, even to bless those who persecute us (Matt. 5:10–12, 38–48; Rom. 12:14–21; 1 Peter 3:8–12). These instructions from Jesus and his apostles are based on the fundamental belief that Christ came to inaugurate an age of grace unparalleled in redemptive history, an age that, however, will end with universal judgment. Jesus foreshadowed this at the inauguration of his ministry in his home synagogue of Nazareth (Luke 4:14–30). There he opened the scroll of the prophet Isaiah and read from Isaiah 61:1–2:

> The Spirit of the Lord is on me,
> because he has anointed me
> to preach good news to the poor.
> He has sent me to proclaim freedom for the prisoners,
> and recovery of sight for the blind,
> to release the oppressed,
> to proclaim the year of the Lord's favor. (Luke 4:18–19)

After rolling up the scroll and giving it back to the attendant and with all eyes on him in that synagogue, he spoke those famous words: "Today this scripture is fulfilled in your hearing." A comparison with Isa. 61:1–2 reveals that Jesus stopped his reading mid-sentence:

> The Spirit of the Sovereign LORD is on me,
> because the LORD has anointed me
> to preach good news to the poor.
> He has sent me to bind up the brokenhearted,
> to proclaim freedom for the captives
> and release from darkness for the prisoners,
> to proclaim the year of the LORD'S favor
> *and the day of vengeance of our God.* (italics added)

Jesus proclaims the year of the Lord's favor, but he stops short of the "day of vengeance of our God." I do not believe that Jesus was ignoring this coming "day of vengeance," especially considering his later teaching on this coming day (e.g., Luke 21). Rather, he was inaugurating an age of grace that proclaimed freedom and forgiveness. Such an age is clearly spiritual as opposed to political, but it does have a political dimension. Therefore, faithfulness to the sovereign Lord means entrusting ourselves into his care even when we are wronged.[29]

Many Christians, even in the West, face persecution for their beliefs and will increasingly do so as Western society becomes secularized. Zechariah's message speaks to those of us today who face such persecution as we seek to live out our faith. But Zechariah's message is also a sober reminder that God's vengeance is a reality for those of us who are involved in injustice, whether on the local level or on the global level. Our divine warrior can come not only to rescue us from the oppressor but also to discipline us as oppressors.

For God's people living today in an era as challenging as those of the Jews of the Persian period, Zechariah 6:1–8 prompts praise for God's past redemption, stimulates hope in his future promises, and provokes faith in his sovereign control of the details of our lives.

---

29. There has been considerable debate over the appropriateness of the cry of vengeance for the Christian believer. See: J. G. Vos, "The Ethical Problem of the Imprecatory Psalms," *WTJ* 4 (1942): 123–38; C. S. Lewis, *Reflections on the Psalms* (London: Geoffrey Bles, 1958), 20–33; M. Chalmers, "Imprecations in the Psalms," in *Classical Evangelical Essays in Old Testament Interpretation*, ed. W. C. Kaiser (Grand Rapids: Baker, 1972), 113–32; J. C. Laney, "A Fresh Look at the Imprecatory Psalms," *BSac* 138 (1981): 35–45; W. Brueggemann, *Praying the Psalms* (Winona, Minn.: Saint Mary's, 1993), 67–80; J. C. McCann and N. R. McCann, *A Theological Introduction to the Book of Psalms: The Psalms As Torah* (Nashville: Abingdon, 1993), 112–24; G. Pauls, "The Imprecations of the Psalmists: A Study of Psalm 54," *Direction* 22 (1993): 75–86; A. M. Harman, "The Continuity of the Covenant Curses in the Imprecations of the Psalter," *RTR* 54 (1995): 65–72

Zechariah 6:9–15

THE WORD OF THE LORD came to me: [10]"Take ⌞silver and gold⌟ from the exiles Heldai, Tobijah and Jedaiah, who have arrived from Babylon. Go the same day to the house of Josiah son of Zephaniah. [11]Take the silver and gold and make a crown, and set it on the head of the high priest, Joshua son of Jehozadak. [12]Tell him this is what the LORD Almighty says: 'Here is the man whose name is the Branch, and he will branch out from his place and build the temple of the LORD. [13]It is he who will build the temple of the LORD, and he will be clothed with majesty and will sit and rule on his throne. And he will be a priest on his throne. And there will be harmony between the two.' [14]The crown will be given to Heldai, Tobijah, Jedaiah and Hen son of Zephaniah as a memorial in the temple of the LORD. [15]Those who are far away will come and help to build the temple of the LORD, and you will know that the LORD Almighty has sent me to you. This will happen if you diligently obey the LORD your God."

Original Meaning

IN 6:9–15 WE LEAVE BEHIND the figurative world of the night visions to return to the "real" world of the early Persian period community. This section has been placed here strategically to round out the night vision complex, continuing the momentum of the final vision in 6:1–8 by describing the result of the divine intervention in Israel's experience, the return of the exiles (cf. 6:10). In this way it completes the earlier oracle in 2:6–13, which brought the first phase of night visions (1:8–2:5) "down to the earth" by inviting the exiles to return to the land where God's presence was promised.[1] It also rounds out the vision-sign-act of chapter 3, by echoing many of the same themes of priestly, royal, and prophetic functions within this renewed community.[2]

Although 6:9–15 concludes 1:7–6:15, it is not part of the night vision. The formula that begins 6:9 ("the word of the LORD came to me") occurs regularly throughout the prophets to introduce or continue a prophetic oracle (Jer. 1:4; 13:8; Ezek. 11:14; 16:1). But it also appears in visionary experiences

1. See Redditt, "Zerubbabel," 76.
2. For detailed analysis of this section of Zechariah, see Boda, "Oil," Art. 10.

(Jer. 1:11, 13) and prophetic sign-acts (Jer. 13:3; Ezek. 12:1). It is this last genre that this formula signals here in Zechariah 6, a genre defined as "non-verbal behaviors ... whose primary purpose was communicative and interactive" (e.g., Jer. 13; Ezek. 3).[3] Sign-acts usually comprise three segments: exhortation, execution, and explanation. This passage contains an exhortation (vv. 10–14) and explanation (v. 15) but omits the middle segment.

In this sign-act the prophet is told to take silver and gold from Jews who have recently returned from Babylon and to bring them to another returnee who is in charge of the growing temple treasure. Zechariah is to oversee the manufacture of two crowns from these metals, one of which is to be placed on the head of the high priest Joshua, who then receives a special message from God. This message concerns a figure who will fulfill Jeremiah's promise of a Davidic descendant (*ṣemaḥ*, "Branch") and rebuild the temple. The priest will have a major role to play when this individual arrives, and they will work together. The crowns are then to be given to the four figures introduced at the outset, who will retain them as a reminder of this experience.

The significance of this sign-act is explained in the final verse. It is a revelation that the building of the temple will not commence until others have joined them, in particular *ṣemaḥ* and his entourage ("those who are far away"). The arrival of *ṣemaḥ* will confirm the prophetic word, and they are urged to heed this prophetic promise.

This sign-act addresses recently arrived priests eager to begin work on the temple. This prophecy reminds them that Zerubbabel, as a Davidic scion, is responsible for the rebuilding project (vv. 12–13) and that along with him will come others to join the project (vv. 15). The two crowns made from the silver and gold are reminders that God will fulfill Jeremiah's promise of the endurance of the royal and priestly lines (Jer. 33). The presence of Joshua (representative of the priestly line) foreshadows the soon arrival of Zerubbabel (representative of the royal line).

Many interpreters have seen in this text evidence of a deep rift in the community between those promoting royal and priestly interests. Although there appears to be evidence of rifts in this community at a later point (hints are given in chs. 7–8 and clearly in chs. 9–14), at this point Zechariah is only carefully delineating the limits of each of the leadership streams within the early Persian period community, possibly noticing or anticipating an overeager priesthood.[4]

---

3. Friebel, *Sign-Acts*, 14. Friebel identifies 6:9–15 as a sign-act; so also Meyers and Meyers, *Haggai*, 338; Hanson, *Dawn*, 256. For this form see esp. R. M. Hals, *Ezekiel* (FOTL 19 Grand Rapids: Eerdmans, 1988), 355; Fohrer, *Handlungen*, 18; Friebel, "Hermeneutical Paradigm," 25–45.

4. Cf. Boda, "Oil," Art. 10; idem, "From Fasts to Feasts: The Literary Function of Zechariah 7–8," *CBQ* 65 (2003): 390–407.

The historical setting of this passage is difficult to pinpoint. The last precise date came in 1:7, a date that merely identifies the day on which the night vision section was proclaimed to the people. Taking 6:9–15 on its own, the context seems to be sometime in the early Persian period, when people are returning to the land from Babylon. Clearly Joshua has returned along with several other figures mentioned in 6:10, including Zechariah. But the absence of Zerubbabel in a context that speaks of the Davidic *ṣemaḥ* seems to indicate that his arrival is still future. Such a historical setting explains why rebuilding the temple appears as a future event here.[5]

Exhortation (6:10–14)

THE LORD INSTRUCTS the prophet to "take ... from Heldai, Tobijah and Jedaiah.... Go to the house of Josiah son of Zephaniah." It is nearly impossible to ascertain the precise identities of these men, although most likely they are priests.[6] Two of the men (Heldai, Josiah) have different names in the second list in verse 14 (Helem, Hen). Perhaps these are merely nicknames for these two individuals (meaning Strength, Grace); however, the second is probably a title for Josiah, designating him as the temple steward who cared for the donations for the temple.[7] This view is strengthened by the fact that Josiah is called the "son of Zephaniah," a powerful priest in the final days of the kingdom of Judah (Jer. 29:24–29; 2 Kings 25:18).

While the name Heldai (Helem) is not found elsewhere, Jedaiah is found in the list of priests who returned in the early Persian period (Ezra 2:36). According to 2:60, "descendants of ... Tobiah" did return in the same period and because of concern over their lineage may have been of Levitical/priestly descent (2:59, 62).[8] Further evidence that these four individuals are of priestly stock is suggested by the later practice of Ezra,[9] who commissioned priests to transport silver and gold from Mesopotamia (8:24–32) into the care of priests at the temple in Jerusalem (8:33–34). Moreover, the introduction of the high priest Joshua in the next verse lends credence to the thesis that these individuals are priests.

---

5. Without this explanation, one is left looking for someone else to build the temple and either identify Jesus Christ as ultimate Davidic Son building the temple, the church, or a third temple in the eschatological age; Baldwin, *Haggai*, 137.

6. See Meyers and Meyers, *Haggai*, 339–46, for an extended discussion.

7. A. Demsky, "The Temple Steward Josiah ben Zephaniah," *IEJ* 31 (1981): 100–103. Another suggestion is that this is an expression meaning: "into the kindness of the son of Zephaniah"; Merrill, *Haggai*, 202.

8. A later Tobiah, an Ammonite official with close links with the Jerusalem temple, is well known for his opposition to Nehemiah (Neh. 12:10; 13:4, 7).

9. See Ezra 1:4, 6, 11; 2:68–69; 7:15–18; 8:24–34.

Heldai, Tobijah, and Jedaiah are "from the exiles" (*haggolah*), a term used for those taken away to Mesopotamia during the first quarter of the sixth century B.C. (e.g., Jer. 29:4; Ezek. 1:1).[10] The phrase "who have arrived from Babylon" actually appears at the end of the verse after Josiah's name, but it is a plural, so it cannot refer to Josiah alone. Perhaps it describes all four men, but its present placement is awkward. This difficulty is easily resolved by translating the Hebrew word *ʾăšer* as "for" (causal particle, cf. 1 Kings 3:19) rather than "who" (relative pronoun). This clause gives the reason why the prophet is to escort the men to Josiah's house (they have arrived from Babylon) and why the command is so vigorous: "Go the same day."[11]

The clear identity of these individuals with the exilic community is key to this message, and thus the characters are introduced before even their precious cargo.[12] This enhances the connection to the final night vision that announced release for the community exiled in "the land of the north" (Babylon; 6:8) and prepares the way for the interpretation in 6:15 that "those who are far away" will come (same verb as "arrived" in 6:10). This passage anticipates further arrivals from the exilic community and provides direction for the activity of those who come.

The prophet is then instructed to make a crown from their silver and gold and set it on the head of the high priest, Joshua son of Jehozadak. Joshua (cf. Ezra 3; Hag. 1–2; Zech. 3) played a significant role in the restoration of the temple service and structure. It is unclear whether Joshua is part of the caravan that just arrived with Heldai, Tobijah, and Jedaiah.

The surprising feature of this verse, therefore, is not the appearance of Joshua, especially in a scene involving a priestly transfer of valuables for the temple project, but rather the symbolic act that is commanded. The prophet is told to make "crowns" (NIV "a crown") and "set it on the head of" Joshua. There is no question that this phrase refers to placing a crown on the head of Joshua,[13] but why would the prophet be asked to place such a symbol on the head of the high priest? Is this suggesting that the high priest will assume royal prerogatives?

---

10. This began as early as 605 B.C. (see Dan. 1) and continued through deportations in 597 and 587 B.C. and beyond. It is uncertain from this text whether Josiah was ever in exile. Clearly he is distinguished from the three other individuals because he already has a "house"; if he did return, it was in an earlier wave.

11. The Heb. text is more energetic than even this translation for it repeats the verb "go" twice and infuses the redundant pronoun and adverbial phrase: "Go, yourself, on that day, go." Such energy may display concern for the safety of this precious cargo in a volatile period in Yehud's history (see 8:9–11).

12. Cf. Petersen, *Haggai*, 273–74; Meyers and Meyers, *Haggai*, 338, on this rhetorical technique, although I think Petersen's link between this rhetoric and fund-raising techniques is misguided.

13. See Boda, "Oil," n. 42.

In order to answer this question, we must examine closely the word "crown" (*ʿaṭarah*).[14] This Hebrew word usually refers to a literal crown on the head of a member of the royal court, usually the king (e.g., Ps. 21:3), but also the queen mother (Jer. 23:18) or an official (Est. 8:15). In most cases, however, the word is used metaphorically to denote honor or beauty (e.g., Isa. 28:1–5). In other words, the act of setting a crown on a high priest does not necessarily signify a royal coronation, even if it suggests a role for the high priest in the royal court.

After making crowns and placing one of them on the head of Joshua, God instructs the prophet to declare a prophetic word to the high priest ("Tell him"). This speech speaks of someone named *ṣemaḥ* ("Branch").[15] This oracle has precipitated even more debate among interpreters than the sign-act that precedes it.

Jeremiah 23:5 and 33:15 use the title *ṣemaḥ* for a future figure who will grow from the royal line of David. Not surprisingly, royal imagery is used repeatedly in the lines associated with this *ṣemaḥ* in Zechariah 6:12–13: "clothed with majesty ... sit ... rule on his throne." Confusing, however, is the apparent identification of Joshua the high priest with this figure, for the oracle about *ṣemaḥ* is directed to Joshua ("Tell him.... Here is the man"; 6:12), the string of descriptions of *ṣemaḥ* ends with the clause ("And he will be a priest on his throne," 6:13), and a "crown" is placed on the head of Joshua (6:11).[16] What one expects here is a reference to someone from the Davidic line and the most likely candidate, contemporary with Joshua, is Zerubbabel, grandson of the Davidic King Jehoiachin. Twice it is claimed that this *ṣemaḥ* will "build the temple of the Lord" (6:12–13), an activity linked to Zerubbabel in the oracle in 4:6b–10a as well as the tradition of the books of Haggai and Ezra.

There have been several approaches to clear up this confusion. Some have suggested oral or rhetorical solutions, in which Joshua's speech is delivered in the presence of Zerubbabel and various sections of the speech are directed towards different people.[17] The majority of scholars, however, have followed a trajectory set by Wellhausen, who posited the activity of editors who either substituted Joshua's name here for the original Zerubbabel[18] or

14. There has been considerable controversy over both the number of crowns referred to in this vision. For my approach see Boda, "Oil," n. 58.

15. For the translation of *ṣemaḥ* and the inappropriateness of "Branch," see Original Meaning section of Zech. 3.

16. The LXX did not see Joshua as king for rather than translating "he will be a priest on his throne," it produces "there will be a priest on his right hand."

17. Cf. Baldwin, *Haggai*, 136; Merrill, *Haggai*, 197–201.

18. J. Wellhausen, *Die kleinen Propheten übersetzt und erklärt*, 2d ed. (Berlin: Reimer, 1893), 185; also J. Wellhausen, "Zechariah," in *Encyclopaedia Biblica*, ed. T. K. Cheyne and J. S. Black (New York: Macmillan, 1903), 5390–95.

inserted the oracle into a passage that originally focused on crowning the high priest or the returned exiles.[19]

The difficulty of this latter approach is that it is intertwined with views of sociological tension within this Jewish community. Some have highlighted the elevation of high priestly control over the civil affairs of the province in the later phases of the Persian period. It has been tempting to see 6:9–15 as "prophetic" legitimization for this later development. Others have been satisfied with a balance of royal and priestly interests here as it fits well with their view of a hierocratic-apocalyptic split in this period.[20] Still others have noted the intense split between Samaritan and Yehudite factions in the Second Temple period and have seen 6:9–15 as an early attempt to heal this rift.[21]

It is not easy to resolve these intricate and intertwined issues, but we must begin with suspension of preconceived ideas about the sociology of this period. Because of the lack of historical evidence from this period, it is tempting to impose evidence from later periods onto this early Persian period, whether that means the Samaritan-Yehudite, the priestly-royal, or the hierocratic-apocalyptic rift of later periods. In addition, attempts to resolve the issue through appeal to scribal mistakes unattested in the textual witness should be avoided, as also should redactional theories that excise material that does not fit with one's theory. Finally, attention must be given to the text itself, its vocabulary and imagery.

(1) Our point of departure is the conclusion of the speech to be delivered to Joshua. At the end of verse 13, Zechariah tells Joshua that "there will be harmony between the two" (lit., "there will be a counsel of peace between the two of them"). The key here is the final piece: "between the two of them," which reveals that the preceding speech is somehow associated with two distinct people (cf. 2 Kings 2:11; Ex. 22:10).[22]

(2) Note the beginning of the speech to "him" (i.e., Joshua, 6:12a). The opening words are: "Behold a man, *ṣemaḥ* is his name" (NIV, "Here is the man whose name is Branch"). When the expression "Behold a man" appears in direct speech, it does not refer to the one addressed but rather to a third party (approaching, 2 Sam. 18:26; present, 1 Sam. 9:17; absent but accessible 9:6). Thus, *ṣemaḥ* cannot be Joshua but someone either present in or absent from the scene. This second possibility is strengthened by the fact that the one instance where the individual is present in the scene uses the article, "Behold *the* man" (1 Sam. 9:17), unlike Zechariah 6:12. That the referent is not in the scene accords well with the only other allusion to *ṣemaḥ* in

19. Petersen, *Haggai*; Redditt, "Zerubbabel," 252–53; idem, *Haggai*, 76–79.

20. Hanson, *Dawn*, 256.

21. Barker, "Two Figures," 33–46.

22. For the use of this phrase in the Old Testament see Boda, "Oil," n. 45.

Zechariah (3:8), in a speech also addressed to Joshua, which refers to *ṣemaḥ* as someone whom the Lord Almighty "is going to bring."

(3) A closer look at the speech reveals the identity and role of both figures. The phrases in 6:12–13 reflect the cadence of poetic verse; that is, they are arranged in couplets of relatively similar length. I have provided my own translation to highlight the Hebrew poetic structure:

> Behold, a man, *ṣemaḥ* is his name//He will grow [*ṣamaḥ*] from his place
> He will build the temple of the LORD//He, indeed, will build the temple of the LORD
> He will be clothed with majesty//He will sit and rule on his throne
> A priest will be on his throne//A counsel of peace will be between them

The first couplet introduces the figure *ṣemaḥ* in the first colon and then plays off the name with the verbal root (*ṣamaḥ*) in the second.[23] The main focus of the activity of this *ṣemaḥ* is provided in the second couplet: He will build the temple. The third couplet makes explicit the royal character of the *ṣemaḥ* figure by using vocabulary often associated with the royal office: to "be clothed with majesty" (e.g., Ps. 21:5); to "sit and rule on his throne" (e.g., 1 Kings 1:46).

These first three couplets share many contacts in vocabulary with the *ṣemaḥ* prophecies of Jeremiah in 23:5–6 and 33:15–16, the only other passages in the Hebrew Bible where *ṣemaḥ* is used to refer to an individual who grows (*ṣamaḥ*).[24] In both Jeremiah passages this individual is identified as a Davidic descendant, the revelation of whom is connected to God's return of a remnant from captivity to a rebuilt and prosperous city filled with inhabitants (Jer. 23:3, 8; 33:7–13). Both Zechariah and Jeremiah (33:7–9) use the verb "build" to refer to the rebuilding of the land with special emphasis on Jerusalem. Jeremiah 22, a passage that prepares the way for the first of the two prophecies of *ṣemaḥ* in Jeremiah (23:5–6), speaks of the loss of "majesty" for Jehoiakim (22:18) and of the condemnation of his son Jehoiachin, whose sons will not "sit on the throne . . . or rule" (22:30).[25] The

---

23. When used with the verb "grow" (*ṣamaḥ*), "from his place" refers to the place from which something grows (Gen. 2:9; Ex. 10:5; Job 5:6; 8:19; Ps. 85:11). For this and other views see Boda, "Oil," n. 50.

24. There are slight differences between Zech. 6:9–15 and Jer. 23, 33 in that Zechariah's presentation transforms the actions of *ṣemaḥ* (grow, build) from passive (God is the subject) to active (Branch is the subject) and focuses the building on the temple rather than city and province; cf. D. K. Stuart, "The Prophetic Ideal of Government in the Restoration Era," in *Israel's Apostasy and Restoration: Essays in Honor of Roland K. Harrison*, ed. A. Gileadi (Grand Rapids: Baker, 1988), 283–92.

25. This is the only other place in the Old Testament where the combination "sit . . . rule . . . throne" appears.

revelation of *ṣemaḥ* in 23:5–6 is the answer to the disaster of the Davidic line proclaimed in Jeremiah 22.

This evidence associates the *ṣemaḥ* figure with rebuilding the land and restoring the Davidic house promised by Jeremiah. But there is still no evidence of the second figure assumed by the final phrase, "between the two" (Zech. 6:13). It is the fourth couplet that introduces this second figure and then defines the relationship between him and the dominant *ṣemaḥ*.

The fourth couplet introduces the second figure as "a priest" who will sit on a throne.[26] Although "throne" is usually associated either literally or figuratively with kings (e.g., 1 Kings 16:11; 22:10; Jer. 1:15), others can occupy this seat, even a priest like Eli (1 Sam. 1:9; 4:13, 18). Interestingly, there are instances in which two people are seated on thrones in the same room, and in each case the king is receiving counsel, from another king (1 Kings 22:10) or the Queen Mother (1 Kings 2:19). In both instances one figure is clearly dominant over the other.

This evidence suggests that the priestly figure will give counsel, a role confirmed by the phrase "counsel of peace" (NIV "harmony") in the second colon of the fourth couplet in 6:13 (cf. 2 Sam. 15:31, 34).[27] The reference to peace suggests that this counsel will be either positive counsel or counsel that results in prosperity.

Such priestly counsel is important in light of the earlier practices of the monarchy. Note how both royal terms associated with the priest in this passage—"crown" (6:11) and "throne" (6:13)—are used of the Queen Mother (1 Kings 2:19; Jer. 13:18), a figure who had considerable political power in preexilic royal courts (1 Kings 15:11–13; 2 Kings 11:1), but also led preexilic Davidic kings away from pure faith (1 Kings 15:13; 18–19). Zechariah 6:12–13 envisions a high priest who will sit with the king to offer advice and keep him faithful to the Lord.[28]

We have argued, then, that the two figures assumed in this prophetic speech are royal and priestly, with the latter offering counsel to the former. Although the identity of these figures is not revealed, the language used implies the imminent arrival of the royal figure while the address to Joshua suggests he is either the priestly figure or a symbol of that figure. Most likely these two figures are Joshua and Zerubbabel, the latter of which has not yet arrived from Babylon.

---

26. This struggle is reflected as far back as the LXX, which translates here that the priest is seated at the right hand of the royal figure. See B. A. Mastin, "A Note on Zechariah VI 13," *VT* 26 (1976): 113–16.

27. Cf. Petersen, *Haggai*, 278.

28. See further Boda, "Oil," n. 62, and great reviews of the Queen Mother by L. S. Schearing, "Queen," *ABD*, 4:585–86, and N. A. Andreasen, "The Role of the Queen Mother in Israelite Society," *CBQ* 45 (1983): 179–94.

This connection between royal and priestly figures has been encouraged by Zechariah's reliance on the prophet Jeremiah. Jeremiah 33:15–26 links the destiny of the Davidic house with the "priests, who are Levites" (see comments on Zech. 3). The arrival of the high priest Joshua presages the arrival of a royal figure, who will rebuild the temple. While assuring the priestly house that they will play a key role in the Davidic court, this prophecy reminds them of the preeminence of the royal line in authority and responsibility.

Instructions from God for the sign-act continue in 6:14. The two crowns are to be given to the four individuals as symbolic reminders of this prophetic action.[29] The word "memorial" (*zikkaron*) is used elsewhere to designate objects that remind the people of someone or something (Ex. 13:9; 28:12, 29; 30:16; 39:7; Num. 10:10). The four men are to keep the crowns in safekeeping because the temple has not yet been constructed, but they are also key witnesses[30] in this sign-act and representative of the community.

Explanation (6:15)

WITH 6:15 WE finally move from exhortation to explanation of the sign-act. The explanation focuses attention on the fact that there are still many to return to the land from Babylon and that when they come, building will begin on the temple. Although the Hebrew word "those who are far away" is used to speak of foreign nations (e.g., Deut. 13:8), it is also used for those who are away from the land in exile (Dan. 9:7; cf. Isa. 66:19), which is likely the case here.

This is not meant to discourage those who have already arrived, but rather to encourage them that God will bring even more resources, both material and human, than those already delivered. Such resources will enable the community to "build the temple of the LORD," echoing the phrase used in 6:12–13 of *ṣemaḥ* and highlighting his key role, while expanding the scope to include a whole community gathered around this royal figure.

The appearance of these material and human resources and the beginning of the temple project is linked to the integrity of the prophet Zechariah: "You will know that the LORD Almighty has sent me to you." This rhetorical technique (cf. 2:9, 11; 4:9) does not function merely as a prediction of future accolades for the prophet. Instead, it is designed to strengthen the prophetic word, subtly reminding the people that these words are not the remarks of a human acting on his own initiative but the declarations of one sent by the Lord.[31]

---

29. These crowns will function as "residual reminders," that is, "the sensory nonverbal items which resulted directly from the original actions but persisted after the communication event had been fully completed"; Friebel, *Sign-Acts*, 459–60.

30. Friebel (ibid., 26) highlights the importance of witnesses in sign-acts (Jer. 19:1, 10; 32:12; 43:9; Ezek. 4:12; 12:3, 4, 5, 6, 7; 21:11; 37:20).

31. See how this word "send" appears regularly in the calls of prophets, often in conjunction with "go": Ex. 3:10–11; Isa. 6:8–9; Jer. 1:7; Ezek. 2:1–4.

But there is a role also for those who see and hear the message of the sign-act. The fulfillment of the prophecy is linked to their obedience: "This will happen if you diligently obey the LORD your God." The Hebrew construction puts great stress on the act of obedience ("diligently obey"), but what is the focus of this obedience? Presumably, the prophet is exhorting them to await the arrival of others—especially the one named *ṣemaḥ*—who must be present before the temple rebuilding project is initiated.[32] It is entirely appropriate for the priests to be passionate about beginning the temple project, especially since it is their livelihood. But the prophet exhorts them to await the fulfillment of his prophecy.

Bridging Contexts

AS ALREADY NOTED, the prophetic sign-act in 6:9–15 is important to the final literary message of the night visions of Zechariah (1:7–6:15), for it brings them "down to earth," accentuating certain aspects of the message for Zechariah's community. This immediately creates a challenge for those seeking to interpret this message for a twenty-first-century audience, for this literature was directed first to an ancient context. Rather than ignoring the ancient context, our goal is to identify the relevance of this message in its ancient context and then identify relevant connections to our experience today.

A message for Joshua. Zechariah 6:9–15 is first directed to a group of priests as they arrive in Palestine from exile in Babylon. The Lord instructs the prophet to perform a sign-act using treasures carried from Babylon. As the priests arrive in the land, the prophet ushers them off to the temple steward, Josiah, who will receive and catalogue gifts for the temple project. The gifts of silver and gold are made into two crowns, one of which is placed on the head of the high priest, Joshua. With this symbol atop Joshua, the prophet declares a message to the high priest in the hearing of these four men that prophesies the coming of another individual, a royal figure of David's line, namely Zerubbabel, who will rebuild the temple and reestablish Davidic rule. The high priest will have a place of honor as chief counselor to Zerubbabel. The crowns are to be kept by the priests and eventually placed in the rebuilt temple as a reminder of this prophetic act.

This sign-act in its original oral context is designed to shape the actions of the priestly caste, who have already begun to return to the land. They must

32. This is not, then, an "ethical" warning, as suggested by Baldwin, *Haggai*, 138. This conclusion fits Friebel's argument that sign-acts were not only oriented to the future but also shaped behavior and fit into contingent prophecy, offering "advice to the people of how they *should* respond to the circumstances, not predictive of how they *would* respond" (Jer. 27; Ezek. 21); Friebel, *Sign-Acts*, 51–57; cf. Friebel, "Hermeneutical Paradigm," 25–45.

await the arrival of Zerubbabel, who will initiate the rebuilding project as representative of the Davidic house, which built the first temple. This timely message affirms the importance of the building project to those returning to the land. It reminds these priests of the need for cooperation between priestly and royal houses for this great project. It also offers hope to those who may be overwhelmed by the challenges of the building project that God will provide many others to assist in the work.

Loosed from that oral context, however, and placed into its present literary context, its meaning is expanded. It now follows the final night vision that describes the release of the exiles from Babylon and shapes the agenda of these returned exiles. God has released the exiles to rebuild the temple. He will provide leadership for this project, a royal figure with a priestly counselor, who signals a new era with the reappearance of figures linked to those responsible for the building of the temple in the early Davidic dynasty (Solomon, Zadok). The status of the priest is an important change from the royal court in the earlier era, for he now takes the rank of chief counselor to the king, an important safeguard to avoid the failures of previous Davidic kings and a strong reminder of the covenant priorities of the Lord.

In its new literary context, this message is appropriate for the community who are in the midst of the rebuilding project. It reveals that God has released them from bondage in Babylon to rebuild the temple, to which his presence will return. This clarifies what was only implicit in the oracle in 2:6–13, which applied the first three visions by calling the people to escape Babylon and rejoice that God's presence was returning. This prophetic sign-act now focuses on the community's role in rebuilding a residence for God's glory.

This section also highlights and sustains the unity between the priestly and royal houses in Israel, an important exhortation as Joshua and Zerubbabel lead the community toward completion of the sanctuary. But it never loses sight of the community as a whole, reminding the leadership that they are not the only ones to return to the land, for it is "those who are far away" who have come and will continue to come to rebuild the temple. The view of the community in Zechariah 1–8 is one that remains hopeful of the ultimate return of the entire community to landed status in Yehud, even though this is not yet a completed reality. Thus, the restoration is not envisioned as a one-time event happening in 538 B.C. under Cyrus, but rather as a series of returns that continue for a time.[33]

---

33. See John Kessler, "Diaspora and Homeland in the Early Achaemenid Period: Community, Geography and Demography in Zech 1-8," in *New Approaches to the Persian Period*, ed. Jon L. Berquist (Semeia Studies; Atlanta: Society of Biblical Literature; Leiden: Brill, 2005).

The emphasis on the prophetic word at the end of the passage (6:15) reminds the audience of the need to obey God's word revealed through the prophets. In this final position in the night vision complex, the conditional clause ("if ...") brings to mind the many lessons learned in the visions and oracles. The night visions have emphasized not only God's grace and mercy toward his covenant people but also his desire for response and repentance. This response involves faith in the One who promised restoration and will protect and be present with them (2:4–5), courage to return to Palestine from the comfort of Babylon (2:6–13), and repentance from oppression of their fellow humanity (5:1–4) and infidelity against their God (5:5–11).

The night visions have consistently placed the prophetic word at the fore. Not only is the prophet the one chosen to reveal God's response to his people, but in the center vision (ch. 4) the prophetic word functions as the oil that fuels the presence and rule of God on earth. This role is depicted in the oracles declared by Zechariah to Zerubbabel as he commences the building of the temple in 4:6b–10a and again is pictured in Zechariah's interaction with Joshua and his priestly associates in chapter 3 and 6:9–15.

A message for today. In what way is this time-bound revelation relevant to the church today? We must start with its redemptive-historical significance. This sign-act signals the reinstatement of priestly and royal houses out of the ashes of the Exile, an act intimately linked to restoration of the temple. For those under the new covenant, it is easy to see the importance of the reinstatement of the royal house because of an emphasis on the Davidic roots of Jesus in the New Testament. But it is difficult to grasp why the priesthood and temple will be resurrected if God's ultimate intention was to transition from a physical temple to a spiritual community and from an exclusive priesthood of Aaron/Levi to a messianic priesthood of Melchizedek (Heb. 4:14–9:28) and an inclusive priesthood of the new covenant community (1 Peter 2:5, 9).[34]

It is important to remind ourselves that the timeline of the history of redemption is not the same as that of the history of revelation. Although the biblical corpus sheds little light on the period after the time of Nehemiah, the covenant community continued to live by faith in what is often dubbed the Intertestamental Period. We must not forget that the temporal interval between Zechariah's time and the coming of Jesus (520 years) is *more* than the interval between Zechariah's time and the kingship of David (450 years).

34. See further J. H. Elliott, *The Elect and the Holy: An Exegetical Examination of I Peter 2:4–10 and the Phrase* basileion hierateuma (NovTSup 12; Leiden: Brill, 2000); idem, *1 Peter: A New Translation with Introduction and Commentary* (AB; New York: Doubleday, 2000).

Although canonically we may feel as if we are on the cusp of the New Testament era, historically we are far from it.

God restores his people to life in the land and provides priests to sustain this remnant community for many years until the arrival of Jesus. The New Testament reveals the role of the temple and its worship in nurturing the messianic hope. Thus in Luke 2:21–40 we meet two individuals in the temple courts who are awaiting the arrival of Christ: Simeon and Anna. They are representatives of the remnant community who were sustained through the ministry of the temple and priests established in Zechariah's time.

Thus, the message of 6:9–15 points to the redemptive-historical acts of God as much as Moses' exodus from Egypt, Joshua's victory in Canaan, David's conquest of Jerusalem, or Solomon's building of the temple. From the ashes of the Exile, God builds a new community by restoring the temple through the priestly and royal lines. Ultimately he will bring his Messiah to supersede temple, priest, and king and create the eschatological people of God, the church.

Through Christ we are linked to Zechariah's community and can listen again to the timeless aspects of his message. The sign-act reveals patterns that are well attested throughout redemptive history and should be incorporated into our lives and communities. (1) The sign-act reveals that we are saved for a purpose. God's salvation from exile is linked in 6:9–15 to the rebuilding of the temple, God's place of residence, from which he exercises his rule on earth. This was true of the Israelites of old, who were saved out of Egypt in order to build a sanctuary for God, the tabernacle, and to worship the Lord God. This was true of David, who, after being given the throne, passionately pursued the establishment of the worship of God in his kingdom by bringing the ark to Jerusalem and preparing materials for the temple. So also Christians are redeemed by God in order to worship him and proclaim his kingship through the gospel.

(2) The sign-act reveals the importance of unity for accomplishing this great purpose. As God calls priestly and royal lines to unite to accomplish the great task of rebuilding, he highlights a principle important throughout the history of redemption: God works through his unified people to accomplish his redemptive work on earth.

(3) Finally, the power of the prophetic word cannot be overlooked. These vignettes remind us that one of God's greatest gifts to his people is his prophetic word, whether that means encouragement or warning, promising or judging. The very fact that God reveals himself to humanity is an incredible expression of grace. God works through communities that pursue his priorities communicated through his Word. For those of us under the new covenant, this Word consists of the canonical expressions of God's servants

in the Old and New Testaments. But God continues to raise up his voices empowered to proclaim and practice this Word with relevance in the present generation. Thus Peter can say with confidence that those with speaking gifts are able to speak "as one speaking the very words of God" (1 Peter 4:11).

Contemporary Significance

SAVED WITH A PURPOSE. It is difficult today to lead the church without using vision, mission, or purpose statements. Trips to various churches reveals, however, the diversity of such statements, which change from community to community. Even in my own church I have seen two different vision statements over the past five years. On one level this shows the incarnational quality of the gospel as it speaks relevantly to various contexts, calling humanity in all of its diversity to God through Christ. On another level, however, it seems to reflect confusion over the purpose of the church.

What is the ultimate purpose of the church? Why has God redeemed us from bondage to sin? For some that purpose is evangelism: to proclaim the gospel to all nations. For many it is worship: to glorify God's name. For others it is service: to provide for the physical needs of the community. For still others it is discipleship: to teach and equip the saints. These and many other priorities are reflected in the variety of statements that accentuate one of these over the others. But is there a purpose that lies at the core of God's redemptive community?

I am convinced that the main purpose of the redeemed people of God is to participate in the restoration of God's rule in this world. Zechariah's community participated in this purpose by rebuilding the temple as the symbol of his presence and rule. Christ came proclaiming this rule of God ("kingdom of God") and inaugurated it through his death, resurrection, and ascension. Today, Christ exercises and extends his rule through the church. Thus, as the church proclaims the gospel, it is fulfilling this purpose by announcing the kingdom. As the church worships the Lord, it attests to this rule on earth. As the church serves its community, it extends the kingdom. As the church equips the saints by teaching them obedience to Christ, it is expanding the rule of God qualitatively deeper into the life of a community of faith.

The early church was well aware of its role in extending the reign of God. They saw themselves as God's temple (1 Cor. 3:16–17; Eph. 2:22), bringing God's rule into everyday life. As they met opposition, they equated it with opposition against the reign of God and his Messiah described in Psalm 2 (Acts 4:23–31). The message of God's rule was on their lips as they proclaimed the gospel. In Romans 10:14–15 Paul links the proclamation of the gospel to that of the messengers in Isaiah 52:7, who declared the victory of God through his powerful arm. That message of peace, good tidings, and salvation was simply: "Your God reigns."

Thus, God's rule is extended through a businesswoman who portrays the qualities of God's character in her work. This means not only sharing the message of the gospel to fellow workers, but more importantly bringing Christian perspective, conscience, and behavior to a world where compromise is often the norm. God's rule is extended through a plumber who exercises the creativity he possesses through the redeemed image of God within to provide the necessities of life. God's rule is extended through the family, which provides for their community an example of God's grace in relationships. We often miss the greatest opportunities for extending the reign of God in our world by limiting our vision to what are often considered vocational ministry positions such as missionaries, pastors, and evangelists. God has called all of us to extend his kingdom, bringing his presence into the entire world through word and deed.

Through the sign-act of 6:9–15, the prophet reminds the people that they have been redeemed from captivity for a purpose. As they give of their resources to the rebuilding project, they are participating in God's redemptive program to bring his presence and rule on earth.

Unified for that purpose. Closely related is the theme of unity, which reminds us of the crucial role that the community plays in accomplishing this purpose. In the early church the reign of God was extended not through lone rangers traipsing across the Roman empire but through groups living and even travelling in fellowship (e.g., Acts 13:1–5). Jesus lay the foundation for this principle by sending out his disciples "two by two" during his earthly ministry (Luke 10:1). He continued this trend after his ascension by inaugurating his mission through the church at a gathering of his followers in Jerusalem on the day of Pentecost (Acts 2). Although several main characters emerged from this community throughout Acts (Peter, John, James, Paul), these characters are firmly rooted in the community from which they were sent to extend the kingdom and to which they returned to find support (e.g., Acts 4:23–31). Their unity extended to even the sharing of financial resources (4:32–35).

Working and living in unity with others to accomplish God's purpose takes humility. Joshua is given special privileges in Zechariah 6:9–15, but he is reminded at the same time that another will soon arrive who will take leadership in the rebuilding project. Obedience to this word means preferring one another for the sake of the kingdom. There is little room for those who grasp after position or honor.

This is a constant temptation for leaders within the church today, young or old. When I was a youth pastor, a key leader and I would take a short canoe outing during our annual pastor's retreat. It was an opportunity to just relax and talk about life, but it also served as teachable moments, at least for me. One year as I contemplated my future, my mentor told me of a lesson he had learned in his life: "Mark, deepen your ministry where you are and allow God to broaden it." To an impatient young man tempted to grasp after "greater" things, this was a poignant reminder that my life and times are in God's hands and that my grasping only distracts me from the most important priority of deepening my life and ministry.

Joshua is exhorted to define himself in terms of another (*ṣemaḥ*); that is, he will have to learn how to play the harmony rather than the melody. Similarly, we are called to do the same in life and ministry, whether that means serving our spouse or children and placing their needs above our own or serving our fellow workers whether above or below us on the corporate or ecclesial flow chart. This echoes the teaching of Jesus on leadership. When a dispute arose among the disciples over who would wield the most authority and power, Jesus contrasted the leadership approach of the Gentiles, who "lord it over them," and his kingdom: "The greatest among you should be like the youngest, and the one who rules like the one who serves" (Luke 22:24–30; cf. Matt. 20:25–28; Mark 10:42–45).

Unity is often thwarted by grasping after position and honor, but it also cannot be assured through vision statements. No doubt one of the greatest priorities of church leadership today is the creation and adoption of vision and mission statements. But such statements do not necessarily guarantee unity within the ranks of the church. If the adoption of these statements is not accompanied by love and humility from leaders, they will be rendered ineffective.

I remember another mentor exhorting me to love my people in the early phases of my ministry in a church. He encouraged me to continue the programs that were presently in place for at least a year and focus attention on loving the people under my care. Although frustrating for a strong leader, such patient shepherding creates the necessary conditions for the transformation of vision and mission. One must earn the right to lead God's people, which comes through competence accompanied by love. In this way vision and mission can move ahead in unity.

Such sensitivity to the issue of unity is important as a community of faith embarks on new phases of ministry. Once I led a pastoral staff through a vision/mission exercise that caught the imagination of many on the staff. They were ready to pursue a unified vision rather than merely sustain past familiar practices. However, not everyone was prepared to sign on, and some noted that key lay leaders needed to participate in the process as well. Although disappointing for those who had embraced new vision, it was wise for this staff to pursue a longer process to ensure that all leadership as well as the congregation would own the vision. It took two more years, but the result was greater ownership and unity within that community of faith.

In the New Testament the apostle Paul spends considerable time speaking to the issue of relationships within the church, for he was convinced of the centrality of the church in furthering Christ's kingdom in this world. Paul was passionate for mission, but he knew that such mission would never be accomplished through disunified communities. This message is echoed in Zechariah 6:9–15 as the prophet calls the priestly community to await the coming *ṣemaḥ* and follow his leadership.

Proclaiming that purpose. Obedience to the prophetic word is strongly urged at the end of 6:9–15. We have already touched on this theme, which appears regularly throughout chapters 1–8. Zechariah traces his word back to the God who sent him. He speaks not on his own authority or initiative but rather as a spokesperson for Almighty God. Similarly, Christ has raised up the church as his prophetic voice in this generation. When he sent forth the church in the power of the Spirit at Pentecost, Peter taught that this was the fulfillment of the prophet Joel (Acts 2). Interestingly, Joel's prophecy speaks of God's pouring out his Spirit so that his people will prophesy. The events of Pentecost, therefore, are interpreted as the ultimate fulfillment of the prophetic office in redemptive history. Through the Spirit-indwelt church God proclaims his rule in Jerusalem, Judea, and Samaria, and to the ends of the earth (Acts 1:8).

Zechariah's confidence is based exclusively on the fact that he has been "sent" by God. He does not act on his own authority but on God's authority. This authority, however, is derived from the fact that his words find their origin in the mind of God. For the church today, commissioned to proclaim his rule in the present generation, this means passionate pursuit of God and his Word. Through Scripture and prayer God invites us into his throne room to shape our minds and fill our tongues with a timely and relevant message for our generation.

This is true for laity in the church as well, on whom the world will look and hopefully echo the Sanhedrin's evaluation of Peter and John: "They took note that these men had been with Jesus" (Acts 4:13). It is also true for those commissioned by God to feed his flock through the preaching and teaching of the Word that their gospel may come "not simply with words, but also with power, with the Holy Spirit and with deep conviction" (1 Thess. 1:5).

Obeying that purpose. Zechariah's message ends with the hope that this "will happen if you diligently obey the LORD your God" (6:15). As we will discover in chapters 7–8, even though there are positive signs in the response of the people in 1:6b, this community is still struggling with disobedience.

This is an important reminder to the new covenant community that they are not only sent to proclaim the prophetic Word of the gospel with faithfulness, but also exhorted to listen to the Word of God with obedience.

God continues to speak through his prophetic Word, the Scriptures, and sends generation after generation of interpreters who are gifted in translating this word into contemporary idiom. As the church we are called to bend our knees before God's Word, to search the Scriptures to check the accuracy of teaching, and to fulfill its demands. God promises much blessing to the kind of community who adopts the posture of submission before his Word, even the blessing of the presence of the ultimate *ṣemaḥ*, Jesus Christ.

This is often difficult in a world that constantly distracts our attention from the message and values of the Word. This explains why the prophet expresses this final phrase so strongly ("*diligently* obey"). He knows how easy it is to lose sight of biblical priorities. Note that this call to diligent obedience is prefaced by an emphasis on the source of the Word; that is, God's people must obey diligently because this is a word from God. This shows us the importance of our theology of Scripture to obedience.

When we accept that these words are "God-breathed," then it is not surprising that they are "useful for teaching, rebuking, correcting and training in righteousness" (2 Tim. 3:16). When we grasp "that no prophecy of Scripture came about by the prophet's own interpretation. For prophecy never had its origin in the will of man, but men spoke from God as they were carried along by the Holy Spirit," then we will "do well to pay attention to it, as to a light shining in a dark place" (2 Peter 1:19–21). Diligent obedience to God's Word is based on acceptance of the authority of the Word.

For the new covenant community, this acceptance and obedience are based on an exciting development in New Testament theology, namely, that the source of the Word, the Spirit of God, indwells us and empowers us to accept it and fulfill its demands (Gal. 5:25). Diligent obedience involves a life of trust in the source of all obedience, the Spirit of Christ, who animates us to reject the "acts of the sinful nature" and to bear "the fruit of the Spirit" (5:19–23).

Zechariah 7

IN THE FOURTH year of King Darius, the word of the LORD came to Zechariah on the fourth day of the ninth month, the month of Kislev. [2]The people of Bethel had sent Sharezer and Regem-Melech, together with their men, to entreat the LORD [3]by asking the priests of the house of the LORD Almighty and the prophets, "Should I mourn and fast in the fifth month, as I have done for so many years?"

[4]Then the word of the LORD Almighty came to me: [5]"Ask all the people of the land and the priests, 'When you fasted and mourned in the fifth and seventh months for the past seventy years, was it really for me that you fasted? [6]And when you were eating and drinking, were you not just feasting for yourselves? [7]Are these not the words the LORD proclaimed through the earlier prophets when Jerusalem and its surrounding towns were at rest and prosperous, and the Negev and the western foothills were settled?'"

[8]And the word of the LORD came again to Zechariah: [9]"This is what the LORD Almighty says: 'Administer true justice; show mercy and compassion to one another. [10]Do not oppress the widow or the fatherless, the alien or the poor. In your hearts do not think evil of each other.'

[11]"But they refused to pay attention; stubbornly they turned their backs and stopped up their ears. [12]They made their hearts as hard as flint and would not listen to the law or to the words that the LORD Almighty had sent by his Spirit through the earlier prophets. So the LORD Almighty was very angry.

[13]"'When I called, they did not listen; so when they called, I would not listen,' says the LORD Almighty. [14]'I scattered them with a whirlwind among all the nations, where they were strangers. The land was left so desolate behind them that no one could come or go. This is how they made the pleasant land desolate.'"

Original Meaning

VERSE 1 SIGNALS the beginning of a new section in Zechariah and catapults the reader forward nearly two years from the date given in 1:7. The fourth day of the ninth month (Kislev) in the fourth year of Darius is December 7, 518 B.C. In terms of the temple rebuilding project this comes near the midpoint between the refounding ceremony (Hag. 2:10–23; cf. Zech. 4:6–10a) and its completion (Ezra 6:14). Although there are allusions to the project in the prophetic response,[1] most likely it is the progress on rebuilding that motivates the delegation's question. As elsewhere in Zechariah, the focus of attention transcends the temple effort.[2]

The appearance of a delegation is not surprising, considering they arrive in 518 B.C., sixty-nine years after the destruction of Jerusalem, close to the end of the seventy years of exile prophesied by Jeremiah (Jer. 29:10; cf. Zech. 7:3, 5). Since a rebuilt temple for the manifest presence of God is clearly a sign of the expected restoration, it is natural to ask a question that is related to the cessation of the fasting ritual that had marked their worship during the Exile. In other words, they are asking about more than just their fasting liturgy; they are also inquiring about the timing of redemptive history: "Is the Exile over?"[3]

A development on the imperial level provides further background to the inquiry and reply in chapters 7–8. One of Darius's great gifts was his administrative abilities that provided lines of accountability. As already noted in the introduction (see Original Meaning section), Darius's use of authorities loyal to the crown is evident in the work of Zerubbabel and Joshua. One example of his administrative prowess is his order for Egyptian laws to be codified, an order that occurred in the fourth year of his reign.[4] Such legal and ritual codification on the Western frontier of the empire may explain the episode found in Zechariah 7–8. The temple authorities are to provide direction for this local legal code, and Zechariah is a key figure for discerning both ritual and moral law.

The historical encounter between prophet and people is encased in the form we now have in chapters 7–8 through a process of editing.[5] We will

---

1. Although the section in which this allusion is found (8:9–13), it is drawn from or refers to an earlier prophetic utterance by Zechariah; see Boda, "Fasts to Feasts," 390–407.

2. See Boda, "Penitential Prophet," 49–69.

3. Notice the link between the seventy years and the practice of fasting and prayer liturgy in Dan. 9:1–4, which is interestingly also set in the period of a king named Darius and, as here, includes a rebuke that discipline will continue because of the presence of sin in the community (9:20–24).

4. See Meyers and Meyers, *Haggai*, 380.

5. For redactional levels in Zech. 7–8 see Boda, "Fasts to Feasts," 390–407.

focus our attention on the rhetoric of this final form. These two chapters are bracketed by two groups of people with foreign origins who "entreat the LORD" (7:2; 8:21). This literary technique (inclusion) binds the pieces as a unit to be read together. This suggests that for Zechariah, the original discussion about fasting is an opportunity for deeper reflection on God's priorities and purposes for this community.

The prophet begins by addressing the intentions of their fasting liturgy since the fall of Jerusalem and subtly links them with the generation that originally invited God's discipline (7:4–14). This functions as implicit motivation for them to break the patterns of the past. The prophet then moves to the future, promising God's salvation of the remnant to fulfill their mission of blessing among the nations. This new era of salvation will be typified by feasting, not fasting, as Yahweh and his people renew covenant relationship, and Yahweh's presence among his people will draw many nations to this renewed community. The inauguration of this new era is linked to God's passion for his people and the obedience of his people to his covenant demands.

These two chapters have been composed with the earlier sections of Zechariah in mind. The opening pericope of Zechariah depicted the prophet echoing the message of the earlier prophets (1:2–6a) and the people responding to this message (1:6b). The next major section (1:7–6:15) presented God's answer to this response, promising and enacting salvation and inviting the people to return and rebuild. In 1:7–6:15, however, there is evidence that not all is right in this community (ch. 5) and that there are outstanding issues.

These first two sections are introduced by historical superscriptions (1:1, 7) with a date formula. Zechariah 7:1, however, diverges from this pattern by affixing the narrative marker *wayehi* (untranslated in NIV; lit., "and it was"). This word is often used in Hebrew narrative to introduce another event in a particular story. In Zechariah this marker signals the next step in the story structured by the historical superscriptions. It appeared that the people's response in 1:6b was a sign of repentance, but 7:1 reopens this issue and reveals that there is cause for concern, although hope for a truly penitent people. Zechariah 7–8 functions as an important transition from Restoration Already in chapters 1–6 to Restoration Not Yet in chapters 9–14.[6]

For the purposes of this commentary we will divide our discussion of chs. 7–8 into three parts (7:1–14; 8:1–13; 8:14–23). However, one must always keep in mind that the two chapters were designed as a complete unit.

---

6. See Boda, "Fasts to Feasts," 390–407.

Narrative Introduction and Question of Delegation— Entreating Yahweh (7:1–3)

ZECHARIAH 7:1 SETS this prophetic passage in the wider context of ancient Near Eastern history and, in particular, the redemptive history of Israel (see above). The use of Darius's reign to orient the reader is a trend already encountered earlier in 1:1 and 7, but 7:1 has two unique characteristics. (1) The text adds the royal designation to Darius's name as "King Darius" and in so doing reminds the reader that this is a particular era in redemptive history, one not defined by the Davidic dynasty but rather by a foreign hegemony.[7]

(2) The date formula is split in two with the year and day/month separated by the messenger formula.[8] This awkward separation is likely related to the close relationship between the actions of Zechariah here and those of Jeremiah. Jeremiah 36 relates how Jeremiah sent Baruch to the temple on a day of fasting to warn the people about God's impending judgment, with hopes that their repentance would avert God's discipline. According to 36:1 this occurred in the fourth year of Jehoiakim and the reading of the message took place in the ninth month (36:9, 22)—two different dates now appearing together in Zechariah 7:1. The significant allusions to the message of the earlier prophets and especially to Jeremiah and the rejection of this message by the former generation, all in the context of inappropriate fasting practices, point to an allusion in Zechariah to Jeremiah's experience. Zechariah is being cast in the line of the earlier prophets as he echoes their message to his own generation.

The scene opens with some people from Bethel[9] approaching the officials at the temple in Jerusalem for a decision on a liturgical matter. The appearance of this delegation of recently returned Jews[10] has significance on both socio-historical as well as theological levels. It reveals the increasing role for Jerusalem as the religio-political center of the province of Yehud. But we should recall that Bethel was one of the two key religious centers of the former idolatrous northern kingdom of Israel (1 Kings 12:28–33). Now "Bethel,

7. See in this vein, Stuhlmueller, *Rebuilding*, 102; Petersen, *Haggai*, 282. Stuhlmueller concludes: "Israel's aspirations are no longer to center upon kingship and its earthly domain but upon the temple and its priesthood."

8. See Boda, "Penitential Prophet," 60 n. 38.

9. Ezra 2:28 (par. Neh. 7:32) attests to a Jewish community at Bethel in the early Persian period. The archaeological record has been much debated. All agree that Bethel was spared in the Babylonian invasion of 597–596 B.C., but the precise date of its demise in the sixth century is uncertain, with dates ranging from 570 to 500 B.C. The site was rejuvenated in the mid-fifth century B.C. (cf. Carter, *Emergence*, 124–26).

10. The name Sharezer is a Mesopotamian name, but his declaration that he has been fasting for so many years reveals his strong adherence to Yahwism.

once in a position to send prophets of the Lord away (Amos 7:13), comes to Jerusalem to ask a question of the Lord."[11] The appearance of this delegation reveals the supremacy of Jerusalem as the central shrine of remnant Jewish faith. It may also suggest a future hope of a renewal of the united kingdom.

This delegation comes "to entreat the LORD" (lit., "to seek the face of Yahweh"), a phrase used in contexts where God's people are seeking relief from difficult circumstances (Ex. 32:11; 1 Sam. 13:12; 1 Kings 13:6; 2 Kings 13:4; Ps. 119:58; Jer. 26:19; Dan. 9:13; Mal. 1:9). Its use in Daniel 9:13 is intriguing for there it is found in the context of a penitential liturgy similar to that alluded to in Zechariah 7. This shows that the question asked here is not a detached query for liturgical direction but a muted plea to God to bring an end to the period of discipline.

The question is posed to the "priests of the house of the LORD Almighty and the prophets," the two sources of revelation in the temple precincts. The priests were commissioned to offer interpretations or rulings for specific situations based on the law[12] and to provide access to direct revelation through the use of Urim and Thummim. The temple prophets provided direct revelation in oracular form.[13] Because the priests are mentioned first and the question posed is binary in character (it can be answered by yes or no),[14] presumably the priests are expected to provide the answer. Instead, the delegation receives a far more complicated answer that deepens the view of their role in inaugurating the new era of restoration (repentance) and expands their view of the eventual goal of this new era (nations).

The question posed in 7:3 concerns liturgical practice, an observation confirmed by the reference to the "fifth month" (a specific time) and "so many years" (a consistent routine). The words for "mourn" (*bakah*, "to weep, cry") and "fast" (*nazar*, "to deny oneself")[15] are not the more technical liturgical terms used in Zechariah's reply in 7:5 but probably reflect the vocabulary of the laity posing the question.[16] Zechariah will clarify the character of this

---

11. E. W. Conrad, *Zechariah* (Readings; Sheffield: Sheffield Academic Press, 1999), 133–34, 138.

12. See the comments on the Torah ruling of Hag. 2:10–14.

13. A. R. Johnson, *The Cultic Prophet in Ancient Israel* (Cardiff: University of Wales, 1962); R. J. Tournay, *Seeing and Hearing God with the Psalms: The Prophetic Liturgy of the Second Temple in Jerusalem* (JSOTSup 118; Sheffield: Sheffield Academic Press, 1991); cf. Boda, "Complaint," 192.

14. See H. Huffmon, "Priestly Divination in Israel," in *The Word of the Lord Shall Go Forth*, ed. C. L. Meyers and M. O'Connor (Winona Lake, Ind.: Eisenbrauns/ASOR, 1983), 355–59.

15. This is a more general word for separation from the unholy and separation to God for holy purposes; see the Nazirite custom (Num. 6; Judg. 13). Its connection to fasting comes through the Nazirites abstaining from certain kinds of foods.

16. *Bakah* is a more general term for weeping, either in a positive sense (Gen. 33:4) or, more commonly, negative (Gen. 21:16; Ex. 2:6), while *sapad* is restricted to mourning rites

practice but will also expand the liturgical routine in view to include fasts during the fourth, seventh, and tenth months as well as the fifth (8:19). His reference to the "seventy years" in 7:5 (cf. "so many years" in 7:3) links this fasting routine to the fall of Judah in 587 B.C., and the citation of these particular months associates them with several crucial events surrounding this demise:[17]

Month	Event	Reference
Tenth (588)	Beginning of siege of Jerusalem	2 Kings 25:1; Jer. 39:1
Fourth (587)	Jerusalem walls breached;[18] leadership fled	2 Kings 25:3–7; Jer. 39:1–10; 52:6–11
Fifth	Jerusalem destroyed	2 Kings 25:8–12; Jer. 52:12–16
Seventh	Assassination of Gedaliah[19]	2 Kings 25:25–26; Jer. 41:1–3

Throughout the Old Testament fasting rituals were regularly practiced but rarely legislated. Although fasting accompanied experiences of revelation from God in the case of Moses and Elijah (Ex. 34:28; 1 Kings 19:6–12), it was usually associated with circumstances of disaster often linked to sin and penitence (1 Sam. 7:6; 2 Sam. 12:16).[20]

Such fasting functioned not only as a penitential act representing the sorrow of the people for sin (Joel 2:12–13) but also as a communicative act, a cry to the God who could transform their circumstances (2 Sam. 12:16;

---

and lamentation (Jer. 49:3; 14:13), but is often linked with *bakah* (Gen. 23:2; 2 Sam. 1:12; Ezek. 24:16; Mic. 1:8–10). *Nazar* is an elusive term, used elsewhere to refer to separation from something, thus in the Nazirite vow the individual is to separate from or abstain from certain liquids (Num. 6:3), but it can refer to other types of separation (see Lev. 15:31; 22:2; Ezek. 14:7). In contrast, *ṣum* refers exclusively to abstaining from food (2 Sam. 12:16–17; Est. 4:16).

17. This is generally accepted by biblical scholars. See Ackroyd, *Exile*, 207 n. 122.

18. It is difficult to determine if the Babylonians breached the wall first, following which the king and his troops (holed up in the palace) fled through the break in the wall (Jer. 39:1–10), or whether the king and his army broke through the wall during the night to escape the famine (2 Kings 25:3–7; Jer. 52:6–11).

19. There is some evidence of a mourning ritual (although no fasting is mentioned) in the seventh month already in place prior to Gedaliah's assassination (Jer. 41:1, 4–6) which had as its destination the "house of the LORD." This may have replaced the Day of Atonement (Lev. 16), which without temple personnel and structure would have been difficult to practice. The assassination of Gedaliah would have given another reason to mourn and fast on this day.

20. The legislation for the Day of Atonement in Lev. 16 uses the term *nazar* found also in Zech. 7:3 in the mouth of the delegation. This probably refers to fasting and in the legislation is linked to the issue of sin to avert disaster for the community.

Isa. 58:3–4, 9; Jer. 14:12). The cries used on such days are preserved in Lamentations, Psalms (Ps. 74; 79; 106), and the Persian period narrative books (Ezra 9; Neh. 1, 9; Dan. 9).[21] These compositions were designed to bring an end to the period of God's discipline of the nation, following the agenda for renewal expressed in Deuteronomy 30, Leviticus 26, and 1 Kings 8. Although there is no mention of fasting in these agenda texts, fasting and weeping were evidently acceptable outward expressions of the repentance and prayer demanded (see Ezra 9:3–5; 10:1; Neh. 1:4; 9:1; Dan. 9:3).

The role of the prophets on these days is difficult to discern from the Persian period narrative books. Although in the Babylonian period the prophet played an important role in fasting liturgies (Jer. 14–15),[22] as the Persian period progressed that role seems to have been replaced by reading the Torah and perhaps also prophetic writings (Neh. 9).[23] Zechariah's strong reliance on the "earlier prophets" as he responds to the delegation's question reveals a fasting liturgy in transition and shows that he is echoing the style of the fasting liturgy. This explains his moving the discussion to the level of intentions and ethical behavior as he seeks to recover the original intention of the fasting liturgy drawn from Leviticus 26, Deuteronomy 30, and 1 Kings 8.

Zechariah's Challenge of Fasting Ritual (7:4–6)

ALTHOUGH THE QUESTION originated with a delegation from Bethel, Zechariah's speech includes all the people of Yehud and priests as well as all the fasting activity of the various communities (7:5; 8:19). He uses the more technical language. His term for fasting (*ṣum*, in contrast to *nazar*) is limited to ritual abstinence from food, while his term for lamentation (*sapad*, in contrast to *bakah*) denotes cries to God in moments of pain. This reveals the communicative nature of the fasting liturgy. It was designed to gain the ear of God and to express the repentance of the people. This is why Zechariah asks whether these liturgies were done for God—that is, as an act of true repentance to help build a relationship with God—or merely to free themselves from the circumstances of discipline. The Hebrew builds up terms to

---

21. See recent work on these compositions and settings in Boda, *Praying*; idem, "Priceless Gain," 51–75; Werline, *Penitential Prayer*; R. J. Bautch, *Developments in Genre Between Post-Exilic Penitential Prayers and the Psalms of Communal Lament* (SBLABS; Atlanta: Society of Biblical Literature, 2003).

22. See Boda, "Complaint," 186–97; cf. Isa 58.

23. This is made explicit in Neh. 9:3 (Torah as written entity) and Dan. 9:2 (Jeremiah as written book), and implicitly through the anthological use of the Torah in all the Persian period prayers. Cf. Boda, *Praying*, 30–32; Newman, "Nehemiah 9," 112–23; Newman, *Praying*.

communicate the passion of this message from God (lit., "really fast ... for me myself").

Zechariah then asks a question directed at eating and drinking (7:6). Some have seen here a reference to the festal schedule of Israel while others interpret it as terms for normal nourishment.[24] The word pair "eating" (*ʾakal*) and "drinking" (*šatah*) is used elsewhere to refer both to normal nourishment (Ex. 34:28; Deut. 2:6, 28; 2 Sam. 19:36; Jer. 22:15) and to celebration (1 Kings 18:41; Isa. 22:13), but in these contexts it does not refer to the celebration of a regular feast. Alluding to Isaiah 22:13,[25] Zechariah expands his message to include those who have not participated in the fasting rituals of the exilic period. There is no difference between those who fasted and those who feasted in this community, for neither display true repentance.

Review of God's Word and Discipline in the Past (7:7–14)

IN 7:7 ZECHARIAH asks one final question as he turns to the past to show the dire consequences of rejecting true repentance. The phrase "the words the LORD proclaimed through the earlier prophets" refers to the amalgamation of phrases in verses 9–10 from Jeremiah, an "earlier prophet," whose prophecies were vindicated by history (contra Hananiah, Jer. 28).

This earlier prophet declared these words during a time of the prosperity and peace in Jerusalem and its surrounding towns and the settlement of the Negev and the western foothills. The Negev was the southern desert region of Yehud, which formed the frontier of the kingdom and needed ideal conditions for civilization (military security, favorable climatic conditions). The western foothills, known as the Shephelah, were the range of hills and valleys lying between the central hill country at the center of Yehud and the coastal plain along the Mediterranean. The Shephelah was often contested between the Israelites and Philistines (here the stories of Samson and David and Goliath take place), and only when the kingdom of Judah reached the pinnacle of political success did it reach its full potential in terms of population and prosperity.

The contrast between this picture and the experience of the Persian period community, assumed in the language used ("when ... at rest and prosperous"), is confirmed by archaeological evidence. In the early Persian period the size

24. For the festal interpretation see Redditt; *Haggai*, 82; for normal nourishment, see Baldwin *Haggai*, 144.

25. Where Isaiah uses the images of eating and drinking to accentuate a lack of repentance by the people of Judah. Instead of engaging in penitential rites (weeping, tearing out hair, and wearing sackcloth) as God instructed, they are fulfilling their appetites and accepting their destiny: "Let us eat and drink for tomorrow we die."

of Yehud was considerably smaller than even the reduced pre-fall size and did not include the Negev or the western foothills.[26] This picture serves two purposes in the overall scope of Zechariah's message in chapters 7–8. (1) It reveals the prosperity and peace that the former generation squandered in their refusal to repent (7:11–14), accentuating their folly. (2) It hints at the conditions the Persian period community should expect if they obey the voice of their prophet Zechariah (8:1–19).

In 7:8–10, Zechariah delivers afresh the message of the earlier prophets. The language reflects standard prophetic speech with a mixture of exhortations and prohibitions that are general, yet also focused on specific vulnerable groups in Israel.[27] The vocabulary is drawn from Jeremiah 7:5–6 (cf. 22:3), where the prophet warns the people about relying too much on the temple in order to avoid God's discipline ("This is the temple of the LORD, the temple of the LORD, the temple of the LORD!" 7:4). Rather, he calls them to "really change your ways and your actions" (7:5), lest God do to the temple what he did to Shiloh (7:12–15). This collection of vocabulary and motifs are striking, considering the temple reconstruction in Zechariah's day.

The message identifies three positive exhortations followed by two prohibitions. These focus attention on the need for social justice as an expression of covenant faithfulness. To "administer true justice" is to hear legal disputes without bias. This word "true" means "faithful" in the Hebrew Bible and often linked to God's character (Ex. 20:6; 34:6). Judging faithfully here speaks of judging with faithful adherence to God's law no matter who stands before the court.[28]

One challenge is to administer true justice, but one can live according to the letter of the law and miss the spirit of the law. This is why the initial exhortation is balanced splendidly by the next two imperatives: "show mercy and compassion." These two characteristics are regularly linked to the character of Yahweh and his people throughout the Old Testament (Ex. 34:6). The first characteristic is the Hebrew word *ḥesed*, which describes the loyalty expected of those who have entered into covenant. The word describes God's loyalty to his covenant people and appears regularly in a phrase translated as "keeps covenant of love" (Ex. 20:6; 34:6–7). This characteristic of Yahweh is to be replicated in the life of God's people (Hos. 6:6; 10:12; 12:6; Mic. 6:8; cf. 2 Sam. 9:1), even if they often failed to live up to this ideal (Hos. 4:1; 6:4).

26. Carter gives a picture of the socioeconomic extent and prosperity of the province of Yehud; C. E. Carter, *The Emergence of Yehud in the Persian Period* (JSOTSup 294; Sheffield: Sheffield Academic Press, 1999), 249–324.

27. Cf. Petersen, *Haggai*, 289–291.

28. Isa. 1:23 reveals that bribes could pervert justice in Israel, tipping the courts in favor of the rich over the poor like the widow and fatherless.

This is also true of the second characteristic: "compassion" (*raḥamim*), which is often paired with *ḥesed* (Ps. 25:6; 40:11; 51:1; 69:16; Jer. 16:5; Hos. 2:21). It is regularly contrasted with the anger of God (Deut. 13:17; Ps. 77:9; Zech. 1:13–16), indicating the emotional character of this term. This character is displayed vividly in 1 Kings 3:26, where it describes the pity of a mother for her threatened child. The earlier prophets called the people to not only administer justice faithfully but to do it with the spirit of faithful loyalty and tender compassion.

These positive exhortations lay the foundation for the prohibitions that follow. The prophets were reflecting a strong theme in the Torah when they prohibited oppression of widows, the fatherless, and aliens. Deuteronomy especially emphasizes God's protection of these types of people (Deut. 10:18) while calling God's covenant nation to the same standard (14:29; 16:11, 14; 24:17–21; 26:12, 13; 27:19). The prophets criticize the people for breaking this covenant value (Isa. 1:17, 23; 10:2; Jer. 7:6; 22:3; Ezek. 22:7).[29] Zechariah expands the list to include the category "poor," which usually appears in tandem with "needy" (*ʾebyon*; e.g., Deut. 15:11) and sometimes with "alien" (e.g., Ezek. 22:29) and widows and fatherless (e.g., Isa. 10:2).

Only in Zechariah, however, do we find the combination of all four categories. This final term "poor" makes it clear that the three other categories are examples of those who were vulnerable within ancient Near Eastern societies, stripped of their socioeconomic safety net. For the fatherless and widow this was caused by the absence of the male provider; for the alien it was the absence of clan protection and connection.[30] These allusions to vulnerable members of the Jewish community, however, are more than just images. Socio-historical research on Zechariah's community reveals economic vulnerability for many within the society.[31]

While the first prohibition makes specific the general tone of the exhortations, the second one focuses on internal threats to covenant justice and loyalty: "In your hearts do not think evil of each other." The Old Testament law was ultimately concerned with the internal life of the people (see Bridging Contexts section of Zech. 5:1–4). "Think" suggests plotting, scheming, and planning. The word "evil" is not a moral term but rather means disaster or harm (cf. Ezek. 38:10), which can have moral implications.[32] Because of

---

29. One sees how abhorrent the nation has become when God even rejects widows and orphans in Isa. 9:17.

30. This vulnerability is vividly displayed in the book of Ruth in which Naomi represents both widow and alien in Ruth 1. This explains the depth of her pain and fear of the future.

31. See Carter, *Emergence*, 285; cf. Neh. 5; Hag. 1–2; Zech. 8:10–12.

32. Thus, Yahweh "plans disaster" on the disobedient: Jer. 26:3 ("the disaster I was planning"); cf. 29:11; 36:3. Notice the way in which Micah plays with this phrase to announce judgment: The people plan disaster (2:1) and thus God will plan disaster for them (2:3).

the context in which this appears, this scheming is to be seen in the context of legal disputes and oppression, something made more clear when it reappears in Zechariah 8:16–17 in connection with giving false testimony (cf. Ps. 10:2; Mic. 2:1).[33] The earlier prophets prohibited even the plotting of harm against one another.

This summary of the teaching of the earlier prophets is not merely a recitation of past facts but is designed to speak to Zechariah's own generation (7:7, "Are these not the words. . . ?"). Here he defines more clearly his concern over the fasting liturgies of his contemporaries and why they are not "for me" (Yahweh). Fasting activity that is supposed to be based on the agenda of Israel's law is missing the main purpose, namely, the renewal of covenant relationship with Yahweh through repentance from the ways of the past.

Having completed his recitation of the themes of the earlier prophets, Zechariah now returns to the main story line. He describes the earlier generation's refusal to respond to the message of the prophets by heaping up several images. (1) He uses an image drawn from animal husbandry ("they stubbornly . . . turned their backs"), in which an animal refuses the yoke (cf. "to stiffen the neck" in Neh. 9:29). (2) Next he depicts their refusal through the image of self-imposed deafness of hearing ("stopped their ears").[34] (3) Finally, he matches two external images with an internal image of the "heart," seen as the seat of the affections, which is turned to a hard stone ("flint").[35] These images depict the willful refusal to listen to God's words communicated through the law and the voices of the earlier prophets (2 Kings 17:13–15), whose words were also direct revelation from Yahweh since they were delivered "by his Spirit."[36]

This willful rejection has resulted in God's becoming "angry" toward that generation (7:12), and his wrath spread quickly from affection to action (7:13–14). The Hebrew text of 7:13 appears at first sight awkward because it begins: "'When he called, they did not listen, so when they called, I would not listen,' says the LORD Almighty." This awkwardness is part of Zechariah's style as he moves from description to quotation.[37] God refuses to listen to those who refuse to listen to him.

But God's discipline involved more than just cutting off communication; he "scattered them with a whirlwind among all the nations." This use of storm imagery is typical of prophetic speech and is used often in connection

---

33. So Baldwin, *Haggai*, 154.

34. Only used elsewhere of people in Isa. 6:10 (cf. 59:1 for God).

35. The LXX translates *šamir* as *apeithe* ("disobedient"), the Vulgate as *admas* ("hard"), showing that neither understood this as a rock.

36. As Petersen aptly expresses: "This notion of spirit enables the prophets to be viewed as direct agents of the deity: to reject them is to reject the deity"; Petersen, *Haggai*, 293.

37. So Merrill and also Baldwin who says that this is "not uncommon in the prophets," Baldwin, *Haggai*, 148; Merrill, *Haggai*, 215–16.

with God's wrath.[38] The image here is most likely of chaff being blown by the wind (cf. Isa. 40:24; 41:16; Hos. 13:3) as the people are scattered among "all the nations."[39] These nations are described here as those "which they did not know" (NIV, "where they were strangers"), a phrase that appears regularly in Deuteronomy and Jeremiah to refer to gods, people, or land, but never to nations (Deut. 13:2; 28:33; Jer. 7:9; 15:14; 16:13; 17:4; 22:28). The phrase highlights the vulnerability of life for those living among the nations.[40]

Thus, God's anger was first expressed through his refusal to listen to his people and then through scattering them among the nations. In the first action he reversed the covenant intimacy promised to Abraham in Genesis 17, so essential to Israel's experience with Yahweh (Gen. 17:7).[41] In the second action he dealt a blow to the seed promised to Abraham who were now scattered as chaff to the nations (17:4–6). In his final action he caused the desolation of the land (17:8), which was so thoroughly ruined that normal human activity could not be pursued, an image typical of the prophetic curses (Jer. 9:9–11; Ezek. 36:33–36).

With the final sentence of the historical overview, Zechariah returns his audience to the point of departure by reminding them of the positive conditions of the earlier generation (cf. 7:7 and 7:14), while juxtaposing this with the devastation they experienced.[42] He makes it clear that although God has been the subject of the verbs describing discipline, the people were ultimately responsible for this by their active refusal to listen.

In summary, in this section Zechariah offers not only the message of the earlier prophets but also a history lesson in the consequences of ignoring or rejecting God's message (cf. Zech. 1:1–6). In doing this, the prophet is not on a tangent unrelated to the original question of the delegation. This review of Israel's story began with his question: "Are these not the words . . ." which were related directly to his concern over the fasting practices during the past seventy years. Furthermore, the language of 7:4–14 displays links to the penitential prayer liturgy of the exilic period[43] and to the vocabulary and style of

---

38. Isa. 29:6; 40:24; 41:16; Jer. 23:19; 30:23.

39. Cf. Petersen, *Haggai*, 148; Merrill, *Haggai*, 216.

40. See Petersen, *Haggai*, 295 and H. Huffmon, "The Treaty Background of Hebrew *yada*ᶜ," *BASOR* 181 (1966): 331–37.

41. See Clines's (*Theme*) excellent view on the themes of the Pentateuch arranged around the three promises to Abraham: promise of covenant, seed, and land.

42. In the Heb. text the word "pleasant" is the penultimate word in the text followed by the word "desolate."

43. This has been noted by several scholars, including W. A. M. Beuken, *Haggai-Sacharja 1–8* (Assen: van Gorcum, 1967), 129–32; Petitjean, *Oracles*, 348, 349; Y. Kaufmann, *The Religion of Israel*, trans. M. Greenberg (Chicago: Univ. of Chicago Press, 1960), 210 n. 17. Baldwin suggests that underlying Neh. 9:30 and Zech. 7:12 may be a well-known psalm; Baldwin, *Haggai*, 147.

the prayer in Nehemiah 9. As already noted in our comments on Zechariah 7:1–3, there is evidence of a strong tradition of penitential prayer underlying this passage.[44] Zechariah is doing something more here than merely reciting the story of Israel and laying the foundation for his challenge to his own generation. He is using the very liturgy from the days of fasting in order to drive home his point about the people's lack of repentance.

Bridging Contexts

AT FIRST GLANCE, the relevance of Zechariah 7–8 seems distant to the modern reader. How does the fasting liturgy of a particular generation in the early Persian period relate to us today? But approaching the Old Testament as Christians means situating ourselves in the larger story of God's redemption. The early Christian community placed the work of Jesus clearly in this broader context (see, e.g., Matt. 1:1). On one level the promises and stories of the Old Testament were interpreted on a redemptive-historical level. They were essential components of the larger story line that ultimately wound its way via the cross into the experience of their community. All Old Testament events and truth were celebrated as part of their heritage, essential to the progress of God's redemption.

On another level, however, these promises and stories were interpreted on a redemptive-experiential level. If these promises and stories were essential to the flow of God's redemption, they contain values helpful for a later community in the same plot to emulate. Highlighting the redemptive-historical character of revelation celebrates the linear progress of redemption; these events and values are unique to their respective age. Emphasizing the redemptive-experiential character of revelation promotes the cyclical recurrence of redemption; these events and values have ongoing significance in every age.[45]

Fasting, feasting, exile, and restoration. The exilic fasting liturgy emerges prominently as the backdrop to the original prophetic message in Zechariah 7–8. Zechariah looks to an age when fasting will be turned to feasting, from mourning to celebration. This could be interpreted literally to mean that there will be specific feasts attached to the fasts observed in each of the months during the exilic period. More likely, however, Zechariah is using the language of the change from fast to feast to point to an approaching restoration. This restoration will make fasting a thing of the past as the community celebrates

44. Boda, "Penitential Prophet," 49–69.

45. This is also seen in the New Testament. No one would question that Christ's death on the cross is a redemptive-historical event that is unique and nonrepeatable. Nevertheless, this same event is also used in the New Testament to call Christians to appropriate modes of behavior (e.g., 1 Peter 2:21–25).

God's redemptive work. It will begin with the Jewish community but will ultimately extend to the nations.

As one reads the various biblical books describing the early Persian period, one may get the impression that the restoration has become a reality. Some scholars attack the optimism expressed in Ezra and Nehemiah as mere ideological rhetoric shaped by the powerful priestly caste in the Jewish community. However, a closer look at these two books shows that their authors were dissatisfied with the progress made during the early Persian period. Ezra 1–6 and Nehemiah 1–7 celebrate the great physical accomplishments of two different communities during this early period. Nevertheless, both depictions are followed by clear evidence of ongoing struggle for the kind of purity demanded in the law and the prophets (Ezra 7–10; Neh. 8–13). Likewise, Haggai portrays a community struggling with lethargy. Zechariah 1–6 has shown a community still struggling with sin, and this trend continues in Zechariah 9–14 and Malachi.

Daniel 9 uses the experience of Daniel in the early Persian period to explain the enduring nature of the Exile. Utilizing a penitential prayer liturgy typical of the exilic period,[46] Daniel cries to God after reading about the seventy-year period of exile in Jeremiah. The fasting liturgy was used as a way to bring an end to the Exile. When he is finished praying, however, an angel approaches him and explains that the length of the Exile has been extended to seventy times seven (9:24) because of the need for cleansing of sin among the people.

Although the date of this account in Daniel 9 is disputed, there is no question that it matches other depictions of the early Persian period. Exile was an ongoing reality because of the sin of the people. This is matched by the practice of intertestamental Judaism in continuing to observe fasts and extending them to twice a week.[47] Thus, the picture of exile and restoration in the Old Testament can be described as "already/not yet." On the one side, exile has come to an end and restoration has begun (2 Chron. 36; Ezra 1); on the other side, there is a not yet side as aspects of exile continue (Dan. 9).

The link between fasting/feasting and exile/restoration in Zechariah 7–8 helps us to understand Christ's allusions to fasting and feasting in the Gospels. His discouragement of fasting is an implicit signal to the Jewish community that the promised restoration was at hand (Matt. 9:15–16; Mark 2:19–22; Luke 5:34–37). As N. T. Wright has so ably asserted:

46. See Boda, *Praying*, 71–72.

47. Luke 18:12. Notice the practice of Anna in Luke 2:36–38, who fasts at the temple awaiting the Messiah. This account follows Simeon, who is "waiting for the consolation of Israel" (2:25). For views of exile and restoration, see J. M. Scott, ed. *Exile: Old Testament, Jewish and Christian Conceptions* (JSJSup 56; Leiden: Brill, 1997); idem, *Restoration: Old Testament, Jewish and Christian Conceptions* (JSJSup 72; Leiden: Brill, 2000).

> Fasting in this period was not, for Jews, simply an ascetic discipline, part of the general practice of piety. It had to do with Israel's present condition: she was still in exile. More specifically, it had to do with commemorating the destruction of the Temple. Zechariah's promise that the fasts would turn into feasts could come true only when YHWH restored the fortunes of his people.
>
> ... In other words, the party is in full swing, and nobody wants glum faces at a wedding. This is not a piece of "teaching" about "religion" or "morality"; nor is it the dissemination of a timeless truth. It is a claim about eschatology. The time is fulfilled; the exile is over; the bridegroom is at hand.[48]

Similarly, when Christ envisions Gentiles joining the Hebrew feast (Matt. 8:11–12), he is alluding to a similar vision in Zechariah 1–8 (2:11; 8:8, 18–23). These intertextual connections remind us that restoration was ultimately fulfilled in the community established by Christ, the church. On one level the cross signaled the end of the Exile and the beginning of restoration, and in an ironic twist this restoration was sealed by the destruction of Jerusalem. On another level, however, the language of exile and restoration continues to inform early Christian theology, revealing a sense of restoration already and not yet. Jesus foreshadows this in his allusions to fasting/feasting, when he predicts that "the time will come when the bridegroom will be taken from them; then they will fast" (Matt. 9:15). In one sense we have experienced the fulfillment of Zechariah 7–8, and yet we still long for its completion when Christ's kingdom is fully realized.

This lays the foundation for ascertaining the role of fasting and feasting within the Christian community. Although we have experienced forgiveness through the cross, we still battle with sin in our lives and communities, and so Christ encouraged fasting as an activity appropriate between his first and second coming (Matt. 9:14–15; Mark 2:19–20; cf. Matt. 6:16–18).[49] It is true that all special days are fulfilled in Christ through whom we have perpetual access to God (Col. 2:16–17), but this does not disqualify the use of special days as part of the rhythm of our experience with God. But they can become as misguided as the fasts of Zechariah 7–8 and thus need to be challenged constantly by the values communicated by Zechariah.

Prophetic witness. In chapter 7 Zechariah points back to the witness of the "earlier prophets." He cites their words and rehearses their example as

48. N. T. Wright, *Jesus and the Victory of God* (Christian Origins and the Question of God 2; Minneapolis: Fortress, 1996), 433–34.

49. In the early church fasting was also used when consecrating individuals for service (Acts 13:1–3; 14:23).

those who proclaimed the word faithfully in their generation. So closely were their words identified with the words of God that Zechariah quotes God as saying, "When I called" (7:13).

In my final year of college in Canada I was separated from my girlfriend (now my wife) by over two thousand miles. In those days with no nickel-a-minute plans available, telephone calls were a financial burden. So an older couple in my church offered to help me make a free phone call. In their backyard was a four-story high amateur radio tower through which they could receive and send radio transmissions across the country. Of course, their radio could not reach my girlfriend's home north of New York City directly; in any case, she did not have an amateur radio. But they did contact a friend one province away, who rebounded the signal to another friend a province away and repeated this process from province to province and state to state until the signal reached a radio operator within local calling range of my girlfriend. After fifteen minutes of repeating the signal, I was able to speak directly to my girlfriend. Of course, the level of privacy was less than desirable for two young people in love, but it was free!

As we read and teach this passage, we replicate the process that linked my girlfriend and me through the amateur radio network, but now linking God's Word to us today. As we seek to communicate the message of 7:1–14, we are proclaiming a message that itself was a message based on another generation of prophets (so similarly 1:1–6; see there). The core values of the prophetic message, although historically removed from Zechariah's audience and even further removed from our audience today, were and continue to be relevant for our communities of faith. As discussed in detail in the Bridging Contexts section of our introduction, the New Testament is witness to this "rebounding" practice of taking up the prophetic message and passing it on as relevant for the church, whether in reference to God's future actions or in reference to God's call to obedience. As Zechariah did not restrict the words of the earlier prophets to a generation long gone, so we cannot afford to restrict Zechariah's words to an ancient context.

Hardness of heart. These words of the prophets (both earlier and in Zechariah) are important to us because we share much in common with the ancient community of faith. It is true that in and through Jesus Christ we have received far greater resources for the life of faith, but this does not free us from the call to purity and obedience, it only enhances that call.

If we were honest, the example of the earlier generation that had "refused to pay attention ... stubbornly ... turned their backs and stopped up their ears ... made their hearts as hard as flint and ... not listen to the law or the words that the LORD Almighty had sent by his Spirit through the earlier prophets" (7:11–12) is not far from our own condition, both individually and corporately. This is why the apostle Paul, reflecting on an even earlier Israelite generation (the desert generation), which he calls "our forefathers" (1 Cor. 10:1), carefully delineates their behavior for the church in Corinth. He knows that the Christian community is capable of replicating these patterns from Israelite history. Therefore, Paul writes to them:

> Now these things occurred as examples to keep us from setting our hearts on evil things as they did. . . . These things happened to them as examples and were written down as warnings for us, on whom the fulfillment of the ages has come. So, if you think you are standing firm, be careful that you don't fall! (1 Cor. 10:6, 11–12)

As Zechariah's generation needed to be reminded of the example of an earlier generation of God's people, so we must remember these examples and learn from their error. As we invite the Spirit to work in our lives, we must place ourselves within earshot of the teaching of God's Word and cultivate spiritual sensitivity to its instruction. This means daily and weekly connection with that Word, but also finding accountability within a community whose hearts are likewise in tune with the Spirit's teaching. This, however, must be done in the context of grace, reciting the faithful love of a God who desires to see us stand firm. Just as Zechariah rehearses the victory that God will bring (ch. 8), so Paul rehearses God's faithfulness:

> No temptation has seized you except what is common to man. And God is faithful; he will not let you be tempted beyond what you can bear. But when you are tempted, he will also provide a way out so that you can stand up under it. (1 Cor. 10:13)

The challenges of the generation described by Zechariah are the challenges we face today ("common"). Zechariah 7 calls us to listen to God and change our ways.

Contemporary Significance

THE ANCIENT MESSAGE of Zechariah is as relevant to our experience today as it was to those who first heard and read these words. Underlying the practice of fasting was the desire to bring an end to the discipline of God (exile) and to experience his blessing (restoration). God had made it clear, however, that what was required was not just the uttering of penitential prayer to him, but rather confession, which was an expression of true repentance in affection and action. Zechariah, however, observes that his contemporaries were fasting "for themselves," not "for God." They were interested in experiencing the blessing of restoration and had set up religious practices to express this interest, but they were not interested in the priorities of Yahweh.

Religious experience. In the same way today we see a generation clambering for religious experience. The other day as I was paying for my gas, the attendant mistakenly gave me too much change. I noticed the error and immediately pointed it out, handing back the extra coins. On my right was a young man in his twenties with the latest hairstyle and fashion. As I extended my hand with the overpayment, he suddenly blurted out: "Cool ... Karma, man, Karma." As I walked away, I thought how much more spiritually aware is our world today than in times past. In one way, this has been a positive development, providing an opportunity for religious dialogue that was difficult in previous generations. But there are dangers that parallel the experience of Zechariah's audience. Religious experiences can become merely extensions of one's own personal agenda. Through them we can create God in our own image, a god from whom we accept promise and salvation but not warning and discipline.

It is instructive that the revelation of Jesus Christ and his grace was preceded by the prophetic call to repentance through John the Baptist. God was serious about a covenant relationship with his people, a relationship based on extending his grace to a sinful people. But such grace required the sincere repentance of his people. This principle is reflected in the hope of Zechariah 7–8 and needs to inform our own experience with God today.

God demands fidelity in relationship and calls us to repentance as he extends grace to us through Christ's death and resurrection. As people are invited to respond to God in faith, they should also reflect deeply over the condition of their hearts and lives, renouncing their past life of sin even as they embrace the Spirit's enabling new life in Christ. In a rush to get people to pray a prayer of faith to God, Christians often present a truncated view of conversion, that is, one that involves a turning to God but not a turning from sin.

Earlier streams of theology are instructive for recovering a fuller view of repentance. For instance, in the Orthodox tradition repentance endures as a key element in conversion, as evident in the renunciation of evil at baptism when the priest, after turning the catechumen to the west, asks: "Do you renounce Satan, and all his angels, and all his works, and all his services, and all his pride?" Then, turning to the candidate to the east (a physical motion that is to parallel an inner turn), asks: "Do you unite yourself to Christ? And do you believe in Him?"[50]

50. See further J. Chryssavgis, *Repentance and Confession in the Orthodox Church* (Brookline: Holy Cross Orthodox, 1988). The theology of repentance within biblical as well as Christian traditions is the focus of a forthcoming book for Liturgical Press that I am editing along with Gordon T. Smith, the result of a two-year consultation at the Society of Biblical Literature/American Academy of Religion. See also the forthcoming volume of A. Firey, ed., *A New History of Penance* (Leiden: Brill, 2005).

In similar fashion the Puritans emphasized repentance in conversion.[51] They considered both repentance and faith as a grace given by God, though both were necessary for salvation. Repentance involved awareness that sin was offensive to God and deserved his judgment, included sorrow for and hatred of sin, entailed turning from sin to God with the intention to be obedient to God's law, and was intermingled with faith resulting in an obedient lifestyle. Like faith, repentance was a lifelong process.

These two traditions challenge us to incorporate a penitential aspect into our presentations of the gospel as well as into communal initiation rites, especially that of baptism. The doctrine of repentance needs to be an enduring theme in the theology of the church, especially in light of the present religious mood in our generation.

Christian liturgy. The greater emphasis on religious experience in society in general can also be discerned in the church, especially with the stress today on recovering the "missing jewel," that is, worship.[52] Many will immediately relate Zechariah's challenge to those Christian traditions that utilize liturgical texts and calendars.

I remember an experience I had with this kind of tradition. I noticed it first on my eldest son, David, because he was sitting next to me at the dining room table. It was 1996, and we had moved into our "new" 1913 home in an older part of our city. Our boys were enjoying their new life at the local school, which happened to be Catholic. It was March, and I noticed a dirty spot on his forehead and on his brother Stephen's forehead. Now my boys are hardly known for their ability to stay out of the mud, but what were the chances that they both had filth in the same spot! As my mouth opened to ask the question, the answer was already forming in my mind, but the question was ventured: "Boys, what is the gray smudge on your forehead?"

"Dad!? [in a tone that sounded like I didn't know how to pronounce the latest rock star's name properly] . . . it's ash from the priest . . . it's Ash Wednesday."

"Of course," I thought to myself, "Ash Wednesday, the first day of Lent," as the boys meticulously explained to me the significance of this day and liturgical season in the life of their school. Although probably unique among their classmates, my two boys were able to fully grasp this liturgical rhythm and even appropriate it into their lives. For them it was not dead ritual but part of a living faith experience.

---

51. For this I am indebted to the superb work on the Puritans in W. R. Hastings, "Repentance in the Evangelical Theological Heritage" (Master's Thesis, Regent College, 1992), 101; cf. T. Watson, *The Doctrine of Repentance* (Edinburgh: Banner of Truth, 1987; reprint of 1668).

52. As Tozer longed for decades ago: A. W. Tozer, *Worship: The Missing Jewel in the Evangelical Church* (Harrisburg, Pa.: Christian Publications, 1961).

This made me reflect on our own tradition and the rituals and traditions that we have. It reminded me that all traditions have a consistent structure to their expressions of worship whether it is admitted or not.[53] This passage is a sincere call to the Christian community to ensure that the rhythms of worship expression fulfill their intended purpose rather than becoming avenues for hypocrisy. This was one of Christ's greatest concerns with his own generation as he highlighted hypocrisy in the worship practices of his contemporaries (e.g., Matt. 6:2–8, 16–18).

As a student I once worked alongside a respected pastor and church growth advisor, helping churches revision their ministries. I remember well an inspiring worship experience in a church in the Canadian Maritimes. Well before the present worship revolution in the evangelical church, this church had made worship top priority in their experience together as a community of faith. Whether they were meeting in a small group in a home, in a prayer meeting in the basement of the church, or in a Sunday service in the sanctuary, worship was not merely "preliminaries" to the main event of preaching, but rather the priority.

While visiting the church I stayed in the home of a young couple with preschool children and enjoyed their perspective on God's work in their church. As I sat with them in the Sunday service, I noticed the children lifting their hands in praise as we sang the songs. At Sunday dinner in their home I asked them about the exuberance of praise in their church and noted the expression of their children. The father then told me that a few months prior he had noticed his young son raising his hands in worship. At home the son proudly told his father that he had "worshiped" God today at church. When his father asked him what he meant by "worshiped," the son informed him that he had lifted his hands in the air. The father proceeded to teach his son that it was not the lifting up the hands that was worship, but rather the attitude of the heart that lay behind the action of the body.

By this I am not playing down the physicality of worship. We are holistic beings of spirit-matter and our worship will be expressed through physical forms that involve our mouths, ears, eyes, noses, and bodies. But these physical forms have meaning because of the reality of our relationship with God. When we separate the physical form from genuine covenant relationship with God, we fall into the hypocrisy that Zechariah and Christ denounced in their generations.

---

53. Although the church in which I grew up was not a "liturgical" church, we could predict the order of service each week with the same cadence of invocation, hymns, pastoral prayer, Scripture reading, offering (with singing of the doxology), sermon, and closing hymn.

Fasting. Zechariah focuses attention on the practice of fasting. At a recent community gathering in my neighborhood I had a fascinating conversation with a family about their practice of fasting for both physical and spiritual health. Through some resources they mentioned, I have discovered that fasting plays an important role in contemporary holistic medicine and spirituality, a movement that has forced us to take seriously that human beings are spirit-matter.[54]

This discovery has forced me to consider seriously the place of fasting within biblical theology and Christian practice.[55] Although Jesus did not require his disciples to fast when he was with them, he did practice fasting himself (Matt. 4:2; Luke 4:2) and said that fasting would be appropriate (Matt. 6:16–18), especially when he was no longer with them (Mark 2:18–20). In the early church fasting is linked to model piety (Acts 6:1; 2 Cor. 6:4–5; 1 Tim. 5:5) and is mentioned in conjunction with commissioning (Acts 13:1–3; 14:23).[56] There are warnings against excessive asceticism in Colossians 2:18, 23, a practice related to the worship of angels.

The Didache (8:1) mentions a twice-weekly Christian fast, while Eusebius in the third century describes a fast on Good Friday, a practice that later was expanded to the annual Lenten fast of penitence. In light of this evidence of fasting in the early church, why is fasting not a core spiritual activity within many Christian traditions?

Although there may be many reasons, one important factor is surely the Reformation reaction to medieval asceticism. Martin Luther's study of the Scriptures led him to revisit the doctrines of salvation, especially the biblical theme of justification by grace through faith, and reconsider the doctrine of penitence, especially the medieval practice of selling indulgences and practicing self-abuse. The medieval church had made repentance an economic

---

54. See, e.g., E. B. Szekely, *The Essene Gospel of Peace: Book One* (San Diego: Academy of Creative Links, 1981); S. Meyerowitz, *Juice Fasting and Detoxification* (Summertown: Book Publishing Company, 1999); S. K. Fines, *Spiritual Fasting: Creating Light Through Cleansing* (Canada: 2001); S. Gabbay, *Nourishing the Body Temple: Edgar Cayce's Approach to Nutrition* (Virginia Beach, Va.: A.R.E., 1999); C. L'Esperance, *The Ancient Cookfire: How to Rejuvenate Body and Spirit Through Seasonal Foods and Fasting* (Santa Fe, N.M.: Bear & Company Publishing, 1998).

55. See further, D. R. Smith, *Fasting: A Neglected Discipline* (Fort Washington, Pa.: Christian Literature Crusade, 1954); A. Wallis, *God's Chosen Fast: A Spiritual and Practical Guide to Fasting* (London: Victory, 1968); J. F. Wimmer, *Fasting in the New Testament: A Study in Biblical Theology* (New York: Paulist, 1982); R. J. Foster, *Celebration of Discipline*, rev. ed. (San Francisco: HarperSanFrancisco, 1988), 47–61; E. L. Towns, *Fasting for Spiritual Breakthrough: A Guide to Nine Biblical Fasts* (Ventura, Calif.: Regal, 1996); J. Piper, *A Hunger for God: Desiring God through Fasting and Prayer* (Wheaton: Crossway, 1997).

56. See J. Muddiman, "Fast, Fasting," in *Anchor Bible Dictionary*, ed. D. N. Freedman (New York: Doubleday, 1992), 2:773–76.

enterprise. People paid for absolution from their sins and the sins of the deceased. In addition, people were required to fulfill certain physical rites in return for forgiveness of sins. Luther tells the story of his trip to Rome in which he climbed the steps of the Vatican on his knees as a penitential rite. Fasting was an essential ritual related to the forgiveness of sins and was thus rejected by Protestant churches.

But in light of the New Testament witness, one should not reject fasting as an important covenant rhythm for the community of God. This rhythm must be founded on a biblical doctrine of salvation and repentance; that is, this practice is not an act that earns our forgiveness; rather, it expresses our hearts' passion for God and mourning for our sins, affords an opportunity to deepen our relationship with God, and affirms our dependence on him for all our needs.

Zechariah's message not only encourages fasting but is designed to shape our fasting experience. He reminds us that fasting is not primarily a self-centered enterprise, focused on improving human health or spiritual well-being. Although fasting can have this effect on us as Christians, Zechariah reminds us of the divine priorities in fasting: an opportunity to examine our relationship with God, reorient us to his priorities, renounce practices that do not conform to kingdom priorities, and embrace those that do. When I served as a leader in my college, a close friend and fellow leader encouraged me to join him on the first Monday of each month to fast and pray over the meal times together. Although a difficult discipline for me, as the year progressed I looked forward to these moments of reorientation in my life as a Christian and as a leader.

For some, the practice of fasting is part of the weekly or monthly rhythm of their lives, taking time over a lunch period to talk with God rather than eat. For those in churches that practice the church calendar, the season of Lent is an annual opportunity to practice fasting. Such fasting can be guided by a passage such as Nehemiah 9–10, where the people read the Scriptures, expressed praise, rehearsed their salvation, confessed their sins, expressed their needs, and finally renewed covenant. This can be a powerful pattern for God's people individually and corporately.

Social justice. For my Dad and his three small kids, it was a last-minute run to the local grocery store for milk, but little did he know the lasting impact this trip would have on his children.[57] The store was only four blocks from our home, and as the four of us boarded our 1965 Ford Falcon, milk in father's hand, we knew the route like the back of our hands: right on Pasqua, left on 4th, right on Connaught.

57. I am thankful to my older brother, Matt, for jogging my memory of this event in our lives.

As we neared the intersection of 4th and Pasqua, however, we all noticed something askew. Lying on the ground between the sidewalk and the curb was a heap of humanity. As we came closer, we could see it was an old man who had fallen in a drunken stupor and lay in a pool of whisky produced by his smashed bottle. My father stopped the car, hopped out, and before our young eyes, helped him to his feet, opened the front door of the car, placed him in the car, and, with our eyes as wide as saucers, delivered the man to his home several blocks away. The picture that endures in my mind's eye is that of my father's arm around this sorry man, helping him up the front walk of his home. A simple act of mercy, compassion in a crisis of need, it was a demonstration of Christian faith in deed, the kind of spirituality Zechariah sought in his day.

The inappropriate nature of the fasting rituals in Zechariah's day was linked to specific ethical demands, a trend discernible in Isaiah 58 as well. In his article on fasting, Mark Buchanan challenges us to see the link between fasting and social justice on a physical level: "The fast God chooses teaches us to have God's heart for the hungry, the oppressed, the naked, the homeless. When we taste a little brokenness ourselves, we have a greater sense of urgency to repair for others what is broken."[58]

In addressing fasting liturgies, Zechariah attacked the social injustice of his day as seen in the abuse of the court systems and the lack of care and compassion for the poor.[59] As we have seen, his concerns echo prophetic voices from the past, who saw the same trends within the preexilic community of God, trends that led ultimately to the Exile and the destruction of Jerusalem. This prophetic witness was based firmly on the covenant foundation in the law.

The New Testament witness continued this call to social justice. Interestingly, Jesus echoed Zechariah's concern when he attacked the teachers of the law for making long prayers for show while abusing widows (Mark 12:38–40; Luke 20:45–47). He also communicated a sincere concern for the poor (Luke 7:22; 12:32–34; 18:22). The early church took seriously their responsibility for those in need (Acts 6:1; 9:36; 10:4, 31; 24:17; Rom. 15:26; 1 Cor. 13:3; Gal. 2:10; 1 Tim. 5:3–16). James was deeply concerned about abuses in his day, highlighting exploitation of the poor and preference for the rich as worthy of judgment. He also defines "true religion" as the care for orphans and widows (James 1:27).

---

58. M. Buchanan, "Go Fast and Live: Hunger as Spiritual Discipline," *Christian Century* (Feb. 28, 2001), 19.

59. For two works that use Zech. 7–8 as a call to justice, see N. E. Williams, "Looking Backward, Living Forward," *Witness* 69 (1986): 18; W. Wink, "Standing on the Rock of the Impossible: From Zechariah 8 Through History to Recent Events—and Hope," *Church and Society* 85 (1995): 3–9.

Although there are some prophets within today's church crying in the wilderness about the social implications of the gospel, the vast majority of white evangelical churches are indifferent to these issues.[60] There are several reasons for the loss of this social emphasis. (1) Sociologically, the location (or relocation) of these churches within the suburban sprawl of North America has led to a distancing from those with the greatest financial and sociological needs. In this the churches represent the general cultural trend of separation of classes.

(2) Politically, there is a strong tendency, especially in North America, to argue for separation between church and state. In the culture at large and in the church as well, this has come to mean that the church should have no voice in the affairs of the culture, a view that was not the original intention of those who first crafted the American constitution.

(3) Theologically, evangelical churches have often distanced themselves from the so-called "mainline" churches, which embraced a social theology considered theologically suspect.[61] Many evangelicals stripped spirituality of its sociological dimension and in doing so violated a major biblical-theological emphasis.[62] In addition, many have reacted against a more culturally engaging postmillennial triumphalism that seeks to establish a Christian nation.[63]

---

60. On this see esp. R. J. Sider, *Rich Christians in an Age of Hunger: A Biblical Study* (Downers Grove, Ill.: InterVarsity Press, 1977) and the response of D. Chilton, *Productive Christians in an Age of Guilt-Manipulators* (Tyler, Tex.: Institute for Christian Economics, 1982).

61. A great example of this is the work of W.Rauschenbusch in the early twentieth century, considered the father of the social gospel. His reworking of the doctrine of atonement in sociological terms does "injustice" to the biblical doctrine (see his *A Theology for the Social Gospel* [Nashville: Abingdon, 1917]). However, his emphasis on the prophetic calls for social justice are accurate and necessary for the church today.

62. Consider the case study of the Christian & Missionary Alliance, which began with a great emphasis on the social aspect of the gospel but ultimately lost this. This is highlighted by N. Magnuson, *Salvation in the Slums: Evangelical Social Work, 1865–1920* (ATLA Monograph Series 10; Metuchen, N.J.: Scarecrow, 1977); J. V. Dahms, "The Social Interest and Concern of A. B. Simpson," in *The Birth of a Vision*, ed. D. F. Hartzfeld and C. Nienkirchen (Beaverlodge, Alta.: Buena Book Services, 1986), 49–74; D. J. Evearitt, *Body and Soul: Evangelism and the Social Concern of A. B. Simpson* (Camp Hill, Pa.: Christian Publications, 1994); idem, "The Social Gospel vs. Personal Salvation: A Late Nineteenth-Century Case Study—Walter Rauschenbusch and A. B. Simpson," in *Alliance Academic Review*, ed. E. Cuccaro (Camp Hill, Pa.: Christian Publications, 1997), 1–18. It is interesting that Rauschenbusch and Simpson served the same community in New York City.

63. For this movement see G. North, *An Introduction to Christian Economics* (no city: The Craig, 1973); D. Chilton, *Paradise Restored: A Biblical Theology of Dominion* (Fort Worth, Tex.: Dominion, 1985); G. North and G. Demar, *Christian Reconstruction: What It Is, What It Isn't* (Tyler, Tex.: Institute for Christian Economics, 1991), and responses by H. W. House and T. Ice, *Dominion Theology: Blessing or Curse?* (Portland, Ore.: Multnomah, 1988); W. S. Barker and W. R. Godfrey, eds. *Theonomy: A Reformed Critique* (Grand Rapids: Zondervan, 1990);

Zechariah called his generation to practice justice with one another. This implies faithful living and speaking with our fellow human beings without favoritism and with compassion. It also means caring for the rights and needs of those with fewer resources than we enjoy. But we cannot restrict this to the individual level. God calls his people both as individuals and as communities to become champions of justice within society. This means taking seriously God's call to become lawyers, social workers, psychologists, and teachers in order to communicate and enact his justice in society as a whole. It also means a realignment of the priorities of the church and possibly also the organization of the church to allow a broader sociological agenda to be addressed. We must show the love of God to our society through our actions as well as words.

As I ministered to teens in Toronto, I began to study the community in which our church was located. I discovered that there was not a single ghetto in the inner-city core (as one often finds in American cities), but rather pockets of low-income housing spread throughout the city. The provincial government had built large housing projects within blocks of middle and upper class single family dwellings. Thus, in my church and local schools the poor attended classes with the rich. In light of this, several members of my youth staff caught a vision for ministry in these areas, running floor hockey clubs to get teens off the streets, events at which they would share the gospel. These activities opened doors for the gospel with these youth.

However, although this was a good start in displaying sensitivity to the community in which we had been placed, if I were to relive that period of ministry, I would like to take our calling to these communities to a deeper level. I encountered an example of this through one of the couples with whom I attended seminary, Steve and Mary Smallman. They have spent the last decade ministering in an inner-city community in Baltimore, Maryland.[64] Rather than plant a church that offers only spiritual instruction and worship experiences, New Song Community Church has initiated ministries that seek to transform their community in all dimensions of life. There are ministries focused on

---

M. G. Moriarty, *The New Charismatics: A Concerned Voice Responds to Dangerous New Trends* (Grand Rapids: Zondervan, 1992), 160–89.

64. See M. R. Gornik, "Between Resurrection and Reconciliation: The Story of New Song Community Church," in *Planting and Growing Urban Churches: From Dream to Reality*, ed. H. M. Conn (Grand Rapids: Baker, 1997), 235–43; N. Harper, "Baltimore: New Song Community Church," in *Urban Churches, Vital Signs: Beyond Charity Toward Justice*, ed. N. Harper (Grand Rapids: Eerdmans, 1998), 11–18; M. R. Gornik and N. Castellanos, "How to Start a Christian Community Development Ministry," in *Restoring At-Risk Communities*, ed. J. M. Perkins (Grand Rapids: Baker, 1995), 220; M. Gornik, *To Live in Peace: Biblical Faith and the Changing Inner City* (Grand Rapids: Eerdmans, 2002).

economic (attracting business, securing loans, creating jobs in their community), infrastructure (building/renovating homes), medical (pediatric and adult health care), educational (after school enrichment, preschool), as well as spiritual development.

Such holistic ministry is as valid in inner-city contexts as it is in the suburban areas, where family and vocational crises are also at issue. For some suburban ministries it will mean finding outlets for ministry in poorer neighborhoods. For some inner-city ministries it will mean remaining and revisioning ministry in light of changing demographics in their community.[65]

This kind of response to the message of Zechariah is important. We need to reach out and communicate the gospel to our communities through word and deed. But the church can also play a role in addressing the roots of dysfunction within our society. As I have already noted, this is not an easy task within societies that celebrate the separation of church and state. A recent news report on charities in Canada highlighted the difficulty of addressing issues of social justice within North American society. According to the report Canadian charities are not allowed to spend more than 10 percent of their budgets on "advocacy," that is, on initiatives designed to address the political system and root causes of the problem their charity is seeking to address. They may spend as much money as they wish on servicing the problem, but are limited in advocating change to the system. If they violate this rule, they risk losing their charitable status.

But if, as Zechariah 7–8 indicates and the New Testament confirms, the gospel has a social dimension, the church must be willing to take risks within their societies, even if that means endangering tax-deductible status. It also means that the church should encourage Christians to participate both in the political process as well as the agencies that carry out government policies in the public sector.

The impact that this kind of holistic approach to ministry can have on a community, culture, and society will be considered in more detail in the commentary on 8:14–23. At this point, however, Zechariah has highlighted God's priority on social justice and the serious consequences of ignoring his call. The urgency of this message to his generation is communicated through his review of the experience of the earlier generation. Their refusal to listen to God's call resulted in the desolation of the "pleasant land." This land of peace and prosperity was destroyed by disobedience, and this would be the perpetual state of Zechariah's generation unless they transcended their ancestors' example. The church needs to hear this message with the same urgency today. We threaten to make the pleasant land desolate, whether that means our lives, our families, our churches, or our communities.

---

65. For many other examples see the case studies in Harper, *Urban Churches*.

Zechariah 8:1–13

AGAIN THE WORD of the LORD Almighty came to me. [2]This is what the LORD Almighty says: "I am very jealous for Zion; I am burning with jealousy for her."

[3]This is what the LORD says: "I will return to Zion and dwell in Jerusalem. Then Jerusalem will be called the City of Truth, and the mountain of the LORD Almighty will be called the Holy Mountain."

[4]This is what the LORD Almighty says: "Once again men and women of ripe old age will sit in the streets of Jerusalem, each with cane in hand because of his age. [5]The city streets will be filled with boys and girls playing there."

[6]This is what the LORD Almighty says: "It may seem marvelous to the remnant of this people at that time, but will it seem marvelous to me?" declares the LORD Almighty.

[7]This is what the LORD Almighty says: "I will save my people from the countries of the east and the west. [8]I will bring them back to live in Jerusalem; they will be my people, and I will be faithful and righteous to them as their God."

[9]This is what the LORD Almighty says: "You who now hear these words spoken by the prophets who were there when the foundation was laid for the house of the LORD Almighty, let your hands be strong so that the temple may be built. [10]Before that time there were no wages for man or beast. No one could go about his business safely because of his enemy, for I had turned every man against his neighbor. [11]But now I will not deal with the remnant of this people as I did in the past," declares the LORD Almighty.

[12]"The seed will grow well, the vine will yield its fruit, the ground will produce its crops, and the heavens will drop their dew. I will give all these things as an inheritance to the remnant of this people. [13]As you have been an object of cursing among the nations, O Judah and Israel, so will I save you, and you will be a blessing. Do not be afraid, but let your hands be strong."

Original Meaning

IN ZECHARIAH 8 there is some confusion over the direction of the prophet's thought. I have argued elsewhere that the original oral continuation of 7:14 is represented in 8:14–19, where the prophet clearly refers to God's discipline on the former generation and then announces a change in intention toward a present generation that responds to the ethical demands rejected by the former generation.[1] This intervening section contains two collections of oracles drawn from two periods in Zechariah's ministry (8:1–8, 9–13). In their present position they begin the transition from the past disaster to future blessing by focusing on God's saving activity (8:7, 13).

The first collection (8:1–8) is drawn from an earlier period of Zechariah's ministry, possibly in connection with the first night vision (cf. 1:14).[2] It speaks in general terms about a glorious future in Jerusalem for those who have returned from exile. The second collection (8:9–13) assumes the challenges experienced by the first waves of exiles. The deliverance mentioned here is not from the nations but rather from the curse the exiles experienced among the nations. There is a hint, however, of something more as the prophet declares that this community "will be a blessing" (8:13). This lays the foundation for 8:14–23, which speaks of a future in which the fasts commemorating the destruction of Jerusalem and the Exile will be replaced with feasts. These feasts will be occasions not only for the Jews but also for all the nations who will join the Jews in Jerusalem. Here the blessing of 8:13 is realized.

God's Salvation of the Remnant—Oracles (8:1–8)

THE MESSENGER FORMULA in 8:1 signals the beginning of a new section. We are then presented with a collection of short oracles that orient us to the coming change in the flow of redemptive history (8:2–8). Each of these is introduced by the formula "This is what the LORD Almighty says." Although these oracles may have come from various periods in Zechariah's ministry, they are drawn together into a unit, offering hope to the skeptics in the community.

Oracle 1. The initial phrase of the first oracle echoes the words of the first night vision in 1:14.[3] In chiastic fashion the prophet pours out a succession of emotional terminology from the heart of Yahweh.[4] We find three

1. Boda, "Fasts to Feasts," 309–407.

2. The reference to the "the countries of the east and the west" (8:7) only makes sense if this oracle is spoken in Jerusalem. The skepticism assumed in 8:6 may suggest that Zechariah spoke it after he communicated the first night vision to his community.

3. The only difference is that the words "for Jerusalem" are left out.

4. The Heb. phrases are arranged in ABBA fashion: "I am zealous for Jerusalem (A) with great zeal (B), and with great wrath (B') I am zealous for her (A')"; cf. Baldwin, *Haggai*, 149.

instances of the root *qana*ʾ. This root is often translated as "jealous" or "zealous" and has a semantic range across these two emotions often distinguished in English. Yahweh's zeal for his people expresses itself in a passionate demand for exclusivity in relationship (Ex. 20:5; Josh. 24:19) and a passionate protection of his people (Isa. 42:13; Ezek. 36:5–6). Zechariah also uses *ḥemah* (NIV, "I am burning"), a word that indicates God's wrath.

Qinʾah and especially *ḥemah* speak of God's judgment on his disobedient people. Thus, after having just encountered 7:4–14 with its description of God's discipline of the former generation, we expect an oracle of judgment directed at Judah. The surprise, however, is that Zechariah follows Ezekiel in using the combination of *qinʾah* and *ḥemah* to speak of Israel's deliverance (Ezek. 36:6). The wrath (*ḥemah*) here is similar to the anger (*qeṣep*) of Zechariah 1:15, which is directed toward the nations who abused Israel.

Oracle 2. The emotional outburst of 8:2 is followed by the purposeful action of 8:3. Again echoing oracles from the night visions (1:16; 2:10–11), Yahweh promises to return and dwell in Jerusalem. He abandoned this city so that it fell to the Babylonians (Ezek. 10), but Ezekiel envisioned his return to the city and temple (43:4). Zechariah's vocabulary of God's return to Jerusalem is closely linked to Exodus 25:8, which uses the same Hebrew phrase to describe God's dwelling in the tabernacle ("God will dwell [*šakan*] in the midst [*betok*]").

God's presence in the city will transform its status, a change typified by its new names. The faithful city ("City of Truth") speaks of faithfulness in contrast to the infidelity of the former generation (7:9–14). "Holy Mountain" reveals the holiness of this site, a place set apart for God's purposes. The allusion here to the mountain (the site of the temple) and the promise of God's dwelling assume a temple structure, but interestingly is not the focus of this oracle. Instead, the prophet is concerned with the renewal of a city (and ultimately its inhabitants) worthy of the God who will reside there.

Oracle 3. The third oracle describes the human element in God's renewal of Jerusalem. The prophet uses two images that represent life at its two extremes (childhood and aged), the periods of greatest vulnerability. The existence and activity of these two types of people paint a picture of renewed prosperity and peace for the city. Old men and women with canes in hand alongside excited young boys and girls playing in the squares symbolize a new day.[5] These images reveal life far above the subsistence level many have known since the judgment of 587 B.C., a life with abundance of provisions and protection from harm.

---

5. In these squares, earlier prophets had seen destruction for the people, esp. the children (Jer. 9:20; Lam. 2:11, 12; Amos 5:16). Cf. Petersen, *Haggai*, 300–301.

Oracle 4. Yahweh's passionate zeal results in his return to dwell in Jerusalem, transforming it into a city with the qualities of his character and with a renewed life of prosperity and peace. This is clearly so beyond the experience of the Jewish community in the early Persian period that Zechariah has to confront the incredulity of his audience in the fourth oracle. Between the fall of Jerusalem in 587 B.C. and the early Persian period (539–520 B.C.), the former state of Judah had shrunk not only in physical size but even more dramatically in population density.[6] The greatest contrast between the two periods is represented in the city of Jerusalem itself, which was merely one-fifth of its pre-fall size in population and in dire need of physical rebuilding.[7]

The great challenge of the renewal of Jerusalem is displayed in the consistent appearance of skeptical and discouraged responses to rebuilding in the literature from this period. Ezra 3:10–13 speaks of the weeping that accompanied the joy at the refounding of the temple. Haggai's questions in Haggai 2:3 and his encouragement in 2:4–9 assumes a community struggling under the weight of the rebuilding burden. Zechariah must also face the challenge of skepticism and doubt.[8] Continuing his focus on the future, he contrasts the reaction of those who will experience this renewal "at that time" with God's reaction, using a chiastic form to accentuate the contrast:

A Thus says the LORD Almighty
  B It will be marvelous
    C In the eyes of the remnant of this people
      D At that time
    C′ In my eyes
  B′ Will it be marvelous
A′ Declares the LORD Almighty

Reference to the "remnant of this people," a term speaking of those who survived the discipline of God, a purified community, provides even greater motivation to trust this miraculous God. Baldwin notes the similarity of this oracle to earlier challenges to the faith of God's people: Abraham (Gen. 18:14) and Jeremiah (Jer. 32:27).[9] In each of these cases the answer to doubt and the challenge to faith is focused on the person of Yahweh in the face of insurmountable circumstances.

---

6. Carter, *Emergence*.

7. Ibid.; see also Neh. 11:1, which reflects the problem of settlement in Jerusalem.

8. Although Zechariah refers to the people "at that time," he is obviously speaking to those in his own period.

9. Baldwin, *Haggai*, 150.

Oracle 5. Having identified the ultimate picture of a renewed Jerusalem, Zechariah now proclaims the means by which this miraculous God will fill his city. He will rescue his people from their exile and return them to Jerusalem. The term "save" (*yašaᶜ*) here is the climactic moment in this collection and matches the similar appearance at the end of the next oracle (8:9–13). This first appearance of "save" reverses one aspect of the discipline of Yahweh in 7:14: the scattering of the people as a whirlwind over the nations. The Hebrew construction here appears elsewhere only in a refrain in Jeremiah, where it anticipates (as in Zechariah) the return from exile (Jer. 30:10–11; 46:27–28).[10]

The image for the nations in 8:7 is a merism (two extremes to refer to all), which utilizes the pattern of the sun to cover the entire cosmos: the land of the rising ("east") and the land of the setting of the sun ("west"). Zechariah is unique in using this idiom for the return of the exiles, but the use of multiple directions is common in Isaiah (Isa. 43:5–6; 49:12). It is more universal in its scope than the idiom Jeremiah uses ("the land of the north"; Jer. 16:15; 23:8; 31:8; cf. Zech. 2:6).[11] These people scattered since the Exile will be saved and return to Jerusalem.

Zechariah uses the identical Hebrew construction here to refer to the returned exiles as he used in oracle 2 to refer to God's return to Jerusalem ("live in Jerusalem," *šakan* + *betok* + Jerusalem). This creates a bracket around the entire complex providing closure to the overall flow of the section and providing the foundation for Zechariah's final statement: "They will be my people, and I will be faithful and righteous to them as their God."

This statement is a familiar formula drawn from the covenant tradition of Israel, emphasizing the relational purpose behind God's redemptive activity (cf. Ex. 6:7; Lev. 26:12; Jer. 7:23; 11:4; 24:7; 30:22; 31:1, 33; 32:38; Ezek. 11:20; 14:11; 34:30; 36:28; 37:23, 27). Zechariah's rendition expands this formula by emphasizing the character of God: He will be "faithful" (*ʾemet*) and "righteous" (*ṣedaqah*). He will consistently hold up his side of the covenant relationship,[12] following his core values. This section closes with God and his people reunited in the city of his presence. Note the contrast to the situation at the end of chapter 7, where the people refused to listen to appeals from Yahweh and were scattered to the nations.

---

10. *hinni* + the participle of *yašaᶜ* + prep. *min*.

11. The reference to the "north" is a designation for Mesopotamian peoples who, because of the desert, always arrived in Israel from the north. Jeremiah's idiom focuses attention on those in Mesopotamia, while leaving room also for those in other areas by adding phrases like "all the countries where he had banished them" (16:15; 23:8), "the ends of the earth" (31:8).

12. Notice the use of the word *ʾemet* to depict the city in 8:3 (NIV "truth").

God's Salvation of the Remnant—Sermon (8:9–13)

THE MESSENGER FORMULA ("This is what the LORD Almighty says") at the beginning of verse 9 signals the beginning of a new oracle. In contrast to verses 1–8 with its staccato style of presentation, verses 9–13 are more prosaic and free of the earlier interjections of the messenger formula.[13] The content of this section also stands in contrast to the setting of chapters 7–8. Here we return to the style familiar from the book of Haggai with its regular use of the phrase "let your hands be strong," "do not be afraid," and an emphasis on rebuilding the temple and agro-economic woe and weal.

The language in the section indicates that Zechariah is reflecting on an earlier message connected with the refoundation ceremony.[14] It is uncertain whether Zechariah includes himself in this group of prophets, although the dating scheme in 1:1 indicates that his work began prior to the refounding ceremony. The rehearsal of the message here is designed to encourage those involved in the rebuilding project. As Haggai encouraged those working between the initial clearing and the refoundation ceremony, Zechariah encourages those active between the refoundation ceremony and completion.

The ceremony of refoundation was a key event in the rebuilding of ancient Near Eastern temples, marking the end of the preparation process and the beginning of the new structure. As in Haggai 2:10–23, the day was to demarcate a turning point in the experience of the early Persian period community. The agro-economic challenges of the community were to be replaced by blessing from Yahweh because of the people's obedience in rebuilding the temple.

The contrast motif between the past curse and the future blessing is presented in verses 10–11. Zechariah depicts a period of economic collapse where there were no employment opportunities for people or their animals. This is linked to the anarchic conditions of this period, which find their ultimate cause in the disciplinary action of God.[15]

Zechariah's depiction, although bearing some similarities to Haggai's, is different. Haggai spoke of economic difficulty because of high inflation and crop failure. Zechariah speaks of economic inactivity and social unrest. To some these depictions may seem to reflect different eras. However, Zechariah is also aware of Haggai's crop failure but only makes this clear in his promise

---

13. The only formula used is "declares the LORD Almighty" at the end of v. 11, which comes at the juncture between past and future.

14. So also Petersen links this to the refoundation ceremony; Petersen, *Haggai*, 305. Zechariah clearly distinguishes between "now" (v. 9; lit., "in these days") and "that time" (v. 10).

15. The reference to "every man against his neighbor" in Heb. means this is internal strife between one's own people, not external attack from enemies. Elsewhere God "sent" (NIV "turned") external punishments against Israel (nations, 2 Kings 24:2; plagues, Ezek. 28:23), but here he uses internal methods (cf. Isa. 19:2).

of verse 12. These two perspectives on the hardships of the early Persian period are easily related. The crop failures mixed with the taxation policy of the Persian rulers caused economic hardship and in turn produced high inflation, reducing the power of any wages acquired and ultimately bringing a halt to economic activity and producing social unrest.[16] Common to both Haggai and Zechariah is the declaration that these conditions are to be interpreted as the discipline of God to awake his community to the priorities of rebuilding.

Verse 11, with its opening construction "but now" (*weᶜattah*) represents a turning point typical in prophetic speeches. As with Haggai, the refoundation day marked a new day in the lives of this community, a point emphasized by the use of the phrase "the remnant of this people." This phrase also appears in Haggai 1:12, 14; 2:2 and is a theological term for the community purified through the exilic discipline.

God's new stance toward the community will be expressed through renewed blessing of the land (8:12). This blessing is typified by a renewal of processes essential for agricultural bounty. The first phrase, "The seed will grow well" (NIV), is *zeraᶜ haššalom* (lit., "seed of peace/prosperity"). Rather than the first of four signs of agricultural bounty, this phrase functions as a general description of the new era as a time of agricultural prosperity, especially considering that "seed" (*zeraᶜ*) can be used for the produce of both tree and plant (cf. Gen. 1:10–11, 29).[17]

Zechariah covers two major kinds of produce in Yehud: the "vines" that grow in the mountainous terrain and the "ground . . . crops" that grow in the valleys and plains (Ex. 22:5; Num. 16:14). Production of fruit from vines is especially noteworthy because it required a significant expenditure of energy and care over a period of time (Isa. 5:1–7). Not only will plants and ground cooperate with humanity in this new era of prosperity, but the heavens will provide the moisture necessary for farming. The "dew" is the result of the overnight temperature differential in Palestine and provides necessary moisture for plants to survive between the rains.[18] These evidences of prosperity are linked to covenant blessing and cursing in Leviticus 26:4, 19–20.[19] Zechariah is prophesying a renewal of covenant relationship in this new era.

In 8:12b Yahweh makes it clear that these will come "to the remnant" from his hand directly. The use of the verb "give . . . as an inheritance" is reminiscent of the conquest of the land (cf. Josh. 1:6; 13:32; 14:1; 16:4) and casts this in Second Exodus and Conquest language so familiar from the prophets Isaiah, Jeremiah, and Ezekiel.

---

16. Cf. Carter, *Emergence*.

17. Contra NIV, which interprets this phrase as an idiom—"the seed will grow well."

18. *TWOT* §807a, 2:348–49.

19. See also Deut. 33:28, where grain, new wine, and dew are signs of blessing.

The final verse repeats the contrast motif in terms of the theme of blessing and cursing and represents the main reason why this prophetic sermon was chosen for this particular place in Zechariah 7–8. Zechariah contrasts their experience among the nations as an object of curse (an example of God's judgment and discipline) with their experience in the coming era in which they will become not only an example of but also a conduit for God's blessing to the nations.

The language in this verse is linked to covenant blessing/curse texts (e.g., Deut. 11:26–28; 28:2, 15; 30:1, 19). Clearly Zechariah is alluding here to the future signs of blessing already reviewed in Zechariah 8:12. Deuteronomy 30:19 defines curse and blessing in the strongest of terms: curse, the result of disobedience, is death, while blessing, the result of obedience, is life. The people are called to obedience and thus to experience life in the blessing of the Creator. God's promise of blessing in Zechariah 8:13 is a promise of life for a community that was once in the position of death among the nations.

Nevertheless, the way the language of blessing and curse is constructed creates an unmistakable link to another tradition of blessing and curse: the Abrahamic tradition. Although the word pair curse/blessing is typical of the Deuteronomic covenant texts, the verbal phrase in which the word "blessing" occurs in 8:13 ("you will be a blessing") is reminiscent of the promise to Abraham in Genesis 12:2. There God promises to bless Abraham, and he will in turn become a source of blessing to the nations. Zechariah represents a similar trend. The people had been an example of curse among the nations, but they will now become a source of blessing to the nations. This is the first sign in this passage of the universal implications of this new era in redemptive history (see also Zech. 8:20–23).

The transformation from curse to blessing is accomplished by the redemptive action of Yahweh ("so will I save you"). As at the end of the previous collection in 8:1–8, so here God declares his intention to "save" (*yašaᶜ*) his people. The nation is referred to as "Judah and Israel." Although this shows the priority of the southern tribe in the new economy of God's people, Zechariah's vision is for the salvation of the entire Jewish community.

Zechariah's sermon, drawn from the refounding ceremony, comes to a close by repeating the first words from 8:9: "Let your hands be strong."[20] In its original oral setting Zechariah encourages the builders by declaring the promises of God's blessing in their present experience and the impact of their faithfulness on the nations as a whole.[21]

---

20. This cannot be seen in the NIV. In the Heb., "let your hands be strong" is the first phrase in 8:9 following "This is what the LORD Almighty says" (8:9).

21. The connection between temple rebuilding and social justice is seen in Mesopotamian ceremonies; cf. J. A. Bewer, "Ancient Babylonian Parallels to the Prophecies of Haggai," *AJSL* 35 (1919): 128–33.

As with the oracle collection in 8:1–8, the sermon in 8:9–13 has been chosen for its suitability to this transition spot between 7:14 and 8:14. Whereas 8:1–8 connected with and transformed the scattering of the people throughout the nations (7:14a), so 8:9–13 connects with and transforms the desolation of the land.[22] The community in the early Persian period is depicted at the tail end of God's discipline on the land. The desolate and impassable land of 7:14, which continued into the recent experience of the remnant community (8:10–11), will now be transformed into its former bountiful state. Verse 13 foreshadows an expansion of a renewed Yehud as it looks to the role God's people will play in the blessing of the nations.

Bridging Contexts

THESE PROPHECIES STAND in stark contrast to the ending of the prophetic sermon in chapter 7. Here we are offered a positive vision of God's intentions for his people, which prepares the way for the prophet's invitation to obedience in 8:16. This positive vision focuses attention on the great saving work of God in delivering his remnant from bondage among the nations, restoring covenant relationship with them, and blessing them in their own land.

Many Christian interpreters have treated 8:1–8 as an idyllic picture of a future millennial kingdom with Jerusalem as its capital.[23] This is based on an approach that links Old Testament passages similar to Zechariah 8 (e.g., Isa. 2; 5; 11; Mic. 4) to the picture of the thousand-year reign of the saints with Christ in Revelation 20:1–6. In the introduction to the commentary (Bridging Contexts section), we have dealt extensively with this issue and have argued that although these passages have implications for the ultimate destination of history, one should not ignore the way they should shape our vision of the community (Israel, Jerusalem) that Christ came to establish through his death and resurrection.

In addition, one should interpret the images in these passages as symbolic of the prosperity of God's community in the era established by Jesus that culminates in his second coming. This hermeneutical orientation to this passage highlights the relevance of this text for Christian communities today as this text describes the reality we can already experience through Christ, rather than only a distant hope for the future. Several themes shared by both

22. Note that the focus in 8:1–8 is on urban prosperity, while 8:9–13 develops the prosperity of rural Yehud.

23. E.g., F. Hartman, *Zechariah: Israel's Messenger of the Messiah's Triumph* (Bellmawr, N.J.: The Friends of Israel Gospel Ministry, 1994); R. B. Gifford, *Zechariah: The Gift of Vision* (Deeper Life Pulpit Commentary; Camp Hill, Pa.: Christian Publications, 1998).

prophetic pieces in 8:1–13 (remnant, salvation, nations) help shape our response to this passage.

Remnant. Both prophecies refer to the "remnant of this people," a phrase used in the Old Testament to describe the community purified from discipline—in this case, the discipline of exile. This theme can be traced into most of the prophetic traditions of the Old Testament,[24] but a closer look at Isaiah 6 provides a good orientation.

In Isaiah 6 the prophet is confronted with the overwhelming experience of the presence of the Holy One of Israel, an experience that will fundamentally shape the content of his message (cf. Isa. 30:10–18). The prophet overhears the proceedings of the divine court and the question of God: "Whom shall I send? And who will go for us?" (6:8a). Isaiah signals his willingness to accept this calling (6:8b) even before he understands fully its details (6:9–13). Then we learn that he is being called to proclaim the destruction of the kingdom (6:11–13a) because of a holy God's discipline of a rebellious people.

This destruction is described in two waves. (1) The land will be ruined, ravaged, and utterly forsaken as well as without inhabitant. (2) The tenth that remains in the land will again be devastated by discipline. However, God does offer one ray of hope: "As the terebinth and oak leave stumps when they are cut down, so the holy seed will be the stump in the land" (6:11b). Although great trees have now been destroyed (the kingdoms of Israel and Judah), there will remain a "holy seed," which represents hope of renewal out of the ashes of discipline.

As an introduction to the great prophetic collection and tradition in the Old Testament (Isaiah to Malachi), Isaiah 6 foreshadows the events that befall this rebellious people. But at the same time it reminds the reader of two important truths. (1) It establishes the prophetic message on the holy character of the God of Israel who is high and lifted up and yet whose robe fills the temple and glory fills the earth. (2) It orients that message toward the creation of a holy people (holy seed), whose character matches their God. This holy seed is the expected remnant of the prophetic tradition, the remnant that is spoken of in Zechariah 8 near the end of this great prophetic collection and tradition.

In the New Testament this remnant is identified with the followers gathered around Jesus. In reviewing the rejection and acceptance of Jesus by the Jewish community, John 12:41 alludes to the prophetic ministry of Isaiah

24. See M. W. Elliott, "Remnant," in *New Dictionary of Biblical Theology*, ed. T. D. Alexander and B. S. Rosner (Leicester: Inter-Varsity Press, 2000), 723–26; and esp. G. F. Hasel, *The Remnant: The History and Theology of the Remnant Idea from Genesis to Isaiah*, 3d ed. (AUMSR 5; Berrien Springs, Mich.: Andrews Univ. Press, 1980).

and claims that Isaiah gazed on Jesus' glory in Isaiah 6. In Jesus, the high and lifted-up One has inhabited the earth in order to create a holy remnant.

Peter makes this clear in his sermon on Pentecost when he links the outpouring of the Spirit with Joel's promise in Joel 2:28–32, where the Spirit is poured out "on Mount Zion and in Jerusalem ... among the survivors whom the LORD calls." So also in Acts 2 the Spirit is poured out on survivors from the nations gathered in Jerusalem for the feast. Joel 2 contains several fascinating links to Zechariah 8 as the promise of the Spirit on the remnant is preceded by the call to genuine repentance (2:12–17) and God's zealous (*qinaʾ*) mercy and restoration of people and blessing (2:18–27). In light of the use of Joel 2 in Acts 2, we understand that the remnant promises of the Old Testament now relate to the church as the community of Christ.

Salvation and blessing. This understanding of the remnant from the New Testament perspective has implications for our appropriation of the message of 8:1–13. In 8:7–8, 13 salvation is clearly a physical salvation from the nations. On one level this has been fulfilled in the early church on the Day of Pentecost as the community returns to Jerusalem for salvation. But in New Testament theology Jerusalem becomes equated with the church (Heb. 12:22–24; Rev. 21:2), which becomes the destination of God's remnant community from among the nations. In this way, then, the image of prosperity is one that needs to be understood in terms relevant to the new Jerusalem. Unquestionably, this is a picture of the ultimate experience of the church when Christ returns. But we should not ignore the opportunity to experience a foretaste of this experience even in this age.

Nation and nations. Both prophecies also share the theme of the nations. However, the emphasis in each of these is not identical. The first piece focuses on the rescue of Israel *from* the nations and God's blessing on them. It is exclusively internal focused. The second piece also emphasizes the blessing of God on the remnant saved from the nations, but at the end foreshadows God's purpose in this blessing: to bring blessing *to* the nations. This prepares the way for 8:14–23, in which we see the impact of God's blessing on the nations of the world. In this Israel fulfills its role in God's great plan of redemption initiated in Genesis 12:1–3.

Character of God. The foundation of all of this hope in 8:1–13 is clearly the character of God, in particular, the intensity of his love for his people, expressed through the explosive expression: "I am very jealous for Zion; I am burning with jealousy for her" (8:1) as well as the reassuring refrain: "I will be faithful and righteous to them as their God" (8:8). It is easy to forget that these are the declarations of the God who seeks true worshipers who will worship "in spirit and truth" (John 4:23). In light of the revelation of Zechariah 8:1–13, we turn now to response.

Contemporary Significance

INTIMACY WITH GOD. Zechariah 8:1 locates Yahweh's intention in moving from discipline to deliverance in his passionate zeal for his people. This reminds us that although this passage emphasizes human response, God is the One who must enact salvation for his people. He does not do so begrudgingly, but rather fervently desires to save and know his people. This revelation of God's heart is the greatest source of hope for every generation. God's discipline flows from the heart of a parent who desires intimate relationship with his children (Heb. 12). He does not take sin lightly, however, for it violates his very character and threatens to destroy his children.

God's zeal also leads to a renewal of covenant relationship (8:7–8). This relationship is possible because God will return to his city and dwell with his returned people (8:2, 8). Such a relationship lies at the core of Old Testament theology. The foundational act of salvation for Israel, the Exodus, also had covenant relationship as its goal (Ex. 3:12) and established a pattern regularly repeated throughout the story and witness of Israel. Christ's death and resurrection represented the climax of this pattern, issuing into the intimacy of the new covenant.

This relational goal is the greatest benefit of salvation for, as the Westminster Catechism reminds us, our chief aim is to glorify God and enjoy him forever. So often we turn covenant relationship into dutiful religion. The fasts of the exilic period lost their way because they did not see this dimension. They had become a ritual to be performed to get one's way rather than to be a means to relationship with the covenant God.

This passage, then, highlights two characteristics in God that support intimate relationship with him. (1) We catch a glimpse of God's passionate engagement in this relationship. Often we view God as a distant Father whose love is assumed but never expressed, and this inevitably impacts our own intimacy with God. (2) We catch a glimpse of God's permanent commitment to this relationship. He reassures his people in 8:8 that he will be "faithful and righteous to them as their God." Not only is his passionate love deep, it is enduring.

On a recent speaking trip to the west coast of the United States, I slipped into the back pew of a church led by a childhood friend. That day he was preaching on the intimacy expressed from the Father to the Son at the baptism of Jesus in Luke 3:21–22: "You are my Son, whom I love; with you I am well pleased." He then shared the story of his own father, who grew up in a home broken apart by my friend's alcoholic grandfather. Because of these experiences, my friend's father expressed little intimacy with his children as they grew up in his home.

While at seminary, however, my friend and his wife joined a Bible study group led by one of his professors. One night while the group was meeting at the professor's home, one of his sons came home. Before going upstairs to bed, the son and father expressed their love for one another in a way that showed it was a natural part of their relationship. That night when my friend went home, he took his one-year-old son in his arms, looked him in the eyes, and slowly said the simple words: "I love you." He admitted that at first this phrase did not come naturally to him, but he persisted each night for the next week until it became a natural part of their relationship.

This kind of passion and intimacy is not alien to the Lord God. He expressed it through his prophet Zechariah to his people, he expressed it to his Son Jesus Christ, and through Jesus he expresses it to his people today. He is passionate for us in relationship, and this kind of vulnerable passion enables us to respond with the same kind of passionate abandon in our relationship with God. Furthermore, for a generation that has experienced not only superficial relationships within their families but also inconsistent relationships because of divorce or separation, this declaration from God is also essential for fostering intimacy in our relationship with God. The Lord is a God who is the same "yesterday, today and forever" (Heb. 12:8), and on that basis invites us into intimate relationship ("they will be my people").

Creation of a community. On the basis of this revelation of God's relational passion the prophet Zechariah discloses the kind of community that God desires for his people. Attainment of the values of this community in their fullness awaits the new Jerusalem at the end of time, but God's intention is to showcase these values in the church today.

According to Zechariah 8 this community is one that accentuates the presence of God, "I will return to Zion and dwell in Jerusalem" (8:1), and a relationship with him, "They will be my people, and I will be faithful and righteous to them as their God" (8:8). This kind of presence and relationship is fostered not only through individuals who pursue intimate relationship with God in their individual lives and homes, but also through communities that make this a priority in their corporate experience.

The early church's impact on their generation is clearly linked to the fact that they were a people marked by the presence of God. The Sanhedrin, astonished by the courage and brilliance of the disciples, "took note that these men had been with Jesus" (Acts 4:13). After being released from prison, they gathered together as a community to seek the face of God. "The place where they were meeting was shaken. And they were all filled with the Holy Spirit and spoke the word of God boldly" (4:31). The impact of this community cannot be separated from the fact that they were a people who not only experienced but also sought God's presence. This should prompt us as leaders of Christian communities to evaluate our corporate experience. Is it characterized by the presence of God? How do we foster intimacy with God in our corporate experience?

The community in Zechariah 8, which is characterized by that presence, is a community portraying the values of their God. Jerusalem is thus called the "City of Truth" and the "Holy Mountain" (8:3). As we noted above, the term "truth" focuses on the fidelity of this community to God's core values, while the term "holy" underlines the fact that this community is set apart for God's purposes. In a way these two values are the same, for they refer to a community that takes seriously their calling as God's sacred people and thus follow him faithfully. Here status and action are intertwined as a holy people walk in holiness.

This community is also a community characterized by new and abundant life. They revel in the salvation they have experienced in God and enjoy the prosperity he offers to them by his grace, expressed in Zechariah 8 through multiple images of life: long human life ("men and women of ripe old age"), new human life ("boys and girls playing"), and abundant agricultural life ("the seed will grow well, the vine will yield its fruits"). The community of God is thus a place where people experience life as God intended it—eternal life, abundant life.

Frederich Nietzsche, in one of his last treatises, *The Twilight of the Idols* (*Götzen-Dämmerung*), caricatured Christianity as "Anti-Nature." He accused the church of never asking: "How can one spiritualize, beautify, deify a desire?" but rather always laying "the emphasis of its discipline on extirpation (of sensuality, of pride, of lust for power, of avarice, of revengefulness)." It is this that Nietzsche despised most, for "to attack the passions at their roots means to attack life at its roots: the practice of the Church is *hostile to life*."[25]

Whether this was true in Nietzsche's church experience is a matter of debate, but it is certainly not true in biblical theology. Here we find a robust view of life presented in its fullness in the Garden of Eden (Gen. 2), rejected through human disobedience (Gen. 3), restored through the sacrificial act of Jesus on the cross, who breathes the re-creative life of the Spirit (John 20:22) into his people destined for the new heavens and earth (Rev. 21–22). Because Christ is "life" (John 14:6) and has been granted "life in himself" (5:26), he invites humanity to "come to me to have life" (5:40). The one who believes has "everlasting life" (6:47), a condition that is not only quantitatively greater (eternal) but also qualitatively greater (life "to the full," 10:10). Through Christ we can truly be fully alive, that is, experience life the way God intended it in creation. But this only is possible as we experience the life-giving touch of the Spirit available to us through the resurrected Christ and become "a new creation" (2 Cor. 5:17).

25. F. Nietzsche, *Twilight of the Idols and The Anti-Christ*, trans. R. J. Hollingdale (New York: Penguin Books, 1990), 52.

Paul Hoon challenges us to consider this qualitative difference that the resurrected Christ offers to us today. In his book *Integrity of Worship*, he reflects on the post-resurrection appearance of Christ with his disciples:

> Jesus Christ continually contradicts us in the way we experience ourselves as alive, and compels us to radically redefine what we mean by life. He encounters us the way he encountered the disciples on Easter Sunday. They were the ones marked out for death. Those who survived him were really the "dead." He the "dead" one was really the living.[26]

It was in that encounter that Jesus breathed into them the re-creative life of the Spirit and they became fully alive, and in the same way the Creator Christ continues to breathe this new life into his people, an act foreshadowed by the images of eternal and abundant life in Zechariah 8.

This description of the community in Zechariah 8 may suggest to some a "holy huddle" cut off from the world and critical of those who are not citizens of this new city. However, this is a people who are well aware that this new status and action is based on the loving grace of the God of salvation. Therefore, there is no room for pharisaism in those who have been rescued from the kingdom of darkness into the kingdom of light. This is suggested by one of the final phrases in 8:1–13: "So will I save you, and you will be a blessing" (8:13). This community of life is destined to be a community of blessing as was promised to Abraham of old. This will be the focus of our attention in 8:14–23.

Beyond our imagination. This description of God's plans for his community and world would have seemed incredulous to Zechariah's audience, as God himself says: "It may seem marvelous to the remnant of this people at that time, but will it seem marvelous to me?" (8:6). Even for those of us living after the first advent of Christ, this vision of a holy and faithful community experiencing abundant and eternal life as they bless the nations is a stretch. However, as God said to Zechariah's audience, he says to us today that he is "able to do immeasurably more than all we ask or imagine, according to his power that is at work within us" (Eph. 3:20).

For Zechariah it was a matter of faith in the promises of God, a response to which we are called in our day and age as we face challenges beyond our human capability, whether that is the evangelization of nations resistant to the gospel, the renewal of inner cities devastated by drugs, or the relief of countries reeling from natural disasters. He is the God of the impossible, who will accomplish his will in us by the power of his Spirit.

---

26. Paul W. Hoon, *Integrity of Worship* (Nashville: Abingdon, 1971), 141. I am grateful to Ravi Zacharias for drawing my attention to this quote, found in *A Shattered Visage: The Real Face of Atheism* (Grand Rapids: Baker, 1990), 162.

Zechariah 8:14–23

THIS IS WHAT the LORD Almighty says: "Just as I had
determined to bring disaster upon you and showed no
pity when your fathers angered me," says the LORD
Almighty, [15]"so now I have determined to do good again to
Jerusalem and Judah. Do not be afraid. [16]These are the things
you are to do: Speak the truth to each other, and render true
and sound judgment in your courts; [17]do not plot evil against
your neighbor, and do not love to swear falsely. I hate all this,"
declares the LORD.
[18]Again the word of the LORD Almighty came to me. [19]This
is what the LORD Almighty says: "The fasts of the fourth, fifth,
seventh and tenth months will become joyful and glad occasions
and happy festivals for Judah. Therefore love truth and peace."
[20]This is what the LORD Almighty says: "Many peoples and
the inhabitants of many cities will yet come, [21]and the inhabi-
tants of one city will go to another and say, 'Let us go at once
to entreat the LORD and seek the LORD Almighty. I myself am
going.' [22]And many peoples and powerful nations will come to
Jerusalem to seek the LORD Almighty and to entreat him."
[23]This is what the LORD Almighty says: "In those days ten
men from all languages and nations will take firm hold of one
Jew by the hem of his robe and say, 'Let us go with you,
because we have heard that God is with you.'"

Original Meaning

ZECHARIAH 8:14–23 IS the final component of the larger literary complex of 7:1–8:23. The messenger formula that begins verse 14 ("This is what the LORD Almighty says") signals a new speech. While the previous section in 8:9–13 represented a sermon to encourage the community to continue rebuilding the temple, 8:14–17 returns to the discussion begun in chapter 7 that broke off in 7:14. Here we find a couple of touch points with the earlier section, including Yahweh's anger with the former generation (8:14; cf. 7:12), similar ethical demands (8:16–17; cf. 7:9–10), and address in the second person ("you"; 8:16; cf. 7:5–6).[1]

1. See Boda, "Fasts to Feasts," 390–407. For an explanation of the historical context of this dialogue, see 7:1–14 (Original Meaning).

God's New Determination (8:14–15)

ZECHARIAH EMPHASIZES GOD'S INTENTIONS in disciplining the former generation. This speech plays off of the oracle in Jeremiah 4, in which the prophet envisions the destroyed city of Jerusalem. In 4:28 he uses the same two verbs as found in Zechariah 8:14: "determined" (*zamam*) and "show pity" (*naḥam*). Jeremiah proclaimed Yahweh's determination to discipline his people, a discipline that in Jeremiah's day would not be revoked through Yahweh's pity. Notice how the former and present generations are indistinguishable in Zechariah's speech. The prophet speaks of disaster on "you" although it is in response to the disobedience of "your fathers."

This is typical of the penitential prayer tradition common on the days of fasting and a source of rhetorical play for Zechariah already in this dialogue with the Bethel group (see 7:1–14). The telescoping of generations is drawn from the key passage Leviticus 26:40, so influential in shaping the agenda of penitential prayer (cf. Ezra 9:7; Neh. 1:6–7; 9:32, 37; Dan. 9:8–11, 16).[2]

Zechariah plays on the term "determined" (*zamam*) to signal a new era of redemptive history. The use of this term emphasizes "divine intentionality" and interestingly is only used elsewhere in the Hebrew Bible in reference to Yahweh's intention to enact discipline (Jer. 4:28; 51:12; Lam. 2:17; Zech. 1:6).[3] In a creative rhetorical move Zechariah plays off this judgment term to signal a turn in the experience of this community. Now instead of disaster ("to bring disaster"; *raᶜaᶜ* in Hiphil), they will experience good ("to do good," *yaṭab* in Hiphil). Yahweh's goodness is directed at Jerusalem and (lit., "the house of") Judah. Because "house of Judah" and "Jerusalem" regularly refer to the remnant community in prophetic literature (Isa. 40), there is no question that the prophet has God's people in mind as the recipients of his goodness. However, it is unlikely that the prophet can place any distance between this remnant community and the physical site of Jerusalem presently under construction.

God's Ethical Demand (8:16–17)

THE COMFORTING WORDS "do not be afraid" bring closure to this oracle of salvation, a regular feature of prophetic speech.[4] The prophet, however, is not finished for now he identifies the part the people must play in order to experience this turn in redemptive history. Verses 16–17 offer a list of admonitions to follow and prohibitions to avoid. Striking similarities between this list and the list ignored by the former generation in 7:9–10 remind the people of the importance of these imperatives in order to avoid the "disaster" of the past. The

2. See Boda, "Penitential Prophet," 49–69; cf. Boda, *Praying*.

3. Petersen, *Haggai*, 309–10.

4. C. Westermann, *Prophetic Oracles of Salvation in the Old Testament* (Louisville: Westminster John Knox, 1991).

introductory phrase ("these are the things," *ʾelleh haddebarim*) is reminiscent of the beginning of the Decalogue (Ex. 20:1), which says that God spoke all "these words" (*haddebarim haʾelleh*).[5] As we saw in Zechariah 7:12, the law is the foundation for prophetic proclamation and is the ultimate source of the list that follows.

The list of ethical demands contains two admonitions (positive) and two prohibitions (negative). The underlying context here is the court system within Yehud, made clear by the use of the phrase "in your gates" (NIV, "in your courts"), the location where justice was carried out in ancient Israel (cf. Deut. 21:19; Ruth 4). The place of relationships takes top priority within the covenant community as is seen in the repeated phrase (lit.) "each with his neighbor" in the first admonition and the first prohibition.[6] The admonitions single out the actions of both those who use and those who administer the justice system. For all parties involved in the justice system, there must be adherence to the "truth."

In the two prohibitions, Zechariah focuses on the thoughts and affections of the heart. As in 7:9–10, Zechariah prohibits plotting the harm of others in the covenant community. He also forbids even the desire or "love" of bearing false witness in the court setting. Such a love of evil contrasts God's negative disposition: "I hate all this." This is highly emotive language that echoes the message of the Law and the Prophets. God's hatred is directed toward idolatry in the Mosaic law (e.g., Deut. 12:31; 16:21–22), but the prophetic tradition extends this also to issues of justice in the context of festal activity (e.g., Isa. 1:13–17; Mal. 2:16).[7] The fact that several of these references to Yahweh's hatred appear in contexts related to festal and sacrificial activity may explain Zechariah's use of this language here as he answers the delegation from Bethel.

Transformation of Fasts to Feasts (8:18–19)

THE MENTION OF GOD'S HATRED of all "these" (NIV "all this") brings closure to the list of ethical demands by repeating the initial word in verse 16: "these." It also brings closure to a much longer section that began in 7:7. To many this may seem to be a long digression from the issue raised by the delegation

5. Petersen (*Haggai*, 310–11) notes Ex. 24:3 and the regular appearance of this vocabulary in the Deuteronomic tradition; cf. M. Weinfeld, *Deuteronomy and the Deuteronomic School* (Oxford: Clarendon, 1972), 65, 152, 261, 304, 336.

6. NIV, "to each other" in v. 16; "against your neighbor" in v. 17.

7. Hosea declares God's hatred of the people's activity at Gilgal (idolatry, 9:15). Jer. 44:1–6 links the fall of Jerusalem to God's hatred of idolatry. Amos 5:18–27 mentions God's hatred in connection with both idolatry and justice. Other references to God's hatred in the prophets are linked to injustice (Isa. 61:8; Mal. 2:16). The last one is esp. interesting because of its link to the injustice of women and children as already seen in 7:9–10. Notice how this is attacked in relation to festal activity (2:13).

from Bethel. However, for Zechariah to give his answer to their question, he has had to set it in the much larger context of redemptive history. He has reminded them that their fasting arose from God's discipline on an earlier generation that did not respond to the ethical demands of God. Zechariah has used this opportunity to call them to transcend the covenant infidelity of those responsible for the disastrous conditions of the Exile and to realize the purpose of the fasting liturgy: covenant fidelity. He has promised them that this will enact a new era of redemptive history, for God is determined to "do good again."

Zechariah signals the climactic nature of his answer in 8:18 by the use of the messenger formula: "The word of the LORD Almighty came to me," a formula only used in the section at the outset of the message in 7:4.[8] He declares that all the fasts practiced by the Jewish community during the exilic period will be transformed into festivals for Judah. We have already noted how these fasts were connected to the various key events leading up to and following the fall of Jerusalem and Judah in the Babylonian period (see Original Meaning on 7:1–3). Zechariah is not attacking the fasting cycle of the Babylonian period communities, as some suggest, but is looking to the future when fasting will be turned to feasting because the new era has been inaugurated.[9]

The purpose of the intervening section has been to shape the fasting liturgy and to call the people to fasting, which will indeed accomplish the purpose for which it was designed: an expression of repentance from infidelity and a commitment to obey God's covenant demands. The previous imperatives in 8:16–17 have shown that this new era will not be inaugurated unless the people obey the ethical demands urged by the earlier prophets.

The term here for festival (*moʾed*) is used in Leviticus 23:2 to refer to the cycle of worship experiences for the Israelites: weekly (Sabbath) or yearly (e.g., Passover). These were joyous times, celebrating God's goodness in harvest and redemption. During the Exile such festivals ceased (Lam. 1:4). The prophet builds up a series of celebrative terms in connection with the festivals: "joyful" (*śaśon*), "glad" (*śimḥah*), and "happy" (*ṭob*). The word *śimḥah* can signify a feast and is used in parallel with festival (*moʾed*) to refer to the festal calendar in Numbers 10:10 (cf. Deut. 12:7; 14:26; 16:11; 26:11; 27:7). The word *ṭob* appears in the idiom "day of happiness," which signifies a feast (1 Sam. 25:8; Est. 8:17).

The terms "joyful" (*śaśon*) and "glad" (*śimḥah*) appear together as a word pair in texts related to the celebration of marriage feasts (Jer. 7:34; 16:9; 25:10;

---

8. The NIV unfortunately masks this by adding the word "again" in 8:18, which is not in the Heb. text, and by adding the phrase "to me" in 8:1, which is also not present. Notice how 7:8 uses "to Zechariah."

9. "The Prophet has maintained that the time for fasting is over and the time of feasting is imminent"; Petersen, *Haggai*, 314.

33:10–11) and the festal cycle of Israel (Isa. 22:13; 33:10–11). On several occasions the word pair appears in connection with the future restoration of the remnant to Israel (Isa. 35:10; 51:3, 11; Jer. 31:13; 33:10–11; cf. Isa. 61:3). Occasionally in the prophets there is a change from mourning to gladness and joy (Isa. 51:3, 11; 61:3). Zechariah is prophesying a period when fasting will no longer be necessary, a period when the tone of the community will be the joy and gladness of the festal calendar.

The final phrase of verse 19, however, reminds the community that this future image of blessing is dependent on their response to the message of those earlier prophets. Zechariah again links the ethical and the ritual: Fasts are to be connected to ethics and future feasts will be dependent on ethics. In contrast to his use of "love" in the prohibition of verse 17, Zechariah now encourages a love of faithfulness (truth) and peace. This more general command sums up the previous ethical messages in 7:9–10 and 8:16–17.

The command to love is found in the covenant base of Israel (Deut. 6:4–5), but there it is linked to the love of Yahweh. Zechariah moves in a complementary yet distinct direction, calling the community to love the qualities demanded by Yahweh. This echoes Amos's call to love good while hating evil in calling his community to justice in the "gates" (Amos 5:15). Here again, Zechariah is drawing on earlier prophets to call his own generation to the priorities of Yahweh.

Impact on the Nations—Entreating Yahweh (8:20–23)

FOLLOWING VERSE 19 we find two additional oracles that expand the scope of the discussion. It is probable that this section belongs to the answer to the Bethel delegation, especially because of two appearances of the idiom "entreat [the face of]" (8:21, 22) found in 7:2.

The first oracle (8:20–22) reflects a strong tradition in the prophetic movement in which the nations are drawn to Jerusalem to seek Yahweh (esp. Isa. 2:2–4; Mic. 4:1–5).[10] These people are not identified as part of the Jewish community, although they use the covenant name of God, Yahweh. The prophet uses the literary device apostrophe (the quotation in 8:21b), giving an exhortation of the foreigners to make the scene more vivid. The language here is extremely passionate, using Hebrew doubling techniques for the verb ("Let us go at once") and pronoun ("I myself"). We do not know how these people have heard about Yahweh, but they not only are drawn to his presence in Jerusalem but also implore others to accompany them.

10. Cf. E. H. Merrill, "Pilgrimage and Procession: Motifs of Israel's Return," in *Israel's Apostasy and Restoration: Essays in Honor of Roland K. Harrison*, ed. A. Gileadi (Grand Rapids: Baker, 1988), 261–72.

The second oracle (8:23–24) highlights the role of the Jewish community returning from exile. It relies on the period described in 8:20–22 ("in those days," v. 23) and is thus reliant on that vision. The image of the "ten men from all languages and nations" expands the vision of the "many peoples and powerful nations" of verse 22. The number "ten" refers to completeness and stresses the universal vision of this pilgrimage (cf. 1 Sam. 1:8). Twice the Hebrew here says that these ten will "take firm hold" of a Jew, seizing whatever they can grasp ("hem," lit., corner). As with the previous oracle, the prophet uses apostrophe to make the oracle more vivid. These people want to accompany the Jew to Jerusalem because they have heard that "God is with you."

This final phrase of Zechariah 1–8 prophesies closure to a key issue introduced at the outset of the book. In Zechariah's initial sermon (Zech. 1:3), God called his people to return to him so that he might return to them. In the first night vision his return to Jerusalem is promised (1:16), a motif appearing in the third vision and accompanying oracle (2:5, 10–11). Now comes the ultimate significance of the response of this community to the cries of Yahweh's prophet. Their obedience will usher in the new era in which Jerusalem will fulfill its original purpose as the place of God's manifest presence on earth, from which his rule will extend over the cosmos and to which all nations will bend their knee either in glad adoration or broken submission.

In sum, the prophetic messages contained within chapters 7–8 have been drawn together to communicate a message of challenge and hope for God's people. The original message was prompted by the fasting practices of the exilic period, which arose in response to the fall and destruction of Jerusalem and Judah. Zechariah challenges his generation to make their fasts appropriate expressions of repentance from the injustices of their ancestors to the covenant agenda proclaimed by the earlier prophets so to avoid extending the Exile indefinitely. While the initial sermon (1:1–6) and vision (1:7–17) proclaimed hope for a penitent people, it is clear from Zechariah 7–8 that at least for some sectors of this community, penitential rites were a mere facade. There was need for true penitence among the people.

Zechariah also engenders hope by linking community obedience to a new vision of salvation. In response to a penitent people pursuing the values of justice, Yahweh has determined to bless Jerusalem and Judah. The sign of this change will be the transformation of the exilic fasts into restoration feasts. Several additional oracles describe more fully the restoration to come. The prosperity of Jerusalem will be realized because of the work of a passionate God, who will once again take up residence in the city. This God will then fill the city with his remnant saved from exile and will shower on this obedient community his blessing. But there is more. This renewed community will fulfill the role promised to Abraham by becoming a blessing to the nations as these are drawn to the city of God's presence.

Bridging Contexts

MUCH OF ZECHARIAH 1–6 focused attention on issues related to the present circumstances of Zechariah's generation. Although this same trend is found in Zechariah 7–8 with its focus on their fasting rituals, one can discern a stronger orientation toward the future.

Jerusalem and Judah. These chapters focus attention on the role of Jerusalem within God's redemptive purposes. For some scholars these prophecies were never fulfilled within the subsequent Jewish communities and therefore they insist these conditions still lie in the future.[11] In one respect these interpreters are correct in arguing that Zechariah's vision was never fully realized in the following generations. Jerusalem did become the destination of many who had been scattered among the nations, but the vision of Gentiles attracted to this city in large numbers was never fulfilled—that is, if one makes a clear demarcation between Jewish and Christian communities. However, if one evaluates this prophecy from the perspective of the early Christian community and its view of Jerusalem, then fulfillment can be shown.

The early Christian community identified A.D. 70 as a key redemptive-historical event that had great implications for their own identity. The second destruction of physical Jerusalem, this time by the Romans, marked the end of one era of redemptive history and the beginning of another (cf. Matt. 23:37–24:31).[12] The early church, as earthly inheritors of the throne of Yahweh, assumed the hopes and dreams of Jerusalem. In this way the writer of Hebrews can claim that Christians have come to "Mount Zion, the heavenly Jerusalem, the city of the living God" and in the same breath declare that they have come to "the church of the firstborn" (Heb. 12:22–23). The writer of Revelation can identify "the bride, the wife of the Lamb" with "the Holy City, Jerusalem" (Rev. 21:9–10; cf. 21:2).

It is no accident that the sending forth of the Spirit occurred during the Feast of Pentecost, when Jews from many nations speaking many tongues were gathered in Jerusalem (Acts 2). Here old and new Jerusalem live concurrently, but only for a time. The book of Acts traces the redemptive-historical action of God who uses the new Jerusalem as the full and faithful expression of his kingship on earth. That is, the church as Jerusalem is the seat from which God exercises his rulership in creation. This mobile city, no

11. E.g., Merrill, *Haggai*, 233–36; Hartman, *Zechariah*, 73–82; Gifford, *Zechariah: The Gift of Vision*, 137–68.

12. Similar to how the first destruction marked a major transition in redemptive history.

longer fixed in one location but rather a living community of people, moves out from physical Jerusalem and penetrates the nations of the world. In this way the prophecies of Zechariah are fulfilled in the church, into which flow the nations as they pursue the presence of God.

From fasts to feasts. Zechariah looks to a period when the present fasts will be replaced by feasts, activities appropriate for the time of restoration. As discussed in our introduction and in our consideration of 7:1–14, Christ's ministry ushered in this anticipated restoration. Jesus saw the restoration breaking in even during the time of his ministry as he discouraged his followers from fasting while he was with him (Matt. 9:15–16; Mark 2:19–22; Luke 5:34–37). This intimates that on one level, this transformation from fast to feast has already taken place now that Christ has come. But Christ also expects that after his departure they will fast. In light of this, one should not forget that restoration has not been fully realized in Christ's first coming, and we look forward to the consummation of all things in his second advent. At this time Christ sees the full realization of the festal message of Zechariah 8:14–23 when, while speaking to the Roman centurion in Matthew 8:10–11, he declares:

> I tell you the truth, I have not found anyone in Israel with such great faith. I say to you that many will come from the east and the west, and will take their places at the feast with Abraham, Isaac and Jacob in the kingdom of heaven.

The already–not yet character of the fulfillment of this transformation from fasts to feasts explains why we still face the kinds of issues that plagued Zechariah's community, and we must consider his message afresh within our generation. As the community that has inherited this message and begun to see its fulfillment in and through Christ, we need the discernment and empowerment of the Spirit to fully embrace and creatively accomplish the prophetic call.

Hermeneutics. Applying Zechariah's message is not an easy task for two reasons. (1) It entails deep reflection on the ways in which social injustice is evidenced within our society in general, but more importantly within our local contexts. God has raised up churches within specific communities in order to have an impact on the needs within that community. What that will mean within a rural community will be different from an urban context. Even within an urban context there will be diversity between inner-city and suburban contexts. So there is no easy, one-size-fits-all application for this passage.

(2) Zechariah's message is a challenge to apply because it may endanger the social privileges on which our lives are based. In Jeremiah 34 the prophet receives news that King Zedekiah and the people have made a covenant to

obey God's law and proclaim freedom for slaves, only to reverse their decision and enslave them again. It is not difficult to see why these people found it difficult to follow through on obedience. These slaves had contributed to the economic prosperity of the upper class. To release them was imperiling their economic system. So also as we reflect on the social issues of the communities in which we live, we run the danger of uncovering issues that, if confronted, may entail discomfort for us today.

As we turn now to consider the contemporary significance of Zechariah's message we do so cognizant of the relevance of this passage to us as a people grafted into the community of God through the sacrifice of Christ, but also keenly aware of the hermeneutical challenges we face and so declare our reliance on the Holy Spirit's power and creativity.

Contemporary Significance

FEASTING. IN CHAPTER 8 Zechariah looks to the future with hope. He envisions a day of restoration when a penitent people rejoice in the presence of their God. This reminds us that fasting is not an end in itself but has covenant relationship as its goal. The Old Testament sacrificial and festal system provided opportunity for such enjoyment of God, in which some sacrifices (fellowship) and nearly all feasts celebrated Israel's relationship with God.

Sin is a serious issue in the Bible, and the fasting liturgy arose among the postexilic community to express remorse over such sins individually and communally. As we have already noted in 7:1–14, Zechariah's prophecy encourages and shapes our rhythms of fasting as Christians today as we continue to live in an imperfect world and struggle with sin in our lives. But we need to remember that the death, resurrection, and ascension of Christ have signaled the beginning of restoration, and God invites us to begin celebrating this new era even prior to the "wedding supper of the Lamb" (Rev. 19:9).

In some revivalistic circles there is a tendency to focus so intently on penitence that there is little opportunity to bask in one's relationship with God, to celebrate joyously the grace we have experienced in and through Jesus Christ. This has implications for the preaching and teaching of Scriptures. Sometimes preachers should end their reflection on Scripture with a call to rejoice and worship the God of redemption and salvation. Rather than identify three steps to success or four points to apply, we should just stop and encourage our people to respond in praise to God for his character or thanksgiving for his salvation.

Churches should not feel guilty celebrating their life together as a community. In some ways this is a major purpose of our weekly gathering as a church, to celebrate all God's goodness to us during the preceding week. But churches should also take opportunities to enjoy fellowship meals together during their yearly rhythm of life as a congregation. These meals can become opportunities to share God's goodness with one another in word and deed. Celebrations on Easter Sunday or Christmas are important to the life of our faith communities.

Missiology. The covenantal aspect of God's community becomes central in 8:20–23, the grand finale of Zechariah's prophetic message. The nations are drawn to the restored community because this is the place where God's presence dwells, the intersection of heaven and earth. The language here is not the language of forced servitude (Ps. 2) but of willing relationship. This functions as both challenge and hope for the Jewish community. It means an expansion of their vision to include the nations, an emphasis established at the beginning of the redemptive story in the promise to Abraham (Gen. 12) and stressed in Isaiah and Jonah. It instills hope that their faithfulness will have cosmic implications and that God desires to fulfill his promise to make Jerusalem the seat of his rule.

This reminds us of God's priorities for the new Jerusalem, the church. The community blessed with God's presence is the one that takes seriously their covenant obligations to one another and the culture in which they dwell. The blessing of the nations typified by feasting is not possible if we do not "love truth and peace" (8:19). Here we see an intimate link between ethics and mission, an emphasis that is fundamental to the identity of Israel as God's covenant people.

C. Wright traces this link through two major covenants in Israel's history.[13] Prior to Abraham's heated dialogue with Yahweh over the fate of the righteous in Sodom, we see this link vividly displayed. In Genesis 18:19 God says: "For I have chosen him, so that he will direct his children and his household after him to keep the way of the LORD by doing what is right and just, so that the LORD will bring about for Abraham what he has promised him." Here is an unmistakable link between keeping the way of the Lord and realizing the promise that includes the blessing of the nations. This blessing is made poignantly clear in the dialogue that follows as Abraham pleads for the salvation of the righteous in this doomed city. Wright expresses it well:

---

13. C. J. H. Wright, "The Ethical Authority of the Old Testament: A Survey of Approaches," *TynBul* 43 (1992): 227–28; idem, *Walking in the Ways of the Lord: The Ethical Authority of the Old Testament*; idem, *Deuteronomy* (NIBCOT; Peabody, Mass.: Hendrickson, 1996); idem, "Old Testament Ethics: A Missiological Perspective," *Catalyst* 26.2 (2000; available at http://catalystresources.org/issues/262wright.html); cf. B. A. Strawn, "The X-Factor: Revisioning Biblical Holiness," *Asbury Theological Journal* 54 (1999): 79–81.

> In the midst of a world characterized by Sodom—whose evil is causing an outcry (vv. 20–21; twice: *ṣeʿaqa*, the technical term for the crying out of those suffering from oppression and cruelty) that can be heard in heaven itself, God wants a community characterized by his own values and priorities—righteousness (*ṣedaqa*: one wonders if the word play is intentional here, as it certainly is in Isa. 5:7) and justice.[14]

So also in the Sinaitic covenant, the Israelites are called to become a community attracting the admiration of the nations (Deut. 4:6–8) and serving as priestly mediators for these peoples (Ex. 19:4–6). Emulating the covenant priorities of the law in God's community was essential to the mission of Israel.

The connection between holiness and mission continues into the New Testament witness. The book of 1 Peter spirals between these twin themes, drawing on the Old Testament witness. The call to holiness, supported by quotations from the Old Testament (1 Peter 1:16; 2:9–10; 3:8–12), is linked to the witness of the church (2:11–12; 3:12–17). The one who makes these two priorities possible is the Holy Spirit: holiness (1:2) and witness (Acts 1:8). Through Jesus, God has created a holy community in which he will display his righteousness and draw the nations to himself. This should motivate us to seek holiness in our communities of faith. This holiness, however, should not be confined to private categories of personal piety, but as we have seen in Zechariah 7–8, needs to extend to the social realm.

Zechariah calls his own generation as well as the Christian community to a life of purity, purity in our relationships with one another and especially in our treatment of the vulnerable, the poor, and the needy. Such purity is powerfully attractive to the community that surrounds us.

In his fascinating book *The Kingdom of God Is a Party*, Tony Campolo illustrates this kind of care. Campolo was attending a Christian conference in Honolulu, Hawaii. The six-hour time differential between Honolulu and his hometown left Campolo awake at about three o'clock in the morning, wandering the streets of Honolulu searching for a place to get something to eat. Eventually he found a tiny coffee shop that was open. He went in and sat down. While there he overheard a conversation between two prostitutes, the one, Agnes, confiding in the other that the next day was her birthday. What caught Tony's attention was the fact that Agnes admitted she had never had a birthday party in her whole life. When the women had all left, Tony turned to Harry, the owner of the diner, and hatched a plan to throw the woman a birthday party the next night, promising to return.

Thus, as planned, Campolo returned at 2:30 A.M. to decorate the coffee shop. Word had spread about the party and by 3:15 the place was wall-to-wall

14. Wright, "Missiological Perspective," online source.

prostitutes. At 3:30 A.M., Agnes walked in the diner to screams of "Happy Birthday!" The woman was so overwhelmed her mouth fell open, her legs weakened, and she had to sit down. When the birthday cake with all the candles was carried out, she openly cried. Unable to blow out the candles, Harry blew them out for her and then offered her a knife to cut the cake. Campolo continues:

> Agnes looked down at the cake. Then without taking her eyes off it, she slowly and softly said, "Look, Harry, is it all right with you if I . . . I mean is it O.K. if I kind of . . . what I want to ask you is . . . is it O.K. if I keep the cake a little while? I mean is it all right if we don't eat it right away?" Harry shrugged and answered, "Sure! It's O.K. If you want to keep the cake, keep the cake. Take it home if you want to." "Can I?" she asked. Then, looking at me she said, "I live just down the street a couple of doors. I want to take the cake home, O.K.? I'll be right back. Honest!" She got off the stool, picked up the cake, and, carrying it like it was the Holy Grail, walked slowly toward the door. As we all just stood there motionless, she left.
>
> When the door closed, there was stunned silence in the place. Not knowing what else to do, I broke the silence by saying, "What do you say we pray?" Looking back on it now, it seems more than strange for a sociologist to be leading a prayer meeting with a bunch of prostitutes in a diner in Honolulu at 3:30 in the morning. But then it just felt like the right thing to do. I prayed for Agnes. I prayed for her salvation. I prayed that her life would be changed, and that God would be good to her.
>
> When I finished, Harry leaned over the counter and, with a trace of hostility in his voice, he said, "Hey! You never told me you were a preacher! What kind of church do you belong to?" In one of those moments when just the right words came, I answered him, "I belong to a church that throws birthday parties for whores at 3:30 in the morning." Harry waited a moment and then almost sneered as he answered, "No, you don't! There's no church like that. If there was, I'd join it. I'd join a church like that!"[15]

What a contrast to the Gentile "Harry" of the final verse of Zechariah 8: "Let us go with you, because we have heard that God is with you. . . ." As the church takes seriously its role within society, not only to initiate birthday parties for prostitutes but also to become an institution that brings deep and lasting transformation to their communities, the Harrys will be drawn to this place where God indeed dwells.

---

15. T. Campolo, *The Kingdom of God Is a Party* (Waco: Word, 1990), 3–9.

The Christian and Missionary Alliance (the denomination in which I was raised) arose from the vision of a man who was burdened for the poor and needy. A. B. Simpson was preaching at an upscale church in New York City, but, burdened for the lost, the young pastor began to slip down to Hell's Kitchen near Times Square. God began to change lives, the lives of the underclass in New York, and so Simpson brought them back to his church. The membership of the church were not prepared to welcome them into that church to sit in their pews.[16]

So Simpson left that church quietly and began a new church in the Times Square area of New York City. There as he taught on the importance of holiness and healing in the life of the Christian believer, his church took seriously its responsibility for social transformation within that area of the city, whether that meant ministering to prostitutes, prisoners, sailors, or the poor. According to Dahms, "the social welfare impact of his movement was both enormous and magnificent. It was the result of lives transformed by the power of the Gospel."[17] Similarly, Magnuson has noted the close relationship between such holiness faith and social consciousness:

> Far from being a hindrance to social Christianity, then, the revivalistic and holiness faith of these people produced extensive social programs and close identification with the needy. Entering the slums in pursuit of the evangelism that remained their chief concern, they gained there an almost unparalleled knowledge of the conditions in which the poor had to live. Encountering that kind of need, they responded with energy and with growing sympathy and indignation.[18]

What is interesting is that at the same time God birthed out of that church a missionary movement in the closing years of the nineteenth century that moved out around the globe. This important connection between the social consciousness of this pastor and his congregation and the birthing of a missionary movement echoes the message of Zechariah 7–8.

There are many missionary stories that one could tell to illustrate this link between social consciousness and missional concern. Senior missionary friends of mine, Jake and Mavis Klassen, tell a story from their time of ministry in Ecuador. While they ministered in a Spanish community at the foot

16. On this story see A. W. Tozer, *Wingspread: A. B. Simpson—A Study in Spiritual Altitude* (Harrisburg, Pa.: Christian Publications, 1943); A. E. Thompson, *A. B. Simpson: His Life and Work* (Harrisburg, Pa.: Christian Publications, 1960); R. K. Niklaus, J. S. Sawin, and S. J. Stoesz, *All for Jesus: God at Work in the Christian and Missionary Alliance over One Hundred Years* (Camp Hill, Pa.: Christian Publications, 1986).

17. Dahms, "Social Interest"; cf. Evearitt, *Body and Soul*; idem, "Social Gospel," 1–18.

18. Magnuson, *Slums*, 178.

of the Andes, they heard about a Qichua Indian chief who had been imprisoned in the local jail. In Ecuador before a trial, responsibility for feeding prisoners does not lie with the government but with the family of the captive. Unfortunately, because this chief came from far up in the mountains, there was no one to feed him in jail, and so this dear couple delivered meals to the jail for him. Through this act of kindness the chief invited this missionary to his village in the mountains.

The missionary drove up the steep mountain roads to the boundary of the chief's land. There, however, he was stopped as the chief approached him with deep concern on his face. The chief asked who was in the vehicle, and the missionary told him that it was a Christian friend from the Spanish village below. The chief informed the missionary that the man was a *Blanco* (white man), to which the missionary replied: "Yes, like me." But the chief contradicted him, declaring that the missionary was *Gringo* (North American) but the man was *Blanco* (Spanish white man). The *Blanco* was from the village that had forced his tribe to maintain an irrigation system that could only be used by the tribe on the two worst days of the week. Jake Klassen was welcome to stay, but he would first have to take the *Blanco* back to the valley below.

This story reminds me of the social implications of the gospel.[19] On the one hand, it demonstrates the positive impact of this simple act of social kindness by these missionaries. This was an important key that opened the door of this village to the gospel. On the other hand, it demonstrates the negative impact that social injustice can have on the spread of the gospel. Christians in that village face hostile resistance to the gospel because of past and present injustice. Christian witness from this village to the Quichua tribes will have to begin by addressing the deep social injustices that undermine their gospel witness.

In a similar way, we need to embrace a vision of holiness that extends to the social plane. The Western suburban church is often accused not only of ignoring the needs of the urban or Two-Thirds World poor but even of encouraging it through active or passive activity. There is the potential of a powerful witness to the "nations" as the church embraces a social agenda that extends beyond its walls. This may mean partnering with churches struggling for survival in the midst of social chaos to provide human, material, and spiritual resources for them. For churches tempted to move to the richer and safer suburbs, it may mean making the hard decision to stay put and changing their mission and vision to meet the needs of the surrounding

19. On social transformation see further H. M. Conn and M. Ortiz, *Urban Ministry: The Kingdom, the City and the People of God* (Downers Grove, Ill.: InterVarsity Press, 2001), 340–57.

community or even challenging members to move back into the area in order to penetrate it with the gospel in word and deed.

It is interesting that the final voice in the message of Zechariah 7–8 is a voice of outsiders attracted to God's presence in the midst of his covenant community (8:23). It is a subtle reminder to those of us feasting in the midst of God's community that he has called us to a mission beyond ourselves. This mission involves the salvation of souls, but also the reclamation of all of creation and culture to the kingdom priorities of Yahweh.

Take your imaginary glass and lean it against the cold stone wall because I want you to listen in on a conversation. This conversation took place nineteen centuries ago as Aristides was describing Christians to the Roman emperor Hadrian:

> They love one another, they never fail to help widows, they save orphans from those who would hurt them. If they have something they give freely to the man who has nothing. If they see a stranger they take him home and are happy as though he were a real brother. They do not consider themselves brothers in the usual sense, but brothers instead through the Spirit in God.[20]

We do not know whom Aristides was talking about. Faceless Christians, no superstars, but yet in one sense stars in Christ's universe. It was faceless acts of kindness to fellow humanity that was so astounding in a cold and ruthless Roman world. So also today, the world will know of Christ's love as they see it demonstrated through a Christian community in deed as well as word.

20. This statement by Aristides, a philosopher from Athens speaking before the emperor Hadrian, is widely available on the Internet: e.g., see "Christian Quotations of the Day" at Oct. 22, 2002, http://cqod.gospelcom.net/cqod0210.htm. The full text is available at http://www.earlychristianwritings.com/text/aristides-kay.html.

Zechariah 9

An Oracle

1The word of the LORD is against the land of Hadrach
and will rest upon Damascus—
the eyes of men and all the tribes of Israel
are on the LORD—
2and upon Hamath too, which borders on it,
and upon Tyre and Sidon, though they are very
skillful.

3Tyre has built herself a stronghold;
she has heaped up silver like dust,
and gold like the dirt of the streets.
4But the Lord will take away her possessions
and destroy her power on the sea,
and she will be consumed by fire.
5Ashkelon will see it and fear;
Gaza will writhe in agony,
and Ekron too, for her hope will wither.
Gaza will lose her king
and Ashkelon will be deserted.
6Foreigners will occupy Ashdod,
and I will cut off the pride of the Philistines.
7I will take the blood from their mouths,
the forbidden food from between their teeth.
Those who are left will belong to our God
and become leaders in Judah,
and Ekron will be like the Jebusites.
8But I will defend my house
against marauding forces.
Never again will an oppressor overrun my people,
for now I am keeping watch.

9Rejoice greatly, O Daughter of Zion!
Shout, Daughter of Jerusalem!
See, your king comes to you,
righteous and having salvation,
gentle and riding on a donkey,
on a colt, the foal of a donkey.
10I will take away the chariots from Ephraim

and the war-horses from Jerusalem,
and the battle bow will be broken.
He will proclaim peace to the nations.
His rule will extend from sea to sea
and from the River to the ends of the earth.
11 As for you, because of the blood of my covenant with you,
I will free your prisoners from the waterless pit.
12 Return to your fortress, O prisoners of hope;
even now I announce that I will restore twice as much to you.
13 I will bend Judah as I bend my bow
and fill it with Ephraim.
I will rouse your sons, O Zion,
against your sons, O Greece,
and make you like a warrior's sword.

14 Then the LORD will appear over them;
his arrow will flash like lightning.
The Sovereign LORD will sound the trumpet;
he will march in the storms of the south,
15 and the LORD Almighty will shield them.
They will destroy
and overcome with slingstones.
They will drink and roar as with wine;
they will be full like a bowl
used for sprinkling the corners of the altar.
16 The LORD their God will save them on that day
as the flock of his people.
They will sparkle in his land
like jewels in a crown.
17 How attractive and beautiful they will be!
Grain will make the young men thrive,
and new wine the young women.

Original Meaning

ZECHARIAH 9 ENVISIONS the triumphant return of God to his residence in Zion, a return that lays the foundation for the reestablishment of his vice-regent and the restoration, triumph, and prosperity of his people. The passage begins with a depiction of God as divine warrior marching north to south in the Levant, defeating Israel's traditional enemies before returning to his temple in Jerusalem (9:1–8).[1] This depiction begins as a prophetic description in the third person (9:1, 4) but transitions into a first-person account of God after 9:6. Following this vision of God's triumph is a series of exhortations in first-person speech ("I," God) directed to the city of God ("Zion," "Jerusalem") that first announce the reestablishment of royal rule (9:9–10). Next comes the restoration of imprisoned exiles, who become weapons in God's hand against the nations (9:11–13). The chapter concludes by shifting back into third person ("the LORD") with a depiction of a future battle in which God's people triumph and enjoy the blessing of their own land (9:14–17).

These shifts in person have ignited much debate over the literary integrity and historical setting of the various sections of this passage. Many have focused attention on the route of the divine warrior in 9:1–8 and on the reference to Greece in 9:13.[2] While there can be no certainty on the issue of literary integrity, evidence from 11:4–16 suggests that the sign-act refers to the end of Zerubbabel's tenure as governor. In light of the positive view of the royal house as well as of a unity of tribes, I consider it likely that chapters 9–10 arose during Zerubbabel's governorship when great hopes were attached to this Davidic ruler.[3]

In other words, I conclude that Zechariah 9 (and 10:3b–12) arose in the late sixth century B.C. (515–510 B.C.) from the prophet Zechariah or at least from the prophetic movement he spawned. The association with chapters 1–8 is demonstrated in the significant links between Zechariah 1–8 and 9–14 as well as the role that chs. 7–8 play in transitioning the reader from chapters 1–6 to chapters 9–14.[4]

---

1. On the divine warrior image in the Bible and ancient Near East see G. von Rad, *Holy War in Ancient Israel*, trans. M. J. Dawn (Grand Rapids: Eerdmans, 1990); S.-M. Kang, *Divine War in the Old Testament and in the Ancient Near East* (BZAW 177; Berlin: de Gruyter, 1989); C. Sherlock, *The God Who Fights: The War Tradition in the Holy Scripture* (Rutherford Studies in Contemporary Theology 6; Lewiston, N.Y.: Mellen, 1993); T. Longman and D. G. Reid, *God Is a Warrior* (SOTBT; Grand Rapids: Zondervan, 1995).

2. Suggestions range from the period of the Neo-Assyrian empire, e.g., E. G. H. Kraeling, "The Historical Situation in Zechariah 9:1–10," *AJSL* 14 (1924–25): 24–33; A. Malamat, "The Historical Setting of Two Biblical Prophecies on the Nations," *IEJ* 1 (1950–51): 149–59; to that of the Greeks, e.g., H. G. T. Mitchell, J. M. P. Smith, and J. A. Brewer, *A Critical and Exegetical Commentary on Haggai, Zechariah, Malachi and Jonah* (ICC; Edinburgh: T. & T. Clark, 1912), 258–60; K. Elliger, "Ein Zeugnis aus der jüdischen Gemeinde im Alexanderjahr 332 vor Christi," *ZAW* 62 (1949–50): 63–115; M. Delcor, "Les allusions a' Alexandre le Grand dans Zach 9:1–8," *VT* 1 (1951): 110–24.

3. M. J. Boda, "Reading Between the Lines: Zechariah 11:4–16 in its Literary Contexts," in *Bringing Out the Treasure: Inner Biblical Allusion and Zechariah 9–14*, ed. M. J. Boda and M. H. Floyd (JSOTSup 304; Sheffield: Sheffield Academic Press, 2003), 277–91.

4. For this see Boda and Floyd, eds. *Bringing Out the Treasure* (see previous note) and Boda, "From Fasts to Feasts," *CBQ* 67 (2005): forthcoming. Differences in literary styles of these chapters are most likely related to divergent genres rather than to authors (see the introduction).

We will approach Zechariah 9 as a prophetic message delivered to the Jewish community in Yehud in the early Persian period. It assumes that a significant portion of the community is still in exile and invites these exiles to return now that God is about to reclaim his temple and city.

God Returns in Triumph (9:1–8)

THE PROPHECY OPENS with the superscription "An Oracle" (*maśśāʾ*). As noted in the commentary introduction, this word also occurs at 12:1 and Malachi 1:1 and functions as an editorial signal at the beginning of a section of prophecy. The phrase "for the eyes of men and all the tribes of Israel are on the LORD," while appearing to break up the flow of theme in 9:1–2, emphasizes the universal character of God's action within both Israel and the world. "The tribes of Israel" foreshadows a major theme in chapters 9–11, which envisions the reuniting of the tribes (chs. 9–10) before announcing judgment through disunity (ch. 11), while "the eyes of men," which forms an inclusio with the reference to God's eye-keeping watch at his temple in 9:8, introduces the global dimension of God's rule from his temple.

Considering that the focus is on "all the tribes of Israel," it is appropriate that traditional enemies of both the northern (Syria, Phoenicia) and southern tribes (Philistia) are mentioned.[5] Both Hadrach and Hamath are on the northern frontier of Syria, with Hamath situated on the eastern side of the River Orontes, the promised northern boundary of Israel (e.g., Num. 13:21; Josh. 13:5; Ezek. 47:15, 20). Damascus was the key city in this northern territory and during the Persian period served as the seat of the Persian satrapy in which Yehud was located (Abar Nahara, "Beyond the River").[6] In this way it is referred to as "its resting place" (NIV, "will rest upon"), or better yet, capital city. Jeremiah 49:23–27 demonstrates how intertwined were the fates of Hamath and Damascus as news of the fall of Damascus results in the dismay of Hamath.

5. On these various cities see the excellent article by C. Meyers, "Foreign Places, Future World: Toponyms in the Eschatology of Zechariah 9," in *Avraham Malamat Volume*, ed. S. Ahituv and B. A. Levine (Eretz Israel 24; Jerusalem: Israel Exploration Society, 1993), 164*–172*. She treats this list as evidence of territorial claim rather than as a military campaign, although in my opinion these two aspects cannot be separated. Schellenberg sees these cities as "within the ideal borders of the Promised Land (Numbers 34)"; A. F. Schellenberg, "One in the Bond of War: The Unity of Deutero-Zechariah," *Didaskalia* 12/2 (2001): 106.

6. See I. Ephʾal, "Syria-Palestine under Achaemenid Rule," in *Persia, Greece and the Western Mediterranean c. 525 to 479 B.C.*, ed. J. Boardman et al. (CAH 4; Cambridge: Cambridge Univ. Press, 1988), 154–55; M. Hengel, "The Political and Social History of Palestine from Alexander to Antiochus III (333–187 B.C.E.)," in *The Cambridge History of Judaism*—Volume Two: *The Hellenistic Age*, ed. W. D. Davies and L. Finkelstein (Cambridge: Cambridge Univ. Press, 1989), 43.

If Hadrach, Hamath, and Damascus represent the interior of the north with Damascus cast as a place of political power, Tyre and Sidon (9:3–4) represent the northern coastal region with these cities cast as centers of commercial enterprise, fostered by their maritime ports and sea vessels (cf. Ezek. 27:3; 28:3–4).[7] Tyre is singled out because of its reputation as an impregnable "stronghold," holding out for five years against the Assyrians (ending 622 B.C.) and for thirteen years against the Babylonians (ending 572 B.C.; cf. Ezek. 29:18). The Persians did gain control of the city but granted the Tyrians home rule through a member of their royal house. Alexander the Great went to great lengths to take Tyre and only succeeded after constructing a causeway to the island. The term "stronghold," used in the Old Testament for a city that can withstand a siege (e.g., 2 Chron. 8:5; 11:5), aptly fits Tyre with its position on an island, isolated from threatening forces while ensuring safe maritime supply lines.

This "stronghold" was necessary to preserve the quantities of silver and gold amassed from mercantile activity. So plenteous are their precious reserves that they are compared to "dust" and "dirt of the streets."[8] But the Lord will strip the city of its material wealth, a feat accomplished through cutting off the Mediterranean supply lines from the city ("destroy her power on the sea") and subsequently storming the city and setting it on fire.

This vision of the sack and burning of Tyre sends shock waves down the coast of the Levant in 9:5–8. To the south along the great coastal highway lie the city states traditionally associated with the Philistines, who realize that they are next in the path of this divine warrior. They know that if invincible Tyre is no match for this warrior, they have little hope.

The Assyrians and the Babylonians dealt a fatal blow to the traditional Philistine culture that had thrived in the cities of Ashkelon, Gaza, Ekron, and Ashdod.[9] By the early Persian period, these cities were considered one of several smaller political entities within the satrapy of Abar Nahara, subsumed under the name Ashdod and distinct from the province of Yehud.

---

7. Besides being a traditional enemy of Israel, Phoenicians were key to Persian hegemony of the ancient Near East with their naval expertise. Their ships contributed to the Persian war effort against the Greeks.

8. Meyers and Meyers compare here Ps. 18:42//2 Sam. 22:43, where the psalmist uses the same comparison ("as dust . . . as dirt of the streets") to refer to the utter devastation of one's enemies; Meyers and Meyers, *Zechariah 9–14*, 101. This, however, does not take into account the verb *ṣabar*, which refers to heaping up a large quantity (Gen. 41:35, 49; Ex. 8:10) with special focus on riches (Job 27:16; Ps. 39:7).

9. Meyers and Meyers (ibid., 104) note that the absence of Gath in prophetic lists is not surprising, considering its close ties with Israel (esp. during the time of David) and its inclusion in Israel (2 Chron. 11:5–12).

Nevertheless, these areas, densely populated in the Persian period,[10] were indistinguishable culturally from the rest of Palestine. Zechariah 9 demonstrates that these cities continue as symbols of the early enemies of Israel, who threaten the realization of the promise of land to Israel (Jer. 25:15–17; Amos 1:6–8; Zeph. 2:4).

Through personification, the predicament of these Philistine cities is made vivid, providing a glimpse of their internal disposition. Filled with fear and writhing in agony these people are left without hope—the same reactions of earlier peoples who heard of the arrival of the Israelites (Deut. 2:25), implying that the conquest is finally reaching its completion. The second phrase "writhe in agony" denotes intense emotional anguish (cf. Isa. 26:17–18)[11] and produces an overwhelming desire to flee (cf. Ps. 55:4–5). Such internal disposition is justified as the cities are stripped of leadership (Gaza) and inhabitants (Ashkelon). Even Ashdod, the "pride" of the Philistines, will be cut off and a foreigner will occupy the seat of rule.[12]

Verse 7 concludes this section of the judgment on the Philistines. Continuing in the first-person speech of verse 6, the Lord promises to eradicate pagan Philistine sacrificial practices. In the Old Testament sacrificial system the ingestion of blood is strongly prohibited (e.g., Lev. 17:10–14). The word for "forbidden food" (*šiqquṣ*, as opposed to the expected term *šeqeṣ*, e.g., Lev. 7:21) is used elsewhere almost exclusively for idolatry.[13] The Philistine eating practices are therefore doubly inappropriate: Not only do they consume inappropriate food, they do so in unacceptable ways (associated with idolatry).

God's removal of these idolatrous practices is not unexpected in this section on the judgment of the Philistines. But the second part of 9:7 introduces a surprising twist, revealing that God's purpose is not merely the cleansing of the land but also the creation of a remnant from the Philistines. In an apparent variation on the Israelite conception of the "ban" (*ḥerem*), in which the Canaanites were to be "devoted to God alone" through their eradication

---

10. E. Stern, *The Material Culture of the Land of the Bible in the Persian Period 538–332 B.C.E.* (Warminster/Jerusalem: Aris and Phillips/Israel Exploration Society, 1982), 243–44; cf. Petersen, *Haggai*, 52.

11. Notice how Isa. 23:5 also uses this word "writhe" when speaking of Egypt's reaction to the fall of Tyre.

12. It is possible that the "pride" here refers to the king of Ashdod (see Zech. 10:11, where pride and scepter are parallel). See Amos 1:8, where one may suggest the reading "king" (the one who sits in Ashdod); cf. Meyers and Meyers, *Zechariah 9–14*, 111. The word here for "foreigner" refers in Deut. 23:3 to a person of mixed race, who was banned from the assembly of Israel.

13. See, e.g., Deut. 29:16; 1 Kings 11:5, 7; 2 Kings 23:13, 24; 2 Chron. 15:8; Isa. 66:3; Jer. 4:1; 7:30; Ezek. 5:11; Dan. 9:27; Hos. 9:10; Nah. 3:6. The only reference that is not linked to idolatry is Nah. 3:6.

(Josh. 6:17, 18; cf. 1 Kings 20:42),[14] this remnant of the Philistines is destined for the community of God, now cleansed by this judgment. As an example, the remnant from Ekron, the Philistine city closest to Judah's territory, is compared to the Jebusites of old,[15] who, although destined for destruction (e.g., Ex. 23:23), were integrated into the Israelite community (Josh. 15:63; 2 Sam. 24:16–25). This remnant is not granted second-class status in Judah but is honored as leaders in Judah.

In 9:8 the divine warrior reaches his destination at the temple in Jerusalem.[16] There God will "defend" (or, better, "encamp," using the vocabulary of an army setting up camp at the end of a march; cf. 1 Sam. 13:5) his house "against marauding forces," that is, from armies that have restricted movement in the land (cf. Zech. 7:14).

The second part of 9:8 promises that there would never be a return to the conditions of the Exile again. Although "oppressor" can have positive connotations of leadership (Isa. 60:17), it is used of Egyptian oppression of the Israelites in Exodus 3:7 (cf. 5:6–14), where the activity of "slave drivers" (Zech. 9:8, "oppressor") is "seen" ("keeping watch") by God. Thus, verse 8 links God's return to the Exodus from Egypt, preparing the way for the return of his people to the Promised Land later in the chapter. As we saw in chapters 7–8, this assumes that the Exile is an ongoing condition for Israel. By returning to the image of the eye (cf. 9:1), this verse brings closure to this section, which has traced the movements of the divine warrior.[17]

The King Receives His Kingdom (9:9–10)

HAVING SECURED THE temple precincts and promised protection for his people, the divine warrior now focuses attention on the restoration of the community in two addresses to the personified city of Jerusalem (9:9–10,

---

14. Another example of late use of ban ideology ("ban as God's portion") according to S. Niditch, *War in the Hebrew Bible: A Study in the Ethics of Violence* (New York: Oxford Univ. Press, 1993), 28–55, esp. 54. Sherlock traces the link between the ban and idolatry (see Deut. 7; 13:15; 20:16–18); cf. Sherlock, *God Who Fights*, 47–105, 240.

15. Hobbs highlights among the evidence for early reconciliation of Philistines, the appointment of Ittai of Gath as general under David (2 Sam. 15:10ff.; 18:2–12); T. R. Hobbs, "The Language of Warfare in Zechariah 9–14," in *After the Exile: Essays in Honour of Rex Mason*, ed. J. Barton and D. J. Reimer (Macon, Ga.: Mercer Univ. Press, 1996), 123; cf. Meyers, "Foreign Places," 169*.

16. Schellenberg argues that in the mythic pattern of the ancient Near East "the arrival of the god at his temple is a sign that he has won the victory and established his kingdom"; Schellenberg, "One," 106.

17. So P. LaMarche, *Zacharie IX-XIV: Structure littéraire et messianisme* (Paris: Librairie Lecoffre, 1961), 42.

11–17).[18] The first address concerns the restoration of a king. Some see this as a reference either to the royal rule of Yahweh himself as king or to the return of the entire community of Judah.[19] However, because this speech is announced by the Lord to the personified city about a third party saved by God (see below), because this figure is called "your king" (that is, Jerusalem's), and because there are clear allusions to Psalm 72:8 (see below), this is more likely a reference to the reestablishment of the royal line of David.[20]

It is not surprising for God to restore Davidic kingship in Jerusalem as the first step after his capture of his capital. During the early Persian Period (520 until around 490 B.C.), governors in the province of Yehud were linked to the Davidic line.[21] As Persian-Greek tensions increased after 490, involvement of the Davidic line in the political structure of Yehud was curtailed. If Zechariah 9 arose in the period following the completion of the temple (515–510 B.C.) (see the commentary introduction), then it offers great hope for the line of which Zerubbabel was the reigning member (cf. Hag. 2:20–23; Zech. 3:8–10; 4:6b–10a; 6:9–13).[22]

The presence of a human king in Jerusalem/Zion is an essential component in God's rule over the nations of the earth (Ps. 2). The Lord installed a human king on Zion and through him exercised his rule on earth. Unlike other kings in the ancient Near East, this human royal figure is not to be the source of military power, for this is God's prerogative as king.[23]

This feature of God's rule is intimated from the outset of Israel's existence. Singing of God's victory over the Egyptians at the Red Sea, Moses begins his

18. This is a typical rhetorical move in Heb. literature. One can see this, for example, throughout Isa. 40–55, Lam. 1–2, and even in Zech. 2. Meyers and Meyers see the use of feminine imagery as a rhetorical strategy emphasizing helplessness; Meyers and Meyers, *Zechariah 9–14*, 138.

19. Contrast C. L. Meyers and E. M. Meyers, "The Future Fortunes of the House of David: The Evidence of Second Zechariah," in *Fortunate the Eyes That See: Essays in Honor of David Noel Freedman in Celebration of His Seventieth Birthday*, ed. A. Beck (Grand Rapids: Eerdmans, 1995), 207–22; A. Leske, "Context and Meaning of Zechariah 9:9," *CBQ* 62 (2000): 663–78.

20. See E. M. Meyers, "Messianism in First and Second Zechariah and the End of Biblical Prophecy," in *'Go to the Land I Will Show You': Studies in Honor of Dwight W. Young*, ed. J. E. Coleson and V. H. Matthews (Altertumskunde des Vorderen Orients 4; Winona Lake, Ind.: Eisenbrauns, 1996), 134–36,142; so also the allusion in 9:10 to Ps. 72:8, a psalm linked in the superscription to the Davidic line. Cf. Meyers and Meyers, "Future Fortunes," 210: "couched in Davidic, royal language"; and F. Laubscher, "The King's Humbleness in Zechariah 9:9. A Paradox?" *JNSL* 18 (1992): 130.

21. See Boda, "Reading," 277–91.

22. Cf. Boda, "Oil," Art. 10.

23. See M. Lind, *Yahweh Is a Warrior: The Theology of Warfare in Ancient Israel* (Kitchener, Ont.: Herald, 1980), 171–72.

song with an exaltation of God as warrior (15:1–3) and ends it with praise of God's kingship (15:18). Such a victory qualifies God as king over Israel and the nations (15:18).[24] This connection between war and kingship explains God's concern over Israel's request for a king in 1 Samuel (see 1 Sam. 8:20; 12:12), for it was fear of military defeat that prompted the people to request a king rather than to trust in God as their warrior. The Israelites' conception of a king was a figure like Saul with physical stature of a great warrior (9:2),[25] while God's idea of a royal figure was insignificant David, who faced the giant with sling and stone "in the name of the LORD Almighty" (ch. 17).

This conception of kingship can be discerned in Zechariah 9:9–10. This king who arrives is not portrayed as a triumphant figure fresh from military success but as an individual faithful to the covenant and reliant on God for salvation.[26] The term "righteous" is one that typifies the rule of an appropriate king in Israel (2 Sam. 23:3; cf. Ps. 72).[27] This king will judge righteously as God's representative on earth. The word underlying "having salvation" is one that elsewhere in the Old Testament refers to someone who is saved by another agent, usually God (e.g., Num. 10:9; Deut. 33:29; 2 Sam. 22:4). Thus, rather than a figure who enacts his own salvation, this king is one who has relied on the Lord for salvation.[28]

In line with the modest description in the first half of 9:9, the king is depicted as a humble figure (NIV "gentle"), using a term often used for the poor and needy of society (Ex. 22:25; Job 12:5; 24:4), an apt descriptor for the condition of the Israelites both in Egypt (e.g., Ex. 3:7, 17; 4:31) and in Exile (e.g., Ps. 107:41).[29] Such a figure enters the city not on stately horse or glorious chariot, symbols of military prowess and success, but rather on lowly

24. Kang notes this trend in the ancient Near East and the Old Testament (Ps. 24:8; 47:3–4); Kang, *Divine War*, 197–98.

25. Lind, *Yahweh Is a Warrior*, 172.

26. See esp. I. Duguid, "Messianic Themes in Zechariah 9–14," in *The Lord's Anointed: Interpretation of Old Testament Messianic Texts*, ed. P. E. Satterthwaite (Carlisle: Paternoster, 1995), 268. Thus these verses with their tone of humility and peace are not in tension with the surrounding divine warrior sections. The king's role was submission and trust in God. On royal humility see Kraeling, "Historical Situation," 30.

27. Laubscher sees *ṣadiq* as the characteristic of one who upholds *ṣedeq*, "the ideal order"; Laubscher, "Humbleness," 131–32.

28. In this we are following the more difficult reading of the Heb. tradition rather than the ancient versions, which suggest an active participle ("Savior"). See also Kraeling, "Historical Situation," 30; Meyers and Meyers, *Zechariah 9–14*, 126; Redditt, *Haggai*, 114; and esp. Duguid, "Messianic Themes," 267 n. 268. On this suffering image of the king, see R. B. Crotty, "The Suffering Moses of Deutero-Zechariah," *Colloquium* 14 (1982): 44–45, although his connection to Moses is a stretch.

29. Laubscher relates this humility to the relationship of the king to God; Laubscher, "Humbleness," 131.

donkey.[30] This verse appears to assume the royal tradition of Genesis 49:10–11,[31] in which Judah will produce a king for Israel who will ride on a "donkey . . . colt."[32] This use of donkey imagery for a royal procession can also be traced into the reign of David (2 Sam. 16:2) and the coronation ceremony of Solomon (1 Kings 1:33, 38), and there is evidence that this imagery is not limited to Israel.[33]

One should not, however, miss elements of contrast between Genesis 49 and Zechariah 9:9, as Duguid has pointed out. Rather than a figure hailing from the warlike tribe of Judah (Gen. 49:8), whose garments drip with blood from battle (49:11), Zechariah 9 presents a humble king. "The warlike language is still present in Zechariah 9 but it has been transferred from the royal figure to the Lord himself."[34]

---

30. This link to humility is not universally accepted. It is true that mules were used in war and that Yadin has concluded that they were "more suited than horses to battle in hill country" (2 Sam. 13:29; 18:9); Y. Yadin, *The Art of Warfare in Biblical Lands: In the Light of Archaeological Study*, 2 vols. (New York: McGraw-Hill., 1963), 2:287. Laubscher claims that because donkeys were associated with kings, the author could not be indicating lowly status; Laubscher, "Humbleness," 130. His argument, however, ignores the possibility that this was indeed the intention for its use with kings in the first place. Hobbs follows Eilberg-Schwartz in seeing in this image the domination of the king over the nations (donkey); Hobbs, "Language," 124–25; H. Eilberg-Schwartz, *The Savage in Judaism: An Anthropology of Israelite Religion and Ancient Judaism* (Bloomington, Ind.: Indiana Univ. Press, 1990), 127–28. Their connection between aliens and donkeys, however, is weak. On the metaphorical level, Eilberg-Schwartz falls into the fallacy that James Barr (on the lexical level) called "illegitimate totality transfer," that is, reading every possible meaning into one instant of the word or image, J. Barr, *The Semantics of Biblical Language* (Oxford: Oxford University, 1961), 217–18; cf. E. A. Nida, "The Implications of Contemporary Linguistics for Biblical Scholarship," *JBL* 91 (1972): 86.

31. So Fishbane, *Biblical Interpretation in Ancient Israel*, 501–2; Duguid, "Messianic Themes," 267; D. Krause, "The One Who Comes Unbinding the Blessing of Judah: Mark 11.1–10 As a Midrash on Genesis 49.11, Zechariah 9.9, and Psalm 118.25–26," in *Early Christian Interpretation of the Scriptures of Israel: Investigations and Proposals*, ed. C. A. Evans and J. A. Sanders (JSNTSup 148; Sheffield: Sheffield Academic Press, 1997), 147. Menken shows how John 12:15 reveals an awareness of this link between Gen. 49:10–11 and Zech. 9; M. J. J. Menken, "The Quotations from Zech 9,9 in Mt 21,5 and in Jn 12,15," in *John and the Synoptics*, ed. A. Denaux (BETL 101; Leuven: Leuven Univ. Press, 1992), 576.

32. The text here suggests that the royal figure is on one animal with the parallel lines denoting the same beast. Matt. 21:1–7, however, cites this passage as the basis for Christ requesting two beasts for his procession into Jerusalem. For various proposals see R. Bartnicki, "Das Zitat von Zach 9:9–10 und die Tiere im Bericht von Matthäus über dem Einzug Jesu in Jerusalem (Mt 21:1–11)," *NovT* 18 (1976): 161–66; see Menken for view that this is a Matthean link to 2 Sam. 16:1–4; Menken, "Quotations," 571–74.

33. Notice how later kings use horses and chariots (Jer. 17:25). For the ancient Near Eastern evidence see Lipinski, "Recherches," 51–52; also J. Sasson, "Ass," in *IDBSup*, 72–73; Laubscher, "Humbleness," 126–27.

34. Duguid, "Messianic Themes," 268.

In line with the use of the donkey for the royal procession, the Lord declares his intention to remove all military equipment from his people. The "chariot," "horse," and "battle bow" are all essential for advanced warfare in the ancient Near East, but they will be unnecessary for this king who relies on the divine warrior for his victory and rule.[35] The Lord expressed disapproval of any royal attempts to rely on horse and chariot in battle strategy (Deut. 17:16; Isa. 31:1–3), even if evidence is plenteous that this was ignored (2 Sam. 15:1; 1 Kings 4:26; 10:26–29). Likewise, the Israelites were not to fear those who challenged them with horse and chariot (Deut. 20:1; cf. Ex. 14:23).

Without this advanced military equipment, this king will exercise peaceful rule over the entire world. While the march of the divine warrior in 9:1–8 was limited to the Levant, the ultimate goal of this military exercise is sovereignty over the entire cosmos. This sovereignty, however, will be characterized by "peace," a feature regularly linked to the rule of God's future royal representative (Isa. 9:6–7; Mic. 5:4–5).[36]

This peace will be proclaimed to the "nations" (9:10b). That this refers to the rest of the world is apparent because his rule will extend "from sea to sea and from the River to the ends of the earth." This phrase is reminiscent of the Lord's promise of land in Exodus 23:31 (cf. 1 Kings 4:21), where the Red Sea is the southern border of Israel, the Sea of the Philistines (the Mediterranean) the western border, while the desert is the eastern and the River Euphrates the northern boundary. Zechariah 9:10 appears to generalize ("sea to sea")[37] and to extend ("to the ends of the earth") the boundaries of Exodus 23:31. The form in Zechariah 9:10 is identical to that found in Psalm 72:8–11, where the extent of the king's rule reveals global domination.[38]

Thus, Zechariah 9:10 "has more than just the boundaries of the Promised Land in view. It envisions nothing less than global peace and sovereignty."[39] In this way it continues the international emphasis that was discerned first in the oracle of 2:6–13 and echoed in 8:20–23.

---

35. See Yadin, *Art.*

36. Meyers and Meyers ("Future Fortunes," 211–12) also see this in ancient Near Eastern literature. One should not miss the key contrast that the king here does not win a military victory with God, but rather God does this alone.

37. See also Amos 8:12 (and possibly Mic. 7:12), where "sea to sea" is a merism for "everywhere."

38. So also Meyers, "Messianism," 135; Duguid, "Messianic Themes," 266–67; K. J. Larkin, *The Eschatology of Second Zechariah: A Study of the Formation of a Mantological Wisdom Anthology* (CBET 6; Kampen: Kok, 1994), 75.

39. See esp. M. Saebø, "From Empire to World Rule: Some Remarks on Psalms 72.8; 89.26; Zechariah 9.10b," in *On the Way to Canon: Creative Tradition History in the Old Testament,* ed. M. Saebø, (JSOTSup 191; Sheffield: Sheffield Academic Press, 1998), 129–30.

This link to Psalm 72 has been helpful to determine the universal extent of the kingdom. But as with Genesis 49 and Zechariah 9:9, Duguid wisely notes a similar contrast between Psalm 72 and Zechariah 9:10: "Whereas in Psalm 72:13 the Davidic king 'saves' (יוֹשִׁיעַ) the lives of the needy, in Zechariah 9:9 he is himself the object of the Lord's salvation."

The People Return to the Kingdom (9:11–17)

WITH VERSE 11 the Lord signals a new section by addressing once again the personified city of Jerusalem ("As for you"). Having secured the Promised Land and having established a political structure, the time has come for the return of a people. The verb "free" is used in the Exodus account to express liberation of the Israelites from Egypt (e.g., Ex. 5:2, "let Israel go"), while the term "prisoners" is used of the exilic community in several texts (e.g., Ps. 107:10; Lam. 3:34) and is thus appropriate for their experience after the fall of Jerusalem.

Most likely 9:11 is a deliberate reminiscence over the story of Joseph, which is the only section in the Old Testament where one finds the various components of the second line of this verse: "prisoner ... waterless pit" (Gen. 37:24; 39:20, 22).[40] The story of Joseph, with its depiction of the rise of an Israelite within the Egyptian court, would have been a great source of hope for this community living under Persia. They would need no less of a miracle in their time.

The basis of this promised liberation is the "blood of my covenant with you." This combination of "blood" and "covenant" constitutes an allusion to Exodus 24:8, which describes the ceremony in which, after the reading of the Book of the Law and the acceptance of the commandments by the congregation, blood was sprinkled on the people to ratify the covenant between God and his people.[41] On the basis of this ancient covenant agreement, God promises salvation for his exiled people.

For a brief moment the speech is directed away from the personified city and onto these released prisoners.[42] As "prisoners of hope" their freedom is a signal of hope for a nation that has experienced the bitter disappointment of the exilic era. Their newfound freedom will result in a return to the city-fortress (Jerusalem), and it is to this personified city that the speech is addressed in the second half of verse 12.[43]

---

40. "Waterless pit" is used for Jeremiah in Jer. 38:6, but not "prisoner." Some see the lack of water as positive (water could have drowned them); Petersen, *Zechariah 9–14*, 60; Meyers and Meyers, *Zechariah 9–14*, 141; some as negative (no drinking water); Baldwin, *Haggai*, 168. Most likely the water is not the issue.

41. See Petersen, *Zechariah 9–14*, 60; Baldwin, *Haggai*, 167.

42. The imperative "return" at the beginning of 9:12 agrees with the word "prisoners."

43. The Heb. pronoun here is feminine singular, as is "Daughter of Zion ... Daughter of Jerusalem" in v. 9.

Emphasizing the dawning of a new day through the phrase "even now," God announces that the return to the city of these prisoners will be accompanied by incredible blessing, for the city will receive twice what they had before the Exile. The language here is that of recompense (e.g., Ex. 21:34), compensating for the pain of exile,[44] through the practice of double blessing (as Isa. 61:7), which reflects the custom of rewarding the firstborn of a family with a double inheritance. In this we may have an allusion again to the Joseph narrative, for it was Joseph, the one who endured the waterless pit and imprisonment, who was rewarded with a double inheritance among the tribes (Gen. 48:5; cf. 48:22; 49:22–26). Specific details of this double blessing are not offered, but the reference to the tribes of "Judah" and "Ephraim" and "sons [of] Zion" in Zechariah 9:13 suggests that it is people who are in view.

Throughout the history of Israel the two tribes of Ephraim and Judah represent the two main power blocks within the nation. Ephraim, as first among the Joseph clans (see Gen. 48:20), represents the northern tribes,[45] with Judah as the inhabitant of the southern region of Israel. Tension between these two tribal groups is discernible throughout the monarchy, whether in the civil war after Saul's death (2 Sam. 2–5) or the schism after Solomon's death (1 Kings 12). David's choice of Jerusalem as his royal seat was most likely related to its position straddling the southern and northern tribal blocks. According to Zechariah 9:11, the royal city of Jerusalem, rejected by Ephraim in an earlier era and abandoned by Judah in the devastation by the Babylonians in 587–586 B.C., will once again overflow with inhabitants.[46] Both north and south will return together to Zion to form a united kingdom under a Davidic monarch.

These freed prisoners will become weapons in God's hands for fighting battles. The imagery in the first half of verse 13 is that of an archer's bow and arrow. God as divine warrior is the archer who bends his bow (Judah) and places his arrows (Ephraim) against the string,[47] an image of unity in the

---

44. Meyers and Meyers, *Zechariah 9–14*, 144.

45. Notice how Ephraim often signifies the entire northern kingdom (e.g., Isa. 7:2, 5, 8, 9, 17; 11:13).

46. The fact that the Babylonians placed their provincial capital in Mizpah after the fall of Jerusalem is suggestive of the magnitude of destruction in Jerusalem (2 Kings 25). Even in the time of Nehemiah the low population in Jerusalem was a serious problem (Neh. 7; 11). Cf. C. L. Meyers and E. M. Meyers, "Demography and Diatribes: Yehud's Population and the Prophecy of Second Zechariah," in *Scripture and Other Artifacts: Essays in Honor of Philip J. King*, ed. M. D. Coogan, J. C. Exum, and L. E. Stager (Louisville: Westminster John Knox, 1994), 268–85, for concern over population in Zech. 9–14 and the early Persian Period.

47. The Heb. constructions here are also used in 2 Kings 9:24; Jer. 51:3. Based on Akkadian expressions, S. Paul demonstrates how the term "bow" does double duty in this verse, as represented in the NIV ("bow . . . it"); S. M. Paul, "A Technical Expression from Archery in Zechariah ix 13a," *VT* 39 (1989): 495–97.

hands of God. This united community is referred to as the "sons [of] Zion," signaling a return to the ideal of David and Solomon's reign. Together these sons of Zion will form another piece of military equipment for the divine warrior: his sword.

One feature of verse 13 that has long mystified interpreters is the reference to "Greece," which many have treated either as a later gloss inserted after the conquest of Asia by Alexander the Great or as evidence that Zechariah 9 was written in the period after Alexander. There is no need to date this text that late. On the one hand, this reference could easily reflect the early Persian period (ca. 539–400 B.C.), when the Persians strove with limited success to incorporate Greece into their empire.[48] On the other hand, the reference here to "sons" of Greece may be an allusion to the ancient Israelite tradition of the table of nations found in Genesis 10.[49] There, among the Japhethites are listed the "sons of Javan":[50] "Elishah, Tarshish, the Kittim and the Rodanim" (Gen. 10:4), who are the forerunners of the "maritime peoples" (v. 5). Three of these names appear elsewhere in key prophetic attacks on Tyre: Elishah, Tarshish, and Kittim/Cyprus (Isa. 23; Ezek. 27). Although in Genesis 10 the Phoenicians (Sidon and presumably Tyre) are traced through Ham's son Canaan (10:15) and the Philistines are traced through his other son Mizraim (Egypt; 10:14), the mention of the sons of Javan (Greece) refers to the Phoenicians' allies who will come from the west via the sea.

These two views are not mutually exclusive. The allusion to the "sons of Javan" here links together the historical tensions of the early Persian period with traditional enemy language in the Old Testament.

With 9:14 the prophecy switches from the first-person address of the Lord to third-person description of a battle involving the Lord and his people. The focus at the outset is on the military action of the divine warrior. He will appear over "them," that is, the sons of Zion of the previous verse. The language here is drawn from traditional formulations of the appearance and activity of the divine warrior, which was known throughout the ancient Near East and prevalent in Israelite literature (Ex. 24; Deut. 33:2; Judg. 5; 2 Sam. 22; Ps. 29; 68; Hab. 3).[51] In these formulations God's march is likened to an approaching storm in which lightning is seen as God's arrow and thunder as God's trumpet.

But there is also a minor role for God's people in this battle. Protected by God, the people gain victory, not with the sophisticated weapons that have

---

48. K. G. Hoglund, *Achaemenid Imperial Administration in Syria-Palestine and the Mission of Ezra and Nehemiah* (Atlanta: Scholars Press, 1992).

49. See R. Weis, "A Definition of the Genre *Maśśa*ʾ in the Hebrew Bible" (Ph.D., Claremont Graduate School, 1986), 183–85.

50. Javan is the same term as Greece in Zech. 9:13.

51. See Schellenberg, "One," 107.

been removed from the kingdom (9:10) but with the lowly sling, an allusion to David's victory over Goliath (1 Sam. 17:40, 50).

The latter half of 9:15 describes the victory in battle through images drawn from drinking and sacrifice. The first image portrays a group of drunken revelers (Prov. 20:1; NIV "brawler"), for which the wine has flowed in great quantities,[52] while the second image draws from the sacrificial realm, where blood is collected in a special bowl for use during cultic ceremonies.[53] The use of drinking and sacrificial imagery is not surprising in a description of battle where blood flows from wounded and dying soldiers (e.g., Deut. 32:42; Isa. 34:1–8).[54]

The beginning of verse 16 is a summary of what God has accomplished in the previous verses: He has saved his people. The phrase "on that day" lends this passage an eschatological tone even as it refers to the day of battle described in 9:14–15. This saved and victorious people are described as the "flock of his people," reliant on God their shepherd. The people are also described as sparkling "jewels in a crown," items of worth and beauty, as 9:17 reads: "attractive and beautiful" or "good [quality] and beautiful" (cf. Song 4:10). The passage closes with images of vitality as the land brings forth plenty (grain, new wine) to sustain a new generation ("young men ... young women").

In sum, at the outset of this prophecy, the prophet grants us a vision of victory and blessing. God will march to his temple to reestablish his royal rule, gaining victory over the enemy and including a remnant from the conquered nations into his kingdom. After installing his human king who will express God's rule over all nations, the Lord will restore his community from their exile. This restoration will include both northern and southern tribes, who will unite in the city of Zion. They will become God's instruments for battle and experience blessed provision in their new land. This prophecy was directed originally to the Jewish community in Yehud during the tenure of Zerubbabel as governor and looked with great hope to the ultimate reunification of the tribes under Davidic kingship.

Bridging Contexts

HERMENEUTICS AND PROPHECY. Zechariah 9, as all of chapters 9–14, presents considerable challenges to those interested in finding out its contemporary relevance. While modern biblical scholars have struggled to discover a historical context that gave rise to the imagery of

52. Here we have an instance of double entendre, for the word "roar" was also associated with the shouts of enemies against their oppressors (Ps. 46:6; 83:2; Jer. 50:42; 51:55).

53. See, e.g., Ex. 27:3; 38:3; Num. 4:14; 7:13, 19; 1 Kings 7:40, 45, 50; 2 Kings 12:14; 25:15; Neh. 7:69; Jer. 52:18–9; Zech. 14:20.

54. On this see Hobbs, who cites Isa. 9:5; 66:24; Hobbs, "Language," 110.

this passage, contemporary preachers have often erred in trying to establish a future context for this imagery, in particular as it relates to the events of the eschaton. This search for the fulfillment of this vision in Zechariah 9 is informed by hermeneutical presuppositions concerning the passage.

These hermeneutical presuppositions are difficult to disentangle, but they involve at least two issues. (1) Does this passage describe a literal fulfillment at a particular time of each of its features or is it speaking in figurative language of God's victory over the cosmos and reestablishment of his kingdom? (2) Are the events spoken of here to be fulfilled during the Persian or Greek periods or do they look to future eschatological events?

Zechariah 9 and fulfillment. Some scholars identify the literal fulfillment of this prophecy as the conquest of the ancient Near East by the young Alexander the Great between 333 and 323 B.C.[55] He is the one who brought Tyre to its knees. But this does not do justice to the message of Zechariah 9, which envisions the conquest of God, the reestablishment of a Davidic monarch, and the restoration of the exilic community. Other scholars, noting the incongruity between Alexander's conquest and Zechariah 9, look to a literal future event in the eschaton.[56]

The New Testament offers some guidance on this matter as each of the Gospel writers either alludes to or cites Zechariah 9 in their description of the triumphant entry of Jesus into Jerusalem prior to Passion Week (Matt. 21:1–11; Mark 11:1–10; Luke 19:28–38; John 12:12–15).[57] As Jesus approached Jerusalem, he sent two of his disciples to find a donkey for him to ride on as he entered the city. The recorded shouts of the people during his entrance made it clear that the royal connection was not lost on them: "Blessed is the coming kingdom of our father David!" (Mark 11:10); "Blessed is the king who comes in the name of the Lord!" (Luke 19:38); "Blessed is the King of Israel!" (John 12:13).

In other words, the New Testament community saw in Jesus the fulfillment of Zechariah 9:9–10 in this arrival in Jerusalem. The enigmatic allusion to

---

55. See Mitchell, Smith, and Brewer, *Haggai*, 260, who see it influenced by the Battle of Issus, while still looking to the future.

56. See, e.g., Crotty, "Suffering in Deutero-Zechariah," 54: "Zechariah ix–xiv is set in an apocalyptic context. It must be read against the background of the end-message of history"; Meyers, "Foreign Places," 165*: "not directed towards specific events of the past or expected events of the immediate future. Rather, all are projected into the eschatological future."

57. See C. H. Dodd, *According to the Scriptures: The Sub-Structure of New Testament Theology* (London: Nisbet, 1952); Bartnicki, "Das Zitat von Zach 9:9–10," 161–66; Menken, "Quotations," 571–78; M. C. Black, "The Rejected and Slain Messiah Who Is Coming with His Angels: The Messianic Exegesis of Zechariah 9–14 in the Passion Narratives" (Ph.D. diss., Emory University, 1990).

the humble and saved Davidic ruler is made clear in the suffering that Jesus endured as he entrusted himself into the hands of his Father in order to bring redemption to the world and to establish God's rule on earth (Phil. 2). God's great victory is not accomplished in its first installment in the way one might have expected by reading Zechariah 9:1–8 literally but rather through the suffering of his royal figure on behalf of the nation.

The New Testament, however, presents Jesus not only as faithful Davidic ruler but also as the divine warrior Yahweh, who will vanquish his foes.[58] In his review of the war tradition in the Old and New Testaments, Sherlock highlights two aspects to this divine warrior tradition. On the one side Yahweh fights for Israel against their enemies, displayed in his rescue from Egypt and conquest of Canaan. On the other side, however, Yahweh fights against Israel when she does not respond as the obedient army of the Lord. These two aspects are also evident in the prophets who presaged the Exile, which "demonstrated the converse of the exodus, what it meant to suffer defeat at Yahweh's hands."[59]

Turning to the New Testament, Sherlock argues that the same two aspects can be discerned in the ministry of Jesus as Messiah, who "recapitulated the exodus and conquest as the (actively) obedient Messiah, and the exilic experience as the (passively) obedient Servant. He lived and died not only as 'priest' and 'victim,' but also as 'victor' and 'vanquished.'"[60]

Thus, the New Testament interprets the Old Testament divine warrior theology as fulfilled ultimately in and through the work of Christ. Christ, as representative of Israel, receives the punishment of the divine warrior for the sins of the people and yet also experiences victory through his actions. Moreover, Christ assumes the role of divine warrior and takes up residence in his temple in Zion. In New Testament theology the location of this residence transcends the physical site of Jerusalem (John 4; Heb. 12). The church with its origins in Jerusalem in the events of Passion Week and the subsequent Pentecost Feast now embodies the values of Zion as the Spirit resides within this redeemed community. From here God's rule extends to all nations.

LaRondelle notes how Christ, rather than "spiritualizing" the kingdom, extends the boundaries of the Davidic kingdom globally in his Sermon on the Mount as he applies Psalm 37:11, 29 to his followers: "Christ is definitely not spiritualizing away Israel's territorial promise when He includes His

---

58. In this I depart from Duguid, who claims that "Jesus overflows the categories of Zechariah 9:9"; Duguid, "Messianic Themes," 277. Zech. 9:9–10 refer to Christ's role as Davidic ruler while 9:1–8 refer to his role as Yahweh. Through the mystery of the Incarnation we see the uniting of both divine and Davidic rule (see Rom. 1:4).

59. Sherlock, *God Who Fights*, 243.

60. Ibid., 244.

universal Church. On the contrary, He widened the scope of the territory until it extended to the whole world."[61]

Not only is Zion equated with the church in the New Testament, but so also are the "sons of Zion." In the New Testament the church as the body of Christ assumes the status of Israel of old and is even addressed as the "twelve tribes" (James 1:1; cf. Matt. 19:28; Luke 22:30). The church is established from the remnant seed of Israel represented first of all in the twelve apostles and then in the community of exiles who returned to the Feast of Pentecost in Acts 2 to receive the full blessing of God. The history of the church is the progressive extension of the rule of God through the community of this Davidic ruler to the ends of the earth, which will reach its fulfillment at the return of Christ.

Thus, Zechariah 9 is relevant to the church fundamentally as a prophecy that has been fulfilled in and through Christ and his community. This redemptive-historical foundation, however, leads us to a secondary relevance of this passage as this prophecy calls us to theological values essential for sustaining this community as they pursue the mission begun at Pentecost. In this we need to transcend chronological speculation and focus on the theological message of this passage. A clue to this is to listen to this prophecy from the perspective of those who first encountered it in the Persian period, most likely in the final decades of the sixth century B.C. Of course, we do this in light of Christ's coming in redemptive history, but as we apply this passage to our community today, we must do so with a view as to its significance to its first hearers. What then is that message in its ancient context?

A message for its time. Zechariah 9 speaks into a particular historical context of Israel's experience. In a world controlled by the greatest empire the ancient Near East had ever known, this chapter reminds God's people of the true ruler of the world. It also reminds them that the capital of the world is not Ecbatana, Susa, Pasargadae, or even Persepolis, the royal cities of the Persian empire, but rather Zion, the seat of the Lord's rule in his temple.

This prophetic message was delivered to a community uncertain about the future of kingship, especially in light of the failure to sustain Davidic rule in this tiny Persian province. This depiction of the king in verses 9–10 is an important reminder to the people that their king will be established by and rule for Yahweh, not the Persians. His rule will transcend the tiny domain of Yehud and exceed even the realm of the Persians. But this will be accomplished by God's work, not their own feeble efforts.

---

61. H. K. LaRondelle, *The Israel of God in Prophecy: Principles of Prophetic Interpretation* (AUMSR 13; Berrien Springs, Mich.: Andrews Univ. Press, 1983), 138.

Zechariah 9 also speaks to a community struggling with their own weakness and poverty, living between the ideal of the prophetic promises of old and the reality of their lives. (1) They are called to return to their fortress, Zion. The place of safety for them is in the presence of God in Zion. (2) God's word to them is one of comfort, promising to use them in his restoration, granting victory and prosperity.

This prophetic message also speaks to a community struggling with issues of identity and community. A key issue in the early Persian period is concern over the purity of the remnant of Israel. Throughout the books of Ezra and Nehemiah one reads of struggles between this remnant and the surrounding peoples—not only Gentile nations but also groups with Yahwistic backgrounds who may have assumed non-Yahwistic religious aspects. Ezra 4 stands as evidence in the early Persian period from at least Cyrus (539 B.C.) until Xerxes (465 B.C.) that there was considerable potential for sectarian fears, especially suspicions between those living in the former northern and southern kingdoms.

Into this context (most likely the late sixth century B.C.), Zechariah 9 introduces the theme of inclusivity. (1) God will transform a remnant from Philistia into his people. Former enemies of Israelite tribes will become full-fledged participants in the life of the Israelite community. (2) This prophecy envisions a remnant that consists of exiles from both the northern and southern tribes. This unity of the tribes has been demonstrated throughout this chapter by subtle allusions to the story and tradition of Joseph. The arrival of the king uses language reminiscent of Jacob's blessing to Judah in Genesis 49 (Zech. 9:9). Ephraim becomes the arrow filling the bow of Judah and joins with Judah as "sons of Zion" (9:13). The release of the exiles is described in terms reminiscent of the imprisonment of Joseph (9:11–12) and possibly of the double blessing of children in Jacob's blessing of Joseph (9:12). (3) Finally, an allusion to Amos 6:6 reminds the reader of the sins of the former generation that had little regard for the imprisonment of the tribes of "Joseph" (Zech. 9:15).

These connections suggest that Zechariah 9 is emphasizing the unity of the tribes and calls the community to consider the plight of the Joseph tribes in exile. Clearly Judah is given a prominent role throughout the chapter with the installation of the king and the role of that tribe as the archer's bow. However, Joseph joins with Judah under this new king, unites with Judah in battle, and assumes the title "son of Zion." By reminding the audience of the Joseph tradition, this chapter is reminding them of the key role that Joseph played in the preservation of the entire Israelite community during an earlier period of "exile" in a foreign land.

The inclusion of the Judah-Tamar narrative in the Joseph novella shows Joseph's special role in rescuing Judah from further disaster in the land of Canaan (Gen. 38). If Zechariah 9 arose in the late sixth century after the first major waves of exiles had returned to the land, it stands as a timely reminder of their need to care about other tribes who are either in exile or who remained in the land. Former enemies, whether from the surrounding nations or from the northern kingdom, will form a united society with the Lord as King and the Davidic monarch as vice-regent, centered around the holy city Jerusalem.

Thus, Zechariah 9 reflects a mediating voice in the clash between Yehud and the peoples around them and between Yehud and Samaria as reflected throughout Ezra and Nehemiah.[62] There is no compromise of the values of purity, for the Philistine remnant is cleansed from its idolatry and all tribes are united around Zion, temple, and king. Nevertheless, God plans to include all peoples in the community he will establish.

Contemporary Significance

AFFIRMING GOD'S SOVEREIGNTY over the nations and expanding our vision of God and his purposes. I caught a glimpse of the photograph on the front cover of *Time* while waiting for a dentist appointment. All I can remember is a picture of burning cars, smashed windows, and tear gas, not shocking scenes to a North American reader barraged daily with images from the war-torn Third World. However, a closer look revealed a surprise: These were scenes from a North American city, rocked by riots over the gathering of major world leaders for discussions on trade. In recent years we have seen a burgeoning youth movement that, frustrated with the processes of government and the influence of industry, has taken to the streets in protest. These young people are demonstrating against two basic problems in our global village: economic injustice and military oppression. In a world run by political and economic systems seemingly beyond their control, these demonstrators are taking their message to the leaders of these systems.

This kind of frustration reflects the powerlessness that many feel today. Does this reflect our own feelings in the church? How do we live in the midst of such a world run by systems propelled by greed and power? In this kind of world the message of Zechariah 9 grants us an eternal perspective. Tyre, representative of the ancient world's material splendor and military prowess, will ultimately collapse before the sovereign Lord.

62. This balance between northern and southern issues is highlighted by LaMarche, *Zacharie IX-XIV*, 42. See also Schellenberg, "One," 107, on the unity of tribes in chs. 9–10.

Zechariah 9 calls us to recognize God's sovereign plan and power, to return to a theme that has often been ignored in the message of a church searching for "relevance." God is in control, and his past record and future promise reveal that he has no patience for the material splendor and military prowess of the nations.

This mention of Tyre should expand our view of God's purposes in this world. It is easy to spiritualize this text away as a reference to the "world," but we should not ignore the military and material aspects of this image. The church should not leave protest to the student movements with their humanistic values but should be at the forefront of the battle against the systems of the world that encourage injustice and oppression. This may involve peaceful protest or political pursuit, but it also will involve the transforming example of Christian business people, the patient labors of social service personnel, and the relevant voice of Christian ministers.

The focus on Philistia highlights a second aspect of God's impatience with this world. He will not tolerate the idolatrous practices of the nations but will purify the Philistines' idolatry before including their remnant in Israel. The message of Zechariah 9 is highly relevant to the present generation living in a cultural context that values tolerance above all else. Fearful to be labeled "fundamentalists" and desirous to win a hearing in our culture, we are tempted to compromise on issues of truth that are not negotiable in Old and New Testament revelation. Of course, "speaking the truth" must always be done "in love" (Eph. 4:15), but it does mean expressing one's own convictions with sincerity and realizing that God desires to purify people of their idolatry as he draws them to worship the one true God.

God's sovereign plan, however, should not be construed in an exclusively negative manner. Zechariah 9 echoes the end of Zechariah 8, namely, that God envisions a community that transcends Israel's borders and ethnicity. The surprising inclusion of Philistines among the tribes of Israel is evidence of God's intention to bless all nations through Abraham's seed.

This was not an easy message for those Jews in the Persian period who had suffered at the hands of foreigners for generations and were struggling to define their identity within the Persian empire. The natural reaction during this period appears to have been exclusion rather than inclusion. God, however, shocks the Israelite community and reminds them of his original intention to bring blessing to all nations.

The same is true for Christians today. In our pursuit of truth, justice, and redemption, we can villainize enemies of the faith to the point that we revel in their damnation. This has been most evident in recent evangelical responses to the homosexual community in North America. Recently as I left my church to drive home, I discovered a pamphlet under the windshield wiper of my van. It was an invitation to a heterosexual pride day in my city. While I did not have a problem with this kind of public expression of biblical values, I was shocked at the tone of the message and the promotion of hatred of the homosexual community throughout the pamphlet.

A far better response was demonstrated to me by a church I once attended in Philadelphia that reached out to the large local homosexual community through a counseling help line and through a regular visitation program to people suffering with AIDS. In this way they incarnated the truth of God in acts of love and compassion. Some may feel ambivalent about implying "acceptance" of lifestyle through compassion, but from God's perspective we possess no moral superiority—that has been given to us by God. As Christ associated with those considered far less than holy, so also we need to reach out in love. We cannot lose sight of God's desire to bring blessing through us to all people.

Celebrating the suffering Messiah and emulating his example. God's methods are not those of the world system. God extends his mighty rule through the weakness of a Davidic king who died on a cross. This message is as shocking to us today as it was to the apostles who first witnessed it and who asked impatiently for the realization of the kingdom (Acts 1:6).

(1) Such a message calls us to stand in awe and wonder at this mysterious feature of redemptive history. When considering the message of the suffering Messiah, we move too quickly to application without pausing for adoration; that is, we are more apt to ask how this will change my patterns of behavior than to be consumed by praise of this divine mystery. I think Christ knew of this temptation when he instituted that central event of Christian worship, the Lord's Supper. In this event we are called regularly as a community to stop and reflect on the wonder of God's grace expressed through Jesus Christ.

(2) This motif of humble suffering is also to inform our methodology as the church. First Peter 2:21 teaches us that Christ's humble suffering is an example that guides us as Christians. As the suffering of Christ brings about the redemption of the world, so the application of that redemption in subsequent generations is through the suffering Christian community.

Evangelicalism, a child of fundamentalism, has sought to move from the periphery to the center of society. This move reflects a healthy growth in the church's conception of mission, from a "come-out-and-be-separate" exclusivism to a movement bringing salt and light into all areas of cultural experience. The danger, however, lies in the subtle tone of arrogance and power, bolstered by financial depth and political weight. We have become "wise as serpents," learning the political systems of this world, while forgetting to be "innocent as doves," portraying the humility of Christ (Matt. 10:16). In local communities as well as on the national scene, churches need to be known for their servanthood and humility, assuming the functions of society abandoned by others and communicating the values of Christ in love.

Why is the church known more for its arrogant demands for tax cuts, military spending, and defense of individual rights and property than for its humble cries for social justice, protection of the poor, and rejuvenation of social conscience? We risk the accusation of God that we are defending the values of Tyre rather than pursuing the suffering servant values of God. As Tyre created an arrogant self-sufficiency, so we are easily enticed to rely on our many financial and technological resources to sustain our ministries and lifestyle. The difficulty is that we become deluded into believing that such resources are signs of God's blessing, even as our hearts are blinded to how much such resources have displaced God as the object of faith.

The greatest challenge for this generation of Christians in the West will be to sustain faith in God in the midst of such plenty. The demographic shift of Christianity from the Western world to the Two-Thirds World is related at least in part, if not in whole, to the power of suffering to nurture faith.

Craving for God's presence and trusting in God's power. Zechariah 9 exhorts the exiled community to return to Zion, their fortress, because it has been secured by their divine warrior God, who has taken up residence in his temple. Confidence for this community, based on God's presence in their midst, catapults them forward as a victorious people among the nations.

For Christians, God's presence now transcends the physical location of Zion, as Zion is now identified as the church, the community of believers (Heb. 12:22–23). For weary Christian "exiles" who long for God's victory in their lives, the first step is the experience of his presence as individuals and communities. In recent years many churches have undergone a transformation in their rhythms of worship with far greater time and thought devoted to these communal experiences. This is an important transformation, for it places recognition of God's presence as a priority in the life of the church. However, these can descend into sentimental celebrations of our "experience of God" rather than adoring encounters with the "God of experience."

This said, we desperately need this focus on God's presence in our church communities. We cannot engineer this through advanced technology or professional creativity. God must show up, and when he does, he may surprise us. A. W. Tozer once spoke of the fear we have about things getting out of control, words written decades ago and yet as relevant today:

> Stamping our feet to start the circulation and blowing on our hands to limber them up, we have emerged shivering from the long period of the theological deep-freeze, but the influence of the frosty years is

still felt among us to such an extent that the words witness, experience and feeling are cautiously avoided by the rank and file of evangelical teachers. In spite of the undeniable lukewarmness of most of us we still fear that unless we keep a careful check on ourselves we shall surely lose our dignity and become howling fanatics by this time next week. We set a watch upon our emotions day and night lest we become over-spiritual and bring reproach upon the cause of Christ. Which all, if I may say so, is for most of us about as sensible as throwing a cordon of police around a cemetery to prevent a wild political demonstration by the inhabitants.[63]

God communicates his presence to us through his Spirit, which enlivens his community. Openness to God's presence is just the beginning; we need also to invite the Spirit's work into our midst both as individuals and communities of faith.

It is not surprising that not only the king but also the people are linked to David in Zechariah 9 as the prophet limits their military action to slinging stones. As David of old, this community must rely on God for victory. The key element here is trust in our sovereign Lord. It is easy to trust in our deep resources as a church or to look on our carefully crafted vision and mission statements as the key to the success of the church. The apostle Paul lived his life with clear vision and mission for his life of ministry: "We proclaim him, admonishing and teaching everyone with all wisdom, so that we may present everyone perfect in Christ" (Col. 1:28). But he was quick to remind us of the key to the fulfillment of his calling: "To this end I labor, struggling with all his energy, which so powerfully works in me" (Col. 1:29).

It was not Paul's strength but rather God's energy communicated through his presence that enabled the apostle to accomplish his mission. As the church we must experience life with the confidence that only God can grant us success. Responding to this truth means incorporating subtle rhythms into our lives and leadership. It may mean introducing into our busy lives, families, and ministries rhythms of prayer in which we are reminded that our lives are reliant on God's grace and action. It may mean setting aside a week or month of prayer and fasting as we embark on a period of strategic planning or begin a new year of ministry.

The need for the power of God through his Spirit is emphasized by Tozer in his book *The Divine Conquest*. Commenting on the work of the church in his day, he writes:

> The Spirit of God may use a song, a sermon, a good deed, a text or the mystery and majesty of nature, but always the final work will

63. A. W. Tozer, *Born After Midnight* (Harrisburg, Pa.: Christian Publications, 1963), 11.

> be done by the pressure of the inliving Spirit upon the human heart. In light of this it will be seen how empty and meaningless is the average church service today. All the means are in evidence; the one ominous weakness is the absence of the Spirit's power. The form of godliness is there, and often the form is perfected till it is an aesthetic triumph. Music and poetry, art and oratory, symbolic vesture and solemn tones combine to charm the mind of the worshipper, but too often the supernatural afflatus is not there. The power from on high is neither known nor desired by pastor or people. This is nothing less than tragic, and all the more so because it falls within the field of religion where the eternal destinies of men are involved.[64]

Tozer's words are as relevant today as they were in his own. It is easy for the church to rely on its own strength and expertise and forget that they are but "slinging stones" in the great battle for human society and souls. Often we have constructed the most beautiful buildings with the latest technology, and we have attended the hottest ministry seminars offering up-to-date strategies from charismatic leaders. Rather than running to the latest seminar or constructing the most audacious building, Zechariah 9 reminds us that the foundation for all ministry and life lies in God's presence and power in our lives and communities as we pursue his kingdom work.

Striving for unity and enjoying God's blessing. In subtle ways we have recognized the call of Zechariah 9 to unity within the restoration community. There is no place in God's kingdom for the division and animosity displayed between tribes throughout the history of Israel. This unity is based on God's use of his people to accomplish his purposes. It is God who strings the bow and fills it with arrows. As a community we are called to work together as we defeat our foes by God's strength and power.

The New Testament record makes it abundantly clear that unity was crucial to the life of the church and the completion of its mission. It is also obvious that disunity threatened its very existence. Each of the New Testament letters addresses this issue in one form or another, rating "love" as the highest value for the redeemed community (cf. 1 Cor. 13). The threat of disunity came from diverse issues: ethnic background (Gal. 2; 3:26), generational insensitivity (1 Peter 5:1–6), gender difference (Gal. 3:28), economic status (Gal. 3:28; James 2:1–9; 5:1–6), spiritual gifting and experience (1 Cor. 12–14), theological affiliation (1 Cor. 1:11–17; 3:4–9), and behavioral patterns (1 Cor. 10).

We are called to unity, but such unity is based not on humanistic values but on our common bond in the Spirit, shared faith in Christ, and mutual worship of God. The picture of the redeemed community in Revelation 7:9 is one

64. A. W. Tozer, *The Divine Conquest* (Harrisburg, Pa.: Christian Publications, 1950), 90.

that reflects the kind of unity we should long for in the church today—"a great multitude that no one could count, from every nation, tribe, people and language, standing before the throne and in front of the Lamb."

To this end we should strive in the church today. We need churches that express the diversity of human life and experience, a goal that will mark communities as countercultural. In a society segmented along ethnic, gender, generational, and economic lines, the church has the potential to showcase God's ultimate design for humanity through the power of the Spirit. Rather than isolating themselves from the poor, affluent congregations should welcome and support ministry alongside the poor of their community. Instead of creating separate worship experiences for various age groups, the church should encourage diverse expressions within a common experience.[65] Church life should account for the perspective and experience of both genders in their hiring of professional staff as well as in the tone and content of their communal experiences. Rather than separating off members of a particular ethnic group within their faith community to plant a church among fellow immigrants, these members should be granted full participation within the church and be encouraged to continue to impact their friends.[66]

The picture of blessing at the end of Zechariah 9 reveals God's intention for his people. He desires that they experience the fullness of life promised

---

65. See the attempt by B. Whitesel and K. R. Hunter, *A House Divided: Bridging the Generation Gap in Your Church* (Nashville: Abingdon, 2000), who suggest a "tri-generational" model, that is, "a holistic congregation with three distinct generational sub-congregations peacefully co-existing under one roof, one name, and one leadership core" (p. 83). With each "sub-congregation" possessing a distinct shepherd (pastor), lay shepherding team, ministries, and artistic expression (pp. 90–91), it appears that strategy accentuates rather than "bridges" the generation gap. The community of God throughout the ages is clearly intergenerational. This generation gap has been emphasized in recent years through distinct worship styles, and several authors have offered suggestions on blending worship. See D. T. Benedict and C. K. Miller, *Contemporary Worship for the 21st Century: Worship or Evangelism* (Nashville: Discipleship Resources, 1994), 96–104; R. E. Webber, *Blended Worship: Achieving Substance and Relevance in Worship* (Peabody, Mass.: Hendrickson, 1996); idem, *Empowered by the Holy Spirit: A Study in the Ministries of Worship* (Peabody, Mass.: Hendrickson, 1998), 28–34; M. Thielen, *Ancient Modern Worship: A Practical Guide to Blending Worship Styles* (Nashville: Abingdon, 2000).

66. On this see Ortiz's practical guide to recovering the diversity of the church in M. Ortiz, *One New People: Models for Developing a Multiethnic Church* (Downers Grove, Ill.: InterVarsity Press, 1996). One serious hurdle to ethnically diverse churches in North America is the pervasive nature of the "homogenous unit principle" within evangelical missiology. The positive side of this principle is that it reminds us that people should be able to hear the gospel in their own cultural forms (language, worship style, etc.). The negative side is that it can promote racism and division in the church. One can discern this tension in Ken Fong's manual for ministry: K. U. Fong, *Pursuing the Pearl: A Comprehensive Resouce for Multi-Asian Ministry* (Valley Forge, Pa.: Judson, 1999), 3–8; cf. H. M. Conn and M. Ortiz, *Urban Ministry: The Kingdom, the City and the People of God* (Downers Grove, Ill.: InterVarsity Press, 2001), 313–39.

to Abraham at the outset of Israel's history and to Adam at the beginning of world history. In each of these instances of blessing, particular emphasis is placed on the blessing of an abundance of people. As already mentioned, this promised blessing is fulfilled ultimately in that "great multitude" of diversity pictured in Revelation 7. Interestingly the members of that great multitude were "holding palm branches in their hands," reminiscent of the entry of Christ in the Gospel at the first fulfillment of Zechariah 9:9–10. The image of abundance is one that sustains the community of God even through times of distress and pain and motivates them to a life of relationship and mission.

Zechariah 10

1 Ask the LORD for rain in the springtime;
it is the LORD who makes the storm clouds.
He gives showers of rain to men,
and plants of the field to everyone.
2 The idols speak deceit,
diviners see visions that lie;
they tell dreams that are false,
they give comfort in vain.
Therefore the people wander like sheep
oppressed for lack of a shepherd.

3 "My anger burns against the shepherds,
and I will punish the leaders;
for the LORD Almighty will care
for his flock, the house of Judah,
and make them like a proud horse in battle.
4 From Judah will come the cornerstone,
from him the tent peg,
from him the battle bow,
from him every ruler.
5 Together they will be like mighty men
trampling the muddy streets in battle.
Because the LORD is with them,
they will fight and overthrow the horsemen.

6 "I will strengthen the house of Judah
and save the house of Joseph.
I will restore them
because I have compassion on them.
They will be as though
I had not rejected them,
I am the LORD their God
and I will answer them.
7 The Ephraimites will become like mighty men,
and their hearts will be glad as with wine.
Their children will see it and be joyful;
their hearts will rejoice in the LORD.

[8]I will signal for them
and gather them in.
Surely I will redeem them;
they will be as numerous as before.
[9]Though I scatter them among the peoples,
yet in distant lands they will remember me.
They and their children will survive,
and they will return.
[10]I will bring them back from Egypt
and gather them from Assyria.
I will bring them to Gilead and Lebanon,
and there will not be room enough for them.
[11]They will pass through the sea of trouble;
the surging sea will be subdued
and all the depths of the Nile will dry up.
Assyria's pride will be brought down
and Egypt's scepter will pass away.
[12]I will strengthen them in the LORD
and in his name they will walk,"
declares the LORD.

Original Meaning

WHILE CONTINUING AND deepening themes introduced in the previous chapter, Zechariah 10 reveals that idyllic conditions have not yet arrived for the community of God in Yehud. This chapter begins with a direct challenge to the present leadership of the community, which has led the people astray into idolatrous practices (10:1–2). God promises to replace this leadership (10:3a) and assume personal responsibility for this community (10:3b). Under his care it will be transformed and new leadership raised to provide security (10:3b–5). This empowering of the community will happen in order to rescue the exiles of the northern tribes from captivity (10:6–12).[1] God has heard their cries for mercy and promises to restore them to their land.

There has been considerable discussion over the literary integrity of Zechariah 10 and its relationship to Zechariah 9–14. Many divide 10:1–2

1. Floyd notes similarity between the address to Judah (10:3b–5) and Ephraim (10:6–12) in the verb "to strengthen" and the noun "mighty ones," but wisely notes the distinctions: Judah is victorious in struggle for good leadership, Ephraim is gathered and brought home; Floyd, *Minor Prophets*, 477.

from the rest of the chapter. Some have suggested that these verses bear the characteristics of an independent prophetic admonition.[2] Others have observed how 10:1–2 break up the closely parallel section in 9:13–17 and 10:3–12.[3] But none of these observations necessarily undermines the integrity of chapter 10. Perhaps the best conclusion is that of Stuhlmueller, Redditt, and Floyd, who have recognized 10:1–2(3) as a piece that creatively stitches the two chapters together.[4]

Elsewhere we have noted that 10:3b–12 arose in the same period as chapter 9 and was later woven together with that chapter with the editorial linkage of 10:1–3a at the end of Zerubbabel's governorship in Yehud (see commentary introduction and comments on ch. 9). With this discussion in mind, we will approach Zechariah 10 as a unity of prophetic messages that carry on themes inaugurated in Zechariah 9. These messages were delivered to the Jewish community in the Persian province of Yehud in the late sixth century B.C. (515–510 B.C.). The main section (10:3b–12) speaks to a community hopeful for the return of all Israel to the land, while 10:1–3a reveals the subsequent frustrations that arose because of inappropriate leadership, expressing God's intention to provide new leadership who will guide the community to victory and bring salvation to all the tribes of Israel.

Transforming Judah (10:1–5)

WITH THE PICTURESQUE SCENE of Jewish youth enjoying the plenteous fruit of the land still vividly in the reader's mind (9:17), 10:1 calls the community to trust God for this abundant harvest by asking him for the rain necessary for crops to flourish. Whether one should add with the LXX the word for "autumn rains" is a matter of debate,[5] but by mentioning the rains of spring (Deut. 11:13–17; Jer. 5:24), the storm clouds (Job 28:25–26; 38:25; Ps. 135:7; Jer. 10:13), and the "showers of rain" (Job 37:6) the prophet is referring to the main water sources for agricultural activity in Canaan.

In Deuteronomy, Moses told the Israelites that an essential distinction between Canaan and Egypt lay in the source of water (Deut. 11:10–12). Rather than using the consistent flow of a great river like the Nile, God's care comes

---

2. See M. Saebø, *Sacharja 9–14: Untersuchungen von Text und Form* (WMANT 34; Neukirchen-Vluyn: Neukirchener Verlag, 1969), 205; R. A. Mason, "Some Examples of Inner Biblical Exegesis in Zech. IX–XIV," in *Studia Evangelica Vol. VII: Papers Presented to the 5th International Congress on Biblical Studies Held at Oxford, 1973*, ed. E. A. Livingstone (Texte und Untersuchungen zur Geschichte der altchristlichen Literatur 126; Berlin: Akademie Verlag, 1982), 344–45.

3. R. C. Dentan, "Zechariah 9–14," in *The Interpreter's Bible*, ed. G. A. Buttrick (New York: Abingdon, 1956), 6:1098–99.

4. Stuhlmueller, *Rebuilding*, 130; Redditt, *Haggai*, 118; Floyd, *Minor Prophets*, 467.

5. So Hanson, *Dawn*, 324–26; Meyers and Meyers, *Zechariah 9–14*, 181.

in the form of rain and results in abundant crops of all types (11:14–15). This care, however, is linked to the faithfulness of the Israelites to his covenant demands (11:13), and they are warned specifically about the temptation "to turn away and worship other gods and bow down to them" (11:16), behavior that will result in God's wrath and discipline expressed through withholding rain and fertility (11:17).

The temptation to serve other gods was especially strong in matters related to agricultural activity. Members of the pantheons of each of the ancient Near Eastern religions were responsible for the provision of rain. In Canaan, this function was delegated to Baal, who is called "the rider on the clouds." This fact explains why Baal religion was so alluring to the Israelites throughout their history.[6]

This connection between rain and idolatry is made explicit in 10:2. Instead of asking God for rain (10:1),[7] the leaders of the community have been looking to other gods for help.[8] The Hebrew term for "idols" here (*terapim*) refers to images representing household gods or possibly images used for ancestral worship.[9] This is the term used of the cultic items that Rachel stole from her father Laban (Gen. 31:34), Micah made for his personal shrine (Judg. 17:5; 18:14, 17, 20), and Michal used to fool Saul's men (1 Sam. 19:13). Such idols were used to ask the spirit world for decisions (Ezek. 21:21; cf. Hos. 3:4; 1 Sam. 15:23)[10] and were condemned in the renewal of King Josiah (2 Kings 23:24).

---

6. See esp. the battle between Yahweh and Baal in the Elijah narratives. Yahweh withholds rain from Israel in order to embarrass Baal and his followers. In the climactic scene in 1 Kings 18 the test focuses on the ability to send down fire from heaven (lightning), and once Baal is defeated rain returns to the land.

7. The verb "ask" (*šaʾal*) elsewhere refers to a prophetic or priestly inquiry of God or idols, but usually the preposition *bet* introduces God (see, e.g., Judg. 20:18, 23, 27; 1 Sam. 10:22; 22:1, 13, 15; 23:2, 14; 2 Sam. 2:1; 5:19, 23), while here the preposition *min* is used. This preposition is normally used for asking someone for something (Ex. 3:22; 11:2), though it is used in Ps. 2:8; 21:5; 27:4 for a request of God. The reference in Zech. 10:1 does not appear, then, to have a prophetic inquiry in mind.

8. The initial imperative ("ask") is addressed to an unknown group, possibly those who wander like sheep (NIV "people") in 10:2, but more likely the "shepherds" of 10:3.

9. Van der Toorn's review of the ancient Near Eastern evidence concludes that *terapim* could refer either to household gods or to ancestral worship, but the analysis of Old Testament evidence convinces him that it refers to images of dead ancestors, esp. as one compares Deut. 18:11 with 2 Kings 23:24, where "dead" and *terapim* stand in the same place; K. van der Toorn, "The Nature of the Biblical Teraphim in the Light of the Cuneiform Evidence," *CBQ* 52 (1990): 203–22; so also Meyers and Meyers, *Zechariah 9–14*, 184–87. Consulting and venerating ancestors was a key feature in the worship of Canaan; cf. M. J. Boda, "Ideal Sonship in Ugarit," *UF* 25 (1994): 9–24.

10. See van der Toorn, "Teraphim," 203–22.

Zechariah 10:2 likewise refers to the cultic personnel responsible for inquiring (diviners) and the means by which messages were received (visions, dreams). Diviners were forbidden by Yahweh (Deut. 18:10, 14; 1 Sam. 15:23), although the Israelites did use them (1 Sam. 12:8; 2 Kings 17:17), as did their neighbors (Num. 22:7; 1 Sam. 6:2; cf. Josh. 13:22). Although the messages received from these idols were, not surprisingly, messages of "comfort," each of them is given a negative evaluation here: "deceit . . . lie . . . false . . . in vain," making explicit the inappropriateness of such inquiries.

Many have noted striking similarities between the vocabulary of Zechariah 10:1–2 and Jeremiah 14:1–15:4,[11] which is a prophetic liturgy from a period of drought in the closing days of the kingdom of Judah.[12] Jeremiah enters into this liturgy as the prophetic mediator for a people crying for salvation from God. The answer they receive is not positive. Instead, it entails the condemnation of a community that has sought answers through inappropriate means. By alluding to such vocabulary, Zechariah is drawing a link between the Babylonian period community that experienced judgment and the Persian period community who is following the same path. By seeking a message from these sources rather than from Yahweh, both communities cut themselves off from their source of truth and hope. Therefore, the people of Zechariah's day are likened to sheep without a shepherd, a community without guidance from their God.

The image of the shepherd and his flock is common in the literature of the ancient Near East in descriptions of the relationship between a king and his people.[13] Psalm 78:70–72 makes this link explicit by tracing David's rise from "tending the sheep" to become "shepherd of his people Jacob." Like David, Yahweh is a shepherd who cares for his flock (Ps. 23:1; Isa. 40:10–11). This pastoral imagery stresses the vulnerability of the community. As domestic sheep are unable to travel or protect themselves without their shepherd, so the

---

11. Identical: Jer. 14:6 "pasture" = Zech. 10:1 "plants"; Jer. 14:14 "lies" = Zech. 10:2 "lie"; Jer. 14:4 "rain" = Zech. 10:1 "rain"; Jer. 14:5 "in the field "= Zech. 10:1 "of the field"; same Heb. root: Jer. 14:14 "divinations" = Zech. 10:2 "diviners"; Jer. 14:14 "visons" = Zech. 10:2 "visions." See R. A. Mason, "The Use of Earlier Biblical Material in Zechariah 9–14: A Study in Inner Biblical Exegesis," in *Bringing Out the Treasure: Inner Biblical Allusion and Zechariah 9–14*, ed. M. J. Boda and M. H. Floyd (JSOTSup 304; Sheffield: Sheffield Academic Press, 2003), 63–69; idem, "Examples," 345; R. Nurmela, *Prophets in Dialogue: Inner-Biblical Allusions in Zechariah 1–8 and 9–14* (Åbo: Åbo Akademi University, 1996), 114–19; R. F. Person, *Second Zechariah and the Deuteronomic School* (JSOTSup 167; Sheffield: Sheffield Academic Press, 1993), 107–8.

12. See Boda, "Complaint to Contrition," 186–97.

13. So in an Egyptian text prior to 2000 B.C. a god-king delivers Egypt as a herdsmen of all men (*ANET*, 443). So also Hammurabi claims he is a shepherd (*ANET*, 164).

people "wander" and are "oppressed" (cf. Judg. 19:24; Ps. 116:10; 119:67). This image in Zechariah 10:2 stands in stark contrast to the picture in Psalm 78:52, which uses the same combination of words to describe God's leadership of his sheep as they escaped from Egypt.

Shepherd imagery appears at regular intervals throughout Zechariah 9–14 as a description of both divine (9:16; 10:2) and human leadership (10:3; 11:3–17; 13:7). This reference to the absence of God's shepherding in 10:2 diverges considerably from the idyllic scene of blessing in 9:16. God's desire is to shepherd his flock, but they have abandoned his leadership. God thus addresses the human shepherds who have led the community astray (10:3).

At the beginning of 10:3 the text switches briefly into the first person as God bursts out in violent judgment against the "shepherds" and "leaders" of his flock. The term "leaders" (*ʿattud*) is used elsewhere for "male goats" (e.g., Gen. 31:10, 12), which apparently were mixed into the flock in ancient times to help guide the sheep (Jer. 50:8). Therefore, shepherds and male goats ("leaders") represent the leadership caste, who have led the people into idolatry.[14]

More details about the identity of these leaders, however, elude us. The subtle hope for restoration of Davidic rule expressed in 9:9–10, a hope that was dashed by the resignation of a Davidic shepherd in 11:4–16, reveals that the most we can say about these inappropriate leaders in 10:1–3a is that they are likely not Davidic. We have associated this section on the shepherds with the period after the tenure of Zerubbabel as governor of Yehud. Thus, it is a leadership group who wrested control of the community after him. The connection to idolatry noted here seems to disqualify the Zadokite priesthood as a candidate, considering it was their purity from idolatry that elevated their status after the Exile (see Ezek. 44).[15]

The Hebrew word for both "punish" and "care" in 10:3 (*paqad*) refers to a person who attends to someone else, either for ill or good. Through God's punishing of the leaders he shows his intention to shepherd and care for his flock. The flock is identified as the "house of Judah," a reference to the Jewish community within Yehud, for whom God had great hopes. In God's care, they will be transformed from an aimless and defenseless community ("flock") into a majestic and mighty force ("horse").

The "proud horse in battle" renders the Hebrew phrase that reads literally: "as the horse of his splendor in battle." The antecedent of "his" is most likely the same as "his flock" in verse 3, that is, the Lord Almighty, not the

14. It is interesting that this term is applied to foreign royal figures in Isa. 14:9, evidence that may suggest that the reference to "male goats" here is a subtle allusion to Persian overlords. Meyers and Meyers sees the image of shepherds/male goats as referring to "two tiers of human leadership"; Meyers and Meyers, "Future Fortunes," 213.

15. See Boda, "Reading," 277–91.

house of Judah, which is referred to as "them." Thus, Judah is pictured as the Lord's majestic steed on which he rides into battle.[16]

This reference to the Lord's war horse signals a transition from pastoral to military imagery. In verse 4 a series of staccato bursts reveals God's provision for his people. The Hebrew text simply reads:

> From him, the corner;
> From him, the peg;
> From him, the battle bow;
> From him, going forth, every ruler together.

As with the final line of 10:3, so here the antecedent of "him" is most likely the Lord Almighty.[17] Therefore, each unit identifies the Lord as the source of the various components, each of which symbolizes the leadership of the community.

The first term (*pinnah*; NIV "cornerstone") refers in the Old Testament to the corner of a structure (e.g., Ex. 27:2; Job 1:19).[18] But this image also applies to leadership in the community (Judg. 20:2; 1 Sam. 14:38; Isa. 19:13). The connection between the corner and leadership is not clear but may be linked to the role of the corner towers in the defense of a city.[19]

A "tent peg" is what secures a tent to the ground and thus lends stability to its structure (e.g., Isa. 54:2). However, this term is also used for a wall peg, from which heavy items could be hung (Isa. 22:23, 25). Although the first sense may be in view here and is thus similar to the term "corner," the reference to future leadership in Isaiah 22 tips the scales in favor of the wall peg as representative of leadership.[20]

The image of the "battle bow" was used in 9:13 to refer to the tribe of Judah. Of the four symbols this is the one with the least connection to leadership. Although some see here simply an image of the military ability of this community,[21] there is evidence that the bow was symbolic of royal power in the ancient Near East.[22]

---

16. So also Merrill, *Haggai*, 272.

17. The NIV follows most interpreters by translating "them," a reference to Judah. Leske uses this to bolster his argument for a corporate interpretation of the royal hope in Zech. 9–14; Leske, "Zechariah 9:9," 673–74.

18. The translation "cornerstone" is not appropriate here because when it refers to this elsewhere, it is linked to the Heb. term for "stone" (*ʾeben*): see Job 38:6; Isa. 28:16; Jer. 51:26.

19. For play on Ps. 118:22 and allusion to kingship, see Mason, "Use," 79–80; Meyers and Meyers, "Future Fortunes," 214.

20. Meyers and Meyers, "Future Fortunes," 214–15.

21. See Meyers and Meyers, *Zechariah 9–14*, 202.

22. See Mason, "Use," 82–83. Egyptian kings used the title "he who repels the nine bows," in which the bows were hostile kings.

The final line in the Hebrew text actually contains the verb that the NIV supplies at the outset of this verse ("will come") and provides the verb for each of the previous phrases.[23] This line should read: "From him [they] will come, every ruler together." In the Hebrew text the word "together" is found at the end of 10:4, not the beginning of 10:5 (cf. NIV text note).[24] It is a term that speaks of a concerted effort by several participants and thus shows that the final phrase ("every ruler together") is a summary of the three images introduced in 10:4. The term "ruler" usually carries negative connotations in the Old Testament, describing the oppressive actions of foreigners against Israel (e.g., Ex. 5:6, 10, 13, 14) as well as those of the rich against the poor (Isa. 58:3). In Isaiah 60:17, however, this term can be used in a positive sense of just rule. God will replace the idolatrous leadership of the shepherds and male goats of Zechariah 10:3 with a new leadership caste for Judah, who will work together.

Verse 5 confirms that the previous verse refers to a group of leaders rather than just one because "*they* will be like *mighty men*." "Mighty men" (*gibborim*) often refers to skilled warriors in the Old Testament (e.g., Josh. 10:2, 7)[25]; combined here with the verb "trampled" (*bus*; Ps. 44:5; 60:12; 108:14; Isa. 14:19, 25; 63:6, 18) and the phrase "muddy streets" (2 Sam. 22:43; Ps. 18:43; Mic. 7:10), it connotes triumphant military conquest. So powerful is this force that they will not only defeat their enemy but humiliate their strongest forces, the cavalry.[26]

The identity of this new leadership caste from Judah is not specified. From our preceding discussion it most likely involves royal leadership, which has led many to see here a reference to a future messianic figure.[27] However, it is also clear that it speaks of a group rather than an individual (as in 9:9–10), which has led others to the conclusion that this refers to a new royal status

---

23. A Heb. technique that Meyers and Meyers call "reverse gapping"; Meyers and Meyers, *Zechariah 9–14*, 199.

24. The NIV follows the suggestion of *BHS* and evidence of Syriac; cf. Petersen, *Zechariah 9–14*, 74; Baldwin, *Haggai*, 174. However, see Meyers and Meyers, who follow the MT and cite a similar list followed by "together" in Jer. 31:8; Meyers and Meyers, *Zechariah 9–14*, 203–4.

25. It is often combined with the term *ḥayil* (as Josh. 10:7), but not always (Josh. 10:2). It is difficult to tell whether a "mighty man" is a general term for military personnel or a technical term for a foot soldier. This term is associated usually with those who carry hand weapons (shield, sword, bow, sling, spear), wear protective clothing (helmets, coats of armor), and proceed on foot (1 Sam. 2:4; 2 Sam. 1:21, 22; 23:8; 1 Chron. 8:40; 12:1–2, 8; 2 Chron. 17:17; 26:12; Joel 2:7). It is less clear in contexts that contain lists whether this is a summary term or not (Ps. 33:16–17; Jer. 46:9; 50:36–37; Ezek. 39:20; Amos 2:14–16). Ps. 45:3–5 is the one context that pictures a "mighty man" (here the king) on a horse.

26. For this term "overthrow" see Ps. 44:7; 53:5 (NIV, "put to shame").

27. See Leske, "Zechariah 9:9," 674 n. 30.

for Judah as a tribe.[28] The tension between these two interpretations can be resolved if one identifies this as a reference to the emergence of a royal court, raised up by God to lead his people to victory.

Such victory is linked here to the presence of Yahweh, who is "with them." This is a reminder of the truth already encountered in 9:14 and indicative of the theology of divine war in the Old Testament.[29] Israel does not gain victory because of superior military tactics or weaponry but rather because of the Lord's overpowering presence. God may secure victory without the participation of Israel's military forces (Ex. 14–15). But there are also instances where God granted victory as Israel fought in the battle (Ex. 17:8–16; 2 Sam. 5:22–25). The key to victory, however, in both scenarios is God's presence with his people.

Restoring Joseph (10:6–12)

ZECHARIAH 10:6 MARKS the transition in the passage from the transformation of Judah to the restoration of Joseph. Up to this point the community in view has been the "house of Judah," the faithful remnant in the Persian province of Yehud. Both the community (10:3b) and its leadership (10:4–5) will be transformed into a powerful fighting force. This transformation is highlighted quickly at the outset of verse 6, using a verb ("strengthen," *gabar*) that echoes the noun "mighty men" (*gibborim*) in verse 5. As God now breaks into the prophetic speech with first-person speech ("I will strengthen"), he emphasizes that the transformation of the house of Judah is linked to the restoration of Joseph, which will be the focus of the latter half of this chapter.

The "house of Joseph" refers to those tribes from the northern kingdom who were taken into exile when Samaria, their capital, fell to the Assyrians in the late eighth century B.C. God here promises to "save" this community and "restore" them to their former state ("they will be as though I had not rejected them"), echoing the promises of several earlier prophets (Isa. 11:11–16; Jer. 3:11–18; 31:1–22; Ezek. 37:15–22).[30]

This promise links God's answer to an assumed cry from the exilic community: "I will answer them." In 10:9 we are told that "in distant lands they will remember me." This kind of remembering is more than just a cerebral exercise, since it involves the religious affections of the community. Deuteronomy 8:18–20 speaks of remembering and forgetting God in terms of covenant fidelity and infidelity. Forgetting God is not just forgetting his

28. Ibid., 673–74, esp. 674 n. 30; Mason, *Haggai*, 100; Hanson, *Dawn*, 331.

29. See further, P. C. Craigie, *The Problem of War in the Old Testament* (Grand Rapids: Eerdmans, 1978); Lind, *Yahweh Is a Warrior*; von Rad, *Holy War*; Longman and Reid, *Warrior*.

30. Leske, "Zechariah 9:9," 674.

great deeds but serving other gods. Therefore, remembering is a covenantal term, indicating a turning to God and a returning to his land (Jer. 51:50). Such penitential cries to God are encouraged in the foundational documents of Israel (Lev. 26:40–45; 1 Kings 8:46–51) and are apparent in the record of the exilic community (Ezra 9, Neh. 1; 9; Lam. 1–5; Dan. 9).[31]

God's restorative action is based on a double foundation: his compassion and his covenant. (1) He will restore this community because of his deep affection for them as his people. Verse 6 reminds us of the declaration of Yahweh's character to Moses following the golden calf incident in Exodus 33:19, where he said: "I will cause all my goodness to pass in front of you, and I will proclaim my name, the LORD, in your presence. I will have mercy on whom I will have mercy, and *I will have compassion on* whom I will have compassion." It points to God's affection for his people, an attribute linked to his promise in Deuteronomy 30:3: "Then the LORD your God will restore your fortunes and *have compassion* on you and gather you again from all the nations where he scattered you" (italics added in both references).

(2) The writer of 2 Kings links this compassion of God for his people to the covenant he made with Israel: "But the LORD was gracious to them and *had compassion* and showed concern for them because of his *covenant* with Abraham, Isaac and Jacob. To this day he has been unwilling to destroy them or banish them from his presence" (italics added). Similarly, Zechariah 10:6 links the compassionate salvation of God to the covenant made with this people through the phrase "for I am the LORD their God" (Ex. 20:2; 29:46; Lev. 26:44–45). God's character of compassion expressed through his commitment of covenant forms the basis of this liberation.

For the exiled community of the northern tribes, referred to by the leading tribe of Ephraim in 10:7 (see comments on 9:10), God's redemption will entail a reversal of their present condition. This defeated, depressed, and decimated people will become skilled warriors (like Judah's leaders in 10:5), who are giddy with joy alongside a new generation. This reversal is expressed in 10:8 through the Hebrew construction translated as "signal for them." This phrase is used in Isaiah 5:26 and 7:18 for God's audible signal (contrast the banner, which is a visual signal) for the nations of Assyria and Egypt to discipline Israel. Now God signals Israel from these same nations (see Zech. 10:10).[32]

31. See Boda, *Praying the Tradition*; idem, "Complaint," 187–97; idem, "Priceless Gain," 51–75; R. A. Werline, *Penitential Prayer in Second Temple Judaism: The Development of a Religious Institution* (SBLEJL 13; Atlanta: Scholars Press, 1998); J. H. Newman, *Praying by the Book: The Scripturalization of Prayer in Second Temple Judaism* (SBLEJL 14; Atlanta: Scholars Press, 1999); R. J. Bautch, *Developments in Genre Between Post-Exilic Penitential Prayers and the Psalms of Communal Lament* (SBLABS; Atlanta: Society of Biblical Literature, 2003).

32. See N. Mendecki, "Deuterojesajanischer und Ezechielischer Einfluss auf Sach 10:8–10," *Kairos* 27 (1985): 340.

He will "gather" and "redeem" this community, actions highlighted regularly in the Old Testament in contexts speaking of the restoration.[33]

Following the Hebrew and Greek text, the word "scatter" in 10:9 should be translated "planted."[34] This is an appropriate word for the experience of the northern tribes, whose long exile resulted in deep roots in their respective locales.[35]

A consistent theme throughout 10:7–10 is the expected increase in the size of the community ("their children ... will be as numerous as before"; "there will not be room enough for them"[36]). Meyers and Meyers have noted that this hope of "extreme demographic growth," which they link to Jeremiah 23:3 and Ezekiel 36:11, evokes the creation and patriarchal promises of fruitfulness and multiplication throughout Genesis.[37]

Recent research on the province of Yehud has confirmed what the biblical text has long asserted, namely, that the population of Yehud was not significant (see Neh. 7; 11).[38] This is expected for a community that has experienced much hardship during the Babylonian period, not least of which was seeing its leadership carted off into exile. If this was true of the southern kingdom of Judah, how much more for the northern tribes, who have endured a far longer exile. These northern tribes will survive and return with children.

We have already noted the indebtedness of 10:10 to Isaiah 7:18 for the mention of Egypt and Assyria. These two nations are often linked in Old Testament literature as they represent the two major threats to Israel's freedom, the former approaching from the south and the latter from the north (Isa. 19:23–25).[39] Although it is most likely that these two nations are representative of the spread of the exiles throughout the world (Mic. 7:12), the image

---

33. "Gather": Deut. 30:3–4; Neh. 1:9; Ps. 106:47; 107:3; Isa. 11:12; 43:5; 49:18; 54:7; 56:8; 60:4; Jer. 23:3; 29:14; 31:8; 31:10; 32:37; Ezek. 11:17; 20:34, 41; 28:25; 34:13; 36:24; 37:21; 39:27; Hos. 2:2; Mic. 2:12; 4:6; Zeph. 3:19, 20; "redeem": Isa. 35:10; 51:11; Jer. 31:11 (used of the Exodus in Deut. 7:8; 9:26; 13:6; 15:15; 21:8; 24:18; 2 Sam. 7:23//1Chron. 17:21; Neh. 1:10; Ps. 78:42; Mic. 6:4).

34. Many have emended the Heb. *zara*ᶜ ("plant") to *zarah* ("scatter, winnow") because the latter often appears in contexts concerned with restoration. Winnowing occurs at the end of the growing season, when farmers separate the wheat from the chaff and the chaff is scattered. After planting, of course, the seed takes root.

35. For this see Meyers and Meyers, *Zechariah 9–14*, 216.

36. The same Heb. idiom is also found in Josh. 17:16.

37. Meyers and Meyers, "Demography," 271; cf. Mendecki, "Einfluss," 341.

38. See Carter, *Emergence*.

39. Assyria's exile of the Israelites is often linked to Egypt's enslavement of them (Isa. 10:24; 11:16; 52:4).

would have had great impact because of the presence of Jewish communities in exile in both Assyria and Egypt (Isa. 11:11; 27:13; Hos. 7:11; 11:5, 11).[40]

These geographical names of Assyria and Egypt are matched by two others, Gilead (on the east side of the Jordan, between the Sea of Galilee and the Dead Sea) and Lebanon (on the northern border of Israel), which are the destination of the return. The choice of these two areas as settlement areas is probably related to the lack of room because of the abundance of people.[41] These northern territories are mentioned because they lie along the boundaries of the land occupied by the northern tribes, who are returning to the land.

In 10:11 the return of the northern tribes is compared to the Israelites' exodus from Egypt, but with an interesting twist.[42] God, rather than the Israelites, "will pass through the sea of trouble," striking the "surging seas" (lit., "sea of waves").[43] Whether the imagery here has been stretched beyond that of the Exodus tradition so that the sea is now equated with the Nile, whether the reference to the drying up of "the Nile" denotes the destruction of Egypt's prosperity as a result of the Exodus, or whether the word here refers to a water body other than the Nile[44] does not matter. In the end God smashes the pride and rule of the nations who held his people captive, which in turn results in liberation for the exiles.

Verse 12 brings closure to this section on the salvation of the northern tribes. Using the same verb with which he introduced the section in verse 6 ("strengthen"), God now promises the same benefits that the house of Judah enjoyed: to be strengthened by God. This strength will enable them to walk in his name. Although the term here for "walk" (Hithpael of *halak*) can be used of generic walking (Gen. 3:8) or of walking in relationship with God (5:22, 24; 6:9; 17:1 etc.), because it is preceded here by a reference to God's strengthening of the Israelites, this word probably refers to the "exercise of dominion over an area" (cf. Gen. 13:17; Josh. 18:4, 8; Job 2:2; Zech. 1:10, 11; 6:7).[45] The restored community will regain control over their land.

---

40. The reference to people in "Assyria" when Mesopotamia was now ruled by Persia is not odd. Not only is Assyria a traditional area of Mesopotamia, it was the name for the area when the Israelites were taken into exile. The Jewish community at Elephantine in "Egypt" may have originated in the northern kingdom; Meyers and Meyers, *Zechariah 9–14*, 220.

41. Mendecki, "Einfluss," 342, claims that Gilead is mentioned first because it was the first area deported.

42. There is an allusion to the Israelite Exodus tradition here, expressed as a polemic against Canaanite myth; Hanson, *Dawn*, 332; Petersen, *Zechariah 9–14*, 78; Merrill, *Haggai*, 279.

43. The verbs "pass through" and "subdue" are both masculine singular forms.

44. Cf. 2 Kings 19:24; Job 28:10; Isa. 7:18; 19:6; 33:21; Ezek. 29:10; Dan. 12:5–7. This word usually refers to the "Nile," but is merely the term "stream."

45. See Merrill, *Haggai*, 282.

Bridging Contexts

THE IDENTITY OF the remnant rescued from the nations has long been a point of contention within the church. Most acknowledge that the books of Ezra and Nehemiah describe the return of several waves of this remnant. However, this is usually identified as the return of a limited portion of the tribes of Judah, Benjamin, and Levi, leaving unfulfilled the return of the northern tribes. These northern tribes, often referred to as "the lost tribes of Israel," have been linked to various ethnic groups around the globe. Although the most prevalent theory connects them with the Anglo-Saxon/Celtic peoples of Britain and America,[46] others have associated them with aboriginal tribes of North America,[47] the Mizos from the Indo-Burma border,[48] and even the Japanese.[49] Some see these tribes as Jewish communities spread across the globe to this day who have returned, are returning, and/or will return to the land of Israel.[50] Finally, a prevalent view within the church is that this remnant is the community of Christ, the church.[51]

Our conclusion on this issue will have a great impact on the implications we draw from this text. It will determine whether this passage has any relevance for the church today or is merely an announcement of God's design for history.

Remnant. We have already argued in detail in the commentary introduction that the New Testament appropriates the Old Testament hope of a purified remnant for its description of Christ and the early church. On one

46. R. Foster, *You Can Understand Bible Prophecy* (Cincinnati: United Church of God, 1999); R. Foster, J. Patton, J. R. Schroeder, and D. Treybig, *The United States and Britain in Bible Prophecy* (Cincinnati: United Church of God, 2001). Note especially the strong influence of the Worldwide Church of God under Herbert W. and Garner T. Armstrong in the past century, who identified the ten lost tribes with Europeans and North Americans.

47. See, e.g., H. M. Bracken, "Bishop Berkeley's Messianism," in *Millenarianism and Messianism in English Literature and Thought 1650–1800* (Publications from the Clark Library Professorship, UCLA 10; Leiden: Brill, 1988); C. H. Gordon, "The Ten Lost Tribes," in *Hebrew and the Bible in America* (Brandeis Series in American Jewish History, Culture and Life; Hanover, N.H.: Univ. of New England Press, 1993), 61–69.

48. An article in *The Asianage* (July 17, 1999) reports the following: The Israeli interior ministry has given its approval in principle to ultra-orthodox rabbi Eliyahu Avishayil's plans to bring to Israel 3,000 Shinlung tribesmen from the Indo-Burmese border. According to him, the Shinlung live like Jews and are probably descended from one of Israel's ten lost tribes.

49. Note the booklet from 1932 entitled, "Who Are The Japanese? 'An address given by Prof. E. Odlum, M.A., B.Sc., in the Oak Room, Hotel Vancouver, Vancouver, B.C., on March 28th, 1932.'"

50. E.g., F. P. Miller, *Zechariah and Jewish Renewal: From Gloom to Glory* (Lithonia, Ga.: Moellerhaus, 1992).

51. See, of course, the classic work of Calvin on Zech. 10:6, J. Calvin, *Commentaries on the Twelve Minor Prophets* (Calvin's Commentaries 13–15; Grand Rapids: Baker, 1989).

level Jesus is presented as the obedient remnant who escapes Egypt (Matt. 2:13–15, 19–21), survives exile (Matt. 2:16–18), and assumes a penitential posture (Matt. 3:13–17). This Jesus then gathers around him twelve disciples as representative of Israel, through whom he gathers a remnant from the nations (Acts 2). In New Testament perspective, in other words, the hoped-for remnant of Zechariah 10 is ultimately fulfilled in the church.

That this remnant is not restricted to those of Jewish lineage is made clear in several passages of the New Testament. (1) In Matthew's description of the encounter between Jesus and the Gentile centurion, Jesus declares:

> I tell you the truth, I have not found anyone in Israel with such great faith. I say to you that many will come from the east and the west, and will take their places at the feast with Abraham, Isaac and Jacob in the kingdom of heaven. (Matt. 8:10b–11)

As already demonstrated in Zechariah 8:7–8, the language of the many who "come from the east and the west" is language connected with the return of the remnant (cf. Ps. 107:3; Isa. 59:19).[52] In Matthew 8, however, this remnant is not restricted to those of Jewish lineage but is extended to all nations.

(2) According to Paul, this expansion of the remnant hope to include Gentiles is evident in Old Testament theology (see comments on 2:11; 8:20–23). As Paul provides the foundation for his ministry among the Gentiles in Romans 15:8–9, 12, he cites three Old Testament passages that describe the praise of God among the Gentiles (in order: 2 Sam. 22:50//Ps. 18:49; Deut. 32:43; Ps. 117:1). Then he paraphrases Isaiah 11:10:

> The Root of Jesse will spring up,
> one who will arise to rule over the nations;
> the Gentiles will hope in him.

Paul's vision of the church is one drawn from a passage that introduces a future Davidic ruler who will raise a banner to draw nations (11:10), an action linked to the reclamation of the remnant of the exiles, both from Ephraim and Judah. Here Paul identifies Christ as this Davidic ruler, who has reclaimed the remnant and is extending his rule to the nations.

(3) This view of the fulfillment of the remnant motif of the prophets informs the foundational narrative of the New Testament community.[53] Acts 2 begins this process as the birth of the church is equated with the return of the remnant from the nations. The experience of Pentecost becomes the

52. G. E. Ladd, *A Theology of the New Testament*, rev. ed. (Grand Rapids: Eerdmans, 1993), 112.

53. Interestingly, the Qumran community also saw themselves as the remnant of Israel, esp. in their division into twelve tribes led by twelve chiefs (1QSa 1.27–2.1).

fulfillment of the hope of Joel 2:28–32. Joel envisioned the return of a remnant from the nations to Jerusalem.

Acts 2 is a key transition point in a story that begins with Israel and ultimately extends to the entire world. Acts as a whole reveals how this remnant community, gathered in Jerusalem at Pentecost, extends God's kingdom to Judea, Samaria, and to the ends of the earth (1:8; cf. ch. 28). Along the way, James cites Amos 9:11–12 in Acts 15:14–21, revealing that Christ came to restore David's tent, resulting in the fulfillment of the remnant promise and the regeneration of the Gentiles.

The restoration and transformation of the tribes in Zechariah 10 are fulfilled, therefore, in the church, which now assumes the status of the "new Israel."

Twelve tribes. The province of Yehud was clearly dominated by those who traced their roots to the tribe of Judah. This prophetic message begins by addressing this community, chiding their leadership and offering the hope of a glorious and triumphant future. But this message does not end at 10:5. The first line of 10:6 summarizes the gracious actions of God toward Judah in 10:3–5 only as a transition into a section accenting God's salvation of the house of Joseph in 10:6–12. In other words, God's action for Judah is for the sake of Joseph, who remains in exile.

As already noted in our discussion of Zechariah 9, this focus on the northern tribes is surprising in light of the animosity evident among significant members of the province of Yehud. Zechariah 10 outlines God's plan for all Israel, a plan in which Judah will play a vital role, especially through its royal house. This hope for "all Israel," gathered around the Davidic king of Judah, is a major theme in another Persian period book: 1–2 Chronicles. Not only does the Chronicler begin his book with genealogies of most of the tribes of Israel (1 Chron. 1–9), but throughout his presentation of Israel's history he constantly refers to "all Israel" (1 Chron. 9:1; 11:1, 10; 12:38; 14:8; 15:3, 28; 18:14; 2 Chron. 1:2; 7:8; 9:30; 10:3, 16; 12:1; 13:4, 15; 18:16; 24:5). Although the focus of the story is on the southern kingdom (i.e., the kingdom of the Davidic kings), many episodes show "all Israel" gathered around that king in Jerusalem (e.g., 1 Chron. 11:1, 10; 2 Chron. 1:1–2; 30:5–14, 25). Both Chronicles and Zechariah 9–10 reveal the hope in the Persian period of the renewal of the united kingdom under a Davidic ruler.

This hope of the restoration of all the tribes continues throughout the Second Temple period as the Diaspora is a continuing reality for the Jews. Clearly, Paul's reference to the "twelve tribes" in his address to Agrippa in Acts 26:7 is meant as a reference to the entire Jewish community. However, there are indications in New Testament theology that the church is the fulfillment of this hope of the return of all the tribes.

As already mentioned, Christ's choice of twelve apostles is clearly an allusion to the twelve tribes of Israel and suggests that Christ considers the community that comes from him as the new Israel (see commentary introduction, Bridging Contexts section). This approach is evident also in one of Christ's key speeches. As he describes the "renewal of all things," Jesus claims that the apostles will rule with him on thrones over the twelve tribes of Israel (Matt. 19:28; Luke 22:30). These are the same apostles who are considered the foundation of the church (Eph. 2:20). It is not odd, then, for the writer of James to address the churches who received his document as the "twelve tribes scattered among the nations" (James 1:1).

This connection between the twelve tribes and the church is confirmed in Revelation. In Revelation 21:12–14 the names of the twelve tribes of Israel are written on the gates of the holy city, the new Jerusalem. So also the twelve foundations contain the names of the twelve apostles. This city is "the bride, the wife of the Lamb" (21:9), a reference to the church. Again we see an intermixing of the language of the tribes and that of the church founded on the apostolic community that followed Jesus.[54] Revelation 7:4–8 describes a group of 144,000 drawn from each of the twelve tribes of Israel. Immediately following this John sees a group of God's people from all tribes and nations (7:9). The close association of these two groups suggests that they are the same group. Crucial to the emergence of this new community in Revelation, however, is Jesus the slain Lamb, who is described as the lion of Judah, the Root of David (5:5).

We conclude, therefore, the biblical theology of "all Israel," of the hope of the reunification of the tribes, is fulfilled in the church. Zechariah 10, addressing a community that has little room for these northern tribes in their future plans, is an important reminder to us of the value of unity within our faith communities.

Therefore, on one level, Zechariah 10 is fulfilled in Christ and the establishment of the church. The abusive shepherds of the community are judged by God, who provides his own pastoral care of his people through Christ. Also through Jesus of Judah, God raises up leadership from David. He rescues his remnant through the transformation of their lives in order that they may fully realize God's kingdom as a community. Transported back to the Persian period community through this redemptive-historical perspective, we listen afresh to Zechariah 10 as the remnant community that trusts in the same God and longs to avoid the mistakes of the community of the past and experience fully the promises of this chapter.

---

54. See also LaRondelle, *Israel of God*, 145.

Contemporary Significance

GOD'S DEMAND OF EXCLUSIVE TRUST. This is not the first time Zechariah 9–14 has highlighted inappropriate idolatrous practices. In 9:7 God cleansed the idolatrous practices of the Philistines before incorporating them into Israel. The difference in 10:1–2 is that these inappropriate spiritual practices have made their way into God's community, encouraged by the leadership and tolerated, if not embraced, by the people. Both of these passages speak strongly against our postmodern spiritual melange. They reveal that the medium is as important as the message; that is, our spiritual sources and practices do matter to God.

God's call to the Christian community today is a call to purity in our practices of listening to his voice. Down the road from my home is a New Age bookstore, which offers certain spiritual services for those within our community: paraphernalia like tarot cards and horoscopes, personnel like palm readers and psychics. These are the diviners of our generation, and people uncertain about their present and future flock to them for advice. Obviously, 10:1–2 prohibits Christians from availing themselves of these resources.

But there are more subtle voices that may have more impact on the church today than the New Age hawkers. It is surprising how often we draw our wisdom from the sources of Wall Street and Harvard Business School. Seeking to insulate ourselves from recession in terms of finances or from downsizing in terms of church growth, we have filled our minds with the advice of a secular world rather than the wisdom of God. By this I am not suggesting that secular sources are devoid of wisdom; as I was taught in college, "All truth is God's truth." However, it is surprising to me how often the church, corporately and individually, treats wisdom from secular sources like "plug-'n'-play" components of a computer, rather than taking the time to reflect Christianly about these sources and configure them according to biblical sensibilities.

This demands wisdom from God, and that wisdom must begin with a mind and a heart filled with the claims and contents of Scripture. By this I do not mean a collection of isolated texts, but rather the foundational and longitudinal themes that shape a Christian perspective on all of life and spirituality. This is as important for the Christian preacher as it is for the Christian carpenter, teacher, and banker. All need spiritual wisdom to walk prudently in this present age.

The connection between the source and shape of our wisdom and the issue of trust is not readily apparent to many of us. But as we face challenges and decisions in life, the one to whom we turn for wisdom and direction and the way in which we process that enlightenment are indicators of whom we ultimately trust. Whether those challenges are uncertain conditions of agricultural enterprise as the community in Zechariah 10 or fluctuating fortunes of financial markets and unpredictable changes in one's physical condition, we must trust God's perspective on these issues, seek counsel from mature Christians, and reflect deeply on God's Word.

God's provision of leadership. Zechariah 10 spoke to a generation led by shepherds who had severed the community from the Lord. God's compassion breaks through in the speech as he promises to punish those shepherds and provide caring guidance for his people. At first this provision is described as God's personal intervention in their circumstances, but as the passage progresses, the Lord reveals that this will be accomplished through leadership he will raise up from Judah, which will not only affect their own tribe but also the northern tribes still in exile.

It is fascinating that in Jesus Christ we see the intertwining of these two aspects of leadership in Zechariah 10. As God, Christ came to care for his flock as the gentle shepherd (John 10), and yet as a child from the royal line of the tribe of Judah he came to reinstate Davidic kingship in Israel (Rom 1:3).

The future Judahite royal leadership is described here with the images of war. These images are echoed in the description of the redemption of Joseph in the latter half of the chapter. Similarly, Christ's work on the cross is described as a battle against the forces of evil. But this is certainly an irony of monumental proportions: Christ does battle through dying on one of the greatest symbols of oppression, the Roman cross. Isaiah 52–53 also envisions the suffering of the Messiah as representative of the exilic community in terms of the victory of God. Isaiah 52:7–10 describes how a messenger declares a victory of God won through the baring of his holy arm. In 53:1, however, the prophet declares his shock as he views this "arm of the LORD." Rather than a mighty armed force, he sees a suffering and dying individual. To this passage the early church turned again and again as they interpreted the cross in light of God's victory presented in Isaiah 52–53. God's victory is accomplished in ways never expected in Zechariah 10.

Zechariah 10, therefore, prompts us to praise God for the victory he accomplished through his messianic leader and shepherd, Jesus, of the line of David and the tribe of Judah. This is the central event of the Christian faith, foreshadowed here in Zechariah 10. God's victory through the cross, however, is not the end. We look for the final consummation of this victory as we await Jesus' second coming (Rev. 19).

In light of these past and future events, we live in the present as those empowered by God to function as Christ-ones who extend this victory incrementally across this globe and within all layers of culture. This is why the royal/messianic promises attached to the line of David can be related so easily by the apostle Paul to the church of Jesus Christ (2 Cor. 6:18). As the body of Christ, we are his incarnation between his two advents as we proclaim and extend his victory. This victory, however, is accomplished through the same kind of suffering that Christ modeled for us (1 Peter 2:13–25; 3:8–18).

God's purposes for all Israel. The theme of the reunification of the tribes of Israel in the Promised Land drives home the prophetic hope of unity for a community that lived in discord for the bulk of its history. It is only through the messianic leadership of the Davidic ruler Jesus that this unity can be realized as he rescues both Jew and Gentile from the kingdom of darkness and delivers them into his kingdom of light. In doing so he creates a community of love and peace, who are united by allegiance to the Father, redemption through Jesus Christ, and empowerment by the Holy Spirit. As the church we can "make every effort to keep the unity of the Spirit through the bond of peace" because there is "one body and one Spirit . . . one Lord, one faith, one baptism; one God and Father of all, who is over all and through all and in all" (Eph. 4:3–6).

God's passion for redemption after discipline. In Zechariah 10 we catch a glimpse of God's passionate love for his people. It is first expressed in his promise to care for his flock, the house of Judah (10:3), the image of a shepherd's intimate protection of his flock. As he turns his attention to the house of Joseph, we learn of God's desire to restore, have compassion, answer, gather, and redeem his people. All of these terms are built up to express the action of God, whose heart is filled with "compassion" for his people. After years in exile this message from his heart brings an incredible comfort for these communities of faith. When one considers the final phases of both the southern and northern kingdoms (2 Kings 17; 25) and the way in which they treated their God with contempt, ignoring the pleas of his prophets and the justice expressed in his law, the promises here are remarkable indeed, highlighting God's grace beyond measure.

In expressing his love, however, God does not conceal his discipline. In the present his anger burns against deceptive shepherds who lead his people astray. In the past he disciplined his people, scattering them abroad. That discipline is not incongruous with his love but is an essential part of his loving plan for them. It is easy to juxtapose these aspects of God's character and action. It is not either the God of love or the God of discipline, but rather the God of loving discipline. His love was expressed to us through Jesus, who took on himself the discipline of the cross. Resting secure in his love through Christ, Christians should expect to be disciplined by their loving God (Heb. 12:7–11).

The compassionate grace that God extends to his people in Zechariah 10 is linked to the cry of the people as God answers them (10:6) and as they "remember" him in distant lands (10:9). These subtle allusions to repentance by the people remind us of our constant need for penitent hearts as we walk with God. This chapter encourages us, then, to experience authentic and consistent relationship with our covenant God. As we are lovingly disciplined, we must cry to him in penitential response, confident that he has promised to answer us—that is, to return to us as we return to him.

God's plan for blessing and joy. Such disciplined love expressed in response to penitence results in a breadth and depth of blessing. (1) God promises a population explosion in this faith community that exceeds all expectations. (2) This blessing is signaled by a depth of gladness and joy as the people revel in the presence and blessing of the Lord. These are images of delight as the people join together from all nations with an abundance of children to celebrate God's salvation and blessing.

The fulfillment of this ingathering is foreshadowed in Acts 2. There the tribes of Israel gather from around the world to attend the Feast of Pentecost. There the Spirit of joy falls on his people, and the restoration community begins its life. But this is just the beginning, and the book of Revelation anticipates an even greater party in the last days as people gather from every tribe and nation to celebrate the salvation of God (Rev. 7:9).

The church needs to be shaped by this vision of the community in Zechariah 10 in the present. The church must be a community open to the kind of growth God envisions for his people. It is easy to become complacent in our church communities, to place priority on those with whom we have fellowshipped over decades, and to become closed to new relationships.

The founding pastor of one of the churches in which I served once told me a story that he said indicated his church was on the verge of a new phase of ministry. The church had grown to a healthy size in its first decade as people were drawn to the relevant preaching, dynamic programs, and warm fellowship. But the test came one Sunday as a tough biker and a few of his friends showed up at the invitation of someone in the church. At the end of the service the founding pastor was distracted by a parishioner with a crisis. Out of the corner of his eye he noticed one of his conservative elders making a beeline for the bikers and waited with baited breath for what would happen. Within moments of their meeting face-to-face, the pastor watched with surprise as the elder embraced the lead biker. This kind of openness to people outside of the community is a core value of the prophetic message in Zechariah 10 as God uses the remnant already saved from exile to extend salvation to those still living among the nations.

Not only is this community known by its openness as they welcome God's redeemed into their midst, but it is also known by a depth of gladness and joy that arises from this community, reveling in God's presence and blessing. Such authentic gladness and joy are communicated through individual and corporate avenues by people who know and experience God's presence in their own lives and express this delight to their friends and neighbors. In this way evangelism is not a presentation of cold facts but the natural expression of one's life, the joyous overflow of one who has experienced the salvation and blessing of God.

I remember when I was involved in an evangelistic program several years ago that the power of the presentation we were taught lay not only in the theological points and Scripture verses, but also in the expression of our own experience with God. This kind of expression need not be restricted to experiences of gladness and joy, for how God sustains us through difficult circumstances is also an important expression. Such experiences form a powerful avenue for communicating and embodying the gospel to those around us.[55]

This is also true on the corporate level. The gospel is proclaimed through communal experiences that facilitate the expression of gladness and joy as we revel in God's presence and blessing. We often view worship as an activity for the saints alone. However, the initial worship experience of the church on Pentecost, in which God's people declared "the wonders of God" in many foreign tongues, led to three thousand baptisms. Furthermore, Paul speaks of unbelievers coming to worship services and through this experience declaring "God is really among you!" (1 Cor. 14:23–25). The expression of gladness and joy in God and his redemptive blessings is a powerful avenue for the salvation of pre-Christians seeking for God.

God's call to dominion in his strength. One key element of the blessing received by the house of Joseph is the return to dominion over their land. The verb used in 10:12 brings to mind Abraham's demarcation and Joshua's subjugation of the Promised Land. As already noted, this verb denotes a breadth of activity as the people extend their influence and authority over all land. For a community living under Persian rulers, this vision was far beyond their greatest dreams. It was the same for the disciples as Christ proclaimed the coming of the long-awaited kingdom, and it is the same today for those of us who live between Christ's first and second advents. God delivers us to execute his dominion over the land. In our world and culture we share a similar calling. God summons us to exercise dominion in all spheres of life on this planet even as we extend his kingdom to all nations and classes, throughout all creation and culture.

Such dominion, however, is only discharged as we are "strengthened in the LORD" (cf. 10:6, 12) and walk "in his name" (10:12). It is only a reality "because

55. See the importance and power of this principle in Leighton Ford's *The Power of Story* (Colorado Springs: NavPress, 1994).

the LORD is with [us]" (10:5). This means that we go not in our strength or power but rather by the Spirit's empowerment in our lives in order to advance his kingdom in this world. He is the One who transforms us as a community from aimless and defenseless sheep into a mighty army. We also go in God's name and for his glory, to build his kingdom and not our own.

Zechariah 10 thus calls us to deeper reliance on God, who graciously offers his Spirit to us for life and ministry. The importance of this strength is stressed consistently through the experience of the early church (Acts) and the teachings of the apostles (the letters).

In our technological world we have become far too reliant on and optimistic of the ability of humans to control their environment. This was driven home to many of us in Canada when in January 1998 freezing rain dropped for four days without stop, wiping out electrical power to the populations of more than half of Quebec and 15 percent of Ontario. People were left in the dark and died of hypothermia while food and fuel shortages were widespread. This kind of experience should not only remind us of how vulnerable we are as humans but should force us into a posture of deeper trust in our God of grace and power. It is only through his strength and the power of the Spirit that we can accomplish anything for the kingdom.

Zechariah 11

1 Open your doors, O Lebanon,
so that fire may devour your cedars!
2 Wail, O pine tree, for the cedar has fallen;
the stately trees are ruined!
Wail, oaks of Bashan;
the dense forest has been cut down!
3 Listen to the wail of the shepherds;
their rich pastures are destroyed!
Listen to the roar of the lions;
the lush thicket of the Jordan is ruined!

4This is what the LORD my God says: "Pasture the flock
marked for slaughter. 5Their buyers slaughter them and go
unpunished. Those who sell them say, 'Praise the LORD, I am
rich!' Their own shepherds do not spare them. 6For I will no
longer have pity on the people of the land," declares the
LORD. "I will hand everyone over to his neighbor and his king.
They will oppress the land, and I will not rescue them from
their hands."

7So I pastured the flock marked for slaughter, particularly
the oppressed of the flock. Then I took two staffs and called
one Favor and the other Union, and I pastured the flock. 8In
one month I got rid of the three shepherds.

The flock detested me, and I grew weary of them 9and said,
"I will not be your shepherd. Let the dying die, and the per-
ishing perish. Let those who are left eat one another's flesh."

10Then I took my staff called Favor and broke it, revoking
the covenant I had made with all the nations. 11It was revoked
on that day, and so the afflicted of the flock who were watch-
ing me knew it was the word of the LORD.

12I told them, "If you think it best, give me my pay; but if
not, keep it." So they paid me thirty pieces of silver.

13And the LORD said to me, "Throw it to the potter"—the
handsome price at which they priced me! So I took the thirty
pieces of silver and threw them into the house of the LORD to
the potter.

14Then I broke my second staff called Union, breaking the
brotherhood between Judah and Israel.

[15]Then the LORD said to me, "Take again the equipment of a foolish shepherd. [16]For I am going to raise up a shepherd over the land who will not care for the lost, or seek the young, or heal the injured, or feed the healthy, but will eat the meat of the choice sheep, tearing off their hoofs.

[17]"Woe to the worthless shepherd,
who deserts the flock!
May the sword strike his arm and his right eye!
May his arm be completely withered,
his right eye totally blinded!"

Original Meaning

IN CHAPTER 11 we return to the issue of leadership, foreshadowed by the announcement of the installment of Zion's king in 9:9–10 and highlighted in the indictment of Judah's shepherds in 10:1–3a. Chapter 11 contains three distinct pieces. (1) Verses 1–3 represents a creative transition between the idyllic description of the return of the northern tribes in 10:3b–12 and the foreboding prediction of leadership in 11:4–16. It uses botanical images drawn from northern territories to announce judgment on the present political structure and turns our attention back to the pastoral issues of 10:1–3a. (2) Then follows an elongated indictment of both leadership and people through the use of a series of prophetic sign-acts (11:4–16). (3) The chapter ends with a woe oracle directed at the leadership (11:17).

These various pieces deliver a message of discipline not only against the leadership of the community as in 10:1–3a, but also against the people themselves, who are indicted for their rejection of God's chosen shepherd. They are responding to the end of Zerubbabel's tenure as governor in Yehud (about 510 B.C.). This prophetic section constitutes an important literary transition to the cataclysmic portraits of chapters 12–14.[1] These later passages will reveal God's plan to deal with the problem of wicked leadership and Israel's place among the nations.

Announcing Judgment (11:1–3)

AFTER 10:3B–12 with its bright hope for all the tribes of Israel, this section snaps the reader back into present reality. There is little question that 11:2 imitates the "call to lament," a prophetic form used to pronounce judgment

1. On this see Boda, "Reading," 277–91.

on nations (e.g., Isa. 14:31; Jer. 6:26; Joel 1:2–14).[2] This form used three key elements: an imperatival call to lament ("wail"), a vocative address of lamenting group ("O pine tree"; "oaks of Bashan"), and a reason for the lament introduced by *ki* ("*for* the cedar has fallen ... the dense forest has been cut down"). The use of this form reveals the negative character of this section. By inviting lament, it implicitly announces judgment.

These three verses share many points of connection. Thematically, they all deal with disaster; rhetorically, they employ a style that demands attention ("open ... wail ... listen"), are interlinked through the anadiplosis technique ("cedars ... cedars"; "wail ... wail"),[3] and use imagery from the botanical world ("cedars ... pine tree ... oaks ... dense forest ... rich pastures ... lush thicket").

These similarities should not veil the fact that each verse uses a unique image. Verse 1 mixes metaphors by envisioning a fiery conflagration of great cedars that are presently protected within the gates of a city called Lebanon.[4] Verse 2 then picks up on the cedar of Lebanon but changes the imagery from fire to cutting as the cedars are fallen, ruined, and cut down; the addressee changes from Lebanon to the pine tree and oaks of Bashan. The addressee in verse 3 is uncertain as the imagery shifts to the destruction of rich pastures and lush thickets in northern Israel used by shepherds and inhabited by lions. A close look at these various images will reveal their significance for the message of 11:1–3.

Lebanon was well known for its cedar forests (e.g., Isa. 14:8), a source of timber for both the palace and temple in Jerusalem (e.g., 1 Kings 5; 7). Because of this use of Lebanon cedar, both Lebanon and cedar occur as images in prophetic indictments of the Davidic kings (e.g., Jer. 22:20–23).[5] Other contexts reveal a broader significance for these images. The Lebanon cedar is used to express the downfall of proud Assyria and Egypt in Ezekiel

---

2. See H. W. Wolff, "Der Aufruf zur Volksklage," *ZAW* 76 (1964): 48–56; Floyd, *Minor Prophets*, 627–28.

3. Anadiplosis is a catchword technique in which a word or root from one verse is carried over into the next verse. This is seen esp. in the Psalms of Ascent. See, e.g., Ps. 121: help (v. 1) ... help (v. 2); watches/slumber (v. 3) ... watches/slumber (v. 4); shade (v. 5) ... shade (v. 6); harm (v. 6) ... harm (v. 7); watch (v. 7) ... watch (v. 8).

4. Hanson identifies this as royal procession imagery, similar to Ps. 24:7–10; Hanson, *Dawn*, 335. Floyd highlights the significance of this ancient urban image here, which envisions a "directive of a sentry to guards below to open the gates at the approach of friendly troops"; Floyd, *Minor Prophets*, 482.

5. The use of Lebanon to signify the temple is common in midrashic literature but is not used in the Old Testament; contra Ryken, Wilhoit, and Longman, *DBI*, 499; cf. Larkin, *Eschatology*, 102–3.

31 while the cedars of Lebanon and oaks of Bashan symbolize the arrogance of humanity in Isaiah 2:12–17.[6]

The Hebrew word behind "stately trees" in 11:2 may be an example of double entendre. This term is used sometimes of God (e.g., Ps. 8:9; Isa. 33:21), often of human leaders (e.g., Jer. 14:3; 30:21), and even once of the glory of the cedar tree (Ezek. 17:23). Most likely this word refers to the cedar tree here while simultaneously playing off of the dominant leadership nuance. In Nahum 3:18 this term for "stately trees" appears together with "shepherds" to describe royal officials attached to the Assyrian court. As discussed under Zechariah 10:1–3, the image of the shepherd is connected with leadership within a nation. It is used for the leaders of Judah in preexilic times, but it can also be used for foreign kings and their courts (see Jer. 25:34–38; Nah. 3:18).

The response of the lions in verse 3 is often identified with the wail of the shepherds in the same verse. However, the image of the roaring lion is not an image of mourning but of attack and victory (Isa. 5:29; Jer. 2:13; Ezek. 19:7; 22:25; Amos 3:4; Zeph. 3:3).[7] This view is confirmed by noting Jeremiah 49:19 and 50:44, in which a lion emerges from the lush thicket of the Jordan to exact judgment on a foreign nation (Edom, Babylon).

The term for "rich pastures" sounds similar to the term for "stately trees" in the previous verse. Although this term is used normally for a man's robe (e.g., Gen. 25:25), in Ezekiel 17:8 it describes botanical fertility in Ezekiel's allegory about the fate of Judah, which sought prosperity and protection from foreign nations. It is this latter sense that is intended here, although it is unclear what botanical feature is in view.[8]

These many images all share in common the destruction of plant life: cedars are burned and felled, fertile pastures destroyed, and lush thickets ruined. This results in the mourning of various trees and shepherds within Israel's territory (oaks of Bashan, shepherds near the Jordan).

Our analysis of the form and imagery of 11:1–3 exposes a passage that has exerted direct influence, namely, Jeremiah 25:34–38.[9] The call to lament (Jer. 25:34 = Zech. 11:2) is followed by the cry to listen to the wailing of

---

6. See Amos 2:9, where cedars are linked to great height and oaks to great strength; in Ezek. 27:5–6 cedars from Lebanon make the mast (height), while oaks of Bashan make the oars (strength) for the ship of Tyre.

7. Cf. Baldwin, *Haggai*, 178; contra Petersen, *Zechariah 9–14*, 83.

8. The best guess is that this refers to the pastures since it is shepherds who are wailing.

9. D. R. Jones, *Haggai, Zechariah, and Malachi: Introduction and Commentary* (Torch Bible Commentaries; London: SCM, 1962), 149; Baldwin, *Haggai*, 178; Mason, "Use," 74; Stuhlmueller, *Rebuilding*, 132; Person, *Second Zechariah and the Deuteronomic School*, 111, 124; Larkin, *Eschatology*, 101, 103; Nurmela, *Prophets in Dialogue*, 133–36.

the shepherds, using the identical Hebrew construction (Jer. 25:36 = Zech. 11:3). The same vocabulary appears in both contexts: wail (verb), listen, wail (noun), shepherds, stately trees, destroyed, lion. Jeremiah 25:34–38 concludes a section envisioning not only the destruction of Judah and surrounding nations (25:9, 15–26a), but also the destruction that will ultimately overtake the Babylonians after seventy years (25:12–14, 26b). The call to wailing at the end of Jeremiah 25 is thus global in character, looking beyond Judah to the kings of the nations who will be destroyed.

Another passage with significant links to Zechariah 11:1–3 is Isaiah 10. In this passage, Isaiah prophesies God's judgment on the Assyrians and the return of a remnant. At the conclusion of Isaiah 10, the prophet speaks of this destruction as God's felling the thick forests of Lebanon (cf. Zech. 11:1–3: Lebanon, cut down, rich pastures).

What is fascinating is that these two passages announce the judgment of the nations that exiled the two kingdoms of Israel and Judah (Assyria, Babylon). By alluding to these passages, Zechariah reminds the people that God is in control of history and that he will bring judgment against foreign nations who subjugate his people. The reaction of the trees and shepherds within Israel's territory probably indicates that this message is directed also against domestic leadership, who operate under the authority of the Persian emperor and contribute to Zerubbabel's demise. Their positions will be threatened by God's coming judgment.

Prophetic Sign-Act of Shepherd and Sheep (11:4–16)

VERSE 4 SIGNALS a transition to a new section.[10] This section constitutes a prophetic sign-act, a form also encountered in 3:1–10 and 6:9–15.[11] This form typically consists of three sections: exhortation (God commands an action), execution (the prophet describes his compliance), explanation (God interprets its significance). Although the exhortation is always the first element, the order and presence of the other two can vary (cf. Jer. 13:1–11; Ezek. 5).

In this section three sign-acts can be discerned, each introduced by an exhortation (11:4, 13, 15). The first sign-act (11:4–12, 14) contains an exhortation (vv. 4–5), explanation (v. 6), and execution (vv. 7–12, 14). The execution of the first sign-act is interrupted momentarily by the second sign-act (11:13), which contains only an exhortation (v. 13a) and an execution (v. 13b). The third sign-act consists of an exhortation (v. 15) and an explanation (v. 16). Because the second sign-act is incorporated into the execution

10. See also Boda, "Reading," 277–91.

11. See Original Meaning section of 6:9–15.

section of the first, the resulting structure indicates two basic reports, one depicting a good and the other a foolish shepherd.

As with all sign-acts, 11:4 begins with an exhortation from God. The phrase "my God" probably emphasizes the intimate relationship between the prophet and God (e.g., Ps. 143:10; 145:1).[12] This exhortation places the prophet in the role of shepherd. Since prophets are not usually associated with shepherding, it is best to understand this as the prophet assuming the role of shepherd in a sign-act, representing God's appointed leadership of his people.

The flock is one "marked for slaughter," that is, a flock destined for complete destruction. This word "slaughter" is restricted elsewhere in the Hebrew Bible to Jeremiah, when he speaks of the destruction of the city of Jerusalem as he preaches against idolatrous practices connected with the temple (Jer. 7:32; 19:6). Such an allusion threatens a recurrence of Jeremiah's earlier judgment of Jerusalem.

Although sheep were raised for food in Israel, this purpose is not part of the positive form of this metaphor in the Hebrew Bible. Good shepherds are those who protect their sheep from destruction while bad shepherds neglect their duties by not caring for the injuries of the sheep and allowing them to be eaten (see further below).

While verse 4 introduces us to the shepherd, verse 5 expands the scene to include buyers, sellers, and shepherds. The terms "buyers" and "those who sell" suggest the marketplace, where ownership is transferred. The buyers are not interested in raising or caring for a flock, but rather in acquiring the sheep to slaughter for food, while the motivation of the sellers is clearly the monetary reward: "Praise the LORD, I am rich!" Although this imagery may only be contributing to the shepherding metaphor, it may indicate the reality to which the sign-act points: economic oppression within the community. The shepherds, hired and paid by these buyers and sellers, stand by and abandon their responsibility of protecting the flock.

Verse 6 represents the explanation of the sign-act. It is directed at the people as much as at their leaders, a focus that can also be discerned in verse 8, when the flock detests the shepherding of God's appointed leader. As their "shepherds" do not show pity (v. 5), so God will not show pity or rescue them from the oppressive hands of "neighbor" and "king." These two terms reveal both vertical and horizontal oppression: abuse from those who live next to them as well as from those who rule over them. That this judgment originates with God is understandable in light of the refusal of this community to follow his appointed leader (v. 8).

12. Baldwin, *Haggai*, 179.

Although the details remain fuzzy, the historical evidence of the early Persian period confirms the depiction and judgment described in verse 6. In Zechariah 7–8 the prophet links the Persian period community to the oppressive practices of Jeremiah's time and calls them to social justice (see 7:8–10; 8:16–17). The horizontal anarchy suggested in chapter 11 is described in 8:10: "No one could go about his business safely because of his enemy, for I had turned every man against his neighbor." In a slightly later period, Nehemiah confronted oppression within his community on both horizontal (Neh. 5:1) and vertical (5:15) levels.[13]

The execution of the sign-act, signaled by the switch to autobiographical style, follows in 11:7–14. The concern of God's appointed shepherd for the "oppressed of the flock" is indicative of good leadership, and most likely good royal leadership since the monarchy was commissioned to care for the "oppressed" (Ps. 72:2, 4, 12; NIV "afflicted").

The positive intention of this shepherd is confirmed by the fact that he takes two staffs, called "Favor" and "Union" (11:7), suggesting the two shepherding implements ("rod and staff," Ps. 23:4) that guided and protected the sheep.[14] The oddity here is that these implements are given names by the shepherd. This feature highlights the close association between this sign-act and that of Ezekiel in Ezekiel 37:13–23, where he takes two sticks and writes names on them.

The word "Favor" (*noᶜam*) is used of God's person (NIV "beauty" in Ps. 27:4) and is linked to divine blessing (90:17) and wisdom (Prov. 3:17). Later in the execution of the sign-act the breaking of this staff is connected to the breaking of the covenant made "with all the nations." In light of the use of the same phrase in Zechariah 12–14 to refer to all the nations of the earth (12:6; 14:12), this reference to a covenant with the nations likely refers to God's manipulation of the nations to bring blessing on Israel, especially as seen in the Persian period with the restoration of the community in Yehud.

The word "Union" is related to the Hebrew root *ḥbl*, which describes the giving of an item in pledge in both verbal (Ex. 22:25; Deut. 24:6, 17; Job 22:6; 24:3; Prov. 20:16; 27:13) and nominal forms (Ezek. 18:12; 33:15) and is also used in connection with the distribution of the land to the various tribes (Josh. 17:5, 14; 19:9; Ezek. 47:13). Later in the execution of the sign-act, this staff is linked to "breaking the brotherhood between Judah and Israel," an act that affects the issue of the inheritance of the land. Therefore, it is appropriate

---

13. Redditt has linked this historically to the oppression in Neh. 5, but there, of course, the oppression is not seen as an act of God's judgment, while here it is; P. L. Redditt, "Nehemiah's First Mission and the Date of Zechariah 9–14," *CBQ* 56 (1994): 664–78.

14. See E. Power, "The Shepherd's Two Rods in Modern Palestine and in Some Passages of the Old Testament," *Bib* 9 (1928): 434–42.

to translate this term as "Inheritance," referring to the redistribution of the land during the restoration from exile.

Although the shepherd has been appointed to care for the flock, he is not alone in this task, for he joins other shepherds already mentioned in 11:5, who have been hired by the buyers and sellers. Verse 8 signals the beginning of trouble for God's appointed shepherd. He must rid the flock of the uncaring shepherds of 11:5, an action that elsewhere refers to physical annihilation (cf. Ex. 23:23; Ps. 83:5). This does not, however, mean a literal event in which God's appointed leader killed other leaders, because the genre used is the "sign-act." This is why the identities of these three shepherds has eluded the historical grasp of scholars.[15] The number three is symbolic of a complete purging of leadership, and the time period of "one month" indicates a short period of time.

The removal of these shepherds appears to cause tension between the flock and the shepherd as the shepherd "grew weary," a phrase used elsewhere to refer to an inability to endure a situation (Num. 21:4; Job 21:4; Judg. 10:16; 16:16), and the flock "detested" their shepherd. This mutual rejection has serious repercussions. The tension is heightened by the switch to dramatic narrative to describe the resignation of the good shepherd, tension intensified further as the shepherd spells out in detail the ramifications of his decision. Abandoning the flock will result in the death of the weak ones and the mutual destruction of those who remain. This "eating one another's flesh" (lit., "each will eat the flesh of his neighbor") alludes back to God's explanation in Zechariah 11:6, where everyone is handed over to his neighbor.

The notice of the shepherd's departure is followed by two symbolic gestures linked to the staffs. (1) Breaking the staff called Favor (11:10), which is linked to his relationship with the nations (the buyers/sellers of v. 5), spells disaster for the flock since this staff represented blessing as well as protection from the hungry buyers/sellers. The comment in verse 11 appears to be a side note bolstering the prophetic word and its implications for the vulnerable.[16]

Before reporting the breaking of the second staff in 11:14, the prophet reports his request for payment of wages. The "them" of verse 12 most likely refers to the "nations" of verse 10, who are the buyers of verse 5. Having terminated his contract with these nations, the shepherd now requests his wages, but he gives them the option of refusal since he has broken the agreement. The amount of payment is "thirty pieces of silver," a measure that is

---

15. See Mitchell for a list of the many possibilities; Mitchell, Smith, and Brewer, *Haggai*, 306.

16. This phrase is common in prophetic literature to bolster the authenticity of the prophetic word: see comments on 6:9–15.

"weighed out" (NIV "paid"), a regular practice in the early Persian period when coinage was not in general use.[17] The low amount of payment indicates disapproval of the shepherd's efforts.[18]

Having received his wages, the prophet quickly reports a second sign-act (11:13). God instructs the shepherd to throw the payment to the "potter," who, according to the execution of this sign-act, is in "the house of the LORD." The Hebrew word *hayyoṣer* is used for those who work with clay as well as metals (Isa. 44:9, 10, 12; Hab. 2:18).[19] Most likely here it refers to the latter—that is, those responsible to smelt coins and precious metals for the temple—but whether "potter" or "smelter," there is no question that the destination of this silver is the temple. The action of throwing implicates temple personnel in the payment. The tone here is one of strong rejection of payment, highlighting the broken relationship with the nations. With this payment, the first symbolic gesture is completed, signaling an end to the covenant with the nations.

(2) In a second symbolic gesture, the shepherd breaks the staff called "Union" (or, better, "Inheritance"; 11:14), an action that, as we have already discussed, represents the shattering of the brotherhood between Judah and Israel. This action represents a reversal of Ezekiel's action in Ezekiel 37, in which the earlier prophet unites two sticks, representing the northern and southern tribes, and dashes hopes of an immediate restoration of the united kingdom, as reflected in Zechariah 9–10.

Verse 15 introduces the final sign-act, where the Lord instructs the prophet to "take the equipment of a foolish shepherd." This equipment is not related necessarily to the staffs already discussed in the first sign-act, since the word "again" does not modify the imperative "take" but the introductory statement ("Then the LORD said to me again").[20] The shepherd's "equipment"

17. Carter, *Emergence*, 283.

18. Whether one makes the argument based on the value of a slave in Ex. 21:32 or based on general ancient Near Eastern evidence. For Sumerian possibilities see E. Reiner, "Thirty Pieces of Silver," *JAOS* 88 (1968): 186–90; on an Akkadian text from Tel el Amarna see Lipinski, "Recherches," 53–55; cf. Larkin, *Eschatology*, 130. Baldwin, however, builds a case for this as a significant sum, based on Nehemiah's comment in 5:15 that the governors had gathered forty shekels from the people, which was oppressive; Baldwin, *Haggai*, 184. Moreover, the reference to the slave in Ex. 21:32 may be showing a high value the Torah placed on human life.

19. On the basis of these prophetic passages, Delcor and Baldwin argue that the silver will become an idol; M. Delcor, "Deux passages difficiles: Zach 12:11 et 11:13," *VT* 3 (1953): 76–77; Baldwin, *Haggai*, 185.

20. Contra NIV. For this see the form in Isa. 8:5 where clearly "again" (*ʿod*) refers to God's speech; cf. Ezek. 8:13; Hos. 3:1. Notice in 2 Kings 4:6 when "again" (*ʿod*) refers to the exhortation that follows it.

(*keli*) means at least a rod and staff (Ps. 23:4).[21] Unlike the shepherd of the first sign-act, whose intention was to care for the sheep, this shepherd is "foolish" (*ʾewili*), a pejorative term marking this final shepherd as corrupt morally (Ps. 107:17), rejecting the fear of the Lord (Prov. 1:7) and counsel (12:15; 15:5) while refusing to make amends for sin (14:9).

The folly of this shepherd is detailed in the explanation that follows in verse 16. The prophet highlights the various types of sheep within the flock. The first three clearly indicate the vulnerable members of the flock: "lost . . . young . . . injured," while the fourth category (NIV "healthy") probably refers to "exhausted ones."[22] In stark contrast to the good shepherd, who protected the vulnerable in the flock (11:7), the foolish shepherd will not only neglect these members of the flock but also turn on the remaining sheep and devour all edible meat.

The situation has become even worse than at the outset. Whereas the shepherds in 11:5 were only guilty of denying the flock protection from ravenous owners, now the shepherd himself is consuming his own flock, echoing Ezekiel's description of the "shepherds of Israel" (34:3–4).[23] These verses are obviously prophesying a return to the conditions that led to exile.

Ezekiel contrasts this dark portrait of the shepherds with that of God's compassionate care for his flock in Ezekiel 34:16, transforming the vocabulary from negative to positive actions. In Zechariah 11:15–16, however, God is the One who has raised up this foolish shepherd over the land. This is the fulfillment of the second warning in verse 6, that God will "hand everyone over to . . . his king" (cf. 11:9 for the fulfillment of the first warning).

The sign-acts in 11:4–16 describe two leaders within the community. The first one is appointed by God, sensitive to his people and equipped with tools appropriate for his task. Tension between leader and people lead to termination of his agreement with the nations and hope of renewal of the united kingdom and his replacement by a second divinely appointed leader, who is foolish because of his irresponsibility and exploitation.

It is difficult to ascertain the precise historical referent of this sign-act report. However, the commentary above has revealed unambiguous links with Ezekiel 34 and 37, two passages that offer a future Davidic ruler as the solution for the coming united kingdom. This suggests that the prophetic

---

21. A similar construction occurs in 1 Sam. 17:40, where David places his stones into a "shepherd's bag" (*keli haroʿim*). Zech. 11:15 is most likely a more general reference to the equipment of the shepherd.

22. See Boda, "Reading," 277–91.

23. Mason, "Use," 115–16; D. A. Witt, "Zechariah 12–14: Its Origins, Growth and Theological Significance" (Ph.D., Vanderbilt University, 1991), 60; Nurmela, *Prophets in Dialogue*, 136–46.

sign-act here is referring to the work of a Davidide who was rejected by both people and empire and replaced by another individual.

Such Davidic hope is expressed elsewhere in this book, particularly in Zechariah 3 and 6:9–15.[24] In these contexts in addresses to priestly figures, Zechariah emphasizes Jeremiah's hope for the Davidic *ṣemaḥ* figure and carefully delineates the role that priestly, royal, and prophetic figures will play in the restoration community. This suggests that the priestly caste may have been vying for responsibilities that were reserved for the royal house. In these contexts Zerubbabel appears to be the focus of Davidic hope. In light of this evidence from Zechariah 1–8 and of the history of the early Persian period, this passage most likely describes the ultimate fate of Zerubbabel, the last Davidic male to participate in the leadership of Yehud.[25]

Judgment on a Leader (11:17)

ALTHOUGH INFLUENCED by the same passage (Ezek. 34), Zechariah 11:17 is not part of the sign-acts of 11:4–16 because of its form and content.[26] In terms of form it represents a complete woe oracle (cf. Isa. 5), a prophetic judgment form that consists of three sections: "woe," recipient, judgment/accusation.[27] In terms of content, its focus is on judgment of leadership rather than on the flock as in the sign-acts. Moreover, it displays affinity with other short pieces in Zechariah 9–14 (10:1–3a; 11:1–3; 13:7–9), which employ declarative language and announce disaster for shepherds and are attributed to the one responsible for assembling Zechariah 9–14 into its final form (see commentary introduction).

As in Ezekiel 34:2, Zechariah 11:17 directs the "woe" oracle against a shepherd. In contrast, however, this shepherd is called "worthless," a term usually employed for idols (cf. 10:1–3).[28] It is interesting that Jeremiah 14:14, from which Zechariah 10:1–3a draws, also uses the term "worthless" to speak of the delusions of the false prophets in Jeremiah's time.

This idolatrous shepherd is one "who deserts the flock," an accusation that echoes Ezekiel 34:8, which delivers judgment against the shepherds of that day because "my flock lacks a shepherd"; as a result, the sheep are plundered by wild animals. It is because of such desertion in Ezekiel 34 that God himself promises to search for the sheep and care for them, that is, gather

---

24. See Boda, "Oil," Art. 10.

25. Boda, "Reading," 277–91.

26. Ibid.

27. See Floyd, *Minor Prophets*, 649.

28. The only other places where this term means "worthless" are Job 13:4 and Jer. 14:14. The latter case, however, can also be linked to idolatrous behavior.

them from the nations (34:11–16). This ingathering will be followed by God's appointment of a Davidic shepherd over the flock, who will faithfully tend them (34:23).

The judgment on the idolatrous and irresponsible shepherd will be severe, with the sword rendering arm and eye useless, two body parts essential for identifying danger and protecting the sheep.[29] Such a sword curse appears elsewhere in the Old Testament only in Jeremiah's judgment on the Babylonians (Jer. 50:35–38), where the prophet attacks officials, wise men, false prophets, fools, warriors, horses, chariots, foreigners, and treasures because of idolatry. Here again we see the connection to false prophecy and idolatry, something noted already in this passage and in 10:1–3a.

In 11:17, the prophet pronounces judgment on shepherds who are compared with the inadequate shepherds of Ezekiel's day. By alluding to Jeremiah, the prophet announces that the idolatrous shepherds of his day will be judged by the sword in the same way that the idolatrous Babylonians with their false prophets were judged at the beginning of the Persian period.

Bridging Contexts

PROPHETIC SIGN-ACTS. FOR those who have studied the books of Jeremiah and Ezekiel, the prophetic sign-act is a familiar form of prophecy. Based on his extensive work on these two prophets, Kelvin Friebel has reviewed various hermeneutical paradigms used by interpreters to grasp the significance of these sign-acts.[30] The dominant approach to sign-acts is what he calls the "inherent efficacious" or "causal link" paradigm, in which the sign-act sets "the depicted event in motion." This view is based either on theories of sympathetic magic or the power of the spoken word and limits the referent of the sign-act to a future event. But there are other views of the sign-act. Some have argued that it merely expresses reality, others interpret sign-acts as acts of power that function within a sociological context, and for still others sign-acts are merely communicative and persuasive, a form of street theater designed to obtain a hearing.

Friebel views a sign-act as "rhetorical nonverbal communication" that is communicative, interactive (persuasive), and informative. This view allows one to see the similarity between verbal and nonverbal prophetic communication. Both forms of communication "give advice, express conviction,

29. Notice the severity of the result: "completely withered . . . totally blinded," expressions formed by building up words from the same root in Heb.

30. See K. G. Friebel, "A Hermeneutical Paradigm for Interpreting Prophetic Sign-Actions," *Didaskalia* 12/2 (2001): 25–45; cf. idem, *Jeremiah's and Ezekiel's Sign-Acts* (JSOTSup 283; Sheffield: Sheffield Academic Press, 1999).

indict" rather than "simply predict." Friebel demonstrates splendidly that sign-acts do not refer only to future events but also to past and present events.

The prophetic sign-act in 11:4–16 does not refer necessarily to a future event. Our exegesis has demonstrated that it interprets the reality of the present, offering reasons for the demise of Zerubbabel. This prepares the ground for the chapters that follow, in which God appears as a judge and savior, offering cleansing and prompting repentance among the community and its leadership. As an interpretation of the present reality of the Persian period community, however, 11:4–16 will have ongoing implications for the Second Temple Jewish community. That this text is connected with the mission of Jesus in the New Testament shows us that the early Christian community treats it as foreshadowing a similar crisis or, better, as a later phase of the same crisis in their own day. As Zerubbabel was rejected, so also a member of his line would be rejected, but this rejection will precipitate the transformation of the world.

Intertextuality. A connection on a formal level to Ezekiel reveals the close relationship between Zechariah 11 and other prophetic books. Research on Zechariah 9–14 has consistently highlighted this trend, cataloguing the variety of ways in which these chapters not only draw on the earlier traditions of Israel but also earlier texts. This trend is foreshadowed in Zechariah's preoccupation with the "earlier prophets" (1:4–6; 7:7), whose message he retransmits to a new generation (1:4; 7:9–10; 8:16–17).[31] In contrast to chapters 1–8, chapters 9–14 do not introduce citations of earlier prophets or texts through explicit references, but they do allude to these texts by using identical words, images, and themes. A wealth of research now exists that not only catalogues the various texts to which chapters 9–14 allude, but also the various ways in which these texts are employed.

Both of these phases are important as one interprets texts like Zechariah 9–14. (1) It is essential to determine which earlier text was in the mind of the writer of the later text. This must be based on multiple aspects of the earlier passage, which should include both lexical stock (identical key words and phrases) and literary forms and themes. This is not always an easy task as Tom Wright has observed from his study of New Testament inner-biblical allusion:

> When is an allusion not an allusion? This question forms a powerful undercurrent in a good deal of New Testament study. The historical question (was Paul, or whoever, alluding to a particular text, and if so

31. See M. J. Boda, "Zechariah: Master Mason or Penitential Prophet?" in *Yahwism After the Exile: Perspectives on Israelite Religion in the Persian Era*, ed. B. Becking and R. Albertz (Studies in Theology and Religion 5; Assen: Royal Van Gorcum, 2003), 49–69, and various articles in Boda and Floyd, eds. *Treasure*.

why) is often intertwined with literary questions about authorial intention and the like; about these things, as the writer to the Hebrews says, we cannot now speak in detail. It is highly probable that writers in Second Temple Judaism alluded to a good many biblical texts, deliberately conjuring up a world of discourse with a word or phrase. It is also highly probable that readers in the twentieth century, alert for such allusions, will hear at least some where none were intended. It is absolutely certain that modern readers who are alert to this danger, and hence unwilling to allow any allusions beyond more or less direct quotations, will radically misread important texts. There are times when the historian needs reminding that history is an art, not a science.[32]

(2) This, however, is only the first step. It is equally important to compare the two texts to determine how a later writer uses the earlier text. Some examples of this include: echoing (arguing for its enduring validity in the present generation, e.g., Zech. 3:8–10; 6:9–15; cf. Jer. 23:5–6; 33:15–16), transforming (slightly changing its validity for the present generation), and reversing (rejecting its validity for the present generation, e.g., Hag. 2:20–23; cf. Jer. 22).[33] This second step is not complete until one asks after the impact of this intertextual allusion on the reading of this passage in its final form.

This intertextual dimension has been compared to the ancient "palimpsests."[34] In an ancient world where writing materials were valuable and scarce, a scroll was recycled if needed. A scribe would scrape off the old markings and write his new text on the recycled page. Remnants of the old markings, however, often remain, and modern scholars have been able to reconstruct ancient texts from the remnants of these underlying marks. In some ways all literature functions like a "palimpsest"; that is, all writers draw from the cultural reservoir of past texts to create a new expression relevant to an emerging generation. Thus, as we read Zechariah 9–14, we can read "between the lines" earlier texts that affect our reading of the prophecy at hand.

Some have taken this intertextual dimension to an extreme by locating it in the mind of the reader; that is, intertextual connections are perceived by creative readers so that whether or not the writer "intended" this is irrelevant. In this case, the dating of literature is unnecessary since the connections are all placed on the same plane in the reader's mind. Although it is true that intertextuality is part of the reading process, intertextuality in the Bible

32. N. T. Wright, *Jesus and the Victory of God* (Christian Origins and the Question of God 2; Minneapolis: Fortress, 1996), 584.

33. See further Meyers and Meyers, *Zechariah 9–14*, 38–39.

34. G. Genette, *Palimpsests: Literature in the Second Degree*, trans. C. Newman and C. Doubinsky (Lincoln: Univ. of Nebraska Press, 1997); Boda, "Reading," 277–91.

is different. It is based on the view that certain texts have inherent priority and authority over other texts, which explains why these texts were chosen for allusion.[35] Therefore, one needs to bring both texts into view, identify the order of causality, and ask what the later text is doing with the earlier.

Some who have studied the intertextual character of Zechariah 9–14 have questioned the validity of these chapters as prophetic literature, contrasting it to the "living voice of prophecy."[36] This is stated succinctly by North when he writes:

> Second Zechariah does not "act like a prophet" in the sense of making independent and original oracles of his own. Instead he seems concerned with gathering up expectations of earlier prophets and interpreting them or showing how they are to be fulfilled.[37]

Such comments reflect the enduring priority given in Christian interpretation to the original and oral declarations of named prophets. However, the prophecies of Zechariah 9–14 are creative and fresh declarations of God's will for a particular community, even as they draw on earlier traditions and texts as a resource for these declarations.

Because of the intertextual character of much of Scripture, intertextuality has been exploited in recent discussions as important to the task of biblical theology. Elmer Martens charts the way ahead when he writes: "A consequence of using the method of intertextuality is to see the two testaments not as sharply discontinuous but as both part of a story with recurring patterns. The canon is interlaced in content but is interconnected also by similar patterning."[38]

Zechariah 9–14, therefore, exists in intertextual relationship with much earlier material in the Old Testament, especially Isaiah, Jeremiah, and Ezekiel. At the same time, however, we must recognize that these chapters exist in an intertextual relationship with the New Testament, which, as we have argued in the commentary introduction (Bridging Contexts section), draws heavily from these chapters to trace Christ's passion. The same intertextual techniques are evident in the New Testament as have been identified in

---

35. See B. D. Sommer, *A Prophet Reads Scripture: Allusion in Isaiah 40–66* (The Contraversions Series; Stanford: Stanford Univ. Press, 1998).

36. Mason, "Use," 208; cf. Person, *Second Zechariah and the Deuteronomic School*, 201.

37. R. North, "Prophecy to Apocalyptic Via Zechariah," in *Congress Volume: Uppsala, 1971*, ed. H. Nyberg (VTSup 22; Leiden: Brill, 1972), 51; cf. Meyers and Meyers, *Zechariah 9–14*, 44–45.

38. E. Martens, "Reaching for a Biblical Theology of the Whole Bible," in *Reclaiming the Old Testament: Essays in Honour of Waldemar Janzen*, ed. G. Zerbe (Winnipeg: CMBC Publications, 2001), 101.

Zechariah. At times there are explicit citations of Old Testament passages introduced by phrases such as "it is written." At other times the connection is implicit, using similar motifs, narrative patterns, and vocabulary.

In our study of Zechariah 9–11 (esp. ch. 11), we have noted intertextual allusions to other passages in the Old Testament. But in light of the preceding discussion, it is important not only to highlight the links but also to allow them to shape our reading of the text at hand.[39] For instance, with Ezekiel 34 and 37 as the backdrop to our reading of the sign-acts in Zechariah 11:4–16, we have been able to see this message in its historical and theological context as a statement concerning the failure of the Davidic line in the early Persian period. The sign-acts place the blame squarely on the shoulders of a community and its temple leaders, who are closely allied with the Persian authorities. The indictments of these leaders in 11:1–3 and 17, with their links to Jeremiah, create an expectation of the kind of discipline from God that the earlier prophets declared.

By drawing on these prophets, Zechariah 11 addressed serious problems in Yehud. The two smaller pieces in 11:1–3 and 17 announce judgment on leaders within the community. While the sign-act section of 11:4–16 enhances the depiction of worthless leaders, it also reveals that the community has rejected appropriate leadership and deserves the kind of leadership it has received. Both leadership and community are implicated here and both are threatened with discipline. This lays the foundation for chapters 12–14, which will reveal God's cleansing of leadership and community, especially the final link in 13:7–9, in which the shepherd will be struck and the flock scattered, images of cleansing for leadership and community.

Redemptive history. In light of this Persian period message, it is not surprising that the New Testament draws on this section in its depiction of Jesus. The most famous verses in this chapter are 11:12–13, used by the Gospel writers in connection with Judas's betrayal of Jesus (Matt. 26:14–16; 27:3–10; cf. Mark 14:10–11; Luke 22:1–6).[40] But the link should not be limited to these two verses, for the Gospel writers have a much larger complex of events in mind.[41] Christ uses shepherd imagery to depict his leadership of Israel (John 10:1–18). He came as the good shepherd with appropriate implements, just like the first shepherd of the sign-act. But the people reject him as their shepherd. The result of this rejection is well known in subsequent Jewish history as the Jewish shepherds lead the people to

---

39. See Boda, "Reading," 277–91.

40. This does not make Judas the "good shepherd" of Zech. 11:4–16; rather, it highlights the fact that money was also used to relieve Jesus as the "good shepherd" of his duties, that is, through betrayal and delivery to the political authorities.

41. Cf. Boda, "Reading," 277–91.

their demise in the climactic revolt against Rome in A.D. 68–70. Upon these shepherds comes the woe of Zechariah 11:17.

Therefore, it is essential to begin with a consideration of redemptive history prompted by intertextual connections between Zechariah 9–14 and the New Testament as we apply chapter 11 to the present day. The grandiose vision of blessing expressed in chapters 9–10 will be realized only through great upheaval within the community that will lead to rejection of good leadership, replacement with bad leadership, and judgment of that leadership. From a Christian perspective, this is fulfilled ultimately through the climactic events connected with and subsequent to the death, resurrection, and ascension of Christ. This text leads us as Christians to celebrate the work of God in and through Christ, who fulfilled Zechariah 11.

As Zechariah 11 echoes the pastoral vision of the book of Ezekiel with its expectation of a Davidic ruler who will rule appropriately, so the New Testament repeats this echo by depicting Christ as this kind of shepherd. Ultimately such leadership is fulfilled in Christ's present leadership of the church from the right hand of the Father. This chapter is a comforting passage because it expresses the qualities of leadership we can expect from our good shepherd as this echo reverberates in our life experience today.

As our shepherd Christ promises to provide pasture and care for the weak. He is a loving shepherd, who shepherds with his staff Favor, acting graciously on their behalf. He is a caring shepherd, who shepherds with his staff Inheritance, providing for the needs of his sheep.

Leadership today. In light of these connections to Christ, is it appropriate to relate Zechariah 11 to leadership issues in the church today? The answer to this is a qualified yes. Since it is a leadership crisis that frustrated the realization of restoration in Zechariah 9–14, and if Christ's leadership initiated restoration for the community of God, a restoration that is an enduring project for the church, then it is not too much to suggest that issues of leadership (and "followership") are important to the realization of the mission of the church.

Contemporary Significance

WORSHIPING OUR SUFFERING SHEPHERD. Zechariah 11 was a key text for the early church's understanding of Christ's ministry. He was God's shepherd, who set out to care for the flock, protecting them from poor shepherds and abusive owners. For thirty pieces of silver he was removed from his leadership, rejected by the flock (Jews), shepherds (priests), and owners (Romans). Yet God used this rejection to bring salvation for his flock. Christ's death was followed by his resurrection and ascension, ushering in a new age for the remnant flock of Israel, the church.

As a foreshadowing of Christ's work, Zechariah 11 stimulates praise of our Shepherd and his sacrifice for us. As we read this chapter, we catch a glimpse of the frustration and betrayal Christ experienced as he sought to lead a rebellious flock. We also catch a glimpse of God's anger toward the rebellious and the power of Christ's forgiveness of those who betrayed him.

As Christians we must return to this story of salvation on a consistent basis and allow it to inform and stimulate our faith and worship. A former pastoral associate of mine set aside time each Friday in his personal reflection to consider afresh the sacrifice of Christ. On a communal level, Christ designed the liturgical rhythm of the Lord's Supper to remind us regularly of his suffering as our shepherd and to provide gracious nourishment for us as his sheep. This is also built into our yearly worship experience through a church calendar that marks the birth, death, and resurrection of our Savior.

Accepting comfort and discipline from our Shepherd. Christ came as the good shepherd who cares for his flock. He not only was willing to sacrifice his life for his sheep but also to offer an intimate relationship with them, as intimate as his own relationship with the Father: "I am the good shepherd; I know my sheep and my sheep know me—just as the Father knows me and I know the Father—and I lay down my life for the sheep" (John 10:14–15).

The pattern of his leadership established in the Gospels can be counted on by those who are members of this flock today. Zechariah 11 focuses particular attention on the concern of the good shepherd for the "oppressed," those who in 11:16 are the "lost ... young ... injured." God expected the royal leaders in ancient Israel to care for these kinds of sheep, an expectation assumed throughout Psalm 72 and linked to the longevity ("he will endure as long as the sun," 72:5), extent ("he will rule from sea to sea," 72:8), and quality ("let grain abound throughout the land," 72:16) of his reign:

> [1]Endow the king with your justice, O God,
> the royal son with your righteousness.
>
> [2]He will judge your people in righteousness,
> your afflicted ones with justice.
> [3]The mountains will bring prosperity to the people,
> the hills the fruit of righteousness.
> [4]He will defend the afflicted among the people
> and save the children of the needy;
> he will crush the oppressor. . . .
>
> [12]For he will deliver the needy who cry out,
> the afflicted who have no one to help.
>
> [13]He will take pity on the weak and the needy
> and save the needy from death.

[14]He will rescue them from oppression and violence,
for precious is their blood in his sight. (Psalm 72:1–4, 12–14)

It is refreshing to hear of the godly king's concern for the weak and afflicted within his flock. Christ reflected this concern throughout his earthly ministry. His depiction of the good shepherd involves risking the entire flock for the sake of one lost sheep (Luke 15:3–7). In Luke 15, the lost sheep is equated with the "sinner," in Matt. 10:6–8 with the sick and dying, leprous, and demon-possessed. These people were often on the outside, failures in the eyes of the Jewish community. But Christ as shepherd had deep compassion for these people.

Within our contemporary society, so enamoured with success, it is easy to deny our weaknesses and failures. This can even be fostered within the church with its penchant for testimonies that sound strikingly similar to the North American dream. One could easily get the impression that the church is a place for the strong and successful, those who have it all together. But Christ invited the weak into his flock, and because of that we must be honest with him about our fears, our weaknesses, our failures, rather than creating a veneer of successful thinking that can easily mask hypocrisy.

I once spoke with a young man who, disillusioned with his flourishing home church, began to attend a struggling church in the inner city. He told me that at this small inner-city church, people were free to express their pain and weakness in a corporate setting. I am finding this view of Christian community more prevalent within the emerging generation in the church. Attraction to Christ is not linked to promises of success or answers to questions but to honest stories of grace in the face of weakness.[42] This latter approach seems closer to the message of Christ, because the good shepherd was one who invited the lost and weak.

Within the contemporary church it is also easy to limit our view of the lost and weak. It is evident in Zechariah 11 and especially in Psalm 72 that God's leader was concerned about the economically oppressed. It is tempting to spiritualize this into those who are spiritually oppressed, that is, those in the clutches of Satan who are trapped in the kingdom of darkness. Although this is true and clearly Christ has come to release such captives from their bondage, we must not lose sight of oppression in all of its forms, even economic ones. Christ cares deeply for the poor, a fact emphasized by his consistent identification with them throughout his earthly ministry. The impact of his death and resurrection will be felt not only in the transformation of individual lives but also in the corporate experience of the societies in which they live. The good shepherd invites the poor to entrust themselves into his care.

42. Tom Beaudoin notes how for this new generation, "Suffering Has a Religious Dimension" and "Ambiguity Is Central to Faith." See T. Beaudoin, *Virtual Faith: The Irreverent Spiritual Quest of Generation X* (San Francisco: Jossey-Bass, 1998), 96–142.

This emphasis on the shepherd's care for the weak should inform our vision of the church community and its mission. The community that bears his name will express his grace and acceptance. It will be a community in which the weak can find understanding, the oppressed can find justice, the afflicted can find refuge, and the hungry can find sustenance.

As his flock today we can entrust ourselves into the care of a shepherd who has known suffering and is sensitive to the needs of the afflicted (Heb. 4:14–16). Through his Spirit of comfort, Jesus not only consoles us but also sustains us through our affliction. But a shepherd will also discipline his sheep for their protection. Christ as caring shepherd cannot be separated from Christ as disciplining shepherd. The gracious care of the shepherd fosters the flock's trust in him. Such trust is needed as he leads his flock through the landscape of their lives. The shepherd knows the path ahead and the sheep must be willing to follow his lead and accept his correction in order to safely arrive at green pastures and quiet waters.

As people saved through Christ's sacrificial act and sustained by relationship with him through the Spirit, we invite the discipline and guidance he brings into our lives as Christians. This does not mean we always have a clear picture of the reasons that lie behind his guidance and discipline, but ultimately we are called to entrust ourselves into the hands of the good shepherd.

Leading the flock with integrity. Zechariah 11 addresses serious leadership issues in the Persian period community in Yehud and is useful for addressing similar concerns in God's community today. Although Christ is the "Chief Shepherd" from whom leadership takes its lead and authority, leaders within the church are also addressed as "shepherds of God's flock" (1 Peter 5:1–4; cf. John 21:15–19). Interestingly, the New Testament is concerned about issues like those mentioned in Zechariah 11, expressing concern both over internal motivations and attitudes and over the external actions and behavior of church leadership (1 Peter 5:2–3; cf. 1 Tim. 3; Titus 1).

Zechariah 11 reveals God's disgust with poor leadership and his commitment to disciplining the "worthless shepherd." It focuses most attention on the questionable motivations of leadership who mark the flock for slaughter (11:4), rejoice in material gain (11:5), and eat the choice sheep (11:16). In similar fashion, the New Testament forbids leadership motivated by lust for money or power (1 Peter 5:2–3). This does not mean that leaders should not discuss issues related to money or power, for God demands that the church care for their needs (1 Tim. 5:17–18) and has granted them appropriate authority (1 Peter 5:2, 5), but this must not constitute the motivation for leadership.

One of the priorities of church leadership, whether clergy or laity, must be honest examination of motivations. Self-examination at regular intervals throughout the year provides an opportunity for reflection on one's motivation.

But one should seek the help of the community here. One's spouse is often the best source for honest evaluation of motivation, though this level of vulnerability can be intimidating and needs to be approached with humility and openness. Church leaders must develop relationships with wise mentors and honest colleagues who can speak to sensitive issues in their lives. In all of this there is great vulnerability, but the leader who invites honest examination displays strength, not weakness, and secures long-term vitality in ministry.

One mentor I had in my life was a pastor who would invite his district superintendent (a pastor over many pastors) to visit his elders' meeting on a yearly basis in order to conduct a review of his ministry. This was an important opportunity in the year for evaluation of his internal motivation and external performance, which afforded this wise pastor the opportunity to grow well into the later years of his ministry.

Another aspect of leadership attacked in Zechariah 11 is that of inappropriate liaisons with foreign nations, that is, leadership that operated under the authority of foreign oppressors (11:1–3) and because of this abused the flock (11:4–16). For those living under the hegemony of the nations there was a constant temptation to capitulate to these foreign powers and follow their patterns of abuse. This pattern, however, is rejected by God, who judges such shepherds (11:17). In light of this, all leaders are challenged to live according to patterns of leadership established by God and not to succumb to the patterns of a secular world.

I have seen one church establish certain patterns among their leadership teams that keep their focus on the Lord and encourage reliance on God for their ministry. Each time a leadership team meets, the members spend the first hour of the meeting in prayer for the church, its members, and its ministries. This is true for committees that are "spiritual" leaders of the church as well as for those whose focus is on care of the physical needs of the church building. By doing this they are reminded that this ministry is one that relies on God, not humans, for its prosperity. It discourages unhealthy reliance on secular leadership techniques alone at the expense of the power and wisdom of the Spirit.

Another way to risk reliance on the world is in our unthinking affirmation of political decisions that have been made by our governments, whether in the domestic or international context. In this scenario the "nations" are our own political bodies for which we have the choice as individuals and communities of faith to support or confront. The church must take its responsibility to be salt and light in the midst of our present generation and ensure that it is reflecting deeply about ways that our societies may be contributing to suffering at home and abroad. Often we affirm injustice by our passivity and failure to speak out even when we know there is abuse. At other times we affirm injustice by our activity, embracing economic systems and encouraging political parties whose value systems do not reflect the compassion of Christ. In such cases we must repent, break liaisons with such sources of abuse, and work actively to become agents of transformation within our communities and nations.

Following the shepherd in obedience. Zechariah 11 not only addresses leaders, it confronts a community that will not submit to good leadership, rebelling against God's provision of a caring shepherd. In similar fashion to the Israelites of old, who demanded a king like the other nations, God granted them the desire of their hearts, which led to disaster. The success of God's community not only depends on godly leaders but also on godly followers. Although the good shepherd in Zechariah 11 pastured this flock with the appropriate implements and gave due attention to the oppressed of the flock, this flock "detested" the shepherd.

There is no question that in the church today there are times when leaders need to be confronted and even removed from their place of authority. But sometimes it is the flock that needs confrontation, for they have fallen into the habit of using well-worn paths that endanger the life of the community and do not lead to green pastures and quiet waters.

I remember one church I pastored for a short period, filling in for the pastor who needed a vacation. I was slated to preach for four Sundays during his absence. After my third sermon I received an anonymous note from a parishioner upset about my interpretation of Scripture. Understandably, as a young leader I was shaken by the note and impatiently awaited the return of the pastor. At our first private moment after his arrival, I showed him the note. He smiled and then led me to his filing cabinet, where he pulled out a file of letters in the same handwriting. He explained that this person had written him letters regularly throughout his few years at the church, complaining about various issues. This individual had been responsible for the removal of nearly every pastor who had served in the church over the past couple of decades. This was an important reminder to a young pastor that the success of God's community is dependent on leader and follower alike. Leaders need to guide the community with wisdom and integrity, but the community needs to follow their shepherds in submission and obedience.

How can the flock of Christ do this within their churches? I think it involves the development of the character of humility. One will never learn to lead if he or she has never learned the humility of following. Humility, however, does not imply passivity. Often leaders mistake a lack of resistance to vision and mission as a sign of successful leading and following. However, such passivity can merely mask a disengagement from the vision. The hope is passionate engagement with God's vision for the church.

Zechariah 12:1–13:6

An Oracle

1This is the word of the LORD concerning Israel. The
LORD, who stretches out the heavens, who lays the foundation
of the earth, and who forms the spirit of man within him,
declares: 2"I am going to make Jerusalem a cup that sends all
the surrounding peoples reeling. Judah will be besieged as
well as Jerusalem. 3On that day, when all the nations of the
earth are gathered against her, I will make Jerusalem an
immovable rock for all the nations. All who try to move it will
injure themselves. 4On that day I will strike every horse with
panic and its rider with madness," declares the LORD. "I will
keep a watchful eye over the house of Judah, but I will blind
all the horses of the nations. 5Then the leaders of Judah will
say in their hearts, 'The people of Jerusalem are strong,
because the LORD Almighty is their God.'

6"On that day I will make the leaders of Judah like a firepot
in a woodpile, like a flaming torch among sheaves. They will
consume right and left all the surrounding peoples, but
Jerusalem will remain intact in her place.

7"The LORD will save the dwellings of Judah first, so that
the honor of the house of David and of Jerusalem's inhabitants
may not be greater than that of Judah. 8On that day the LORD
will shield those who live in Jerusalem, so that the feeblest
among them will be like David, and the house of David will
be like God, like the Angel of the LORD going before them.
9On that day I will set out to destroy all the nations that
attack Jerusalem.

10"And I will pour out on the house of David and the
inhabitants of Jerusalem a spirit of grace and supplication.
They will look on me, the one they have pierced, and they
will mourn for him as one mourns for an only child, and grieve
bitterly for him as one grieves for a firstborn son. 11On that
day the weeping in Jerusalem will be great, like the weeping of
Hadad Rimmon in the plain of Megiddo. 12The land will
mourn, each clan by itself, with their wives by themselves: the
clan of the house of David and their wives, the clan of the
house of Nathan and their wives, 13the clan of the house of
Levi and their wives, the clan of Shimei and their wives, 14and
all the rest of the clans and their wives.

**13:1"On that day a fountain will be opened to the house of
David and the inhabitants of Jerusalem, to cleanse them from
sin and impurity.**
**2"On that day, I will banish the names of the idols from the
land, and they will be remembered no more," declares the
LORD Almighty. "I will remove both the prophets and the
spirit of impurity from the land. 3And if anyone still prophe-
sies, his father and mother, to whom he was born, will say to
him, 'You must die, because you have told lies in the LORD's
name.' When he prophesies, his own parents will stab him.**
**4"On that day every prophet will be ashamed of his
prophetic vision. He will not put on a prophet's garment of
hair in order to deceive. 5He will say, 'I am not a prophet. I am
a farmer; the land has been my livelihood since my youth.' 6If
someone asks him, 'What are these wounds on your body?' he
will answer, 'The wounds I was given at the house of my
friends.'"**

Original Meaning

WITH 12:1 WE enter into a new section of Zechariah signaled by the Hebrew term *maśśaʾ* (NIV "oracle"), which also appeared in 9:1. In the commentary introduction, we presented the overall shape of chapters 9–14, including points of continuity and discontinuity between chapters 9–11 and 12–14. There we argued that chapters 12–14 describe the consequences of the crisis described in the sign-act of 11:4–16, which shattered the hopes of chapters 9–10. Chapters 12–14 present God's plan to cleanse his people and defeat the nations in a future day.

One can discern three distinct units within Zechariah 12–14, namely, 12:1–13:6, 13:7–9, 14:1–21. The first and last units use a similar editorial style as they are introduced by the Hebrew term *hinneh* ("behold," untranslated in NIV) at 12:2 and 14:1. The middle unit (13:7–9), however, is distinguished from the other two on the rhetorical level by its use of the vocative ("O sword") and the imperatives ("awake . . . strike"), and on the thematic level by its use of shepherd/sheep imagery, showing its affinity with other short editorial transitions throughout chapters 9–14.[1]

Zechariah 12:1–13:6 represents an oracle from God that outlines his comprehensive plan for the renewal of his people. Not only will he make his city, Jerusalem, a fortress impenetrable by the nations, but he will also use

1. On 13:7–9 and its role in chs. 12–14, see comments on 13:7–9.

Judah to strike at these foreign forces before transforming Jerusalem and his Davidic king into a mighty army. This salvation from God is only the first step in his plan for his people. He promises to produce penitence, provide cleansing, and remove idolatry and false prophecy from the land.

The global dimension of 12:1–13:6 makes it challenging to ascertain the precise historical context in which this oracle was delivered to Judah. Its placement in chapters 9–14 suggests that it reflects the perspective of a prophet who has great hope for the future of Jerusalem, its people, and Davidic leadership. Clearly Jerusalem is in need of political salvation and spiritual renewal, while Judah is seen as not only supportive of, but essential to, God's purposes for Jerusalem. But the writer does not exclude the house of David or the city of Jerusalem from God's redemptive purposes, even though mention of the Levitical line of Shimei rather than that of Zadok in 12:13 may be evidence of a negative stance toward the Zadokite priesthood in Jerusalem.

In light of these aspects, we have isolated the period after the tenure of Zerubbabel as governor in the Persian province of Yehud. This prophecy could have arisen soon after this (just after ca. 510 B.C.), when Jerusalem had attained heightened status with the restoration of the temple structure, or even as late as the time of Nehemiah (after 445 B.C.), when Jerusalem received much attention with its rebuilt wall and repopulation of the city. The sociological perspective of the one(s) writing these oracles is clearly the province of Yehud as it grappled with the relationship between province and capital and the function that both would play in the ultimate reign of Yahweh over the earth. If it is from the earlier date, the author could easily be the prophet Zechariah, but if the latter one (after 445 B.C.), then it would have arisen from the prophetic community he spawned.

The appearance of the formula "on that day" at regular intervals throughout this passage is a significant rhetorical feature that should not be overlooked, but this does not mean that every appearance of this formula has structural significance.[2] Indeed 12:1 serves as a superscription to chapters 12–14 as a whole. The Hebrew word *hinneh* at the beginning of 12:2 and 14:1 indicates the start of a new section within these chapters, while the form of "on that day" found in 12:3, 9; 13:2, 4 marks the structural skeleton for the passage that follows.[3] This identifies 12:2 as an introduction to 12:2–13:6 with its focus on the victory of Jerusalem over the nations. Then, 12:3–8

2. For a superb review of various approaches to the structure of this passage see E. J. C. Tigchelaar, *Prophets of Old and the Day of the End: Zechariah, the Book of Watchers and Apocalyptic* (OtSt 35; Leiden: Brill, 1996), 116–20; but also Petersen, *Zechariah 9–14*, 109–10; Redditt, *Haggai*, 128–32; Floyd, *Minor Prophets*, 495.

3. This form precedes "on that day" with an untranslated Heb. verb (*hayah*).

relates various aspects of this victory, and 12:9 with its structural formula signals the end of God's victory for Israel and provides the transition realized in 12:10 to God's new work within Israel as he pours out his Spirit, which produces mourning (12:10–14) and cleansing (13:1).

Then in 13:2 with its structural formula, we transition to the issue of idolatry and prophecy that will be removed from the land. Finally, 13:4 with its structural formula shows how false prophecy will be squelched, showing the enduring legacy of God's judgment on idolatry.

Introducing the God of the Oracle (12:1)

THE TERM "ORACLE" signals the beginning of a new section of prophecy (see comments at 9:1). As in 9:1, a prophetic utterance with universalistic overtones unexpectedly interrupts the flow of speech—here, "who stretches out the heavens, who lays the foundation of the earth, and who forms the spirit of man within him." This phrase foreshadows the global dimensions of God's dominion and is reminiscent of participial praise expressions found in the Psalter (e.g., Ps. 18:47–48), Job (e.g., Job 5:9–16), Amos (e.g., Amos 4:13), and Isaiah (e.g., Isa. 40:22).

The first two divine actions in 12:1 refer to God's creation of the cosmos (see esp. Isa. 51:13), while the third action alludes to God's formation of the spirit of humanity by breathing into the human being the breath of life (Gen. 2:7). By using these snippets of praise, especially connected to God's role as Creator, the prophet establishes Yahweh's right to proclaim the message and his ability to act against or for the recipients.[4]

Victory for Jerusalem and Judah Against the Nations (12:2–8)

THE PROPHECY THAT verse 1 introduces begins by describing a siege of Jerusalem and Judah by opposing forces. The antagonists are described as "all the surrounding peoples" (vv. 2, 6) and "all the nations [of the earth]" (vv. 3, 4, 9)—terms that point to a force of global proportions.[5]

The protagonists here are mainly Jerusalem and Judah, with some mention of the house of David. Both Jerusalem and Judah are besieged (12:2). Before being used by God to defeat their enemies, the leaders of Judah remind themselves that the origin of the strength of Jerusalem is "the LORD Almighty ... their God" (12:5). God then uses these leaders to bring the

4. In the wisdom context it is used to explain why one cannot contest God's sovereign will (9:14) or to encourage people to turn to God for help (5:8).

5. Smith suggests this is an allusion to the Persian army and cites Herodotus 7.60–99; Smith, *Micah-Malachi*, 273.

first phase of victory for Judah and Jerusalem, with no participation from the inhabitants of Jerusalem (12:6). The Lord will save the "dwellings" (lit., "tents") of Judah first, granting them the same honor as the royal house and city (12:7). In the second phase of victory, God uses Jerusalem and the house of David as a fighting force, shielding the inhabitants of the city so that the weakest fighters will be like David and the Davidic house like God, who went before the armies of Israel through the angel of the Lord (12:8).

The way these protagonists are described suggests a distinction between Jerusalem and Judah, between Davidic leadership and Judean leadership. Neither Jerusalem nor its inhabitants (royal and otherwise), however, are denigrated in this prophecy. Nevertheless, one cannot miss the way in which the prophecy lifts the status of non-Jerusalemite Judeans, whom God will use to bring victory first and thus obtain the same level of status as Jerusalem and the royal house.

Throughout this initial section the author uses a variety of images to describe the triumph of Jerusalem and Judah. (1) Jerusalem is identified as "a cup that sends . . . reeling" (12:2),[6] the image being of a cup of strong wine that makes those who drink it stagger like a drunkard (Ps. 75:9; Isa. 51:17, 22; Jer. 25:15–29; 51:7; Lam. 4:21; Ezek. 23:31–34; Hab. 2:16).[7] Tigchelaar has shown how this image is "bound up with Yahweh's judgment, and that the drinking from this cup brings about either a situation of unpleasant intoxication (tottering, vomiting, shame) or of destruction."[8] Those who attack Jerusalem will be rendered incapacitated like a drunkard.

(2) The next image of Jerusalem is that of "an immovable rock" (12:3) that injures all who try to "move" it, a verb that describes the heavy load carried by a pack animal (Gen. 44:13; Neh. 13:15). The word for "injure" is used in Leviticus 21:5 for cutting oneself; thus, it refers not to a muscle strain but to a bloody gash.[9]

(3) With the third image (12:4) the focus shifts to God's protection of the house of Judah as the nations advance as cavalry against Judah.[10] Using three

---

6. Merrill, *Haggai*, 313; Redditt, *Haggai*, 129; Floyd, *Minor Prophets*, 519; Tigchelaar, *Prophets*, 120–21.

7. See further W. McKane, "Poison, Trial by Ordeal and the Cup of Wrath," *VT* 30 (1980): 474–92.

8. Tigchelaar, *Prophets*, 120.

9. See Petersen, *Zechariah 9–14*, 112; Redditt, *Haggai*, 132; Mason, "Use," 145–46, although Mason goes too far in linking this term to the proper order of the cultus in the Second Temple.

10. Nearly every time "horse" and "rider" are linked in the Old Testament, they refer to a military scene: Ex. 15:1, 21; 2 Kings 9:18–19; 18:23; Job 39:18; Isa. 36:8; Jer. 6:23; 50:42; 51:21; Ezek. 23:6, 12, 23; 38:15; Hos. 14:3; Amos 2:15; Hab. 3:8; Hag. 2:22; Zech. 1:8. In some cases it denotes a royal image, which is most likely a subset of the military sense, as Ezek. 23:6, 12, 23 shows (see Est. 6:8, 9, 11; 8:10; Jer. 17:25; 22:4).

words restricted elsewhere to the list of curses in Deuteronomy 28:28,[11] the prophecy envisions a scene of mass confusion with senseless riders mounted on bewildered and blinded horses.

(4) The final image (12:6) continues the theme of victory for Judah by comparing its leaders to two common images of fire (a wood fire under a fire-pot, a grass fire in a field). In these images the enemy is the wood and sheaves, which are entirely consumed ("right and left"). Taken together these four images emphasize God's victory over the surrounding nations through Jerusalem and Judah.

Grace and Supplication for Repentance and Cleansing in Victorious Jerusalem (12:9–13:1)

AS NOTED ABOVE, 12:9 begins with the structural formula that signals the transition to a new section. On one level this verse summarizes 12:2–8, emphasizing that it is God who will destroy this global coalition against Jerusalem. However, it also functions as a key transition to the next phase of God's redemptive work, reminding the people that repentance and cleansing are prerequisite to God's promised victory over the nations on behalf of Jerusalem and Judah.

This promise is not new in the Old Testament. Psalm 48 reminds us of God's pleasure for the city of Jerusalem, that is, Zion, the seat of his rule (cf. Ps. 2). Although the kings amassed their forces to attack the city, they were overwhelmed by the mere sight of God's majestic city. What makes this city secure is the presence of God (48:3, 8), who is characterized by "unfailing love" (48:9) and "righteousness" (48:10).

This promise to Zion became an important part of the city's tradition. Theological distortions of this tradition led to the belief that Zion's security was guaranteed apart from covenantal relationship with Yahweh (cf. Jer. 7:4; 21:13). Thus, in Lamentations 2:15 we find an allusion to Psalm 48 in the surprised cry from those who pass by: "Is this the city that was called the perfection of beauty, the joy of the whole earth?" Similarly in Lamentations 4:12 one finds this statement: "The kings of the earth did not believe, nor did any of the world's people, that enemies and foes could enter the gates of Jerusalem." Overlooked in this distortion was the necessity of God's presence in this city, a presence threatened by the disobedience of the people: "But it happened because of the sins of her prophets and the iniquities of her priests, who shed within her the blood of the righteous" (4:13).[12]

11. Interestingly Deut. 28:28 is not related to a military engagement.

12. On the importance of the Zion tradition in Lamentations see Boda, "Priceless Gain," 51–75.

These voices from the Exile reveal how important was a reevaluation of the status of Jerusalem/Zion in God's plan for those who lived in the wake of its destruction. The message of Lamentations guides the community toward a repentance based on God's grace (Lam. 3:40–42). What is fascinating about Zechariah 12:1–13:6 is that God offers victory and salvation for Zion simultaneously with his transformation of the people through his Spirit.

In 12:10–14 the prophet reveals that accompanying this salvation from external forces will be an internal renewal of the nation as God transforms their affections to seek him in repentance. This renewal begins with the initiative of Yahweh, who will "pour out . . . a spirit of grace and supplication." The pouring out (*šapak*) of a spirit (*ruaḥ*) is an expression that appears in two other contexts of the Old Testament, both in prophetic literature (Ezek. 39:29; Joel 2:28–29). In these other instances this spirit is referred to as "my Spirit," thus indicating more than just "a persuasion or conviction from YHWH that prompts a course of action."[13] God's pouring out his Spirit is a declaration of his placing his unique and manifest presence upon his people.

This Spirit of God is one of "grace and supplication." "Grace" (*ḥen*) is often used to denote the favor a person receives and enjoys with another person (e.g., Gen. 30:27), even someone in authority over them, such as the king (e.g., Est. 8:5) or God (e.g., Gen. 6:8). "Supplication" (*taḥanunim*) is linked to the same root as the first term, but in this case denotes seeking favor from God (e.g., Ps. 28:2, 6), which in the later period of Israel's history appears in texts guiding the penitential response of the people (2 Chron. 6:21; 31:9; Dan. 9:3, 17, 18, 23). These terms highlight two aspects of the ministry of God's Spirit: granting his people favor with himself through renewed relationship and invigorating them to respond to him in penitence.[14]

The remainder of 12:10–14 describes the impact of God's Spirit on the community. Most of the terms and imagery in this section are drawn from the context of mourning for the dead. The people mourn over the fact that they had "pierced" someone. This raises two key questions: To what action and to which person does this "piercing" refer?

First of all, the term "pierced" is one used elsewhere for a fatal wounding (e.g., Num. 25:18) and thus indicates that the person here is experiencing

---

13. Merrill argues against equating this reference with the third person of the Trinity; Merrill, *Haggai*, 318.

14. So also Tigchelaar, who notes: "This spirit effects two complementary aspects: being favourable and asking someone to look in favour"; Tigchelaar, *Prophets*, 124–25. Ap-Thomas misses these two aspects by interpreting the "and" as signaling an explanation: "a spirit of favour, or rather, of supplication for favour"; D. R. Ap-Thomas, "Some Aspects of the Root ḤNN in the Old Testament," *JSS* 2 (1957): 128–48.

death.[15] This view is supported by presence of vocabulary and images that are clearly linked to Israelite responses to death. Zechariah 12:10 uses images drawn from the mourning rites of families in ancient Israel. While the death of "a firstborn son," who was considered special in the ancient patriarchal societies, would have been difficult, the death of "an only child," on whom rested the hope of the continuance of the family, would have been devastating.[16]

While these two initial images are clear, the image found in 12:11 has attracted much controversy. Some have interpreted this verse as an allusion to mourning rites connected to the untimely death of Josiah in the "plain of Megiddo" (2 Chron. 35:25), with "Hadad Rimmon" identified either as an unknown town[17] or a textual mistake for "son of Amon."[18] If this interpretation is accepted, the image here is the same as those in 12:10, only on a national level.

Many interpreters, however, have noticed conspicuous similarities between this verse and the myth and ritual of Canaanite religion.[19] The word Hadad Rimmon is an Aramaic epithet for the god Baal (1 Kings 15:18; 2 Kings 5:18). Baal's death and resurrection figures prominently in Canaanite mythology and religion. Although it is difficult to determine the relationship between this myth and Canaanite agricultural rhythms and religious rituals, it is significant that mourning is associated with the cult of Baalism in Old Testament texts. In 1 Kings 18, which describes the famous battle between Elijah and Baalism on Mount Carmel above the plain of Megiddo, when Baal does not

---

15. The LXX offers an interesting perspective on the Heb. text here at the word "pierced" (*daqar*). We find here the verb *katorcheomai*, a word not found elsewhere in the LXX. This has typically been translated as "treated spitefully," thus taking this piercing as metaphorical for the Israelites' treatment of God and displaying the uncomfortability of the ancient translators with a reference to the death of God. It is interesting, however, that at three places in the LXX the Heb. verb *raqad* ("to stamp about/dance") is translated with *orcheomai* (1 Chron. 15:29; Eccl. 3:4; Isa. 13:21). Furthermore, in Eccl. 3:4 this "dancing" is the opposite of "mourning" (*sapad*), the very next Heb. term in Zech. 12:10 (Jerome also suggested that the LXX had a text with *raqad*, see M. Delcor, "Un probleme de critique textuelle et d'exegèse: Zach 12:10," *RB* 58 [1951]: 189–99). Thus, what is in view here is "those who danced will mourn for him as one mourns for. . . ."

16. Some have interpreted this as a reference to child sacrifice related to the siege of the city in 12:1–9, similar to 2 Kings 3:27, where Mesha's son is sacrificed to stop the siege; Petersen, *Zechariah 9–14*, 121. Interestingly, in the sacrifice of Isaac stress is laid on the special character of Isaac as the "only son" (Gen. 22:1–2). The difficulty with this interpretation is that Zech. 12 emphasizes God's salvation of Jerusalem.

17. Merrill, *Haggai*, 324.

18. Delcor, "Deux passages difficiles: Zach 12:11 et 11:13," 70–73.

19. See S. Ackerman, *Under Every Green Tree: Popular Religion in Sixth-Century Judah* (HSM 46; Atlanta: Scholars Press, 1992), 79–93, esp. 89–91; J. Day, *Yahweh and the Gods and Goddesses of Canaan* (JSOTSup 265; Sheffield: Sheffield Academic Press, 2000), 71.

respond to their cries, his prophets perform mourning rites, cutting themselves in similar fashion to El in the Baal myth (1 Kings 18:28).[20]

Although the evidence is stronger for this second strain of interpretation, many have rejected it because of its association with pagan religion, considered inappropriate in a passage that will go on to reject idolatry and its practices (see 13:2–6).[21] But one should not dismiss the connection to Canaanite religion too quickly. Rather than affirming pagan practices, this passage may simply be drawing on two vivid examples of mourning in Israel: family and religious mourning.

What must not be forgotten is that these various examples are introduced as similes ("as one mourns ... as one grieves ... like the weeping") to express the depth of mourning that will follow the pouring out of God's "spirit of grace and supplication."[22] Thus, it is not speaking directly of the death of someone; rather, it is using mourning to describe penitential response to God. As in the past the Israelites mourned their children, so now they will mourn in repentance for their treatment of God. As in the past they mourned their pagan gods, so "piercing" Yahweh, they will now mourn penitently their mistreatment of God.[23]

While this answers the first question (to what action does this piercing refer?), the second of our key questions is more challenging (to whom does this piercing refer?). The recipient of this piercing is referred to as "me" in one phrase ("they will look on *me* the one they have pierced") while in the following phrases the person is referred to as "him" ("they will mourn for *him* ... grieve bitterly for *him*"). Suggestions to alleviate this disagreement abound, with some altering the Hebrew text and others dividing the phrase differently.[24] The former approach lacks textual support as the best manuscripts in Hebrew and the ancient versions all have "me." The latter approach is possible but renders an awkward word order.

Several approaches can be discerned in past study of this verse.[25] Some see here an allusion to the suffering servant of Isaiah 53 (either as an individual or communal figure), to a representative (often messianic) figure who takes

20. Similar rites were connected with the cult of Tammuz in the Mesopotamian context (see Ezek. 8:14).

21. See Merrill, *Haggai*, 323.

22. So similarly Witt, "Zechariah 12–14", 48.

23. A similar technique is used in Ps. 48:2, in which Mount Zion is compared to the "heights of Zaphon," the dwelling place of Baal and the highest mountain in Syria. For other examples see Day, *Gods and Goddesses*, 91–127.

24. See discussion in Mason, "Use," 160–67. M. Dahood, "A Note on the Third Person Suffix -y in Hebrew," *UF* 4 (1972):163–64, argues that no emendation is needed, suggested that *ʿly* is a variant of *ʿlyw*.

25. See the excellent discussion in Mason, "Use," 160–67.

the piercing directed at Yahweh, to some unknown figure, to some historical figure in the eighth to second century B.C.,[26] to the king as royal figure in a preexilic ritual,[27] or to someone killed in the war of Zechariah 12:1–8.

Those who stress connections to the suffering servant of Isaiah 52–53 do not take into account some clear differences, especially the fact that the death there is vicarious while here it is not; moreover, the death here leads to mourning while in Isaiah 52–53 it leads to salvation.[28] Most of the other views assume that there are references to two distinct figures in this verse or presuppose a ritual for which there is little evidence.

Throughout 12:1–9 first-person speech is consistently attributed to Yahweh (see 12:1), and thus it appears that Yahweh is the "me" of 12:10. While the switch to the third person ("him") in the following phrase is awkward, examples of such switches can be found in the Old Testament and is probably merely a feature of style.[29] In this verse, God likens the people's past treatment of him as "piercing"—disregarding and abandoning him to the point that his existence was irrelevant to their lives.[30]

While 12:10–11 reveals the depth of this mourning, 12:12–14 reveals its breadth. Up to here, the focus has been on the house of David and the inhabitants of Jerusalem, but with 12:12 this mourning impacts the entire land as each family feels the pain of the mourning generated by this new Spirit from God. Notably women and men are separated for this activity, an action probably related to the abandonment of decorum in ancient mourning customs.[31]

Although this mourning is clearly universal in the land (12:14), certain families are singled out. While this listing may be of the entire leadership caste of the community (royal, David; prophetic, Nathan; priestly, Levi; sapiential, Shimei),[32] more likely this list represents two specific lines within the royal (David/Nathan) and priestly (Levi/Shimei) houses.

Solomon and his descendants are the ones who sat on David's throne and through them the royal line is traced (1 Chron. 3), but Nathan is another

---

26. Suggestions range from Uriah, Josiah, Gedeliah, Jeremiah, Zerubbabel, Onias III, Simon Maccabeus, Judas Maccabeus.

27. See Otzen, *Studien*, 173–83. This explains the reference to "me" as an oral piece from the ritual.

28. See further Petersen, *Zechariah 9–14*, 121; Mason, "Use," 163–64.

29. See GKC §144p; Merrill, *Haggai*, 320. This use of "him" may have arisen because of the construction of the phrase "the one whom they have pierced."

30. For this metaphorical approach see Delcor, "Un problème," 189–99; Merrill, *Haggai*, 320; cf. Prov. 12:18, so possible reason for LXX and Vulgate.

31. This separation may be reflected in 2 Chron. 35:25, which refers to lamenting male and female singing groups. Certainly women played a special role separate from men in mourning rituals, see Jer. 9:17–26. This gender separation is picked up in the *m. Sukk.* 51–52.

32. Smith, *Micah-Malachi*, 277; Stuhlmueller, *Rebuilding*, 149.

of David's sons (2 Sam. 5:14). Luke's genealogy in Luke 3 reveals that at a later date, at least Nathan's line could be used for tracing the promised line, a line that went through Zerubbabel. Perhaps Nathan's line was raised in status because of the sinful behavior of Solomon's line, though certainty is beyond our grasp.

The focus on Levi and Shimei is more difficult to explain. The leading family of priests in the Persian period, the Zadokites (see comments on Hag. 1:1–12; Zech. 3), traced their lineage through Aaron to Levi's son Kohath (1 Chron. 6:1–15).[33] Shimei, however, was the child of Levi's other son, Gershom (1 Chron. 6:17; cf. Ex. 6:16–17; Num. 3:17–18). The absence of reference to the Zadokite line here is reminiscent of the trend suggested for the house of David, that is, that the founder of the line is mentioned (David, Levi), but a different descendant is used to trace the legitimate line.

It appears that this verse envisions the future royal and priestly leadership as emerging from Davidic and Levitical lines that includes the line of Zerubbabel but not the Zadokites, who were presently in charge. With this, however, we should not lose the focus of this section of 12:1–13:6, that is, that God's Spirit will bring about a depth and breadth of mourning that will encompass the depths of the people's being and the breadth of the community.

God's grace has led to penitence for the house of David and the people of Jerusalem, but even this does not complete his work. In the final phase, God will provide cleansing for the behavior of this people. The term "fountain" here speaks of a spring that brings forth "fresh water" (lit., "water of life"; e.g., Jer. 2:13).[34] Such a spring was an important source for water needed for ritual cleansing described in the Torah (e.g., Lev. 14:5, 50).[35]

This connection to ritual cleansing appears to be in view throughout this verse. Although the first term, "sin" (*ḥaṭṭa*ʾ*t*), is a more general term for human behavior that breaks God's will (e.g., Deut. 9:18), it is nuanced here by its connection to the "fountain" (spring) and to the second term for sin, "impurity" (*niddah*). These two terms for sin are found together in only one other context in the Old Testament (Num. 19:9), where they are linked to water as here. Numbers 19:9 speaks of the "water of impurity, sin." The phrases "water of impurity" and "water of sin" are stock terms in the Torah for the waters that bring ritual cleansing: 8:7 (water of sin); 19:13, 20, 21; 31:23 (water of

---

33. See Num. 4 for the responsibilities of the various sons of Levi and of the Kohathites.

34. See the similar phrase (lit.) "well of living water" in Gen. 26:19; Song 4:15.

35. It is interesting that the term for "fountain" (*maqor*) here is also used for the flow of fluids connected with childbirth and menstruation (Lev. 12:7; 20:18; Prov. 5:18), fluids that also brought impurity (*niddah*) because of their connection to death (Lev. 12:2, 5; 15:19, 20, 24, 25, 26, 33; Lam. 1:17; Ezek. 18:6; 22:10). However, the "fountain" in this case caused the impurity, while in Zech. 13:1 the "fountain" brings cleansing.

impurity). In all of these cases the term refers to purification from ritual impurity. These waters are usually related to the impurity that arises from contact with dead bodies (cf. 31:23), but in 8:7 it is used in the consecration of the Levites for service in the temple.

Some have connected this ritual cleansing from defilement by a corpse to the involvement of the inhabitants of Jerusalem and the house of David in the siege of 12:1–8.[36] Although this is possible, more likely this alludes to the contact with death in 12:10, where there is mention of the same characters.[37] The community that has slain their God has received the "spirit of grace and supplication" in order to mourn their actions and be ritually cleansed, a symbol of God's acceptance.

Judgment on Idolatry and False Prophecy (13:2–3)

THIS SLAYING OF GOD has still not been defined. We know that this metaphorical slaying has brought defilement, but what is the nature of this slaying? Zechariah 13:2–6 brings clarity to this question, showing that the people have rejected their God by turning to idolatry. Verse 2 continues the close association with the language of ritual impurity already encountered in 13:1, in particular using the words "cut off" (*karat*) and "unclean" (*ṭumʾah*), terms that appear together elsewhere only in connection with the state of ritual impurity (e.g., Lev. 7:20, 21).[38] As Zechariah 13:1 does, so also 13:2 alludes to Numbers 19:13, with its focus on the contact with the dead. In Zechariah 13:2, however, the impurity is clearly defined as idolatry and divination.

This connection between idolatry and impurity is bolstered by the fact that the word *niddah* ("impurity") is used for one other human activity in the Old Testament: idolatry (e.g., Ezek. 36:17). Ezekiel 36 has often been noted for its influence on Zechariah 13:1–6.[39] Ezekiel 36 highlights the sorrowful state of the land of Israel that has been conquered and possessed by the nations (36:1–4), and the prophet promises judgment against the nations and restoration of God's people to the land (36:5–15). It traces the dispersion of the people into exile to their unclean behavior of idolatry (36:16–21) but promises to return them, cleanse them with water from their idolatry, give them a new heart and spirit to follow the law, and provide bountiful provisions (36:22–30). The people will respond to this gracious act of Yahweh by loathing their sins, being ashamed and disgraced for their conduct (36:31–32).

These same aspects are apparent in Zechariah 12:1–13:6. The nations that have besieged Jerusalem are defeated (12:1–9), the gift of God's Spirit (12:10)

36. E.g., Floyd, *Minor Prophets*, 528.

37. E.g., Conrad, *Zechariah*, 184; Tigchelaar, *Prophets*, 127.

38. So also Otzen, *Studien*, 195.

39. See, e.g., Mason, "Use," 168–69; Baldwin, *Haggai*, 195; Redditt, *Haggai*, 134.

leads to deep mourning for their sin (12:11–14), and God provides cleansing for the impurity (13:1), which is identified as the slaying of God through idolatry (12:11; 13:2–6).

This idolatry is the focus of 13:2–6. Here we see the same combination of idolatry and false prophecy first encountered in 10:1–3. This is not an odd connection since divination was closely related to the practice of religion, as people delivered requests and expected answers from their gods.[40] The words "spirit of impurity" sum up the impact of this idolatry and false prophecy. Such practices have left their stain on the land, which will be cleansed from it. This "spirit" stands in contrast to the Spirit of God graciously poured out in 12:10.

God will "banish the names of the idols." The "name" is representative of the idol itself, which will be destroyed. The verb "banish" (*karat*, "to cut off") is usually the punishment of the idolater, but with the transformation of the community envisioned in 12:10 and 13:1, all that will remain are the idols and their attendants. The promise that these idols will "be remembered no more" refers to more than just cerebral amnesia in the Old Testament. It describes the religious affection of the Old Testament worshiper: To remember is to serve a god, while to forget is to abandon it (see comments on 10:9; cf. Deut. 8:18–20).

Not only idols, but also their religious attendants, the prophets, will be removed from the land.[41] Many have interpreted this as the end of the prophecy in the Old Testament.[42] However, similar to Zechariah 10:1–2, these prophets are linked to idolatry, not to the religion of Yahweh. Furthermore, the prophets are described in terms used for false prophecy: "told lies in the LORD's name" (13:3), "to deceive" (13:4). Thus, the removal is restricted to idolatrous prophets.

These prophets are the focus of the final verses in 13:3–6. Here we see either the fate of false prophets who will arise after God's removal of false prophecy from the land or the means by which God removes such false prophets. The people will be so transformed by God that parents will enact the Torah's judgment against their own child. In Deuteronomy 13 there was to be no toleration of false prophecy connected with idolatry, as the people are commanded to put the person to death (13:5), a practice obeyed in Zechariah 13:3 as the parents "stab" him (same Heb. word as "pierced" in 12:10). Here we see a reversal of the people's actions toward God in 12:10. As they have "pierced" God, abandoning him through their idolatry, so now they will cleanse

40. See Tigchelaar, who cites Jer. 23:9–40 and Deut. 13; Tigchelaar, *Prophets*, 131.

41. The same construction ("remove from") is used in 1 Kings 15:12 for expelling male prostitutes who served alongside idols.

42. Cf. Mason, who links this to Jeremiah's vision of a new covenant in which there will be no need for teaching the word of God since all will know God; Mason, "Use," 170.

the land of idolatry by piercing their prophets. This word not only plays off of 12:10 but also off of Numbers 25:8, in which an Israelite man and Midianite women, participating in idolatrous behavior through sexual intercourse, were "pierced" by Phinehas, grandson of Aaron the high priest.[43]

Enduring Eradication of False Prophecy (13:4–6)

SUCH DRASTIC MEASURES will make false prophets fear their vocation. They will be ashamed of their visions,[44] and such shame will lead them to try to conceal their vocation. The description of this cover-up alludes to four "earlier scriptural types."[45] The reference to "garment" certainly alludes to the garment or cloak worn by prophets in the past (e.g., 1 Kings 19:13; cf. 2 Kings 1:8). But the full phrase "garment of hair" adds another nuance by suggesting the tradition of Jacob and Esau. The only other time this phrase occurs in the Hebrew Bible is in Genesis 25:25 to describe the condition of Esau's skin, a condition that Rebekah seeks to replicate on his brother, Jacob, in the blessing deception in Genesis 27. The use of "deceive" in Zechariah 13:4 suggests this story is also in mind.

Verse 5 moves from implicit visual denial to explicit verbal dismissal of prophetic status. Again, allusion to two traditions in the Hebrew Bible can be discerned. The first is Amos's defense of his prophetic calling to Amaziah in Amos 7:14 ("I was neither a prophet ...") followed by a claim of agrarian vocation. While Amos explains that God had called him to prophesy, the opposite is the case in Zechariah 13:5. The second tradition is the description of Cain and his birth in Genesis 4:1–2. There "Cain worked the soil" ("I am a farmer," Zech. 13:5). Furthermore, the Hebrew text behind the phrase "the land has been my livelihood since my youth" consists of three words that read: "A man acquired me in my youth." Two of these three words are found in Genesis 4:1, the first ("a man") is Adam who impregnates Eve, the second ("acquired") the word on the lips of Eve at the birth of Cain ("have brought forth," Gen. 4:1).[46]

One can see, then, that both the visual denial and verbal dismissal follow the same pattern. Both draw on two earlier traditions, one a reversal of a

---

43. Note how this narrative follows the account of the prophet Balaam and when the narrative resumes in Num. 31, reference is made to the death of Balaam and to the idolatrous affair at Peor. This may account for the idolatry-prophecy connection in Zech. 13:1–6.

44. The noun form (*bošet*) of this verb "ashamed" (*bwš*) is used throughout the prophetic literature to refer to the worship of Baal (Hos. 9:10; Jer. 3:24; 11:13).

45. Floyd, *Minor Prophets*, 532–33.

46. This last phrase has been a great challenge to translators and interpreters. The NIV translation is based on a change to the word divisions in the Heb. text, based on the fact that the particular form of the verb here (*qanah* in the Hiphil) is not attested elsewhere. Other suggestions include allusions to illicit seduction (Petersen, *Zechariah 9–14*, 107) and hallucinatory activity (H. L. Ginsberg, "The Oldest Record of Hysteria with Physical Stigmata,

positive prophetic tradition intimately related to the calling of a prophet who attacks inappropriate pagan religion and its officials in the northern kingdom (Elijah/Elisha putting on a cloak, Amos defending his calling), the other a negative sibling tradition from Genesis that involved deception and resulted in the deceiver roaming the earth (Esau/Jacob and the stolen birthright, Cain/Abel and the attempted deception of God).[47] Through this play on earlier traditions, the author is driving home God's rejection of this idolatrous prophetic stream; they will not be able to appeal to the ancient legitimizing traditions, and their deceptive lives will result in devastating consequences.

Verse 6 brings this section on false prophecy to a close. Continuing the Hebrew rhetorical technique of apostrophe begun in 13:5, the deception is uncovered. Without the hairy robe to cover his body, the false prophet will expose his "wounds." The term here for "wound" can refer to both fatal (e.g., 1 Kings 22:35) and nonfatal injuries (e.g., Deut. 25:3). The location of the wounds is "between your arms," a construction similar to the wound of King Joram in 2 Kings 9:24, which was "between the shoulders" (lit., "between the arms").

Some have insisted that this wound refers to the injury inflicted by the parents in 13:3 and that the Hebrew phrase behind "the house of my friends" (lit., "the house of those who love me") is a reference to the family home.[48] The problem with this approach is that the wound in 13:3 is fatal and the Hebrew construction behind "my friends" is never used for a parental home. Elsewhere it refers to the allies of the Israelites (e.g., Jer. 22:20, 22) or the illicit lovers (prostitutes) of the Israelites in contexts speaking of idolatry (e.g., Ezek. 16:33–37; Hos. 2:5–13). Thus, many conclude that this refers to wounds connected with illicit religious rites.[49] The cutting of the body is linked to idolatrous practices connected with Baal religion (1 Kings 18:28) and the cult of the dead (Lev. 19:28; Deut. 14:1; Jer. 16:6; 47:5).[50] The false prophet who tries to deceive will ultimately be discovered.

Zech. 13:2–6," in *Studies in Bible and the Ancient Near East*, ed. Y. Avishur and J. Blau [Jerusalem: E. Rubinstein, 1978], 23–27) among others, but these are unnecessary once the connection to Cain is recognized; see Floyd, *Minor Prophets*, 533.

47. It is also possible that these two Genesis sibling traditions are referring to deception (Jacob/Esau) and murder (Cain/Abel), the second being an allusion to Zech. 12:10 and the piercing of God or his representative.

48. Redditt, *Haggai*, 136; Floyd, *Minor Prophets*, 533.

49. So Mason, *Haggai*, 122; Baldwin, *Haggai*, 197; Petersen, *Zechariah 9–14*, 127; Witt, "Zechariah 12–14", 53.

50. Interestingly, Jer. 5:7 contains the verb often used for pagan ritual cutting, but here it is often translated as "gather together" (NIV "throng"). If this is another reference to ritual practice, it would show the connection between idolatry, prostitution, and cutting ritual; see Ackerman, *Green Tree*, 88–89.

As already noted, this message is likely delivered by a member of Judah critical of activities in Jerusalem and yet hopeful of a renewal for this city and its leadership. It is significant that the community that reconstructed the temple and settled around its sacred precincts receives this message. Speaking in language familiar to the temple community, this prophet not only reminds them of the causes of the Exile but also of the hope for transformation envisioned by Ezekiel. In all of this, however, there is never a hint of rejection neither of Jerusalem nor of the Davidic line. There is an enduring hope of victory over external enemies as well as anticipation of internal renewal.

What should not be missed in all this is that these various aspects of renewal are inaugurated through the initiative of God. Although there are serious issues in view, human ability is not the way ahead. Rather, Yahweh brings victory and salvation for Israel, pours out the spirit of grace and supplication, provides a fountain of cleansing, and finally removes idolatry and false prophecy from the land.

Bridging Contexts

ZECHARIAH 9–14 AND apocalyptic. Zechariah 9–11 possesses characteristics typical of classic prophecy. One finds the hope of an idealized future for a united Israel, focus on localized enemies with some allusions to universal rule, and plenty of allusions to earlier prophecy. Announcements of salvation and judgment, woe oracles, and prophetic sign-acts are some of the forms used to express both comfort and warning.

After 12:1, however, the tone changes considerably. Chapters 12–14 focus attention on a future "day" on which God will battle against "all the nations" who have gathered against his people. Additionally, on this day God will remove sin as well as its patterns and structures from his people and establish Jerusalem as his prosperous capital, from which he will rule the earth.

In light of these characteristics, it is not surprising that chapters 12–14 are often mentioned in discussions of apocalyptic literature.[51] This type of

51. See D. Mathewson, "Revelation in Recent Genre Criticism: Some Implications for Interpretation," *TrinJ* ns13 (1992): 193–213, for a superb review of the study of apocalyptic. For more detailed discussion of the definition and interpretation of apocalyptic, see J. J. Collins, ed., *Apocalypse: The Morphology of a Genre* (Semeia 14; Missoula., Mont.: Scholars Press, 1979); idem, *The Apocalyptic Imagination: An Introduction to the Jewish Matrix of Christianity* (New York: Crossroad, 1984); S. L. Cook, *Prophecy and Apocalypticism: The Postexilic Social Setting* (Minneapolis: Fortress, 1995); P. D. Hanson, *Old Testament Apocalyptic* (Interpreting Biblical Texts; Nashville: Abingdon, 1987); D. S. Jacobsen, *Preaching in the New Creation: The Promise of New Testament Apocalyptic Texts* (Louisville: Westminster John Knox, 1999).

literature, displayed in its mature form (e.g., the book of Revelation), has been defined in the following way:

> "Apocalypse" is a genre of revelatory literature with a narrative framework, in which a revelation is mediated by an otherworldly being to a human recipient, disclosing a transcendent reality which is both temporal, insofar as it envisages eschatological salvation, and spatial, insofar as it involves another, supernatural world.[52]

The fact that many of the elements of apocalyptic literature can be traced back to passages found in prophetic books (Isa. 24–27; 56–66; Ezek. 38–39; Joel 2:28–3:21; Zech. 1–6; 12–14) suggests that one of its key roots is to be found among the prophetic movement.[53] Although not all apocalyptic works have arisen from persecuted communities, the prophetic passages that have provided the building blocks for this form have been linked to such contexts, implying that oppression was key to this transformation within prophetic speech forms.[54] Apocalyptic forms with their use of symbols on a heavenly plane not only granted a divine perspective on the situation but protected the writers from their oppressors.

It is obvious that Zechariah 12–14 does not fit the definition of apocalyptic precisely.[55] The narrative framework is not as developed as one finds in apocalyptic literature, and there is no otherworldly being or supernatural world. But one does find a key characteristic that ultimately dominates in

---

52. J. J. Collins, "Introduction: Towards the Morphology of a Genre," in *Apocalypse: The Morphology of a Genre*, ed. J. J. Collins (Semeia 14; Missoula, Mont.: Scholars Press, 1979), 9.

53. Cf. Hanson, *Apocalyptic*, 35–38. For the key role of prophetic literature, see D. S. Russell, *The Method and Message of Jewish Apocalyptic* (Philadelphia: Westminster, 1964); idem, *Divine Disclosure: An Introduction to Jewish Apocalyptic* (Minneapolis: Fortress, 1992); idem, *Prophecy and Apocalyptic Dream: Protest and Promise* (Peabody, Mass.: Hendrickson, 1994). Even Collins says: "Postexilic prophecy undoubtedly supplied some of the codes and raw materials utilized by the later apocalypses"; Collins, *Imagination*, 26. This does not preclude, however, the influence of other key streams represented in the Old Testament, esp. that of the wisdom tradition. The emphasis on interpretations of mysterious symbols and numbers has often been linked to the wisdom tradition of Babylon, esp. as represented in Daniel; see Larkin, *Eschatology*; Hanson, *Apocalyptic*, 26.

54. There is a growing uneasiness with linking apocalyptic to oppression, with many scholars opting for the term "crisis"; see Hanson, *Apocalyptic*, 29; J. J. Collins, *Daniel: With an Introduction to Apocalyptic Literature* (FOTL 20; Grand Rapids: Eerdmans, 1984), 22.

55. As Carroll so poignantly stated: "It is not easy to differentiate between prophetic discourses and apocalyptic language"; R. P. Carroll, "Deportation and Diasporic Discourses in the Prophetic Literature," in *Exile: Old Testament, Jewish and Christian Conceptions*, ed. J. M. Scott (JSJSup 56; Leiden: Brill, 1997), 63–85; cf. D. C. Olson, "Jeremiah 4.5–31 and Apocalyptic Myth," *JSOT* 73 (1997): 81–107. Petersen identifies Zech. 9–14 as prophetic literature, not apocalyptic; Petersen, *Zechariah 9–14*, 24, esp. n. 65.

apocalyptic literature and is described in the above definition: "temporal, insofar as it envisages eschatological salvation." One can tag Zechariah 12–14 as proto-apocalyptic literature, displaying the transformation from classic forms of prophecy, rooted in the particular and historical, to apocalyptic forms, dominated by the universal and eschatological.

But it is important to note that Zechariah 12–14 can only be called proto-apocalyptic in their eschatological outlook. These chapters look to "that day" with a cosmic perspective ("all the nations"). The image of armies gathered around Jerusalem where God fights for Israel will become an important motif in apocalyptic eschatology, but this does not mean that we have here apocalyptic material. To call this "proto-apocalyptic" only means that the prophetic style found here later joins with other stylistic features to form apocalyptic.[56]

This discussion of genre orients us to the interpretive issues at play as we approach Zechariah 9–14. Because this prophetic material shares much in common with apocalyptic material as a result of their common eschatological perspective, lessons learned from the interpretation of apocalyptic can help shape our reading strategy.

Apocalyptic. Apocalyptic literature offers both "consolation and exhortation in the face of some crisis" by providing "a comprehensive view of the cosmos through the order of the heavens or the predetermined course of history."[57] It speaks primarily to communities undergoing a difficulty, promising hope and exhorting faithfulness through offering a vision of divine justice. This vision comes through symbolic language that communicates more like an impressionistic painting than a photograph. The various symbols are rich and need to be understood in their original context, but together they form a general impression of the ideal future of the community. This general impression usually consists of several key themes:[58] God will rescue his people, bring justice to this world, purify his people and the earth from sin, and establish his reign on earth.

This view of apocalyptic is different from that adopted by many evangelicals in North America.[59] For them apocalyptic literature provides a

---

56. So similarly in Zech. 1–6 we find visionary experiences with otherworldly guides and a cosmic dimension. However, the items encountered in these visions are drawn from the natural world and interpreted, and lacking from these visions is the "characteristic worldview"; Collins, *Daniel: With an Introduction to Apocalyptic Literature*, 20. One can discern similar visionary experiences in prophetic literature; cf. S. Niditch, *The Symbolic Vision in Biblical Tradition* (Chico, Calif.: Scholars Press, 1983). To call this "proto-apocalyptic" only means that the prophetic style found here later combines with other stylistic features to create apocalyptic.

57. Collins, *Daniel: With an Introduction to Apocalyptic Literature*, 22.

58. See Russell, *Prophecy*, 110–21.

59. Esp., but not limited to, the dispensational traditions.

photograph of events at the end of time, and by studying the various passages, one can construct a detailed picture of these events. Beasley-Murray has identified the error of this approach:

> Even the best apocalyptic cryptographer could not produce an account of the birth, life, death and resurrection of Jesus from the mythic picture of Revelation 12 alone, nor from the vision of the lamb in Revelation 5. Why then should we suppose that anyone would be able to produce an account of the parousia from Revelation 19:11ff., in which the Word of God rides down from heaven on a white horse followed by armies of heavenly cavalry and treads the wine press of God's wrath alone, slaying men with the scimitar that issues out of his mouth?[60]

When apocalyptic passages are treated like newspaper stories, one displays little sensitivity to the symbolic value of the images. Another problem with this approach is the disregard of the way this literature functioned within the communities to which it was first addressed. One focuses less on the comfort and warning functions of this literature with so much energy expended on time lines of the eschaton.

This approach to apocalyptic, however, is also different from that adopted by many historical and literary critics who ignore the future orientation of these passages. Historical critics have traditionally focused exclusively on the function of this literature within an ancient context. Collins, for instance, in his discussion of the "apocalyptic technique" argues:

> This apocalyptic technique does not, of course, have a publicly discernible effect on a historical crisis, but it provides a resolution in the imagination by instilling conviction in the revealed "knowledge" that it imparts. The function of the apocalyptic literature is to shape one's imaginative perception of a situation and so lay the basis for whatever course of action it exhorts.[61]

Recent literary critics have distanced themselves from the attempt by historical critics to root apocalyptic literature in objective historical contexts, stressing instead the function of such literature to "evoke a social world, the shared reality among us."[62] In this way this ancient literature becomes relevant to the reader today within his or her own "social world."

---

60. G. R. Beasely-Murray, *Jesus and the Kingdom of God* (Grand Rapids: Eerdmans, 1986), 341–42.

61. Collins, *Imagination*, 32.

62. See Jacobsen, *Preaching*, 61.

The historical and literary approaches to apocalyptic stress the past and present and with their focus on the sociological setting of the writing and reading of apocalyptic texts have become a theological source for many oppressed, encouraging them as they seek a new world.[63]

One must question, however, whether the ancient writer of apocalyptic intended that this literature merely have "a resolution in the imagination" or "evoke a social world." Indeed, this literature did serve to comfort and exhort and did encourage hope and expectation of God's kingdom to come, but it was not merely therapeutic literature. One cannot avoid the presence in this ancient literature of a sincere expectation that nothing less than God's breaking into history would transform the circumstances of his people. Thus, although not providing a detailed, literal photograph of the future, apocalyptic literature does anticipate future events.

New Testament use of apocalyptic. The use in the New Testament of eschatological passages from the prophets confirms the approach outlined above.[64] In his study of the use of such passages in the New Testament, C. H. Dodd cautions the modern interpreter with the following words:

> The passages to which reference is made are in general couched in the symbolic language characteristic of apocalyptic literature. We should do less than justice to their authors, and certainly to the New Testament writers who quote them, if we insisted on the kind of crudely literal understanding to which our western minds are prone. Exactly where the attempt at literal description ends and symbolism begins, the writers themselves probably did not know, and we can hardly guess. But we shall be wise to treat the entire scheme of imagery as language appropriate to describe that which lies upon the frontier of normal experience, which therefore cannot be directly communicated in plain speech. But the prophets seriously believed that what they spoke of (in however cryptic terms) would happen.[65]

---

63. See M. L. King, "Our God is Marching On," in *A Testament of Hope*, ed. J. M. Washington (San Francisco: Harper, 1986), 230; A. A. Boesak, *Comfort and Protest: Reflections on the Apocalypse of John of Patmos* (Philadelphia: Westminster, 1987); E. Schüssler Fiorenza, *Revelation: Vision of a Just World* (Minneapolis: Fortress, 1991); P. Richard, *Apocalypse* (Maryknoll, N.Y.: Orbis, 1995), cited in Jacobsen, *Preaching*, xii–xiv; cf. A. Y. Collins, *Cosmology and Eschatology in Jewish and Christian Apocalypticism* (Leiden: Brill, 2000), 15–16.

64. See Mathewson, "Revelation," 193–213.

65. Dodd, *According to the Scriptures*, 72–73; see also Wright, *Victory*, and the heated debate between Wright and Allison; D. C. Allison, "Jesus and the Victory of Apocalyptic," in *Jesus and the Restoration of Israel: A Critical Assessment of N. T. Wright's Jesus and the Victory of God*, ed. C. Newman (Downers Grove, Ill.: InterVarsity Press, 1999), 126–41; N. T. Wright, "In Grateful Dialogue: A Response," in *Jesus and the Restoration of Israel*, 244–77.

Here Dodd rejects both extremes described above—that is, an interpretation that confines the prophetic expectation to a literal future or to a metaphorical past.

Such passages were addressed to communities in crisis, offering hope and exhorting faithfulness through a symbolic vision of God's ordering of the future. In New Testament perspective, they anticipate the eschatological redemption of Jesus Christ, through whom God entered into the history of his people. They also grant us perspectives on how to live faithfully in hope as we experience crises today and await Christ's second coming.

Biblical theology. There is little question that 12:1–13:6 presents considerable challenges to application in our contemporary context. On the surface it uses imagery that is foreign to our modern senses and assumes a historical context for which there is scanty evidence. Nevertheless, this passage was important to the early church, who saw in it hints of the ministry of Jesus on earth, as evidenced in the allusions to 12:10 in the New Testament witness.

New Testament relevance, however, should not be limited to this single verse. The New Testament authors used this allusion to refer to the entire complex of events found in 12:1–13:6 as well as chapters 9–14 as a whole. Because of this, it is important to consider the message of 12:1–13:6 to its ancient hearers and highlight the various expectations for the community of God.

Zechariah 12:1–13:6 was addressed originally to the Jewish inhabitants of the Persian province of Yehud. In this period the Persians tightened their control over the various provinces as they sought to extend their empire into Europe. The Davidic line no longer ruled the tiny province, and the priests in Jerusalem were afforded a key role in its administration. This prophecy addresses issues within the community and yet looks to the future with hope. The prophet, distanced from the Jerusalem power structures and deeply concerned over Persian idolatrous practices, still fixed his hopes on Jerusalem, envisioning both external and internal transformation for the city. God will deliver her from all her external enemies, using the people of the province and city to bring victory. God also will transform the community from within, granting grace, inducing penitence, cleansing sin, and removing idolatrous prophecy.

Celebrating the past. The New Testament community saw in the Roman soldiers' piercing of Jesus on the cross, the fulfillment of Zechariah 12:10. The ultimate offense against God would be this disregard for his Son by the Gentile soldiers encouraged by the Jewish community. In Revelation 1:7 and Matthew 24:30 the mourning connected to this piercing is attributed to the "nations" who will see Christ at his return. Most Christians see this return as a future experience at the eschaton, others believe that this refers to Christ's judgment on Jerusalem in A.D. 70. Most likely both events are in view; the judgment in A.D. 70 is a foretaste of God's final victory in history.

The destruction of Jerusalem in A.D. 70 is an important event in redemptive history. It signals a major transition in God's redemptive plan as hopes connected to the physical city are ended and transferred to the communal city of Jerusalem, the new Jerusalem—that is, the church. This new entity made up of Jews and Gentiles (the nations) now assumes the ancient promises of Jerusalem. In an ironic twist, God's rescue of Jerusalem and defeat of the nations was already accomplished prior to A.D. 70. Although unknown to the Jews and Gentiles at the time, Christ's death on the cross was God's means of delivering Jerusalem. Through this victory God pours out his spirit of grace and penitence, drawing his people to himself through Jesus.

Zechariah 12:1–13:6 is thus relevant to Christians today, primarily because it anticipates the great victory of God through Jesus and the fundamental transformation that resulted.

Living in the present. Since this passage relates to us as Christians through Christ's great work of redemption, this text offers guidance for our life in the present, especially in 12:10–13:6. God promises to pour out a "spirit of grace and supplication." Through Christ's death and by his Spirit he has first of all offered his grace to humanity. But such grace is accompanied by the spirit of "supplication," that work of the Spirit of softening the heart and bending the knee in submission before God. It is not surprising that a key theme of the early church is to "repent," to return to God in covenant relationship. Zechariah 12:10 reveals that this is not a human work but a divine operation on hearts and communities. The accompanying imagery of mourning shows the depth of such repentance, as deep a pain as that which attends the loss of a child. This imagery also shows the breadth of such repentance as it moves throughout the entire community of God.

God not only offers grace and forgiveness but also cleansing from the impure stains of past rebellion, especially in connection with false prophecy and idolatry. The challenge of false prophecy and idolatry was fundamentally a challenge to God's sovereignty. Through such means, the people were desirous of spiritual knowledge without the "constraints" of relationship with their covenant God. In the New Testament this cleansing is provided through the sacrifice of Christ on the cross applied through the work of the Holy Spirit.

Contemporary Significance

AS 12:1–13:6 SPOKE to the Persian period Jewish community and to the Roman period Christian community, both of whom needed to live faithfully in their context, so it speaks to the church today.

Celebrating the victory of God. We must begin by celebrating the redemptive work of Christ on the cross, through which God has inaugurated a new era of salvation for his people. This era will reach its culmination in the second advent of Christ, who will come as divine warrior and bring closure to the defeat of the nations. With our bent toward pragmatism, it is easy to overlook the significance of this vision of victory both past and future.

The New Testament community saw here a revelation of Jesus and paused to consider the mystery of God's redemptive plan—that divine piercing would inaugurate a new era of salvation. We encounter this truth regularly through the Lord's Supper, a rhythm established by Christ to force us to reflect on the mystery of the suffering God and on the grace extended to us through his supreme act of sacrifice. As Jesus inaugurated the rhythm of celebrating his death within his community, he reminded them of a hope: "I tell you, I will not drink of this fruit of the vine from now on until that day when I drink it anew with you in my Father's kingdom" (Matt. 26:29).

As Jesus closed the first Eucharist, he anticipated an eschatological supper, engendering hope in his followers. This future dimension was obviously important to the celebration of Christ's death in the Lord's Supper as reflected in the Pauline instructions: "For whenever you eat this bread and drink this cup, you proclaim the Lord's death until he comes" (1 Cor. 11:26). Zechariah 12:1–13:6, offering us a picture of God's victory, should engender hope in his final victory inaugurated through Christ's death, resurrection, and ascension.

Declaring the praise of God. The salvation promised in 12:1–13:6 is founded on the revelation of God as Creator (12:1), subtly setting the tone for the entire passage. Because God is Creator, he has the prerogative, power, and passion to save and judge humanity. The final shape of the Christian canon, with Genesis 1–2 as its introduction and Revelation 22 as its conclusion, reveals that the history of redemption serves a larger purpose: restoration of faithful relationship between God and humanity within a renewed cosmos.

As already noted, there is a close association between the theological statements in 12:1 and participial phrases in the Psalter and Isaiah. The regular appearance of similar phrases among the praise psalms of Israel reveals the importance of the rhythm of praise for the life of faith. Certainly praise of God is the natural expression of the redeemed to their Redeemer and of the created to their Creator. In addition, it orients believers for a life of faithfulness, reminding them of their dependence on God and his authority over him. This secondary role of praise is displayed in the prophetic messages of the latter part of the book of Isaiah, where the people are called to trust in God in the face of the nations and their idols (e.g., Isa. 44:6–28). In this way praise sets the tone for the declaration of the promises and exhortations of God.

This is why praise is such an important rhythm within the life of the community of God and necessary to the reception of his Word. From one perspective the Christian sermon is an expression of worship. If preaching the gospel is declaring God's victory and establishing his rule in the hearts of humanity (Isa. 52:7–10; Rom. 10:14–15),[66] it is one of the key rhythms in our communal praise of God, both as the preacher declares the Word and as the community responds in word and deed. From another perspective, our worship is an expression of revelation as we rehearse the creative and redemptive works of Yahweh and respond to him in word and deed. In either case, the worship of God should not be relegated to the status of "preliminaries" before the main event of the sermon.

The revelation of God and response through worship also should not be viewed as impractical. Fundamentally, the life of faith is a continuous discovery of God, our Creator and Redeemer. (1) Therefore, theological reflection and response are worthy pursuits because through them we explore the infinite character of our covenant partner and express our love to him.

(2) Such reflection and response are practical because of their influence on our attitudes and actions. Our comprehension and celebration of the character of our God will have a profound impact on our hope for the future and our response in the present. Increasing our grasp of revelation will mean pursuing opportunities to deepen our theological knowledge, whether in a formal learning environment like a seminary or in one of the many informal opportunities afforded by churches for discipleship. As leaders we must take seriously our role as teachers and facilitators of teaching within our local communities of faith. Zechariah 12:1 serves as an important gateway to the prophetic message that follows, a message that seeks to engender hope and stimulate obedience within the community of God.

Using all God's people. The fact that Yahweh is the subject of the verbs of action throughout 12:2–9 shows that future victory will be accomplished through his sovereign actions. But clearly human instruments are used in the hands of this sovereign God. Three entities in particular are highlighted: the house of David, the people of Jerusalem, and the house of

66. See J. Piper, *The Supremacy of God in Preaching* (Grand Rapids: Baker, 1990).

Judah. On a sociological level this text appears to be written from the perspective of the last entity and indicates some tension between the house of Judah and the other two groups. In all of this, however, there is no suggestion that the house of David and people of Jerusalem will be rejected; rather, the house of Judah will play a major part in God's victory over the nations.

On a theological level this evidence highlights a major theme within biblical theology. In the call of Abraham in Genesis 12, Yahweh expresses his desire to create a "nation." God's focus is not on the creation of covenant leaders but on the formation of covenant community. True, he does raise up leaders to foster community, but these leaders are not the focus; instead, it is the community defined by relationship with God.

Moses, for instance, was the first leader of this community, and the biblical accounts of the Exodus and desert wanderings focus much attention on this central figure. But even Moses hoped for a larger role for the people of God. In Numbers 11, after the Spirit that had rested on Moses was extended to the seventy elders, Moses declares: "I wish that all the LORD's people were prophets and that the LORD would put his Spirit on them!" (11:29).

Although royal leadership in Israel was part of God's plan for the nation, one of the dangers inherent in kingship was the accumulation of power within the monarchial family and limitation of communal participation. This balance between covenant leader and community is echoed in the New Testament. Christ comes as covenant leader, who secures victory for God's people and continues to lead this community at the right hand of the Father. But he has formed a covenant community on whom have fallen promises and responsibilities formerly exercised by Old Testament covenant figures. In Acts 2 Peter tells us that the prophetic office has been extended to all God's people. In 2 Corinthians 6:18 the promise to the Davidic royal line is now extended to the entire Christian community.

Zechariah 12:2–9 affirms an ongoing role for covenant leadership while asserting the full participation of the entire community. It is a warning to those who accentuate a split between clergy and laity in the church today. Surely the New Testament witness affirms the development of leadership within the church as well as the release of gifted individuals to focus their attention on various leadership roles. But these leaders need to define themselves in terms of the community that God indwells and uses to accomplish his purposes. Similarly, the community must not view their leaders as ministers but as equippers of a community of ministers.

This temptation is not unique to a certain size of church. I remember ministering in a church in the Canadian Maritimes during my college internship. One afternoon I spent a couple of hours reading past annual reports of the church. I noticed that during one period, the pastor's name appeared at the head of nearly every ministry (except the Women's Prayer Group). This struggling church had adopted a philosophy of ministry that excused the laity from ministry.

Large churches face similar challenges. The larger the church becomes, the larger the ministerial staff grows. The presence of a large professional staff in a church can lead to passivity on the lay level not only because of these deeper resources, but also because the quality of ministries increases dramatically, intimidating those without professional training. In addition, there is a tendency in large churches to concentrate decision-making in a small executive group. This may be efficient, but it will create unproductive disjuncture between leadership and community. Leaders must think creatively about ways to draw on the considerable resources of the community as a whole for the ministry of the church, and members of churches must take seriously their gifting and resist the temptation to abandon ministry to the professionals.

This "clericalization" of the church, however, is not only linked to patterns of those in vocational ministry. To sustain our modern urban lifestyle there seems to be an expectation that families have to maintain a sixty-hour or more work week, distributed between both spouses. With these kinds of demands, there is little time to devote to family, church, or community, which thus encourages passivity among the laity. Such economic realities have serious implications for spreading the gospel and force us to consider deeply our priorities and calling as Christians, even if that means adopting a simpler lifestyle that is countercultural.

Submitting to God in repentance. While 12:1–9 presents God's victory over the nations on behalf of his people, 12:10–13:6 focuses on the result of this victory and its implications for God's people. Whereas one might have expected 12:10–13:6 to present a victory march around his freed city for the victorious divine warrior, followed by a massive banquet feast in his honor, instead one finds mourning and weeping. This is clearly linked to the fact that the people rescued by God were a people who had rejected him.

In the contemporary church we know little of the message of 12:10–14 with its focus on God's work and a penitential depth of his people. In an era of "easy-believism," we preach a faith that requires intellectual acceptance of key tenets of doctrine rather than the transformation of our affections. At the same time we often preach a faith that becomes another human work, not a work of God on human hearts. We must teach the doctrine of deep repentance as God's work.

The kind of repentance encouraged in 12:10–14 is rooted in covenant relationship. The focus here is not on turning from a list of inappropriate behaviors but on mourning over our treatment of God through our rebellion. It is primarily a relational issue arising from our infidelity to God, a theme introduced at the beginning of Zechariah and captured in the simple cry of God through his prophet: "Return to me ... and I will return to you" (1:3).

Some theological streams within Christianity have emphasized the transcendence of God over his immanence and in the process have caricatured him as a distant God unaffected by the behavior of and indifferent to a relationship with his people. However, God's revelation in his Word and through his Son highlights his passion for relationship with us and his vulnerability when such relationship is thwarted. Hosea 11 provides a window into the tender love of God for his people, a people described as his dear child whom he sought to love, taught to walk, strove to heal, guided with kindness, released from slavery, and bent to feed (Hos. 11:2–4). The emotions of the divine heart release in 11:8–9 with the impassioned cry:

> How can I give you up, Ephraim?
> How can I hand you over, Israel?
> How can I treat you like Admah?
> How can I make you like Zeboiim?
> My heart is changed within me;
> all my compassion is aroused.
> I will not carry out my fierce anger,
> nor will I turn and devastate Ephraim.
> For I am God, and not man—
> the Holy One among you.
> I will not come in wrath.

This cry comes from the heart of the Transcendent One, the Creator of the universe, who has entered into vulnerable relationship with his people as a sovereign choice of his will. Such vulnerability demands response from his people, and Zechariah 12:10–14 guides us in this response by calling us to penitential mourning for our rejection of God in the past and present.

Furthermore, this penitential mourning is motivated and sustained by God's work. Within Christian traditions guilt is often used to motivate penitential response. But 12:10 declares that it is the Spirit "of grace and supplication" that stimulates such response. This means that it is an operation of God within the heart of his community, which in New Testament perspective means the work of the Holy Spirit within the life of believers. We do not conjure up this response to God; rather, it is his work. This is an important truth for preacher as well as hearer of the gospel, both of whom must rely on God for this divine work.

The emphasis on "grace" here matches the prominence of God's grace within the penitential traditions of the Old Testament.[67] Essential to the revelation of God in the Old Testament is the character creed encountered in Exodus 34:6–7:

> The LORD, the LORD, the compassionate and gracious God, slow to anger, abounding in love and faithfulness, maintaining love to thousands, and forgiving wickedness, rebellion and sin. Yet he does not leave the guilty unpunished; he punishes the children and their children for the sin of the fathers to the third and fourth generation.

This revelation of God's "glory ... goodness ... name" (Ex. 33:18–19) is one of the most intimate revelations of God's person and character in the Old Testament, one that is echoed throughout its history as an essential summary of Old Testament revelation and faith (cf. Num. 14:18; Neh. 9:17; Ps. 86:15; 103:8; 145:8; Joel 2:13; Jonah 4:2; Nah. 1:3; cf. 2 Chron. 30:9; Ps. 111:4). (1) What is instructive for our response to Zechariah 12 is the priority of position and proportion of emphasis on God's grace in this self-revelation. A review of the echoes of this revelation in the Old Testament shows that the more limited phrase "the compassionate and gracious God, slow to anger, abounding in love," focusing on his mercy, is the constant (Neh. 9:17; Ps. 86:15; 103:8; 145:8; Joel 2:13; Jonah 4:2), and sometimes only a portion of this more limited phrase is used (Num. 14:18; Ps. 111:4; Nah. 1:3).

(2) What is also instructive is the preponderance of these echoes in contexts dealing with the forgiveness of sin. This is true in the initial self-revelation that occurs in the aftermath of the famous golden calf rebellion in Exodus 32. Functioning as mediator between God and people, Moses cries out to God to forgive his people and remain with them. The foundation of the renewal of covenant between God and people (Ex. 34) is this self-revelation of God. This pattern is replicated throughout the Old Testament—as Moses pleads for forgiveness of a later rebellion in the desert (Num. 14:18–19), as David cries to God (Ps. 86:5, 15) and praises him for his forgiveness (Ps. 103:8), as Jonah observes the repentance of sinful Nineveh (Jonah 4), as Joel calls his generation to repentance (Joel 2:12–14), or as the priests reflect on God's forgiveness toward an earlier generation (Neh. 9:16–21).

This trend is displayed most poignantly within the penitential prayer tradition of the Persian period, which focuses attention on the faithful grace of the God who keeps covenant (Ezra 9:8–9, 13, 15; Neh. 1:10; 9:33, 35; Dan. 9:9, 13, 15, 17–18). This same focus on grace as a catalyst for penitence is echoed in the New Testament statement in Romans 2:4, "God's kindness

67. See Boda, "Priceless Gain," 51–75.

leads you toward repentance," and the assurance of 1 John 1:9, "if we confess our sins, he is faithful and just to forgive us our sins and cleanse us from all unrighteousness."

Thus, it is important not to miss the accent in Zechariah 12 and in the entire Scriptures on God's grace in contexts of forgiveness and repentance. Through his grace displayed in Christ on the cross and communicated to us through his gracious Spirit who indwells us and softens our hearts, we are called to respond in a depth of penitence.

Repentance played an important role at the outset of the Christian church. It was the message of John the Baptist as he prepared the way for Jesus. Christ also called his generation to repentance, as did the early church. The declaration of the gospel must thus include the call to repentance and must consider deeply the ways we have rejected God so that we can turn to embrace the living God. To the early church this was not additional to the call to faith in Christ; rather, it was inseparable from it (e.g., Acts 2:38; 3:19, 26).

Repentance is not restricted to this initial period but is necessary throughout our Christian journey. John stresses this in the letters to the churches in Revelation. These communities are challenged to repent of forsaking their first love (Rev. 2:4–5), endorsing false teaching (2:14–16), encouraging sexual immorality and idolatry (2:20–21), and displaying lukewarm devotion (3:15–19). These letters remind us of the need for rhythms of repentance throughout our lives as Christians, but do so always based on the revelation of grace in Jesus (1:5–6; cf. chs. 4–5).

Such rhythms should not be restricted to the individual Christian. One should not miss the communal dimension of the repentance described in Zechariah 12:10–14, where whole clans mourn together before God. Those of us who have grown up in the West with our individualistic approach to life often miss this. This passage envisions penitential communities, that is, communities that practice and foster the rhythms of penitence.

Although the communal penitential tradition was a reality throughout the history of Israel and Judah, the Babylonian destruction of Jerusalem provided greater impetus for its practice. It is clear that throughout the Babylonian exile and down to the time of Christ, the Jewish community regularly set apart time for communal expressions of penitence (Zech. 7–8). Nehemiah 9–10 offers some insights into the components of such a day:

1. gathering together apart from those outside the community (9:1–2)
2. fasting, wearing sackcloth, sprinkling dust on the head (9:1–2)
3. confession of sins of community, present and past (9:2, 3, 16–37)
4. reading from the Torah (9:3)
5. worshiping (9:3–15)

6. reviewing the story of redemption (9:6–31)
7. entering into covenant agreement (9:38–10:39)

Such a model is instructive for the church today as we take seriously penitential rhythms within our faith community. I know of at least one church that sets aside one week early in January as a time of sacred assembly. During this week all church events are cancelled and the people meet each evening to seek their God together as they begin their year. Some churches capitalize on the traditional season of Lent in the lead-up to Easter as a period to consider the message of repentance in a special way. These kinds of communal experiences are invitations to the community to live "penitentially" throughout the year.

Cleansing from sin. God's victory for his people, demonstrated in 12:1–9, leads to the penitential response of his people in 12:10–14. Then 13:1–6 opens with the refreshing picture of a cleansing fountain provided for a people dirtied by sin. God promises cleansing from the sin that stains our lives, consciences, relationships, and societies, disqualifying us from his holy presence. This promised fountain is fulfilled in and through Christ's redemptive work and the ongoing application of this work to our lives by the Holy Spirit.

Zechariah 13:1 affirms God's desire to cleanse his penitent people. Such a desire is echoed in the promise of 1 John 1:9: "If we confess our sins, he is faithful and just to forgive us our sins and cleanse us from all unrighteousness." So also in 1 Corinthians 6:11, after providing a list of those excluded from the kingdom of God, the apostle Paul declares: "And that is what some of you were. But you were washed, you were sanctified, you were justified in the name of the Lord Jesus Christ and by the Spirit of our God."

At the beginning of this same letter, Paul notes the dual character of this kind of cleansing sanctification when he writes: "To the church of God in Corinth, those sanctified in Christ Jesus and called to be holy" (1 Cor. 1:2). Through faith in Christ Jesus these believers were "sanctified" (past), and yet in the same breath Paul reminds them that they are "called to be holy" (future). In Christ we are cleansed and yet we are also in the process of being cleansed by the work of the Spirit.

The promise of cleansing in Zechariah 13:1 thus reminds us of God's provision for cleansing through Christ's death on the cross and of our need to embrace this provision through faith in him. But this cannot be separated from the ongoing process of cleansing so essential to our walk in the Spirit. We are cleansed, we are being cleansed, and we will be cleansed.

Renouncing idolatry. Zechariah 13:1–6 also reminds us of God's abhorrence of sin, in particular the sin of idolatry and its attendant divination.

So serious was God about such actions that capital punishment was required. While it is true that Western Christians are not often tempted to worship divine images, we must not forget that at the heart of idolatry is the pursuit of one's agenda apart from reliance on and submission to God. Even as the prohibition of idolatry endures in New Testament writings (1 Cor. 6:9; 10:7, 14; 12:12; Gal. 5:20; 1 Thess. 1:9; 1 Peter 4:3; 1 John 5:21; Rev. 9:20), one can discern a broader definition of idolatry in Paul's treatment of evil behavior:

> But among you there must not be even a hint of sexual immorality, or of any kind of impurity, or of greed, because these are improper for God's holy people. Nor should there be obscenity, foolish talk or coarse joking, which are out of place, but rather thanksgiving. For of this you can be sure: No immoral, impure or greedy person—*such a man is an idolater*—has any inheritance in the kingdom of Christ and of God. (Eph. 5:3–5, italics added)

> Put to death, therefore, whatever belongs to your earthly nature: sexual immorality, impurity, lust, evil desires and greed, *which is idolatry*. (Col. 3:5, italics added)

Our idols may take different forms, such as hedonism, materialism, or domination, but they are as idolatrous as ancient forms. In light of the seriousness with which God treats idolatry in the Old Testament as well as the New, we need to examine our lives and seek the cleansing waters and motivating Spirit of God to live righteously as his people.

Zechariah 12:1–13:6 has emphasized God's passion to remove sin from his people and reminds us of the importance of penitential rhythms in our lives. The deceptive nature of sin can be illustrated by the following story that radio personality Paul Harvey once told on his show, in which he vividly describes the method of the sly Eskimo seeking to kill an Arctic wolf.

First, the Eskimo coats his knife blade with animal blood and allows it to freeze. Then he adds another layer of blood, and another, until the blade is completely concealed by frozen blood. Next, the hunter fixes his knife in the ground with the blade up. When a wolf follows his sensitive nose to the source of the scent and discovers the bait, he licks it, tasting the fresh frozen blood. He begins to lick faster, more and more vigorously, lapping the blade until the keen edge is bare. Feverishly now, harder and harder the wolf licks the blade in the Arctic night. So great becomes the craving for blood that the wolf does not notice the razor sharp sting of the naked blade on his own tongue, nor does he recognize the instant at which his insatiable thirst is being satisfied by his own warm blood. His carnivorous appetite just craves more until the dawn finds him dead in the snow![68]

This applies to our world today with its enticing message of lifestyles that are sure to satisfy. Promised as paths of "life," they end in disappointment, despair, and even death. There are many pursuits that can be mentioned within our present culture. One is the hedonistic pursuit of pleasure through sex, food, and drugs that has left our society physically and emotionally scarred. Another is the relentless pursuit of amusement through entertainment and travel, which Neil Postman has succinctly described as "amusing ourselves to death."[69] Still another is the materialistic pursuit of things, the latest technology, clothes, cars, and homes that insulates us for a time from the realities of the world around us and the Spirit that indwells us. Finally, there is the arrogant pursuit of power, the ability to heartlessly knock off all those in line in front of us so that we can advance in status in this world. These are but a sampling of those sinful pursuits that ultimately will destroy us not only as individuals but also as a culture.

God came through Christ to give us life, not death, and Zechariah 12:1–13:6 reminds us not only of the life-giving work of Jesus for us and in us, but also of God's design to enliven us by his Spirit. Walking in step with this Spirit of life is truly a matter of life and death.

---

68. C. Swindoll, *The Tale of the Tardy Oxcart And 1,501 Other Stories* (Nashville: Word, 1998), 565.

69. N. Postman, *Amusing Ourselves to Death: Public Discourse in the Age of Show Business* (New York: Penguin, 1986).

Zechariah 13:7–9

AWAKE, O SWORD, against my shepherd,
against the man who is close to me!"
declares the LORD Almighty.
"Strike the shepherd,
and the sheep will be scattered,
and I will turn my hand against the little ones.
8In the whole land," declares the LORD,
"two-thirds will be struck down and perish;
yet one-third will be left in it.
9This third I will bring into the fire;
I will refine them like silver
and test them like gold.
They will call on my name
and I will answer them;
I will say, 'They are my people,'
and they will say, 'The LORD is our God.'"

Original Meaning

THERE IS LITTLE QUESTION about striking similarities between 11:4–17 and 13:7–9. Both use shepherd imagery, refer to a sword striking the shepherd, allude to smelting, and use covenant concepts.[1] Based on this, some have treated 13:7–9 as a unit displaced from its original position at the end of Zechariah 9–11.[2] This, however, displays insensitivity to the role played by this short unit in chapters 9–14 as a whole and chapters 12–14 in particular. (1) Those shaping the final form of Zechariah 9–14 saw 13:7–9 with its focus on shepherding as the final installment of a series of short redactional seams that reminded the community of the crisis in leadership.

(2) Zechariah 13:7–9 is intimately related to the surrounding sections.[3] The consistent mention of the house of David in 12:1–13:1 indicates that

1. Mason, "Use," 129–30.

2. See Mitchell, Smith, and Brewer, *Haggai*, 316–17; Hanson, *Dawn*, 368–69.

3. See, e.g., Plöger, who points out how vv. 7–9 acts as development on vv. 1–6 and transition to ch. 14; O. Plöger, *Theocracy and Eschatology*, trans. S. Rudman (Oxford: Blackwell,

leadership is a key concern of those responsible for this piece. Furthermore, the closing section (13:2–6), which cannot be separated from 12:1–13:1, identifies idolatry-false prophecy as a key problem, the same problem identified in the earlier shepherd transition in 10:1–3. Also 13:7–9 foreshadows the remnant theme, which will be taken up in 14:2. This evidence thus allows for the connection of 13:7–9 to chapters 9–11 without ripping it out of its present literary position.

This short piece begins with an appeal to the "sword." The sword is a regular metaphor in prophetic literature, an image of death and judgment (Isa. 34:5–6; Ezek. 5:1). In Jeremiah 47:6 and Ezekiel 21:16, as in Zechariah 13:7, the sword is addressed directly—in the former by humans, in the latter by God. The phrase "awake ... against" is used for wielding a weapon in battle (2 Sam. 23:18) as well as for raising up an army against a nation (Isa. 13:17; Jer. 50:9).[4] The fact that this imperative is directed at a weapon ("sword") suggests the first sense. However, one cannot completely discount the second sense since the sword is personified. In either case, this shepherd is doomed, for the awaking is only the first of two imperatives directed to this sword. The second is devastating for the shepherd—the sword is instructed to "strike."[5]

This shepherd is called "my shepherd" and "the man who is close to me." The phrase "who is close" translates the Hebrew term *ᶜamit*, used elsewhere only in Leviticus, where it refers to one's neighbor, friend, or fellow citizen (Lev. 6:2; 18:20; 19:11, 15, 17; 24:19; 25:14, 15, 17). In a surprising twist, both phrases use the possessive pronoun "my," emphasizing the close association between the Lord and the one who is struck by the sword.

Because the image of the sword is connected with God's judgment, this Shepherd is apparently someone who is struck as a result of some offense. This is not surprising in light of the many negative depictions of shepherds elsewhere in Zechariah 9–14. However, precise identification of this shepherd is difficult to attain.

The phrase "my shepherd" is used of leadership on two other occasions in the Old Testament (cf. Zech. 11:17). In Isaiah 44:28 it refers to Cyrus, whom God raised up to accomplish his purposes. Ezekiel 34:8 contains a reference to "my shepherds," as the prophet attacks the leadership of his day.

1968), 87. Baldwin and Petersen integrate vv. 7–9 into chs. 12–14 to the point that 13:7–9 serves as a further elaboration of 12:1–13:6; Baldwin, *Haggai*, 197; Petersen, *Zechariah 9–14*, 129.

4. The root is the same in each passage, but the stem is different: 2 Sam. 23:18 (Polel); Isa. 13:17 and Jer. 50:9 (Hiphil), Zech. 13:7 (Qal). But Joel 3:9 does show that the Qal can be used in the same way as the Hiphil.

5. See 2 Sam. 23:18: "raised ... killed"; Isa. 13:17–18: "stir up ... strike down"; cf. Jer. 50:9–10.

In light of the close relationship between Zechariah 13:7–9 and 11:4–16 where, because of clear reliance on Ezekiel 34 and 37, evil shepherds were identified as non-Davidic leadership in Yehud, the shepherd may be a reference to a leadership figure within this group. This seems true also for the woe oracle against the shepherd in Zechariah 11:17.

Because of the loss of the shepherd, the flock will be scattered, the expected result of a flock without leadership (1 Kings 22:17//2 Chron. 18:16; Ezek. 34:5, 6, 12, 21). This scattering leaves the "little ones" (cf. Jer. 49:20; 50:45)[6] vulnerable to attack. The attack comes from God, who turns his hand against them, a phrase used elsewhere to refer to his judgment (Ps. 81:14; Isa. 1:25; Ezek. 38:12; Amos 1:8). The reference in Isaiah 1:25 is significant because there one finds a reference also to "refining," as in Zechariah 13:7–9. This indicates that God will discipline the flock ("little ones") in order to purify them.

The process of purification is described in verses 8–9 as the community is divided into thirds (cf. Ezek. 5, where the prophet's hair is divided into thirds, with a third burnt [representing those who die of the plague or perish by famine inside the city], a third struck with the sword [representing those who fall by the sword outside the city], and a third scattered to the wind [representing those exiled]). Both passages reveal that the majority of the flock will be eliminated from the outset as two-thirds "will be struck down and perish."

The final third in both cases survives but then undergoes further discipline. In Ezekiel 5 a sword pursues this final third. In Zechariah 13:9, this final third is refined, using terminology drawn from the practice of metallurgy, a common image in prophetic literature (e.g., Isa. 1:25; Jer. 6:27–30; Ezek. 22:18–22). The process involves the powerful agent of "fire," which will "refine ... and test" (Ps. 17:3; 26:2; 66:10; Jer. 9:7) as "silver" and "gold." Such a process removes the impurities from deposits containing these precious metals.

The second half of Zechariah 13:9 reveals the result of this refining process. The covenant relationship between God and his people will be restored. Calling on God's name is used for several types of interchange between God and his people, including sacrifice (Gen. 12:8; 13:4; Ps. 116:17; cf. Gen. 21:33), thanksgiving (1 Chron. 16:8; Ps. 80:18; 105:1), and petition (1 Kings 18:24–26), but also for general seeking of God (Gen. 4:26; Ps. 99:6; Joel 3:5; Zeph. 3:9; cf. Ps. 79:6). Having been refined by God, they will now seek him, and to this people God promises to respond. He will declare them

---

6. The word in Jer. 49:20; 50:45 is a noun of the same root as the participle here in Zech. 13:7. When the verb appears elsewhere, it refers to becoming insignificant (Job 14:21, "brought low"; Jer. 30:19, "disdained").

"my people" while they affirm that he is "our God."[7] These declarations echo covenantal declarations throughout the history of Israel (Jer. 24:7; 31:33; 32:38; Ezek. 11:20; 14:11; 34:30; 37:23, 27; Hos. 1:9; 2:23; Zech. 8:8).

Bridging Contexts

THIS SECTION IS the final installment in a series of intervening pieces that set the future prophecies of hope (9:1–17; 10:4–12; 12:1–13:6; 14:1–21) against a backdrop of crisis in leadership in Persian period Yehud (10:1–3; 11:1–3; 11:17; 13:7–9). These pieces have become increasingly violent—at first threatening God's punishment for the shepherds (10:3), then envisioning the destruction of their pastures (11:3), then calling for serious injury against the shepherd (11:17), and now advocating a fatal injury (13:7).

The precise identity of the shepherd(s) is difficult to ascertain. It is hard to imagine that this refers to the Zadokite priesthood who controlled the temple in Jerusalem because of the connection to idolatry in 10:1–3.[8] Most likely this refers to political leadership, namely, Jews who ruled Yehud under Persian authority and who may have assumed aspects of Persian religion that compromised Yahwistic faith.

It is important that the New Testament uses 13:7 to interpret the death of Christ and its effect on the disciples, especially Peter's denial of Jesus (Matt. 26:31; Mark 14:27; cf. John 16:32). One can conclude that Jesus was merely using Zechariah 13:7 as an illustration of a principle, that when a leader (shepherd) is struck down, it has an effect on the followers (sheep). But in light of the way that Zechariah 9–14 is used to shape the narrative of Christ's passion in the Gospels (see commentary introduction, Bridging Contexts section), it is more likely that Christ saw his death and the disciples' scattering as a fulfillment of the expectations of Zechariah 9–14. The difficulty with this conclusion, however, is that it places Jesus into the role of the inappropriate leadership that led Yehud astray.

But this need not cause difficulty for Christian interpreters. Just as Christ assumed the role of the covenant community, walking in obedience before taking on himself their sins, so here Christ assumes the role of the covenant leader of this community, leading as a good shepherd before taking on

---

7. In the Heb. text this section is cast in the third-person singular rather than plural, as in NIV: "He will call on my name and I will answer him; I will say, 'He is my people,' and he will say, 'The LORD is my God.'" Obviously the statement "he is my people" shows that this singular form signifies the voice of the people as a whole.

8. In Ezek. 44:10–16 Ezekiel contrasts the "Levites" in general with the Levitical Zadokite clan. What disqualified the non-Zadokite clans was syncretistic behavior.

himself their sins and redeeming the community and its leadership. The surprising twist in the New Testament rereading of Zechariah 9–14 is that the good shepherd of 11:4–16, rejected by his people in favor of a bad shepherd, takes the punishment of the bad shepherd in order to achieve the transformation expected throughout chapters 9–14, that is, the creation of a restored, united, and victorious Israel as the center of God's rule over the cosmos.

This transformation is not only linked to the work of Jesus, who bore the brunt of divine punishment through the sword of Rome, but also to the reaction of the disciples. Zechariah 13:7–9 depicts a new "exile," the scattering and subsequent slaughter of the sheep to create a remnant that will be refined and ultimately enter into covenant relationship with God. In rereading 13:7–9, the Gospels not only cite the striking of the shepherd but also the scattering of the sheep. This shows us that the scattering of the disciples after the arrest of Jesus is identified by Christ and the Gospel writers as a reenactment of the Exile of Israel.

According to Christ's comment following the citation of Zechariah 13:7–9, the gathering of the remnant is connected somehow to Galilee: "But after I have risen, I will go ahead of you into Galilee" (Matt. 26:32; cf. Mark 14:28). This gathering in Galilee is described in the final paragraph of the Gospel of Matthew as the disciples meet and worship Jesus on "the mountain where Jesus had told them to go" (cf. Matt. 28:7, 10; Mark 16:7), where they receive his commission to "go and make disciples of all nations" (Matt. 28:16–20). The remnant community is identified as the disciples of Jesus, an identification echoed in Acts, where the remnant community are the followers of Jesus filled with God's Spirit on the day of Pentecost (Acts 2).

On the one hand, in Christian perspective 13:7–9 reminds us of the role of Jesus as leader of his people, who received God's judgment and inaugurated a final exile that would produce a new community. As Christians we celebrate the Christ event and the creation of the remnant community in his followers.

On the other hand, however, the New Testament shows us that the creation of this remnant community is an enduring project as we live as exiles in this world and continue to see people enter into this community. This approach can be discerned in the teaching of the latter part of John, a section that also contains an allusion to Zechariah 13:7–9 (John 16:32). This section, immediately preceding the arrest and crucifixion of Jesus, prepares the way for life after Christ's death and resurrection. In his prayer of John 17 that follows almost immediately, Jesus prays for God's care for his disciples through the approaching darkness. This prayer, however, is uttered not only for the disciples but also "for those who will believe in me through their message" (John 17:20), showing that the experience of the disciples following Christ's death, as a remnant community scattered and gathered, will be the enduring experience of the remnant community that is formed by and through their teaching throughout the ages.

In light of this, the themes of 13:7–9, so essential in the formation of the early Christian community, endure as themes for the church, not only as we celebrate the foundational events of Christ's death and his community's creation, but also as we seek to live in faithfulness to him.

Contemporary Significance

THROUGH 13:7–9 WE observe, with the early church, the redemptive work of Jesus, who suffered as covenant leader to create a remnant community. With the early church, then, we celebrate this act of sacrifice on our behalf. But we also are attentive to the way in which 13:7–9 shapes the experience of the church today, considering the church is the enduring fulfillment of the hopes of this prophetic message. In the following section we will focus on two key themes that define the remnant community in this passage.

Refining. A key theme throughout biblical theology is that of the remnant, namely, that from sinful humanity God forms a holy community.[9] The basic trajectory of this activity is set in the early chapters of Genesis. From thoroughly sinful humanity (Gen. 6:5), God sets apart one family as a remnant (9:1–17) and establishes covenant with them. Similarly, from the clan of Shem, God again sets apart one family, that of Abraham and Sarah (12:1–7) and establishes covenant with them (chs. 15; 17). Although this family grows into a blessed and powerful nation (Israel), it also falls into sin and ultimately is disciplined by God through exile (2 Kings 17).

The Law and the Prophets teach that God's design is not the eradication of Israel; rather, it is the purification of his people. For instance, Leviticus 26:14–46 describes the curses that will fall on Israel when they break covenant with their God. These curses are designed to turn Israel to their God. Ultimately, this list envisions a scattering among the nations, but this exile is not an end in itself. Rather, God does this in order that his people may repent and confess their sins (26:40–45). Similarly, the prophet Isaiah, after experiencing God's holy presence, receives his prophetic commission. Central to it is the theology of the remnant, filled out in answer to Isaiah's question, "For

9. G. F. Hasel, *The Remnant: The History and Theology of the Remnant Idea from Genesis to Isaiah*, 3d ed. (AUMSR 5; Berrien Springs, Mich.: Andrews Univ. Press, 1980); L. Ryken, J. C. Wilhoit, and T. Longman, "Remnant," in *Dictionary of Biblical Imagery* (Downers Grove, Ill.: InterVarsity Press, 1998), 703–4.

how long, O Lord?" God says that after "a tenth remains in the land," even this group will be purified further until there is only "the holy seed" (Isa. 6:11–13). A key to the biblical theology of remnant is the purification of God's people.

In the New Testament Jesus is presented as the remnant of Israel, the embodiment of the nation (see Matt. 2:15; Gal. 3:16), as well as the remnant of the Davidic line (Matt. 1:1–17). His death is the ultimate expression of exile at the hands of foreign nations. In his death he takes on himself the punishment of his clan and nation. But we also enter into this same exilic experience, called by Christ to take up our cross daily to follow him (Mark 8:34). In this we see the enduring character of this theme as the church undergoes refining through suffering. The New Testament stresses this theme both through example and exhortation. To follow Christ will mean suffering, and such suffering is to refine us (Heb. 12; 1 Peter 2:20–25; 4:1–6).

It has often been easy for the church to embrace a remnant theology that ultimately distances itself from any danger of suffering and refinement. Remnant theology can become an excuse for creating Christian enclaves that provide a measure of insulation from surrounding secularism. But such insulation can frustrate the purpose of the remnant agenda. God desires to refine his people through suffering, and this will mean living in "detached attachment" to the surrounding culture—in other words, as Christ teaches, to be in the world and yet not of it (John 17). This will mean fully entering into our community as Christ entered into his, something that brought God with us and yet ultimately meant God crucified. It will mean that as we face opposition and pain, we should reflect deeply on how God is refining us and look to the One who endured so much suffering on our behalf and through it "learned obedience" (Heb. 5:8).

The gospel challenges the Western church's penchant for the health and wealth gospel. In the New Testament account, when people devote their lives to Christ, they are greeted more often with suffering rather than success. We should not be surprised, then, at suffering but rather embrace it as part of God's purification of his remnant community (Rom. 8:18–39; 1 Peter 4:17).

Relationship. In 13:7–9, the purpose of this refining is clearly covenantal, as we hear the commitments of both parties to one another: "They are my people.... The LORD is our God" (13:9). The covenant language of this verse weaves its way like a scarlet thread throughout the fabric of Old and New Testaments.[10]

Covenant language is first encountered near the end of the account of the Flood. In Genesis 9, God establishes a covenant with Noah in words

10. See, W. J. Dumbrell, *Covenant and Creation: A Theology of the Old Testament Covenants* (Nashville: Nelson, 1984).

reminiscent of the initial commission to humanity in Genesis 1.[11] God establishes a redemptive covenant with Abraham in Genesis 15 and 17, promising land, descendants, and relationship with his family.[12] At Mount Sinai this promised relationship with the nation is ratified again through covenant as Israel is about to enter the Promised Land (Ex. 19–20; Deut. 5–6). Finally, God establishes covenant with David as covenant leader of Israel (2 Sam. 7).

These various covenants are all based on God's grace and reflect his desire for a relationship with his people. When Israel broke the terms of the Sinai covenant, God reveals his plan for a "new covenant" (Jer. 31:31–34), confirming his enduring passion for relationship.[13] This new covenant is fulfilled in and through Christ's death and resurrection, and by the Spirit we are empowered to fulfill covenant demands as well as enjoy relationship with Yahweh.

This review reminds us that ultimately the Christian life is about relationship with God, a relationship that has several key characteristics. (1) This relationship is intimate and personal. Parallel to the covenant declaration in 13:9 is God's promise that "they will call on my name and I will answer them." To be in relationship with God through Christ grants us the privilege of access to him. We can cry to him in the midst of our distress, and he promises to answer.

(2) This relationship is exclusive; it involves fidelity to God's covenant demands. Israel's struggle was that it loved the privileges of this relationship but rejected the responsibilities. In Christ we have the resource of the Spirit, who empowers to fulfill God's covenant demands.

(3) This relationship is communal; that is, covenant is never seen as something between me and God, but always between us and God: "They are my *people*. . . . The LORD is *our* God." The early church viewed their lives in these terms. After being released from prison, Peter and John returned immediately to the believing community to report their experiences and join together in prayer (Acts 4). This was never a "me and God" religion; rather, it was "us and God."

The relational destination of 13:7–9 reminds us that the refining process has this as its goal. It is this that comforts us in trials and tribulations. Such challenges are intricately related to our relationship with a loving almighty God, who desires to reform his image within us.

---

11. After the fall of humanity, covenant is necessary to structure the relationship between God and humanity.

12. See D. J. A. Clines, *The Theme of the Pentateuch* (JSOTSup 10; Sheffield: Sheffield Academic Press, 1978).

13. Notice also Jer. 33:14–26, which shows the enduring nature of the Davidic covenant.

Zechariah 14

A DAY OF the LORD is coming when your plunder will be divided among you.

2I will gather all the nations to Jerusalem to fight against it; the city will be captured, the houses ransacked, and the women raped. Half of the city will go into exile, but the rest of the people will not be taken from the city.

3Then the LORD will go out and fight against those nations, as he fights in the day of battle. 4On that day his feet will stand on the Mount of Olives, east of Jerusalem, and the Mount of Olives will be split in two from east to west, forming a great valley, with half of the mountain moving north and half moving south. 5You will flee by my mountain valley, for it will extend to Azel. You will flee as you fled from the earthquake in the days of Uzziah king of Judah. Then the LORD my God will come, and all the holy ones with him.

6On that day there will be no light, no cold or frost. 7It will be a unique day, without daytime or nighttime—a day known to the LORD. When evening comes, there will be light.

8On that day living water will flow out from Jerusalem, half to the eastern sea and half to the western sea, in summer and in winter.

9The LORD will be king over the whole earth. On that day there will be one LORD, and his name the only name.

10The whole land, from Geba to Rimmon, south of Jerusalem, will become like the Arabah. But Jerusalem will be raised up and remain in its place, from the Benjamin Gate to the site of the First Gate, to the Corner Gate, and from the Tower of Hananel to the royal winepresses. 11It will be inhabited; never again will it be destroyed. Jerusalem will be secure.

12This is the plague with which the LORD will strike all the nations that fought against Jerusalem: Their flesh will rot while they are still standing on their feet, their eyes will rot in their sockets, and their tongues will rot in their mouths. 13On that day men will be stricken by the LORD with great panic. Each man will seize the hand of another, and they will attack each other. 14Judah too will fight at Jerusalem. The wealth of

all the surrounding nations will be collected—great quantities
of gold and silver and clothing. [15]A similar plague will strike
the horses and mules, the camels and donkeys, and all the ani-
mals in those camps.
[16]Then the survivors from all the nations that have attacked
Jerusalem will go up year after year to worship the King, the
LORD Almighty, and to celebrate the Feast of Tabernacles. [17]If
any of the peoples of the earth do not go up to Jerusalem to
worship the King, the LORD Almighty, they will have no rain.
[18]If the Egyptian people do not go up and take part, they will
have no rain. The LORD will bring on them the plague he
inflicts on the nations that do not go up to celebrate the Feast
of Tabernacles. [19]This will be the punishment of Egypt and
the punishment of all the nations that do not go up to cele-
brate the Feast of Tabernacles.
[20]On that day HOLY TO THE LORD will be inscribed on the
bells of the horses, and the cooking pots in the LORD's house
will be like the sacred bowls in front of the altar. [21]Every pot
in Jerusalem and Judah will be holy to the LORD Almighty, and
all who come to sacrifice will take some of the pots and cook
in them. And on that day there will no longer be a Canaanite
in the house of the LORD Almighty.

Original Meaning

IN OUR INTRODUCTION, we presented affinities between 12:1–13:6 and 14:1–21 while remaining sensitive to their distinctive character. There we argued that these are two depictions of the future renewal necessary to see God's community fully realize the potential presented in chapters 7–8 as well as chapters 9–10, in light of the disappointing response of people and leadership as presented in the shepherd pieces in 10:1–3a; 11:1–3, 4–16, 17; and 13:7–9.[1]

As we now approach chapter 14 in detail, we must admit that grasping the structure of this fascinating passage has always been a challenge. Some have sought to explain the divergent elements by using the tools of form criticism and its focus on genre,[2] redaction and tradition criticism and its focus

1. See Boda, "Reading," 277–91.

2. Hanson sees here "the most advanced example of apocalyptic" and traces the structure of the ancient conflict myth on ch. 14: Threat (vv. 1–2), conflict and victory (v. 3), theophany and procession (vv. 4–5), peace (vv. 6–8), manifestation of Yahweh's universal reign (vv. 9–11), covenant curses (vv. 12–15), procession of the nations (vv. 16–19), sacrifice and banquet (vv. 20–21); Hanson, *Dawn*, 372; see also Schellenberg, "One," 111–13.

on additions and revision,[3] rhetorical criticism and its focus on structural markers ("on that day"),[4] "narrative" flow,[5] or chiastic design.[6] Some have abandoned this search for structural unity, describing the chapter as a montage or loose thematic collection.[7]

Although our work on the text must ultimately deal with its final form, one cannot ignore the evidence that this text has undergone some form of revision prior to its inclusion in the book of Zechariah.[8] At a couple of points in 14:1–21 one can discern an awkward flow. (1) Although the focus of the chapter is on Jerusalem and its inhabitants, one finds an odd interjection at 14:14a—"Judah too will fight at Jerusalem"—in the midst of a section that features God's gaining victory alone over the nations on behalf of Jerusalem.[9] (2) Although parts of this chapter are addressed directly to a feminine singular party "you" (14:1, "among you"; 14:5b, "with [you]"),[10] 14:5a twice addresses a plural masculine party "you" ("you will flee"). These features may reflect a complicated editorial history of the text that we now possess. They suggest that this chapter was originally focused on Jerusalem (feminine singular) but was expanded by later hands to include the inhabitants of the entire province (masculine plural) as well.[11]

By contrast P. L. Redditt, "Zechariah 9–14, Malachi, and the Redaction of the Book of the Twelve," in *Forming Prophetic Literature: Essays on Isaiah and the Twelve in Honor of John D. W. Watts*, ed. J. W. Watts and P. R. House (JSOTSup 235; Sheffield: Sheffield Academic Press, 1996), 137, and Floyd, *Minor Prophets*, 557, see here a prophecy of salvation; cf. C. Westermann, *Prophetic Oracles of Salvation in the Old Testament* (Louisville: Westminster John Knox, 1991), 195–96, 211–12.

3. Witt, for instance, suggests three stages: Stage 1 (vv. 1–11, pessimistic, conflict with cultic leadership in Jerusalem), Stage 2 (vv. 2b, 3ab, 12–15, more positive view of Jerusalem, cult, and leadership), Stage 3 (vv. 16–21, enlarge theme of holiness, round off unit): "In this final form of chapter 14, the focus has completely shifted from an extreme polemic attack against Jerusalem to an affirmation of the cleansing and renewing action of Yahweh to be anticipated at the end of history"; Witt, "Zechariah 12–14", 93–94.

4. Clark, "Skeleton," 64–80.

5. Floyd, *Minor Prophets*, 544 (see vv. 1–5, 6–7, 8–12, 13–21).

6. See LaMarche for his view on 14:1–15: a = vv. 1–2a; b = vv. 2a–b; c = vv. 3–5; d = v. 6; e = v. 7a; d' = vv. 7b–8; c' = vv. 9–10a; b' = vv. 10b–11; a' = vv. 12–15; LaMarche, *Zacharie IX–XIV*, 11.

7. Petersen identifies ten vignettes in his montage (vv. 1–3, 4–5, 6–7, 8, 9, 10–11, 12+15, 13–14, 16–19, 20–21); Petersen, *Zechariah 9–14*, 137–39. Saebø tags it as *sui generis* (unique); Saebø, *Sacharja 9–14*, 66, 282, 307–9; cf. Witt, "Zechariah 12–14," 65.

8. This comment does not allow the interpreter to discredit the later canonical form in favor of an earlier oral or written kernel.

9. Notice the striking similarity to the awkward interjection at 12:2.

10. See below for the discussion of the final phrase of 14:5, "with him," which reads in the Heb. text, "with you."

11. In this it is similar to 12:2–13:6.

Despite these subtle indications of redactional activity, the final text does preserve a basic overall structure. This structure does not appear to be dependent on the phrase "on that day" in the same way as 12:2–13:6. The passage begins in 14:1–2 with a depiction of God's discipline of Jerusalem through the nations. Verse 3 signals a transition in God's discipline as he turns around and fights against the nations. Verses 4–15 disclose the specifics of this discipline of the nations, revealing God's appearance and entrance into his royal city (vv. 4–11) followed by his awful punishment of the nations (vv. 12–15). The defeat of the nations leads to their submission to this cosmic king, demonstrated in their yearly pilgrimage to Jerusalem for the Feast of Tabernacles (vv. 16–19). Both this royal city (Jerusalem) and its surrounding territory (Judah) are transformed by the presence of Yahweh assuming the holy character of their king (vv. 20–21).

Although this chapter is difficult to place historically, indications from other sections of chapters 9–14 suggest the late sixth century to the mid–fifth century B.C. (possibly as early as the period following the end of Zerubbabel's tenure in ca. 510 B.C. until the tenure of Nehemiah after 445 B.C.). The province of Yehud lived in the midst of the turmoil of the Greco-Persian wars as Darius I (from 513 B.C. on) and then his son Xerxes (486–465 B.C.) and grandson Artaxerxes (465–424 B.C.) sought to extend Persian hegemony into the European continent. Persia's earlier lax political control over the internal affairs of the provinces was tightened as "military garrisons were stationed along strategic routes and in the major cities."[12]

Evidence from Ezra 2–6 reveals consistent challenges for Jews and their leaders in Yehud from the time of Cyrus until Artaxerxes, many times with appeals going directly to the emperor (4:5, 6, 8, 23, 24; 5:6; 6:14). Leaders in Jerusalem would have capitulated to these new Persian initiatives, dashing any nationalistic hope for the residents of Yehud.

Judgment on Jerusalem (14:1–2)

AS IN 12:2, so 14:1 begins with the Hebrew word *hinneh* ("behold," untranslated in NIV), introducing the second major section of chapters 12–14. The phrase "a day of the LORD is coming" emphasizes the doom about to strike the city (Joel 1:15; 2:1).[13]

The description of the day as one "when your plunder will be divided among you" does not announce victory for Israel, because in every other

12. Meyers and Meyers, "Future Fortunes," 222.

13. Mason notes that close similarities between Joel and Zech. 14 (similarities in vocabulary and style as well as content of the day of Yahweh, threat against Jerusalem, the phrase "Lord my God") "suggest that they may have originated in circles which showed at least some aspects in common"; Mason, "Use," 174–75.

case in which this form of the verb "divided" occurs (Pual), possessions of the person addressed are distributed to others (Isa. 33:23; Amos 7:17).[14] Thus, Zechariah 14:1 is an apt foreshadowing of the traumatic events described in 14:2.

These events are traced to the action of Yahweh, who will "gather all the nations to Jerusalem" (cf. Zeph. 3:8). No reason is offered for the fact of this action, but one must assume that it is linked to the misdeeds of the people in the city. The incidents described are typical in the capture of a city whose male population has been lost as possessions are confiscated (Isa. 13:16; cf. Judg. 2:14; 1 Sam. 17:53; Jer. 30:16) and women are molested (Isa. 13:16). Connections between Zechariah 14 and Isaiah 13 suggest that the prophet is identifying Jerusalem with its former enemy Babylon.[15] In the end half the inhabitants of the city are taken off into exile while a remnant is left behind in the city.[16]

Appearance of Yahweh (14:3–5)

WHILE 14:1–2 ENVISION DISASTER for Jerusalem and its inhabitants, 14:3 signals a reversal of fortunes for the city as the Lord marches out against the same nations that he previously sent against Jerusalem.[17] He enters the fray as one who "fights on the day of battle" (Job 38:23; Ps. 78:9), but creation's violent response reveals that he is no ordinary adversary.[18]

Theophanies (or divine appearings) of Yahweh throughout the Old Testament are often associated with mountains, whether that is Mount Sinai (Ex. 19:18; Deut. 33:1–5) or Mount Zion (Ps. 50:2–3). This appearance on the Mount of Olives, a strip of hills across the Kidron Valley from Jerusalem and its temple, is unique and may be related to Ezekiel's vision of God's abandonment of and return to Jerusalem via the same route (Ezek. 11:23; 43:1–5).[19]

---

14. Notice Amos 7:17 ("your land") has, as Zech. 14:1, the construction "your xxx" to signify the plundered possession; cf. K. R. Schaefer, "The Ending of the Book of Zechariah: A Commentary," *RB* 100 (1993): 171.

15. Witt, "Zechariah 12–14", 78; K. R. Schaefer, "Zechariah 14: A Study in Allusion," *CBQ* 57 (1995): 68.

16. The differences between the percentages in 13:7–9 and 14:2 should not be magnified. Both refer to significant discipline for the people.

17. When the Heb. preposition *b* (NIV "against") follows the verb "fight" (*laḥam*) in the Heb. Bible, it usually denotes the opponent (Ex. 1:10; 14:25; 17:9; Num. 21:1, 23, 26; Judg. 1:3, 5, 8, 9; etc.). However, it can also denote the location of the battle (1 Kings 20:25; 2 Chron. 35:22) or the means of defeat (Jer. 21:5, "with an outstretched hand").

18. There is no need to separate vv. 4–5 from vv. 1–3 because the focus in vv. 4–5 is on theophany rather than battle (so Petersen, *Zechariah 9–14*, 142). Theophany is an important aspect of divine warrior scenes. For the effect of the divine warrior on creation, see Miller, *The Divine Warrior*, 140–41.

19. Mason, "Use," 176–78.

Ezekiel links God's abandonment to the idolatrous behavior of his generation (8:5–18), a connection that may explain the reference to "east of Jerusalem," the site of much idolatry throughout the history of Israel (1 Kings 11:7; 2 Kings 23:13).[20]

God's descent on the Mount of Olives wreaks havoc in the natural order. His appearance causes an earthquake (Mic. 1:3–5; Hab. 3:3–10), splitting in two the line of hills running north-south along the eastern edge of Jerusalem and creating a great east-west chasm that extends to "Azel." There has been much speculation about the location of Azel, a name found only here in the Old Testament. Suggestions have ranged from changing the text to reflect a known location such as the town "Beth Ezel" (Mic. 1:11) or the Kidron tributary Wadi Yasoul,[21] or changing the text to suggest a nonspecific location such as "the side of it" (the eastern extent of the valley)[22] or "the ends [of the earth or Israel]" (Isa. 41:9). All one can conclude is that this valley would extend toward the east.

This newly created valley will serve two purposes. (1) It will be an escape route for those who have remained behind in Jerusalem. East was the direction for a quick escape from the city in times of siege, as demonstrated by David in 2 Samuel 15:16, 23, 30 and Zedekiah in 2 Kings 25:4.[23] The earthquake in the days of King Uzziah is documented in Amos 1:1–2, an event linked by this prophet to the activity of God (1:2; 6:11; 8:8; 9:1–5). An earthquake generally produced great destruction in an ancient city and led to a mass exodus from the city. This image suggests that the people will leave in a hurry, the valley providing an escape route for the remnant to find safety from the impending battle.

(2) The valley will serve another purpose, providing a path for the triumphal return of Yahweh to his seat of rule. Accompanying God will be "the holy ones." Some have seen here a reference to heavenly beings who will accompany God in his battle against the nations (Ps. 89:6–8; cf. Job 5:1; 15:14).[24] The difficulty with this view is that the final phrase of verse 5 in the Hebrew text is "with you" (NIV, "with him").[25] Some have suggested that the prophet, overwhelmed by God's appearance, turns the description into a prayer to God.[26] Unfortunately, however, the "you" in the Hebrew text cannot be

20. See 2 Sam. 15:32, which shows that the Mount of Olives was used for worship.

21. See F.-M. Abel, "ʾAṣal in Zechariah xiv, 5," *RB* 45 (1936): 385–400.

22. See RSV and Baldwin, *Haggai*, 202.

23. A journey east of Jerusalem places a person in the environs of the desert of Judah. With its abundance of caves and dearth of water, it was a safe haven from armies.

24. Merrill, *Haggai*, 350; Schellenberg, "One," 112.

25. The NIV, along with most modern versions, follow the LXX at this point, which has "with him."

26. Baldwin, *Haggai*, 202–3.

God since it is a feminine singular pronoun. This is the same form already encountered in 14:1 ("your plunder"; "among you"), a reference probably to the city of Jerusalem. Thus, the "holy ones" here are the remnant that has fled from danger and now return under the protection of their Almighty God.[27]

Transforming the Cosmos, Assuming His Rule (14:6–11)

THE EFFECT OF GOD'S APPEARANCE on the natural order continues in verses 6–7 with the transformation of the cycle of light. The Hebrew text reads here "there will be no light of splendor, they will congeal" (NIV, "there will be no light, no cold or frost").[28] The term here for "splendor" is used in Job 31:26 to describe the light emanating from the moon. In Zechariah 14:6 it is rendered in the plural, probably referring to the sun and moon. The term "congeal" is used for thickening a liquid (Ex. 15:8; Job 10:10; Zeph. 1:12). The normally translucent bodies of light in the sky (sun and moon) will be congealed and no longer emanate light.

The vocabulary of 14:7 is reminiscent of the account of creation in Genesis 1, in particular, the account of the first day in 1:3–5: "unique day" (= "first day"), "day," "night," "evening."[29] The "congealing" of the heavenly lights will return the cosmos to the conditions of the first day of the creation account, a day known only to the God who created the world.[30] On this day light was created and later it was distinguished from darkness, creating "daytime" and "nighttime." Zechariah 14:6 stops the creative process partway through this day, for when "evening" arrives, light continues; there is no darkness. This image of a future era with perpetual light is a regular feature of apocalyptic literature (cf. Isa. 60:19, 20; Rev. 21:25; 22:5).[31]

The transformation of the cosmos continues in 14:8 as Jerusalem becomes a perpetual source of water for the entire land, supplying the seas to the east and west. "Living water" is used for fresh water originating in a well or spring

27. This could also be a reference to Judah as a whole; Mason, *Haggai*, 126; Leske, "Zechariah 9:9," 677.

28. The Kethib is the verbal form ("to congeal"), while the Qere is the nominal form ("congelation").

29. Cf. Merrill, *Haggai*, 351; Redditt, *Haggai*, 141; Petersen, *Zechariah 9–14*, 145; Floyd, *Minor Prophets*, 546.

30. Many see this as a reference to a future day (only God knows when this day will come), cf. Redditt, *Haggai*, 141; Merrill, *Haggai*, 351. Others see this as a scribal gloss, cf. Witt, "Zechariah 12–14", 68; Fishbane, *Biblical Interpretation*, 46–48. Floyd translates this as "familiar," thus a day only familiar to God who dwells in perpetual light; Floyd, *Minor Prophets*, 547. However, our interpretation is suggested by the theme of the return to the first day of creation, when only God was there.

31. Merrill (*Haggai*, 351) sees this as chaos out of creation (a sign of judgment), which leads to re-creation.

(e.g., Gen. 26:19; Jer. 2:13). Jerusalem contains such a spring, the Gihon, which lies below the city in the Kidron Valley (e.g., 2 Kings 20:20). This spring made settlement possible in Jerusalem, but it was vulnerable to attacking armies and inadequate for the needs of the growing city.[32] This verse envisions a flow of water from within Jerusalem that will exceed the needs of the city, running throughout the land and emptying into the Eastern Sea (Dead Sea) and the Western Sea (Mediterranean Sea).

The reference to "summer and . . . winter" is a merism denoting all seasons (Gen. 8:22; Ps. 74:17) and signifying that the flow of water will no longer fluctuate according to seasonal patterns (Ps. 32:4). This image of a future era with abundant water flowing from Jerusalem is a consistent feature in apocalyptic literature (Ezek. 47:1–20; Joel 3:18), one that is drawn from the description of Eden in Genesis 2:10–14.[33]

This great upheaval in the cosmos has been caused by the arrival of Yahweh, and to Yahweh the prophecy returns in 14:9. He now assumes his universal rule over "all the earth."[34] As sovereign Lord of the earth, he is declared as "one" and his name is "the only name." This echoes the credal Shema of Deuteronomy 6:4–5: "Hear, O Israel: The LORD our God, the LORD is one. Love the LORD your God with all your heart and with all your soul and with all your strength." This declaration stresses exclusive worship of Yahweh (see 6:13–14). So here he is declared as sole king over the cosmos, a theme developed throughout the Psalms (e.g., Ps. 47).

God's right to rule the earth is intimately linked to his subjugation of the cosmos and nations. As conquering divine warrior, he takes his legitimate place as king of the earth. This can be seen throughout the history of Israel, most notably in the inaugural event of the Exodus in which God as warrior is praised as the God who reigns (Ex. 15). This focus on the kingship of God does not necessarily mean a rejection of the Davidic line that has been highlighted in Zechariah 9–13 (9:9–10; 11:4–16; 12:10–14).[35] As Meyers and Meyers have argued: "Certainly the eschatological vision of chap. 14 focuses on Yahweh's universal sovereignty, not on that of a restored Davidide. But the

---

32. Even Hezekiah's tunnel, built to bring water from the Gihon within the city walls, was not enough to provide for the city.

33. See Clifford on the cosmic mountain motif in the ancient Near East and life-giving waters, which may explain 14:10 and the raising of Jerusalem; R. J. Clifford, *The Cosmic Mountain in Canaan and the Old Testament* (HSM 4; Cambridge, Mass.: Harvard Univ. Press, 1972), 51, 102, 158–60.

34. Janzen highlights the link between kingship and water (cf. Isa. 6–7; 8:8; 23–24; cf. Ps. 66:4–5; 72:8; 89:26; also Joel 3:17–21); Janzen, "Shema," 298 n. 19.

35. See Leske, "Zechariah 9:9," 677.

difference between the two chapters [chs. 9, 14] may be one of emphasis rather than contradiction."[36]

Verse 10 envisions further transformation of the cosmos. The land from Geba, six miles north of Jerusalem and representing the northern boundary of Judah (e.g., 1 Kings 15:22), to Rimmon (probably En-Rimmon), about thirty-five miles southwest of Jerusalem and marking the southern boundary of Judah (Josh. 15:32; 19:7), will be turned into "a plain." This term "plain" is Arabah, a word used to denote the rift valley that extended from the Sea of Galilee to the Red Sea (Deut. 3:17; 2 Kings 14:25) and is lower and flatter than the surrounding land.

As the surrounding land drops and levels, Jerusalem will tower over the land, producing a picture similar to Psalm 48:2; Isaiah 2:2–4//Micah 4:1–3, passages depicting the establishment of God's universal rule over the earth and of Jerusalem as the center, to which all nations stream. The dimensions of the city are those of the eighth-century capital in its prime, with mention of the Benjamin (e.g., Jer. 20:2), First and Corner (e.g., 31:38) Gates, the Tower of Hananel (e.g., 31:38), and the royal winepresses (39:4).

According to verse 11, this elevated and spacious city will be filled with inhabitants who will enjoy security. The term "destroyed" is the one used for the destruction of the inhabitants of the land in the conquest accounts of Joshua (*ḥerem*). In the Conquest the Canaanites were to be totally destroyed (Josh. 6:17–18), an instruction linked to God's judgment on their idolatry and to his desire to keep his people pure from it. The city of Jerusalem, at that time a city of the Jebusites, was also included in this command (Deut. 7:1–2; 20:16–18), although this command was never accomplished (Judg. 1:21).[37]

This verse suggests that finally Jerusalem will have been cleansed from such idolatry and no longer in need of the radical cleansing of *ḥerem*, since God has brought his judgment on the city (14:1–2). God's presence in this city generates unprecedented conditions of security, security both from the internal judgment of a holy God (*ḥerem*) and from the external threat of foreign invasion. The final blow to this latter threat is now the focus of 14:12–15.

Defeating the Nations (14:12–15)

THE DEPICTION OF GOD'S BATTLE against the nations,[38] anticipated in 14:3 but deferred until after the description of God's arrival and acquisition of his base of operations in Jerusalem (14:4–11), is now provided. God strikes his

36. Meyers and Meyers, "Future Fortunes," 221.

37. Notice how this kind of destruction was also required for Israelite cities who participated in idolatry (Deut. 13:12–18, esp. v. 15, 17).

38. Because of the use of identical vocabulary in 14:2 and 12, these opponents are apparently the same ones who attacked Jerusalem in 14:2.

opponents with an unprecedented plague. Their bodies will disintegrate on the spot: flesh, eyes, and tongues. This plague will generate overwhelming panic among the armies of these nations,[39] and in the ensuing confusion, they will engage one another in hand-to-hand combat (cf. Judg. 7:22).

While the focus to this point has been on Jerusalem and its inhabitants, verse 14 quickly mentions that Judah will join in the battle, and one assumes in support of Jerusalem.[40] The defeat of the armies is confirmed by the collection of plunder, including gold, silver, and clothing. The animals will not join this collection, for they will suffer the same plague as the soldiers.

Worshiping Yahweh (14:16–21)

THE DEFEAT OF these nations who attacked Jerusalem results in an annual pilgrimage of all these nations to Jerusalem. They will come to worship Yahweh as King (Ps. 24:10; Isa. 6:5), affirming the sovereignty already declared in Zechariah 14:9. Specific mention is made of the Feast of Tabernacles. This feast is a celebration of God as Creator and Redeemer, the One who provided the harvest (Deut. 16:13–17) and also rescued his people from Egypt (Lev. 23:39–43). Those nations, especially Egypt, who do not participate will have no rain to nourish their crops.[41]

The participation of the nations in the festal celebration is not the only surprising feature of the final section of Zechariah 14. There is a significant shift in perspective on ritual holiness in 14:20–21. Although there remains a "house of the LORD Almighty" (14:21b), utensils and items in Jerusalem and Judah will be considered "holy to the LORD," the title inscribed formerly only on the head plate of the high priest (Ex. 28:36–38). The reference to "bells of the horses" is interesting, especially considering that the horse is a ritually unclean animal (Lev. 11:1–8).[42] In this new Jerusalem that which was unclean will be made clean.

Furthermore, the cooking pots in the temple will share the status of the sacred bowls at the altar, and common pots throughout Jerusalem and Judah will share the status of the cooking pots. These verses transform the ritual categories of Torah, a change necessitated not only by the increased number of

---

39. Such panic is found elsewhere in plague (1 Sam. 5:9, 11) and military settings (Deut. 7:23; 1 Sam. 14:20; 2 Chron. 15:5; Isa. 22:5).

40. While in 14:3 the combination of *laḥam* ("fight") with the preposition *b* was interpreted as adversative ("to fight against"), here the same combination should be taken as locative ("to fight at"). There is precedence for both in the Old Testament.

41. The point of v. 18 is that Egypt, which is not seriously affected by a lack of rain because of its reliance on the Nile for agriculture, will be judged also by a plague, as in days of old.

42. Merrill, *Haggai*, 365. The Heb. term for "bells" is only found here in the Heb. Bible.

worshipers in the city,[43] but possibly also by a shift necessitated by a new phase of redemptive history, that is, a shift in the operation of the cult in the coming age.[44]

This new ritual condition of Jerusalem and Judah in which everything is consecrated for worship will eliminate the need for merchants in the temple precincts. The term here "Canaanite" is one used for the inhabitants of the land of Israel prior to their conquest (e.g., Gen. 12:6).[45] But it also can denote the merchant class that bought and sold goods (cf. Isa. 23:8; Prov. 31:24), a role necessary in a temple context for those who needed proper utensils for their sacrifices or who did not want to transport their offering to the feast in kind. This verse indicates, then, that there will be no more room for such merchants, who may have abused worshipers through exorbitant prices, or there will be no more need for them because of the availability of sacred utensils or the expansion of the types of offerings acceptable to Yahweh.

This final oracle brings not only Zechariah 9–14 but also the entire book of Zechariah to a climactic end. Its cosmic vision of the institution of the kingship involves the appearance of the divine warrior, whose very presence shakes the cosmos and, as a result, stirs the submission of both creation and culture to his mighty rule from his place of manifest presence, the temple in Jerusalem. God's people will be cleansed, and the nations will bend their knee before this mighty king and express their allegiance through annual worship of this Lord of the universe at the place of his holy presence. While the book began with a focus on human obedience as the people are called to repent and respond, at the end the book is consumed by a vision of the divine whose presence demands nothing short of total obedience and surrender. To a people who have lived under the abusive thumb of the superpowers of their day, this is a word of comfort indeed.

Bridging Contexts

IN ITS ORIGINAL context, Zechariah 14 addressed a community under the oppressive rule of the Persians and those Jews who had capitulated to their rule in and through the capital Jerusalem. Members of the prophetic community who perpetuated the tradition of their founder Zechariah and lived in the territory surrounding Jerusalem did not,

43. Redditt, *Haggai*, 144; Petersen, *Zechariah 9–14*, 160; Mason, "Use," 91; Witt, "Zechariah 12–14," 91.

44. Mason, "Use," 195; Mason, *Haggai*, 133. Leske and Hanson see here an attack on the priesthood at the Jerusalem temple; Hanson, *Dawn*, 387–88; Leske, "Zechariah 9:9," 677.

45. Merrill sees this as an ethnic reference and suggests that even Canaanites will be allowed in the holy temple precincts: "There is, in that sense, no longer a Canaanite, for

however, reject the ancient city but envisioned a future in which God would cleanse the city and bring all nations to their knees in submission to his universal rule.

Eschatological future or redemptive past? Many have used Zechariah 14 as the basis for the events of the eschaton. It is often linked to events that precede the establishment of the millennial kingdom with Jerusalem as its center. Although there are clearly eschatological implications that can be drawn from this chapter, one should not try to build a literal picture of end-time events from its eschatological language and imagery.

The New Testament writers found in Zechariah 14 a basis for understanding Christ's mission to Israel (see the introduction, Bridging Contexts section). In particular, one should note the way in which the description of Christ's entrance into Jerusalem and cleansing of the temple in Mark 11 alludes to Zechariah 14, depicting Christ as the divine warrior Yahweh who comes from the Mount of Olives to defeat Israel's enemies and cleanse the city.[46]

Through these allusions to Zechariah 14 in Mark 11, we can discern the conviction of the early Christian community that Christ's first coming is related to the expectation of this chapter. However, the flow and outcome of Mark 11, with its use of the fig tree motif to signify rejection, clearly shows that the Jerusalem of Jesus' day does not represent the ideal of Zechariah 14. Christ's parable at the outset of Mark 12 foreshadows the rejection of the divine warrior of Zechariah 14.

Although rejected by the leaders of Jerusalem in his day, the divine warrior Jesus will still accomplish the mission described in the apocalyptic imagery of Zechariah 14. Through his death and resurrection he will fight against the enemies of God and his people, inaugurating a new creation over which he rules as King. The nations of the earth will submit to his rule, drawn to his throne to worship him. The story of the early church describes the initial phase of the submission of the nations to Christ's rule as the church carried the message of salvation to the ends of the earth. The story of the

---

all alike will be the people of YHWH"; Merrill, *Haggai*, 366; see a similar line of thought in Floyd, *Minor Prophets*, 556. Considering the festal and temple context of these verses, the other gloss for this word is more likely.

46. See esp. P. B. Duff, "The March of the Divine Warrior and the Advent of the Greco-Roman King: Mark's Account of Jesus' Entry Into Jerusalem," *JBL* 111 (1992): 55–71; cf. R. M. Grant, "The Coming of the Kingdom," *JBL* 67 (1948): 297–303; C. F. Evans, "I Will Go Before You into Galilee," *JTS* ns5 (1954): 3–18; C. Roth, "The Cleansing of the Temple and Zechariah xiv 21," *NovT* 4 (1960): 174–81. Bruce notes a connection between Zech. 14 and John's account of the cleansing of the temple in John 2; F. F. Bruce, "The Book of Zechariah and the Passion Narrative," *BJRL* 43 (1960–61): 167–90.

church today is a later chapter in this same narrative plot, which will reach fulfillment with the return of Christ.

Through Zechariah 14 we celebrate the work of God in and through Christ at the beginning of church history. On this basis is built all that we are and do in the church today. But because of this foundation, we must return to this chapter to discover those elements that challenge us in the church today.

Victory against, for, and through his people. Zechariah 14:1–3 juxtaposes two different military pictures of God. In the first picture (14:1–2) God is depicted as an army general who musters his troops (all the nations) against his enemy (Jerusalem). In the second picture (14:3–5) God is depicted as a warrior who fights against his enemy (all the nations). The greatest distinction between these two images is not in the fact that in the first he is a general while in the second a warrior, but in the fact that in the first he fights against Israel while in the second against the nations.

These two approaches to battle can be traced throughout the history of redemption.[47] In Exodus 15, for example, the Lord is depicted as the mighty warrior who fights on behalf of a defenseless Israel against their enemies. Similarly in Joshua 5:13–15 the "commander of the army of the LORD" sketches out the divine battle plan for the defeat of Jericho. In the exchange, however, between the commander and Joshua, one can discern another vantage point on divine battle. In response to Joshua's query, "Are you for us or for our enemies?" the commander declares: "Neither" (5:13–14). This suggests that God's protection of Israel is not unqualified. He is not Israel's mercenary but rather Israel's king, and he is "for them" if they are "for him." When Israel rebelled against their king throughout their history, he turned against them as an enemy, often handing them over to other nations, to discipline them for their disobedience (Judges). In this way, the prophets drew on the divine warrior motif to speak not only of God's promised salvation of Israel but also of God's discipline of his people.

Zechariah 14:1–3 highlights these two modes of battle, displaying God's passion for purity among his people as well as for relationship with these people. The Lord is a God who will accomplish his purpose of purity, creating a holy remnant (see Isa. 6). His love for his people is demonstrated in his desire to fight on their behalf. These two passions intersect at the cross as Christ suffers the discipline of God through the nations against Israel while at the same time fighting against the forces of oppression that caused his death. His resurrection is the firstfruits of his victory over all forces of oppression in this world, both spiritual and physical.

---

47. See Sherlock's excellent account of these two modes; Sherlock, *God Who Fights*, 218, 243.

It is interesting that the Lord appears at the end of 14:5 with "all the holy ones." The community of Christ, purified through his sacrificial act, appears to rule with him. The church is purified through the cross, as a once-for-all redemptive event in Christ but also as a daily experience of submission to this Christ (cf. "take up your cross daily"). The church is Christ's representative on earth to complete his victory over the forces of oppression.

God's kingdom come. Zechariah 14 also pictures the restoration of the kingship of God on earth (14:6–21). The One who brings military victory is the One who rules over the earth, and God is clearly depicted as victorious in this chapter. His kingship is declared in 14:9, a declaration at the center of a section that depicts a transformation in the created order with a return to the first day of creation. God's seat of rule, secure and populated, is raised above the land as water flows out to nourish the land. The nations are not only defeated through God's superior military tactics, but they are then drawn to a purified Jerusalem to worship him. What a vision this is at the end of Zechariah! The nations of the earth will be defeated, but this defeat is not an end but a means. God's desire is for the nations to worship him.

There is no question that this chapter expands the theological vision of the Jewish community. Longing for release from the oppression of their Persian lords, they would have applauded the defeat of the nations. But Zechariah 14 reveals that the defeat of the nations will be followed by their submission to Yahweh and participation in the Jews' exclusive festival. Further evidence of theological development can be discerned in the expansion of the theology of ritual holiness, in which utensils in the entire land are sanctioned for holy use.

These elements of Zechariah 14 foreshadow the great mission instituted by Jesus through his death and resurrection. Through his redemptive act he makes possible the vision God always had for Israel, to bring the blessing of God to all nations (Gen. 12:1–3) as a kingdom of priests (Ex. 19:5–6), to serve as the seat of God's rule on earth. The church, as the fulfillment of Israel, is this kingdom of priests, made holy by the redemptive work of Jesus and the sanctifying work of his Spirit (1 Peter 2:9–10). The church, as the fulfillment of the temple, is the place of God's presence and vehicle of God's worship on earth (1 Peter 2:1–8). The church, as the fulfillment of Jerusalem, is the seat of God's rule on earth, and through the church God extends his kingdom to the ends of the earth.

While reminding the community of God today of our great privilege, Zechariah 14 also challenges this community. It reminds the church of the key role they are called to play in this world. The defeat of the nations has been accomplished through the surprising work of Christ on the cross (Isa. 52–53), and Christ commands his community to extend his rule to the nations through the proclamation of the gospel to the ends of the earth (Matt. 28:18–20; Acts

1:8). Jerusalem and Judah have now been embodied in the church, and the nations are drawn to God's seat of rule wherever the community of his Spirit is represented (John 4:21–24). The expansion of holiness categories near the end of Zechariah 14 does remind the church of the fulfillment of the ritual law in Christ, who has made all things holy. But this truth continues to remind the church of the fact that as priests and temple they are set apart for God's use.

Finally, this section also reminds us of the cosmic character of this vision of God's ultimate intervention on earth. God's actions shake the entire cosmos, transforming the very structure of his creation by his mere appearance. Related to this is the manifest extension of his power and authority over the nations, which results in the realization of the goal of redemptive history, that is, the transformation of all creation and the submission of all humanity to his rule. This cosmic vision is a powerful depiction of the implications of Christ's work, which include the transformation of all creation and culture.

Contemporary Significance

ZECHARIAH 14 SPEAKS to the church today, first as a revelation of God's work inaugurated in and through Christ. In that way it has enduring relevance to us today as we celebrate this work, but also as we take to heart the way this passage shaped this community's vision of God's design for them in this world (a holy community for the nations) and the way it ministered to the community of God in its time (offering hope as well as warning).

Holiness and mission. Throughout Zechariah 14 two theological themes come consistently to the fore: purity of God's community and establishment of God's rule. Placed into the larger plot of redemptive history, these two themes have been linked to the work of Christ on the cross with enduring implications for the vision and mission of the church.

This link between holiness and mission can be discerned in many traditions within Protestantism, which McClung has called "renewal/missions movements." They include "Pietism, Puritanism, Moravianism, the Evangelical revival in England and the related Wesleyan revival, and the Great Awakening in the American colonies."[48] This can be illustrated from the life and teaching of the young German, Nicholaus Ludwig von Zinzendorf (1700–1760).[49] Trained under the German Pietist August Hermann Francke, Zinzendorf established on his estate the famous missionary community that we today

48. L. G. McClung, "'Try to Get People Saved': Revisiting the Paradigm of an Urgent Pentecostal Missiology," in *The Globalization of Pentecostalism: A Religion Made to Travel*, ed. M. W. Dempster, B. D. Klaus, and D. Petersen (Oxford: Regnum, 1999), 35.

49. F. M. DuBose, ed. *Classics of Christian Missions* (Nashville: Broadman, 1979), 289–300.

know as the Moravians. In Zinzendorf's sermon entitled "Concerning the Proper Purpose of the Preaching of the Gospel," preached on September 4, 1746 on Matthew 22:2 and Luke 14:17, this godly missionary statesman, declared:

> My friends! We must establish this principle, that the blessed, fruitful, and almost irresistible "calling in" of many thousands of souls presupposes a little flock in the house which cleaves to the Saviour with body and soul, souls which are already there, united with the Saviour, so that one may point to these very people with the finger when one wants to invite others. It is an advantage, a blessing, a sound preaching of the Gospel, when one can say, "Come, everything is ready. I can show you the people who are already there; just come and see."... One perceives a people of God with whom the bridegroom concerns himself, people who glory in him, as he does in them. Thus it has come so far that the city on the hill can no longer be hidden, and it is a light which one does not put under a bushel but sets upon a candlestick. Thus a preaching of the Gospel must come out of this little flock."[50]

This same mix of pietism and mission can be discerned in the life of John Wesley (1703–1791) who, after establishing his famous "Holy Club" in Oxford, later traveled to North America as a preacher and missionary. It was through this experience that he came in contact with the Moravians and after returning to Europe traveled to meet Zinzendorf. There he was thoroughly saved and went forth to preach with power. Similarly, Whitefield, who was also part of the earlier "Holy Club," was impacted by Zinzendorf's teacher, Francke.[51] These figures and their related movements laid the foundation for the combination of renewal and mission among what is often considered the "holiness" movement of the late nineteenth and early twentieth centuries, which in turn shaped the great evangelical mission enterprise of the twentieth century.

In the latter part of the nineteenth century these two themes inspired a Presbyterian pastor named A. B. Simpson, who experienced a revival in his own life through the Holy Spirit's filling and physical healing and at the same time caught a vision for the unreached millions across the globe.[52] Passionate

50. DuBose, ed. *Classics*, 291.

51. Ibid., 92–93.

52. See esp. Thompson, *A. B .Simpson*; M. J. Boda, "The Christian and Missionary Alliance," in *An Encyclopedia of Religions in the United States*, ed. W. B. Williamson (New York: Crossroads/Continuum, 1992), 64–67.

to share these newfound theological emphases with the church, he began two interdenominational movements. The one he called the Christian Alliance (1887), a society committed to deeper Christian experience through sanctification and healing; the other, the Evangelical Missionary Alliance (1887, later called International Missionary Alliance, 1889), a society promoting world missions and sending missionaries to unreached peoples.

Soon, however, Simpson merged these two societies into the Christian and Missionary Alliance (1897), not only because both shared common board members and adherents, but more so because their emphases cannot be separated: mission emanates from holiness. As A. W. Tozer wrote of Simpson's passion for the Alliance: "He wanted the Alliance to be a spiritual association of believers who hungered to know the fullness of the blessing of the Gospel of Christ, working concertedly for the speedy evangelization of the world."[53] The link between holiness and mission is aptly described in McGraw's description of Simpson's writings:

> This interrelationship between sanctification and missions pervades the Simpson literature, demonstrating that those anointed with the Spirit must logically be missionary enthusiasts but that missions has too often floundered for lack of the Holy Spirit's enduement.[54]

This same combination can be discerned in the twentieth-century explosion of mission among the Pentecostal movement.[55] This movement, whose roots are often traced to the revivals on Azusa street in Los Angeles in the early twentieth century, now encircles the globe.[56] A movement that began with a passion for a greater experience of God and the filling of the Holy

53. Tozer, *Wingspread*, 103.

54. G. E. McGraw, "The Doctrine of Sanctification in the Published Writings of Albert Benjamin Simpson" (Ph.D., New York University, 1986), 580, see 577–82.

55. Cf. Cox, *Fire from Heaven*. For Pentecostal missiology see P. A. Pomerville, *The Third Force in Missions: A Pentecostal Contribution to Contemporary Mission Theology* (Peabody, Mass.: Hendrickson, 1985); McClung, "Pentecostal Missiology," 30–51; L. G. McClung, ed., *Azusa Street and Beyond: Pentecostal Missions and Church Growth in the Twentieth Century* (South Plainfield, N.J.: Bridge, 1986). For the related charismatic movement, see its global culture in K. Poewe, *Charismatic Christianity As a Global Culture* (Studies in Comparative Religion; Columbia, S.C.: Univ. of South Carolina Press, 1994), and the call to missiology in E. K. Pousson, *Spreading the Flame: Charismatic Churches and Missions Today* (Grand Rapids: Zondervan, 1992); D. Shibley, *A Force in the Earth: The Charismatic Renewal and World Evangelism* (Altamonte Springs, Fla.: Creation House, 1989).

56. For the global culture of Pentecostalism see W. J. Hollenweger, *Pentecostalism: Origins and Developments Worldwide* (Peabody, Mass.: Hendrickson, 1997); M. W. Dempster, B. D. Klaus, and D. Petersen, eds., *The Globalization of Pentecostalism: A Religion Made to Travel* (Oxford: Regnum, 1999), 127–260.

Spirit for service and holiness now has more adherents overseas than in North America.[57] Pomerville has demonstrated the close link between renewal and missiology in Pentecostalism:

> The notion that Pentecostalism provides direction for contemporary missions is based on its emphasis on the experiential dimension of the Christian faith, the dynamic experience of the Spirit. As a renewal movement, emphasizing a neglected dimension of the Holy Spirit's ministry, Pentecostalism sets the subtle influence of post-Reformation Protestant Scholasticism in bold relief. . . . It is at this point that Pentecostalism's "God with us" experience makes its major contribution to contemporary missions. Paradoxically, the chief criticism of the Movement, the distinct, dynamic experience of the Spirit, reveals its chief contribution for contemporary missions.[58]

This view is echoed by McClung: "At the heart of the early Pentecostals' missiology was their personal experience with the Holy Spirit found around an altar of prayer with fellow seekers"[59] As with Zinzendorf, Wesley, Whitefield, so with Simpson and Pentecostalism, in generation after generation one can see the power of the fusion of these two themes.

The two theological themes of holiness and mission have often been juxtaposed in the minds of Christians. Christ anticipates this tension in his prayer of John 17 when he reveals that his people are "not of the world" (John 17:14), even as he sends them "into the world" (17:18). To be in the world and yet not of the world is one of the greatest challenges of the Christian community.

Some Christian movements err by emphasizing holiness at the expense of mission, a fundamentalism that withdraws from society into exclusive community. This error is not limited to Christian movements that have physically separated themselves from society by establishing communes or monasteries. They occur in churches in towns and cities through weekly programs that absorb the resources of their members so that they have little time to participate in their culture as transformative agents. The vision of these

---

57. As Hollenweger wrote in 1997: "By the year 2000 85–90 percent of the Christians in the Third World will be Pentecostal/Charismatic"; Hollenweger, *Pentecostalism*, 289.

58. Pomerville, *Third Force*, 79.

59. McClung, "Pentecostal Missiology," 36. In his earlier review of Pentecostal missiological practice he placed two principles at the forefront: emphasis on the Holy Spirit and worship: "It should be noted from the outset, however, that the very heartbeat of Pentecostal missions is their experience with the power and Person of the Holy Spirit. . . . Pentecostal worship allows the participant to be involved in a personal and direct way with the manifestation of God among His people in the congregation," L. G. McClung, "Spontaneous Strategy of the Spirit: Pentecostal Missionary Practices," in *Azusa Street and Beyond*, 72–73.

communities is often limited to what happens within the walls of the church, with little sense of how God will use the church in the culture at large.

Other Christian movements err by emphasizing mission at the expense of holiness, only calling their communities to be "in the world." This error can be traced through the story of many mainline churches in North America in the past century. In their desire to address society's needs they loosened their grasp on the theological foundations that define the church as a holy community. But this is not limited to mainline churches. There is a constant temptation to reach out in mission and forget the key tenets of holiness.

Christ calls us to balance these two aspects of faith. Such balance is often attempted by focusing attention on the two aspects in isolation from one another, but a more healthy approach, prompted by the examples provided above, is to see the intimate connection between holiness and mission. In Zechariah 14 God purifies his community and establishes them as a holy community through which the nations enter into communion with God. God brings the nations to their knees through his sovereign acts of power, but then draws them into the life of his holy community for worship before his throne.

Our mission of the church is often abstracted from our vision of a holy community. We train specialists in evangelism and mission to take the message to another culture or generation. These kinds of people are distinguished from others whose primary concern is the pastoral care of the church, seeking to build the faith community up in holiness. Zechariah 14 challenges us to bring these two aspects of the church together: to see how a holy community of worship is an essential ingredient in, rather than a constant impediment to, the mission of the church.

Some recent approaches to evangelism have capitalized on the power of the witness of the gathered community of faith on unbelievers. Rather than creating a user-friendly church experience that feels more like a nightclub than a church, they have borne witness to the church's experience of God's grace and invited unbelievers to come and experience God.[60] When I was a pastor in Toronto, I met a high school campus worker who, after participating in the classic "relevant" evangelistic methods of his interdenominational movement, opted to follow the example of Christ and focus on a smaller group of unchurched teens to whom he imparted the strong message of discipleship and sought to incorporate into his local church.

The creation of a vibrant holy community into which others are invited to experience God is an important implication that can be drawn from

60. An example of this is the ALPHA program that began in England but has now spread throughout North America.

Zechariah 14. But our view of holiness needs to be expanded in a way that complements our mission to a decaying culture. Such expansion can be seen in this chapter as ritual holiness extends to what was formerly considered "common" in Jerusalem and Judah. Zechariah 14 opens the way for a vision of holiness that culminates in Christ, in which God's holiness is extended to all the world through his people. With this kind of vision before us, mission and holiness are more easily integrated.

What does this broader vision of holiness mean for us today? It means an expansion of our vision of holiness beyond the private and ecclesial realms to the social and communal spheres of our culture. God desires nothing less than a transformation of all culture and creation, set apart for his use and glory.

Recently over a period of three years I participated in a Strategic Vision Task Force for my denomination in Canada. As we sought God for his call on our community of faith in our nation, we were moved to produce a vision prayer. This prayer stresses the kinds of values identified in our application of Zechariah 14, so let me share this prayer:

> O God, with all our hearts we long to be: a movement of churches transformed by Christ, transforming our nation and world. By Your grace and for Your glory: Renew and empower us through a fresh encounter with Yourself; release us to be strategic in service, kingdom-connected in practice, passionate in pursuit of Your mission and mercy; use us to fulfill Your purpose for Canada and the world.

Hope and warning. Zechariah 14 was written to a community with little reason for hope. Reduced to a small community within an insignificant province in a world controlled by Persians and Greeks, the Jewish community had to strain to imagine the world described in Zechariah 14. But this chapter was written to raise their vision beyond their present circumstances, that they might see the world from God's eternal perspective and live accordingly.

Zechariah 14 grants a vision of hope to this community, hope that God will fulfil his purposes, that the oppression they presently experience will not be their eternal lot, but rather that God has chosen them and will ultimately establish his rule in and through them. As Christians we need to hear this message of triumphant hope, not so that we can vindictively anticipate the demise of our enemies, but that we may be encouraged to live by faith in the present age, confident in our transforming message. As the Persian period community longed for God's arrival, so also we long for the arrival of Christ, who has come and will come again. Zechariah 14 grants us hope that our lives are not lived in vain, that God will someday transform the cosmic and political structures of our world.

Past approaches to apocalyptic literature, with their schematization of history and predictions of the future, have created a ubiquitous skepticism within the church today toward this form of literature. At the same time, we live in a media-saturated and often tabloid-exploited culture where a constant stream of negative messages and stories bombard our lives, reminding us that we live in a world filled with evil, injustice, and perversion. This dangerous mix of loss of this literature base together with the gain of this media blitz has led to the undermining of the fundamental disposition of Christian faith: hope. In such a world it is easy to forget that we are to be purveyors of hope because we are convinced of the message of Zechariah 14, that God's kingdom will come, as Jesus prayed, "on earth as it is in heaven."

At the same time this apocalyptic passage functions as a warning to the community of faith. It warns us to remain faithful to this divine warrior who not only judges the nations but also disciplines his people. By foreshadowing the ultimate destination of history, Zechariah 14 provides perspective on living each day in the power of the Spirit. Some have sought to contrast the God of the Old Testament with the God of the New Testament—the former the God of law, justice, and punishment, the latter the God of grace, love, and forgiveness. But this contrast is easily dismissed by a closer look at the revelation of God's character and action in the two Testaments. God is a God of grace and justice in the Old Testament, as his revelation to Moses in Exodus 34 makes clear. This same balance can be seen in the New Testament as Christ comes both as the Christ of grace and the Christ of justice (Rev. 19). Zechariah 14 thus warns us to remain faithful and pursue holiness as we live with confidence in and reliance on God's grace.

A climactic ending. Zechariah 14 brings us to the end not only of chapters 9–14 but also of the entire book of Zechariah. We began this book with the prophetic sermon of 1:1–6, which called the people to return to God in repentance in order that he might return to them. An initial positive response in 1:6b launched the prophetic complex of 1:7–6:15, which offered a powerful vision of God's planned return of presence and people to Yehud. However, chapters 7–8 revealed an enduring dysfunction within this community. Insincerity in repentance reaching back into the exile itself necessitated an elongation of exilic conditions as the people awaited the return of God's presence as well as the full company of God's people, renewals only possible when repentance was a reality among them.

The hope for the return of God and his people is expressed more fully in the prophecies of chapters 9 and 10, where the prophet offers the future vision of God's return to his temple and the rescue of all Israel from the nations to live in prosperity in Israel. Although foreshadowed in 10:1–3a, this picture of prosperity and peace is deeply disturbed in chapter 11 with the revelation of serious problems among both leadership and community. This revelation serves as a segue to chapters 12–14, which present an agenda for God's universal reign over the nations after cleansing his people from their sin and idolatry.

There is a clear shift in the book as a whole from more focused attention on the human at the outset to the divine. It becomes clear that although there are some who are sensitive to the prophetic call for repentance, ultimately hope lies with the revelation and action of the Lord God, who will cleanse the community and personally intervene to institute his kingship on earth. While some take this shift from the human to the divine as discouragement for human participants in covenant relationships, at the end of the day it is to be appropriated as a signal of God's gracious intervention to make possible the kind of salvation that will last for eternity.

A similar shift is apparent in the latest era of prophetic reflection in the preexilic era. In Jeremiah hope lies not in a new opportunity for Israel in the future but in the divine promise that God will take the initiative to ensure that covenant relationship is possible. Indeed he will "forgive their wickedness and will remember their sins no more" (Jer. 31:34), but he will even go further and "put my law in their minds and write it on their hearts" (31:33). Although Ezekiel called his people to repent, defined as "rid yourselves of all the offenses you have committed and get a new heart and a new spirit" (Ezek. 18:30–31), as he looked to the future, he promised an ingathering of his people from the nations after which God will "give them an undivided heart and put a new spirit in them" so that "they will follow my decrees and be careful to keep my laws" (11:17–20; cf. 36:26–28; 37:1–14).

This does not mean that there is no room for human response, an aspect that has not been ignored throughout Zechariah, even in chapters 12–14. However, the clear shift to the dominance of God and his actions first through discipline and later through salvation echoes a stream of theology that will be articulated most fully in the new covenant era. God took initiative by sending his Son to enter creation and culture and ultimately transformed it through his death and resurrection. He sent forth his Spirit to fill his church and give to them the promised "new heart and new spirit" that would enable them to fully embrace covenant relationship.

As we await the return of the Son in glory we are reminded that ultimately our hope rests on the work of the sovereign Creator of the universe. It is not surprising that Zechariah ends in a similar way to the New Testament (Revelation), with the accent on God's final climactic history-fulfilling, cosmos-shaking appearance to make all things right. It is not a celebration of humanity's potential that ultimately brings hope to God's people and creation but a celebration of God's promised intervention at the end of time.

Scripture Index

Daniel

Romans

1 Corinthians

Subject Index

Author Index